The predominant forms of religions in the world today

Legend:

- Indigenous religions
- Hinduism and Islam
- Buddhism
- China: Remnants of Confucianism, Buddhism, Taoism
- Japan: Shinto, Buddhism, Sects
- Christianity (Roman Catholicism, Protestantism, Eastern Orthodox)
- Islam
- Varied religions

COMMONWEALTH OF INDEPENDENT STATES
(Formerly USSR)

Kazakhstan

Kyrgyzstan

MONGOLIA

NTH. KOREA

STH. KOREA

JAPAN

NORTH PACIFIC OCEAN

Georgia

Uzbek.

Turk.

Tajikistan

Azerbaijan

Armenia

URKEY

LEB.

RAEL

IRAQ

IRAN

AFGHANISTAN

PAKISTAN

CHINA

TAIWAN

Sikhism

INDIA

MYANMAR

HONG KONG

KUWAIT

SAUDI
ARABIA

Parsism
(Zoroastrianism)

THAILAND

LAOS

KAM.

VIETNAM

PHILIPPINES

SOUTH PACIFIC OCEAN

SRI LANKA

ETHIOPIA

SOMALIA

GANDA

KENYA

MALAYSIA

TANZANIA

INDONESIA

PAPUA
NEW
GUINEA

AWI

INDIAN OCEAN

MOZAMBIQUE

MADAGASCAR

WE

SWAZILAND

LESOTHO

AUSTRALIA

NEW ZEALAND

LIVING
RELIGIONS

LIVING RELIGIONS

THIRD EDITION

MARY PAT FISHER

SPECIALIST CONSULTANTS
Deepali Bhanot, Delhi University
Robert Carter, Trent University
David Chappell, University of Hawaii
Homi Dhalla, Bombay University
Kathleen Margaret Dugan, San Diego University
John A. Grim, Bucknell University
Sheldon R. Isenberg, University of Florida
Timothy Miller, University of Kansas
Anand Mohan, Queens College of the City University of New York
Basheer Nafi, International Institute of Islamic Thought, Virginia
Bhai Kirpal Singh, Gobind Sadan Institute of
Advanced Studies in Comparative Religion

PRENTICE HALL
Upper Saddle River, N.J. 07458

Prentice Hall, Inc.
Simon & Schuster/A Viacom Company
Upper Saddle River, N. J. 07458

10 9 8 7 6 5 4 3 2 1

ISBN 0-13-254806-2

This book was designed and produced by
CALMANN AND KING LTD., LONDON

Designer (3rd edition): Karen Osborne
Picture researcher (3rd edition): Julia Hanson
Maps: Eugene Fleury

Printed in Hong Kong

Cover: MC34749 *St. Clemente — Gateway to the Hills*
Chase, Michael (living artist),
Private Collection/Bridgeman Art Library, London

Half title: Praying in Tibet.

Frontispiece: Caodai Temple near Hochiminh City, Vietnam.

CONTENTS

CHAPTER NINE

JUDAISM
page 216

CHAPTER TEN

CHRISTIANITY
page 265

PREFACE

Religion is not a museum piece. At the turn of the century, it is alive in people and places around the world. *Living Religions* is a sympathetic approach to what is living and significant in the world's religious traditions. It provides a clear and straightforward account of the development, doctrines, and practices of the major faiths practiced today. The emphasis throughout is on the personal consciousness of believers and their own account of their religion and its relevance in contemporary life.

New features in this edition

The collapse of communism in Eastern Europe has reopened doors long closed to overt religious practice. Almost all living religions are found in these countries and are affected by this sea change. This edition explores the nuances of this new historical situation, as seen by believers who were witness both to repression and to today's greater freedom of belief.

This third edition of *Living Religions* appears at the end of the twentieth century and the beginning of the twenty-first, a time anticipated in many religions as a period of major change. I have therefore developed a new chapter to end the book, "Religion at the Turn of the Century," to survey global trends found in all religions. These include both an increase in fundamentalist rigidities and softening of historical boundaries between people of different faiths. The chapter also looks at religious principles in business, government, and courageous individual acts of faith among those who are trying to live by the teachings of their religion.

Because students are often unfamiliar with terms from other cultures, a guide to pronunciation has been added to the glossary.

Special features updated

This third edition of *Living Religions* preserves and improves upon the features which make *Living Religions* special. One of these is personal interviews with followers of each faith, providing first-person accounts of each religion as perceived from within the tradition. These are presented at length in boxes and also in excerpts woven throughout the text.

This edition includes a rare and fascinating interview with a Siberian shamaness in Chapter 2, together with other new interview material from the former Soviet Union which I have gathered during several visits there.

In addition, the book incorporates extensive quotations from primary sources to give a direct perception of the thinking and flavor of each tradition. Particularly memorable brief quotations are set off in boxes.

The teaching stories from each faith, introduced in the second edition, have been retained and two new stories included. Each boxed narrative is told without analysis, just as a person within the faith would hear it, so that the stories can work on many levels. They could be take-off points for group discussion about the values they encourage which are central to that religion.

New photographs have been added to the extensive illustration program to convey a living sense of each tradition. The book incorporates 58 color and 187 black and white illustrations, with an emphasis on contemporary religious life. Narrative captions accompanying them offer a deepened insight into the characteristics and orientation of each tradition and the people who practice it.

Four chapters are especially unique. One is the new final chapter described above, "Religion at the Turn of the Century." The first chapter – "The Religious Response" – explores religion in general. Religion is presented as a valid account of reality that takes many forms. This chapter includes a discussion of women and the feminine in religions, an area to which little attention has been paid in past surveys of world religions, but which is a recurring theme in *Living Religions*. It also examines the controversial side of religions, for they have at times evoked the lowest as well as the highest aspects of human nature.

The second chapter portrays the little-understood indigenous religions. I have tried to bypass the many misleading accounts of indigenous traditions written by outsiders, and to get at the heart of how real people experience their close-to-nature spiritual ways. As our world totters on the brink of ecological collapse, it is especially important that these surviving members of the ancient ways be heard correctly.

The penultimate chapter is an original framework for understanding new religious movements. It is an up-to-date discussion of the novel and important religious trends of the late nineteenth and twentieth centuries in the context of the continual arising and developing of new religious movements throughout human history.

Learning aids

I have tried to present each tradition clearly and without a clutter of less important names and dates. Key terms, highlighted in bold or italics, are defined when they first appear and also in an extensive glossary. Maps are used to give a sense of geographical reality to the historical discussions, as well as to illustrate the present distribution of the religions.

The history of each of the major religions is recapitulated in a time-line in the history section of that chapter. The simultaneous development of all religions can be compared in the overall time-line on the end pages.

I assume that readers will want to delve further into the literature. At the end of each chapter, I offer an annotated list of books that might be particularly interesting and useful in deeper study of that religion.

Acknowledgements

In order to try to understand each religion from the inside, I have been travelling for many years to study and worship with devotees and teachers of all faiths, and to interview them about their experience of their tradition.

In preparing this edition I have worked directly with a team of authorities in specific traditions who have offered detailed suggestions and resources for its revision. They are Deepali Bhanot of Delhi University, Robert Carter of Trent University, Homi Dhalla of Bombay University, David Chappell of the University of Hawaii, Kathleen Margaret Dugan of San Diego University, John A. Grim of Bucknell University, Sheldon R. Isenberg of the University of Florida, Timothy Miller of the University of Kansas, Anand Mohan of Queens College of the City University of New York, Basheer Nafi of the International Institute of Islamic Thought, and Bhai Kirpal Singh of the Gobind Sadan Institute of Advanced Studies in Comparative Religions. All have been extraordinarily helpful and enthusiastic about this book. For breadth of scholarship, I worked with two different teams of scholars in preparing the first and second editions, and their considerable help is acknowledged therein. I am very grateful for the generous help of all my consultants; responsibility for the content of the book nonetheless rests with me, and I continue to welcome constructive remarks from all scholars in anticipation of the fourth edition.

Living Religions has been extensively reviewed by professors teaching courses in world religions. Reviewers of the first edition included: George Braswell of Southeastern Baptist Theological Seminary, Howard R. Burkle of Grinnell College, James Carse of New York University, Frances Cook of University of California, Ronald Flowers of Texas Christian University, Rita Gross of University of Wisconsin, Willard Johnson of San Diego State University, Anjum Khilji of Institute of Para-psychology at Durham Technical Community College, Dennis Klass of Webster University, Robert Minor of University of Kansas, Kusumita P. Pederson of New York University, Lynda Sexson of Montana State University, Paul Schwartz of San Francisco State University, and Herb Smith of McPherson College. In addition, Reverend Stan Possell, Rabbi Steven Razin, Mohammad T. Mehdi, and Prajapati O'Neill have read and commented on specific chapters.

Reviewers of the second edition included: Gary Alexander of University of Wisconsin, Stevens Point, Howard R. Burkle of Grinnell College, Francis H. Cook of University of California, Riverside (retired), Ronald B. Flowers of Texas Christian University, Eugene V. Gallagher of Connecticut College, John A. Grim of Bucknell University, Marcia K. Hermansen of San Diego State University, Wayne R. Husted of Penn State University, John P. Keenan of University of Pennsylvania, Lynn Ross-Bryant of University of Colorado, Boulder, Larry D. Shinn of Bucknell University, H. Michael Simmons of Center for Zoroastrian Research, Maurine Stein of Prairie State College, James D. Tabor of University of North Carolina, Charolotte. In addition, Robert Carter of Trent University and Balkar Singh of Punjabi University at Patiala offered suggestions on the chapters on Shinto and Sikhism, respectively, and S. A. Ali of Hamdard University and R. P. Jain of Delhi were very helpful in guiding me to literature on Islam and Jainism.

Reviewers for this third edition of *Living Religions* include: William R. Goodman, Jr. of Lynchburg College, Robert Imperato of Saint Leo College, Barbara Ring Kotowski of University of Texas at El Paso and El Paso Community College, Scott Lowe of University of North Dakota, Elizabeth Neumeyer of Kellogg Community College, Maurine Stein of Prairie State College. Lee Bailey of Ithaca College was also generous in his help. Many Russian scholars have reviewed the text, and their comments have been very helpful in preparing additions particularly with concern to the contemporary and historical situations in the former Soviet Union. The many suggestions, insights, and resources which all of these scholars have offered have been extremely valuable, and I would like to thank them all.

Probably most important to the spiritual validity of the book are those many devotees, teachers, and scholars from each religion who were enthusiastic about the possibility of presenting their path truthfully and who gave generously of their own time, insights, and books. Some are quoted in the text; many more have helped. I would particularly like to thank those who appear in the featured interview boxes. All these people have shared great richnesses of information and experience, and for this I am sincerely grateful.

It is my good fortune that my editor again for this edition is Melanie White of Calmann and King in London. Her brilliance and orderly way with details of production have once again given birth to an aesthetically appealing book. Heather Gross has worked with me to develop the pronunciation guide and the symbols used at the beginning of each chapter. Some are traditional; some are the products of her enlightened imagination.

Finally, I cannot adequately express my gratitude to my own revered teacher, Baba Virsa Singh of Gobind Sadan. Under his inspiration both the common people and the great scholars of all religions are moving toward more profound understanding and practice of their own faiths.

May God guide us all in our search for truth.

Mary Pat Fisher
Gobind Sadan Institute for Advanced Studies
in Comparative Religions, New Delhi

CHAPTER 1
THE RELIGIOUS RESPONSE

Before sunrise, members of a Muslim family rise in Malaysia, perform their purifying ablutions, spread their prayer rugs facing Mecca, and begin their prostrations and prayers to Allah. In a French cathedral, worshippers line up for their turn to have a priest place a wafer on their tongue, murmuring, "This is the body of Christ." In a South Indian village, a group of women reverently anoint a cylindrical stone with milk and fragrant sandalwood paste and place around it offerings of flowers. The monks of a Japanese Zen Buddhist monastery sit crosslegged and upright in utter silence, broken occasionally by the noise of the *kyosaku* bat falling on their shoulders. On a mountain in Mexico, men, women, and children who have been dancing without food or water for days greet an eagle flying overhead with a burst of whistling from the small wooden flutes they wear around their necks. By a stream in Iowa, a young woman sits with her eyes closed, praying to the universe that her life may serve some sacred purpose.

These and countless other moments in the lives of people around the world are threads of the tapestry we call "religion." The word is probably derived from the Latin, meaning "to tie back," "to tie again." Despite the rich diversity of its expressions, all of religion shares the goal of tying people back to something behind the surface of life — a greater reality which lies beyond, or invisibly infuses, the world that we can perceive with our five senses.

Attempts to connect with this greater reality have taken many forms. Many of them are organized institutions, such as Buddhism or Christianity, with leaders, sacred scriptures, and historical traditions. Others are private personal experiences of individuals who belong to no institutionalized religion but nonetheless have an inner life of prayer, meditation, or direct experience of an inexplicable presence.

In this introductory chapter, we will try to develop some understanding of religion in a generic sense — why it exists and what general forms it takes — before studying the characteristics of the particular group religions that are practiced today.

Why are there religions?

We could account for the universality of religions from two different points of view: Firstly, that there is actually an underlying reality that cannot be readily perceived but which some people in all cultures have experienced. Ways of acknowledging it and accommodating one's life to this reality have become institutionalized as religions. The second point of view is that there is no reality except the material

Spiritual experience may be private or communal. Members of the Krishna Consciousness movement become ecstatic in their praises of Krishna, a much-loved Hindu god.

world; humans everywhere have invented religions to satisfy their own personal needs. The twentieth-century psychoanalyst Sigmund Freud described religion as a "universal obsessional neurosis," depicting it as a cosmic projection and replaying of our love/fear relationships with our parents. Others believe that religions have been created or at least used to manipulate people. Historically, religions have often supported and served centers of secular power. The nineteenth century socialist philosopher Karl Marx argued that a culture's religion — as well as all other aspects of its social structure — spring from its economic framework. Rather than being a response to spiritual reality, religion is, in Marx's view, a tool for oppressing people, a mirror of an unjust economic structure:

> *Man makes religion: religion does not make man.... The religious world is but the reflex of the real world.... Religion is the sigh of the oppressed creature, the sentiment of a heartless world, and the soul of soulless conditions. It is the opium of the people....*[1]

Marx observed that religious authorities claim to possess absolute truth and then permit that claim to be wielded as a weapon by contemporary social and political forces. For instance, he charged Christian authorities of his times with supporting "vile acts of the oppressors" by explaining them as due punishment of sinners by God. Other critics have made similar complaints against Eastern religions which blame the sufferings of the poor on their own misdeeds in their previous lives. Such interpretations and uses of religious teachings lessen the perceived need for

society to help those who are oppressed and suffering.

Yet others have rejected religion on the grounds that it is unscientific. This tendency arose with the glorification of Western science. From the seventeenth century onward, Western science considered mind and spirit separate from matter. The physical realities of the universe were approached as a world unto themselves, a giant machine that could presumably be taken apart, understood, and used however humans chose. The belief that spirit creates, permeates, or intervenes in the material world was set aside because spirit was not tangible, not scientifically verifiable. Religious concepts were not honored as they had been in all previous times and all places, for they seemed irrational. There were predictions that religions would fall by the wayside, since science was now on the verge of explaining everything.

In recent times, however, there has been a return to a more religiously sympathetic worldview, and some of the leaders of this shift have been our most respected scientists. Cynicism about religion is giving way to a search for spirituality, though not necessarily to the same faiths that sustained our ancestors.

Fulfillment of basic human needs

Many human needs are not met by the outer aspects of our life on earth. One of these is the difficulty of accepting the commonsense notion that this life is all there is. We are born, we struggle to support ourselves, we age, and we die. If we believe that there is nothing more, fear of death may inhibit enjoyment of life and make all human actions seem pointless. Confronting mortality is so basic to the spiritual life that, observes the Christian monk Brother David Steindl-Rast, whenever monks from any spiritual tradition meet, within five minutes they are talking about death.

> It appears that throughout the world man has always been seeking something beyond his own death, beyond his own problems, something that will be enduring, true and timeless. He has called it God, he has given it many names; and most of us believe in something of that kind, without ever actually experiencing it.
>
> Jiddu Krishnamurti[2]

Many of us seek an assurance that life continues in some form beyond the grave. But we may also want this present life to have some meaning. For many, the desire for material achievement offers a temporary sense of purposefulness. But once achieved, these material goals may seem hollow. The Buddha said:

Look!
The world is a royal chariot, glittering with paint.
No better.
Fools are deceived, but the wise know better.[3]

All religions help to uncover meaningfulness in the midst of the mundane. They do so by exploring the *transpersonal* dimension of life — the eternal and infinite, beyond limited personal or communal concerns. In doing so, some religions totally deny the value of earthly life; others seek to bring heaven to earth, infusing each moment with awareness of the sacred.

Opposite *The huge monument to space travel built in Moscow under Soviet rule reflected a reverence for science as the hope of the world.*

Some religions try to transcend the mundane, glimpsing what lies beyond. Others, such as the Zen Buddhism that influenced this 18th-century drawing of The Meditating Frog, *find ultimate reality in the here and now intensely experienced.*

There is in some of us a desire for perfection, but that which is absolute, ultimate, and perfect does not seem to exist in the world that we perceive with our five senses. For example, if we look for perfection in human love, or justice within the inequities of human societies, we are likely to be disappointed. Yet religious practices may offer us insight into perfect Love, Justice, and Eternal Truth existing in vaster dimensions of time and space.

Some of us also have a strong sense of our own imperfections and long to outgrow them. Religions describe ideals which can radically transform people. Mahatma Gandhi was an extremely shy, fearful, self-conscious child. His transformation into one of the great political figures of our time occurred as he meditated single-mindedly on the great Hindu scripture, the Bhagavad-Gita. Gandhi was particularly impressed by the second chapter, which he says was "inscribed on the tablet of my heart."[4] It reads, in part:

> He lives in wisdom
> Who sees himself in all and all in him.,
> Whose love for the Lord of Love has consumed
> Every selfish desire and sense-craving
> Tormenting the heart. ...
>
> He is forever free who has broken
> Out of the ego-cage of I and mine
> To be united with the Lord of Love.
> This is the supreme state. Attain thou this
> And pass from death to immortality.[5]

People long to escape from personal problems. Those who are suffering severe physical illness, privation, terror, or grief often turn to the divine for help. Agnes Collard, a Christian woman near death from four painful years of cancer, reported that her impending death was bringing her closer to That which she called God:

I don't know what or who He is, but I am almost sure He is there. I feel His presence, feel that He is close to me during the awful moments. And I feel love. I sometimes feel wrapped, cocooned in love.[6]

Religious literature is full of stories of miraculous aid which has come to those who have cried out in their need. But sometimes help comes as the strength and philosophy to accept burdens. The eighteenth-century Hasidic Jewish master, the Baal Shem Tov, taught that the vicissitudes of life are ways of climbing toward the divine. Islam teaches patience, faithful waiting for the unfailing grace of Allah.

Despite his own trials, the Christian apostle Paul wrote of "the peace of God, which passeth all understanding."[7] Gandhi was blissful in prison, for no human could bar his relationship with the Lord of Love.

Rather than seeking help from without, an alternative approach is to seek freedom from problems by changing our ways of thinking. According to some Eastern religions, the concept that we are distinct, autonomous individuals is an illusion; what we think of as "our" consciousnesses and "our" bodies are in perpetual flux. From this point of view, freedom from problems lies in recognizing and accepting the reality of temporal change and devaluing the "small self" in favor of the eternal

Nostalgia for perfection has inspired the creation of intricate temples such as Hagia Sophia in Istanbul. Built as an immense Christian church, it was transformed into a Muslim mosque when the city was taken over by Turks in 1453.

self. The ancient sages of India referred to it as "This eternal being that can never be proved, ... spotless, beyond the ether, the unborn Self, great and eternal, ... the creator, the maker of everything."[8]

Many contemplative spiritual traditions teach methods of turning within to discover and eradicate all attachments, desires, and resentments associated with the small self, revealing the purity of the true self. Once we have found it within, we begin to see it wherever we look. This realization brings a sense of acceptance in which, as philosopher William James observed:

> *Dull submission is left far behind, and a mood of welcome, which may fill any place on the scale between cheerful serenity and enthusiastic gladness, has taken its place.*[9]

Kabir, a fifteenth-century Indian weaver who was inspired alike by Islam and Hinduism and whose words are included in Sikh scripture, described this state of spiritual bliss:

> *The blue sky opens out farther and farther,*
> *the daily sense of failure goes away,*
> *the damage I have done to myself fades,*
> *a million suns come forward with light,*
> *when I sit firmly in that world.*[10]

Some people feel that their true selves are part of that world of light, dimly remembered, and long to return to it. The nineteenth-century Romantic poet William Wordsworth wrote:

> *Our birth is but a sleep and a forgetting;*
> *The Soul that rises with us, our life's Star*
> *   Hath had elsewhere its setting*
> *   And cometh from afar;*
> *   Not in entire forgetfulness,*
> *   And not in utter nakedness,*
> *But trailing clouds of glory do we come*
> *   From God, who is our home.*[11]

When we encounter nature in all its original beauty, or humans acting in pure love, we may be struck by another religious impulse — appreciation for this extraordinary creation. Ray Fadden, an elder of the Mohawk Nation, speaks of the native spiritual traditions as the "thank-you religion." For those who honor the miracles seen in all created beings, each day is begun in gratitude. Brother David Steindl-Rast observes that gratitude is the basis of the spiritual life. Religions teach us that there is a "someone" or "something" to thank for all of this. The Christian St. Francis of Assisi offered a beautiful Canticle to God for all creation:

> *... Be praised, my Lord, with all your created things. Be praised, brother Sun, who brings the day and gives us light. He is fair and radiant with shining face and he draws his meaning from on high.*

> *Be praised, my Lord, for sister moon and the stars in the heavens. You have made them clear and precious and lovely.*

Storm system north of
Hawaii, as seen from the
Apollo 9 spaceflight,
March 1969.

*Praised be my Lord for our brother Wind, and for the air and the clouds and calm
days and every kind of weather, by which you give your creatures nourishment.*

*Praised be my Lord for our sister Water, which is very helpful and humble, precious
and pure.*

*Praised be my Lord for our brother Fire, by which you light up the darkness; he is
fair, bright and strong.*

*Praised be my Lord for our sister, Mother Earth, for she sustains and keeps us and
brings forth all kinds of fruits together with grasses and bright flowers.*

*Praised be my Lord for our sister, bodily death, from which no living person can flee,
praised be my Lord for all your creatures. We give you thanks. ...*[12]

Behind the miracle of creation, there may be an intelligence. Some of us want
to know who or what it is. We look to religions for understanding, for answers to
our many questions about life. Who are we? Why are we here? What happens
after we die? Why is there suffering? Why is there evil? Is anybody up there
listening? For those who find security in specific answers, some religions offer
dogma – systems of doctrines proclaimed as absolutely true and accepted as such,
even if they lie beyond the domain of one's personal experiences. Absolute faith
provides some people with a sense of relief from anxieties, a secure feeling of
rootedness, meaning and orderliness in the midst of rapid social change. Religions
may also provide rules for living, governing everything from diet to personal
relationships. Such prescriptions are seen as earthly reflections of the order that
prevails in the cosmos. Some religions, however, encourage people to explore the
perennial questions by themselves, and to live in the uncertainties of not-knowing
intellectually, always breaking through old concepts until nothing remains but
truth itself.

A final need that draws some people to religion is the discomforting sense of
being alone in the universe. This isolation can be painful, even terrifying. The divine

The existential loneliness some feel is hauntingly depicted by the sculptures of Alberto Giacometti, such as his Walking Man, *c. 1947–48.*

may be sought as a loving father or mother, or as a friend. Alternatively, some paths offer the way of self-transcendence. Through them, the sense of isolation is lost in mystical merger with the One Being, with Reality itself.

Realities beyond the visible world

Religion therefore may be embraced because of personal needs — such as longings for immortality, meaningfulness, perfection, personal growth, escape from problems, happiness, peace, understanding, and order, or the sense of gratitude or isolation. But the faithful would deny that the supernatural is simply a wishful projection of these needs. Either they have directly experienced a greater reality or they believe the words of a teacher who has done so. As we shall see, even Western science, long a bastion of religious scepticism, is now confirming that there is far more to life than the material world that we can touch and see with our normal senses.

MYSTICAL ENCOUNTERS WITH THE SACRED   Religious belief often springs from mystical experience — the overwhelming awareness that one has been touched by a reality that far transcends ordinary life. Those who have had such experiences find it hard to describe them, for what has touched them lies beyond the world of time and space to which our languages refer. These people usually know instantly

> *… the things which are seen are temporal; but the things which are not seen are eternal.*
>
> *II Corinthians 4:18*

and beyond a shadow of doubt that they have had a brush with spiritual reality. Teilhard de Chardin, a highly respected French paleontologist and Jesuit priest, became convinced that God is "the heart of All" because of his fiery personal encounters with "the unique Life of all things."[13] George William Russell, an Irish writer who described his mystical experiences under the pen name "AE," was lying on a hillside:

> *not then thinking of anything but the sunlight, and how sweet it was to drowse there, when, suddenly, I felt a fiery heart throb, and knew it was personal and intimate, and started with every sense dilated and intent, and turned inwards, and I heard first a music as of bells going away … and then the heart of the hills was opened to me, and I knew there was no hill for those who were there, and they were unconscious of the ponderous mountain piled above the palaces of light, and the winds were sparkling and diamond clear, yet full of colour as an opal, as they glittered through the valley, and I knew the Golden Age was all about me, and it was we who had been blind to it but that it had never passed away from the world.[14]*

Encounters with a transcendent reality are given various names in spiritual traditions: enlightenment, God-realization, illumination, kensho, awakening, self-knowledge, gnosis, ecstatic communion, coming home. They may arise spontaneously, as in near-death experiences in which people seem to find themselves in a world of unearthly radiance, or may be induced by meditation, fasting, prayer, chanting, drugs, or dancing.

A sense of the presence of the Great Unnamable may burst through the seeming ordinariness of life. (Samuel Palmer, The Waterfalls, Pistil Mawddach, North Wales, 1835–36.)

[The "flash of illumination" brings] a state of glorious inspiration, exaltation, intense joy, a piercingly sweet realization that the whole of life is fundamentally right and that it knows what it's doing.

Nona Coxhead[15]

There are degrees of realization, just as there seem to be many levels of consciousness. In his classic study, *The Varieties of Religious Experience*, William James concluded:

Our normal waking consciousness, rational consciousness as we call it, is but one special type of consciousness, whilst all about it, parted from it by the flimsiest of screens, there lie potential forms of consciousness entirely different …

No account of the universe in its totality can be final which leaves these other forms of consciousness quite disregarded.[16]

Science, religion, and the new understanding

Like religion, science searches for universal principles that explain the facts of nature. Actually, the distinction made today between science and religion was less clear cut in ancient times. In both Eastern and Western cultures, there was a universal attempt to seek to understand Reality as a whole.

In ancient Greece, source of many "Western" ideas, a group of thinkers who are sometimes called "nature philosophers" tried to understand the world through their own perceptions of it. By contrast, Plato distrusted the testimony of the human senses. He thus made a series of distinctions: between what is perceived by the senses and what is accessible through reason, between body and soul, appearance and reality, objects and ideas. In Plato's thought, the soul was superior to the body, and the activity of reason preferable to the distraction of the senses. This value judgment dominated Western thought through the Middle Ages, with an underlying belief that all of Nature had been created by God for the sake of humanity's salvation.

With the Renaissance of fourteenth- to sixteenth-century Europe, science and religion parted ways in Western thought. A new conception of the universe as a vast set of facts that no one planned with any end in view came to be readily accepted. Renaissance thinkers were confident that physical observation and mathematical analysis would yield all the principles of nature, and that scientific instruments revealed the whole truth about the universe. Since microscopes and telescopes did not reveal God or souls or immortality, these were all dismissed as subjective fancy. The success of physics and Isaac Newton's genius in explaining the operation of matter in motion encouraged people to believe that the world itself was like a massive machine.

During the eighteenth-century Enlightenment, the Deists allowed for the possibility that the world might have been created by God, but dispensed with any plausible role for the Divine in the operation of the material universe or in human history. Then in mid-nineteenth century, the naturalist Charles Darwin developed the theory of gradual evolution by survival of the fittest, contradicting a literal reading of the Judeo-Christian biblical book of Genesis, in which God is depicted as creating, from the void, heaven and earth and all plants and creatures thereon in six "days." By the end of the century, all Western values linked to the Judeo-Christian tradition were being questioned, and Neitzsche, the German philosopher, proclaimed, "God is dead!"

To some scientists, the perfection of features that make it possible for a bird to fly suggests the existence of an unseen organizing force or Creator.

At the dawn of the twenty-first century, religious dogmatism is increasing in some quarters, but it seems that scientific dogmatism is on the wane. Many scientists have come to the conclusion that "scientific truth" in any area of research is at best only finite, relative, and limited to the narrow range of human perception and understanding. We can see only a narrow group of electromagnetic energies, for instance. Scientific instruments extend the limits of human perception, but scientists acknowledge that more lies beyond what we have been able to measure.

This realization of the inadequacy of empirical inquiry came long ago in Eastern religious traditions. They recognized the value of perception and reason for the acquisition of ordinary, utilitarian knowledge, but discounted their use for the acquisition of transcendent knowledge of the mystery of Being. This mystery, they hold, can be apprehended only through spiritual experience.

Science is limited in its questions as well as its answers. As Professor Anand Mohan of The City University of New York explains,

> *No matter how ably and diligently the exploration of the universe around us is undertaken by science, one core issue will always retain its centrality. And it is this: The systematic search for descriptive facts, measurement of data, and quantitative analysis, which constitute the tools of empirical science, rule out, by definition, the consideration of all qualitative aspects, such as meaning, value, and purpose in nature as well as in human life. These, precisely, are the questions that have remained traditionally in the realm of religion.*[17]

Biologists find that the natural world is an intricate harmony of beautifully elaborated, interrelated parts. Scientists are struck with wonder as they push their research into previously unknown realms. They have found, for instance, that stars could never have formed if the force of gravity were ever so slightly stronger or weaker. The geneticist Lucien Cuenot points out that "birds that fly can do so because a thousand details converge: long wing and tail feathers, pneumatic bones, air sacs, breast bone and pectoral muscles, design of the ribs, neck, feet, spinal column, pelvis, automatic hooking of feather barbules, etc."[18] The question arises: Can the convergence of so many characteristics be the consequence of chance arrangements of atoms, or is it the result of deliberate design by some First Cause? After surveying the intelligence that seems to pervade the organic world, biologists Robert Augros and George Stanciu conclude:

> *Nature wastes neither function nor structure. She provides all the equipment needed for each organism to live but does not burden it with useless organs … Every cell, every tissue, every organ serves a purpose. Every animal, every plant directs its activities to an end. The whole of nature is ordered by purpose.*[19]

Transformation of the scientific point of view is particularly striking in twentieth-century quantum physics. In place of a machine-like universe separate from the human observer, those probing the world of subatomic particles have found that their behaviors can only be described in terms of a dynamic, interdependent whole. Furthermore, what we perceive with our five senses is not ultimate reality. For instance, the inertness and solidity of matter are only illusions. Each atom consists mostly of empty space with tiny particles whirling around in it. These subatomic particles — such as neutrons, protons, and electrons — cannot even be described as "things." In experiments they behave like energy as well as like mass, wavelike interconnections as well as separate particles. They have no precise location and may be found in several places at one time. And the interconnections do not exist separately from the mind of the person who is observing them. Human consciousness is inextricably involved in what it thinks it is watching. As physicist David Bohm puts it: "Everything interpenetrates everything."[20]

Conventional notions of matter are now being discarded by scientists. Students were traditionally taught that all matter takes one of three distinct forms: solid, liquid, or gas. But in 1985, scientists created a bizarre type of matter, the "Bose-Einstein condensate," in which the point where one atom ends and another begins is lost, so that they form a cloud.

Numerous scientifically unorthodox, but spiritually possible, explanations of the universe are now being proposed by highly respected scientists. Quantum physicist David Bohm suggests that the universe is multi-dimensional. The dimension we see and think of as "real" is the *explicate* order, but behind it lies the *implicate* order, in which separateness resolves into unbroken wholeness. Beyond may lie other subtle dimensions, all merging into an infinite ground that unfolds itself as light.

The world is not as it appears to be on the surface. Our bodies appear relatively solid, but they are in a constant state of flux and interchange with the environment. Our eyes, ears, noses, tongues, and skin do not reveal absolute truths. Rather, our sensory organs may operate as filters, selecting from a multi-dimensional universe only those characteristics that we need to perceive in order to survive. Imagine how difficult it would be simply to walk across a street if we could see all the electromagnetic energy in the atmosphere, such as X-rays, radio waves, gamma rays, and infrared and ultraviolet light, rather than only the small band we see as the colors of the visible spectrum. Scientific devices can perceive a greater range of energies, but we know that more lies beyond what we have yet been able to measure. And even our ability to conceive of what we cannot sense is limited by the way our brain is organized. To accept the possibility, if not the certainty, that ultimate reality lies beyond the scope of our empirical experience or rational thought is no longer considered unscientific.

> The most beautiful and profound emotion that we can experience is the sensation of the mystical. It is the sower of all true science. He to whom this emotion is a stranger, who can no longer wonder and stand rapt in awe, is as good as dead. To know that what is impenetrable to us really exists, manifesting itself as the highest wisdom and the most radiant beauty which our dull faculties can comprehend only in their most primitive forms — this knowledge, this feeling is at the center of true religiousness.... A human being is part of the whole.... He experiences himself, his thoughts and feelings as something separated from the rest — a kind of optical delusion of his consciousness.... Our task must be to free ourselves from this prison by widening our circle of compassion to embrace all living creatures, and the whole [of] nature in its beauty.
>
> *Albert Einstein*[21]

Modes of encountering Ultimate Reality

We have two basic ways of knowing what is: rational thought and direct intuition. To reason is to establish abstract general categories from the data we have gathered with our senses, and then organize these abstractions to formulate seemingly logical ideas about reality. Reason may lead different people to different conclusions, however. The seventeenth-century English rationalist philosopher, Thomas Hobbes, reasoned that God is simply an idea constructed by the human imagination from ideas of the visible world. His contemporary, the rationalist French philosopher, René Descartes, asserted that his awareness of his own existence and his internal reasoning were proofs of the existence of God.

Some people come to religious convictions through unquestioning belief in what has been uttered by great religious figures or what has been established as doctrine by religious tradition. The Prophet Muhammad was instructed by divine revelation to say, "I believe in whatever Book Allah has sent down,"[22] including not only the Holy Qur'an but also the revelations given through previous messengers in the Judeo-Christian tradition, such as Jesus and Moses.

Other people develop faith only after their own questions have been answered. Martin Luther, father of the Protestant branches of Christianity, says he searched for faith in God through storms of doubt, "raged with a fierce and agitated conscience."[23]

In some religions, people are encouraged to develop their own intuitive abilities to perceive spiritual truths directly, beyond the senses, beyond the limits of human reason, beyond blind belief. This way is often called **mysticism**, from the Greek word for rejoining the two sides of a wound, because a person may thus be reunited with the underlying Reality. In the ancient Upanishads (teachings given by great Indian masters of meditation to their students), the pupils are urged to sit in deep meditation and, with mind fully absorbed in love, direct their consciousness like an arrow toward the target, the eternal One. In indigenous traditions, people may be taught to undergo austerities and then cry out for a sacred vision from the unseen to help guide their actions.

Many religions have developed meditation techniques that encourage intuitive wisdom to rise from the depths — or the voice of the divine to descend into individual consciousness. Whether this wisdom is perceived as a natural faculty within or an external voice, the process is similar. The consciousness is initially turned away from the world and even from one's own feelings and thoughts, letting them all go. Often a concentration practice, such as watching the breath or staring at a candle flame, is used to collect the awareness into a single unfragmented focus. Once the mind is quiet, distinctions between inside and outside drop away. The seer becomes one with the seen, in a fusion of subject and object where the inner nature of things often seems to reveal itself.

Our ordinary experience of the world is that our self is separate from the world of objects which we perceive. But this dualistic understanding may be transcended in a moment of enlightenment in which the Real and our awareness of it become one. The Mundaka Upanishad says, "Lose thyself in the Eternal, even as the arrow is lost in the target." For the Hindu, this is the prized attainment of *moksha*, or liberation, in which one enters into awareness of the eternal reality known as Brahman. This Reality is then known with the same direct apprehension with

which one knows oneself. The Sufi Muslim mystic Abu Yazid said, "I sloughed off my self as a snake sloughs off its skin, and I looked into my essence and saw that 'I am He.' "[24]

This enlightened awareness cannot be communicated to those who have not had a similar experience, although our sacred literature is full of attempts to do so. Neither human language nor human logic, both of which deal with the experience of a world of separate forms, is adequate to describe the unitary experience of Ultimate Reality.

Understandings of the Ultimate Reality

Approached by different ways of knowing, by different people, from different times and different cultures, the sacred has many faces. The Ultimate Reality may be conceived as **immanent** (present in the world) or **transcendent** (existing above and outside of the material universe). Many people perceive the sacred as a personal Being, as Father, Mother, Teacher, Friend, Beloved, or as a specific Deity. Religions based on one's relationship to the divine Being are called **theistic**. If the Being is worshipped as a singular form, the religion is **monotheistic**. If many attributes and forms of the Divine are emphasized, the religion may be labeled **polytheistic**.

Some people believe that the sacred reality is usually invisible but occasionally appears visibly in human **incarnations**, such as Christ or Krishna, or in special manifestations such as the flame Moses reportedly saw coming from the center of a bush but not consuming it. Or the deity which cannot be seen is described in human terms. Theologican Sallie McFague thus writes of God as Lover by imputing human feelings to God:

> God as lover is the one who loves the world not with the fingertips but totally and passionately, taking pleasure in its variety and richness, finding it attractive and valuable, delighting in its fulfilment. God as lover is the moving power of love in the universe, the desire for unity with all the beloved.[25]

Throughout history, there have been religious authorities who have claimed that the deity they worship is the true one and that all others are worshipping false gods. They have labeled others as "pagans" or "nonbelievers." For their part, the others apply similar negative epithets to them. When these rigid positions are taken, often to the point of violent conflicts or forced conversions, there is no room to consider the possibility that all may be talking about the same indescribable thing in different language or referring to different aspects of the same unknowable Whole.

Atheism is the non-belief in any deity. Following Karl Marx, many communist countries in the twentieth century discouraged or suppressed religious beliefs, attempting to replace them with secular faith in supposedly altruistic government. The distinguished Protestant theologian Reinhold Neibuhr described atheistic communism as "an irreligion transmuted into a new political religion, canonized precisely in the writings of Marx (and the later Lenin) as sacred scripture" with Marx cast as "the revered prophet of a new world religion."[26] It was not uncommon for people of all faiths in all continents of the world to embrace as a new religion of sorts Marx's message of collectivism in contrast to the dehumanizing effects of

Opposite *Many religions use ritual cleansing with water to help remove inner filth that obscures awareness or Ultimate Reality.*

modern industry and capitalism, and with it, his stinging criticism of oppression of the people in the name of religion.

Atheism may also arise from within, in those whose experiences give them no reason to believe that there is anything more to life than the mundane. One American college student articulates a common modern form of unwilling atheism:

> *To be a citizen of the modern, industrialized world with its scientific worldview is to be, to a certain extent, an atheist. I myself do not want to be an atheist; the cold mechanical worldview is repugnant to my need for the warmth and meaning that comes from God. But as I have been educated in the secular, scientistic educational system — where God is absent but atoms and molecules and genes and cells and presidents and kings are the factors to be reckoned with, the powers of this world, not a divine plan or a divine force as my ancestors must have believed — I cannot wholly believe in God.*
>
> *If I want to find God I have got to go looking for him (or her) in books or nature or within, but never on TV, in the schools, in the shopping malls — in short nowhere in the mainstream. To the extent that this mainstream attitude, which is Godless, is reiterated to my mind over and over again, day after day, the part of me that is atheistic is reinforced.*[27]

Agnosticism is not the denial of the divine but the belief that if it exists it is impossible for humans to know it. Ultimate reality may, on the other hand, be conceived in **nontheistic** terms. It may be experienced as a "changeless Unity," as "Suchness," or simply as "the Way." There may be no sense of a personal Creator God in such understandings.

These categories are not mutually exclusive, so attempts to apply the labels can sometimes confuse us rather than help us understand religions. In some "polytheistic" traditions there is a hierarchy of gods and goddesses with one highest being at the top. In Hinduism, each individual deity is understood as an embodiment of all aspects of the divine. In the paradoxes that occur when we try to apply human logic and language to that which transcends linear thought, a person may believe that God is both a highly personal being and also present in all things. Or mystics may have deep personal encounters with the divine and yet find it so unspeakable that they say it is beyond human knowing. The eleventh-century Jewish scholar Maimonides asserted that:

> *…the human mind cannot comprehend God. Only God can know Himself. The only form of comprehension of God we can have is to realize how futile it is to try to comprehend Him.*[28]

Jaap Sahib, the great hymn of praises of God by the Tenth Sikh Guru, Guru Gobind Singh, consists largely of the negative attributes of God, such as these:

> *Salutations to the One without colour or hue,*
> *Salutations to the One who hath no beginning.*
> *Salutations to the Impenetrable,*
> *Salutations to the Unfathomable …*
> *O Lord, Thou art Formless and Peerless*
> *Beyond birth and physical elements.*

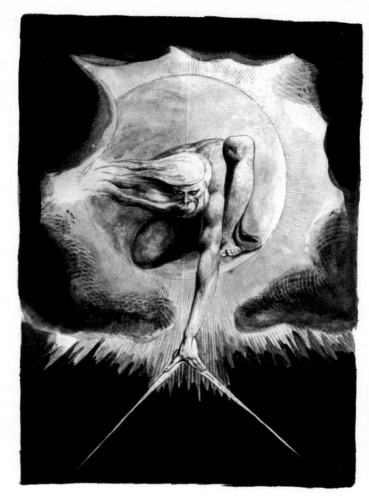

The concept of God as an old man with a beard who rules the world from the sky has been supported by the art of patriarchal monotheistic traditions, such as William Blake's frontispiece to "Europe," The Act of Creation, *1794.*

Beyond description and Garbless
Thou art Nameless and Desireless.
Thou art beyond thought and ever Mysterious.
Thou art Unconquerable and Fearless.[29]

Some people believe that the aspect of the divine that has revealed itself to them is the only one. Others feel that there is one being with many faces, that all religions come from one source. Father Bede Griffiths, a Catholic monk who lived in a community in India that attempts to unite Eastern and Western traditions, was among those who feel that if we engage in a deep study of all religions we will find their common ground:

In each tradition the one divine Reality, the one eternal Truth, is present, but it is hidden under symbols.... Always the divine Mystery is hidden under a veil, but each revelation (or "unveiling") unveils some aspect of the one Truth, or, if you like, the veil becomes thinner at a certain point. The Semitic religions, Judaism and Islam, reveal the transcendent aspect of the divine Mystery with incomparable power. The oriental religions reveal the divine Immanence with immeasurable depth. Yet in each the opposite aspect is contained, though in a more hidden way.[30]

Worship and symbol

No matter how believers conceive of the Ultimate Reality, its greatness inspires their reverence. The outer forms of religions consist in large part of human attempts to express this reverence and perhaps enter the sacred state of communion with that which is worshipped. Around the world, rituals, sacraments, prayers, and spiritual practices are used to create a sacred atmosphere or state of consciousness in which people hope to touch or be touched by whispers of the eternal.

Our religious ceremonies are but the shadows of that great universal worship celebrated in the heavens by the legions of heavenly beings on all planes, and our prayers drill a channel across this mist separating our earthbound plane from the celestial ones through which a communication may be established with the powers that be.

Pir Vilayat Inayat Khan[31]

Group ceremonies often include sharing of food, fire or candles, purification with water, flowers, fragrances, and offerings of some sort. All have inner meanings. In reference to offerings, for instance, Professor Antony Fernando of Sri Lanka explains,

Even the most illiterate person knows that in actual fact no god really picks up those offerings or is actually in need of them. What people offer is what they own. Whatever is owned becomes so close to the heart of the owner as to become an almost integral part of his or her life. Therefore, when people offer something, it is, as it were, themselves they offer. People offer themselves because they know that the general tendency they have of "owning" themselves is based on a wrong understanding of life. Nobody can really own anything — material goods, spouse and children, or even one's own breath. Sacrifices and offerings are a dramatic way of proclaiming that they are not the ultimate possessors of their life and also of articulating their determination to live duty-oriented lives and not desire-oriented lives.[32]

That which religions attempt to approach is beyond human utterance. Believers build statues and buildings through which to worship the divine, but these forms are not it. Because people are addressing the invisible, it can only be suggested through metaphor. Deepest consciousness cannot speak the language of everyday life; what it knows can only be suggested in images.

Many peoples have used similar images to represent similar sacred meanings. The sun is frequently honored as a symbol of the divine because of its radiance; the sky is the abode of many gods, for it is elevated above the earth. Great spiritual leaders are often said to have been born of virgin mothers, for their seminal source is not human but rather the Invisible One.

It is now common to interpret such symbols metaphorically rather than literally and to see them as serving functions for the society or the individual. For example, Joseph Campbell speculated that the sacred myths of a group serve basic social purposes: awakening a sense of wonder at creation, incorporating the group's ethical codes, and helping individuals pass harmoniously through life-cycle changes. Following psychoanalyst Carl Jung's lead, Campbell interpreted legends of the hero's journey (stories of separation, initiation, and return bearing truth to the people) as a form of psychological instruction for individuals:

> It is the business of mythology to reveal the specific dangers and techniques of the dark interior way from tragedy to comedy. Hence the incidents are fantastic and "unreal": they represent psychological, not physical, triumphs. The passage of the mythological hero may be overground, [but] fundamentally it is inward — into depths where obscure resistances are overcome, and long lost, forgotten powers are revivified, to be made available for the transfiguration of the world.[33]

On the other hand, scholars have sometimes interpreted metaphorically that which believers find literally true. Indigenous medicine people experience their spirit allies as real, albeit often invisible. When we encounter the symbols of unfamiliar religions we may find them strange or unpleasant unless we can enter into the mystical truths they embody, empathize with those who believe in them, or develop an intellectual understanding of their metaphorical content.

An early image of what appears to be the Great Mother, creator and sustainer of the universe. (Tel Halaf, 5th millennium BCE.)

Women and the feminine in religions

Many of the myths surviving in today's religions may be related to the suppression of early female-oriented religions by later male-oriented religious systems. Archaeological evidence from many cultures has recently been re-interpreted, suggesting that worship of a female high Goddess was originally widespread. Although there were, and are now, cultures that did not ascribe gender or hierarchy or personality to the divine, some that did may have seen the highest deity as a female.

Just as today's male high deity goes by different names in different religions (God, Allah), the Great Goddess had many names. Among her many identities, she was Danu or Diti in ancient India, the Great Mother Nu Kwa of China, the Egyptian Cobra Goddess Ua Zit, the Greek Creator Goddess Gaia, the Sun Goddess Arinna of Turkey, Coatlique the Mother of Aztec deities, Queen Mother Freyja of the Scandinavians, Great Spider Woman of the Pueblo peoples of North America, and Mawu, omnipotent creator of the Dahomey. A reverent address to Ishtar, supreme deity of ancient Babylon, dating from the eighteenth to seventh centuries BCE suggests some of the powers ascribed to her:

> Unto Her who renders decision, Goddess of all things. Unto the Lady of Heaven and Earth who receives supplication; Unto Her who hears petition, who entertains prayer; Unto the compassionate Goddess who loves righteousness; Ishtar the Queen, who suppresses all that is confused. To the Queen of Heaven, the Goddess of the Universe, the One who walked in terrible Chaos and brought life by the Law of Love; And out of Chaos brought us harmony.[34]

Temples and images that seem to have been devoted to worship of the Goddess have been found in almost every Neolithic and early historic archaeological site in Europe and the Near and Middle East. She was often symbolically linked with water, serpents, birds, eggs, spirals, the moon, the womb, the vulva, the magnetic currents of the earth, psychic powers, and the eternal creation and renewal of life.

Some who worshipped her claimed knowledge about techniques of spiritual rebirth and illumination — or raising the lower earth energy represented by the serpent up the spine into the wings of higher spiritual knowledge and ecstatic communion with life. Sexuality was often a part of this process, with ritual intercourse honored as a means of accessing spiritual energies.

In these agricultural cultures that may have worshipped the Goddess, women frequently held strong social positions. Hereditary lineages were often traced through the mother, and women were honored as priestesses, healers, agricultural inventors, counselors, prophetesses, and sometimes warriors.

What happened to these apparently Goddess-oriented religions? Contemporary scholars are now trying to piece together not only the reality, extent, and characteristics of Goddess worship, but also the circumstances of its demise. A recent cross-cultural survey by Eli Sagan *(The Dawn of Tyranny)* indicates that male-dominant social and religious structures accompanied the often violent shift from communal kinship groups and tribal confederations to centralized monarchies. In these kingdoms, social order was based on loyalty to the king and fear of his power. In Europe and the Middle East worship of the Goddess was suppressed by invading Indo-European groups (most probably from the steppes of southern Russia) in which males were dominant and championed worship of a supreme male deity. These conquests took place throughout the third and second millennia BCE with the help of horse-drawn chariots, a more devastating war technology than any previously used.

The Indo-Europeans' deity was often described as a storm god residing on a mountain and bringing light (seen as the good) into the darkness (portrayed as bad and associated with the female). Mythical accounts of the struggle between this male god and the female goddess for supremacy often involve a male god grappling with a serpent or dragon, as in the early Hebrew myth of Yahweh's defeat of the serpent Leviathan (an alternative name for Lotan, the Goddess of Canaan). In India, the Aryan god Indra, "he who overthrows cities," kills the Mother Goddess Danu and her son, who are described in the Vedic scriptures of the invaders as serpents and then as a dead cow and her calf.

In some cases, worship of the Goddess co-existed with or later surfaced within male deity worship. In India, the new gods often had powerful female consorts or counterparts or were androgynous, both male and female.

Durga, represented as a beautiful woman riding a lion, is worshipped as the blazing splendor and power of the Godhead. In Christianity, some scholars feel that devotion to Mary, Mother of Jesus, is in some ways a substitute for earlier worship of the Goddess.

Nevertheless, as worship of the Goddess was suppressed, so was spiritual participation of women. In patriarchal societies, women often became property and were expected to be obedient to the rule of men. Although Christ had honored and worked with women, his later male followers limited the position of women within the Christian church.

Not only was women's spiritual contribution cast aside; in replacing the Goddess, patriarchal groups may also have devalued the "feminine" aspect of religion — the receptive, intuitive, ecstatic mystical communion which was seemingly allowed freer reign in the goddess traditions. Fears of the force latent in the unconscious, unknown, and uncontrolled aspects of the psyche led to witch hunts, in which

In Hindu tradition, the great goddess Durga (left) is understood as the active principle that can vanquish the demonic forces. She carries symbols of the cosmic energies of other aspects of the Divine (Durga slaying the Buffalo Demon, India, c. 1760).

women were the major victims, and to a distrust of mystics of both sexes who dared to reveal their ecstatic and personal relationship with the divine.

Although women are still barred from equal spiritual footing with men in many religions, this situation is now being widely challenged. As we explore specific religions throughout this book, we will look at the position of women and any changes that seem to be taking place. Feminist Christian theologian Rosemary Ruether feels that the movement toward greater religious participation by women may transcend gender issues to heal other fragmentations in our spiritual lives:

> *The feminist religious revolution ... reaches forward to an alternative that can heal the splits between "masculine" and "feminine," between mind and body, between males and females as gender groups, between society and nature, and between races and classes.*[35]

Fundamentalist and liberal interpretations

Within each faith people often have different ways of interpreting their traditions. The labels given to these modes of interpretation are often burdened by negative judgments, but the labels themselves are neutral and descriptive rather than judgmental.

The **orthodox** stand by an historical form of their religion. They try to be strict followers of its established practices, laws, and creeds. **Fundamentalists** are in general those who try to resist contemporary influences and affirm what they perceive as the historical core of their religion. In our times, many people feel that their distinctive identity as individuals or as members of an established group is threatened by the sweeping social changes brought by modern industrial culture.

The breakup of family relationships, loss of geographic rootedness, decay of clear behavioral codes, and loss of local control may be very unsettling. To find stable footing, some people may try to stand on selected religious doctrines or practices from the past. Religious leaders may encourage this trend toward rigidity by declaring themselves absolute authorities or by telling the people that their scriptures are literally and absolutely true. They may encourage antipathy or even violence against people of other religious traditions.

The term "fundamentalism" is often applied to this selective insistence on parts of a religious tradition and to violence against people of other religions. This use of the term is misleading, for no religion is based on hatred of other people, and because those who are labeled "fundamentalists" may not be engaged in a return to the true basics of their religion. A Muslim "fundamentalist" who insists on the veiling of women, for instance, does not draw this doctrine from the foundation of Islam, the Hoy Qur'an, but rather from historical cultural practice in some Muslim countries. A Sikh "fundamentalist" who concentrates on externals such as wearing a turban, sword, and steel bracelet overlooks the central insistence of the Sikh Gurus on the inner rather than outer practice of religion. A Hindu "fundamentalist" who objects to the presence of Christian missionaries working among the poor ignores one of the basic principles of ancient Indian religion, which is the tolerant assertion that there are many paths to the same universal Truth. Rev. Valson Thampu, editor of the Indian journal *Traci*, writes that this selective type of religious fundamentalism "absolutises what is spiritually or ethically superfluous in a religious tradition. True spiritual enthusiasm or zeal, on the other hand, stakes everything on being faithful to the spiritual essence."[36]

Those who are called religious **liberals** take a more flexible approach to religious tradition. They may see scriptures as products of a specific culture and time rather than the eternal voice of truth, and may interpret passages metaphorically rather than literally. If activists, they may advocate reforms in the ways their religion is officially understood and practiced. Those who are labeled **heretics** publicly assert controversial positions that are unacceptable to the orthodox establishment. **Mystics** are guided by their own spiritual experiences, which may coincide with any of the above positions, from fundamentalist understandings to heresy.

The negative side of organized religion

Tragically, religions have often split rather than unified humanity, have oppressed rather than freed, have terrified rather than inspired.

Since the human needs that religions answer are so strong, those who hold religious power are in a position to dominate and control their followers. In fact, in many religions leaders are given this legitimized authority to guide people's spiritual lives, for their wisdom and special access to the sacred is valued. Because religions involve the unseen, the mysterious, these leaders' guidance may not be verifiable by everyday physical experience. It must more often be accepted on faith. While faith is one of the cornerstones of spirituality, it is possible to surrender to spiritual leaders who are misguided or unethical. Religious leaders, like secular leaders, may not be honest with themselves and others about their inner motives. They may mistake their own thoughts and desires for the voice and will of God.

Angels Weep

Wherever there is slaughter of innocent men, women, and children for the mere reason that they belong to another race, color, or nationality, or were born into a faith which the majority of them could never quite comprehend and hardly ever practice in its true spirit; wherever the fair name of religion is used as a veneer to hide overweening political ambition and bottomless greed, wherever the glory of Allah is sought to be proclaimed through the barrel of a gun; wherever piety becomes synonymous with rapacity, and morality cowers under the blight of expediency and compromise, wherever it be — in Yugoslavia or Algeria, in Liberia, Chad, or the beautiful land of the Sudan, in Los Angeles or Abuija, in Kashmir or Conakary, in Colombo or Cotabatu — there God is banished and Satan is triumphant, there the angels weep and the soul of man cringes; there in the name of God humans are dehumanized; and there the grace and beauty of life lie ravished and undone.[37]

Dr. Syed Z. Abedin, Director of the Institute for Muslim Minority Affairs

Some people believe, however, that the most important thing for the disciple is to surrender the ego; even an unworthy leader can help in this goal simply by playing the role of one to whom one must surrender personal control.

Because religions paint pictures of life after death, they may play on people's fear of death or fears of punishment, both here and hereafter. This excerpt from a sermon by the New England Calvinist minister Jonathan Edwards illustrates the terrifying images that can be conjured:

> You are thus [sinners] in the hands of an angry God; 'tis nothing but his mere pleasure that keeps you from being this moment swallowed up in everlasting destruction. The God that holds you over the pit of hell, much as one holds a spider or some loathsome insect over the fire, abhors you, and is dreadfully provoked; his wrath towards you burns like fire; he looks upon you as worthy of nothing else, but to be cast into the fire.[38]

Religions try to help us make ethical choices in our lives, to develop a moral conscience. But in people who already have perfectionist or paranoid tendencies, the fear of sinning and being punished can be exaggerated to the point of neurosis or even psychosis by blaming, punishment-oriented religious teachings. If they try to leave their religion for the sake of their mental health, they may be haunted with guilt that they have done a terribly wrong thing. Religions thus have the potential for wreaking psychological havoc in their followers.

Because some religions, particularly those that developed in the East, offer a state of blissful contemplation as the reward for spiritual practice, the faithful may use religion to escape from their everyday problems. Psychologist John Welwood observes that Westerners sometimes embrace Eastern religions with the unconscious motive of avoiding their unsatisfactory lives. He calls this attempt "spiritual bypassing":

Spiritual bypassing may be particularly tempting for individuals who are having difficulty making their way through life's basic developmental stages, especially at a time when what were once ordinary developmental landmarks — earning a livelihood through dignified work, raising a family, keeping a marriage together — have become increasingly difficult and elusive for large segments of the population. While struggling with becoming autonomous individuals, many people are introduced to spiritual teachings and practices which come from cultures that assume a person having already passed through the basic developmental stages.[39]

Because religions may have such a strong hold on their followers — by their fears, their desires, their deep beliefs — they are potential centers for political power. When church and state are one, the belief that the dominant national religion is the only true religion may be used to oppress those of other beliefs within the country. As the 1991 World Conference of Religions in Kochi, India, concluded:

We found that interpretation of religious teachings has often been used to support social injustices, such as the oppression of women, racial oppression, human rights abuses, genocide, and marginalization of the poor. Religion has been misused to manipulate, exploit and divide people, rather than to draw us into compassionate unity.[40]

Religion may also be used as a rallying point for wars against other nations, casting the desire for control as a holy motive. Throughout history, huge numbers of people have been killed in the name of eradicating "false" religions and replacing them with the "true" religion. Our spirituality has the potential for uniting us all in bonds of love, harmony, and mutual respect. But often it has served instead to divide us by creating barriers of hatred and intolerance.

Because institutionalized religions attempt to follow the teachings of their founders, there is also the danger that more energy will go into preserving the outer form of the tradition than into maintaining its inner spirit. The living nature of any spiritual path can only be experienced. It cannot be solidified into dogma. If rituals are carried out without genuine inner experience, they become empty shells.

No religion is free from these distortions. To keep religion alive, true, and vibrant requires a genuine connection with the unseen, scrupulous honesty, and pure-heartedness. As we survey the various contemporary manifestations of the religious impulse, we will find people and groups who are keeping the spark of the divine alive today. They can be found in all traditions.

Suggested reading

Campbell, Joseph, *The Hero with a Thousand Faces*, second edition, Princeton, New Jersey: Princeton University Press, 1968. Brilliant leaps across time and space to trace the hero's journey — seen as a spiritual quest — in all the world's mythologies and religions.

Campbell, Joseph with Bill Moyers, *The Power of Myth*, New York: Doubleday, 1988. More brilliant comparisons of the world's mythologies with deep insights into their common psychological and spiritual truths.

Capra, Fritjof, *The Tao of Physics*, New York: Bantam Books, 1977, and London: Fontana, 1983. A fascinating comparison of the insights of Eastern religions and contemporary physics.

Carter, Robert E., ed., *God, The Self, and Nothingness — Reflections: Eastern and Western*, New York: Paragon House, 1990. Essays from major Eastern and Western scholars of religion on variant ways of experiencing and describing Ultimate Reality.

Eliade, Mircea, *The Sacred and the Profane*, translated by William R. Trask, New York: Harper and Row, 1959. Encompassing all religions, a study of religious myth, symbolism, and ritual as ways of creating a place for the sacred within a secular environment.

Hick, John, *An Interpretation of Religion*, New Haven: Yale University Press, 1992. A leading philosopher of religion offers a rational justification for seeing the major world religions as culturally conditioned forms of response to the great mystery of Being.

Hixon, Lex, *Coming Home: The Experience of Enlightenment in Sacred Traditions*, Garden City, New York: Anchor/Doubleday, 1978. An exploration of the enlightenment experience in religious teachings from Plotinus to recent Hindu gurus.

Otto, Rudolf, *The Idea of the Holy*, second edition, London: Oxford University Press, 1950. An important exploration of "non-rational" experiences of the divine.

Sharma, Arvind, ed., *Women in World Religions*, Albany, New York: State University of New York Press, 1987. Analyses of the historic and contemporary place of women in each of the major religions.

Shinn, Larry D., ed., *In Search of the Divine: Some Unexpected Consequences of Interfaith Dialogue*, New York: Paragon House Publishers, 1987. Scholars from varied religions present a tapestry of understandings of the Sacred Reality.

Stone, Merlin, *When God was a Woman*, San Diego, California: Harcourt Brace Jovanovich, 1976. Pioneering survey of archaeological evidence of the early religion of the goddess.

CHAPTER 2

INDIGENOUS SACRED WAYS

"Everything is alive"

Here and there around the globe, pockets of people still follow local sacred ways handed down from their remote ancestors and adapted to contemporary circumstances. These are the traditional *indigenous* people — descendants of the original inhabitants of lands now controlled by political systems in which they have little influence.

Indigenous people comprise at least four percent of the world population. Some who follow the ancient spiritual traditions still live close to the earth in non-industrial small-scale cultures; many do not. But despite the disruption of their traditional lifestyles, many indigenous people maintain a sacred way of life that is distinctively different from all other religions. These enduring ways, which indigenous people may refer to as their Original Instructions on how to live, were almost lost under the onslaught of genocidal colonization, conversion pressures from global religions, mechanistic materialism and destruction of their natural environments by the global economy of limitless consumption.

Much of the ancient visionary wisdom has disappeared. There are few traditionally trained elders left and few young people willing to undergo the lengthy and rigorous training necessary for spiritual leadership in these sacred ways. Nevertheless, in our time there is a renewal of interest in these traditions, fanning hope that what they offer will not be lost.

> *To what extent can [indigenous groups] reinstitute traditional religious values in a world gone mad with development, electronics, almost instantaneous transportation facilities, and intellectually grounded in a rejection of spiritual and mysterious events?*
>
> *Vine Deloria, Jr.*[1]

Barriers to understanding

Outsiders have little known or understood the indigenous sacred ways. When threatened with severe repression, many of these traditions have long been practiced only in secret. In Mesoamerica, the ancient teachings have remained hidden for five hundred years since the coming of the conquistadores, passed

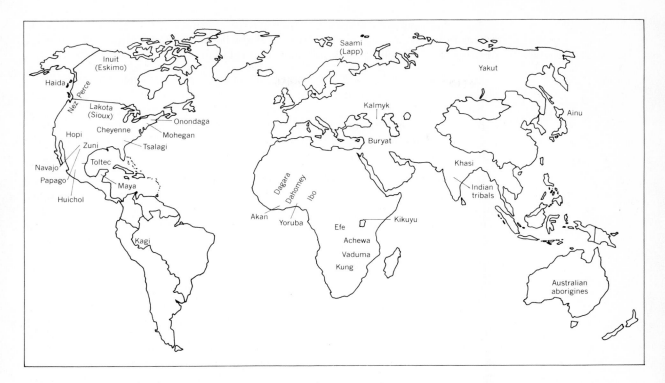

down within families as a secret oral tradition. The Buryats living near Lake Baykal in Russia were thought to have been converted to Buddhism and Christianity centuries ago; however, few attended the opening of a Buddhist temple after the fall of communism, whereas almost the entire population of the area gathered for indigenous ceremonies on Olkhon Island in 1992 and 1993.

In parts of aboriginal Australia, the real teachings have been underground for two hundred years since white colonialists and Christian missionaries appeared. As aborigine Lorraine Mafi Williams explains:

We have stacked away our religious, spiritual, cultural beliefs. When the missionaries came, we were told by our old people to be respectful, listen and be obedient, go to church, go to Sunday school, but do not adopt the Christian doctrine because it takes away our cultural, spiritual beliefs. So we've always stayed within God's laws in what we know.[2]

Not uncommonly, the newer global traditions have been blended with the older ways. For instance, Buddhism as it spread often adopted the existing customs, such as the recognition of local deities. Now many indigenous people sincerely practice one of the global religions while still retaining many of their traditional ways.

Until recently, those who attempted to ferret out the native sacred ways had little basis for understanding them. Most were anthropologists who approached spiritual behaviors from the non-spiritual perspective of Western science. Knowing that researchers from other cultures did not grasp the truth of their beliefs, the native peoples have at times given them information that was incorrect in order to protect the sanctity of their practices from the uninitiated.

The approximate distribution of indigenous groups mentioned in this chapter.

Academic study of traditional ways is now becoming more sympathetic and self-critical, however, as is apparent in this statement by Gerhardus Cornelius Oosthuizen, a European researching African traditional religions:

[The] Western worldview is closed, essentially complete and unchangeable, basically substantive and fundamentally non-mysterious; i.e. it is like a rigid programmed machine.... This closed worldview is foreign to Africa, which is still deeply religious.... This world is not closed, and not merely basically substantive, but it has great depth, it is unlimited in its qualitative varieties and is truly mysterious; this world is restless, a living and growing organism.[3]

Indigenous spirituality is a lifeway, a particular approach to all of life. It is not a separate experience, like meditating in the morning or going to church on Sunday. Rather, spirituality ideally pervades all moments, from reverence in gathering clay to make a pot, to respect within tribal council meetings. As an elder of the Huichol in Mexico puts it:

Everything we do in life is for the glory of God. We praise him in the well swept floor, the well weeded field, the polished machete, the brilliant colors of the picture and embroidery. In these ways we prepare for a long life and pray for a good one.[4]

In most native cultures, spiritual lifeways are shared orally. Teachings are experienced rather than read from books. There are therefore no scriptures of the sort that other religions are built around (although there once existed some texts which were destroyed by conquering groups, such as the Mayan codices). This characteristic helps to keep the indigenous sacred ways dynamic and flexible rather than fossilized. It also keeps the sacred experience fresh in the present. However, outside investigators have only within the latter part of the twentieth century begun to understand and study the oral narratives as clues to the historical experiences of the individuals or groups.

In the Kikuyu indigenous tradition of Kenya, it is very important to know intimately the land on which one lives, including its orientation to the sun and to Mt. Kenya, the sacred "mountain of brightness."

Lifeways of many small-scale cultures are tied to the land on which they live and their entire way of life; they are only meaningful within this context. The people respect the rights of others to their own ways and make no attempt to convert outsiders to theirs.

Traditional world views are not inevitably linked to materially simple ways of life. When Tsalagi (Cherokee) priestess Dhyani Ywahoo lived in Brooklyn, her family continued their ceremonial cycles in their backyard gardens. Their neighbors thought their fireplaces were barbecue pits. She asserts:

The idea that to be a traditional Indian you have to go back into the past and throw everything away is not a realistic vision. A traditional Indian has a traditional state of mind that is respectful for the land and is always considering how to benefit as many people as possible.[5]

Despite the hindrances to understanding of indigenous forms of spirituality, the doors to understanding are opening somewhat in our times. Firstly, the traditional elders are very concerned about the growing potential for planetary disaster. Some are beginning to share their basic values, if not their esoteric practices, in hopes of preventing industrial societies from destroying the earth. Secondly, those of other faiths are beginning to recognize the value and profundity of indigenous ways which were in the past viewed as abhorrent and suppressed by organized religions. Thirdly, many people who have not grown up in native cultures are attempting to embrace indigenous spiritual ways, finding their own traditions lacking in certain qualities for which they long, such as love for the earth. However, even outsiders who value the sacred teachings may disrupt or alter the indigenous practices. Osage theologian George Tinker describes what often happens in North America:

The first Indian casualty today in any such New Age spiritual–cultural encounter is most often the strong deep structure cultural value of community and group cohesion that is important to virtually every indigenous people.... Well-meaning New Agers drive in from New York and Chicago or fly in from Austria and Denmark to participate in annual ceremonies originally intended to secure the well-being of the local, spatially configured community. These visitors see little or nothing at all of the reservation community, pay little attention to the poverty and suffering of the people there and finally leave having achieved only a personal, individual spiritual high.[6]

Indigenous traveling teachers who have revealed themselves are swamped with eager students. But many native peoples are wary of this trend. They feel that their sacred ways are all they have left and worry that even these may be sold, stolen, and ruined. Dhyani Ywahoo warns that outsiders themselves may be hurt in the process:

Caution: Native American religion is like fire. It's the fire that burns away confusion. It is the fire that warms the body and relieves suffering, and it is also the fire that destroys illusions. These are very powerful teachings. Native American teachings on the surface appear very simple. As one grows older, one realizes just how subtle and how deeply penetrating this wisdom is. There are certain rituals that people are very attracted to. They can really cause nervous breakdowns in someone who is not properly prepared, because Native American teaching is an internal process as well as an external process.[7]

Cultural diversity

In this chapter we are considering the faith-ways of indigenous peoples as a whole. These traditions have evolved within materially as well as religiously diverse cultures. Some are descendants of civilizations with advanced urban technologies that were needed to support concentrated populations. When the Spanish "conqueror" Cortes took over Tenochtitlan (which now lies beneath Mexico City) in 1519, he found it a beautiful clean city with elaborate architecture, indoor plumbing, a highly accurate calendar, and advanced systems of mathematics and astronomy. The Tsalagi people had an advanced theocracy before the time of Christ. Former African kingdoms were highly culturally advanced with elaborate arts such as intricate bronze casting.

At the other extreme are those few cultures that still maintain a survival strategy of hunting and gathering. For example, some Australian aborigines continue to live as mobile foragers, though constricted to government-owned stations. A nomadic survival strategy necessitates simplicity in material goods; whatever can be gathered or built rather easily at the next camp need not be dragged along. But material simplicity is not a sign of spiritual poverty. The Australian aborigines have a complex **cosmogony**, or model of the origins of the universe and their purpose within it, as well as a working knowledge of their own bioregion.

Some traditional people live in their ancestral enclaves, somewhat sheltered from the pressures of modern industrial life, though not untouched by the outer world. Tribal peoples have lived deep in the forests and hills of India for thousands of years, utilizing the trees and plants for their food and medicines, although within the twentieth century their ancestral lands were encroached upon by groups which are more politically and economically powerful, rendering some of the fifty million Indian tribal people landless laborers. The Hopi Nation has continuously occupied a high plateau area of the Southwestern United States for eight hundred to one thousand years; their sacred ritual calendar is tied to the yearly farming cycle.

Other indigenous people visit their sacred sites and ancestral shrines but live in more urban settings because of job opportunities. The people who participate in ceremonies in the Mexican countryside include subway personnel, journalists, and artists of native blood who live in Mexico City. Lorraine Mafi Williams is a filmmaker living in Sydney, Australia, but her people return to their sacred sites (some of them owned by non-native people) for spiritual and cultural renewal "whenever the industrial white world gets a bit too much for us."[8]

In addition to variations in lifestyles, indigenous traditions vary in their adaptations to dominant religions. Often native practices have become interwoven with those of global religions, such as Buddhism, Islam, and Christianity. In Southeast Asia, household Buddhist shrines are almost identical to the spirit houses in which the people still make offerings to honor the local spirits. The Dahomey tradition from West Africa was carried to Haiti by thousands of African slaves and called "Voodoo" from *Vodu*, one of the names for the chief non-human spirits. Forced by the European colonialists to adopt Christianity, worshippers of Voodoo fused their old gods with their images of Catholic saints.

While interaction with larger state societies or colonial powers has been extremely detrimental to indigenous peoples around the world, adaptation of the dominant religions has at times allowed the traditional people to survive. Indigenous people sometimes earnestly try to practice the dominant religion, and in doing so they bring new life into it, as in the lively practice of Christianity in rural Africa. In other places, forced converts may practice the new religion only indifferently. A third outcome is the mixing of traditions to produce a new hybrid.

Despite their different histories and economic patterns, indigenous sacred ways do tend to have some characteristics in common. Perhaps from ancient contact across land-bridges that no longer exist, there are linguistic similarities between the languages of the Tsalagi in the Americas, Tibetans, and the aboriginal Ainu of Japan.

Certain symbols and metaphors are repeated in the inspirational art and stories of many traditional cultures around the world, but the people's relationships to and concepts surrounding these symbols are not inevitably the same. Nevertheless, the following sections look at some recurring themes in the spiritual ways of diverse small-scale cultures.

The circle of right relationships

For many indigenous peoples, everything in the cosmos is intimately interrelated. A symbol of unity among the parts of this sacred reality is a circle. This symbol is not used by all indigenous people; the Navajo, for instance, regard a completed circle as stifling and restrictive. However, many other indigenous people hold the circle sacred because it is infinite — it has no beginning, no end. Time is circular rather than linear, for it keeps coming back to the same place. Life revolves around the generational cycles of birth, youth, maturity, and physical death, the return of the seasons, the cyclical movements of the moon, sun, stars, and planets.

Among the gentle Efe Pygmies of Zaire's Ituri Forest, children learn to value the circle by playing the "circle game." With feet making a circle, each names a circular object and then an expression of roundness (the family circle, togetherness, "a complete rainbow").

This understanding of life as a complex of circles is thought to be the perfect framework for harmony. As Lame Deer, a Lakota (Sioux) holy man, explains:

Nature wants things to be round. The bodies of human beings and animals have no corners. With us the circle stands for the togetherness of people who sit with one another around the campfire, relatives and friends united in peace while the pipe passes from hand to hand. The camp in which every tipi had its place was also a ring. The tipi was a ring in which people sat in a circle and all the families in the village were in turn circles within a larger circle, part of the larger hoop which was the seven campfires of the Sioux, representing one nation. The nation was only a part of the universe, in itself circular and made of the earth, which is round, of the sun, which is round, of the stars, which are round. The moon, the horizon, the rainbow — circles within circles within circles, with no beginning and no end.[9]

To maintain the natural balance of the circles of existence, indigenous peoples are taught that they must develop right relationships with everything that is. Their relatives include the unseen world of spirits, the land and weather, the people and creatures, and the power within.

Relationships with spirit

Many indigenous traditions worship a Supreme Being who they believe created the cosmos. This being is known by the Sioux as "Wakan tanka" or "Great Mysterious" or "Great Spirit."

African names for this One are attributes such as "All-powerful," "Creator," "the one who is met everywhere," "the one who exists by himself," or "the one who began the forest." The aChewa of Malawi use the same word for all of creation (*moyo*) and for its divine source (*moyo*). The supreme being is often referred to by male pronouns, but in some groups the supreme being is a female, such as Ala, earth mother goddess of the Ibo. Many traditional languages make no distinction between male and female pronouns, and some see the divine as androgynous, a force arising from the interaction of male and female aspects of the universe.

Awareness of one's relationship to the Great Power is thought to be essential, but the Power itself remains unseen and mysterious. An Eskimo shaman described his people's experience of:

… a power that we call Sila, which is not to be explained in simple words. A great spirit, supporting the world and the weather and all life on earth, a spirit so mighty that [what it says] to mankind is not through common words, but by storm and snow and rain and the fury of the sea; all the forces of nature that men fear. But Sila has also another way of [communicating]; by sunlight and calm of the sea, and little children innocently at play, themselves understanding nothing. Children hear a soft and gentle voice, almost like that of a woman. It comes to them in a mysterious way, but so gently that they are not afraid; they only hear that some danger threatens.... When all is well, Sila sends no message to mankind, but withdraws into endless nothingness, apart.[10]

To traditional Buryats of Russia, the chief power in the world is the eternally blue sky, Tengry. In many cultures, the Great Mysterious is thought to have been less distant at one time. African myths suggest that the High God was originally so close to humans that they became disrespectful. The All-Powerful was like the sky, they say, which was once so close that children wiped their dirty hands on it, and women (blamed by men for the withdrawal) broke off pieces for soup and bumped it with their sticks when pounding grain. Although southern and central Africans believe in a high being who presides over the universe, including less powerful spirits, they consider this being either too distant, too powerful, or too dangerous to worship or call on for help.

More accessible to humans and more involved in the daily workings of life are many unseen powers. Some of these are perceived without form, as mysterious and sacred presences. Others are perceived as having more definite, albeit invisible, forms and personalities. These may include deities with human-like personalities, the nature spirits of special local places such as venerable trees and mountains, animal spirit helpers, personified elemental forces, ancestors who still take an interest in their living relatives, or special beings such as the spirit keepers of the four directions.

Ancestors may be extremely important. Traditional Africans understand that even the person is not an individual, but a composite of many souls — the spirits of one's parents and ancestors — resonating to their feelings. As Rev. William Kingsley Opoku, organizer of the African Council for Spiritual Churches, explains:

Our ancestors are our saints. Christian missionaries who came here wanted us to pray to their saints, their dead people. But what about our saints? We have come to know them in prayer, for inspiration, to continue developing our civilization and everything around ourselves, rather than relying on far-away theology. If you are grateful to your ancestors, then you have blessings from your grandmother, your grandfather, who brought you forth. If you neglect them because they are dead or call them evil people — non-Africans came in and said we should not obey our ancestors, should not call upon them at all, because they are evil people. This has been a mental bondage, a terrible thing.[11]

Continued communication with the "living dead" is extremely important to traditional Africans. These are ancestors who have died sufficiently recently that some people still remember them personally. Food and drink are set out or poured for them, acknowledging that they are still in a sense living and engaged with the people's lives. Failure to keep in touch with the ancestors is a dangerous oversight which may bring misfortunes to the family.

The Dagara of Burkina Faso in West Africa are familiar with the *kontombili* who look like humans but are only about one foot tall, because of the humble way they express their spiritual power. Other West African groups, descendants of hierarchical ancient civilizations, recognize a great pantheon of deities, the *orisa* or *vodu*, each the object of special cult worship. This worship is most highly elaborated among the Yoruba, who honor seventeen hundred divinities. The orisha are embodiments of the dynamic forces in life, such as Oya, goddess of death and change, experienced in tornadoes, lightning, winds, and fire; Olokun, ruler of the mysterious depths of consciousness; Shango, a former king who is now honored as the stormy god of electricity and genius; Ifa, god of wisdom; and Obatala, the source of creativity, warmth, and enlightenment.

The spirits are available to reverent seekers as helpers, as intermediaries between the people and the power, and as teachers. Their teachings may come in frightening

YORUBA TEACHING STORY

Osun and the Power of Woman

Olodumare, the Supreme Creator, Who is both female and male, wanted to prepare the earth for human habitation. To organize things, Olodumare sent the seventeen major deities. Osun was the only woman; all the rest were men. Each of the deities was given specific abilities and specific assignments. But when the male deities held their planning meetings, they did not invite Osun. "She is a woman," they said.

However, Olodumare had given great powers to Osun. Her womb is the matrix of all life in the universe. In her lie tremendous power, unlimited potential, infinities of existence. She wears a perfectly carved, beaded crown, and with her beaded comb she parts the pathway of both human and divine life. She is the leader of the *aje*, the powerful beings and forces in the world.

When the male deities ignored Osun, she made their plans fail. The male deities returned to Olodumare for help. After listening, Olodumare asked, "What about Osun?" "She is only a woman," they replied, "so we left her out." Olodumare spoke in strong words, "You must go back to her, beg her for forgiveness, make a sacrifice to her, and give her whatever she asks."

The male deities did so, and Osun forgave them. What did she ask for? The secret initiation that the men used to keep women in the background. She wanted it for herself and for all women who are as powerful as she. The men agreed and initiated her into the secret knowledge. From that time onward, their plans were successful.[12]

forms, such as thunder and lightning which test one's faith and courage. But right relationship with these spirit beings can be a sacred partnership. Sincere seekers respect, silently listen for, and learn from them and also purify themselves in order to engage their services for the good of the people. As we will later see, those who are best able to call on the spirits for help are the medicine men and women who have dedicated their lives to this service.

Teachings about the spirits also help the people to understand how they should live together in society. Professor Diedre Badejo observes that in Yoruba tradition there is an ideal of social balance between the awesome potential and creativity of women who give and sustain life, and the power of men who protect life. Under various internal and external pressures, this balance has swung towards male dominance, but the stories of feminine power and the necessity for men to recognize it remain in the culture, teaching an ideal symmetry between female and male roles.

Kinship with all creation

In addition to the unseen powers, all aspects of the tangible world are imbued with spirit and spiritually interconnected. Everything is therefore experienced as family. The community is paramount, and it may extend beyond the living humans in the area. Many traditional peoples know the earth as their mother. The land one lives on is part of her body, loved, respected, and well-known. Oren Lyons, an elder of the Onondaga Nation Wolf Clan, speaks of this intimate relationship:

[The indigenous people's] knowledge is profound and comes from living in one place for untold generations. It comes from watching the sun rise in the east and set in the west from the same place over great sections of time. We are as familiar with the lands, rivers and great seas that surround us as we are with the faces of our mothers. Indeed we call the earth Etenoha, our mother, from whence all life springs …. We do not perceive our habitat as wild but as a place of great security and peace, full of life.[13]

In contrast to the industrial world's attempts to use and dominate the earth, native people now consider themselves caretakers of their mother, the earth. They are raising their voices against the destruction of the environment. Their prophecies warn of the potential for global disaster, and the visionaries say they hear the earth crying. Contemporary Australian aboriginal elder Bill Neidjie speaks of feeling the earth's pain:

I feel it with my body,
with my blood.
Feeling all these trees,
all this country…
If you feel sore…
headache, sore body
that mean somebody killing tree or grass.
You feel because your body in that tree or earth.
Nobody can tell you,
you got to feel it yourself.
Tree might be sick…
you feel it.
You might feel it for two or three years.
You get weak…
little bit, little bit…
because tree going bit by bit…
dying.[14]

The earth abounds with living presences, in traditional worldviews. Rocks, bodies of water, and mountains — considered inanimate by other peoples — are personified as living beings by indigenous peoples. Before one can successfully climb a mountain, one must ask its permission. Visionaries can see the spirits of a body of water and many traditional cultures have recognized certain groves of trees as places where spirits live, and where specially trained priests and priestesses can communicate with them. As a Pit River Indian explained, "Everything is alive. That's what we Indians believe."[15]

All creatures are perceived as kin, endowed with consciousness and the power of the Great Spirit. Many native peoples have been raised with an "ecological" perspective: They know that all things depend on each other. They are taught that they have a reciprocal, rather than dominating, relationship with all beings. Hawaiian *kahuna* (shaman-priest) Kahu Kawai'i explains:

How you might feel toward a human being that you love is how you might feel toward a dry leaf on the ground and how you might feel toward the rain in the forest and the wind. There is such intimacy that goes on that everything speaks to

Many traditional peoples learn a sense of reverence for and kinship with the natural world, as suggested in this image from Botswana created by Elisabeth Sunday.

you and everything responds to how you are in being — almost like a mirror reflecting your feelings.[16]

Even the dreams of indigenous peoples are often intimately related to their particular environment and are understood as providing guidelines for proper ways to act.

Trees, animals, insects, and plants are all to be approached with caution and consideration. If one must cut down a tree or kill an animal, one must first explain one's intentions and ask forgiveness of the being. Scientific research now verifies that there can be a sort of communication between human and non-human species. Plants may actually grow better when loved and talked to; if a person even thinks of harming a plant, some polygraph tests show that the plant experiences a "fear" reaction.

Indigenous people feel that one who harms nature may himself be harmed in return. When a Buryat cuts a tree to build a house, he must first offer milk, butter, rice, and alcohol to the spirits of the forest and ask their forgiveness, or he is likely to fall ill. In 1994, a half-French, half-Buryat businessman returned to Buryatia and started to build a guesthouse in a picturesque place, Svyatoy Nos, which had long been considered sacred to the god Huushan-baabay. When the businessman began cutting trees, he was warned by the traditional people that he would not be successful. Nonetheless, he proceeded and finished the guesthouse. Three months later, it burned down.

Respect is always due to all creatures, in the indigenous world view, but sometimes a degree of coercion is also necessary. In traditional Eskimo whale hunts by kayak through rough, icy seas, the odds were stacked so heavily in favor of the whale that it was necessary to use song and ritual to charm and befuddle the whale.

There are many stories of indigenous people's relationships with non-human creatures. Certain trees tell the healing specialists which herbs to use in curing the people. Australian aboriginal women are adept at forming hunting partnerships with dogs. Birds are thought to bring messages to the people from the spirit world. A Hopi elder said he spent three days and nights praying with a rattlesnake. "Of course he was nervous at first, but when I sang to him he recognized the warmth of my body and calmed down. We made good prayer together."[17]

Relationships with power

A second common theme is developing an appropriate relationship with spiritual energy.

> All animals have power, because the Great Spirit dwells in all of them, even a tiny ant, a butterfly, a tree, a flower, a rock. The modern, white man's way keeps that power from us, dilutes it. To come to nature, feel its power, let it help you, one needs time and patience for that.... You have so little time for contemplation.... It lessens a person's life, all that grind, that hurrying and scurrying about.
>
> Lame Deer, Lakota nation[18]

In certain places and beings, the power of spirit is believed to be highly concentrated. It is referred to as *mana* by the people of the Pacific islands. This is the vital force that makes it possible to act with unusual strength, insight, and effectiveness. Those who have developed their sensitivities can feel it and channel it for useful purposes.

Tlakaelel, a contemporary spiritual leader of the descendants of the Toltecs of Mexico, describes how a person might experience this power when looking into an obsidian mirror traditionally made to concentrate power:

> When you reach the point that you can concentrate with all your will, inside there, you reach a point where you feel ecstasy. It's a very beautiful thing, and everything is light. Everything is vibrating with very small signals, like waves of music, very smooth. Everything shines with a blue light. And you feel a sweetness. Everything is covered with the sweetness, and there is peace. It's a sensation like an orgasm, but it can last a long time.[19]

Sacred sites may be recognized by the power that believers feel there. Concentrated power spots were known to ancient as well as contemporary peoples of the earth. Some sacred sites have been used again and again by successive religions, either to capitalize on the energy or to co-opt the preceding religion. Chartres Cathedral in France, for instance, was built on an ancient ritual site.

When indigenous people have been forced off their ancestral lands, many have felt the loss of access to their sacred power sites as a great tragedy. But when outsiders offer to buy these lands or mining rights to them, there is often a conflict

At a remote shrine used by indigenous people in New Mexico, a ring of stones protects the sacred area where sun-bleached antlers and offerings have been placed around two stones naturally shaped like mountain lions.

within tribes between those of spiritual values and those who want the money.

Because power can be built up through sacred practices, the ritual objects of spiritually developed persons may have a lot of power. Special stones and animal artifacts may also carry power. A person might be strengthened by the spiritual energy of the bear or the wolf by wearing sacred clothing made from its fur. Power can also come to one through visions or by being given a sacred pipe or the privilege of collecting objects into a personal sacred bundle.

In some cultures — such as the traditional peoples of the North American plains — women are thought to have a certain natural power; men have to work harder for it. Women's power is considered mysterious, dangerous, uncontrolled. It is said to be strongest during their menstrual period.

Women's reproductive power is viewed as different from men's versions of power. In certain rituals in which both men and women participate, women's menstrual blood is often thought to diminish or weaken the ritual or the men's spiritual power. In most native American nations that have *sweat lodge* ceremonies for ritual purification, menstruating women are not allowed to enter the lodge. Nevertheless, a few cultures such as the Ainu of Japan have prized menstrual blood as a most potent offering returned to the earth.

Gaining power is both desirable and dangerous. If misused for personal ends, it becomes destructive and may turn against the person. To channel spiritual power properly, native people are taught that they must live within certain strict limits. Those who seek power or receive it unbidden are supposed to continually purify themselves of any selfish motives and dedicate their actions to the good of the whole. A pipe carrier must be ethically impeccable and must never turn away anyone who asks for help.

Power is not an end in itself. The goal of indigenous spiritual practices, which tend to develop power secondarily, is, according to Tlakaelel:

> *to identify yourself with nature, and to organize yourself with everything that exists so that you can use it for your service — to conserve life on this planet and to create the superior being of the future.*[20]

Spiritual specialists

In a few of the remaining hunting and gathering tribes, religion is a relatively private matter. Each individual has direct access to the unseen. Although spirit is invisible, it is considered a part of the natural world. Anyone can interact with it spontaneously, without complex ceremony and without anyone else's aid.

More commonly, however, the world of spirit is thought to be dangerous — the fire that can burn those who are unprepared for its power, as Dhyani Ywahoo said. Although everyone is expected to observe certain personal ways of worship, such as offering prayers before taking plant or animal life, many ways of interacting with spirit are thought best left to those who are specially trained for the roles. These specialists are gradually initiated into the secret knowledge that allows them to act as intermediaries between the seen and the unseen. They sacrifice themselves through ritual purification and emptying practices in order to be clean vessels for the sacred knowledge and the sacred role.

Various sacred roles

Specialists' roles vary from one group to another, and the same person may play several of these roles. One specialization often present is that of storyteller. Because the traditions are oral rather than written, these people must memorize long and complex stories and songs so that the group's sacred traditions can be remembered and taught, generation after generation. It is very important to Australian aborigines that their children learn about the origin of the people and the local creatures, and that they understand the weather and the patterns of the stars. Songs about these matters may have a hundred verses or more. The orally transmitted epics of the indigenous Ainu of Japan are up to ten thousand "lines" long. Chants of the Yoruba orisa comprise two hundred and fifty-six "volumes" of eight hundred long verses each.

What is held only in memory cannot be physically destroyed, but if a tribe is small and all its storytellers die, the knowledge is lost. This happened on a large scale during contacts with colonial powers as native people were killed by war and imported diseases. Professor Wande Abimbola, who is trying to preserve the oral tradition of the Yoruba, has made thousands of tapes of the chants, but there must also be people who can understand and interpret them.

There are also bards who carry the energy of ancient traditions into new forms. Rather than memory, they cultivate the muse. In Africa, poets are considered "technicians of the sacred," conversing with a dangerous world of spirits. They are

A storyteller of the Kung people of Botswana, Africa, entertains an audience while passing on the oral teachings of the distant past.

associated with the flow and rhythms of water. Players of the "talking drums" are highly valued as communicators with the spirits, ancestors, and Supreme Being. As the Akan say:

> *The thumb, finger with mouth, wake up and speak!*
> *The thumb armed with sticks for drumming*
> *Is more loquacious and more eloquent*
> *Than a human being sleeping;*
> *Wake up and come!* [21]

"Tricksters" such as foxes often appear in the stories of indigenous traditions. They are paradoxical, transformative beings. Similarly, sacred clowns may endure the shame of behaving as fools during public rituals in order to teach the people through humor. Often they poke fun at the most sacred of rituals, keeping the people from taking themselves too seriously. A sacred fool, called *heyoka* by the Lakota, must be both innocent and very wise about human nature, and must have a visionary relationship with spirit as well.

> *Life is holiness and everyday humdrum, sadness and laughter, the mind and the belly all mixed together. The Great Spirit doesn't want us to sort them out neatly.*
> Leonard Crow Dog, Lakota medicine man[22]

A more coveted role is that of being a member of a secret society. Some indigenous cultures include groups in which one can participate by initiation or invitation only, whether to enhance one's prestige or to draw closer to the spirit world. When serving in ceremonial capacities, members often wear special costumes to hide their human identities and help them take on the personas of spirits they are representing. In African religions, some members of secret societies periodically appear as impersonators of animal spirits or of dead ancestors, helping to demonstrate that the dead are still watching the living and are available as awe-inspiring protectors of villages. The all-male Oro secret society in some Yoruba tribes uses this authority to enforce male domination; when Oro appears, "roaring" by swinging a piece of wood on a cord, women stay inside their huts.

Women also have their secret societies, whose activities are yet little known by outsiders. Among aboriginal peoples of Australia, the men's and women's groups initiate members into separate but interrelated roles for males and females. For instance, when boys are separated from the tribe for circumcision by the men's secret society, the women's secret society has its own separation rituals and may stage mock ritual fights with the men's society. Men's and women's rituals ultimately refer to the eternal Dream Time, in which there is no male–female differentiation.

Sacred dancers likewise make the unseen powers visible. Body movements are a language in themselves expressing the nature of the cosmos, a language which is understood through the stories and experiences of the community. Such actions keep the world of the ancestors alive in the consciousness of succeeding generations.

In some socially stratified societies there are also priests and priestesses. These are specially trained and dedicated people who carry out the rituals that ensure proper functioning of the natural world, and perhaps also communicate with particular spirits or deities. Though West African priests or priestesses may have part-time earthly occupations, they are expected to stay in a state of ritual purity and spend much of their time in communication with the spirit being to whom they are devoted, paying homage and asking the being what he or she wants the people to do. In West Africa, there are also mediums associated with the temples; they enter a state of trance or allow themselves to be possessed by gods or spirits in order to bring messages to the people.

Black Elk, visionary and healer.

Shamans

The most distinctive spiritual specialists among indigenous peoples are the **shamans**. They are called by many names, but the Siberian word "shaman" is used as a generic term by scholars for those who offer themselves as mystical intermediaries between the physical and the non-physical world for specific purposes, such as healing. According to archaeological research, shamanic methods are extremely ancient — at least twenty to thirty thousand years old. Ways of becoming a shaman and practicing shamanic arts are remarkably similar around the globe.

Shamans may be helpers to society, using their skills to benefit others. They are not to be confused with sorcerers, who practice black magic to harm others or promote their own selfish ends, interfering with the cosmic order. Spiritual power is neutral; its use depends on the practitioner. A shaman may thus be either a causer or healer of sickness. In either case, what Native Americans call "medicine power" does not originate in the medicine person. Black Elk explains:

Of course it was not I who cured. It was the power from the outer world, and the visions and ceremonies had only made me like a hole through which the power could come to the two-leggeds. If I thought that I was doing it myself, the hole would close up and no power could come through.[23]

There are many kinds of medicine. One is the ability to heal physical, psychological, and spiritual problems. Techniques used include physical approaches to illness, such as therapeutic herbs, dietary recommendations, sweatbathing, massage, cauterization, and sucking out of toxins. But the treatments are given to the whole person — body, mind, and spirit, with special emphasis on healing relationships within the group — so there may also be metaphysical divination, prayer, chanting, and ceremonies in which group power is built up and spirit helpers are called in. If an intrusion of harmful power, such as the angry energy of another person, seems to be causing the problem, the medicine person may attempt to suck it out with the aid of spirit helpers and then dry vomit the invisible intrusion into a receptacle.

These shamanic healing methods, once dismissed as quackery, are now beginning to earn respect from the scientific medical establishment. Medicine people are permitted to attend indigenous patients in some hospitals, and in the United States, the National Institute of Mental Health has paid Navajo medicine men to teach young Indians the elaborate ceremonies that have often been more effective in curing the mental health problems of Navajos than has Western psychiatry.

In addition to healing, certain shamans are thought to have gifts such as talking with plants and animals, controlling the weather, seeing and communicating with the spirit world, and prophesying. A gift highly developed in Africa is that of divination, using techniques such as reading patterns revealed by a casting of cowrie shells. According to Mado Somé of the Dagara:

Divination is a way of accessing information that is happening now, but not right where you live. Divination is something like your possession of a television. Thanks to that, you can know what is going on outside your immediate area or how something that is going on now is going to end up being. The cowrie shells work like an intermediary between us and the other world. Divination is actually the inscription of information on those physical things, allowing the shaman — whose eyes have been modified through the course of her various medicine journeys — to be able to read and interpret them.[24]

Shamans are contemplatives, Lame Deer explains:

The wicasa wakan *[holy man] wants to be by himself. He wants to be away from the crowd, from everyday matters. He likes to meditate, leaning against a tree or rock, feeling the earth move beneath him, feeling the weight of that big flaming sky upon him. That way he can figure things out. Closing his eyes, he sees many things clearly. What you see with your eyes shut is what counts.*

The wicasa wakan *loves the silence, wrapping it around himself like a blanket — a loud silence with a voice like thunder which tells him of many things. Such a man likes to be in a place where there is no sound but the humming of insects. He sits facing the west, asking for help. He talks to the plants and they answer him. He listens to the voices of the wama kaskan — all those who move upon the earth, the animals. He is as one with them. From all living beings something flows into him all the time, and something flows from him.*[25]

The role of shaman may be hereditary or it may be recognized as a special gift. Either way, training is rigorous. In order to work in a mystical state of ecstasy, moving between ordinary and non-ordinary realities, shamans must experience physical death and rebirth. Some have spontaneous near-death experiences. Uvavnuk, an Eskimo shaman, was spiritually initiated when she was struck by a lightning ball. After she revived, she had great power, which she dedicated to serving her people.

> *The great sea has set me in motion*
> *Set me adrift,*
> *Moving me as the weed moves in a river.*
> *The arch of sky and mightiness of storms*
> *Have moved the spirit within me,*
> *Till I am carried away*
> *Trembling with joy.*
>
> *Uvavnuk, Netsilik Eskimo shaman*[26]

Left *Traditional diviners of Mali rake sand and leave it overnight. The tracks of animals which run over it are interpreted the next day for information the client seeks.*
Right *Mexican* curandera *(healer) Maria Sabina has eaten hallucinogenic mushrooms to enter an ecstatic state. She chants, "I am a doctor woman ... I am the morning star woman ... I am the moon woman ... I am the heaven woman ... they say it is like softness there."*

Other potential shamans undergo rituals of purification, isolation, and bodily torment until they make contact with the spirit world. Igjugarjuk from northern Hudson Bay chose to suffer from cold, starvation, and thirst for a month in a tiny snow hut in order to draw the attention of Pinga, a helping female spirit:

My novitiate took place in the middle of the coldest winter, and I, who never got anything to warm me, and must not move, was very cold, and it was so tiring having to sit without daring to lie down, that sometimes it was as if I died a little. Only towards the end of the thirty days did a helping spirit come to me, a lovely and

Living Indigenous Sacred Ways

One of the remaining traditional shamans of Buryatia, Nadezhda Ananyevna Stepanova comes from a family of very powerful shamans. Her mother tried to prevent her becoming a shaman. Buddhist lamas had spread the impression that shamans were to be avoided, saying that they were ignorant, primitive servants of dark, lower spirits. The reputation of shamans has also been recently damaged by pseudo-shamans — some of whom have certain extrasensory powers and others of whom are simply cheats. But when a shaman receives a true spiritual call, to deny that pull is dangerous. Nadezhda explains:

"As a child I knew when I would fall ill, and I could repeat by heart anything the teacher said or anything I read in a book, but I thought that was normal. When I was twenty-six, I was told I would be a shaman, a great shaman. When I told Mother, she said, 'No, you won't.' She took a bottle, went to her native town, and then came back. 'Everything will be taken away; you won't become a shaman,' she said. I didn't understand. The year I was said to become a shaman, I became seriously ill, and Mother was paralyzed. Usually paralyzed people have high blood pressure, but hers was normal. The doctors were surprised, but I understood then: We were both badly ill because she went against the gods.

Nobody could heal me. Then one seer said, 'You must cure.' I replied, 'I don't know anything about curing.' But a voice inside me said, 'If you don't become a shaman, you will die. You will be overrun by a lorry with a blue number.' I began to collect materials about medicine, about old rites. Then I could do a lot, for all we need is seeing and feeling. I was initiated by the men shaman of all the families, each praying to his god in a definite direction, for every god has his direction. I sat in the middle. Every shaman asked his gods to help me, to protect me, to give me power. The ritual was in early March. It was very frosty and windy, and I was only lightly dressed, but I wasn't cold at all. The wind didn't touch me. I sat motionless for about four hours, but I was not cold.

I began to cure. It is very difficult. You go through pain, through the tears of children and adults. I am able to see whether I will be able to cure a specific person. The main thing to me is to help a person if I can. I pray to my gods, ask them for mercy, I ask them to pay attention, to help. I feel the pain of those who come to me, and I want to relieve it. I have *Yodo* — bark from a fir tree scratched by a bear; its smoke purifies. I perform rituals of bringing back the soul; often they work. My ancestors are very close to me; I see them as well as I see you.

Last year in the island Olechon in Lake Baikal, there was a great gathering of shamans from Tchita, Irkutsk, Ulan-Ude, Yakutiya, and Buryatia to pray to the great spirits of Baikal about the well-being and prosperity of the Buryat land. For a long time these spirits were not turned to. They were forgotten by the people, and they fell asleep. They could not take an active part in the life of people; they could not help them any more. *Teylagan*, the prayer of the shamans for the whole Buryatia, was to awaken the great spirits.

It was a clear, clear sunny day, without a cloud. When the prayer began, it started to rain. It was a very good sign. There had been a long drought before. The Olechon shamans had tried to call rain, but they couldn't. But when everyone gathered and three sheep were sacrificed, then they could, and the shamans of that district were grateful.

We had always prayed to thirteen northern nainkhats, the great spirits of this area. But when the Buddhists came, persecution began, and people prayed secretly, only for their families. They could not pray for the whole Buryat nation, and they did not. They forgot. Shamans were killed. Then the atheistic Soviet regime tried to make us forget the faith, and we forgot. The most terrible thing about them was that they wanted to make people forget everything, to live by the moment and forget their roots. And what is man without roots? Nothing. It is a loss of everything. That is why now nobody has compassion for anybody. Now we are reaping the fruit: robbery, drinking, drugs. This is our disaster. That is why we must pray to our own gods.

When we had the teylagan, on the first day three blue pillars rose from earth to the sky — it was a prayer to Ehon-Bahve, the head spirit of Baikal, and to all three gods. The second day we prayed to the bird-god, and there were very many birds flying and a rainbow in the sky."[27]

beautiful helping spirit, whom I had never thought of; it was a white woman; she came to me whilst I had collapsed, exhausted, and was sleeping. But still I saw her lifelike, hovering over me, and from that day I could not close my eyes or dream without seeing her.... She came to me from Pinga and was a sign that Pinga had now noticed me and would give me powers that would make me a shaman.[28]

In addition to becoming a familiar with death, a potential shaman must undergo lengthy training in shamanic techniques, the names and roles of the spirits, and secrets and myths of the tribe. Novices are taught both by older shamans and reportedly by the spirits themselves. If the spirits do not accept and teach the shaman, he or she is unable to carry the role.

The helping spirits that contact would-be shamans during the death-and-rebirth crisis become essential partners in the shaman's sacred work. Often it is a spirit animal who becomes the shaman's guardian spirit, giving him or her special powers. The shaman may even take on the persona of the animal while working. Many tribes feel that healing shamans need the powers of the bear; Lapp shamans metamorphosed into wolves, reindeer, bears, or fish.

Not only do shamans possess a power animal as an alter-ego, they also have the ability to enter parallel, spiritual realities at will in order to bring back knowledge, power, or help for those who need it. An altered state of consciousness is needed. Techniques for entering this state are the same around the world: drumming, rattling, singing, dancing, and in some cases hallucinogenic drugs. The effect of these influences is to open what the Huichol shamans of Mexico call the *Narieka* — the doorway of the heart, the channel for divine power, the point where human and spirit worlds meet. It is often experienced and represented artistically as a pattern of concentric circles.

Left *Many traditional peoples feel that women have special spiritual powers, so they often serve as priestesses and shamans.*
Right *The drum, "voice of the ancestors," is used by shamans around the world to help enter a trance state in which they can commune with the spirit world, as in this historical photograph of an East Siberian Yakut shaman.*

The "journey" then experienced by shamans is typically into the Upperworld or the Lowerworld. To enter the latter, they descend mentally through an actual hole in the ground, such as a spring, a hollow tree, cave, animal burrow, or special ceremonial hole regarded as a navel of the earth. These entrances typically lead into tunnels which if followed open into bright landscapes. Reports of such experiences include not only what the journeyer saw but also realistic physical sensations, such as how the walls of the tunnel felt during the descent.

The shaman enters into the Lowerworld landscape, encounters beings there, and may bring something back if it is needed by the client. This may be a lost guardian spirit or a lost soul, brought back to revive a person in a coma. The shaman may be temporarily possessed by the spirit of departed relatives so that an afflicted patient may finally clear up unresolved tensions with them that are seen as causing illness. Often a river must be crossed as the boundary between the world of the living and the world of the dead. In West African tradition, there are three rivers separating these worlds and one must cross them by canoe. In another common variant, the journeyer crosses the underworld river on a bridge guarded by some animal. Often a kindly old man or woman appears to assist this passage through the underworld. This global shamanic process is retained only in myths, such as the Orpheus story, in cultures that have subdued the indigenous ways.

Contemporary rituals

Although the forces of life honored by traditional peoples are unseen, one can communicate with these forces in symbolic non-verbal ways, such as sprinkling cornmeal in thanks for the offerings of the earth or using pipe smoke to carry prayers up to the spirits. The people have also observed that life operates according to strict natural laws. Humans can help to maintain the harmony of the universe by their ritual observances.

In order to maintain the natural balance and to ensure success in the hunt or harvest, ceremonies must be performed with exactitude. For instance, there is a specific time for the telling of specific stories. Chona, a Tohono O'odham (Papago) medicine woman, told anthropologist Ruth Underhill:

> *I should not have told you this [the origin of Coyote, who helped to put the world in order, with a few mistakes]. These things about the Beginning are holy. They should not be told in the hot time when the snakes are out. The snakes guard our secrets. If we tell what is forbidden, they bite.*[29]

Ritual precision is not just an exercise in remembering the old traditions. According to Dhyani Ywahoo, there are strong psychological, as well as spiritual, reasons for doing things the right way. Paying attention to the proper forms brings clarity of attention and creates a sacred space in which many things can happen:

> *What's important about ritual is that it has a beginning. And before that beginning there has been a preparation, so that people's bodies and minds are brought to a certain level of vibrancy. [After] abstaining from certain things, doing certain exercises, and living and behaving in a certain way, the sleepiness, the illusions that may veil our true nature are more transparent, more ready to let go. Also one is*

cultivating a more peaceful nature by having certain prescriptions about speech and behavior with other people.

Then there is the beginning where everyone comes together, and there is the beginning of the family bonding. You also see what you need to correct in yourself in terms of relationship.

Then the actual ceremonies begin, which [involve] much purifying, pacifying, and visioning — knowing what one's purpose is and seeing what needs to happen. And then there is generating of the energy through the ritual itself, so that vision can manifest for the benefit of family, clan, nation, all beings.[30]

Group observances

Indigenous ways are community-centered. Through group rituals, traditional people not only honor the sacred but also affirm their bonds with each other and all of creation.

Rituals often take people out of everyday consciousness and into awareness of the presence of the sacred. When participants return from such altered states, they typically experience a heightened group consciousness that powerfully binds individuals together as a community. Each group has its own special ways of ritual dedication to the spirits of life, but they tend to follow certain patterns everywhere. Some honor major points in the human life cycle, such as birth, naming, puberty, marriage, and death. These rites of passage assist people in the transition from one

Concentric circles and spirals appear throughout the visionary art of the world, including Australian aborigines' paintings of the Dreaming, a parallel and original reality. These patterns often suggest a journey through spiritual levels toward union with the Great Holy.

state to another and help them become aware of their meaningful contribution to life. When a Hopi baby is twenty days old, it is presented at dawn to the rays of Father Sun for the first time and officially given a name. Its face is ritually cleansed with sacred cornmeal, a ceremony that will be repeated at death for the journey to the Underworld.

There are also collective rituals to support the group's survival strategies. In farming communities these include ways of asking for rain, of insuring the growth of crops, and of giving thanks for the harvest. In the Great Drought of 1988, Sioux holy man Leonard Crow Dog was asked by three non-native Midwestern communities to perform rainmaking ceremonies for them, thus honoring the power of the traditional medicine ways. Dhyani Ywahoo explains, "When Native American people sing for the rain, the rain comes — because those singers have made a decision that they and the water and the air and the Earth are one."[31]

Ritual dramas about the beginnings and sacred history of the people engage performers and spectators on an emotional level through the use of special costumes, body paint, music, masks, and perhaps sacred locations. These dramas provide a sense of orderly interface among humans, the land, and the spiritual world. They also dramatize mysticism, drawing the people toward direct contact with the spirit world. Those who have sacred visions and dreams are supposed to share them with others, and often this is done through dramatization.

The Plains Indians were given, according to legend, the sacred pipe by White Buffalo Calf Woman as a tool for communicating with the mysteries and understanding the ways of life. The bowl of the pipe represents the female aspect of the Great Spirit, the stem the male aspect. When they are ritually joined, the power of the spirit is thought to be present as the pipe is passed around the circle for collective communion with each other and with the divine.

Groups also gather for ritual purification and spiritual renewal of individuals. Indigenous peoples of the Americas "smudge" sites and possessions, cleansing them with smoke from special herbs, such as sage and sweetgrass. Many groups make an igloo-shaped "sweat lodge" into which hot stones are carried. People huddle together in the dark around the stone pit. When water is poured on the stones, intensely hot steam sears bodies and lungs. Everyone prays earnestly. Leonard Crow Dog says of the *inipi* (sweat lodge):

> The inipi *is probably our oldest ceremony because it is built around the simplest, basic, life-giving things: the fire that comes from the sun, warmth without which there can be no life;* inyan wakan, *or* tunka, *the rock that was there when the earth began, that will still be there at the end of time; the earth, the mother womb; the water that all creatures need; our green brother, the sage; and encircled by all these, man, basic man, naked as he was born, feeling the weight, the spirit of endless generations before him, feeling himself part of the earth, nature's child, not her master.*[32]

Pilgrimages to sacred sites are often communal. Buryats gather atop Erde, the mountain where the spirit of the earth lives, and all join hands to encircle it, playing games; a great energy is said to appear in the huge circle. The Huichol Indians of the mountains of western Mexico make a yearly journey to a desert they call Wirikuta, the Sacred Land of the Sun. They feel that creation began in this place.

Above left *To the Pygmies of the Ituri rainforest, the Great Spirit is embodied in the forest itself, a benevolent presence that is both Mother and Father. Pygmy men perform a dance of gratitude to the forest for the animal food it provides.*

Above right *In West Africa, the gods and the spirits of the dead appear to the living in masquerade. The mysteries of spirit are made semi-visible by costumed initiates.*

Left *This altar in the home of a Mexican healer illustrates the blending of indigenous ways with those of later religions. The serpent, masks, vegetables, eggs, and "bird's nest" derive from indigenous sacred ways, but are juxtaposed with Christian symbols.*

And like their ancestors, they gather their yearly supply of peyote cactus at this sacred site. To them, the psychotropic peyote is "the little deer," a spirit who helps them to communicate with the spirit world.

When indigenous groups are broken up by external forces, they lose the cohesive power of these group rituals. Africans taken to the New World as slaves lost not only their own individual identity but also their membership in tight-knit groups. In an attempt to re-establish a communal sense of shared spiritual traditions among African-Americans, Professor Maulana Ron Karenga created a contemporary celebration, *Kwanzaa*, based on indigenous African "first fruits" harvest festivals. Using symbolic objects to help create a special atmosphere (such as candles, corn, fruits and vegetables, and a "unity cup," all called by their Swahili names), families and groups of families meet from December 26 to January 1 to explore their growth over the past year. They look at their own experiences of the Seven Principles — unity, self-determination, collective work, family-centeredness, purpose, creativity with limited resources, and confidence — and reward each other for progress by giving gifts.

Individual observances

In indigenous sacred ways, it is considered important for each person to experience a personal connection with the spirits. The people acknowledge and work with the spirits in many everyday ways. For instance, when searching for herbs, a person is not to take the first plant found; an offering is made to it, with the prayer that its relatives will understand one's needs. Guardian spirits and visions are sought by all the people, not just specialists such as shamans. The shaman may have more spirit helpers and more power, but visionary experiences and opportunities for worship are available to all. Indigenous traditions have therefore been called "democratized shamanism."

Temples to the spirits may exist, but one can also worship them anywhere. Wande Abimbola observes:

> You go to Sao Paulo, Brazil, ride the elevator to the twenty-fourth floor of an apartment building, and meet a friend. He takes you to a corner of his house and says, "Come and salute my Shango." It is contained in a small bowl. Big temples aren't necessary to worship the orisa, even though there are temples for most orisa in Africa. If you are a devotee of Ifa, you can carry the objects of Ifa in your pocket. If you want to make an offering to Ogun, put any piece of iron on the floor and make an offering to it. It's just like a Christian would carry a Bible or maybe a cross.[33]

To open themselves for contact with the spirit world, individuals in many indigenous cultures undergo a **vision quest**. After ritual purification, they are sent alone to a sacred spot to cry to the spirits to reveal something of their purpose in life and help them in their journey. This may also be done before undertaking a sacred mission, such as the Sun Dance. Indigenous Mexican leader Tlakaelel describes the vision quest as he observes it:

> You stay on a mountain, desert, or in a cave, isolated, naked, with only your sacred things, the things that you have gained, in the years of preparation — your eagle feathers, your pipe, your copal [tree bark used as incense]. You are left alone four days and four nights without food and water. During this time when you are

looking for your vision, many things happen. You see things move. You see animals that come close to you. Sometimes you might see someone that you care about a lot, and they're bringing water. You feel like you're dying of thirst, but there are limits around you, protection with hundreds of tobacco ties. You do not leave this circle, and this vision will disappear when they come to offer the water or sometimes they will just drop in on the ground. Or someone comes and helps you with their strength and gives you messages. [34]

In the traditional sacred ways, one is not supposed to ask for a vision for selfish personal reasons. The point of this individual ordeal, which is designed to be physically and emotionally stressful, is to ask how one can help the people and the planet.

Contemporary Issues

Sadly, traditional spiritual wisdom has been largely obliterated in many parts of the world by those who wanted to take the people's lands or save their souls with some other path to the divine. Under the slogan "Kill the Indian and save the man," the American founder of the boarding school system for native children took them away from their families at a young age and transformed their cultural identity, presenting the native ways as inferior and distancing them from normal participation in the traditional sacred life. In Africa, the traditional interest in the flow of the past into the present, with value placed on the intensity of present experience, has been rapidly replaced by a Westernized view of time, in which one is perpetually anxious about the future. This shift has led to severe psychological disorientation and social and political instability. Those whose spiritual cultures have been merged with world religions such as Islam, Buddhism, or Christianity are now examining the relationship of their earlier tradition to the intercultural missionary traditions.

Indigenous peoples have also been recent victims of well-meaning but disastrous development projects. In Zimbabwe, for example, thousands of traditional self-sufficient Vaduma people were displaced from their ancestral lands, when the lands were flooded to create a huge artificial lake for irrigating an area hundreds of kilometers away. Jameson Kurasha of the University of Zimbabwe describes the effects on the Vaduma:

When the "idea" of development was imposed on them, families were separated by a massive stretch of water. Now the Murinye Mugabe families are alienated from each other. They are now peoples without a tangible past to guide and unite them because their past (i.e. ancestors) are either buried or washed away by the lake. They are basically a people without a home to point to. The separation has left a cultural damage that will never be restored.

Economically they are worse off. The wetlands were taken away from them. Since they were moved to dry reservations, if they want to fish they have to pay authorities. All this was done in the name of development and national interest. That national interest was an irrigation scheme hundreds of kilometers away in Chiredzi. The scheme ensures constant water supply for cash crops that would earn the nation foreign currency. To these victims of development, "forex" is meaningless. In 1992, because of drought, most of the Murinye and Mugabe people were lonely and starving in the reservations, and animals and trees were drowned in thousands. [35]

The Sun Dance Way of Self-Sacrifice

Sacrificing oneself for the sake of the whole is highly valued in most indigenous traditions. Through purification ceremonies, the people attempt to break through their small selves in order to serve as clear vehicles for the energy of the Great Spirit. In the Americas a powerful ceremony for these purposes is the Sun Dance. Among the Oglala Lakota, participants may dance for four days without food or water, looking at the sun and praying for blessings for the people. They say the ceremony as they practice it was first given to them through a vision received by a man named Kablaya.

In diverse forms, Sun Dances are now performed at many sites each spring and summer, most of them on the midwestern and northern plains of North America. In theory, only those who have had visions that they should perform the dance should do so. Some come in penance, for purification; others offer themselves as vehicles to request blessings for all people or for specific people who need help. It is not considered proper to dance for one's own needs.

Dancers make a commitment to do the dance for a certain number of times. Some Sun Dances include women dancers; some who dance are children. Non-indigenous people are generally barred from dancing.

The power of the Sun Dance requires that everything be handled in a sacred way. Dancers must do vision quests and purify themselves in sweat lodges before the ceremony begins. In spite of thirst and exhaustion, those in some Sun Dances continue to participate in sweat lodges each day of the dance. A tree is chosen to be placed at the center of the circle (among the Lakota, it is always a cottonwood, which when cut crosswise reveals a multi-pointed star pattern representing the sun).

Sweat lodges are used for physical and spiritual purification. A pole frame is covered with skins or blankets and heated rocks are splashed with water to create searing steam.

The tree's sacrifice is attended with ritual prayers. Participants may string prayer flags onto its branches before it is hoisted in the center of the dancing circle.

During the dance itself, the participants are guided through patterns with symbolic meanings. The choreography varies from one group to another. The Sioux Sun Dancers do not move around the circle except to shift slightly during the day so that they are always facing the sun. In Mexico the patterns continually honor the powers of the four directions by facing each one in turn.

As they dance, the dancers blow whistles traditionally made from the wing bones of the spotted eagle, but now often whittled from hollow sticks. When giving instructions for the dance, Kablaya reportedly explained, "When you blow the whistle always remember that it is the voice of the Spotted Eagle; our Grandfather, Wakan-Tanka, always hears this, for you see it is really His own voice."[36]

A group of people support the dancers by singing special sacred songs and beating a large drum. If their energy flags, so does that of the dancers. A woman Sun Dancer says that after a while, "The drum is no longer outside of you. It is as if in you and you don't even know that you're dancing." The dancers also support each other in ways such as using the feathers they carry to fan those whose energy seems low. There may also be communal vision ceremonies.

Each dancer is the carrier of a sacred pipe. Between rounds, these may be shared with group onlookers who are led into the circle and who pass the pipes around among the dancers to strengthen them with the power of the smoke.

Non-dancers may also be led into the circle for a special healing round on the third or fourth day. By that time, the dancers have been so purified and empowered that they can all act as healers, using their eagle feathers as instruments to convey the divine power.

The suffering which each dancer willingly undergoes is heightened during piercing. For those whose visions suggest it — and whose tribes use piercing, for some do not — at some point during the dance incisions are made in the skin of their chest, back, or arms and sharpened sticks are inserted. There are then various ways of tearing through the skin. One reserved for chiefs is to drag buffalo skulls from ropes attached to the piercing sticks, symbolizing their carrying of the burdens of the people. More often, ropes are thrown over the trees and attached to the piercing sticks. Each person who pierces is then pulled upward, "flying" by flapping eagle wings, until the sticks break through the skin. It is thought that the more one asks when making the sacrifice the more difficult it will be to break free. One Lakota dancer was instructed in a vision that he should be hung from the tree for a whole night. They had to pierce him in many places in order to distribute his weight, and then pull him down in the morning.

Why must the dance involve so much suffering? A Lakota Sun Dancer explains, "Nobody knows why, but suffering makes our prayers more sincere. The sun dance tests your sincerity, pushes your spirit beyond its limits." And as the dance goes on, many of the dancers transcend their physical agony and experience an increasing sense of euphoria. A Mexican dancer explains:

> It's not pain. It's ecstasy. We get the energy from the sun and from the contact with Mother Earth. You also feel the energy of the eagles [who often fly overhead], all the animals, all the plants that surround you, all the vegetation. That energy comes to sustain you for the lack of food and water. Also when you smoke the pipe it serves as food or energy; the smoke feeds you energy so that you can continue. And every so often we put our palms to the sun to receive the energy from the sun. You can feel it in your whole body, a complete bath of energy.

*Names of individual dancers interviewed are not given here, to preserve their privacy and the sacredness of the Dance.

One way of communicating with unseen spirits is to make material offerings to them. This woman is making offerings to the spirits involved in the rice crop in Bali.

Modern development schemes are being called into question by land-based traditional peoples around the world and attempts have begun to revive the ancient wisdom by acknowledging its validity. For example, in 1995 damage from rainy season floods and sedimentation in northern Thailand was so severe that villagers whose houses and fields had been destroyed revived an ancient indigenous ritual to apologize to the Mae Chaem River. Respectful relationships with the river had lapsed with the introduction of modern water control technologies, such as dams and irrigation projects. At dawn, in the rain, villagers made altars in the river, filling them with sweets, nuts, bananas, sugar cane, foods, and cigarettes as offerings to the spirits of the forest, the earth deities, and the guardian spirits of the river. In their prayers, the people asked forgiveness of the river for misuse of the water and requested that the water level be lowered.

Some indigenous people feel that their traditional sacred ways are not only valid, but actually essential for the future of the world. They see these under-standings as antidotes to mechanistic, dehumanizing, environmentally destructive ways of life. Rather than regarding their ancient way as inferior, intact groups such as the Kogi of the high Columbian rainforest feel they are the Elder Brothers of all humanity, responsible for keeping the balance of the universe and re-educating their Younger Brothers who have become distracted by desire for material gain.

Personal visions and ancient prophecies about the dangers of a lifestyle that ignores the earth and the spiritual dimensions of life are leading native elders around the world to gather internationally and raise their voices together. They assert indigenous spiritual insights and observations about the state of the planet, political matters, and contemporary lifestyle issues. At international gatherings about the fate of the planet, it is often the voices of the native elders which help to ground the lofty abstractions in sacred reality. The indigenous delegates to the 1993 Parliament of World Religions in Chicago noted that

> One hundred years ago during the 1893 Parliament of World Religions, the profoundly religious Original Peoples of the Western Hemisphere were not invited. We are still here and still struggling to be heard for the sake of our Mother Earth and our children.[37]

Indigenous elders who are now speaking out seek converts not to their path but to a respect for all of life which they feel is essential for the harmony of the planet. And they seek freedom to practice their Original Instructions. A 1989 communique from the Traditional Circle of Indian Elders and Youth, meeting in the Queen Charlotte Islands, included these reminders of their spiritual rights and needs:

> Increasingly, the world is beginning to recognize the integrity of indigenous religions. Our spiritual visions are gaining equality and support in international affairs.... Yet we must remind all people that the practices of our spiritual ways require certain elements. We need access to sacred sites, which must be protected. We need access to sacred animals, which must be kept from regulatory interference. We need the return of sacred objects, many of which are now in museums, historical societies, universities and private collections.
>
> Indigenous people around the world have a birthright and a responsibility to their ancestral lands. Our cultural and spiritual identity is dependent upon a land base. If the nations remain truthful to their traditional philosophy and values toward the land, their future is secure.[38]

Rigoberta Menchú of the K'iché Maya, a Nobel Laureate, asserts:

> Many people have said that indigenous peoples are myths of the past, ruins that have died. But the indigenous community is not a vestige of the past, nor is it a myth. It is full of vitality and has a course and a future. It has much wisdom and richness to contribute. They have not killed us and they will not kill us now. We are stepping forth to say, "No, we are here. We live."[39]

Suggested reading

Beck, Peggy V. and Walters, Anna L., *The Sacred: Ways of Knowledge, Sources of Life*, Tsaile (Navajo Nation), Arizona: Navajo Community College Press, 1977. A fine and very genuine survey of indigenous sacred ways, particularly those of North America.

Berger, Julian, *The Gaia Atlas of First Peoples: A Future for the Indigenous World*, New York: Anchor Books, 1990. An illustrated survey of contemporary survival issues facing the original inhabitants of many lands, with particular reference to threats to their environment from invading cultures.

Brown, Joseph Epes, *The Sacred Pipe*, 1953, New York: Penguin Books, 1971. Detailed accounts of the sacred rites of the Oglala Sioux by Black Elk, a respected holy man.

Eliade, Mircea, *Shamanism: Archaic Techniques of Ecstasy*, translated from the French by Willard Trask, London: Routledge and Kegan Paul, 1964. The first scholarly book to examine shamanism as an authentic religious form rather than an anthropological oddity.

Ewen, Alexander, *Voice of Indigenous Peoples*, Santa Fe, New Mexico: Clear Light Publishers, 1994. Speeches and writings from indigenous speakers at the 1992 United Nations Human Rights Day, analyzing the political conditions facing indigenous peoples.

Gill, Sam D., *Native American Religions*, Belmont, California: Wadsworth, 1982. A sensitive academic survey of indigenous sacred ways in the United States.

Gleason, Judith, *Oya: In Praise of the Goddess*, Boston: Shambhala Publications, 1987. A complex exploration of the Yoruba goddess which gives some insight into African traditions.

Halifax, Joan, *Shamanic Voices: A Survey of Visionary Narratives*, New York: E. P. Dutton, 1979, and Harmondsworth, London: Penguin, 1980. First-hand accounts of shamanistic visionary experiences.

Lame Deer, John and Richard Erdoes, *Lame Deer: Seeker of Visions*, New York: Pocket Books, 1976. Fascinating first-hand accounts of the life of a rebel visionary who tried to maintain the old ways.

Mbiti, John S., *African Religions and Philosophy*, second edition, Oxford, England: Heinemann, 1990. Update of a classic on traditional African spirituality, including its interface with global religions.

Olupona, Jacob K., *African Traditional Religions in Contemporary Society*, New York: Paragon House, 1991. A rich collection of papers by African scholars affirming and analyzing the contemporary characteristics and impacts of indigenous African sacred ways.

CHAPTER 3
HINDUISM

"With mind absorbed and heart melted in love"

In the Indian subcontinent there has developed a complex variety of religious paths. All those that honor the ancient scriptures called the Vedas are commonly grouped under the term "Hinduism." This label is derived from a name applied by invaders to the people living in the region of the Indus River. The indigenous term for the Veda-based traditions in the entire Indian region is **Sanatana Dharma** ("eternal religion"). Sanatana, "eternal" or "ageless," reflects the belief that this religion has always existed. **Dharma** is derived from the word meaning "support." It is often translated as "religion," but its meaning encompasses matters of duty, natural law, social welfare, ethics, and direction of all activities in life toward transcendental realization.

The spiritual expressions of Sanatana Dharma range from extreme asceticism to extreme sensuality, from the heights of personal devotion to a deity to the heights of abstract philosophy, from metaphysical proclamations of the oneness behind the material world to worship of images representing a multiplicity of deities. According to tradition, there are actually thirty-three million gods in India. The feeling is that the Divine has countless faces, and all are divine. The extreme variations within Sanatana Dharma are reflections of its great age. Few of the myriad religious paths that have arisen over the millennia have been lost. They continue to co-exist in present-day India.

> *Truth is one; sages call it by various names.*
>
> Rig Veda

One avenue into understanding this mosaic of beliefs and practices is to trace the supposed chronological development of patterns which co-exist today. But this approach is offered simply as an organizational framework. Historians of religion and devotees of the various forms have widely variant ideas about the historical origin of the threads that now compose Hinduism. The archaeological evidence is fragmented and Indians have not traditionally emphasized historical accuracy, readily interweaving reports of actual events and people with mythological embellishments and symbolism. This is because in Sanatana Dharma, the life of the human body is regarded as very transitory, and the world as illusory. Human accomplishments have never been recorded with any accuracy, for they are regarded as unimportant. What is important is the life of the soul.

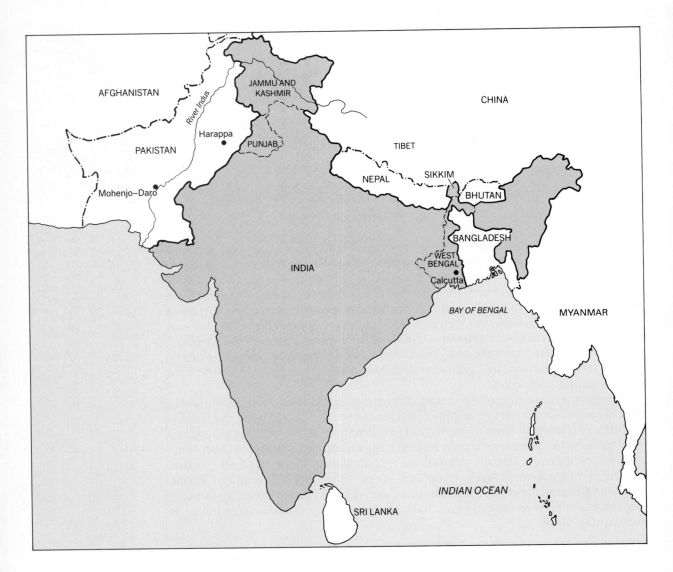

The Indian subcontinent includes areas that are now politically separate from India. The Indus Valley, for instance, lies in what is now the largely Muslim state of Pakistan.

Pre-Vedic religion

Many of the threads of contemporary Hinduism may have existed in the religions practiced by the aboriginal peoples of India. Some of the ways of the ancient Dravidian people seem to have persisted in southern Indian villages. There were also advanced urban centers in the Indus Valley of what is now Pakistan from about 2500 BCE or even earlier until 1500 BCE. Major fortified cities were found by archaeologists at Harappa and Mohenjo-Daro; the culture they represent is labeled "Harappan."

Archaeologists have found little conclusive evidence of temples in the Harappan cities, but the people clearly lavished great care on their plumbing systems. Houses had wells, bathing rooms or drained bathing floors, and even built-in latrines.

Wastes were carried off in an elaborate system of communal brick drains. And the major structure at Mohenjo-Daro has been called the Great Bath by archaeologists. A large lined tank with steps leading down into it is surrounded by an open courtyard; an adjoining structure has what appear to be private bathing rooms. Historians speculate from this evidence that the early Indus people placed a religious sort of emphasis on hygiene and/or ritual purification.

They also seemed to venerate life-giving power. Although few pieces of ritual art remain seals have been found depicting an ascetic male figure in cross-legged yogic posture. He has an erect phallus, wears a great horned headdress, and is surrounded by strong animals such as bulls and tigers. There were also stone lingams, natural elongated oval stones or sculptures up to two feet tall.

Both the seals and the lingams suggest that the early Indus people knew about meditation practices and were worshippers of a deity who bore the attributes of the later god Siva,[1] who is still one of the major forms of the Divine worshipped today. The word used in India to signify ritual worship, *puja*, is derived from an ancient Dravidian word meaning "to anoint." Worshippers may have reverently anointed the lingams, as people still do in India today.

Even more prominent among the artefacts are pieces that seem to honor a great goddess. Sacred pots, like those still used in south Indian village ceremonies honoring the goddess, may have been associated then, as now, with the feminine as the receptacle of the primeval stuff of life. There is also considerable evidence of worship of local deities by stone altars placed beneath sacred trees. Each tree is still popularly believed to be the home of a tree spirit, and many are honored with offerings.

The river goddess Ganga. Appreciation of the feminine as a symbol of plenty, of sacred trees, and of the purifying powers of rivers may have been of pre-Vedic origin, but has persisted in Indian art and ritual practices.

Vedic religion

Western historians think that the highly organized cultures of the Indus Valley and the villages in other parts of the subcontinent were gradually overrun by nomadic invaders from outside India. Those whose influence became predominant were the *Aryans* (their Sanskrit word meaning "noble," or "one who knows the value of life"). They were among the Indo-European tribes who migrated outward from the steppes of southern Russia during the second millennium BCE.

The Aryans' material culture was relatively simple, and they were probably illiterate. They had organized themselves into patriarchal tribes worshipping gods of nature (such as fire and sky). Their advantage over the local populations was their emphasis on war technologies, primarily horse-drawn chariots.

The Vedas

The evidence used by archaeologists to piece together the theory of the Aryan invasion shows that the Indus Valley civilization was followed by a materially crude culture. But the sacred literature that is traced back at least to this time reaches great spiritual heights. The works are called the *Vedas* ("body of knowledge") and are still held in greatest reverence as revealed scriptures which are believed to form the basis of all later scriptures.

The Vedas include four parts which appear to have evolved over time. The earliest are the Samhitas, praises and worship of the deities. Then appeared the

HINDUISM

HISTORIANS' STANDARD VIEW		INDIAN TRADITION
	6000 BCE	*Vedas* heard by rishis, carried orally c.8000–6000
	5000	
	4000	
Harappan civilization c.3500–1500		Beginning of Kali Yuga: Vishnu incarnates as Vyasa, who writes down the *Vedas* c.3102
	3000	
Aryan invasions of north India c.2000–900	2000	
Early *Vedas* first written down c.1500		
Upanishads recorded c.1000–500	1000	
Brahmanas written down c.900–700		
Jainism: Mahavira's life c.599–527		
Buddhism: Buddha's life c.563–483	500	
Ramayana (present form) 400 BCE – 200 CE		
Mahabharata (present form) 400 BCE – 400 CE		
Patanjali systematizes Yoga Sutras by 200 BCE		Yoga practices are ancient, indigenous
	CE	
Code of Manu compiled before 100 CE		
Tantras written down c.300		*Tantras* are as old as the *Upanishads*
Sankara reorganizes Vedanta c.500–800	500	
Bhakti movement flourishes 600–1800		
Muslim invasions begin 711		
Purana of the Lord written down c.800–900		
	1000	
Mughal Empire 1556–1707	1500	
Brahmo Samaj revitalization 1828		
Ramakrishna's life 1836–1886		
Arya Samaj reform 1875		
British rule of India 1857–1947	2000	

The Vedas include hymns praising the cow, who is still beloved and treated as sacred by Hindus. The cow is our Mother, for she gives us her milk. The traditional diet is vegetarian; cows are raised for dairy products rather than killed for their flesh.

Brahmanas, directions about performances of the ritual sacrifices to the deities. Perhaps on finding that these rituals did not inevitably achieve the desired results, some people went to the forests to meditate as recluses; their writings form the Aranyatas, or "forest treatises." The latest of the Vedas are the Upanishads, consisting of teachings from highly-realized spiritual masters. Their major subject is realization of the oneness of the godhead, a supreme formless reality behind the world of transitory appearances.

These sacred teachings seem to have originated by 1500 to 1000 BCE, though the Indian people and some scholars feel that they are far older. We know that the Vedas are much older than their earliest written forms; they were originally transmitted orally from teacher to student and may then have been written down over a period of eight or nine hundred years.

According to orthodox Hindus, the Vedas are not the work of any humans. They are believed to be the breath of the eternal, as "heard" by the ancient sages, or *rishis*. The scriptures are thought to transcend human time and are thus as relevant today as they were thousands of years ago. The *Gayatrimantra*, a verse in a Vedic hymn, is still chanted daily by the devout as the most sacred of prayers:

Aum [the primordial creative sound],
Bhu Bhuvah Svah [the three worlds: earth, atmosphere, and heaven],
Tat Savitur Varenyum,

Bhargo Devasya Dheemahe [adoration of the glory, splendor, and grace that radiate
    from the Divine Light that illuminates the three worlds],
Dhiyo Yo Nah Prachodayat [a prayer for liberation through awakening of the light
    of the universal intelligence].²

The oldest of the known Vedic scriptures — and perhaps the oldest of all the world's existing scriptures — is thought to be the *Rig Veda*. This praises and implores the blessings of the **Devas** — the "shining ones," the controlling forces in the cosmos. They were referred to as deities who consecrate every part of life. The major deities seem to have included Indra (god of thunder), Agni (god of fire), Soma (associated with a sacred drink), and Ushas (goddess of dawn). The devas included both opaque earth gods and transparent deities of the sky and celestial realms. But behind all the myriad aspects of divinity, the sages perceived one unseen Reality, beyond human understanding, ceaselessly creating and sustaining, encompassing all time, space, and causation.

Sacrifices

Vedic worship centered around the fire sacrifice. Communities seem to have gathered around a fire placing offerings in it to be conveyed to the gods by **Agni**, the being of fire. The Vedic hymns sung to Agni are spiritually complex invocations of the power of truth against darkness.

Vedic worship with fire is still significant in contemporary rituals.

Ritual use of fire to offer clarified butter *(ghee)* and grains to the devas is still central to contemporary Hindu worship. The twentieth-century seer Sri Aurobindo has written extensively about the metaphorical significances of Agni. His insights include these:

> The Vedic deity Agni is the first of the Powers that have issued from the vast and secret Godhead. Agni is the form, the fire, the forceful heat and flaming will of this Divinity. [The word Agni] means a burning brightness, whence its use for fire. When man, awakened from his night, wills to offer his inner and outer activities to the gods of a truer and higher existence and so to arise out of mortality into the far-off immortality, it is this flame of upward aspiring Force and Will that he must kindle; into this fire he must cast the sacrifice.[3]

Over time elaborate fire rituals were created, controlled by Brahmin priests. The *Brahmanas* gave detailed instructions for the performance of the fire sacrifices. Specified verbal formulas, sacred chants, and sacred actions were to be used by the priests to invoke the breath behind all of existence (later known as **Brahman**, the Absolute, the Supreme Reality). The verbal formulas were also called **mantras**, sacred verse whose sound was believed to evoke the reality they connoted. The language used was Sanskrit (meaning "well-formed"), which was considered a re-creation of the sound-forms of objects, actions, and qualities, as heard by ancient sages in deep meditation.

The fire rituals were apparently held in the open air. The most auspicious places for their performance were at the confluence of two rivers. The junction of the major rivers of the early Aryan settlements, the sacred Ganga and the Jumna, was considered extremely sacred. The feeling that special blessings are available there continues today; the confluence is still a major pilgrimage spot for worshippers.

Offerings to Agni usually consisted of melted butter, grains, soma, and sometimes animals. Soma was a drink apparently made of a specific plant that grew in mountainous, windy places; its juice seemed to confer great vigor. It was so potent that only the god Indra could drink it undiluted, for strength in his battles against the demons. Human worshippers mixed it with water or milk for their own ritual consumption. Despite considerable contemporary interest in recreating this drink, the soma plant has not been identified.

Vedic worship was primarily sacrificial. The sacrifice offered by humans was metaphorically linked with the original personal sacrifice by which the universe was created, namely the dismemberment of the *Purusha*, the primal Being, by the gods. His mind, for example, became the moon, his eyes the sun, his breath the wind.

The Vedic principle of sacrifice was based on the idea that generous sacrifices to a deity will be rewarded by some specific result. This attitude toward giving has remained in Indian culture. Hospitality to guests is highly stressed. To turn someone away from your door without feeding him is considered a great sin, for the person could be the deity incarnate. Even today, there are huge ceremonies for making offerings to a deity and feeding the public. Professional beggars take advantage of belief in sacrifice by suggesting that those who give to them will be blessed. But the most important sacrifices are considered to be inner sacrifices — giving one's entire self over to God, symbolized as cutting off one's head and humbly offering it.

Castes and social duties

Earthly sacrifices were designed to mirror the original cosmic sacrifice of Purusha and thus keep the world in proper order. If the sacrifices were offered correctly, the gods would be guided by the people's requests. Because the sacrifices were a reciprocal communion with the gods, priests who performed the public sacrifices had to be carefully trained and maintain high standards of ritual purity. Those so trained — the Brahmins — comprised a special occupational group or **jati**. According to Vedic religion, the orderly working of society included a clear division of labor among four major occupational groups, which later became entrenched as **castes**. The Brahmins were the priests and philosophers, specialists in the life of the spirit. They had even higher status than the next group, later called *kshatriyas*. These were the nobility of feudal India: kings, warriors, and vassals. Their general function was to guard and preserve the society; they were expected to be courageous and majestic. *Vaishyas* were the economic specialists: farmers and merchants. The *shudra* caste were the manual laborers and artisans.

Some of the shudras carried on such impure functions that for hygienic reasons they were somewhat isolated from the rest of society. Work such as removing human wastes and corpses and sweeping streets made their bodies and clothing potential carriers of disease, so in time they were considered "untouchable" by others. Most who carried on these lowly but necessary functions were members of the conquered black-skinned indigenous population.

Religion was increasingly controlled by the ritually pure and carefully trained priests, and contact between castes was limited. Caste membership became hereditary rather than a reflection of each individual's talents. This system became as important as the Vedas themselves in defining Hinduism until its social injustices were attacked in the nineteenth century. One of its opponents was the courageous leader Mahatma Gandhi, who renamed the lowest caste *harijans*, "the children of God." In 1948 the stigma of "untouchability" was legally abolished, though many caste distinctions still linger in modern India. Marriage across caste lines, for instance, is still often disapproved in India. If a boy and girl—one of whom is from lowest caste—fall in love, sometimes the families from both sides will kill them rather than allow their marriage, to prevent disgrace or retribution.

Despite its abuses, the division of labor represented by the caste system is part of Sanatana Dharma's strong emphasis on social duties and sacrifice of individual desires for the sake of social order. Dharma's purpose is to uplift people from worldly concerns and to encourage them to behave according to higher laws. The Vedas, other scriptures, and historical customs have all conditioned the Indian people to accept their social roles. These were set forth in a major document known as the *Code of Manu*, compiled by 100 CE. In it are laws governing all aspects of life, including the proper conduct of rulers, dietary restrictions, marriage laws, daily rituals, purification rites, social laws, and ethical guidance. It enjoins hospitality to guests and the cultivation of such virtues as contemplation, truthfulness, compassion, non-attachment, generosity, pleasant dealings with people, and self-control. The Code of Manu also specifies the reciprocal duties of men and women. Women are expected to be dependent on men at all times; men are to revere women in their household settings. Of ancient origin, such dharmic laws still have a strong impact in Indian culture.

Transcendent Reality

Of the four parts of the Vedas, the Upanishads are thought to have evolved last, around 1000 to 500 BCE or later. They represent the mystical insights of rishis who sought Ultimate Reality through their meditations in the forest. Many people consider them the cream of Indian thought, among the highest spiritual literature ever written. They were not taught to the masses but rather were reserved for advanced seekers of spiritual truth.

Diagram of Brahman and Atman.

CONTEMPLATION OF THE LUMINOUS SELF The word "Upanishad" embraces the idea of the devoted disciple sitting down by the teacher to receive private spiritual instruction about the highest reality, loosening all doubts and destroying all ignorance. Emphasis is placed not on outward ritual performances, as in the earlier Vedic religion, but on inner experience as the path to realization and immortality.

The rishis explain that the bodily senses are made for looking outward; the eyes, ears, nose, tongue, and skin are enticed by sensory pleasures. But ultimately these are fleeting, impermanent. They pass away and then one dies, never having experienced what is of greater value because it is infinite, everlasting. What is real and lasting, they found, can only be discovered by turning away from worldly things. They taught their pupils to turn their attention inside, and thus discover a transcendent reality from within. This unseen but all-pervading reality they called Brahman, the Unknowable:

Him the eye does not see, nor the tongue express, nor the mind grasp.[4]

From Brahman spring the multiplicity of forms, including humans. The joyous discovery of the rishis was that they could find Brahman as the subtle self (**Atman**) within themselves. Existence was like a wheel, with the One in the center and the individual selves radiating outward like spokes. One of the rishis explained this relationship thus:

In the beginning there was Existence alone — One only, without a second. He, the One, thought to himself: Let me be many, let me grow forth. Thus out of himself he projected the universe, and having projected out of himself the universe, he entered into every being. All that is has its self in him alone. Of all things he is the subtle essence. He is the truth. He is the Self. And that, … THAT ART THOU.

Chandogya Upanishad[5]

The rishis declared that when one discovers the inner self, Atman, and thus also its source, Brahman, the self merges into its transcendent source, and one experiences unspeakable peace.

REINCARNATION In addition to these profound descriptions of contemplation of the Absolute, the Upanishads express several doctrines that are central to all forms of Sanatana Dharma. One is the idea of **reincarnation**. In answer to the universal question, "What happens after we die?" the rishis taught that the soul leaves the dead body and enters a new one. In later scriptures, this process would be likened to shedding old clothes and donning new ones. One takes birth again and again in countless bodies — perhaps as an animal or some other life form — but the self remains the same. Birth as a human being is a precious and rare opportunity for the soul to advance toward its ultimate goal of liberation from rebirth and merging with the Absolute Reality.

KARMA An important corollary to the idea that we are reborn into another body is the concept of **karma**. It means action, and also the consequences of action. Every act we make, and even every thought and every desire we have, shapes our future experiences. Our life is what we have made it. And we ourselves are shaped by what we have done: "As a man acts, so does he become.... A man becomes pure through pure deeds, impure through impure deeds."[6] Not only do we reap in this life the good or evil we have sown; they also follow us after physical death, affecting our next incarnation. Ethically, this is a strong teaching, for our every move has far-reaching consequences.

The ultimate goal, however, is not creation of good lives by good deeds, but a clean escape from the karma-run wheel of birth, death, and rebirth, which is called samsara. To escape from **samsara** is to achieve **moksha**, or liberation from the limitations of space, time, and matter through realization of the immortal Absolute. Many lifetimes of upward-striving incarnations are required to reach this transcendence of earthly miseries. This desire for liberation from earthly existence is one of the underpinnings of classical Hinduism, and of Buddhism as well.

Devotional religion of the epics and Puranas

It is difficult to pray to the impersonal Absolute, for it is formless and is not totally distinct from oneself. More personal worship of a divine Being can be inferred from the goddess and proto-Shiva statues of ancient India. It probably persisted during the Vedic period and was later given written expression. **Bhakti** — intense devotion to a personal manifestation of Brahman — became the heart of Hinduism as the majority of people now experience it.

Although there are many devotional passages in the Upanishads, personal love for a personal deity flowered in the spiritual literature that followed the Vedas. Two major classes of scriptures that arose after 500 BCE (according to Western scholarship) were the *epics* and the *Puranas*. They were helpful vehicles to popularize spiritual knowledge and devotion through myths and legends of national events. They were particularly useful in spreading Hindu teachings to the masses at times when Buddhism and Jainism — movements born in India but not recognizing the authority of the Vedas — were winning converts.

In contrast to the rather abstract depictions of the Divine Principle in the Upanishads, the epics and Puranas are highly theistic. That is, they represent the Supreme as a Person. In fact, the Supreme is presented as various human-like deities. As T. M. P. Mahadevan explains:

> *The Hindu mind is averse to assigning an unalterable or rigidly fixed form or name to the Deity. Hence it is that in Hinduism we have innumerable god-forms and countless divine names. And, it is a truth that is recognized by all Hindus that obeisance offered to any of these forms and names reaches the one supreme God.[7]*

Two great epics, the *Ramayana* and the *Mahabharata*, present the Supreme usually as Vishnu, who intervenes on earth during critical periods in the cosmic cycles. In the unthinkable vastness of time as reckoned by Hindu thought, each world cycle lasts 4,320,000,000 years, the equivalent of one day in the life of Brahma, the Creator god. Each world cycle is divided into four ages, or *yugas*.

Dharma — moral order in the world — is natural in the first age. The second age is like a cow standing on three legs; people must be taught their proper roles in society. During the darker third age, revealed values are no longer recognized, people lose their altruism and willingness for self-denial, and there are no more saints. The final age, **Kali Yuga**, is as imbalanced as a cow trying to stand on one leg. The world is at its worst, with egotism, ignorance, recklessness, and war rampant. According to Hindu figuring, we are in the midst of Kali Yuga, an age which began on a Friday in 3102 BCE. Such an age is described thus:

> *When society reaches a stage where property confers rank, wealth becomes the only source of virtue, passion the sole bond of union between husband and wife, falsehood the source of success in life, sex the only means of enjoyment, and when outer trappings are confused with inner religion …[8]*

Each of these massive cycles witnesses the same turns of events, with the balance inexorably shifting from the true dharma to dissolution and then back to the dharma as the gods are again victorious over the anti-gods. The Puranas list the many ways that the Lord has incarnated in the world when dharma is decaying, to help restore virtue and defeat evil. For instance, Vishnu is said to have incarnated as Vyasa at the beginning of Kali Yuga to write down the Vedas, for humans no longer had good memories. It is considered inevitable that Vishnu will continually return in answer to the pleas of suffering humans, and equally inevitable that he will meet with resistance from "demonic forces" who are also part of the cosmic cycles.

THE RAMAYANA The epics deal with this eternal play of good and evil, symbolized by battles involving the human incarnations of Vishnu. Along the way, they teach examples of the virtuous life, which is a life of responsibilities to others defined by

During the north Indian festival Ram-lila, giant effigies of Ravana and the demons from the epic Ramayana are dramatically burned to the delight of the crowds.

one's social roles. One is first a daughter, sister, wife, mother, or friend in relationship to others, and only secondarily an individual.

The *Ramayana*, thought to have been composed by about 100 or 200 BCE, is much beloved and is acted out with great pageantry throughout India every year. It lovingly brings out the duties of relationships, portraying ideal characters such as the ideal servant, the ideal brother, the ideal wife, the ideal king. In the story, Vishnu incarnates as the virtuous prince Rama in order to kill Ravana, the ten-headed demon king of Sri Lanka. Rama is heir to his father's throne, but the mother of his stepbrother compels the king to banish Rama into the forest for fourteen years. Rama, a model of morality, goes willingly, observing that a son's duty is to obey his parents implicitly, even when their commands seem wrong. He is accompanied into the ascetic life by his wife Sita, the model of wifely devotion in a patriarchal society. She refuses his offer to remain behind in comfort:

> *O my Lord! A father, mother, son, brother or daughter-in-law indeed abide by the results of their actions; but a wife, O best of men, shares in her husband's fate. Therefore I have been ordered no less than thou, to exile in the forest. If thou goest there I shall go before thee, treading upon thorns and prickly grass. I shall not cause thee trouble but will live on roots and fruits. And there will be pools, with wild geese and other fowl and bright with full-blown lotus flowers, where we may bathe. There I shall be happy with thee even for a hundred or a thousand years.*[9]

Eventually Sita is kidnapped by Ravana, who wooes her unsuccessfully in his island kingdom, guarded by all manner of terrible demons. Although Rama is powerful, he and his half-brother Lakshman need the help of the monkeys and bears in the battle to get Sita back. Hanuman the monkey becomes the hero of the story. He symbolizes the power of faith and devotion to overcome our human frailties. In his love for the Lord he can do anything.

The bloody battle ends in single-handed combat between Ravana and Rama. Rama blesses a sacred arrow with Vedic mantras and sends it straight into Ravana's heart. In one traditional version of the *Ramayana*, when Rama and Sita are reunited, he accuses her of possible infidelity, so to prove her innocence she successfully undergoes an ordeal by fire in which Agni protects her. After Rama's kingship is restored, he asks Sita to prove her purity several more times in order to preserve the integrity of his rule from the people's suspicions. After many ordeals, she utters these final words, becomes a field of radiance, and disappears into the ground:

> *O Lord of my being, I realize you in me and me in you. Our relationship is eternal. Through this body assumed by me, my service to you and your progeny is complete now. I dissolve this body to its original state.*
> *Mother Earth, you gave form to me. I have made use of it as I ought to. In recognition of its purity may you kindly absorb it into your womb.*[10]

Indian arts are designed to be interpreted on many levels. One way of interpreting the Ramayana is to see all the characters as parts of ourself. Rama, for instance, is the innate principle of goodness, while Ravana is our dark side, or ego — that which tends to greed, jealousy, and selfishness. Sita represents our devotion to the Supreme. If our good side loses its Sita, we will see evil all around, like the demons whom Rama had to confront. To restore our devotional connection with Brahman, we must kill the ego.

*Rama and Lakshman
shoot arrows into the
breast of the demon
Ravana, with Hanuman
and the monkeys in the
background. Sita waits
within Ravana's
compound, guarded by
his demons. (North
India, c. 19th century.)*

Sita's role in the story also illustrates two features of Hindu women's spirituality. One is the ideal of marriage, in which couples are spiritual partners. Marriage is a vehicle for spiritual discipline, service, and advancement toward a spiritual goal, rather than a means of self-gratification. Men and women are thought to complement each other, although the ideal of liberation has traditionally been intended largely for the male.

Second, the female is highly venerated in Hinduism, compared to many other religions. Women who follow role models such as Sita make major contributions to the good earthly life, consisting of dharma (order in society), material wealth (by bearing sons in a patriarchal society), and the aesthetics of sensual pleasure. Women are auspicious beings, mythologically associated with wealth, beauty, splendor, and grace. As sexual partners to men, they help activate the spiritualizing life-force. No ceremonial sacrifice is complete unless the wife participates as well as the husband.

Despite their idealization, women are not encouraged to seek liberation through their own spiritual practices; their role is usually linked to that of their husband, who takes the position of their god and their guru. For many centuries, there was even the hope that a widow would choose to be cremated alive with her dead husband in order to remain united with him after death. This supreme self-sacrifice was called *sati*, meaning "good woman." It was treated as a religious ceremony, with the widow wearing her bridal sari, being blessed and bowed down to by the elders.

Historically, there were apparently some women who died thus. But this extreme ideal of duty and devotion was in some cases forced upon them rather than willingly chosen. Widowhood put women in a difficult position as well; widows tended to be regarded as impure and unwanted by society unless they became strict ascetics. Sati was finally outlawed in 1829, and remarriage of widows was legalized in 1856.

Women's roles have been and still are ambiguous in India. In early Vedic times, women were relatively free and honored members of Indian society, participating

An Indian woman prepares a protective rice paste pattern, honoring the ancient tradition by which her female ancestors created intuitive designs to bring spiritual protection for their families.

TEACHING STORY

Hanuman, the Monkey Chief

Hanuman was of divine origin and legendary powers, but he was embodied as a monkey, serving as a chief in the monkey army. When Rama needed to find his wife Sita after Ravana abducted her, he turned to the monkey king for help. The monkey king dispatched Hanuman to search to the south.

When the monkeys reached the sea dividing India from Sri Lanka, they were dismayed because monkeys do not swim. A vulture brought word that Sita was indeed on the other side of the water, a captive of Ravana. What to do? An old monkey reminded Hanuman of the powers he had displayed as an infant and told him that he could easily jump to Lanka and back if only he remembered his power and his divine origin.

Hanuman sat in meditation until he became strong and confident. Then he climbed a mountain, shook himself, and began to grow in size and strength. When at last he felt ready, he set off with a roar, hurling himself through the sky with eyes blazing like forest fires.

When Hanuman landed in Lanka, he shrunk himself to the size of a cat so that he could explore Ravana's forts. After many dangerous adventures, he gave Sita the message that Rama was preparing

to do battle to win her back, and then he jumped back over the sea to the Indian mainland.

During the battle of Lanka, Rama and Lakshman were mortally wounded. Nothing would save them except a certain herb that grew only in the Himalayas. In his devotion to Rama, Hanuman flew to the mountains, again skirting danger all the way. But once he got there, he could not tell precisely which herb to pick, so he uprooted the whole mountain and carried it back to Lanka. The herb would only be effective before the moon rose. From the air, Hanuman saw the moon about to clear the horizon so he swallowed the moon and reached Lanka in time to heal Rama and Lakshman.

After the victory, Rama rewarded Hanuman with a bracelet of pearls and gold. Hanuman chewed it up and threw it away. When a bear asked why he had rejected the gift from God, Hanuman explained that it was useless to him since it did not have Rama's name on it. The bear said, "Well, if you feel that way, why do you keep your body?" At that, Hanuman ripped open his chest, and there were Rama and Sita seated in his heart, and all of his bones and muscles had "Ram, Ram, Ram" written all over them.

equally in important spiritual rituals. By the time the British took control of India in the nineteenth century, wives had become virtual slaves of the husband's family, and worship of the goddess had in many places been superseded by worship of gods, with goddesses playing a secondary role as their spouses. With expectations that the girl will take a large dowry to the boy's family in a marriage arrangement, having girls is such an economic burden that many female babies are intentionally aborted or killed at birth. Nevertheless many women in contemporary India have been well-educated and many — including Indira Gandhi — have attained high political positions.

THE MAHABHARATA The other famous epic is the **Mahabharata**. Fifteen times as long as the Bible and apparently semi-historical, it may have been composed by about 300 BCE. The story revolves around the struggle between the sons of a royal family for control of a kingdom near what is now Delhi. Lessons inculcated in the course of the story revolve around the importance of sons, the duties of kingship,

Lord Krishna and Arjuna discuss profound philosophical questions in a battle chariot, as represented in this archway above the sacred Ganges River in Rishikesh.

the benefits of ascetic practice and righteous action, and the qualities of the gods. In contrast to the idealized characters in the Ramayana, the *Mahabharata* shows all sides of human nature, including greed, lust, intrigue, and desire for power. It is thought to be relevant for all times and all peoples. A serial dramatization of the *Mahabharata* continues to draw huge television audiences in contemporary India, and many people replay the episodes on home videotape. Throughout its episodes, the *Mahabharata* teaches one primary ethic: that the happiness of others is essential to one's own happiness. This consideration of others before oneself is the basis of dharma.

A portion of the *Mahabharata* that is of particular importance is the **Bhagavad-Gita** ("The teaching given in song by the Supreme Exalted One"). Krishna, one of the incarnations of Vishnu, appears as the charioteer of Arjuna, who is preparing to fight on the virtuous side of a battle that will pit brothers against brothers. The battle provides the occasion for a theological treatise on the nature of faith, which opposes our earthly duties and our spiritual aspirations. Before they plunge into battle, Krishna instructs Arjuna in the arts of self-transcendence and realization of the eternal. The eternal instructions are still central to Hindu spiritual practice.

Arjuna is enjoined to withdraw his attention from the impetuous demands of the senses, ignoring all feelings of attraction or aversion. This will give him a steady, peaceful mind. He is instructed to offer devotional service and to perform the prescribed Vedic sacrifices, but for the sake of discipline, duty, and example alone rather than reward — to "abandon all attachment to success or failure … renouncing the fruits of action in the material world."[11]

Actually, Lord Krishna says those who do everything for love of the Supreme transcend the Vedic notion of duty. In offering everything they do to the Supreme, "without desire for gain and free from egoism and lethargy,"[12] knowing that their eternal self is separate from the experiences of the body, they feel peace, freedom from earthly entanglements, and unassailable happiness.

This yogic science of transcending the "lower self" by the "higher self" is so ancient that Krishna says it was originally given to the sun god and through his agents, to humans. But in time it was lost, and Krishna is now renewing his instructions pertaining to "that very ancient science of the relationship with the Supreme."[13] He has taken human form again and again to teach the true religion:

Whenever and wherever there is a decline in religious practice … and a predominant rise of irreligion — at that time I descend Myself.

To deliver the pious and to annihilate the miscreants, as well as to re-establish the principles of religion, I advent Myself millennium after millennium.[14]

Krishna says that everything springs from his being:

There is no truth superior to Me. Everything rests upon Me, as pearls are strung on a thread.…

I am the taste of water, the light of the sun and the moon, the syllable om *in Vedic mantras; I am the sound in ether and ability in man.…*

All states of being — goodness, passion or ignorance — are manifested by My energy. I am, in one sense, everything — but I am independent. I am not under the modes of this material nature.[15]

This Supreme Godhead is not apparent to most mortals. The Lord can only be known by those who love him, and for them, it is easy, for they remember him at all times: "Whatever you do, whatever you eat, whatever you offer or give away, and whatever austerities you perform — do that … as an offering to Me." Any

Krishna is often pictured as drawing humans to the divine by the power of love, symbolized by the lure of his flute.

Above *Legends about Krishna as a child are often reenacted by children as part of a holiday honoring Krishna's birthday, Janmashtami.*
Right *A sannyasin, also referred to as a sadhu, renounces most possessions and lives only for the spiritual life.*

small act of devotion offered in love for Krishna becomes a way to him: "If one offers Me with love and devotion a leaf, a flower, fruit, or water, I will accept it."[16] Sincere worship creates a direct path to the Divine: "To those who are constantly devoted and worship me with love, I give the understanding by which they come to Me."[17]

KRISHNA OF THE PURANAS **Bhakti** — the way of devotion so beloved by the masses in India, and said to be the best path for Kali Yuga — is even more evident in the *Tales of the Lord (Bhagavata Purana)*. Most Indologists think it was written about the eighth or ninth century CE, but some Indians feel it was one of the works written down at the beginning of Kali Yuga by Vyasa. According to tradition, Vyasa had written down all the Vedas, Puranas, and the *Mahabharata*, but still he felt dissatisfied, as though something were missing. When he asked his spiritual master why this was so, his master said that the missing element was love of the Divine. What Vyasa then wrote describes the Supreme as a Person to be adored.

The Supreme Personality of Godhead is portrayed first in its vast dimensions: the Being whose body animates the material universe. For instance:

> *His eyes are the generating centers of all kinds of forms, and they glitter and illuminate. His eyeballs are like the sun and the heavenly planets. His ears hear from all sides and are receptacles for all the Vedas, and His sense of hearing is the generating center of the sky and of all kinds of sound.*[18]

This material universe we know is only one of millions of material universes. Each is like a bubble in the eternal spiritual sky, arising from the pores of the body of Vishnu, and these bubbles are created and destroyed as Vishnu breathes out and in. This cosmic conception is so vast that it is impossible for the mind to grasp it. It is much easier to comprehend and adore Krishna in his incarnation as Krishna the cowherding boy. Whereas he was a wise teacher in the Bhagavad-Gita, the Lord Incarnate of the Puranas is a much-loved child raised by cowherds in an area called Vrindavan near Mathura on the Jumna River. This area was actually home to a cowherding tribe, but whether the stories about Krishna have any historical basis is unclear.

The mythology is rich in earthly pleasures. The boy Krishna mischievously steals balls of butter from the neighbors and wanders garlanded with flowers through the forest, happily playing his flute. Between episodes of carefree bravery in vanquishing demons that threaten the people, he playfully steals the hearts of the *gopis*, the cowherd girls, many of them married. Through his magical ways, each thinks that he dances with her alone. He is physically beautiful.

Eventually Krishna is called away on a heroic mission, never returning to the gopis. Their grief at his leaving, their loving remembrances of his graceful presence, and their intense longing for him serve as models for the *bhakti* path — the way of extreme devotion.

In Hindu thought, the emotional longing of the lover for the beloved is one of the most powerful vehicles for concentration on the Supreme Lord. The Divine is known as a person rather than an impersonal principle.

Spiritual disciplines

Another thread of Sanatana Dharma is spiritual discipline. The process of attaining spiritual realization or liberation is thought to take at least a lifetime, and probably many lifetimes. Incarnation in this world is prized as a chance of advancing toward spiritual perfection. The techniques seem to have been known in ancient India.

In the past, spiritual training was usually available to upper-caste males only; women and shudras were excluded. It was preceded by an initiation ceremony in which the boy received the *sacred thread*, a cord of three threads to be worn over the shoulder.

Many gurus migrated to the West to spread Sanatana Dharma there. Paramahansa Yogananda's book Autobiography of a Yogi *continues to attract Western followers to Indian religious traditions.*

A Hindu male's lifespan is idealized or divided into four periods of approximately twenty-five years each. For the first twenty-five years he is a chaste student at the feet of a teacher. Next comes the householder stage, in which he is expected to marry, raise a family, and contribute productively to society. After this period, he begins to withdraw into semi-retirement, starting to detach himself from worldly pursuits and to turn to meditation and scriptural study. By the age of seventy-five, he is able to withdraw totally from society and become a **sannyasin**.

Living as a renunciate, the sannyasin is a contemplative who ritually cuts himself off from wife and family, declaring, "No one belongs to me and I belong to no one." Some sannyasins take up residence in comfortable temples; others wander alone with only a water jar, a walking staff, and a begging bowl as possessions. Some wandering sannyasins wear no clothes. In silence, the sannyasin concentrates on practices that will finally release him from samsara into cosmic consciousness.

The majority of contemporary Hindu males do not follow this path to its sannyasin conclusion in old age, but sannyasins still exist in great numbers. Some of them have renounced the world at a younger age and joined one of the many monastic orders within Hinduism, living in an **ashram** or retreat community that has developed around a guru.

The guru

Those who choose the path of study and renunciation often place themselves at the feet of a spiritual teacher, or guru. In Sanskrit, **guru** means "the venerable" or "the one who leads the disciple out of the darkness of ignorance." He or she does so not by academic teaching, but by being enlightened. Gurus do not declare themselves as teachers; people are naturally drawn to them because they have achieved spiritual states to which the seekers aspire.

> *Anyone and everyone cannot be a guru. A huge timber floats on the water and can carry animals as well. But a piece of worthless wood sinks, if a man sits on it, and drowns him.*
>
> *Ramakrishna*[19]

Ramana Maharshi, who died in 1951, lived on a holy mountain in south India, so absorbed in Ultimate Consciousness that he neither talked nor ate and had to be force-fed by another holy man. But the needs of those who gathered around him drew out his compassion and wisdom, and he spontaneously counseled them in their spiritual needs. His glance alone was said to have illuminated many who visited him.

The Siddha tradition of south India specializes in "teaching" by the power of a glance, word, touch, or thought (called *shaktipat*). A disciple of the late Swami Muktananda (whom he calls "Baba," an endearing "Father" term for a holy man) describes the effect:

> *When a seeker receives* shaktipat, *he experiences an overflowing of bliss within and becomes ecstatic. In Baba's presence, all doubts and misgivings vanish, and one experiences inner contentment and a sense of fulfillment.*[20]

The great nineteenth-century saint Ramakrishna observed that no guru is necessary for the person who approaches God with sincere longing and earnest prayer. But such people are rare, he said — most seekers need a teacher.

When seekers find their guru, they love and honor him or her as their spiritual parent. The guru does not always behave as a loving parent; often the disciples are treated harshly, to test their faith and devotion or to strip away the ego. True devotees are nevertheless grateful for opportunities to serve their guru, out of love. They often bend to touch the feet or hem of the robe of the guru, partly out of humility (placing the dust from the guru's feet on top of their heads, signifying utter submission) and partly because great power is thought to emanate from the guru's feet. Humbling oneself before the guru is considered necessary in order to receive the teaching. A metaphor commonly used is that of a glass and a pitcher of water. If the glass (the disciple, or *chela*) is already full, no water (spiritual wisdom) can be poured into it from the pitcher (the guru). Likewise, if the glass is on the same level as the pitcher, there can be no pouring. What is necessary is for the glass to be empty and below the pitcher; then the water can be freely poured into the glass.

Behaviors that outsiders often interpret as worship of the guru are ideally directed to that which comes through the guru. Swami Satchidananda explains:

> *Even if you find someone who is the right teacher for you, you should still know who the real guru is. Remember, it is not the physical body, but the Self, the light within. What you wish to acquire is the way he lives, the serenity he has…. Ultimately all these forms and names should disappear into a formless and nameless One, who is the Absolute Guru.*[21]

Above *Yogic adepts have developed extreme control of their bodies to amplify meditation efforts.*

Yogic practices

Spiritual seekers are generally encouraged to engage in disciplines that clear the mind and support a state of serene, detached awareness. This desired state of balance, purity, wisdom, and peacefulness of mind is described as *sattvic*, in contrast with active, restless states or lethargic, dull states.

The practices for increasing sattvic qualities are known collectively as **yoga**, which means "yoke" or "union" of the individual consciousness with the Infinite Consciousness. According to a modern classification system, there are four main yogic paths, suited to different kinds of human personalities — *raja, jnana, karma,* and *bhakti*.

RAJA YOGA The physical and psychic practices of raja yoga are those with which non-Hindus are most familiar, as they have been popularized in the West. They are not so common within India today, although they are thought to be extremely ancient. Some believe that the **sadhanas**, or practices, were known as long ago as the Paleolithic Age and were the basis for the great Indus Valley culture.

Included in this path are **asanas** — sustained physical postures used to cleanse the body and develop the mind's ability to concentrate. Regulated breathing exercises are used to calm the nerves and increase the body's supply of **prana**, or invisible life energy. Breath is thought to be the key to controlling the flow of this energy within the subtle energy field surrounding and permeating the physical body. Its

Below *In Kundalini yoga, the body is thought to exist within a field of energy, which is most concentrated at the major chakras — subtle centers along the vertical axis of the body.*

Above *The OM symbol, representing the original sound of creation, is topped by the sun and the moon, harmonized opposites. To chant OM is to commune with this cosmic sound vibration.*
Right *Sacred musicians tune their inner beings to the subtle resonances they hear in classical Indian instruments.*

major pathway is through a series of **chakras**, or subtle energy centers along the spine. To raise the energy from the lowest, least subtle chakra at the base of the spine to the highest, most subtle energy center at the crown of the head is the goal of **kundalini** yoga practices, with kundalini referring to the latent energy at the base of the spine. Ideally, opening of the highest chakras leads to the bliss of union with the Sublime. In its fully open state, the crown chakra is depicted as a thousand-petaled lotus, effulgent with light.

In addition to these practices using the body and breath, Indian thought has long embraced the idea that repetition of certain sounds has sacred effects. It is said that some ancient yogic adepts could discern subtle sounds and that **mantra** (chanted sacred sounds) express an aspect of the Divine in the form of sound vibration.

Mystics say that the word "mantra" (or "mantram") comes from the Sanskrit roots "man," or mind, and "tri," to cross. Chanting sacred syllables allows the consciousness to ride over the sea of the mind, calming and raising the vibration of the devotee, stilling the mind and attuning him or her to the Divine Ground of Existence. Indians liken the mind to the trunk of an elephant, always straying restlessly here and there. If an elephant is given a small stick to hold in its trunk, it will hold it steadily, losing interest in other objects. Just so, the mantra gives the restless mind something to hold, quieting it by focusing awareness in one place. If chanted properly, with full concentration and devotion, the mantra is also meant to invoke the presence and blessings of the deity who is being praised.

Many forms of music have also been developed in India to elevate one's attunement. Concerts may go on for hours if the musicians are spiritually absorbed. The most cherished sound vibrations are the "unheard, unstruck" divine sounds which cannot be heard with our outer ears.

Another way of steadying and elevating the mind is on some visual form — a candle flame, the picture of a saint or guru, the OM symbol, or **yantras**. The latter are linear images with cosmic symbolism. The yantra to the right shows the physical core of the universe as a large dot surrounded by three rings representing the three qualities of nature: balance, activity, and inertia. Beyond these rings, two triangles are superimposed, symbolizing the linked male and female qualities of the Divine. The lotus petals symbolize the love and beauty of spirit manifesting as matter. The outer square is open on all sides, reminding the devotee that creation expands infinitely. Large yantras are also created as designs of colorful grains for ritual invocations of specific deities.

In the state of meditation that ideally follows concentration, all wordly thoughts have dissipated. Instead of ordinary thinking, the clear light of awareness allows insights to arise spontaneously as flashes of illumination. There may also be phenomena such as colored lights, visions, waves of ecstasy, or visits from immortal beings. The mind, heart, and body may gradually be transformed.

None of these phenomena are considered goals in themselves. The ultimate goal of yogic meditation is **samadhi**: a super-conscious state of union with the Absolute. Swami Sivananda attempts to describe it:

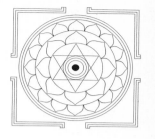

A yantra, cosmic symbol and focus for concentration.

Hindu pandits worship Durga after constructing an elaborate yantra to invoke her presence.

Words and language are imperfect to describe this exalted state… Mind, intellect and the senses cease functioning.… It is a state of eternal Bliss and eternal Wisdom. All dualities vanish in toto.… All visible merge in the invisible or the Unseen. The individual soul becomes that which he contemplates.[22]

JNANA YOGA Another yogic path uses the rational mind rather than trying to transcend it by concentration practices. This is *jnana yoga* — "the way of wisdom." In this path, ignorance is considered the root of all problems in the world. Our basic ignorance is our idea of our selves as being separate from the Absolute. A method advocated by Ramana Maharshi is continually to ask, "Who am I?" Through intellectual effort, the seeker discovers that the one who asks the question is not the body, not the senses, not the pranic body, not the mind, but something eternal beyond all these:

After negating all of the above-mentioned as "not this," "not this," that Awareness which alone remains — that I am.… The thought "Who am I?" will destroy all other thoughts, and, like the stick used for stirring the burning pyre, it will itself in the end get destroyed. Then, there will arise Self-realization.[23]

In the jnana path, the seeker must also develop the spiritual virtues (calmness, restraint, renunciation, resignation, concentration, and faith) and have an intense longing for liberation. By cutting through all doubts and mental habits, the seeker finally graduates from theoretical knowledge of the self to direct experience of it. The ultimate wisdom is spiritual insight rather than intellectual knowledge.

Spiritual knowledge is the only thing that can destroy our miseries for ever; any other knowledge removes wants only for a time.

Swami Vivekananda[24]

KARMA YOGA In contrast to ascetic and contemplative practices, another way involves action in the world. *Karma yoga* is service rendered without any interest in its effects and without any personal sense of giving. The yogi knows that it is the Absolute who performs all actions, and that all actions are gifts to the Absolute. This consciousness leads to liberation from the self in the very midst of work. Krishna explains these principles in the Bhagavad-Gita:

A person in the divine consciousness, although engaged in seeing, hearing, touching, smelling, eating, moving about, sleeping and breathing, always knows within himself that he actually does nothing at all. Because while evacuating, receiving, opening or closing his eyes, he always knows that only the material senses are engaged with their objects and that he is aloof from them.

The steadily devoted soul attains unadulterated peace because he offers the results of all activities to Me; whereas a person who is not in harmony with the Divine, who is greedy for the fruits of his labor, becomes entangled.[25]

BHAKTI YOGA The final type of spiritual path is the one embraced by most Indian followers of Sanatana Dharma. It is the path of devotion, *bhakti yoga*. "Bhakti"

The love between Radha and Krishna is the model for bhaktas' devotion to the Supreme Person.

means "to share," to share a relationship with the Supreme. The relationship is that of intense love. Bhakta Nam Dev described this deep love in sweet metaphors:

> *Thy Name is beautiful, Thy form is beautiful, and very beautiful is Thy love, Oh*
>   *my Omnipresent Lord.*
> *As rain is dear to the earth, as the fragrance of flowers is dear to the black bee,*
>   *and as the mango is dear to the cuckoo, so is the Lord to my soul.*
> *As the sun is dear to the sheldrake, and the lake of Man Sarowar to the swan, and*
>   *as the husband is dear to the wife, so is God to my soul.*
> *As milk is dear to the baby and as the torrent of rain to the mouth of the sparrow-*
>   *hawk who drinks nothing but raindrops, and as water is dear to the fish,*
> *so is the Lord to my soul.*[26]

Bhaktas' devotion is considered more dear to the Supreme than ritualistic piety. The story is told that a pious Brahmin came daily to offer ritual worship to a stone statue of Siva. One day he was horrified to see wild flowers and partly-eaten pork decorating the shrine. These had been left by a hunter who stopped to worship Siva in his own fashion. Hoping to teach the Brahmin a lesson, Siva appeared to him in a dream commanding that he watch from hiding while the hunter expressed his devotion. When the hunter then came to worship, he saw blood oozing from the eye of the statue. Without hesitation, he plucked out his own eye to place it on that of the idol. The bleeding stopped, but then the statue's other eye started bleeding. The hunter prepared to pull out his other eye when Siva manifested himself, healed the hunter, and took him as one of his chosen devotees, thenceforth called "the beloved of the eye."

The story of Siva's actually appearing to the devotee who loved him is what the bhakta ultimately expects. Bhakta Ravi Das, a shoemaker who became a highly regarded spiritual teacher because of his intense devotion, implored his Beloved, "I am a sacrifice unto You, my Omnipresent Lord. Why are you silent? For many births I have been separated from you. This life I dedicate to You. I live only with the hope of you. It is so long since I have seen You."[27] Mirabai, a fifteenth-century Rajput princess, was married to a ruler at a young age, but from her childhood she had been utterly devoted to Krishna. When she continued to spend all her time in devotions to Krishna, her infuriated husband tried to poison her. It is said that Mirabai drank the poison while laughingly dancing in ecstasy before Krishna; in Krishna's presence the poison seemed like nectar to her and did her no harm. Such is the devotion of the fully devoted bhakta that the Beloved One is said to respond and to be a real presence in the bhakta's life.

In the bhakta path, even though the devotee may not transcend the ego in samadhi, the devotee's whole being is surrendered to the deity in love. Ramakrishna explains why the bhakti way is more appropriate for most people:

> *As long as the I-sense lasts, so long are true knowledge and Liberation impossible....*
> *[But] how very few can obtain this Union (Samadhi) and free themselves from this*
> *"I"? It is very rarely possible. Talk as much as you want, isolate yourself*
> *continuously, still this "I" will always return to you. Cut down the poplar tree today,*
> *and you will find tomorrow it forms new shoots. When you ultimately find that this*
> *"I" cannot be destroyed, let it remain as "I" the servant.*[28]

Living Hinduism

Sarala Chakrabarty, a Calcutta mother whose children are now grown, has undertaken spiritual studies with a guru in the Ramakrishna tradition. Her love for the Supreme, in many forms, is highly personal.

"In our Hindu religion, we worship God in some form. God is infinite, but we cannot imagine of infinite. We must have some finite person — whom I love like friend, like father, like son, like lover. We make a relation with God like this. When I think he is my lover, I can always think of him. When I think he is my father, when I am in trouble, I pray to him, ask him to save me.

And I always pray to the Holy Mother [Ramakrishna's spiritual bride and successor, Sarada Devi]. When I have a problem, Mother will save me. She has given word when she was leaving her body (you say 'dying') — she said, 'I am blessing all who have come, who are coming, who have not come yet but are coming, blessings for all.' Only Mother can say this — so big heart, so much affection for us.

I feel something. Somebody is standing behind me. I feel always the hands on my shoulders, guarding me. Everybody is protected by God, everyone. I am not his only child. But I think God is only mine.

I want everything from God. God does not want anything from me. He wants bhakti — devotion.

A mother wants nothing from a child but love. She says only, 'Pray to me, call me, and I will do everything for you.' When I am traveling I say to Her, 'I am talking to you,' and this is done.

As we love God, God loves us. Our Lord Krishna says Love is the rope. It ties God and pulls him down to you.

I have a very powerful guru, a swami of the Ramakrishna Mission. He just passed on. He gave me a mantram, and it gives me very much peace. When I chant, I cannot leave it. Time is over, somebody is calling, I have to cook, I have to work — then I get up and still I am chanting in my mind. After bedding, I worship and chant. After that I realize I am pleased, I am quiet. There is no trouble in body and mind. I am very happy, very blissful. Whatever that problem is, all goes away."

Major theistic cults

After a period when Brahmanic ritual and philosophy dominated Sanatana Dharma, the Bhakti approach came to prominence around 600 CE. It opened spiritual expression to both shudras and women, and has been the primary path of the masses ever since. It may also have been the initial way of the people, for devotion to personal deities is thought to predate Vedic religion.

Of all the deities worshipped by Hindus, there are three major groupings: **Vaishnavites** who worship the Divine as Vishnu, **Saivites** who worship the Divine as Siva, and **Saktas** who worship the female creative power. Each devotee has his or her own "chosen deity," but will honor others as well.

Ultimately, Hindus rest their faith in one genderless deity with three basic aspects: creating, preserving, and destroying. The latter activity is seen as a merciful act that allows the continuation of the cosmic cycles.

Right *At the end of the Durga Puja, images of the ten-armed vanquisher of evil are carried to the river and consigned to the deep, so that she may return to her mate Siva, who awaits her in the Himalayas.*
Far right *Kali is the archetype of the transcendental power of the Kundalini earth energy, and destroyer of hypocrisy and selfishness.*

Saktas

An estimated fifty million Hindus worship some form of the goddess. As we have seen, worship of the feminine aspect of the Divine probably dates back to the pre-Aryan ancient peoples of the Indian subcontinent. Her power is called *sakti* and is often linked with the kundalini energy. Lushly erotic, sensual imagery is frequently used to symbolize her abundant creativity.

The feminine principle is worshipped in many forms, including those representing the totality of deity — eternal creator, preserver, destroyer. **Durga** is often represented as a beautiful woman with a gentle face but ten arms holding weapons with which she vanquishes the demons who threaten the dharma; she rides a lion (see page 33). She is the blazing splendor of God incarnate, the ultimate light and power in benevolent female form.

Kali, by contrast, is the divine in its fierce form. She may be depicted dripping with blood and skulls symbolizing her aspect as the destroyer of evil. Her worship has had its dark "left-hand" side, with sacrifices of animals and purportedly even humans. A "right-hand" version of devotion to Mother Kali consists of asking her help in transforming oneself. What appears as destruction is actually a means of transformation. With her merciful sword she cuts away all personal impediments to realization of truth, for those who sincerely desire to serve the Supreme. At the same time, she opens her arms to those who love her. Two of her eight arms hold a sword and a severed human head; the third arm gestures "Fear not" and the other offers boons to her devotees.

Fearsome to evil doers, but loving and compassionate as a mother to devotees, Kali wears a mask of ugliness. The divine reality is a wholeness encompassing both the pleasant and the unpleasant, creation and destruction. In Hindu thought, death and birth are linked, each giving way to the other in eternal cycles. All beings, all phenomena, are inter-related parts of the same divine essence. Sanskrit scholar Leela Arjunwadkar observes that there is a deeply sensed unity among all beings in classical Indian literature:

*That is why we find all types of characters in Sanskrit literature — human
beings, gods and goddesses, rivers, demons, trees, serpents, celestial nymphs, etc.,
and their share in the same emotional life is the umbilical cord that binds all to
Mother Nature.[29]*

From ancient times, worship of the divine female has therefore been associated
with worship of nature, particularly great trees and rivers. The Ganges River is
considered especially sacred, an extremely powerful female presence, and her
waters which flow down from the Himalayas are thought to be extraordinarily
purifying. Pilgrims reverently bathe in Mother Ganga's waters so that their sins
will be washed away.

Sacred texts called **Tantras** instruct worshippers how to honor the feminine
Divine. "Right-handed" tantra is well established in mainstream Hinduism. "Left-
handed" tantra is a cluster of secret practices, including ritual sexual intercourse
and sacramental use of otherwise forbidden foods such as meat and wine in order
to inflame the passions. Ideally, these stimulants are used under strict controls, not
for pleasure but as a means of transcending the limited personal consciousness and
riding the potential energy of the body into sublime union with the ultimate Power.

Sakti worship has also been incorporated into worship of the male deities. Each
is thought to have a female consort, shown in close physical embrace signifying
the eternal unity of male and female principles in the oneness of the Divine. In
these pairs, the female is often conceived as the life-animating force; the transcendent
male aspect is inactive until joined with the productive female energy.

Saivites

Also quite ancient is worship of **Siva**, a personal, many-faceted manifestation of
the attributeless supreme deity. In older systems he is one of the three major aspects
of deity: Brahma (Creator), Vishnu (Preserver), and Siva (Destroyer). Saivites
worship him as the totality, with many aspects. As Swami Sivasiva Palani, Saivite
editor of *Hinduism Today*, explains: "Siva is the unmanifest; he is creator, preserver,
destroyer, personal Lord, friend, primal Soul"; and he is the "all-pervasive underlying
energy, the more or less impersonal love and light that flows through all things."[30]
Siva is often depicted dancing above the body of the demon he has killed, reconciling
darkness and light, good and evil, creation and destruction, rest and activity in the
eternal dance of life.

Siva is also the god of yogis, for he symbolizes asceticism. He is often shown in
austere meditation on Mount Kailas, clad only in a tiger skin, with a snake around
his neck. The latter signifies his conquest of the ego. In one prominent story, it is
Siva who swallows the poison which threatens the whole world with darkness,
neutralizing the poison by the power of his meditation.

Siva has various saktis or feminine consorts, including Durga. He is often shown
with his devoted spouse Parvati. Through their union cosmic energy flows freely,
seeding and liberating the universe. Nevertheless, they are seen mystically as
eternally chaste. Siva and his sakti are also expressed as two aspects of a
single being. Some sculptors portray Siva as androgynous, with both masculine
and feminine physical traits. This unity is often expressed abstractly, as lingam
within yoni.

*Siva as Lord of the
Dance, trampling the
demon of evil and
bearing both the flame
of destruction and the
drum of creation. One
of his two free hands
gestures "Fear not;"
the other points to his
upraised foot,
connoting bliss.*

A large lingam from the 6th century CE honors Siva as the unmanifest creative force beyond time and space.

Lingams are naturally-occurring or sculpted cylindrical forms honored since antiquity in India (and apparently in other cultures as well, as far away as Hawaii). Those shaped by Nature, such as stones polished by certain rivers, are most highly valued, with rare natural crystal lingams considered unspeakably precious. While the lingam has often been interpreted sexually, as a phallic symbol, most Siva-worshippers do not perceive it as such and consider the sexual attribution the opposite of their beliefs. They feel that the original and pure understanding is that the lingam is a nearly amorphous, "formless" symbol for the unmanifest, transendent nature of Siva — that which is beyond time, space, cause, and form — whereas the yoni represents the manifest aspect of Sivaness.

Siva and his family — his spouse Parvati, their son Ganesh with the head of an elephant, the bull Nandi, and the cobra whose hood is often shown arching over the head of Siva — were the subject of an extraordinary miracle which happened in temples in many parts of India, as well as in Hindu temples in other parts of the world. On September 21, 1995, statues devoted to these deities began drinking milk from spoons, cups, and even buckets of milk offered by devotees. Crowds queued up at temples to see if the Divine would accept their offering. Many who came out of curiosity over the reports, which spread like wildfire, had the thrilling experience of watching the milk slowly drain out of their spoon as they held it to the lips of the statue or vanish as they poured it over a Siva lingam. Sceptics tried to offer scientific explanations, such as mass hysteria or capillary action in the stone, but the phenomenon lasted only one day and was fully convincing to all who experienced it. Contrary to caste expectations, the statues accepted milk from members of the lowest castes. It is quite likely that love and devotion for Siva's family will increase following this miraculous phenomenon.

Milk slowly drains from a spoon held to the trunk of a Ganesh statue, on one miraculous day in 1995.

The auspicious blessings of Ganesh are invoked for all occasions. Here his image has been painted on a wall before a marriage celebration.

Vaishnavites

In contrast to Sakti and Siva, Vishnu is beloved as the tender, merciful Deity. In one myth a sage was sent to determine who was the greatest of the gods by trying their tempers. The first two, Brahma and Siva, he insulted and was soundly abused in return. When he found Vishnu, the god was sleeping. Knowing of Vishnu's good-naturedness, the sage increased the insult by kicking him awake. Instead of reacting angrily, Vishnu tenderly massaged the sage's foot, concerned that he might have hurt it. The sage exclaimed, "This god is the mightiest, since he overpowers all by goodness and generosity!"

Vishnu's incarnation as Krishna is especially beloved. The ecstatic sixteenth-century Bengali saint and sage Sri Caitanya inflamed popular love for Krishna, adored as the flute-playing lover. Like Sri Caitanya, the devotee plays the role of Radha, Krishna's favorite among the gopis, making himself (if a male) like a loving female in order to experience the bliss of Lord Krishna's presence. It is this form of Hindu devotion that was carried to America in the 1960s and then to other countries, and whose followers are known as Hare Krishnas.

Vishnu is often linked with his consort, Sri Lakshmi, who is also an ancient goddess worshipped in her own right. She is associated with the presence of prosperity and glorious regal power. Lakshmi is often depicted as a radiant woman sitting on a water-borne lotus flower. The lotus floats pristine on the water but has its roots in the mud, thus representing the refined spiritual energy which rises above worldly contamination. The lotus also symbolizes the fertile growth of organic life, as over the eons the world is continually reborn on a lotus growing out of Vishnu's navel.

Major philosophical systems

Although the majority of followers of Sanatana Dharma are bhaktas, the spiritual wisdom of India has also expressed itself in elaborate intellectual systems of philosophy. Many distinct systems have evolved, but they all have certain features in common:

1 All have deep roots in the Vedas and other scriptures but also in direct personal experiences of the truth through meditation;
2 All hold ethics to be central to orderly social life — they acknowledge the existence of suffering and attribute it to the law of karma, thereby suggesting incentives to more ethical behavior;
3 All hold that the ultimate cause of suffering is people's ignorance of their true nature, the Self, whch is omniscient, omnipotent, omnipresent, perfect, and eternal.

Two of the major philosophical systems born in India do not acknowledge the authority of the Vedas but nevertheless draw on many of the same currents as Sanatana Dharma. These two, Jainism and Buddhism, will be considered in the following two chapters. Prominent among the others are Samkhya, Yoga, and Advaita Vedanta.

Samkhya

The Samkhya system is thought to be the oldest in India, but no definite date has been set as its origin. Its founder, the partially mythical sage Kapila, was mentioned in the *Mahabharata*, which apparently took its current form somewhere between 400 BCE and 400 CE. But Buddhism and Jainism, which developed simultaneously in the sixth century BCE, both include Samkhya principles, so the system probably preceded them and may be of pre-Vedic origin.

Samkhya philosophy puts forward two states of reality. One is the **Purusha**, the Self which is eternally wise, pure, and free, beyond change, beyond cause. The other is **Prakriti**, the cause of the material universe. All our suffering, which is the focus of Kapila's concerns, stems from our false confusion of Prakriti with Purusha, the eternal Self. A dualistic understanding of life is essential, according to this system, if we are to distinguish the ultimate transcendent reality of Purusha from the temporal appearances of Prakriti, which bring us happiness but also misery and delusion.

An illuminating story is told about Indra, once king of the gods. He was forced by the other devas to descend into the body of a pig, and once there, began to enjoy the life, wallowing in the mud, mating, and siring baby pigs. The devas were aghast; they came down to try to convince him to return, but Indra had forgotten his kingly state and insisted on remaining as a pig. Unable to talk him out of his delusion, the devas tried killing his babies; he was distraught but simply mated to have more piglets. Then the devas killed his mate. Indra grieved his loss but stayed in the mud. They finally had to kill him as well to bring him back to his senses. His soul could then see the body of the pig it had been inhabiting and was glad to return to heaven. The moral is that we, too, are like gods who forget the heights from which we came, so intent are we on the joys and sorrows of earthly life.

Yoga

Yoga as a philosophy is a system for recognizing earthly life for what it is and identifying with our eternal being. The system is closely linked to Samkhya philosophy, as the practical way of gaining direct experience of the distinction between Purusha (spirit) and Prakriti (material energy).

As indicated earlier, the yoga sadhanas, or methods, are extremely ancient. By 200 BCE, a yogi named Patanjali (or perhaps a series of people taking the same name) had gathered them into a coherent system for attaining the highest consciousness. The 196 terse sayings are called **sutras**, "threads" on which meaning can be strung. For example, Book 2:5 contains this sutra: "Ignorance is regarding the impermanent as permanent, the impure as pure, the painful as pleasant, and the non-Self as the Self."

Yogis say that it is easier to calm a wild tiger than it is to quiet the mind, which is like a drunken monkey that has been bitten by a scorpion. The problem is that the mind is our vehicle for knowing the Self. If the mirror of the mind is disturbed, it reflects the disturbance rather than the pure light within. The goal of yogic practices is to make the mind absolutely calm and clear.

The mind is easily distracted from this clarity by the obstacles encountered by anyone who attempts to meditate: physical disease, dullness, doubt, carelessness, laziness, sensuality, false perception, failure to reach firm ground, and slipping from the ground gained. Patanjali prescribes the *eight limbs of yoga* as an integrated system for the seeker to outgrow the distractions:

1 *yama* (abstinence in our relationships with others; non-violence, truthfulness, non-stealing, celibacy, non-greed)
2 *niyama* (personal observances: purity, contentment, mortification, study, and devotion)
3 *asana* (postures)
4 *pranayama* (breath control)
5 *pratyahara* (withdrawal of attention from the senses)
6 *dharana* (concentration)
7 *dhyana* (meditation)
8 *samadhi* (contemplation or absorption in the superconscious state).

To attain samadhi, the yogi must steadily practice control of the mind and body, making them still and steadfast, one-pointedly concentrated on the divine. In samadhi, awareness of material existence ceases and one is absorbed into the "spiritual sky." Gerard Blitz, contemporary leader of yoga teachers in Europe, describes the effects:

The "I" disappears. Then you live with the stream of life every moment. You live without yourself. You have fantastic energy and an open heart and are full of love and you have intelligence and consciousness. [It is] being in life at every moment, completely, without fear, without being tired. You are always filling your batteries, so: action. You obtain siddhis — *a larger state of consciousness in which you have more capacities. But this power [may be] an obstacle, and [you may use it to] influence people. You have to disappear. You have to become nothing. You have to serve.*[31]

Advaita Vedanta

Whereas Samkhya and Yoga are dualistic systems, Advaita ("not two") Vedanta is generally **monistic**, positing a single reality. It is based on the Upanishads (called Vedanta, or "the end of the Vedas"). Its founder is said to be Vyasa, systematizer of the Upanishads sometime between 1000 and 500 BCE; Shankara reorganized the teachings many centuries later, probably between the sixth and ninth centuries CE. He is said to have been initiated by a thousand-year-old south Indian yogi (some hidden sages are thought to have become semi-immortal through inner alchemical processes). He received the tradition from the student of the student of Vyasa's son.

According to Shankara, our material life is an illusion. It is like a momentary wave arising from the ocean, which is the only reality. Ignorance consists in thinking that the waves are different from the ocean. The absolute spirit, Brahman, is the essence of everything, and it has no beginning and no end. It is the eternal ocean of bliss within which forms are born and die, giving the false appearance of being real. That which makes us think the physical universe has its own reality is maya, the power by which the Absolute veils itself.

In Shankara's philosophical system, maya refers to the illusion that the world as we perceive it is real. He uses the metaphor of a coil of rope that, at dusk, is mistaken for a snake. The physical world, like the rope, does actually exist but we superimpose our memories and subjective thoughts upon it. Moreover, he says, only that which never changes is truly real. Everything else is changing, impermanent. Apparent phenomenal existence is not the same thing as reality.

In our ignorance we think that we exist as individuals, superimposing the notion of a separate ego-self on the underlying absolute reality of pure being, pure consciousness, pure bliss. It is a mistake to identify with the body or the mind, which exist but have no unchanging reality. When a person reaches transcendent consciousness, superimposition stops and the monistic oneness of reality is experienced.

Popular forms of worship

In Hindu worship, personal and public opportunities abound for serving and celebrating the Supreme in many forms.

Devotions and rituals

There are sixteen rites prescribed in the ancient scriptures to purify and sanctify the person in his or her journey through life, including rites at the time of conception, the braiding of the pregnant mother's hair, birth, name-giving, first leaving the family house, beginning of solid foods, starting education, investing boys with a sacred thread, starting studies of Vedas, marriage, and death. The goal is to continually elevate the person above his or her basically animal nature.

Pilgrimages to holy places and sacred rivers are also thought to be special opportunities for personal purification and spiritual elevation. Millions of pilgrims yearly undertake strenuous climbs to remote mountain sites that are thought to be blessed by the divine.

The devout make pilgrimages to sacred rivers, particularly the Ganges, for ritual ablutions and prayers to the sun. Here Hindu women bathe in a river at the commencement of an eclipse.

Many Hindu families have a special room or place for puja to their favorite deities.

Millions of Hindus undertake difficult pilgrimages to worship at mountain shrines each year.

Nearly every home in India has a shrine with pictures or small statues of various deities, and many have a special prayer room set aside for their worship. For **puja**, or worship, ritual purity is still emphasized; the time for prayer and offerings to the deities is after the morning bath or after one has washed in the evening. Puja is an everyday observance, although among orthodox families, women are considered unclean when menstruating and are not allowed to approach the shrines at that time. Typically, a small oil lamp and a smoldering stick of incense are waved in a circle before the deities' images. If the devotee has a guru, a picture of him or her is usually part of the shrine, and one honors the guru as well as the deities as an adored guest.

In public worship ceremonies, the sacred presence is made tangible through devotions employing all the senses. Siva-lingams may be anointed with precious substances, such as ghee (clarified butter), honey, or sandalwood paste, with offerings of rose water and flowers. In a temple, devotees may have the great blessing of receiving **darsan** (visual contact with the Divine) through the eyes of the images. One hears the sounds of mantras and ringing bells. Incense and flowers fill the area with uplifting fragrances. **Prasad**, food that has been sanctified by being offered to the deities and/or one's guru, is passed around to be eaten by devotees, who experience it as sacred and spiritually charged.

The deity image is treated as if it were a living king or queen. Fine-haired whisks are waved before it, purifying the area for its presence. Aesthetically pleasing meals are presented on the deity's own dishes at appropriate intervals; fruits must be perfect, without any blemishes. During visiting hours, the deity holds court, giving audience to devotees. In the morning, the image is ritually bathed and dressed in sumptuous clothes for the day; at night, it may be put to rest in bedclothes. If it is hot, the deity takes a nap in the afternoon, so arrangements are made for its privacy. For festivals, the deity is carefully paraded through the streets.

To an outsider, such observances look like children playing with dolls. But for the devout, loving service to the Divine makes It real and present. The statue is not a symbol of the deity; the deity may be experienced through the statue, reciprocating the devotee's attentions. According to Swami Sivasiva Palani:

> It is thought that the subtle essences of these things given in devotion are actually absorbed by the Divine, in an invisible and rather mystical process. It's as though we are feeding our God in an inner kind of way. It's thought that if this is done properly, with the right spirit, the right heartfulness, the right mantras, that we capture the attention of the personal Lord and that he actually communes with us through that process, and we with him. Of course, when I say "us" and "him" I connote a dualism that is meant to be transcended in this process. One uses the dualism of the puja to find the monism that is at the heart of it.[32]

In addition to worshipping the Divine through services to images, orthodox Brahmins observe many days of fasting and prayer, corresponding to auspicious points in the lunar and solar cycles or times of danger, such as the four months of the monsoon season.

Festivals

Sanatana Dharma honors the Divine in so many forms that almost every day a religious celebration is being held in some part of India. Sixteen religious holidays are honored by the central government so that everyone can leave work to join in the throngs of worshippers. These are calculated partially on a lunar calendar, so dates vary from year to year. Most Hindu festivals express spirituality in its happiest aspects. Group energy attracts the gods to overcome lurking evils, and humorous abandon helps merry-makers transform their fears.

On a mid-winter night, people happily celebrate *Lohari* by building a bonfire and throwing popcorn, peanuts, and sesame candies into it. The feeling is that one is symbolically throwing away one's evils, and at the same time invoking blessings for the year to come. In particular, families who have given birth to a male child during the past year perform this ceremony for his auspicious future.

Holi is the riotously joyful celebration of the death of winter and the return of colorful spring. In northern Indian areas where Vaishnavism is strong, the holiday is associated with Krishna, for as an infant he is said to have killed a demon employed by the king of winter. Pilgrims flock to Mathura for re-enactments of Krishna's playful exploits with the gopis. The festivities are probably of ancient indigenous origin, and in some areas, the two-day craziness is dedicated to Kama, the god of sexual love. Whatever the excuse, bands of people take to the streets with pistols for squirting colored liquids at anyone they meet. At the end of this uninhibited gaiety, everyone hugs and old grudges are dropped as the new year begins.

In July or August a special day, *Naga panchami*, is devoted to the *Nagas*, or snakes. Snakes were considered powerful gods by the indigenous peoples, and the tradition persists. In south Indian villages, where they are especially honored, thousands of live snakes are caught and exhibited by brave handlers. Worshippers sprinkle vermilion and rice on the hoods of cobras, considered especially sacred.

On Naga Panchami, farmers abstain from ploughing to avoid disrupting any snake-holes.

In August or September, Vaishnavites celebrate Krishna's birthday (*Janmashtami*). At his birthplace, Mathura, Krishna's devotees fast and keep a vigil until midnight, retelling stories of his life. Elsewhere, pots of milk, curds, and butter are strung high above the ground to be seized by young men who form human pyramids to get to their prize. They romp about with the pots, drinking and spilling their contents like Krishna, playful stealer of these milk products he loved.

At the end of the summer, it is Ganesh who is honored, especially in west and south India, during *Ganesh Chaturti*. Special potters make elaborate clay images of the jovial elephant-headed remover of obstacles, son of Parvati, who formed him as a boy from the residue of her bathing tub and set him to stand guard while she bathed. Since he wouldn't let Siva in, her angry spouse smashed the boy's head into a thousand pieces. Parvati demanded that the boy be restored to life with a new head, but the first one found was that of a baby elephant. To soothe Parvati's distress at the peculiarity of the transplant, Siva granted Ganesh the power of removing obstacles. The elephant-headed god is now the first to be invoked in all rituals. After ten days of being sung to and offered sweets, the Ganesh images are carried to a body of water and bidden farewell with prayers for an easy year until Ganesh Chaturti comes around again.

In different parts of India, the first nine or ten days of Asvina, the lunar month corresponding to September or October, are dedicated either to the *Durga Puja* (in which elaborate images of the many-armed goddess celebrate her powers to vanquish the demonic forces) or to *Dussehra* (in which huge effigies of the wicked Ravana and his helpers may be burned, re-enacting the climax of the Ramayana and the triumph of Rama, his brother Lakshman, and the beloved monkey Hanuman). Or both aspects may be incorporated into the ceremonies, in which the same theme is the triumph of good over evil.

Twenty days later is *Divali*, the happy four-day festival of lights. Variously explained as the return of Rama after his exile, the puja of Lakshmi (goddess of wealth, who visits only clean homes), and the New Year of those following one of the Indian calendars, it is a time for tidying business establishments and financial records, cleaning and illuminating houses after the mess of the monsoon season, wearing new clothes, gambling, feasting, honoring clay images of Lakshmi and Ganesh, and setting off fireworks.

Initially more solemn is *Mahashivaratri*, in which a day of fasting and a night of keeping vigil to earn merit with Siva are followed by gaiety and eating. During the ascetic part of the observance, many pilgrims go to sacred rivers or special tanks of water for ritual bathing. Siva lingams and statues are venerated, and the faithful chant and tell stories of Siva to keep each other awake. A reformist group, Arya Samaj, decries what it considers superstition and idolatry and honors the day as the end of a weeklong celebration of their reform. They carry out Vedic fire sacrifices and hold spiritual talks, throwing personal offerings into the fire on the last day.

Approximately every twelve years, millions of Hindus of all persuasions gather for the largest festival in the world. The occasion is the *Kumbha Mela*; the place is the confluence of the Ganges and Jumna rivers and the invisible Saraswati river of enlightenment. In addition to masses of the general public, throngs of ascetics converge to discuss matters of religion and to purify themselves in the sacred waters.

Modern world Hinduism

Great numbers of ascetics gather for a procession to the sacred river Ganges during Kumbha Mela.

Hinduism did not develop in India in isolation from other religions and national influences. Groups continued to flow into the subcontinent from outside. Muslims began taking over certain areas beginning in the eighth century CE; during the sixteenth and seventeenth centuries CE a large area was ruled by the Muslim Mogul Emperors. Islam and Hinduism generally co-existed, despite periods of intolerance on the part of Muslim leaders, along with Buddhism and Jainism which had also grown up within India. Indian traders carried some aspects of Sanatana Dharma to Java and Bali, where Hinduism survives today with unique Balinese flavor.

When the Mughal Empire collapsed, European colonialists moved in. Ultimately the British dominated and in 1857 India was placed under direct British rule. Christian missionaries set about to correct abuses they perceived in certain Hindu practices, such as sati (widow-burning) and the caste system. But they also taught those who were being educated in their schools that Hinduism was "intellectually incoherent and ethically unsound."[33] Some Indians believed them and drifted away from their ancient tradition. Others felt that this accusation was untrue, but wondered how to make Hinduism palatable to modern tastes, how to reconcile it with contemporary life.

Ramakrishna, the great nineteenth century mystic, recognized the Divine as being both formless and manifested in many forms, and also as transcending both form and formlessness.

To counteract Western influences, *Mahatma* ("Great Soul") *Gandhi* (who died in 1948) encouraged grassroots nationalism, emphasizing that the people's strength lay in awareness of spiritual truth and in non-violent resistance to military-industrial oppression. He claimed that these qualities were the essence of all religions, including Hinduism, which he considered the universal religion.

In addition to being made a focus for political unity, Hinduism itself was revitalized by a number of major figures. One of these was *Ramakrishna*, who lived from 1836 to 1886. He was a devotee of the Divine Mother in the form of Kali. Eschewing ritual, he communicated with her through intense love. He practiced Tantric disciplines and the *bhavanas* (types of loving relationships). These brought him spiritual powers, spiritual insight, and reportedly a visible brilliance, but he longed only to be a vehicle for pure devotion:

> *I seek not, good Mother, the pleasures of the senses! I seek not fame! Nor do I long for those powers which enable one to do miracles! What I pray for, O good Mother, is pure love for Thee — love for Thee untainted by desires, love without alloy, love that seeketh not the things of the world, love for Thee that welleth up unbidden out of the depths of the immortal soul!*[34]

Ultimately, Ramakrishna worshipped the Divine through many Hindu paths, as well as Islam and Christianity, and found the same One in them all. Intoxicated with the One, he had continual visions of the Divine Mother and ecstatically worshipped her in unorthodox, uninhibited ways. For instance, once he fed a cat some food that was supposed to be a temple offering for the Divine Mother, for she revealed herself to him in everything, including the cat. He also placed his spiritual bride, Sarada Devi, in the chair reserved for the Deity, honoring her as the Great Goddess.

The pure devotion and universal spiritual wisdom Ramakrishna embodied inspired what is now known as the Ramakrishna Movement, or the Vedanta Society. A famous disciple named *Vivekananda* (1863–1902) carried the eternal message of Sanatana Dharma to the world beyond India, and excited so much interest in the West that Hinduism became a global religion. He also reintroduced Indians to the profundities of their great traditions.

Within India Hinduism was also influenced by reform movements such as *Brahmo Samaj* and *Arya Samaj*. The former defended Hindu mysticism and bhakti devotion to an immanent Deity. The latter advocated a return to what it saw as the purity of the Vedas, rejecting image worship, devotion to a multiplicity of deities, priestly privileges, and popular rituals. Though different, both movements were designed to convince intellectuals of the validity of "true" Hinduism. Today many liberal Hindus practice only those portions of the traditions which they find meaningful. They refuse to follow the old ways out of fear of the Deity or blind habit.

> *Do not care for doctrines, do not care for dogmas, or sects, or churches, or temples; they count for little compared with the essence of existence in each [person], which is spirituality.... Earn that first, acquire that, and criticise no one, for all doctrines and creeds have some good in them.*
>
> *Ramakrishna*[35]

The Swadhyaya Movement

Today there are said to be twenty million people in a hundred thousand villages in India who are beneficiaries of a silent social revolution based on the principles of the ancient Hindu scriptures, especially the *Bhagavad-Gita*. The movement is called Swadhyaya. The term means self-study, using traditional scriptural teachings as means for critically analyzing oneself in order to improve. On this basis, villagers and village life have been profoundly improved.

The work began in the 1950s, as scriptural scholar Shri Pandurang Vaijnath Athavale Shastri, known by his followers as "Dada" (elder brother), determined that the Gita was "capable of resolving the dilemmas of modern man and solving the problems of material life, individual and social."[36] He founded a school near Bombay, refusing until today to accept any financial help from the government or outside funding agency, insisting that "those institutions which depend upon others' favors are never able to achieve anything worthwhile or carry out Divine work."[37] He named the buildings for the ancient sages who have inspired people to live according to Vedic principles. It was they who recognized that within each person is a divine spark whose realization gives them the energy and guidance with which to uplift themselves. As Dada once observed, the sage who wrote the Ramayana is

virtually urging us to take Ram — the awareness that the Lord is with us and within us all the time — to every home and every heart, as this alone will provide the confidence and the strength to the weakest of the weak and will bring joy and fragrance into the life of every human being.[38]

Realization of the divine within themselves also leads to realization of the divine within others, which is the beginning of social harmony and cooperation.

The principle upon which Dada's social development work is centered is bhakti, or selfless devotion. He inspired his students to pay devotional visits to poor villages in Gujarat state. They carried their own food and asked for nothing from the people. They simply held meetings to teach dharmic principles. Then they began using local materials to build simple hut temples for villagers of all castes and creeds, as places not only for nonsectarian devotion but also for village meetings. The responsibilities of taking care of the temple are

rotated among the village families, and all who are able bring a portion of their income there to be distributed among the most needy. They are taught that it is the Divine who gives them the energy to work, so they readily offer back a portion of their income.

Believing in work as worship, the villagers were also inspired to set aside a portion of land to be farmed in common, as "God's farm." All give a certain number of days of volunteer service on the farm, in grateful service to God. The harvests are treated as "impersonal wealth." One-third of the money is distributed directly to the needy; two-thirds is put into a community trust for larger purchases of machinery and such to help people stand on their own feet.

The movement spreads from village to village, as missionaries who have seen the positive results of the program voluntarily go to other areas to tell the people there about it. When swadhyaya volunteers first appeared in fishing villages on India's west coast, they found the people were spending what income they had on gambling and liquor. Now, the same people place a portion of their earnings from fishing and navigation at the feet of God, as it were. Since they no longer waste money on gambling and liquor, they have created such a surplus that they have been able to purchase community fishing boats. These are manned by volunteers on a rotation basis, with everyone eager to take a turn, and the income is distributed impersonally as God's donation to those in need.

In addition, swadhyayas have also created "tree temples," in which trees are planted in formerly barren lands and cared for in a spirit of devotion to God. The volunteers are so dedicated in this service that one hundred percent of the trees reportedly survive. Swadhyayas have also developed cultural programs, sports clubs, family stores, dairy produce centers, children's centers, centers for domestic skills, and discussion centers for intellectuals and professionals.

Throughout the growing network of swadhyayas, there is no hierarchy and no paid staff. Those whose lives have been improved by inner study and devotional service become enthusiastic volunteers and living demonstrations that people are happiest when dharmic principles are placed ahead of self interest.

Gurus have kept the teacher-to-pupil transmission alive, training the many contemporary gurus, both male and female, who now offer training in Hindu thought and practice in ashrams and study centers around the globe. Beginning in the 1960s and 1970s, **Transcendental Meditation**, a technique taught by the Indian teacher Maharishi Mahesh Yogi, claimed great benefits for practitioners. By simply spending twenty minutes twice each day repeating a secret mantra which they were given, TM followers were supposed to be able to work more efficiently, become more satisfied with their lives, be better athletes, be more creative, end drug addiction, and learn more effectively. The advanced TM program includes the claim that people can be taught to levitate.

TM research also indicated that crime rates declined in areas where groups were meditating strongly; meditation groups have therefore been rushed to troubled areas (such as places of rioting) to spread an atmosphere of peacefulness. They are now promoting this service to cities for fees in the millions of dollars. Thousands of TM's meditators traveled to Washington, D.C. in summer 1993 to meditate for two months there in an effort to alleviate crime in the nation's capital. Records indicate that crime rates did indeed drop by approximately eighteen percent.[39] TM has also been taught to prison inmates, with indications that the number who returned to crime within three years after leaving the prison was reduced by twenty percent. Use of TM as therapy for ending alcoholism and drug abuse reportedly has a success rate of sixty-five percent.[40]

Some of the self-proclaimed Hindu "gurus" turn out to be fraudulent, with scandalous private behavior or motives of accumulating wealth and personal power. Nevertheless, in the process of propagation of the ancient teachings, many of the major scriptures of Sanatana Dharma have been translated into other languages. Yoga has a wide following, though many outside India learn the asanas and breathing practices without knowing anything of the spiritual framework of their traditional use. At the other extreme, Western-born ascetics of the Krishna Consciousness movement renounce their possessions, wear the orange robes of sannyasins, study all the literature about Krishna, and humbly offer chants and devotional services to the Lord. Theirs is the only example of bhakti Hinduism being transplanted onto non-Indian soil, complete with Indian dress, food, rituals, and traditional values.

In 1965, the Indian guru A.C. Bhaktivedanta Swami Prabhupada arrived in the United States, carrying the asceticism and bhakti devotion of Sri Caitanya's tradition of Krishna worship from India to the heart of Western materialistic culture. By the time he died in 1977, he had initiated several thousand followers worldwide. Adopting the dress and diet of Hindu monks and nuns, they lived in temple communities. Their days began at 4 a.m. with meditation, worship, chanting of the names of Krishna and Ram, and scriptural study, with the aim of turning from a material life of sense gratification to one of transcendent spiritual happiness. During the day, they chanted and danced in the streets to introduce others to the bliss of Krishna, distributed literature (especially Swami Prabhupada's illustrated and esteemed translation of *Bhagavad-Gita*), attracted new devotees, and raised funds.

The movement has continued since Swami Prabhupada's death, and is growing in strength in various countries. However, Krishna Consciousness devotees in Russia assert that worship of Lord Krishna is not new to Russian soil — that Vedic culture existed throughout Russia thousands of years ago, long before Christianity. In the heart of Moscow, a large group of monks in saffron robes, as well as lay followers, gathers every morning in their temple building to chant the holy name of Krishna and to hear talks designed to lift them from material desire to love for the "Supreme Godhead," Whom they know as Lord Krishna. The Temple president of the Moscow branch of the International Society for Krishna Consciousness, Krishna Kaumar Das, was a student during the years of Soviet persecution of the movement. He says,

> *Some of the followers were sent to labor camps, some to psychiatric hospitals. I was threatened that I would be the next on the list. We met secretly, but almost always followed by KGB people. But then Gorbachev came to power, and by Krishna's mercy, everything is okay now for [our work of] uplifting humanity to the transcendental level, so that humans can associate with the Supreme Lord.*[41]

The international *Vedanta Society* and the *Ramakrishna Movement* teach a simplified version of Sanatana Dharma, based on these central principles:

> *Truth or God is One.*
> *Our real nature is divine.*
> *The purpose of our life is to realize the One in our own soul.*
> *There are innumerable spiritual paths, all leading to this realization of divinity.*[42]

There is a highly ecumenical spirit of tolerance in many of the ways that Sanatana Dharma is being shared with the world. For example, Swami Sivananda (1887–1963) wrote 340 books and pamphlets to disseminate spiritual knowledge in English. He founded the Yoga-Vedanta Forest Academy for research and practice of Hindu philosophies, yoga sadhanas, comparative religion, and mysticism, as well as the nonsectarian Divine Life Society for "anyone devoted to the ideals of truth, non-

A family visits a temple together seeking spiritual blessings for the family members.

violence, and purity." At the same time, India is now experiencing violent clashes between its own Hindus, Muslims, and Sikhs; some have turned to religious fundamentalism and intolerance as an antidote to the insecurities of rapid modernization, as well as a thousand years of rule by foreign powers.

Inter-religious disharmony is being fanned into violent hatreds by those using the name of religion for divisive, power-amassing political purposes. Late in 1992, Hindu mobs stormed and destroyed the Babri Masjid, a Muslim mosque built in the sixteenth century by the Muslim emperor Babar in Ayodhya on the site where his army had torn down a temple thought to mark Lord Rama's birthplace. The extensive Hindu–Muslim violence that ensued throughout India revealed deep communal antipathies that have been strengthened by fundamentalist organizations. One of these is the RSS — Rashtriya Svayamsevak Sangh — which arose early in the twentieth century, espousing Hindu cultural renewal. It gave organized expression to the ideals of V. D. Savarkar, who wrote of an ancient Hindu Nation and Hindu-ness, excluding Muslims and Christians as aliens, in contrast to the history of Sanatana Dharma as an evolving composite of variegated ways of worship, with as many ways to the Ultimate as there are people.

The RSS maintains tens of thousands of branches in Indian villages and cities where Hindu men and boys meet for group games, martial arts training, songs, lectures, and prayers to the Hindu Nation, conceived as the Divine Mother. They greet each other by saying, "Ram, Ram!"

Political affiliates of the RSS — including the BJP — are becoming increasingly visible and strident in Indian politics, and its religious affiliate — the Vishva Hindu Parishad ("World Hindu Society") — has sponsored "unity processions" throughout the country, featuring Mother India as a goddess.

Those who had for some years been agitating for replacement of the Babri Masjid with a new temple to Lord Ram espouse restoration of the rule of Ram, a legendary time when Hindu virtues were maintained by a perfect ruler. But many Hindu intellectuals feel that the emotions of the common people are thus being used cynically by vested interests and power-seeking politicians. They feel that the ancient philosophy of India has no place for dogma or exclusivity.

Despite the politically motivated appearance of Hindu fundamentalism, Brahmanic orthodoxy is on the wane, and many modern Indians are less in touch with their traditions than were their parents and grandparents. Some "untouchable" Hindus have converted to Christianity or Islam because those religions do not make caste distinctions. The Indian government has tried to woo the former out-castes back to Hinduism by reserving government posts for what are now called "Scheduled Castes" but poor Christians are now demanding the same advantage. An estimated fifty percent of all Christians in India were formerly of scheduled caste origin.

Women in Hindu society, where the feminine is religiously venerated as Sakti, are often nevertheless by social custom bound to their husband's families as near-servants. Their low status has been investigated and legislation created to raise them socially and to decrease the burden of dowry on their own families, but many cases of oppressive treatment of women persist.

Social problems notwithstanding, the multifaceted traditions of Sanatana Dharma are being kept alive by interest both inside and outside India. Hindu scholar and statesman Karan Singh observes that the vast understandings of the ancient Vedas will always make them relevant to the human condition:

We, who are children of the past and the future, of earth and heaven, of light and darkness, of the Human and the divine, at once evanescent and eternal, of the world and beyond it, within time and in eternity, yet have the capacity to comprehend our condition, to rise above our terrestrial limitations, and, finally, to transcend the throbbing abyss of space and time itself. This, in essence, is the message of Hinduism.[43]

Suggested reading

The Bhagavad-Gita, available in numerous translations. Central teachings about how to realize the immortal soul.

Eck, Diana, *Darsan: Seeing the Divine Image in India*, second edition, Chambersburg, Pennsylvania: Anima Books, 1985. A lively explanation of deity images and how the people of India respond to them.

Jayakar, Pupul, *The Earth Mother*, New Delhi: Penguin Books, 1989. Explorations of ways of worshipping the Goddess in rural India.

Mahadevan, T. M. P., *Outlines of Hinduism*, second edition, Bombay: Chetana Limited, 1960. One of the clearest general introductions to the intricacies of Sanatana Dharma.

Sahi, Jyoti, *The Child and the Serpent*, London: Routledge and Kegan Paul, 1980. An artist's attempt to rediscover the inner meanings of traditional visual symbols by living in the villages of south India.

Sastri, *The Cultural Heritage of India*, Calcutta, 1962. A classic survey of the social aspects of Sanatana Dharma.

Singh, Karan, *Essays on Hinduism*, New Delhi: Ratna Sagar, 1987 and 1990. An excellent and concise introduction of the many facets of Hinduism, interpreted in modern terms.

Swami Prabhavananda, *The Spiritual Heritage of India*, Hollywood, California: Vedanta Press, 1979. A scholarly summary of the complexities of Hindu philosophy, with relatively little emphasis on bhakti or popular ways of worship.

Swami Satchidananda, trans., *Integral Yoga: The Yoga Sutras of Patanjali*, Yogaville, Virginia: Integral Yoga Publications, 1984. An opportunity to compare literal translations of the terse Sanskrit sutras with interpretation of their meaning, plus interesting commentaries.

The Upanishads. Sublime scriptures about the highest reality, as apprehended through meditation.

Swami Vivekananda, *Essentials of Hinduism*, Calcutta: Advaita Ashrama. A valuable small booklet by the great scholar and devotee of Ramakrishna who introduced Hinduism to the West.

Yogananda, Paramhansa, *Autobiography of a Yogi*, Los Angeles: Self-Realization Fellowship, 1956, and London: Rider and Company, 1987. First-hand account of the growth of a great spiritual leader, with explanations of many aspects of Sanatana Dharma.

Zimmer, Heinrich, *Philosophies of India*, New York: Bollingen Foundation/Pantheon Books, 1951. An advanced analysis of Indian philosophies (including Jainism and Buddhism) which assumes some prior knowledge of the traditions.

CHAPTER 4

JAINISM

"Be careful all the while!"

Although the majority of Indians who are religious continue to follow the Hindu paths, Mother India has given birth to several other religions which are not based on the Vedas. One of them is Jainism. Until recently, it has been little known outside India. Even within India it is practiced by a small minority. Yet its gentle ascetic teachings offer valuable clues to our global survival.

Earlier descriptions of Jainism by Western observers were strangely negative. It was accused of having an "empty heart," because it has no personal savior and no Creator God as First Cause. But now interest in Jainism is reviving, for it is becoming recognized as a complete and fruitful path with the potential for uplifting human awareness and inculcating high standards of personal ethics. It has never condoned war, the caste system, or the killing of animals for any reason. Jain teachings recognize that we humans are imperfect, but hold out the promise that through strict control of our senses and thoughts we can attain perfection, freedom, and happiness.

The Tirthankaras and Ascetic Orders

Jainism's major teacher is **Mahavira** ("The Great Hero"). He was a contemporary of the Buddha who died approximately 526 BCE. Like the Buddha, he was the prince of a kshatriya clan and renounced his position and his wealth at the age of thirty to wander as a spiritual seeker. The austerities he tolerated are legendary. For example, when he was meditating, villagers are said to have treated him miserably to make him leave:

> *Once when he [sat in meditation], his body unmoving, they cut his flesh, tore his hair, and covered him with dirt. They picked him up and then dropped him, disturbing his meditational postures. Abandoning concern for his body, free from desire, the Venerable One humbled himself and bore the pain.*[1]

Finally after twelve years of meditation, silence, and fasting, Mahavira achieved liberation and perfection. For thirty years until his death at Pava, now a sacred pilgrimage site, he spread his teachings. His community is said to have consisted of 14,100 monks, 36,000 nuns, and 310,000 female and 150,000 male lay followers. They came from all castes, as Jainism does not acknowledge the caste system.

The Jain teachings are not thought to have originated with Mahavira, however. He is considered the last of twenty-four **Tirthankaras** ("Fordmakers") of the current era. In Jain cosmology, the universe is without beginning or end. Eternally it passes through long cycles of progress and decline. At the beginning of each downward cycle, humans are happy, long-lived, and virtuous; they have no need for religion. As these qualities decline, humans look at first to patriarchs for guidance but as things get worse Tirthankaras must create religion in order to steer people away from the growing evilness of the world.

The first Tirthankara is said to have been the ancient Lord Rishabha. He introduced civilizing social institutions such as marriage, family, law, justice, and government, taught the arts of agriculture, crafts, reading, writing, and mathematics, and built villages, towns, and cities. Twenty-three more Tirthankaras followed over a vast expanse of time. The twenty-second is generally acknowledged by scholars as an historic figure, Lord Krishna's cousin, renowned for his compassion toward animals. During his wedding procession, it is said that he heard the groans of animals who were to be slaughtered, and immediately decided not to marry since so many innocent animals would be killed to feed the wedding guests; he became an ascetic who preached religion for many years. His betrothed princess made the same decision and became an ascetic nun. The twenty-third Tirthankara, a prince who became an extreme ascetic and a great preacher of Jain principles, lived from 877 to 777 BCE.

The extreme antiquity of Jainism as a non-Vedic, indigenous Indian religion is well documented. Ancient Hindu and Buddhist scriptures refer to Jainism as an existing tradition which began long before Mahavira.

After Mahavira's death, his teachings were not written down at first because the monks lived as ascetics without possessions; they were initially carried orally by memory. In the third century BCE, the great Jain saint Bhadrabahu predicted that there would be a prolonged famine where Mahavira had lived, in what is now Bihar in northeast India. He led some twelve thousand monks to South India to avoid the famine, which lasted for twelve years. When they returned to their original home, they discovered that two major changes had been introduced by the monks who had remained in the area. One was relaxation of the requirement of nudity for monks; the other was the convening of a council to edit the existing Jain texts into an established canon of forty-five books.

Eventually the two groups split over their differences into the **Digambaras** who had left and did not accept the changes as authentic to Mahavira, and the **Svetambaras** who had stayed near his original location. Two major differences remain between the ascetic orders today. Digambara ("sky clad") monks wear nothing at all, symbolizing their innocence of shame and their non-attachment to material goods. They do not consider themselves "nude"; rather, they have taken the environment as their clothing, thus damaging it as little as possible by stoically enduring all kinds of weather. They have only two possessions: a broom of feathers dropped by peacocks and a gourd for drinking water. The Svetambaras ("white-clad") feel that wearing a piece of white cloth does not prevent them from attaining liberation.

The two orders also differ over the subject of women's abilities. Digambaras believe that women do not have the strong body and willpower needed to attain liberation; they can only be liberated if they are reborn in a man's body. Svetambaras feel that women are capable of the same spiritual achievements as men, and that the nineteenth Tirthankara was a woman.

Rishabhadeva, the First Tirthankara of the present era. The Tirthankaras are always depicted either in cross-legged lotus position or standing up, a form of deep meditation for enlightened beings who are said never to sleep. (Northeast India, 12th-13th century.)

The new Jain symbol: Ahimsa is inscribed on the open palm. The swastika represents the wheel of samsara. The three dots symbolize insight, knowledge, and conduct. The crescent and dot above symbolize the liberated soul in the highest region of the universe.

The influence of Jainism was overshadowed by the growing popularity of devotional bhakti ways in India, but the tradition has never died out. Jain merchants, monks, and nuns still practice teachings which have not changed much in two thousand years, with the monastics practicing much stricter forms of the religion than lay people.

Freeing the soul: the ethical pillars

In the midst of a world of decline, as they see it, Jains are given great room for hope. The **Jiva** — the individual's higher consciousness, or soul — can save itself by discovering its own perfect, unchanging nature and thus transcend the miseries of earthly life. This process may require many incarnations. Jains, like Hindus and Buddhists, believe that we are reborn again and again until we finally free ourselves from **samsara**, the wheel of birth and death and of life's ups and downs.

The gradual process by which the soul learns to extricate itself from the lower self and its attachments to the material world involves purifying one's ethical life until nothing remains but the purity of the jiva. In its true state, it is omniscient, shining, self-contained, and blissful. One who has thus brought forth the highest in his or her being is called a **Jina** (a "winner" over the passions), from which the term Jain is derived. The Tirthankaras were Jinas who helped others find their way, regenerating the community by teaching inspiring spiritual principles.

Karma

The soul is covered by the debris of karmic accumulations. Like Hindus and Buddhists, Jains believe that our actions influence the future course of our current life, and of our lives to come. But there is a difference: in Jain belief, karma is actually subtle matter — minute particles that we accumulate as we act and think. Mahavira likened karma to coats of clay that weigh down the soul.

Jains are very careful to avoid accumulating karma. Three of the chief principles to which they adapt their lives are **ahimsa** (non-violence), **aparigraha** (non-possessiveness), and **anekantwad** (non-absolutism).

Ahimsa

The principle of non-violence — ahimsa — is very strong in Jain teachings. Jains believe that every centimeter of the universe is filled with living beings, some of them minute. A single drop of water contains three thousand living beings. All of them want to live. Humans have no special right to supremacy; all things deserve to live and evolve as they can. To kill any living being has negative karmic effects.

All breathing, existing, living, sentient creatures should not be slain, nor treated with violence, nor abused, nor tormented, nor driven away. This is the pure, unchangeable, eternal law.... Correctly understanding the law, one should arrive at indifference for the impressions of the senses, and not act on the motives of the world.[2]
Akaranga Sutra, IV: Lesson 1

It is difficult not to do violence to other creatures. As we walk, we squash insects unknowingly. Even in breathing, Jains feel, we inhale tiny organisms and kill them. Jains avoid eating after sunset, so as not to inadvertently eat unseen insects who might have landed on the food, and some Jain ascetics wear a cloth over their mouth to avoid inhaling any living organisms.

Human life is inevitably destructive; the best that can be hoped for is to do as little damage as possible. The higher the life-form, the heavier the karmic burden of its destruction. Levels of life are determined by their degree of sensitivity. The highest group of beings are those with many senses, such as humans, gods, and higher animals (such as horses, snakes, monkeys, and elephants). Lower forms have fewer senses. The "one-sensed" beings have only the sense of touch. They include plants and the elements: the earth-bodies in soil, minerals, and stones, the water-bodies in rivers and lakes, fire-bodies in fires and lightning, and wind-bodies in winds and gases. The Jain sutras describe the suffering of even these one-sensed beings: Their agony at being wounded is like that of a blind and mute person who cannot see who is hurting him or express the pain.

Jains are therefore strict vegetarians, and they treat everything with great care. Jain benefactors have established a unique hospital for sick and wounded birds in Delhi. Great attention is paid to their every need, and their living quarters are air-conditioned in the summer. Jains also go to markets where animals for sale are usually bound with wire, packed into hot trucks, and driven long distances without water, to then be killed as meat. To prevent their sufferings, Jains buy the animals at any price and then raise them in comfort as orphans. Even to kick a stone while walking is to injure a living being.

Ahimsa also extends to care in speaking and thinking, for abusive words and negative thoughts can injure another. One's profession must also not injure beings, so most Jains work at jobs considered harmless, such as banking, clerical occupations, education, law, and publishing. Agriculture is considered harmful, for in digging into the soil one harms minute organisms in the earth; in harnessing bullocks to plows or water buffalos to carts, one would harm not only the bullock or buffalo but also the tiny life forms on its body.

Jain nuns wearing mouth-cloths to prevent injury to inhaled minute beings; they are carrying all their worldly possessions.

Prescriptions for Monks and Nuns

The Jain sutras are filled with detailed prescriptions for every aspect of the lives of monks and nuns, lest they commit acts which are impure or pose a threat to any kind of being. For example, the sections on begging for food point out considerations such as these:

A monk or a nun on a begging-tour should not accept food which has been placed on a post or pillar or beam or scaffold or loft or platform or roof or some such-like elevated place; for such food fetched from above is impure and unacceptable. The Kevalin says: This is the reason: The layman might fetch and erect a stool or a bench or a ladder or a handmill, get upon it, and getting upon it fall or tumble down. Thus he might hurt his foot or arm or breast or belly or head or some other part of his body; or he might kill or frighten or bruise or smash or crush or afflict or pain or dislocate all sorts of living beings....

A monk or a nun on a begging-tour should not accept food which is kept in earthenware. The Kevalin says: This is the reason: The layman might, for the sake of the mendicant, break the earthen vessel containing the food and thereby injure the earth-body; in the same way he might injure the fire-body, the wind-body, plants and animals....

When a monk or a nun on a begging-tour smells, in travellers' houses or garden houses or householders' houses or baths, the scent of food or drink or sweet scents, they should not smell them, being indifferent against smell, and not eager or desirous or greedy or covetous of the pleasant smell.[3]

Monks and nuns must move slowly with eyes downward, to avoid stepping on any being. In general, they will do the least harm if they devote their time to sitting or standing in meditation rather than moving around.

Aparigraha

Another central Jain ideal is non-attachment to things and people. One should cut one's living requirements to a bare minimum. Possessions possess us; their acquisition and loss drive our emotions. Some Jain monks wear no clothes; the Tirthankaras are always depicted as naked, and therefore free. Even attachments to our friends and relatives bind us to samsara. Jainism advocates compassion for all beings, but this is not the same as dependent love. We are to live helpfully and consciously within the world but not be drawn into its snares.

Aparigraha, or non-acquisitiveness, is considered the way to inner peace. If we can let go of things and situations, moment by moment, we can be free. The story is told of a **muni** (monk) who saw twelve stray dogs chasing another dog who was racing away with a bone he had found. When they caught him, they attacked him to wrest it from his jaws. Wounded and bleeding, he let go of it. The others immediately abandoned him to chase the one who picked it up. The monk saw the scene as a moral lesson: So long as we cling to things, we have to bleed for them. When we let them go, we will be left in peace.

A Jain nun of the Rajasthan desert, Samani Sanmati Pragya, belongs to an order in which the nuns' clothing and bedding is limited to four white saris, one white shawl, and one woolen cloth. She explains,

> In the winter we do not have a quilt for warmth at night, for it would be too bulky to carry. In the summer we use no fan. It is so hot that we cannot sleep at night. We bear any kind of circumstances. In fact, we remain very happy. Our happiness comes from inside.[4]

Aparigraha is of value to the world community as well. Contemporary Jains point out that their principle of limiting consumption offers a way out of the global poverty, hunger, and environmental degradation that result from unequal grasping of resources by the wealthy. As His Holiness Acharya Sushil Kumar explained:

> If we live simply, limit our needs and do not try to fulfill every desire, collecting more and more, automatically we will protect the environment. Because we will not need so many things, we will not need big industries to produce unnecessary things.... If we live simply, automatically the environment will stay clean.[5]

Anekantwad

The third central ethical principle is anekantwad, roughly translated as "relativity." Jains try to avoid anger and judgmentalism, remaining open-minded by remembering that any issue can be seen from many angles, all partially true. They tell the story of the blind people who are asked to describe an elephant. The one who feels the trunk says an elephant is like a snake hanging from the sky. One feeling a leg argues that an elephant is a tree trunk. The one holding the tail is sure that neither of the others is right, that an elephant is a long hairy thing. The one feeling an ear argues that an elephant is not at all like any of the above. Each has a different version, each a partial grasp of the truth.

In the Jain way of thinking, the fullness of truth has many facets. There is no point in finding fault with others; our attention must be directed to cleansing and opening our own vision. Shree Chitrabhanu, a contemporary Jain teacher, describes the results of eliminating false impressions and allowing the pure consciousness to flow in:

> Once you have closed the open gates, dried up the polluted water, and cleaned out all the debris, then you can open them again to receive the fresh, clean rainfall. What is that rainfall? It is the flow of maitri — pure love, compassion, and communication. You feel free and flowing with all.... You meet to share. See how easily you meet people when there is no feeling of greater or lesser, no scar or bitterness, no faultfinding or criticism.[6]

Spiritual practices

Jainism is an ascetic path and thus is practiced in its fullest by monks and nuns. In addition to practicing meditation, monks and nuns adopt a life of celibacy, physical penance and fasting, and material simplicity. They may sleep on the bare ground or wooden slabs, and are expected to endure any kind of weather with indifference. At initiation, they may pull their hair out by the roots rather than be shaved. They must learn to accept social disapproval, to depend on others for their food, and to feel no pride at being more spiritually advanced than others.

Jain monks and nuns carry ahimsa to great extremes in their wariness of injuring one-sensed beings. Among the many activities they must avoid are digging in the ground (because of the earth-bodies there), bathing, swimming, or walking in the rain (because of the water-bodies they might injure), extinguishing or lighting fires (because even to light a fire means that a fire-body will eventually be destroyed), fanning themselves (to avoid sudden changes in air temperature that would injure air-bodies), and walking on vegetation or touching living plants.

In New Delhi, a wealthy sixty-year-old Jain businessman, head of a large construction company, recently astounded the populace by moving from lay austerities such as eating and drinking only once in twenty-four hours to the utterly renunciate life of a naked Digambara monk. Before a huge celebration in which he shed his clothes and his possessions, Lala Sulekh Chand announced:

I have no interest in life. I have found that life just means one remains agitated for twenty-four hours and there is no peace of mind. I have fulfilled all my responsibilities and obligations in life and handed over my business to my son and family. I am not taking this path due to some problem.[7]

He then sat unflinching as his mentor, Muni Amit Sagar, pulled all the hairs from his head, a process which took an hour and a half. Afterward, Muni Amit Sagar admonished the crowd that the way to spiritual liberation lies in non-attachment and patient, indifferent forbearance of all difficulties. "We cannot change anything, but we can change our attitude of expectation," he said. "The peace one gets from renunciation cannot be gained by reading a lot of religious books."[8]

Difficult to conquer is oneself; but when that is conquered, everything is conquered.
Uttaradhyayana Sutra 9.34-36

Most householders cannot carry renunciation as far as monks and nuns, but they can nonetheless purify and perfect themselves. Jains believe that the universe is without beginning and that it has no creator or destroyer. Our lives are the results of our own deeds; only by our own efforts can we be saved. Padma Agrawal explains:

In Jainism, unlike Christianity and many Hindu cults, there is no such thing as a heavenly father watching over us. To the contrary, love for a personal God would be an attachment that could only bind Jainas more securely to the cycle of rebirth. It is a thing that must be rooted out.[9]

The world operates by the power of nature, according to natural principles. Jains do believe in gods and demons, but the former are subject to the same ignoble passions as humans. In fact, one can only achieve liberation if one is in the human state, because only humans can clear away karmic accumulations on the soul. Until it frees itself from karmas, the mundane soul wanders about through the universe in an endless cycle of deaths and rebirths, instantly transmigrating into another kind of being upon death of its previous body. Acharya Shri Kund Kund asserts, "Nowhere throughout the space in the entire universe is there any place in its course where the mundane soul has not taken birth in many forms, big and small."[10]

TEACHING STORY

The Story of Bahubali

Rishabha, the First Tirthankara of this era, had one hundred sons from one wife and one son — Bahubali — from the other. He gave his eldest son, Bharat, the lion's share. Bharat was eager to be the supreme king, and he wanted his other brothers who had been given smaller portions of land to come under his subjugation. All the people surrendered to his sovereignty, except for Bahubali, who refused to surrender his kingdom. He said to Bharat, "You are independent, I am independent. Why should I come under your rule?"

The armies of the two sides were drawn upon the battleground. The wise men from the two sides came forth and said, "In the clash of two brothers, millions of people will be killed. Millions of innocent people will be killed to satisfy the egos of two brothers. Why should this happen?" So it was decided that the two would fight it out between themselves. They would fight in three ways to see who was defeated.

First, they looked into each other's eyes, concentrating until one looked away. Bahubali knocked out Bharat in this combat. Then they fought underwater, and again Bahubali was victorious. Thirdly, Bahubali picked up Bharat physically and held him overhead, ready to dash him to the ground. That is how he got the name Bahubali — "He whose arms are very powerful."

As Bahubali was holding Bharat aloft, a thought crossed his mind: "Whom am I throwing? My own brother. For what? For this parcel of land? For this kingdom? Only for that, I would kill my brother?" He put Bharat down.

At that point, Bahubali felt like renouncing the world. He ceased to make war, and he went standing into meditation. For twelve years he meditated, standing. Vines grew on his legs. Snakes made their homes around his body. Many people tried to convince him to come out of his meditation, but he was unmoved. Nevertheless, he could not attain ultimate liberation.

Rishabha, his father, was asked why Bahubali was not attaining liberation. From his omniscient knowledge, Rishabha said that just before Bahubali started his meditation, he had a thought left in his mind: "I am standing on my brother's soil." So Bharat went and prayed to him: "This soil is universal, not yours or mine." The moment that thought entered Bahubali's mind, he was liberated.

Birth as a human is prized by Jains as the highest stage of life short of liberation. One should therefore lose no time in this precious, brief period in human incarnation.

Householders can journey toward the final state by passing through fourteen stages of ascent of the soul, or *gunasthana*. The first four are efforts to remove false mental impressions. Moral effort to purify oneself begins with the fifth stage. Jains attempt to plumb the depths of what psychoanalysts call the "shadow self" in order to free themselves from emotional problems. Then as spiritual inertia is overcome, self-control and relinquishing of the passions follow. Throughout this process, the veils of karma are lifting and the soul experiences more and more of its natural luminosity. In the highest state of perfection, known as *kevala*, all gross activities have come to an end, and the liberated being has "boundless vision, infinite righteousness, strength, perfect bliss, existence without form, and a body that is neither light nor heavy."[11]

Although severe vows of renunciation can be taken by householders, lay spiritual life is more likely to consist of six duties: the practice of equanimity through meditation, praise of the Tirthankaras, veneration of teachers (who live as

A monk at the feet of the Jain statue of Gomateshvara (renunciate son of the first Tirthankara) in Mysore in India.

mendicants), making amends for moral transgressions, indifference to the body (often by holding a particular position for a length of time), and renunciation of certain foods or activities for specific periods.

> *Just as a fire quickly reduces decayed wood to ashes, so does an aspirant who is totally absorbed in the inner self and completely unattached to all external objects shake to the roots, attenuate, and wither away his karma-body.*
>
> Samantabhadra, Aptamimamsa 24-27

The Tirthankaras are honored through images. They all look alike for the perfect soul is non-particularized; symbols such as the bull always shown with the first Tirthankara are used to help worshippers identify each of the twenty-four.

The worshipper's feeling is one of reverence rather than supplication; the Tirthankaras are elevated beyond the human plane and are not available as helpers. They are instead models for one's own life and since there can be no divine intervention, there is not a great emphasis on priesthood. Laypeople can carry out worship services themselves, either alone or in groups.

When participating in *devapuja* (worship of the Tirthankara images), a Jain has to feel that he or she is approaching a living Jina, radiant and omniscient, with teachings issuing from his body in the form of a divine sound. People pay their respects with offerings and waved lamps, but unlike Hindu pujas, Jain rituals do not expect any reciprocation from the object of veneration. Liberation from samsara is a result of personal effort, often portrayed by a symbolic diagram laid out with rice grains.

Living Jainism

R. P. Jain's family runs two charitable free dispensaries of homeopathic remedies in Delhi. He himself spends much of his time arranging Jain speakers for international audiences, as Indian Coordinator for Jainism Abroad. He says,

"We believe that Jainism was not born at a certain time. It is timeless, and it is timely. We cherish the preservation of our religion — the religion which shows the maximum penance, the highest sacrifice, and the biggest contribution to humanity.

I've had the chance to travel in twenty-two countries of the world. After a mental debate within my own mind, I've come to this conclusion: I must keep on striving to become a better Jain. If the world would follow Jain principles, with or without the label of Jainism, this planet would survive.

I pray, but not to God as understood in other religions. The twenty-four Tirthankaras are pathfinders. By their philosophy, they guide us in how we should live our life. In Jainism we pray to the Lord, 'I would like to be like you, and no different. I would like to be no less than what you are.' Coming from that wisdom, my prayer is, 'Show me the right way.' I do not pray, 'God, give me this motorcar. Give me this house. Give me this woman.' I ask that I may be helped in following the right path.

Jainism is a difficult faith, but if mankind is to survive, and if this planet is to remain habitable for human beings, this is the only answer, in my mind. I'll give you some small mundane examples from my own life. First of all, I am a strict vegetarian, because we do not believe in doing violence to even the lowest level of life for our own existence. Secondly, I have a self-imposed limit on my worldly goods, in terms of the number of clothes, the number of shoes, the amount of furniture I will have. I wear a PVC sandal; it is not made of leather. In the modern affluent community, it is laughed at. They think that I am being a miser or

that I cannot afford leather. I tell them, 'I pity your mind. Let your God give you better vision. Why do you have to use leather? The world knows that leather comes out of the slaughter of innocent animals. How would you feel if you were born an animal and used for leather? How would you feel if you were used for making hamburgers for MacDonald's or pizzas for Pizza King?'

I used to wear silk. On my eighteenth birthday I was telling one of my distant relatives not to eat a chocolate because it had egg powder in it. He said 'Turn around — you're wearing silk. What are you preaching? Do you know that to make one yard of silk, nearly fifty thousand to one hundred thousand silkworms are boiled alive? To wear silk is a sin!' When I learned that is the way natural silk is made, I said, 'R. P. Jain, what are you doing to your own soul? Shame on you!' From that day, I took a vow never in my life to wear natural silk or to buy it for anyone else, despite the fact that my sister would like a silk sari.

Similarly, I try to use minimal water. If I am driving my car and see a dog or a cow or a buffalo on the road, which often happens in India, I would go out of my way to avoid hitting it. I used to be very fond of horseback riding. One day my grandfather told me, 'Look here; in my youth there were no cars. But times have changed. You are blessed with a car. Why do you want to have fun horseback riding? One day you will be born as a horse and all the others will ride on you.' That day was the last day I wore my riding breeches.

I have donated blood somewhere between fifty to one hundred times, never for my own relatives or because the recipient would be a Jain, but because it was the need of the needy. I have no right to let my body grow until from my body I can contribute something. There is a debt of this planet Earth on me, and I must repay that debt. I breathe air, I drink water, I eat food. What am I doing?"

In Jain worship, images of the Tirthankara are ideally to be venerated without expectation of a personal response to their prayers or help for the worshippers.

World Jainism

Through the centuries, Jainism managed to survive as a small heterodox minority within largely Hindu India. In the twentieth century, it has been carried to the outside world by several teachers. One of them, Shree Chitrabhanu, was for twenty-nine years a monk who walked barefoot over 30,000 miles (48,279 km) of Indian soil to teach Jain principles to the populace. When he was invited to address the Temple of Spiritual Understanding Summit Conferences in Switzerland and the United States in 1970 and 1971, his controversial decision to attend in person marked the first time in Jain history that a Jain monk had traveled outside India. He has now established Jain meditation centers in the United States, Brazil, Canada, Kenya, England, and India.

Acharya Shri Sushil Kumar likewise established Jain centers in the United Kingdom and the United States as well as India. He pointed out that the Jain scriptures consider as "Jains" all those who practice Jain principles:

If somebody is a real symbol of non-violence, love, compassion, peace, harmony, oneness, then he is the perfect Jain. We can't convert any Jains, but you can convert your habits, your mind.[12]

In this spirit, the Anuvrat Movement was begun by the revered Acharya Tulsi in 1949 to enlist people of all faiths and nationalities to commit themselves to Anuvrats ("small vows"). He developed these to help people rejuvenate strong moral standards of self-restraint in the midst of ethically unhealthy society. The small vows include these: to avoid wilfull killing of any innocent creature, to refrain from attacks and aggression and to work instead for world peace and disarmament, to avoid discrimination on the basis of caste or race, to eschew religious intolerance, to avoid false business and political practices, to limit acquisition of possessions, to eschew addictive substances, and to avoid wasting water or cutting down trees.

In 1995, Acharya Tulsi renounced even his own position as the leader of his order by installing Acharya Mahapragya as his successor. The latter's self-description is an indication of the internal qualities which keep Jain faith alive:

> I am an ascetic. My asceticism is not bound by inert rituals. My faith is in that asceticism which is not lifeless. I have faith in that asceticism which is a veritable ocean of joy. I have faith in that asceticism which has a perennial source of energy. I follow a tradition, but do not treat its dynamic elements as static. I derive benefit from the scriptures, but do not believe in carrying them as a burden....

> In my consciousness there is no bondage of "yours and mine." It is free from it. My spiritual practice is not to "worship" truth, but to subject it to minute surgery.

> The only mission of my life is boundless curiosity to discover truth.... It is not an external accoutrement. Like a seed it is sprouting out of my being.[13]

Suggested reading

Chitrabhanu, Gurudev Shree, *Realize What You Are: The Dynamics of Jain Meditation*, New York: Jain Meditation International Center/Dodd, Mead and Company, 1978. A useful introduction to a path of meditation designed to overcome negativity, release blocks to fulfilling one's potential, and to identify the eternal in oneself.

Chitrabhanu, Gurudev Shree, *Twelve Facets of Reality: The Jain Path to Freedom*, New York: Jain Meditation International Center/Dodd, Mead and Company, 1980. Classic Jain reflections on the realities of life with many teaching tales.

Fischer, Eberhard, and Jain, Jyotindra, *Jaina Iconography*, parts 1 and 2, Leiden: E. J. Brill, 1978. An inside look at Jainism through the visual representations of its beliefs.

Jaini, Padmanabh S., *The Jaina Path of Purification*, Berkeley: University of California Press, 1979. An appreciative, scholarly analysis of the Jaina path.

Kumar, Acharya Sushil, *Song of the Soul*, Blairstown, New Jersey: Siddhachalam Publishers, 1987. Insights into Jain mantra practice, as taught by a twentieth-century contemporary monk.

Muller, F. Max, ed., *Jaina Sutras*, vols. XLV and XXII of *Sacred Books of the East*, Oxford: Clarendon Press, 1884 and 1895. Engaging translations of various sorts of sutras, including both philosophical treatises and rules of conduct for Jain ascetics.

Rosenfield, Clare, and Segall, Linda, "Ahimsa is not a religion: It is a way of life," New York: Jain Meditation International Center. A brief but profound explanation of Jain tenets in contemporary terms, relating the principles to planetary concerns.

Sangave, Vilas A., *Aspects of Jaina Religion*, New Delhi: Bharatiya Jnanpith, 1990. Concise, accurate discussions of Jain antiquity, principles, practice, relationships to other religions, and cultural contributions.

Tobias, Michael, *Life Force: The World of Jainism*, Berkeley, California: Asian Humanities Press, 1991. A highly appreciative and readable account of Jain practices and philosophy by a Western observer.

CHAPTER 5

BUDDHISM

*"He will deliver by the boat of knowledge
the distressed world"*

At the same time that Mahavira was teaching the way of Jainism, the man who came to be known as the Buddha preached another alternative to the ritual-bound Brahmanism of sixth-century BCE India. His teachings generally focus on earthly suffering and its cure. Many religions offer comforting supernatural solutions to the difficulties of earthly life. In its early forms, Buddhism was quite different: It held that our salvation from suffering lies only in our own efforts. The Buddha taught that in understanding how we create suffering for ourselves we can become free.

We might imagine that the discomfort of having to face ourselves and take responsibility for our own liberation would be an unappealing path that would attract few followers. But the way of the Buddha spread from his native India throughout the Far East, becoming the dominant religion in many Eastern countries. In the process, it took on devotional and mystical qualities from earlier local traditions, with various deity-like buddhas to whom one could appeal for help. And now, more than two and a half thousand years after the Buddha's death, the religion that he founded is also attracting considerable interest in the West.

The life of the Buddha

What we know about the Buddha himself is sketchy. His prolific teachings were probably not collected in written form until at least four hundred years after his death. In the meantime they were apparently held, and added to, as an oral tradition chanted from memory by monks, groups of whom were responsible for remembering specific parts of the teachings. Only a few factual details of the Buddha's own life have been retained. Most of what is usually taught about the life of the Buddha is rich in symbolic meanings but not verifiable as historical fact.

The one who became the Buddha (a title that means "Enlightened One") was born about 563 years before the beginning of the Christian calendar. His father was apparently a wealthy landowner serving as one of the chiefs of a kshatriya clan, the Shakyas. They lived in the foothills of the Himalayas and could probably see these great mountains looming in the distance.

Legends describe a miraculous conception in which his mother dreamed that she was taken up the Himalayas by guardian spirits and placed on a divine couch in a golden mansion. The Future Buddha came to her in the form of a white elephant and entered her womb. He had incarnated many times before and was drawn to

BUDDHISM

	600 BCE — Life of Guatama Buddha c.563–483 BCE
	400
Development of Theravada Buddhism 200 BCE – 200 CE	**200** — King Asoka begins spreading Buddhism outward from India c. 258 BCE
	Pali Canon written down in India 80 BCE?
	CE — Perfection of Wisdom scriptures originally developed c.100 BCE – c.300 CE
Buddhism transmitted to China and then East Asia c.50 CE	
Development of Mahayana Buddhism 1st C CE	**200** — Nagarjuna expounds concept of voidness c.200s CE
	400
Peak of Chinese Buddhism 589–845	**600** — Buddhism enters Japan c.550
Songstan declares Buddhism the national religion of Tibet 700s	
Persecution of Buddhism begins in China 845	**800**
	1000
Ch'an Buddhism of China carried to Japan as Zen 13th C	**1200** — Life of Milarepa 1079–1153
Buddhism declines in northern India 13th C	Life of Nichiren 1222–1282
Buddhism declines in southern India 15th C	**1400**
	1600
	1800
	2000 — Communist Chinese repress Buddhism in Tibet 1959

The Buddha gives his first sermon, using the mudra (sacred gesture) representing the karmic wheel of birth, death, and rebirth.

The region where Siddhartha grew up is in full view of the high peaks of the Himalayas.

earth once again by his compassion for all suffering beings. Legends also tell of the Brahmins' interpretation of his mother's dream (and of marks on the baby himself): A son would be born whose greatness would lead to his either becoming king of all India or one who retires from earthly life to become an enlightened being, sharing his own awakening with the world.

The heralded birth occurred in Lumbini, a garden retreat. The boy was named Siddhartha*, "wish-fulfiller," or "He who has reached his goal." His family name, Gautama, honored an ancient Hindu sage whom the family claimed as ancestor or spiritual guide. It is said that Siddhartha's father, hoping to encourage his son's kingship, tried to make the boy's earthly life so pleasant that he would not chose to retire from it. Siddhartha later described a life of fine clothes, white umbrellas for shade, perfumes, cosmetics, a mansion for each season, the company of female musicians, and a harem of dancing girls. He was also trained in knightly sports and married to at least one wife, who bore a son.

In the midst of this life of ease, Siddhartha was apparently unconvinced of its value. An early indication of his future direction had occurred as a mystical experience during his youth. While sitting beneath a rose-apple tree, he spontaneously entered an extremely blissful state of meditation. By contrast, he was struck by the stark fact that despite its temporary pleasures, life always leads to decay and death. According to the legend, the gods arranged for him to see the "Four Sights" that his father had carefully tried to hide from him: a bent old man, a sick person, a dead person, and a monk seeking eternal rather than temporal pleasure. Increasingly dissatisfied with the futility of sensual delights, at the age of twenty-nine Prince Siddhartha renounced his wealth and position as heir to the throne, left his wife and baby, shaved his head, and donned the coarse robe of a wandering ascetic.

The new role he had adopted was not unique. Many Indian sannyasins were already leading the homeless life of poverty considered appropriate for seekers of spiritual truth. Although the future Buddha would later develop a new religion that departed significantly from certain orthodox Hindu beliefs, he initially tried the traditional methods. He headed southeast to study with a famous Brahmin teacher who had many followers. Although Siddhartha is said to have achieved the Sphere of No-thing-ness under his teachings, he resumed his search, apparently feeling that a still higher state of realization lay beyond. His next Brahmin teacher helped him to realize an even higher level, the Sphere of Neither-Perception-nor-non-Perception. But again he moved on, unsatisfied that he had reached his ultimate goal: the way of total liberation from suffering. He sought out temple priests but was disturbed by the cruelty of their animal sacrifices to the gods. Before leaving them, he tried to teach them that it was hypocritical and futile to try to atone for misdeeds by destroying life.

Still searching, Siddhartha found five pupils of his second teacher living as ascetics in the forest. Admiring their efforts to subdue the senses, he decided to try their

---

*Buddhist terms have come to us both in Pali, an Indian dialect first used for preserving the Buddha's teachings (the Buddha himself probably spoke a different ancient dialect), and in Sanskrit, the language of Indian sacred literature. For instance, the Pali **sutta** ("that which is heard or learned") is equivalent to the Sanskrit **sutra**. In this chapter Sanskrit will be used, as it is more familiar to Westerners, except in the section on Theravada, which uses the Pali.

practices himself as an experiment in liberation. For six years he outdid them in extreme self-denial techniques: nakedness, exposure to extreme heat and cold, breath retention, a bed of brambles, severe reduction of food. Finally he acknowledged that this extreme ascetic path had not lead to enlightenment.

Siddhartha then shifted his practice to a Middle Way of neither self-indulgence nor self-denial. To the disillusionment of the five ascetics, who left him, he revived his failing health by accepting food once more and taking reasonable care of his body. Placing his faith in clarity of mind, he began a period of reflection. On the night of the full moon in May as he sat in deep meditation beneath a sacred fig tree at Gaya, he finally experienced Supreme Enlightenment.

After passing through four states of serene contemplation, he first recalled all his previous lives. Then he had a vision of the wheel of deaths and rebirths, in which past good or bad deeds are reflected in the next life. Finally, he had a revelation of the existence of suffering, its source, and the means for removing suffering. After this supreme experience, it is said that he literally radiated light. According to the legend, he was tempted by Mara, the personification of evil, to keep his insights to himself, for they were too complex and profound for ordinary people to understand. But the Buddha, as he now knew himself, compassionately determined to set the wheel of teaching in motion, even if only for the sake of a few who would understand: those with "only a little dust" in their eyes.

The first people with whom the Buddha shared the essence of his insights were the five ascetics who had abandoned him, thinking he had given up. In his famous Deer Park sermon at Sarnath, he taught them what became the essence of Buddhism: The Four Noble Truths about suffering and the Eightfold Path for liberation from suffering. Convinced, they became the first disciples of the new techniques.

The Buddha continued to teach the **Dharma** (Pali: **Dhamma**) — which in his system means the truths of reality, and the right conduct for each person's state of evolution — for forty-five years. As he walked through the northern Indian countryside, still as a voluntarily poor teacher with a begging bowl, he gave sermons and converted people of all sects and classes. Some became **bhikshus** (Pali: **bhikkus**), monks emulating his life of poverty and spiritual dedication; others continued as householders. One who became a lay disciple was his father; his son joined the order of bhikshus.

The order was not dependent on caste; people from all levels of society became Buddhists and bhikshus. His stepmother and his wife became **bhikshunis** (Pali: **bhikkhunis**), members of the order of nuns that the Buddha founded. In contrast to the suppression of women in Indian culture of the times, there are many evidences of the Buddha's egalitarian attitude toward women (the rules which make Buddhist nuns subservient to monks were apparently created by monks long after he died). He also forbade animal sacrifice and admonished his followers to be kind to all living beings.

The circumstances of the Buddha's death at the then extraordinary age of eighty bespeak his selfless desire to spare humankind from suffering. His last meal, served by a blacksmith, seemingly included some poisonous mushrooms or tainted pork. Severely ill and recognizing his impending death, the Buddha nevertheless pushed on to his next teaching stop at Kusinara, converting a young man along the way. He sent word back to the blacksmith that he must not feel remorse or blame himself for the meal, for his offering of food brought him great merit.

When he reached his destination, he lay down on a stone couch, at which point, it is said, the trees above rained blossoms down upon him. As his monks came to pay their last respects, he urged them to tend to their own spiritual development:

You must be your own lamps, be your own refuges.... A monk becomes his own lamp and refuge by continually looking on his body, feelings, perceptions, moods, and ideas in such a manner that he conquers the cravings and depressions of ordinary men and is always strenuous, self-possessed, and collected in mind.[1]

He designated no successor, no one to lead the order. But it survived and spread because, as his closest helper, Ananda, explained, "We are not without support. We have a support: Dharma is the support."[2]

The Dharma

Buddhism is often described as a "nontheistic religion." There is no personal God who creates everything and to whom prayers can be directed. The Buddhists at the Chicago Parliament of the World's Religions in 1993 found it necessary to explain to people of other religions that they do not worship Buddha:

Shakyamuni Buddha, the founder of Buddhism, was not God or a god. He was a human being who attained full Enlightenment through meditation and showed us the path of spiritual awakening and freedom. Therefore, Buddhism is not a religion of God. Buddhism is a religion of wisdom, enlightenment and compassion. Like the worshippers of God who believe that salvation is available to all through confession of sin and a life of prayer, we Buddhists believe that salvation and enlightenment are available to all through removal of defilements and delusion and a life of

The Buddha's final liberation into Nirvana when he physically died is symbolized by this enormous Sri Lankan statue in which he is serenely lying down with eyes closed to the world.

meditation. However, unlike those who believe in God who is separate from us, Buddhists believe that Buddha which means "one who is awake and enlightened" is inherent in us all as Buddhanature or Buddhamind.[3]

Unlike other Indian sages, the Buddha did not focus on descriptions of ultimate reality, the nature of the soul, life after death, or the origin of the universe. He said that curiosity about such matters was like a man who, upon being wounded by a poisoned arrow, refused to have it pulled out until he was told the caste and origin of his assailant, his name, his height, the color of his skin, and all details about the bow and arrow. In the meantime, he died.

Being religious and following Dhamma has nothing to do with the dogma that the world is eternal; and it has nothing to do with the other dogma that the world is not eternal. For whether the world is eternal or otherwise, birth, old age, death, sorrow, pain, misery, grief, and despair exist. I am concerned with the extinction of these.[4]

The Buddha spoke of his teachings as a raft to take us to the farther shore, rather than a description of the shore or something to be carried around once we get there. The basic planks of this raft are insights into the truths of existence and the path to liberation; **Nirvana** (Pali: **Nibbana**) is the farther shore, the goal of spiritual effort.

The basic facts of existence

In his very first sermon, the "Deer Park" sermon preached to the five ascetics, the Buddha set forth **The Four Noble Truths** around which all his later teachings revolved. These were:

1 that life inevitably involves suffering, is imperfect and unsatisfactory;
2 that suffering originates in our desires;
3 that there is a state in which there is no suffering; and
4 that there is a way to realize this state.

The Buddha is therefore neither pessimistic nor optimistic about our human condition. Sri Lankan monk and scholar Walpola Rahula speaks of medical practice as a metaphor for spiritual teaching: In giving the diagnosis and prognosis for a sick patient, one doctor may feel that the patient will surely die, that the situation is hopeless. Another doctor may falsely encourage the patient to think that nothing is wrong. A third doctor takes the most useful middle way:

…diagnoses the symptoms correctly, understands the cause and nature of the illness, sees clearly that it can be cured, and courageously administers a course of treatment, thus saving the patient. The Buddha is like the last physician. He is the wise and scientific doctor for the ills of the world.[5]

To look at the diagnosis and treatment of our human condition one step at a time, the Buddha's First Noble Truth is the existence of **dukkha**, which means suffering, impermanence, emptiness. We all experience grief, unfulfilled desires, sickness, old age, physical pain, mental anguish, and death. We may be happy for a while, but happiness is not permanent. Even our identity is impermanent. There is no continual "I". What we regard as our self is simply an ever-changing bundle of fleeting feelings, sense impressions, ideas, and evanescent physical matter.

We have no eternal, unchanging soul; one moment's identity leads to the next like one candle being lit from another. These are the realities to which Buddhist teachers are referring when they begin their dharma talks by saying, "We are all human beings."

The Second Noble Truth is that dukkha has its origin in desire—desire for sensory pleasures, for fame and fortune, for things to stay as they are or become different than they are — and in attachment to ideas. The reason that desire leads us to suffering, the Buddha taught, is that we do not understand the nature of things, of that which we desire. Everything is actually impermanent, changing all the time. We seek to grasp and hold life as we want it to be, but we cannot, since everything is in constant flux.

In Buddhism, unhappiness is understood as the inevitable companion of happiness. The sun will give way to rain; a lovely flower will decay; beloved friends will die; our bodies will surely age. As the contemporary monk Ajahn Sumedho points out, "trying to arrange, control and manipulate conditions so as to always get what we want, always hear what we want to hear, always see what we want to see, so that we never have to experience unhappiness or despair, is a hopeless task."[6]

What a Buddhist strives for instead is the recognition of dukkha (the fact of suffering: of discomfort and frustration with our life situations), **anicca** (impermanence), and **anatta** (no eternal self). Suffering is actually useful to us because it helps us to see things as they really are. When our attention is drawn to the fact that everything changes and passes away, moment by moment, we can become aware that nothing in this world has an independent, solid character. There are only momentary configurations within a continual process of change. Once we have grasped these basic facts of life, we can be free in this life, and free from another rebirth.

The Third Noble Truth is that dukkha can cease, revealing Ultimate Reality, or Nirvana (Pali: Nibbana). This is a state in which desire and illusion are no more. One lives happily and fully in the present moment, free from self-centeredness and full of compassion for others. One can serve them purely, for in this state there is no thought of oneself.

The Fourth Noble Truth is that only through a life of morality, concentration, and wisdom — which the Buddha set forth as the Noble Eightfold Path — can desire and therefore suffering be extinguished.

The Eightfold Path of liberation

The Buddha set forth a systematic approach by which dedicated humans could pull themselves out of suffering and achieve the final goal of liberation. The Eightfold Path offers ways to burn up all past demerits, avoid accumulating new demerits, and build up merit for a favorable rebirth. Perfection of the path means final escape from the cycle of death and rebirth, into the peace of Nirvana.

The first factor is **right understanding**. Initially this means seeing through illusions, such as the idea that a little more wealth could bring happiness. Gradually one learns to question old assumptions in the light of the Four Noble Truths. Everything we do and say is governed by the mind. The Buddha said that if our mind is defiled and untrained, suffering will follow us just as a chariot follows the horse. If we think and act from a purified, trained mind, happiness will always follow us.

Second is **right thought or motives**. The Buddha encourages us to uncover any "unwholesome" emotional roots behind our thinking, such as a desire to hide our imperfections or avoid contact with others. As we discover and weed out such emotional blocks, our thought becomes free from the limitations of self-centeredness — relaxed, clear, and open.

Third is **right speech**. The Buddha cautions us to relinquish our propensity to vain talk, gossip, tale-bearing, harsh words, and lying, and to use communication instead in the service of truth and harmony. He also advises us to speak in a positive manner to our own minds — to say to ourselves, "May you be well and happy today."

The fourth factor, **right action**, begins for the layperson with observing the five basic precepts for moral conduct: avoid destroying life, stealing, sexual misconduct, lying, and intoxicants. Beyond these, we are to base our actions on clear understanding. "Evil deeds," said the Buddha, are those "done from motives of partiality, enmity, stupidity, and fear."[7]

Fifth is r**ight livelihood** — being sure that one's way of making a living does not violate the five precepts. One's trade should not harm others or disrupt social harmony.

Right effort, the sixth factor in the Eightfold Path, bespeaks continual striving to cut off "unwholesome states," past, present, and future. This is not a way for the lazy.

The seventh factor, **right mindfulness**, is particularly characteristic of Buddhism, for the way to liberation is said to be through the mind. We are urged to be aware in every moment. In *The Dhammapada*, short verses about the way of truth, said to have been uttered by the Buddha, there appears this pithy injunction:

Check your mind.
Be on your guard.
Pull yourself out
as an elephant from mud.[8]

The eighth factor, **right meditation**, applies mental discipline to the quieting of the mind itself. "It is subtle, invisible, treacherous,"[9] explains the Buddha. Skillful means are therefore needed to see and transcend its restless nature. When the mind is fully stilled, it becomes a quiet pool in which the true nature of everything is clearly reflected. The various schools of Buddhism that have developed over the centuries have taught different techniques of meditation, but this basic principle remains the same.

Try to be mindful, and let things take their natural course. Then your mind will become still in any surroundings, like a clear forest pool. All kinds of wonderful, rare animals will come to drink at the pool, and you will clearly see the nature of all things. You will see many strange and wonderful things come and go, but you will be still. This is the happiness of the Buddha.
Achaan Chah, meditation master, Wat Ba Pong, Thailand[10]

TEACHING STORY

The Monkeys take Care of the Trees

The king's park-keeper wanted to celebrate a festival in the city. Therefore he wanted to find some people to water the trees so that he could take a leave for a week or so. He wondered to himself, "How can I find some people to look after the trees?" Then he thought of the monkeys in the park.

He summoned the chief monkey. "Can you water the trees for me during my leave?"

The chief monkey said, "Oh, sure."

The park-keeper said to him, "Here are the watering pots. Please tell the monkeys in this park to water the trees while I am gone." Then he went away.

When the time came for watering the trees, the chief monkey said to the other monkeys who had gathered to take the watering pots, "One moment, please. We have to use water economically. How can we do so? We have to water the trees according to their needs. How can we know the needs of the trees? The tree with long roots needs much water;

the tree with short roots needs less water. We should make a division of labor by dividing the monkeys into groups. Two monkeys to a group: One monkey pulls up the tree to see if it has long or short roots. The other monkey, when he sees — 'Oh, this one has short roots' — waters it less. If it has long roots, he should water it more."

The monkeys divided their labor in this way. They watered all the trees in the garden park, and all the trees died.

Then a wise man came and saw what the monkeys were doing. The chief monkey, who considered himself very wise, explained his orders. Then the wise man uttered this stanza:

A foolish person, even when he wants to do something good, may instead do something that leads to destruction.

(A tale from one of the Buddha's previous lives, as retold by Phra Depvedi)

The wheel of birth and death

Buddhist teachings about reincarnation are slightly different from those of Hindu orthodoxy, for there is no eternal soul to be reborn. In Buddhism, one changing state of being sets another into motion: every event depends on a cause. The central cause in this process is **karma** (Pali: **kamma**) — our acts of will. These influence the level at which that personality-developing process we think of as "me" is reborn. The impressions of our good and bad actions help to create our personality moment-by-moment. When we die, this process continues, passing on the flame to a new life on a plane that reflects our past karma.

There are thirty-one planes of existence, interpreted as psychological metaphors by some Buddhists. Metaphors or metaphysical realities, these include hells, "hungry ghosts" (beings tormented with unsatisfied desires), animals, humans, and gods. Like the lower levels, the gods are imperfect and impermanent. Round and round we go, life after life, caught in this cycle of **samsara** (worldly phenomena), repeatedly experiencing ageing, decay, suffering, death, and painful rebirth, unless we are freed into Nirvana, which is beyond all the cause-and-effect-run planes of existence.

The Wheel of Life: In the center are animals representing lust, hatred, and delusion. The next circle shows the fate of those with good karma (left) and bad karma (right). The third circle represents the six spheres of existence from the gods to the infernal regions. The outer rim shows the chain of cause and effect. Grasping the wheel is a monster representing death, impermanence.

Nirvana

About the goal of Buddhist practice, Nirvana, the Buddha had relatively little to say. The word itself refers to the extinguishing of a flame from lack of fuel. The only way to end the cycle in which desire feeds the wheel of suffering is to end all cravings and lead a passion-free existence which has no karmic consequences.

For the **Arhant** (Pali: **Arhat** or **Arahat**), or saint, who has found Nirvana within this life:

No suffering for him
who is free from sorrow
free from the fetters of life
free in everything he does.
He has reached the end of his road....

Like a bird invisibly flying in the sky,
he lives without possessions,
knowledge his food, freedom his world,
while others wonder....

He has found freedom —
peaceful his thinking, peaceful his speech,
peaceful his deed, tranquil his mind.[11]

What happens when such a being dies? One enters a deathless, peaceful, unchanging state that cannot be described. Individuality disappears and one enters the realm of ultimate truth, about which the Buddha was silent. Why? At one point he picked up a handful of leaves from the forest floor and asked his disciples which were more numerous, the leaves in his hand or those in the surrounding forest. When they replied, "Very few in your hand, lord; many more in the grove," he said:

Exactly. So you see, friends, the things that I know and have not revealed are more than the truths I know and have revealed. And why have I not revealed them? Because, friends, there is no profit in them; because they are not helpful to holiness; because they do not lead from disgust to cessation and peace, because they do not lead from knowledge to wisdom and Nirvana.[12]

Buddhism south and north

As soon as he had attracted a small group of disciples, the Buddha sent them out to help teach the Dharma:

Walk, monks, on tour for the blessing of the manyfolk, for the happiness of the manyfolk, out of compassion for the world, for the welfare, the blessing, the happiness of devas and men.... There are beings with little dust in their eyes who, not hearing Dhamma, are decaying, but if they are learners of Dhamma they will grow.[13]

This missionary effort spread in all directions. Two hundred years after the Buddha died, a great Indian king, Asoka, developed appreciation of many religions. Under his leadership Buddhism was carried throughout the kingdom and outward to other countries as well, beginning its development as a global religion. After Asoka's death, Brahmins reasserted their political influence and Buddhists were persecuted in parts of India. By the time of the twelfth-century Muslim invasions of India, Buddhism nearly died out and never became the dominant religion in the Buddha's homeland.

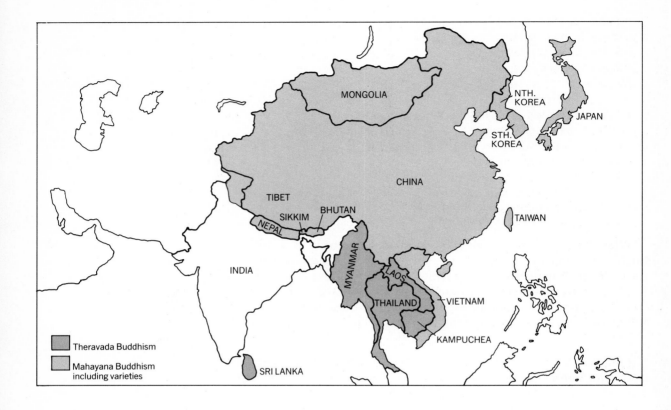

Map showing the approximate distribution of Theravada and Mahayana Buddhism in the world today.

Many Buddhist sects have developed as the Buddha's teachings have been expanded upon and adapted to local cultures in different areas. There are two primary divisions. The remaining form that tries to adhere closely to what it considers the original teachings is called **Theravada**, or Teaching of the Elders. It is prevalent in the south Asian countries of Sri Lanka, Myanmar (Burma), Thailand, Kampuchea (Cambodia), and Laos and is therefore referred to as the Southern School. The other major grouping is the Northern School, which is the dominant Buddhist path in Nepal, Tibet, China, Korea, Mongolia, and Japan. Those of this group call it **Mahayana**, the "Greater Vehicle," because they feel that theirs is a bigger raft that can carry more people than the stark teachings of the Theravadins, which they call the **Hinayana**, or "Lesser Vehicle." Both groups are in general agreement about the Four Noble Truths, the Eightfold Path, and the teachings about karma and Nirvana described above.

Theravada: the path of mindfulness

Theravada is noted for its adherence to early scriptures, its emphasis on the monastic life of renunciation, and its mindfulness meditation teachings. These characteristics are more obvious among the intellectuals and monastics; the common people are more devotional in their practices.

THE PALI CANON The doctrine and quotations cited thus far all come from the **Pali Canon**, the "Bible" of Theravada Buddhism. Because the Buddha taught tirelessly for decades, sayings attributed to him fill forty-five volumes in the Thai edition of the canon. This compilation is also referred to as the **Tipitaka** (Sanskrit: **Tripitaka**)— "the three baskets of the law." The teachings were collected immediately after the Buddha's death by a council of five hundred Elders, monks who had studied directly with him. From memory, the Venerable Ananda recited his discourses and another close disciple rehearsed the discipline of the order. Then the Elders agreed upon a definitive body of the Buddha's teachings which were carried orally until the first century BCE, when they were written down on palm leaves and were stored in baskets.

The "three baskets" were: rules for monks and nuns, discourses of the Buddha, and "the basket of further discipline." According to legend, the last pitaka was preached by the Buddha to the gods in heaven, but scholars think that this highly philosophical, academic part of the canon probably represents later attempts to systematize the Buddha's ideas.

In addition to the Tipitaka, Theravadins also honor other non-canonical Pali works, such as later commentaries and commentaries-on-the-commentaries. The 547 lively Jataka Tales, such as the story of the foolish monkeys, appear in the commentaries as explanations of the context of the pithy sayings found in the discourses ("A foolish man, even when he tries to do good…"). These folk tales are said to have been told by the Buddha and to represent scenes from his own previous incarnations, but they are also used to demonstrate Buddhist virtues, such as wisdom and compassion.

Training of Buddhist monks often begins at an early age, with study of the ancient scriptures.

THE TRIPLE GEM Like all Buddhists, those of the Southern School soften the discipline of the mind with devotion to the **Triple Gem**: Buddha (the Enlightened One), Dhamma (the doctrine he taught, ultimate reality), and Sangha (the order of his disciples). To become a Buddhist, and then afterwards to reassert the basis of one's faith, a person "takes refuge" in these three jewels by reciting the Pali formula, *Buddham saranam gacchami* ("I go to the Buddha for refuge"), *Dhammam saranam gacchami* ("I go to the Dhamma for refuge"), *Sangham saranam gacchami* ("I go to the Sangha for refuge").

One takes refuge in the Buddha not by praying to him for help but by paying homage to him as supreme teacher and inspiring model. In a sense, taking refuge in the Buddha is honoring the Buddha-wisdom within each of us.

The Dhamma is like a medicine, but it will not cure our suffering unless we ourselves take it. In the Pali chanting, the Dhamma is described as immediate, timeless, leading to calmness, and only known through our direct experience and personal effort.

The Sangha is the order of bhikkus and bhikkunis who have renounced the world in order to follow, preserve, and share the Dhamma. The Buddha established one of the world's first monastic orders, and this core remains strong in Theravada. There are presently about half a million Theravadin monks in Southeast Asia. To simplify their wordly lives and devote themselves to studying and teaching the Dhamma, monks must shave their heads, dress in simple robes, own only a few basic material items, eat no solid foods after noon, practice celibacy, and depend upon the laity for their food, clothing, and medical supplies. Early every morning they set forth with begging bowl, and the laypeople regard it as a merit-making opportunity to set up sidewalk kitchens to feed them. In this interdependent system, the monks reciprocate by offering spiritual guidance, chanted blessings, and various social services, often including secular advice and education. Monks offer discourses on the Dhamma in monasteries and also, when invited, in private homes.

Buddhist monasteries are at the center of village life, rather than separated from it. The monasteries are open, and people come and go. The monks hold a revered social position as models of self-control, kindness, and intelligence; no one can sit on a higher level than a bhikkhu. In Theravadin countries it is common for young men to take temporary vows of monkhood — often for the duration of the rainy season when little farmwork can be done. They wear the saffron robes, set forth with shaven heads and begging bowls, and receive religious instruction while they practice a life of simplicity.

By contrast, there has traditionally been little social support for bhikkunis, or Buddhist nuns, in Southeast Asia. Provisions were made during the time of the Buddha for women monastics to live in the same monasteries as men, with the same lifestyle, but the order of fully ordained nuns disappeared completely in Theravadin countries about a thousand years ago. Many of the early Buddhist scriptures take an egalitarian position toward women's capacity for wisdom and attainment of Nibbana, but spiritual power was kept in the hands of monks. Nuns were by rules of the order forever subservient to the monks, seniority notwithstanding, so there was little opportunity for them to grow into positions of leadership.

Nevertheless, some women's desire for spiritual freedom is strong today. As part of attempts to revive fully ordained orders of nuns in Theravadin countries such

In Southeast Asia a large population of monks is supported by laypeople, who offer food daily.

as Sri Lanka, a landmark meeting occurred in Bodh Gaya in 1987: The First International Conference of Buddhist Nuns. At a 1995 seminar on the role of Buddhist nuns and laywomen in the reconciliation of Cambodia, So Mouy, founder of a nunnery, explained the effects of women's subordination to men in monasteries:

> *When we stay in the temples, we spend too much time cooking and cleaning for the monks, and not enough time on our own spiritual practice. If we are to have a greater role in social and development work, first we must have a more solid spiritual foundation.[14]*

VIPASSANA MEDITATION In addition to trying to preserve what are thought to be the Buddha's original teachings, Theravada is the purveyor of mindfulness meditation techniques. **Vipassana** literally means "insight" but the meditation methods used to develop insight begin by increasing one's attentiveness to every detail as a way of calming, focusing, and watching the mind. As taught by the Burmese meditation master Mahasi Sayadaw, the beginning vipassana practice is simply to watch oneself breathing in and out, with the attention focused on the rise and fall of the abdomen. To keep the mind concentrated on this movement, rather than dragged this way and that by unconscious, conditioned responses, one continually makes concise mental notes of what is happening: "rising," "falling." Inevitably other mental functions will arise in the restless mind. As they do, one simply notes what they are — "imagining," "wandering," "remembering" — and then returns the attention to the rising and falling of the breath. Body sensations will appear, too, and one handles them the same way, noting "itching," "tight," "tired." Periods of sitting meditation are alternated with periods of walking meditation, in which one notes the exact movements of the body in great detail: "lifting," "moving," "placing."

Living Buddhism

In Thailand, over ninety-three percent of the population is Buddhist, and there are historically close ties between State and Sangha. Although consumerism is beginning to erode traditional values the people have been unusually happy and free, perhaps partly because of their Buddhist faith. Below are interviews with two women from Bangkok.

Komkai Charoensuk, a grandmother who practices meditation and studies with monks and nuns:

"I'm just beginning to become a good Buddhist. I practice meditation, but not continuously. It needs a lot of patience and great attention. Not time. The present moment — that's the most important thing we must know.

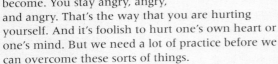

When somebody else is angry and starts to curse us, it is very easy for us to feel that we are hurt by them. But we can try to find out what is the cause of their suffering, their anger. The longer you keep the pain in yourself, the worse it will become. You stay angry, angry, and angry. That's the way that you are hurting yourself. And it's foolish to hurt one's own heart or one's mind. But we need a lot of practice before we can overcome these sorts of things.

We don't want to start and end and come back and start and end again and come back and start again. We don't want to be born again and suffer, another time be happy, another time suffer. You laugh and you cry, and you laugh and you cry all your life. That's why we want to go to Nirvana: No more happiness, no more unhappiness. And then when anyone scolds you, you are smiling, you understand why they are scolding you. You understand everything. Nobody can hurt you."

Prachoomsuk Achava-Amrung, a professor of educational research with a background in chemistry, and past president of the International Association of Educators for World Peace:

"I am a scientist and Buddhism is very scientific. Everything is cause and effect relationships. There is no God or anything holy. You have to help yourself.

In some other religions, you pray for God to help you, but not in Buddhism. Buddha said, 'I can guide you. I cannot help you. I can point your way, but you have to do it yourself. Not me.'

The whole Buddhist teaching is peace, peace of mind. You know the word 'Thai' means 'free.' This is a very interesting case history: Thailand was never colonized during the period of European colonization. Did Thailand have powerful weapons? Huge armies? Not a bit. We can stay free because we have Buddhism in our hearts. We are smiling. We see everybody as a friend. We have a proverb that you can find friends everywhere, but you cannot find enemies anywhere unless you make them.

In that time it was very funny that the British battleship sailed to Bangkok through the Gulf of Thailand, and also the French, and the Thai people said, 'What a big ship! Let's everybody go and see!' instead of shooting at them. Just, 'What can we do for you? What's wrong with your ship?' And the captain came down and they signed a contract, a treaty of friendship. They made that treaty so that the British had the advantage. We didn't know — we just signed. We are friendly, so we didn't fall, we were not colonized. But other countries had fighting and the Europeans had more powerful weapons and conquered them.

So when I work with the peace movement, I try to let people know that peaceful mind, like we have in Thailand. We have freedom and peaceful mind and right attitude toward people. We see everybody as friend. This is the way we are trying to teach the world to help children develop peaceful minds."

This same mindfulness is carried over into every activity of the day. If ecstatic states or visions arise, the meditator is told simply to note them and let them pass away without attachment. In the same way, emotions that arise are simply observed, accepted, and allowed to pass away, rather than labeled "good" or "bad." By contrast, says dharma teacher Joko Beck, we usually get stuck in our emotions:

> That's where everybody's stuck. Everyone's fascinated by their emotions because we think that's who we are. We're afraid that if we let our attachment to them go, we'll be nobody. Which of course we are! When you wander into your ideas, your hopes, your dreams, turn back — not just once but ten thousand times if need be, a million times if need be.[15]

The truths of existence as set forth by the Buddha — dukkha, anicca, anatta — will become apparent during this process, and the mind becomes calm, clear, attentive, and flexible, detached from likes and dislikes.

THE LAITY Although meditators from all over the world are now traveling to Southeast Asia to study with the masters of meditation, their demanding discipline is embraced by relatively few Theravadins. The majority of monasteries are not meditation centers. Most laypeople's religious lives are more devotional than intellectual. Recognizing this natural tendency, Theravada developed two separate paths for bhikkhus and the laity: the path for monks and nuns was based on development of morality, concentration, and wisdom, leading to freedom, whereas the laity was expected only to give alms and to observe the Three Refuges and the Five Precepts, with some attention to the development of tranquility. Laypeople

Stupas such as these bell-shaped monuments at the Great Stupa complex in Borobudur, Java, may house relics or statues of the Buddha and are sacred places for pilgrimage. The Buddha's long ears signify wisdom; the topknot represents higher consciousness.

Left *Buddhists sit on the floor in their temples, honoring statues of the Buddha as an eternal principle in the universe.*
Right *In Southeast Asia roadside shrines of the Buddha, some of them on busy city streets, are visited by laypeople bringing offerings such as food and drink, elephant figures, flowers, candles, and incense. They are quite similar to the earlier spirit shrines.*

are not expected to know much about the Buddha's teachings; few of them try to gain Enlightenment.

Even within the relatively austere Theravada path there have arisen a number of ways of worship. One is the veneration of relics thought to be from the Buddha. These are placed in **stupas**, architectural mounds reaching into the sky, perhaps derived from the indigenous spiritual traditions. A tiny bone chip from the Buddha, for instance, is enshrined at Doi Suthep temple near Chiang Mai in Thailand. To share this sacred relic with the people, the ruler was said to have placed it on the back of a sacred white elephant — legendary symbol of the Buddha — so that it would choose the best place for the temple. The elephant climbed a nearby hill until it reached the auspicious spot, where it circled three times and then went down on its knees. Thousands of pilgrims climb the 290 steps to the temple today, praying for blessings by acts such as pressing squares of gold leaf onto an image of the Buddha, lighting three sticks of incense to honor the Triple Gem, lighting candles, and offering flowers to the Buddha images.

Loving images of the Buddha proliferate in the temples and roadside shrines (which are almost identical to the indigenous spirit shrines, still quite common in Southeast Asia for Theravada has related itself to indigenous ways rather than displacing them). These physical images of the Buddha give a sense of his protective, guiding presence even though according to Theravadin orthodoxy the Buddha no longer exists as an individual, having entered Nibbana. Even the monks are regarded as magical protectors of sorts, and the faithful can request chantings of blessings for protection. For instance, in the books of Pali chants there is a special prayer for protection from unwanted crawling creatures, such as spiders and rats. It addresses them in a spirit of loving-kindness (*metta*) and then requests, "May those beings go away!"[16]

Mahayana: the path of compassion and metaphysics

Further Buddhist practices and teachings appeared in a wide range of scriptures dating from the first century BCE. These innovations in thought and practice beyond the Pali scriptures became grouped together and called *Mahayana*, the Great Vehicle. Rather than enforcing a gap between monastics on one hand and the common people on the other, these new scriptures take a more liberal approach designed to encompass everyone. They honor the scriptures in the Pali Canon but claim that they express more advanced teachings of the Buddha. They are explained by Mahayanists as esoteric teachings given only to the Bodhisattvas, the compassionate enlightened beings described below.

The Mahayana **sutras** (teachings) are open-ended, and emphasize the importance of religious experience. The Dharma is not embodied only in scriptures; for the Mahayanist it is the source of a conversion experience that awakens the quest for enlightenment as the greatest value in life.

Each school, and there are many branches within Mahayana, offers a special set of methods, or "skillful means," for awakening. They are quite varied, in contrast

Buddhist nuns have traditionally been given lower status than monks, but as a group they are growing in strength today.

Kuan-yin, "hearer of cries," Bodhisattva of mercy.

to the relative uniformity of Theravada, but most Mahayana traditions have a few characteristics in common.

BODHISATTVAS An early Mahayana scripture, the *Lotus Sutra*, defended its innovations beyond the Pali Canon by claiming that the earlier teachings were merely skillful means for those with lower capacities. They were ideally to be replaced by the true Dharma of the Lotus. The idea that the Buddha geared his teaching to his audience, and that his teachings were at different levels of completeness depending on the readiness of his audience to hear the full truth, is explained by some researchers as a way to give credit to earlier teachings while going beyond them, and also a way to include helpful popular practices, mythology, and local customs.

In contrast to the earlier goal of individual liberation from suffering by those who were capable, the Lotus Sutra claimed that a higher goal was to become like the Buddha by seeking enlightenment for the sake of saving others. In fact, it asserted that we are called not just to individual liberation but to Buddhahood itself. Contrary to earlier teachings, the Lotus Sutra says that all beings have the capacity for Buddhahood and are destined to attain it eventually. Members of the new Mahayana communities dared to call themselves **Bodhisattvas**, beings dedicated to attaining enlightenment. Both monastics and laity took the Bodhisattva vow to become enlightened.

Today Mahayana Buddhists often express this commitment in the Four Great Bodhisattva Vows compiled in China in the sixth century CE by Tien-t'ai Chih-i:

Beings are infinite in number, I vow to save them all;
The obstructive passions are endless in number, I vow to end them all;
The teachings for saving others are countless, I vow to learn them all;
Buddhahood is the supreme achievement, I vow to attain it.

As His Holiness the Fourteenth Dalai Lama says:

The motivation to achieve Buddhahood in order to save all sentient beings is really a marvelous determination. That person becomes very courageous, warm-hearted, and useful in society.[17]

> *You are not just here for yourself alone, but for the sake of all sentient beings. Keep your mind pure, and warm.*
>
> *Soen Nakagawa-roshi*[18]

Bodhisattvahood is not just an ideal for earthly conduct; numerous heavenly Bodhisattvas are available to hear the pleas of those who are suffering. The heavenly Bodhisattvas are seen as aspects of the eternal Buddha. Each has a specific attribute, such as wisdom or compassion, and worshippers can pray to them for help.

The most popular Bodhisattva in East Asia is Kuan-yin, who symbolizes compassion and refuses help to no one. Although this being is depicted as a male (Avalokitesvara) in Indian images, the Lotus Sutra says that Kuan-yin will take any form that is needed to help others, and it lists thirty-three examples. In East Asia, Kuan-yin is typically represented as female, often as the giver or protector of babies. An image with a baby has become especially popular in East Asia as a refuge for aborted fetuses and their mothers.

THE THREE BODIES OF BUDDHA In Theravada, Buddha is an historical figure who no longer exists but who left his Dharma as a guide. By contrast, Mahayana regards the Buddha as a universal principle. Metaphysically, Buddha is said to be an eternal presence in the universe with three aspects, or "bodies": The essence of knowledge and compassion, "Consciousness merged in the Universal Consciousness"; the body of bliss, that radiant aspect of Buddhahood that communicates the Dharma to Bodhisattvas; and the body of transformation, by which the Buddha principle becomes human to help liberate humanity. It was in this third body that the Buddha appeared for a time on the earth as the historical figure Siddhartha Gautama of the Shakyas. He is called Shakyamuni Buddha by Mahayanists to distinguish him from other manifestations of the Buddha.

Whereas Theravada is non-theistic, Mahayana has thus elevated Buddhahood to almost theistic status. The common people therefore recognize a multitude of Buddhas and Bodhisattvas to whom they can pray for help. But some Mahayanists interpret teachings about the Bodhisattvas and the three bodies of the Buddha symbolically rather than literally, as metaphors for aspects of consciousness within the mysteries of the cosmos. From this point of view, Nirvana can be described as the state of pure, blissful, and radiant consciousness.

EMPTINESS Mahayana scriptures portray Buddhas moving swiftly through intergalactic space and time, cloning and appearing at different places simultaneously, dematerializing and materializing at will. However, practitioners at higher stages are not to be attached to these appearances. Many schools within Mahayana also affirm, along with Theravadins, that there is an eternal reality, the transcendent "Suchness," Truth, or Law by which the universe is governed. In the Udana scripture from the Pali Canon, the Buddha stated, "O monks, there is an unborn, undying, unchanging, uncreated. If it were not so, there would be no point to life, or to training." However, as contemporary teacher Roshi Jiyu Kennett explains, "Buddhism states what the Eternal is not.... It does not state what it is because if it did, then we would be stuck with a concept."[19]

Some of the most complex and paradoxical of Mahayana teachings concern the concept of **sunyata**, meaning voidness or emptiness. They were elaborated by the brilliant Indian philosopher Nagarjuna around the second century CE on the basis of the earlier Perfection of Wisdom scriptures.

According to Nagarjuna, all earthly things arise and pass away, as a process of events dependent on other events, having no independent origin and no eternal reality. The world of phenomena — **samsara** — is therefore empty. As the Dalai Lama says,

> If we really want to find that Tibetan being called Dalai Lama, we cannot find it. There is something if we pinch our skin, but we cannot find it.[20]

Nirvana is also empty in the sense that it is a thought construct, even though it is not dependent on conditions. Nirvana is not an eternal reality that can be acquired. In the paradoxical analyses of voidness, even Ultimate Reality is called Sunyata because it transcends all thought constructs.

In the Perfection of Wisdom scriptures, the student to whom the lengthy teachings on Sunyata are given is at last asked if he has understood the teachings. "In truth, nothing has been taught," he declares.

The Perfection of Wisdom scriptures that celebrate the liberating experience of emptiness are foundational texts for most of Mahayana. What is distinctive and startling about Mahayana is the application of the idea of emptiness to all things, even including the teachings of the Buddha. In the popular *Heart Sutra* that is used liturgically throughout East Asia, the core doctrines of traditional Buddhism are systematically shattered: Bodhisattva Kuan-yin sees that the five aggregates of a person (form, sensation, perception, reaction, and consciousness) are each empty, and thereby becomes free of all suffering. Next, birth and death, purity and defilement, increase and decrease are seen as empty; the six sense objects, the six sense organs, and the six sense awarenesses are seen to be empty; the Wheel of Life is seen as empty; the Four Noble Truths and Eightfold Path are seen as empty. Even knowledge and attainment are proclaimed to be empty. With this "perfection of wisdom," there are no obstacles, and therefore no fear, and going beyond delusions one attains Nirvana, having emptied Buddhism of its central objects. The Heart Sutra replaces the doctrines with a mantra which it proclaims as supreme: *Gate, Gate, paragate, parasamgate, bodhi, svaha!* (Gone, gone, gone beyond, gone to the other shore. O enlightenment, all hail!) As Professor David Chappell observes,

> *The systematic emptying of the central doctrines of the tradition is unparalleled in religious history. (Imagine a Christian saying that the Ten Commandments and Lord's Prayer and Apostles' Creed are empty!) And yet, insight into the impermanence of all things, and their connectedness, gives Mahayana a self-critical profundity and an inclusive acceptance of diversity, which provides balance in the midst of movement, and peace in the midst of compassion.*[21]

Tibetan Vajrayana: short-cut to the Palace of Unity

Of the many branches of Mahayana Buddhism, perhaps the most prolific in creating elaborations developed in Tibet. Prior to the introduction of Buddhism, the mountainous region may have been home to a shamanistic religion called Bon (pronounced "pern"). In the seventh century CE a particularly powerful king of Tibet, Songtsan, became interested in the religion that surrounded his isolated kingdom. He sent a group of students to study Buddhism in India, but they all died in the searing heat of the plains. Only one member of a second group survived the arduous trip across the Himalayas, returning with many Sanskrit texts. After some of these works were translated into Tibetan, Songtsan declared Buddhism the national religion and encouraged Buddhist virtues in his subjects.

The Bon shamans are said to have kept trying to sabotage this threat to their power until a tantric adept, Padmasambhava, was invited to the country from Kashmir in the eighth century CE. Along the way, it is said, he subdued and converted the local Bon deities. He — and perhaps his consort, Yeshe Tsogyel — developed Tibetan Buddhism by splicing elements of the Bon ways and esoteric tantric practices into Mahayana Buddhism. Many of the Bon gods and goddesses were adopted as lower-grade tantric guardian deities, but animal sacrifice was replaced with symbolic forms of worship and black magic gave way to inner purification practices. When people interpreted tantric teachings literally, indulging freely in alcohol and sex in the name of spirituality, another teacher named Atisha from the great center of Buddhist learning at Nalanda, India, was called in to set things right.

Under Atisha, Tibetan Buddhism became a complex path with three stages, said to have been the **yanas** — vehicles, means of progress, or responsibilities — prescribed by the Lord Buddha. While the Buddha did not develop them to their current state, he is said to have supported the idea of different levels of teachings for the less and more evolved. The first of these is called Hinayana by the Tibetans: quieting of the mind and relinquishing of attachments through meditation practices. The second is Mahayana: training in compassion and loving-kindness. The third is an advanced esoteric path called **Vajrayana** ("the indestructible diamond vehicle") or **Tantrayana**, said to be the speeded-up path that allows enlightenment within a single lifetime. It includes extremely rigorous practices derived from the tantric yoga of India. Adepts in this path attempt to construct a "diamond-body" for themselves that will allow them physically to sustain entries into the intense energies of higher levels of consciousness.

The "Hinayana" part of this process is similar to Vipassana meditation. Meditators are advised to watch their emotions rising and falling, without attachment to them, without judgment. But whereas Theravadins doing this practice tend to emphasize revulsion over the emptiness of samsara, Tibetans use the center of emotions as a source of energy. Lama Tarthang Tulku explains:

Any experience is fresh and valuable when we let go of our expectations and resistances, our judgments and conceptualizations. With an attitude of acceptance, even our negative emotions have the potential to increase our energy and strength. Concentrate on the feeling, not on thoughts about it. Concentrate on the center of the feeling; penetrate into that space. There is a density of energy in that center that is clear and distinct. This energy has great power, and can transmit great clarity. Our consciousness can go into the emotion, contacting this pure energy so that our tension breaks. With gentleness and self-understanding we control this energy.

The Buddhist framework for life in Tibet revolved around mountain monasteries until they were closed by the Chinese, who also killed a large proportion of the monks.

We are always rejecting ourselves, blaming ourselves for one thing or another. Instead of rejecting ourselves, it helps to realize that our negativities have no solidity. When our thoughts and concepts change, our attitude changes, and a free-floating energy is released. The more we loosen our concepts and tightness, the more this energy flows.[22]

After then developing tranquility, freedom, and loving-kindness, as encouraged in Mahayana Buddhism, dedicated Vajrayana aspirants are guided through a series of tantric practices by gurus. The highest of these are **lamas**, who are revered as teachers. Some are considered as incarnate Bodhisattvas and carefully trained from a young age for their role as those who have realized the Supreme Truth and can help others advance toward it. As in Hinduism, submission to the guru in gratitude for the teachings is the only way to receive them.

Tantric meditations always begin and end with dissolving into emptiness, the enlightened awareness of how things are. With this understanding, initiates are given practices in **deity yoga**: meditating on one of the many deities who embody various manifestations of energy in the universe. These radiant forms are themselves illusory, like the moon's image on water. But meditating on them is considered a way of reflecting on and thus bringing forth one's own true nature. Some of the deities are wrathful, such as Mahakala, defender of Dharma. Buddhists understand that wrathful acts without hatred are sometimes socially necessary to protect truth and justice.

The highest form of vajrayana is the use of the subtle vital energies of the body to transform the mind. A very high state of consciousness is produced after lengthy practice in which the "gross mind" is neutralized and the "subtle mind" manifests powerfully, "riding" on what Tibetans call "the clear light of bliss." This innermost subtle mind of clear light is considered the only aspect of existence that is eternal. Once it is uncovered, one is said to be capable of attaining Buddhahood in a single lifetime.

The practices used to transform the mind also have as side-effects such abilities as levitation, clairvoyance, meditating continuously without sleep, and warming the body from within while sitting naked in the snow. Milarepa, the famous Tibetan poet-saint whose enlightenment was won through great austerities, once sang this song:

Blissful within, I don't entertain
The notion "I'm suffering,"
When incessant rain is pouring outside.

Even on peaks of white snow mountains
Amidst swirling snow and sleet
Driven by new year's wintry winds
This cotton robe burns like fire.[23]

Tibetans have suffered persecution by the communist Chinese, who overran the country in 1951, destroying ancient monasteries and scriptures and killing an estimated one-sixth of the people over decades of occupation. Hundreds of thousands of Tibetans have escaped into exile. Among them is the highest of the lamas — the beloved fourteenth Dalai Lama, spiritual and political leader of the people. His speaking appearances around the world have been a major factor in the

The fourteenth Dalai Lama, spiritual leader of Tibetan Buddhists from his government-in-exile in Dharamsala, in the Himalayan foothills of northern India, is also revered around the world as a compassionate voice for global peace.

contemporary revival of interest in Buddhism. One of the most universally respected of all religious leaders, he is a model of the peace and compassion that he preaches. He works ceaselessly for an end to Chinese occupation of his country, but when asked how he keeps his composure in the face of the Tibetan situation, he replies,

> *Oh, anger still comes. But only like lightning, only for an instant. Hatred, ill-feeling, hardly ever. But there's an ill-feeling against negative emotion because that is the root of all suffering. When you think of the suffering of samsara, it's worse than the situation of Tibet.... The enemy teaches you inner strength. Your mind by nature is very soft, but when you have troubles, your mind gets strong.*[24]

One of the most beloved of Tibetan Buddhist deities is Tara. She is savior and mother of the world; she protects us and helps us to achieve our spiritual longings. (Detail of Tibetan thang-ka, 18th/19th century, tempera on cotton.)

Despite persecution, religious fervor and ceremony still pervade every aspect of Tibetan life, from house-raising to ardent pilgrimages. Monks and laypeople alike meditate on **thang-kas** and **mandalas**, visual aids to concentration and illumination which portray a Buddha or Bodhisattva surrounded by deities in a diagram symbolically representing the universe. Both also chant mantras. A favorite one is the phrase associated with the beloved Tibetan Bodhisattva of mercy, Avalokitesvara: *Om mani padme hum.* It evokes awareness of the "jewel in the lotus of the heart," that beautiful treasure lying hidden within each of us. Because some emphasis is placed on the number of repetitions, mantras are written out thousands of times and spun in prayer wheels or placed on prayer flags which continue the repetition of the mantra as they blow in the wind.

Zen: the great way of enlightenment

As Buddhism was transmitted to China around 50 CE and thence to Japan, Korea, and Vietnam, absorbing elements of Taoism along the way, another radical form

The purpose of Zen meditation and arts such as archery, the tea ceremony, calligraphy, garden design, and flower arrangement is to train the mind to return to its original unselfconscious union with ultimate reality.

of the religion developed that came to be called Zen (*Ch'an* in Chinese — which in turn is derived from the Sanskrit *dhyana*, the yogic stage of meditation). It claims to preserve the essence of the Buddha's teachings through direct experience, triggered by mind-to-mind transmission of the Dharma. It dismissed scriptures, Buddhas, and Bodhisattvas in favor of training for direct intuition of cosmic unity, known as the Buddha-nature or the Void.

A central way of directly experiencing the underlying unity is **zazen**, sitting "meditation." "To sit," said the Sixth Zen Patriarch, "means to obtain absolute freedom and not to allow any thought to be caused by external objects. To meditate means to realize the imperturbability of one's original nature."[25]

> *The Great Way is not difficult*
> *for those who have no preferences.*
> *When love and hate are both absent*
> *everything becomes clear and undisguised.*
> *Make the smallest distinction, however,*
> *and heaven and earth are set infinitely apart.*
>
> *Sengtsan*[26]

Prescriptions for the manner of sitting are quite rigorous: One must take a specific upright posture and then not move during the meditation period, to avoid distracting the mind. Skillful means are then applied to make the mind one-pointed and clear. One beginning practice is simply to watch and count each inhalation and exhalation from one to ten, starting over from one if anything other than awareness of the breath enters the mind. Although this explanation sounds simple, the mind is so restless that many people must work for months before finally getting to ten without having to start over. Getting to ten is not really the goal; the goal is the process itself, the process of recognizing what comes up in the mind and gently letting it go without attachment or preferences.

As one sits in zazen, undisturbed by phenomena, the natural mind is revealed. This "original mind" is spacious and free, like an open sky. Thoughts and sensations may float through it like clouds, but they arise and then disappear, leaving no trace. What remains is reality, "True Thusness." In some Zen schools, this perception of thusness comes in a sudden burst of enlightenment, or **kensho**.

When the mind is calmed, action becomes spontaneous and natural. Zen practitioners are taught to have great confidence in their natural functioning, for it arises from our essential Buddha-nature. It is said that two Zen monks, upon becoming enlightened, ran naked through the woods scribbling on rocks.

On the other hand, the Zen tradition links spontaneity with intense, disciplined concentration. In the art of calligraphy, the perfect spontaneous brushstroke — executed with the whole body, in a single breath — is the outcome of years of attentive practice. Giving ourselves fully to the moment, to be aware only of pouring tea when pouring tea, is a simplicity of beingness that most of us have to learn. Then whatever we give ourself to fully, be it painting, or serving tea, or simply breathing, reveals the Thusness of life, its unconditioned reality.

Another tool used in one Zen tradition is the *koan*. Here the attention is focused ardently on a question that boggles the mind, such as "What is the sound of one hand clapping?" or "What is your face before your parents' birth?" As Roshi [venerable teacher] Philip Kapleau observes, "Koans deliberately throw sand into the eyes of the intellect to force us to open our Mind's eye and see the world and everything in it undistorted by our concepts and judgments." To concentrate on a koan, one must look closely at it without thinking about it, experiencing it directly. Beyond abstractions, Roshi Kapleau explains, "The import of every koan is the same: that the world is one interdependent Whole and that each separate one of us is that Whole."[27]

The aim of Zen practice is enlightenment, or **satori**. One directly experiences the unity of all existence, often in a sudden recognition that nothing is separate from oneself. As one Zen master put it:

The moon's the same old moon,
The flowers exactly as they were,
Yet I've become the thingness
Of all the things I see![28]

All aspects of life become at the same time utterly precious, and utterly empty, "nothing special." This paradox can only be sensed with the mystically expanded consciousness; it cannot be grasped intellectually.

Enlightenment is not an end in itself, however. As Zen master Seung Sahn explains, one first attains an empty, "don't know" mind. This mental emptiness brings the direct experience of truth — "Sky is blue, tree is green, sugar is sweet" — and of the "mystical energy" of life. The true goal lies even beyond this:

The correct function of mystical energy is only to help other people. Somebody
is hungry — What? Somebody is suffering — What? Moment to moment, keep
correct situation, correct function, correct relationship. That is the human being's
original job.[29]

The Zen Oxherding Pictures illustrate the stages along the spiritual path. The ox represents our true nature. By the sixth stage the seeker has found the ox and rides it home. In the eighth stage both ox and self are forgotten: "Whip, rope, Ox and man alike belong to Emptiness." And in the tenth stage, the enlightened one happily returns to everyday life, "entering the marketplace with helping hands." (Brush and ink drawings by Gyokusei Jikihara.)

Pure Land: calling on Amida Buddha

Zen is essentially an inner awareness in which great attention is given to every action; it has little appeal for the laity. Other forms developed in India and the Far East have much greater popular appeal. One of the major trends is known as Pure Land Buddhism. At times of great social upheaval (for instance, when the old Japanese feudal aristocracy was falling apart), it was widely thought that people had become so degenerate that it was nearly impossible for them to attain enlightenment through their own efforts. Instead, many turned to Amida Buddha to save them. Amida (Sanskrit: Amitabha) is the Buddha of Boundless Light. According to scriptures, he had vowed to prepare a special place of bliss, the Pure Land, for all those who called on his name with total faith and devotion.

Amida appears to welcome the faithful to the Western Paradise. (Konkai Komya-ji, Kyoto, 14th century.)

Many people contributed to the growth of Pure Land Buddhism into a mass movement. In the tenth century, for example, a Japanese monk named Kuya encouraged others to join him as he danced through the streets with a bell about his neck, singing songs of devotion and calling on Amida Buddha by chanting praise of Amida Buddha.

The results of loving trust in Amida Buddha were described very vividly by the monk Genshin. After graphic depictions of the eight hells, such as the burning vat in which people are cooked like beans, he describes the ineffable pleasures of being reborn into the Pure Land upon death:

> *Rings, bracelets, a crown of jewels, and other ornaments in countless profusion adorn his body. And when he looks upon the light radiating from the Buddha, he obtains pure vision, and because of his experiences in former lives, he hears the sounds of all things. And no matter what color he may see or what sound he may hear, it is a thing of marvel.*[30]

Many believers interpret these passages literally, anticipating that if they are sufficiently faithful they will enjoy a beautiful life after death. But some understand the Pure Land as a state that can be achieved in this life; a metaphor for the mystical experience of enlightenment, in which one's former identity "dies" and one is reborn into an expanded state of consciousness. According to this view, the lotus symbolizes the blooming of the pure lotus from the mire of ignorance and suffering, which the Buddha identified as the human condition. As contemporary Pure Land Buddhist priest and scholar Taitetsu Unno explains:

> *To be reborn into that state one has to be reborn here and now in awakening. There is no such thing as after death. Buddhism sees time not past, present, and future, but as present to present to present … When one's life is fulfilled in this moment, the next moment is fulfilled. And if death is the next moment, that, too, is fulfilled. One can't be in total confusion and say, "When I die I will be saved and be reborn in Pure Land." You've got to be careful because that may not be true. But if you have some understanding, some major awakening now, then even if people say "That's a bunch of baloney!" you don't care, because each moment is fulfilled, each moment.*[31]

In pragmatic China, Ch'an Buddhism—with its emphasis on personal effort and meditation—has often been combined with Pure Land Buddhism—with its devotional emphasis on salvation by Amida Buddha. Although reliance on "self-power" and reliance on "other power" seem contradictory, the combination of meditation and devotion is considered a practical way to single-minded concentration on the Buddha and thus to the Pure Land of enlightenment.

Nichiren: salvation through the Lotus Sutra

While some Pure Land Buddhists despair of purifying themselves by their own efforts, and therefore humbly submit to the grace of Amida Buddha, a thirteenth-century Japanese fisherman's son, who named himself Nichiren, stressed the importance of striving to reform not only ourselves but also society. He blamed the political struggles of the time on false Buddhist paths, including the Pure Land focus on the next life rather than this one. For Nichiren, the highest truths of Buddhism were embodied in the Lotus Sutra, a large compilation of parables, verses, and descriptions of innumerable forms of beings who support the teachings of the World-Honored One, the Buddha. Nichiren gave particular attention to two of these beings: the Bodhisattva of Superb Action, who staunchly devotes himself to spreading the Perfect Truth, even in evil times, and the Bodhisattva Ever-Abused, who is persecuted because of his insistence on revering everyone with unshaken conviction that each person is potentially a Buddha. Nichiren himself was repeatedly abused by authorities but persisted in his efforts to reform Buddhism in Japan and then spread its purified essence, the Bodhisattva ideal, to the world.

The phrase chanted by Nichiren and his followers, *"Namu myoho rengekyo,"* refers to faith in the entire Lotus Sutra. Today it is chanted by Nichiren monks and nuns

Peace pilgrims fast and pray in Bosnia on their way from Auschwitz to Nagasaki and Hiroshima to call attention to the need for nonviolence.

by the hour, slowly revealing its depths as it works inwardly, beyond thought. In our time, some in the Nichiren tradition undertake long peace walks, such as one sponsored by Nipponzan Myohoji in 1995. People walked from Auschwitz in Poland to Hiroshima and Nagasaki in Japan, to commemorate the 50th anniversary of the end of World War II with a plea for nonviolence and respect for all of life. They beat small hand drums while chanting *"Nanu myoho rengekyo,"* and hope to contribute to world peace by truly bowing to the Buddha in each person, even if they encounter abuse. As the Most Venerable Nichidatsu Fujii, who passed away in 1985 at the age of one hundred and influenced Gandhi's doctrine of nonviolence, has explained:

> We do not believe that people are good because we see that they are good, but by believing that people are good we eliminate our own fear and thus, we can intimately associate with them. To believe in the compassionate power of the Supreme Being which we cannot see is a discipline in order to believe in the invisible good in others.[32]

The chanting of *"Namu myoho rengekyo"* has also caused seventy Peace Pagodas to arise thus far in Japan, England, Austria, and the United States, in fulfillment of the prophecy in the Lotus Sutra that wherever this Scripture of the Lotus Blossom of the Fine Dharma is preached, a beautiful stupa will spontaneously emerge as a physical reminder of the Buddha's "supernatural penetrations." These pagodas are built with donated materials and labor by people of all faiths who support the belief expressed by Nichidatsu Fujii, in hopes of world peace.

Another new offshoot of Nichiren Shoshu is **Soka Gakkai**, based in Japan but claiming over twenty million members around the world. Its leader, Daisaku Ikeda, calls for a peaceful world revolution through transformation of individual consciousness. The order emphasizes chanting of *"Namu myoho rengekyo"* for earthly happiness. According to a pamphlet distributed by the group:

> One who chants is able to gain the power and wisdom to live with confidence, overcome any problem, and develop a happy future.... Such benefits include better jobs, places to live and cars to drive. Buddhism maintains that all realms are essential to happiness.[33]

This focus on material benefits may be a selective interpretation of classical Buddhism, which seems to have emphasized detachment from earthly concerns. But Soka Gakkai's strategy is to help people gain earthly power first and then lead them toward higher goals. The leaders explain:

> When enough people passionately embrace the viewpoint that life is sacred and inviolable, peace will ensue.[34]

Yet another new branch of Buddhism inspired by the Lotus Sutra is **Rissho Kosei-kai**, founded in the 1930s by Rev. Nikkyo Niwano and Myoko Naganuma to bring the message of the Lotus Sutra to the world in practical ways in order to encourage happiness and peace. Members meet to discuss ways of applying the Buddha's teachings to specific problems in their own lives. The organization, which is active in international inter-religious activities, asserts that "The Eternal Buddha, invisible but present everywhere, is the great life-force of the universe, which sustains each of us."[35]

Life in a Western Zen Monastery

Side-by-side in still rows, with birdsong and sunlight streaming in through the tall windows, sit the monks and laypeople of Zen Mountain Monastery. For thirty-five minute blocks separated by periods of attentive walking, they support each other by practicing zazen together in silence. With this group structure, many find it easier to carry on the rigorous discipline of serious Zen training than they would by themselves.

This particular monastery, located in the Catskill Mountains near Mount Tremper, New York, reflects the changing face of religion in the United States. A hundred years ago the main building was handcrafted of stone as a Benedictine Monastery; later it became a Lutheran summer camp. Now back-to-back with the Christ on the cross on the outside of the building is a statue of Buddha on the altar in the zendo. The monastery houses eleven fully ordained monastics who have taken lifetime vows of service (six of them women), several novices and postulants in training (an aspect adopted from Western monasticism), lay residents who stay for up to a year, and groups of people who come for special retreats and classes. Increasingly these are professionals and family people from the mainstream culture, rather than the hippies who embraced Buddhism in the 1960s and 1970s. They do not come for a comfortable vacation, for zazen is hard work and the teachers are dedicated to creating snags that help people discover the places where they are not free. They are expected to practice intensely and then leave, carrying what they have learned back into the world. As the monk Shugen observes, "If Zen doesn't work in the world, it's not working."

In addition to long sessions of silent sitting and walking, Dharma talks by the resident Zen master John Daido Loori Sensei (an American ordained in both authentic Zen lineages), and private coaching by the monks, monastery residents participate in structured non-theistic liturgical services designed to foster attentiveness and appreciation. They chant in Japanese and English, with frequent bowing to each other, to their meditation cushions, and to the Buddha on the altar in identification with all beings and gratitude for the teachings. Zen master Daido notes that liturgy reflects the innards of a religion: "In Catholicism, cathedrals are awe-inspiring, the chants expansive; in Zen the form is simple and the chanting is grounded, not other-worldly."

The rest of the day is devoted to caretaking of the buildings and two hundred-acre nature sanctuary, mindful practice done in silence, and to work practice. Those with office jobs combine ancient and modern arts: They sit cross-legged on low cushions before their computers and use calligraphic skills to hand-letter signs. Meals are simple and include coarse breads donated by a nearby whole-grain bakery. Every action — even brushing one's teeth — is treated as liturgy, in the sense of bringing total attentiveness to the sacredness of even the most "mundane" activity as a teaching that enlightenment takes place in one's everyday experience.

Following the lead of their teacher Daido, who is at once highly disciplined in the pure mind-to-mind Dharma transmission and very down-to-earth, approachable, compassionate, and married, monastery residents are human, playful, and loving. The women monks shave their heads when ordained and keep it very short thereafter, but for them near-baldness feels like freedom rather than self-sacrificing asceticism. The monk Myotai observes:

I could feel every breeze, and being bald definitely altered the way I saw the habit patterns I brought to my interactions with other people, clarifying how much "extra" was still there, to a degree that surprised me. There is a several-year entry period before ordination, to get clear on what it means, but one aspect of actually having no hair was that it really opened up the male-female dynamic. I no longer felt myself relating to men as a woman. That was very freeing. It was also wonderful to have this daily reminder of what I was doing with my life.

Above *The stillness of the zendo at Zen Mountain Monastery.*

Above right *Oriyoki, a ceremonial meal, at Zen Mountain Monastery.*

Right *John Daido Loori Sensei, abbot of Zen Mountain Monastery.*

Buddhism in the West

Images of the Buddha are now enshrined around the world, for what began in India has gradually spread to the West as well as the East. Much of this transmission has occurred in the twentieth century, with the United States becoming a vibrant center of Buddhism. Scholars are studying Buddhist traditions in great depth at many universities, and many people are trying to learn Buddhist meditation practices.

A number of the highest Tibetan lamas, forced out of Tibet, have established spiritual communities in the United States, complete with altars full of sacred Tibetan artefacts. Intensive vipassana retreats of up to three months are carried out in centers such as the Insight Meditation Society in rural Barre, Massachusetts. Theravadin teachers from Southeast Asia and Europe make frequent appearances to conduct retreats, and American teachers undertake rigorous training in Southeast Asia under traditional meditation masters. In addition to numerous Zen centers where Westerners who have undergone training in the East serve as teachers to lay practitioners of meditation, there are a number of Zen monasteries giving solid training in zazen and offering a monastic lifestyle as a permanent or temporary alternative to life in the world. In Chithurst, England, the American monk Ajahn Sumedho guides a monastic forest community in the Thai Theravada style in which he was trained.

Many Buddhist centers in the United States are led by women, in contrast to the cultural suppression of females in the East. Leading women in American Buddhism have deeply imbibed traditional Buddhist teachings and are explaining them to Westerners in fresh, contemporary ways.

Buddhism has often been embraced by Westerners because of their longing for the peace of meditation. In the midst of a chaotic materialistic life, there is a desire to discover emptiness, to let the identity with self fall away, or to become familiar with the mind's tricks in the still simplicity of a **zendo**, a Zen meditation hall. Many psychotherapists are studying Buddhism for its insights into the mind and human suffering. Richard Clarke, who is both a Zen teacher and a psychotherapist, feels that a discipline such as Zen should be part of the training of therapists:

> [We must] come holding to nothing. Zen is to guide people into experiencing the realm of emptiness and to let that experience penetrate all of life and be the ground from which one lives. Then a person could be very effective anywhere, not just as a therapist, but particularly as a therapist. Any human interaction becomes more than superficial interaction.
>
> Emptiness is also the source of infinite compassion in working with people: to really feel a person without any agenda, to be spacious to that person, to will that they be the way they are. When a person experiences that in someone's presence, then they can drop away those things that they've invented to present themselves with. Those faces, those armors, those forms of the self become unnecessary.[36]

The growing interest in Buddhism in the West, where new books on Buddhism and translations of traditional scriptures are rapidly appearing, is helping to revitalize Buddhism in Asia. As Asia entered the modern world, many of its peoples lost interest in their traditional religions, which became superficial re-enactments of ceremonial practices. But as Westerners themselves are taking strong interest in

Buddhism, those who have grown up as Buddhists are reassessing their religion and finding new depths in it.

Buddhist women from West and East have joined hands to hold international gatherings to enhance the role of women in Buddhism. The international Association of Buddhist Women, or "Daughters of the Buddha," established in Bodhgaya in 1987, continues to work to improve conditions for women's Buddhist practice and education, full ordination of women, and training of women as teachers of Buddhism.

Socially engaged Buddhism

An emerging focus in contemporary Buddhist practice is the relevance of Buddhism to social problems. Contrary to popular assumptions, the Buddha did not advise people to permanently leave society to seek their own enlightenment. Sri Lankan Buddhist monk Walpola Rahula explains:

> It may perhaps be useful in some cases for a person to live in retirement for a time in order to improve his or her mind and character, as preliminary moral, spiritual, and intellectual training, to be strong enough to come out later and help others. But if someone lives an entire life in solitude, thinking only of their own happiness and salvation, without caring for their fellow beings, this surely is not in keeping with the Buddha's teaching which is based on love, compassion, and service to others.[37]

The Buddha's teachings on retraining and purifying the mind are far better known than his social commentaries, but he did make many pronouncements about the ways in which social suffering is to be corrected. No holy wars have been conducted in his name, for he preached non-violence:

> Hatred is never appeased by hatred. It is appeased by love. This is an eternal law. Just as a mother would protect her only child, even at the risk of her own life, even so let one cultivate a boundless heart towards all beings. Let one's thoughts of boundless love pervade the whole world above, below, and across, without any obstruction, without any hatred, without any enmity. Whether one stands, walks, sits, or lies down, as long as one is awake, one should maintain this mindfulness.[38]

Buddhists have therefore often been non-violent social activists, protesting and trying to correct injustice, oppression, famine, cruelty to animals, nuclear testing, warfare, and environmental devastation. E. F. Schumacher preached what he called "Buddhist economics," to restore willingness to live simply, generously, and humanely with each other. During the Vietnam War, many Buddhist monks set themselves on fire to bring public attention to the need for an end to the suffering. In Sri Lanka, a Buddhist schoolteacher has started the Sarvodaya Shramadana Sangamaya movement which has now spread to five thousand villages. It engages people in working together to eliminate social decadence and poverty, through developing schools, nutrition programs, roads, and irrigation canals, and propagating the Four Noble Truths and the Eightfold Path.

Sulak Sivaraksa, Director of the International Network of Engaged Buddhists, explains that socially engaged Buddhism does not mean promoting Buddhism per se:

The presence of Buddhism in society does not mean having a lot of schools, hospitals, cultural institutions, or political parties run by Buddhists. It means that the schools, hospitals, cultural institutions, and political parties are permeated with and administered with humanism, love, tolerance, and enlightenment, characteristics which Buddhism attributes to an opening up, development, and formation of human nature. This is the true spirit of nonviolence.[39]

Not to respond to the suffering around us is a sign of an insane civilization, according to Vietnamese monk Thich Nhat Hanh:

While the rest of the human family suffers and starves, enjoying false security and wealth can only be seen as a sign of insanity.… We have built a system which we cannot control. This system imposes itself upon us, and we have become its slaves and victims. Most of us, in order to have a house to live in, a car to drive, a refrigerator, television, and so on, must pledge our time and our lives in exchange. We are constantly under the threatening pressure of time. In former times, we could afford three hours for one cup of tea, enjoying the company of our friends in a serene and spiritual atmosphere. We could organize a party to celebrate the blossoming of one orchid in our garden. But we can no longer afford to do these things. We say that time is money. We have created a society in which the rich become richer and the poor become poorer, and in which we are so caught up in our own immediate problems that we cannot afford to be aware of what is going on with the rest of the human family.[40]

Buddhism is thus as relevant today, and its insights as necessary, as in the sixth century, when Siddhartha Gautama renounced the life of a prince to save all sentient beings from suffering.

Suggested reading

Conze, Edward, Horner, I.B., Snellgrove, David, and Waley, Arthur, ed. and trans., *Buddhist Texts through the Ages*, Oxford, England: Oneworld Publications, 1995. A fine new collection of Buddhist scriptures translated from the Pali, Sanskrit, Chinese, Tibetan, and Japanese.

de Bary, William Theodore, ed., *The Buddhist Tradition in India, China, and Japan*, New York: Modern Library, 1969. An excellent survey with useful commentaries and selections from Buddhist scriptures.

Eppsteiner, Fred, ed., *The Path of Compassion: Writings on Socially Engaged Buddhism*, Berkeley, California: Parallax Press, 1988. A highly readable and relevant collection of essays by leading contemporary Buddhist teachers about the ways in which Buddhism can be applied to social problems.

Fernando, Antony, *Buddhism Made Plain*, Maryknoll, New York: Orbis Books, 1995. A very perceptive introduction to Buddhism for people of Western religions.

Fremantle, Francesca, and Trungpa, Chogyam, trans., *The Tibetan Book of the Dead*, Boston and London: Shambhala Publications, 1975. The classic Tibetan Buddhist scripture on the projections of the mind and the practices of deity yoga to attain enlightenment.

Friedman, Lenore, *Meetings with Remarkable Women: Buddhist Teachers in America*, Boston and London: Shambhala Publications, 1987. Wisdom from Buddhist traditions shared in very personal, perceptive interviews.

Kitagawa, Joseph M. and Cummings, Mark D., eds., *Buddhism and Asian History*, New York: Macmillan, 1989. A collection of articles drawn from the sixteen-volume Macmillan *Encyclopedia of Religion*, covering topics across the full range of Buddhism.

Lal, P., trans., *The Dhammapada*, New York: Farrar, Straus and Giroux, 1967. A basic book attributed to the Buddha that covers the essentials of the Dharma in memorable, pithy verses.

Levine, Stephen, *A Gradual Awakening*, Garden City, New York: Doubleday, 1979 and London: Rider and Company, 1980. Gentle, poetic presentation of vipassana techniques in their relevance to contemporary life.

Lopez, Donald S., Jr., ed., *Buddhism in Practice*, Princeton: Princeton University Press, 1995. Annotated translation of original sources dealing with Buddhist practice around the world, organized around the Triple Jewels of Buddha, Dharma, and Sangha.

Rahula, Walpola Sri, *What the Buddha Taught*, New York: Grove Press, 1974. The classic introduction to Buddhist teachings — an accurate and clear guide through the complexities of Buddhist thought and practice, with representative texts.

Suzuki, Shunryu, *Zen Mind, Beginner's Mind*, New York and Tokyo: Weatherhill, 1970. A beautiful book leading one gracefully and seemingly simply through the paradoxes of Zen.

CHAPTER 6

TAOISM AND CONFUCIANISM

The unity of opposites

While India was giving birth to Hinduism, Jainism, and Buddhism, three other major religions were developing in East Asia. Taoism and Confucianism grew largely in China, and later spread to Japan and Korea; Shinto was distinctively Japanese. These religions have remained associated primarily with their homelands. In this chapter we will explore the two that developed in China from similar roots but with different emphases: Taoism and Confucianism. Shinto will be the subject of Chapter 7. Buddhism also spread to East Asia and its practice has often been mixed with the native traditions.

In East Asia, religions that will be treated as separate entities in this chapter and the next are in fact more subtly blended and practiced. Taoism and Confucianism, though they may seem quite opposite to each other, co-exist as complementary value systems in East Asian societies, and a person's thought and actions may encompass both streams. Twentieth-century political shifts in China, however, have made it difficult to pin-point or predict the continued existence of religious ways there.

Ancient traditions

Indigenous spiritual ways permeate all later religious developments in China, Korea, and Japan. One major feature is the veneration of ancestors. The spirits of deceased ancestors remain very closely bonded to their living descendants for some time. Respect must be paid to them — especially the family's founding ancestor and those recently deceased — through funerals, mourning rites, and then continuing sacrifices. The sacred rituals are called *li* and are essential because the ancestors will help their descendants, if treated with proper respect, or cause trouble if ignored.

In addition to veneration of family ancestors, there are also shrines and temples to other deities, from nature spirits to charismatic humans who have died but are still available to help the people. For instance, coastal peoples in China honor "The Holy Mother in Heaven" as a guardian of the sea. She is said to have been born in the tenth century CE, and as a teenager apparently used her miraculous powers to save her father and brother from drowning when their boat sank.

From ancient times, there are references to a male deity called *Shang-ti*, the Lord-on-High, ruler of the universe, the supreme ancestor of the Chinese as deity of the ancient Shang Dynasty. Deities governing aspects of the cosmos and the local environment were subordinate to him. One can make offerings to these deities and seek their aid with personal problems. Sometimes their help can be sought through the mediumship of a man or woman who enters trance states in order to commune with the supernatural beings.

In addition to these personal entities, there has long existed in China a belief that the cosmos is a manifestation of a self-generating force called *ch'i*, rather than the work of a Creator. This force has two aspects whose interplay causes the ever-changing phenomena of the universe. **Yin** is the dark, receptive, "female" aspect; **yang** is the bright, assertive, "male" aspect. Wisdom lies in recognizing their ever-shifting, but regular and balanced, patterns and moving with them. This creative rhythm of the universe is called the **Tao**, or "way."

As traditionally diagrammed, yin and yang interpenetrate each other (represented by the small circles). As soon as one aspect reaches its fullest point, it begins to diminish, while its polar opposite increases.

To harmonize with the ancestors and gods, and yin and yang, the ancients devised many forms of divination. One system was eventually written down as the *I Ching*, or *Book of Changes*. It was highly elaborated with commentaries by scholars beginning in the Han Dynasty (202 BCE–220 CE). To use this subtle system, one respectfully purifies the divining objects — such as yarrow stalks or coins —, asks a question, casts the objects six times, and then consults the *I Ching* to find advice and guidance by interpreting its symbolic responses.

The pattern of throws is diagrammed in the *I Ching* as a hexagram, with yin represented as a broken line and yang by a straight line. Commentaries on the sixty-four possible hexagrams revolve around personal attributes, natural phenomena, and family relationships. For example, hexagram number 46, called "Pushing Upward," has been likened by some commentators to a tree emerging from the earth, growing slowly and invisibly:

> *Thus the superior person of devoted character*
> *Heaps up small things*
> *In order to achieve something high and great.*[1]

Another set of commentaries is based on the two trigrams within the hexagram: the upper pattern of three yin lines can be interpreted as devotion and yielding, and the lower pattern of two yang lines atop one yin line suggests gentleness. According to the commentaries, these non-aggressive qualities will ultimately lead to supreme success.

By studying and systematizing the ways of humans and of nature, the ancient Chinese tried to order their actions so that they might steer a coherent course within the changing cosmos. They recognized that any extreme action will produce its opposite as a balancing reaction and thus they strived for a middle way of subtle discretion and moderation.

Taoism — The Way of Nature and Immortality

Taoism is as full of paradoxes as the Buddhist tradition it influenced: Ch'an or Zen Buddhism. It has been adored by Westerners who seek a carefree, natural way of life as an escape from the industrial rat race. Yet beneath its words of the simple

The hexagram Sheng is a visual symbol of the various meanings attached to "pushing upward."

life in harmony with nature is a tradition of great mental and physical discipline. Taoism includes both efforts to align oneself with the unnamable original force, and ceremonial worship of deities from the Jade Emperor to the Kitchen god. Some Taoist scriptures counsel indifference about birth and death; others teach ways of attaining physical immortality. These variations developed within an ancient tradition that had no name until it had to distinguish itself from Confucianism. "Taoism" is actually a label invented by scholars and awkwardly stretched to cover both a philosophical tradition and an assortment of religious sects whose relationship to the former is complex, but which probably developed at least in part from the early philosophical texts and practices.

Teachings of Taoist sages

Aside from its general basis in ancient indigenous ways, the specific origin of Taoist philosophy and practices is unclear. In China, tradition attributes the publicizing of these ways to the Yellow Emperor, who supposedly ruled from 2697 to 2597 BCE. He was said to have studied with an ancient sage and to have developed meditation, health, and military practices based on what he learned. After ruling for a hundred years, he ascended to heaven on a dragon's back and became one of the immortals.

The philosophical basis of Taoism is expounded in the famous scripture, the **Tao-te Ching** ("The Classic of the Way and the Power"). It is second only to the Bible in number of translations, for its ideas are not only fascinating but also elusive for

Lao-tzu, one of the major conveyers of the Taoist tradition, is often depicted as a humorous old man riding off into the mountains after reportedly drawing the five thousand characters of the Tao-te Ching.

translators working from the terse ancient Chinese characters. One recent translation, by Stephen Mitchell, alternately refers to sages as "she" and "he," for there are no gender distinctions in the Chinese. Another problem is that extant Chinese copies of the book vary in places.

Even the supposed author of the *Tao-te Ching* is obscure. According to tradition, the book was dictated by Lao-tzu (or Lao-tse), a curator of the royal library of the Chou dynasty, to a border guard as he left society for the mountains at the reported age of 160. The guard recognized Lao-tzu as a sage and begged him to leave behind a record of his wisdom. Lao-tzu reportedly complied by inscribing the five thousand characters now known as the *Tao-te Ching*. This is traditionally said to have happened during the sixth century BCE, with Lao-tzu purportedly fifty-three years older than Confucius. But some historians date the *Tao-te Ching* at c. 300 BCE and claim it was a reaction to Confucianism. Some think the *Tao-te Ching* was an oral tradition derived from the teachings of several sages and question whether Lao-tzu ever existed. Others maintain that the author was one Lao T'an, who may or may not have been the same person as Lao-Tzu.

The book's central philosophy, which shines through widely varying translations, is that one can best harmonize with the natural flow of life by being receptive and quiet.

These teachings were elaborated more emphatically and humorously by a sage named Chuang-tzu. He, too, was a minor government official for a while but left political involvement for a hermit's life of freedom and solitude. Unlike Lao-tzu, whose philosophy was addressed to those in leadership positions, Chuang-tzu asserted that the best way to live in a chaotic, absurd civilization is to become detached from it.

FLOWING WITH TAO At the heart of Taoist teachings is *Tao*, the "unnamable," the "eternally real."[2] Contemporary Master Da Liu asserts that Tao is so ingrained in Chinese understanding that it is a basic concept that cannot be defined, like "goodness." Moreover, Tao is a mystical reality that cannot be grasped by the mind. The *Tao-te Ching* says:

> *The Tao that can be told of*
> *   Is not the Absolute Tao,*
> *The Names that can be given*
> *   Are not Absolute Names.*
> *The Nameless is the origin of Heaven and Earth;*
> *The Named is the Mother of All Things ...*
> *These two (the Secret and its manifestations)*
> *   Are (in their nature) the same; ...*
> *They may both be called the Cosmic Mystery:*
> *Reaching from the Mystery into the Deeper Mystery*
> *Is the Gate to the Secret of All Life.*[3]

Chapter 25 of the *Tao-te Ching* is more explicit about the mysterious Unnamable:

> *There is a thing confusedly formed,*
> *Born before heaven and earth.*
> *Silent and void*
> *It stands alone and does not change,*

Goes round and does not weary.
It is capable of being the mother of the world.
I know not its name
So I style it "the way."
I give it the makeshift name of "the great."[4]

Although we cannot describe the Tao, we can live in harmony with it. Ideally, says Lao-tzu:

Humans model themselves on earth,
Earth on heaven,
Heaven on the way,
And the way on that which is naturally so.[5]

There are several basic principles for the life in harmony with Tao. One is to experience the transcendent unity of all things, rather than separation. Professor Chang Chung-yuan observes that "the value of Tao lies in its power to reconcile opposites on a higher level of consciousness."[6] This higher level can only be attained when one ceases to feel any personal preferences. Everything has its own nature and function, says Chuang-tzu. But disfigured or beautiful, small or large, they are all one in Tao. Taoism is concerned with direct experience of the universe, accepting and cooperating with things as they are, not with setting standards of morality, not with labeling things as "good" or "bad."

Chuang-tzu asserts that herein lies true spirituality:

Such a man can ride the clouds and mist, mount the sun and moon, and wander beyond the four seas. Life and death do not affect him. How much less will he be concerned with good and evil![7]

TEACHING STORY

Three in the Morning

Whether you point to a little stalk or a great pillar, a leper or the beautiful Hsi-shih, things ribald and shady or things grotesque and strange, the Way makes them all into one.... Only the man of far-reaching vision knows how to make them into one. So he has no use [for categories], but relegates all to the constant. The constant is the useful; the useful is the passable; the passable is the successful; and with success, all is accomplished. He relies upon this alone, relies upon it and does not know he is doing so. This is called the Way.

But to wear out your brain trying to make things into one without realizing that they are all the same — this is called "three in the morning." What do I mean by "three in the morning"? When the monkey trainer was handing out acorns, he said, "You get three in the morning and four at night." This made all the monkeys furious. "Well, then," he said, "you get four in the morning and three at night." The monkeys were all delighted. There was no change in the reality behind the words, yet the monkeys responded with joy and anger. Let them, if they want to. So the sage harmonizes with both right and wrong and rests in Heaven the Equalizer.

Chuang-tzu[8]

Sites for Taoist and Buddhist temples in China were traditionally chosen according to the ancient art of feng-shui, or geomancy, the awareness of the presence and movement of natural energies. The energies of waterfalls and mountains were considered conducive to spiritual practices. (Buddhist Temple Amid Clearing Mountain Peaks, *Northern Sung, c. 940–967* CE.)

In addition to experiencing oneness, the Taoist sage takes a low profile in the world. He or she is like a valley, allowing everything needed to flow into his or her life, or like a stream. Flowing water is a Taoist model for being. It bypasses and gently wears away obstacles rather than fruitlessly attacking them, effortlessly nourishes the "ten thousand things" of material life, works without struggling, leaves all accomplishments behind without possessing them. Lao-tzu observes:

Water is the softest thing on earth,
Yet its silken gentleness
Will easily wear away the hardest stone.

Everyone knows this;
Few use it in their daily lives.
Those of Tao yield and overcome.[9]

This is the uniquely Taoist paradox of **wu wei** — "doing nothing," or taking no action contrary to nature. Chuang-tzu uses the analogy of a butcher whose knife always stays sharp because he lets his hand be guided by the natural makeup of the carcass, finding the spaces between the bones where a slight movement of the blade will glide through without resistance. Even when difficulties arise, the sage does not panic and take unnecessary action.

> *Do you have the patience to wait*
> *till your mud settles and the water is clear?*
> *Can you remain unmoving*
> *till the right action arises by itself?*
>
> *Lao-tzu*[10]

The result of wu-wei is non-interference. Much of Lao-tzu's teaching is directed at rulers, that they might guide society without interfering with its natural course. Nothing is evil, but things may be out of balance. The world is naturally in harmony; Tao is our original nature. But according to tradition, the Golden Age of Tao declined as humans departed from the Way. "Civilization," with its intellectual attempts to improve on things and its rigid views of morality, actually leads to world chaos, the Taoists warn.

How much better, Lao-tzu advises, to accept not-knowing, moving freely in the moment with the changing universe rather than trying to control it. In describing this state, Lao-tzu paradoxically suggests the hidden power of wu wei:

My mind is that of a fool — how blank!
Vulgar people are clear.
I alone am drowsy.
Vulgar people are alert.
I alone am muddled.
Calm like the sea;
Like a high wind that never ceases.
The multitude all have a purpose.
I alone am foolish and uncouth.
I alone am different from others
And value being fed by the mother.[11]

Thirdly, Taoism places great value on withdrawal from the madding crowd to a contemplative life in nature. Whether in a peaceful or chaotic environment, the Taoist seeks to find the still center, save energy for those times when action is needed, and take a humble, quiet approach to life. Things of importance to the worldly are seen as having little value. Chuang-tzu even goes to some lengths to point out that it is the useless who survive; the tree which is good for nothing does not get chopped down.

> *Sweet music and highly seasoned food*
> *Entertain for a while,*
> *But the clear, tasteless water from the well*
> *Gives life and energy without exhaustion.*
>
> *Lao-tzu[12]*

SPIRITUAL ALCHEMY Flowing with Tao is easy and natural. But paradoxically, it is based on masterful spiritual discipline. Lao-tzu describes the appearance of mastery:

> *The ancient Masters were profound and subtle.*
> *Their wisdom was unfathomable....*
> *They were careful*
> *as someone crossing an iced-over stream.*
> *Alert as a warrior in enemy territory.*
> *Courteous as a guest.*
> *Fluid as melting ice.*
> *Shapable as a block of wood.*
> *Receptive as a valley.*
> *Clear as a glass of water.[13]*

One of the goals of esoteric Taoist practice is to separate the spirit from the body so that the former can operate independently, both before and after death.

The mastery to which Taoist writers refer may be the result of powerful unknown ascetic practices traditionally passed down secretly from teacher to pupil. These teachers lived in the mountains; Taoist teachers are said to be still hidden in the remote mountains of China and Korea.

The aim of the ascetic practices is to use the energy available to the body in order to intuitively perceive the order of the universe. Within our body is the spiritual microuniverse of the "three treasures": generative force *(ching)*, vitality *(ch'i)*, and spirit *(shen)*. Using breath and the subtle energy channels in the body, the practitioner builds a reservoir of *ching* energy in the "cauldron" several inches below the navel, whence it rises up the spine as a vapor, transmuted into *ch'i* energy. *Ch'i* is in turn transmuted into *shen* in an upper cauldron in the head (an area similar to the Third Eye of Indian yogic practice), drops down to illuminate the heart center, and then descends to an inner area of the lower cauldron. There it forms what is called the Immortal Fetus, which adepts can reportedly raise through the Heavenly Gate at the top of the head and thus leave their physical body for various purposes, including preparation for life after death. In addition, the adept learns to draw the *ch'i* of the macrouniverse of heaven and earth into the microuniverse of the body, unifying and harmonizing inner and outer, heaven and earth. This process, called **ch'i-kung**, takes many years to complete.

> *The secret of the magic of life consists in using action in order to attain non-action.*
> *The Secret of the Golden Flower[14]*

THE LURE OF IMMORTALITY It is unclear whether Taoist texts are to be taken allegorically or literally. Literal readings have long lured those desiring physical longevity or spiritual immortality to discover Taoist secrets. Chuang-tzu had counseled indifference to birth and death: "The Master came because it was time. He left because he followed the natural flow. Be content with the moment, and be willing to follow the flow."[15] Lao-tzu referred enigmatically to immortality or long life realized through spiritual death of the individual self, the body and mind transmuted into selfless vehicles for the eternal. However, as Professor Huai-Chin Han puts it, people who are interested in Taoist practices:

> *usually forget the highest principles, or the basis of philosophical theory behind the cultivation of Tao and the opening of the* ch'i *routes for longevity.... Longevity consists of maintaining one's health, slowing down the ageing process, living without illness and pain, and dying peacefully without bothering other people. Immortality does not mean indefinite physical longevity; it indicates the eternal spiritual life.*[16]

A quiet contemplative life in natural surroundings, with sexual abstinence, peaceful mind, health-maintaining herbs, practices to strengthen the inner organs and open the meridians (subtle energy pathways known to Chinese doctors), and ch'i-kung breath practices to transmute vital energy into spiritual energy, does seem to bring a marked tendency to longevity. Chinese literature and folk knowledge contain many references to venerable sages thought to be centuries old. They live hidden in the mountains, away from society, and are said to be somewhat translucent. Their age is difficult to verify. The Chinese sage Li Ch'ing Yuen claimed that he was two hundred and fifty years old, shortly before he died early in the twentieth century, apparently from the effects of being exposed to "civilization." The most famous of the legendary long-lived are the Eight Immortals, humans who were said to have gained immortality, each with his or her own special magical power.

Another way of flowing with Tao, and thereby living long and effectively, is the body-centered practice of **T'ai-chi chuan**. Of unknown origin, it appeared in China

Al Huang embodies the fluidity of T'ai-chi chuan, practiced both for physical health and for teaching the mind to flow with change so that action is effortless.

by the tenth century as a martial art and is still practiced daily by many Chinese at dawn and dusk for their health. It looks like slow swimming in the air, with continual circular movement through a series of dance-like postures. They are ideally manifestations of the unobstructed flow of ch'i through the body. According to the *T'ai-chi Ch'uan Classics*, "In any action the entire body should be light and agile and all of its parts connected like pearls on a thread."[17] Ch'i is cultivated internally but not expressed externally as power. In combat, the practitioner of T'ai-chi is advised to "yield at your opponent's slightest pressure and adhere to him at his slightest retreat,"[18] using mental alertness to subtle changes rather than muscular strength in order to gain the advantage.

T'ai-chi is also a physical way of becoming one with the eternal interlocking of yin and yang, and of movement and stillness. T'ai-chi master Al Chung-liang Huang says:

> Think of the contrasting energies moving together and in union, in harmony, interlocking, like a white fish and a black fish mating. If you identify with only one side of the duality, then you become unbalanced.... Movement and stillness become one. One is not a static point. One is a moving one, one is a changing one, one is everything. One is also that stillness suspended, flowing, settling, in motion.[19]

Despite the development of these techniques for body-mind harmony with Tao, the desire for shortcuts to longevity has persisted from ancient times to the present. From aristocrats to peasants, the Chinese people sought to prolong life through the advice and potions of Taoist alchemists. Some of them have been frauds; others have taken the allegorical references to spiritual alchemy literally, trying to compound actual chemical formulas to make the body immortal. These efforts persist. In 1988 "Laoshan Taoist Beverage" went into mass production. The secret brew's lifespan-lengthening formula is said to have been guarded by the chief priest of Mount Laoshan for a thousand years.

Immortals Taoism

Under the umbrella of what scholars call "Taoism" lies not only philosophical Taoism but also religious sects sometimes known collectively as Hsien ("Immortals") Taoism. They are characterized by belief in numerous gods and ancestral spirits, magic-making, ritual, and the aid of priests.

Practices such as alchemy, faith-healing, sorcery, and the use of power objects seem to have existed from ancient times in China, but their conversion into institutionalized and distinctive social movements with detailed rituals, clergy, and revealed texts dates from the second century CE. At that time, the Han Dynasty was declining amidst famine and war. An array of revelations and prophecies predicted the end of the age and finally led to the rise of religious/political organizations. For example, Yu Chi received a visionary revelation that yin and yang were no longer in balance in heaven or on earth, for the rulers had forgotten to follow the ways of nature, and that in 184 CE the blue heaven of the Han would be replaced by the yellow heaven. In that year, hundreds of thousands of followers of a leader who was known as a faith healer and advocate of egalitarian ideals rebelled in eight of China's twelve provinces; their rebellion took ten months to suppress.

In ancient Chinese tradition, the universe arises from the interplay of yin and yang. They are modes of energy commonly represented as interlocking shapes, with dominance continually shifting between the dark, receptive yin mode and the bright, assertive yang mode.

Simultaneously, in western China, Chang Tao Ling had a vision of Lao-tzu as the heavenly Lord Lao. He advocated similar practices of healing by faith and developed a quasi-military organization of religious officials. After thirty years of dominance in their region, they abandoned political goals to focus on spiritual practices. Once Chang Tao Ling ascended to the heavens, they referred to him as the first Celestial Master. The older Han religion had involved demons and exorcism, belief in an afterlife, and a God of Destinies who granted fortune or misfortune based on heavenly records of good and bad deeds. These roles were now ascribed to a pantheon of celestial deities, who in turn were controlled by the new Celestial Master priesthood led by Chang's family. This hereditary clergy performed imperial investitures as well as village festivals, with both men and women serving as libationers in local dioceses.

After the sack of the northern capitals early in the fourth century, the Celestial Masters and other aristocrats fled south and established themselves on Dragon-Tiger Mountain in southeast China. Today the 64th patriarch in the lineage lives in Taiwan, although practices are being revived on Dragon-Tiger Mountain in mainland China.

Approximately 365 CE another aristocratic family in exile in southern China began receiving revelations from a deceased member, Lady Wei. These revelations of the names and powers of newly discovered deities, meditation methods, alchemy, and rituals, were recorded in exquisite calligraphy and transmitted to only a few advanced disciples. This elite group of celibates residing on Mount Mao called their practices "*Highest Purity Taoism.*" They looked down on the Celestial Master tradition and its sexual rituals as crude, and they avoided village rituals and commoners. Instead, they focused on personal immortality through meditations for purifying the body with divine energies so as "to rise up to heaven in broad daylight." Although the Highest Purity Taoism did not reach the mass of the people, its texts and influence continue to be revered today as the elite tradition of Taoism.

The assimilation of Buddhism into Chinese culture added a great medley of new meditation practices, divine beings, rituals, scriptures, heavens and hells to Chinese cosmology. Various Taoist movements freely borrowed from these resources. During the last eight hundred years, the most successful tradition has been *Complete Perfection Taoism*. It unites Taoist inner alchemy with Ch'an Buddhist meditation and Confucian social morality, harmonizing the three religions. Actively monastic, it focuses on meditation and non-attachment to the world. Today its major center is the White Cloud monastery in Beijing, the headquarters of the government-approved Chinese Taoism Association. It is also the foundation for most Hong Kong Taoist temples and martial arts groups.

The many revealed scriptures of Taoist movements were occasionally compiled and canonized by the court. The present Taoist canon was compiled in 1445 CE. Containing over one thousand sophisticated scriptures, it has only recently begun to be studied by non-Taoist scholars.

Popular Taoism Today

In addition to Taoist ways traced to Lord Lao and the supreme Tao, popular Taoist-related rituals and beliefs are in current practice both within communist mainland China and in Chinese communities elsewhere such as Taiwan, Hong Kong, and

Southeast Asia. Since approximately 1000 CE, the Chinese peoples have practiced rituals associated with a period of testing and purification of the soul after death. Either Taoist or Buddhist priests may be hired by private families to perform rituals to help the deceased appear before the Ten Hell Judges, as well as to join in communal rituals of grave-cleaning in April and of universal liberation and feeding of hungry ghosts in August. Every temple has a side shrine to T'u-ti Kung, Lord of the Earth, who can transport offerings to deceased loved ones at any time. Written prayers and paper money are burned to send them to the other world.

New revelations and scriptures continue to be produced today in new temples in Taiwan. They are identified as "precious scrolls" emanating from deities such as the Golden Mother of the Celestial Pool. It is believed that in the past the Divine Mother sent Buddha and Lao-tzu as Her messengers, but that now the crisis of the present world requires Her direct intervention.

Popular religion also follows the ancient practice of worshipping certain people as divine, appointed to heavenly office after they died. There are many examples, such as the valiant and loyal late Han Dynasty general Kuan-kung, who is honored everywhere in China as the righter of wrongs and supporter of justice. As indicated earlier, a virtuous daughter of the Lin family saved members of her own family and others in distress during the Sung Dynasty, and now she is worshipped as Tien-hou, the Holy Mother in Heaven, especially in coastal regions. Recently in mainland

Left *Taoist priest.*
Right *Taoist religion is still practiced in non-communist Chinese areas. At the Matsu Yen Tao Temple in Anping, Taiwan, Taoist elements are incorporated into worship of the goddess Matsu.*

China, worship has revived for the Great Emperor Who Protects Life, who is traced back to an inspired eleventh-century doctor. The reverence that is still shown to the twentieth-century liberator of China, Mao tse-Tung, who died in 1976, likewise reflects the Chinese pattern of recognizing certain humans as possessing divine power to help and save the people.

Historically, whenever the central Chinese government has been strong, it has tended to demand total allegiance to itself as a divine authority and to challenge or suppress competing religious groups. The Emperors of ancient China either claimed divine origin or referred to themselves as the Sons of Heaven appointed from on high. Confucian scholars were suppressed and their books were burned by the Ch'in Dynasty (221–206 BCE), shamans were forbidden during the Han Dynasty, Buddhists were persecuted during the T'ang Dynasty, the T'ai-p'ing rebellion of the nineteenth century attempted to purge China of Taoism and Buddhism, and during the Cultural Revolution of 1966 to 1976, zealous young Red Guards destroyed Taoist, Buddhist, and Confucian temples and books. However, during the economic liberalization of the late twentieth century in mainland China, in spite of an atheistic communist ideology, temples have been maintained as historic sites, pilgrimages to temples in natural sites and religious tourism from abroad have been encouraged, and in some areas remote from the capital an explosion of temple building has occurred.

Domestic rituals continue in every home, such as the farewell party to the god of the kitchen at the end of the lunar year (often in late January). In hopes that the god of the kitchen, who sits in the corner watching what the family does, will speak well of them in his annual report to the Jade Emperor, god of the present, families offer sweets, incense, and paper horses, with the prayer, "When you go to heaven you should report only good things, and when you come down from heaven you should protect us and bring peace and safety to us."[20]

Confucianism — the practice of virtue

The sixth century BCE was a period of great spiritual and intellectual flourishing in many cultures. It roughly coincided with the life of the Buddha and perhaps of Lao-tzu, the Persian empire, the Golden Age of Athens, the great Hebrew prophets, and in China, with the life of another outstanding figure. Westerners call him Confucius and his teaching Confucianism. His family name was Kung; the Chinese honored him as Kung Fu-tzu ("Master K'ung") and called his teaching *Juchiao* ("the teaching of the scholars"). This philosophy became highly influential in China and still permeates the society despite great political changes. For two thousand years Taoism, Buddhism, and Confucianism co-existed in China, contributing mutually to the culture. Both Taoism and Buddhism emphasize the ever-changing nature of things in the cosmos, whereas Confucianism focuses on ways in which people can live together harmoniously and develop a just and orderly society.

Individuals often harmonize the apparently opposite characteristics of Taoism and Confucianism in their own lives. For example, elderly Taoist Master An speaks on one hand of the fact that he and his fellows sweep the temple when they feel like it — "We're not caught up in routines" — and on the other of the ways that his father's teaching of Confucian maxims shaped his life:

My father was very cultured and adamant about teaching us the true Tao. He mastered the classics, and would write out quotations all the time. Over on the wall there is a quotation by Confucius he wrote:

If I'm not generous with those below me,
If I'm disrespectful toward the proprieties,
Or if I do not properly mourn at a funeral,
How can I have self-esteem?

He'd paste these quotations on our wall above the bed. I'd turn my head and there it was, sinking in my brain.... Confucius also said, "One who seeks the Tao cannot be deficient in manners."[21]

Professor Yu Yingshi explains that Taoism and Confucianism can coexist because in Chinese tradition there are no major divisions between mind and matter, utopian ideals and everyday life:

For Chinese, the transcendental world, the world of the spirit, interpenetrates with the everyday world though it is not considered identical to it. If we use the tao to represent the transcendental world and the Confucian ideal of human relationships to represent the human world, we can see how they interface. The tao creates the character of these human relations. For these relations to exist as such, they must follow the tao, they cannot depart from the tao for a moment. These two worlds operate on the cusp of interpenetration, neither dependent on or independent of the other. So mundane human relationships are, from the very beginning, endowed with a transcendental character.[22]

Master K'ung's life

Young K'ung Ch'iu was born in approximately 551 BCE, during the Chou dynasty, into a family whose ancestors had been prominent in the previous dynasty. They had lost their position through political struggles, and Ch'iu's father, a soldier, died when the boy was only three years old. Although young Ch'iu was determined to be a scholar, the family's financial straits necessitated his taking public service jobs to earn a living. His responsibilities included such humble work as overseeing granaries and livestock. He married at the age of nineteen and had at least two children.

Ch'iu's mother died when he was twenty-three, sending him into three years of mourning. During this period he lived ascetically and studied ancient ceremonial rites (**li**) and imperial institutions. When he returned to social interaction, he gained some renown as a teacher of *li* and of the arts of governing.

It was a period of political chaos, with the stability of the early Chou dynasty having given way to disorder. Feudal lords held more power than kings of the central court, ministers assassinated their rulers, and sons killed their fathers. Confucius felt that a return to classical standards of virtue was the only way out of the chaos, and he earnestly but unsuccessfully sought rulers who would adopt his ideas.

Confucius turned to a different approach: training young men to be wise and altruistic public servants. He instructed them in the "Six Classics" of China's cultural heritage: the I Ching, poetry, history, rituals, music and dance, and the Spring and

Confucianism idealized gentlemen-scholars, who became the highest class in China until the 20th-century revolution.

Autumn Annals of events in his state, Lu. According to tradition, it was Confucius who edited older documents pertaining to these six areas and who put them into the form now known as the *Confucian Classics*. There are now only five; the treatises on music were either destroyed or never existed. Of his role, Confucius claimed only:

> *I am a transmitter and not a creator. I believe in and have a passion for the ancients.*[23]

Although great value was later placed on study of the Confucian Classics in China, Confucius's work and teachings were considered relatively insignificant during his lifetime. After his death in 479 BCE, interstate warfare increased to the point that ancient family loyalties were replaced by increasingly large and impersonal armies, and personal virtues were replaced by laws and state control. After the brutal reunification of China by the Ch'in and Han dynasties, however, rulership required a more cultured class of bureaucrats who could embody the virtues advocated by Confucius. In the second century BCE the Confucian Classics thus became the basis of the civil service examinations for the scholar–officials who were to serve in the government. The life of the gentleman-scholar devoted to proper government became the highest professed ideal. Eventually temples were devoted to the worship of Confucius himself as the model for unselfish public service, human kindness, and scholarship. From a skeptical point of view, however, the official state use of the Confucian Classics can be seen as a political device to give the government a veneer of civility and the appearance of relief from brutality.

The Confucian virtues

Foremost among the virtues that Confucius felt could save society was **jen**. Translations of this central term include innate goodness, love, benevolence, perfect virtue, humaneness, and human-heartedness.

In Chapter IV of the *Analects*, Confucius describes the rare person who is utterly devoted to *jen* as one who is not motivated by personal profit but by what is moral, is concerned with self-improvement rather than public recognition, is ever mindful of parents, speaks cautiously but acts quickly, and regards human nature as basically good.

The prime example of jen should be the ruler. Rulers were enjoined to rule not by physical force but by the example of personal virtue:

> *Confucius said: If a ruler himself is upright, all will go well without orders. But if he himself is not upright, even though he gives orders they will not be obeyed.... One who governs by virtue is comparable to the polar star, which remains in its place while all the stars turn towards it."*[24]

Asked to define the essentials of strong government, Confucius listed adequate troops, adequate food, and the people's confidence. But of these, troops are least important, he said, followed by food. The only true necessity is that the people have faith in their rulers. To earn this faith, the ruling class should "cultivate themselves," leading lives of virtue and decorum. They should continually adhere to jen, always reaching upward, cherishing what is right, rather than reaching downward for material gain.

The Chinese character for jen is a combination of "two" and "person," conveying the idea of relationship. Those relationships emphasized by Confucius are the interactions between father and son, older and younger siblings, husband and wife, older and younger friend, ruler and subject. In these relationships, the first is considered superior to the second. Each relationship is nonetheless based on distinct but mutual obligations and responsibilities. Reciprocity is the key to this web of human relationships, which supports the individual like a series of concentric circles.

At the top, the ruler models himself on Heaven, serving as a parent to the people and linking them to the larger cosmic order through ritual ceremonies. Confucius says that this was the source of the greatness of Yao — a sage king of c. 2357 BCE: "It is Heaven that is great and Yao who modelled himself upon it."[25]

In Confucius's ideal world, there is a reciprocal hierarchy in which each knows his place and respects those above him. Social order is based on this system of appropriate conduct according to status. As the *Great Learning* states it, peace begins with the moral cultivation of the individual and order in the family. This extends outward to society, government, and the universe itself like circular ripples in a pond:

> *The ancients who wished clearly to exemplify illustrious virtue throughout the world would first set up good government in their states. Wishing to govern well their states, they would first regulate their families. Wishing to regulate their families, they would first cultivate their persons. Wishing to cultivate their persons, they would first rectify their minds. Wishing to rectify their minds, they would first seek sincerity in their thoughts. Wishing for sincerity in their thoughts, they would first extend their knowledge. The extension of knowledge lay in the investigation of things.*[26]

The heart of moral rectification is the practice of filial piety to one's parents. Confucius also supports the ancient Chinese custom of ancestor veneration, as an extension of filial piety:

> *Filial piety is the force that continues the purposes and completes the affairs of our forefathers.... To gather in the same place where they earlier have gathered; to perform the same ceremonies which they earlier performed; to play the same music which they earlier have played; to pay respect to those whom they honored; to love those who were dear to them; in fact, to serve those now dead as if they were living, and those now departed as if they were with us still. This is the highest achievement of filial piety.*[27]

Confucius said relatively little about the supernatural, preferring to focus on the here-and-now: "While you are not able to serve men, how can you serve the ghosts and spirits?"[28] He made a virtue of *li* (the rites honoring ancestors and deities), but with the cryptic suggestion that one make the sacrifices "as if" the spirits were present. According to some interpreters, he encouraged the rites as a way of establishing earthly harmony through reverent, ethical behavior. The rites should not be empty gestures; he recommended that they be outwardly simple and inwardly grounded in jen.

Although Confucius did not speak much about an unseen Reality, he asserted that *li* are the earthly expressions of the natural cosmic order. Not only formal rituals but also everyday actions become *li* if they spring from *jen*. Everything should be done with a subtle sense of propriety. Continually eulogizing the paradigmatic gentleman of China's ancient high civilization as the model for proper conduct, Confucius used examples such as the way of passing someone in mourning. Even if the mourner were a close friend, the gentleman would assume a solemn expression and "lean forward with his hands on the crossbar of his carriage to show respect; he would act in a similar manner towards a person carrying official documents."[29] Even in humble surroundings, the proprieties should be observed:

> *Even when a meal consisted only of coarse rice and vegetable broth, [the gentleman] invariably made an offering from them and invariably did so solemnly.*[30]

Divergent followers of Confucius

The Confucian tradition has been added to by many later commentators. Two of the most significant were Mencius and Hsun Tzu, who differed in their approach.

A little over a hundred years after Confucius died, the "Second Sage" Meng Tzu (commonly latinized as Mencius) was born. During his lifetime Chinese society became even more chaotic. Like his predecessor, the Second Sage tried to share his wisdom with embattled rulers, but to no avail. He, too, took up teaching, based on his studies of stabilizing aspects of the earlier feudal system.

Mencius's major additions to the Confucian tradition were his belief in the goodness of human nature and his focus on the virtue of *yi*, or righteous conduct. Mencius emphasized the moral duty of rulers to govern by the principle of humanity and the good of the people. If rulers are guided by profit motives, this self-centered motivation will be reflected in all subordinates and social chaos will ensue. On the other hand, "When a commiserating government is conducted from a commiserating heart, one can rule the whole empire as if one were turning it in one's palm."[31] This is a natural way, says Mencius, for people are naturally good: "The tendency of human nature to do good is like that of water to flow downward."[32] Heaven could be counted on to side with the righteous, empowering their good cause.

Another follower quite disagreed with this assessment. This was Hsun Tzu, who seemingly was born when Mencius was an old man, and whose life as a would-be reformer resembled that of his predecessors. He argued that human nature is naturally evil and that heaven is impersonal, operating according to natural laws rather than intervening on the side of good government or responding to human wishes ("Heaven does not suspend the winter because men dislike cold....."[33]) Humans must hold up their own end. Their natural tendency, however, is to envy, to hate, and to desire personal gain and sensual pleasure. The only way to constrain these tendencies is to teach and legally enforce the rules of *li* (rites and rules of decorum) and *yi* (guides to righteous conduct). Though naturally flawed, humans can gradually attain sagehood by persistent study, patience, and good works and thereby form a cooperative triad with heaven and earth.

Hsun Tzu's careful reasoning provided a basis for the new legalistic structure of Chinese government. The idealism of Mencius was revived much later as a Chinese response to Buddhism and became required for the civil service examinations from the thirteenth to the twentieth centuries. However, their points of agreement are basic to Confucianism: the appropriate practice of virtue is of great value; humans can attain this through self-cultivation; and study and emulation of the ancient sages are the path to harmony in the individual, family, state, and world.

Confucianism as a state cult

During the Han dynasty (202 BCE to 220 CE) Confucius's teachings were at last honored by the state. The Han scholar Tung Chung-shu set up the educational system based on the Confucian Classics that lasted until the twentieth century. He used Confucian ideals to unite the people behind the ruler, also noting that the ruler himself should be subject to Heaven.

It was during this period that civil service examinations were first established as a means of attaining government positions. These examinations were based on the Confucian Classics, which were later systematized into the Four Books by the Sung

Neo-Confucian scholar, Chu Hsi (1130–1200 CE). His *Reflections on Things at Hand* gave a metaphysical basis for Confucianism: The individual is intimately linked with all of the cosmos, "forming one body with all things." According to Chang Tsai's *Western Inscription*:

> *Heaven is my father and earth is my mother and even such a small creature as I finds an intimate place in their midst. Therefore, that which extends throughout the universe I regard as my body and that which directs the universe I regard as my nature. All people are my brothers and sisters and all things are my companions.*[34]

By becoming more humane one can help to transform not only oneself but also society and even the cosmos. The Neo-Confucianists thus stressed the importance of spiritual practice — meditation and dedication to becoming a "noble person."

Women were encouraged to offer themselves in total sacrifice to others. Confucian women had previously been expected to take a subordinate role in the family and in society, but at the same time to be strong, disciplined, wise, and capable in their relationships with their husbands and sons. In Neo-Confucianism, such virtues were subsumed under an extreme ideal of self-sacrifice, especially for widows.

Although Confucius had counseled restrained use of *li*, Neo-Confucianism also included an increased emphasis on sacrifice, as practiced since ancient times and set forth in the traditional *Book of Rites* and *Etiquette and Ritual*, which had been reconstructed during the Han Dynasty. These rites were thought to preserve harmony between humans, heaven, and earth. At the family level, offerings were made to propitiate the family ancestors. Government officials were responsible for ritual sacrifices to beings such as the gods of fire, literature, cities, mountains, waters, the polar star, sun, moon, and former rulers, as well as spirits of the earth and sky.

The most important ceremonies were performed by the emperor, to give thanks and ask blessings from heaven, earth, gods of the land and agriculture, and the dynastic ancestors. Of these, the highest ritual was the elaborate annual sacrifice to Shang Ti at the white marble Altar of Heaven by the emperor. He was considered Son of Heaven, the "high priest of the world." Both he and his retinue prepared themselves by three days of fasting and keeping vigil. In a highly reverent atmosphere, he then sacrificed a bull, offered precious jade, and sang prayers of gratitude to the Supreme, such as this one:

> *With reverence we spread out these precious stones and silk, and, as swallows rejoicing in the spring, praise Thy abundant love.... Men and creatures are emparadised, O Ti, in Thy love. All living things are indebted to Thy goodness, but who knows whence his blessings come to him? It is Thou alone, O Lord, who art the true parent of all things.*[35]

The performance of rituals was a time-consuming major part of government jobs, carried out on behalf of the people. But as China gradually opened to the West in recent centuries, a reaction set in against these older ways. The last of the imperial dynasties was overthrown in 1911, and the New Culture movement of the 1920s Republic glorified science and social progress. Under the Communist regime established in 1949, Communism took the place of religion, attempting to transform the society by secular means. Party Chairman Mao tse-Tung was venerated almost as a god, with the little red book of quotations from Chairman Mao replacing the Confucian Classics.

During the Cultural Revolution (1966–1976), Confucianism was attacked as one of the "Four Olds" — old ideas, culture, customs, and habits. The Cultural Revolution attempted to destroy the hierarchical structure that Confucianism had idealized and to prevent the intellectual elite from ruling over the masses. Contrary to the Confucian virtue of filial piety, young people even denounced their parents at public trials, and scholars were made objects of derision. An estimated one million people were attacked. Some were killed, some committed suicide, and millions suffered.

Mao said that he had hated Confucius from his childhood. What he so disliked was the intellectual emphasis on study of the Classics and on rituals. But in some respects, Confucian morality continued to form the basis of Chinese ethics. Mao particularly emphasized the (Confucian) virtues of selfless service to the people and of self-improvement for the public good:

All our cadres, whatever their rank, are servants of the people, and whatever we do is to serve the people. How then can we be reluctant to discard any of our bad traits?[36]

For decades, Communist China prided itself on being the most law-abiding country in the world. The streets were safe, and tourists found that if they could not understand the currency, they could trust taxi drivers to take the exact amount, and no more, from their open wallets. But recently there has been a rise in crime

During the years of Mao tse-Tung's ascendency, the Chairman was treated as a larger-than-life hero of a grand drama that replaced but also resembled religion.

and official corruption. The society has changed abruptly since China opened its doors to the West in 1978, undermining traditional Confucian virtues. The government blames the influx of materialistic values, from indiscriminating embrace of the underside of Western culture and the rapid shift toward a free market economy. In early 1989, Zhao Ziyang, then Communist Party leader, urged officials to maintain Confucian discipline (without naming it that) in the midst of the changes: "The Party can by no means allow its members to barter away their principles for money and power."[37] But when the people picked up this cry, ageing leaders chose brutally to suppress popular calls for greater democracy and an end to official corruption; they did so in the name of another Confucian value: order in society.

For their part, the intellectuals of the democracy movement had tried to do things in the proper way but were caught on the horns of the poignant Chinese dilemma. Under Confucian ethics, it has been the continuing responsibility of scholars to morally cultivate themselves and properly remonstrate with their rulers, to play the role of upright censors. On the other hand, scholars had to remain loyal to the ruler, for they were subjects and observing one's subservient position as a subject preserved the security of the state. The leaders of the democracy movement tried to deal with this potential conflict by ritualized, respectful action: They formally walked up the steps of The Great Hall of the People in Tiananmen Square to present their written requests to those in power. But they were ignored and brutally suppressed.

Again, in 1995, forty-five of China's most distinguished scholars and scientists delivered a petition to the government urging freedom of thought and accountability of the government to the public, in order to end socially corrosive corruption. Some observers speculate that slow transformations will bring a new form of Confucian tradition as the foundation of a non-Communist China.

After two thousand years of ascendency, Confucius's teachings are no longer the primary texts of Chinese schoolchildren. They may only encounter his teachings as college students if they happen to major in the study of Chinese philosophy or literature. Only a few old Confucian scholars remain from the old days. But Confucian values are passed on in the family. As Chinese scholar Ann-ping Chin asserts:

> Children live according to the Confucian rules and rites without having to learn them from texts. Confucianism is a living tradition in China.[38]

The Communist Chinese government still calls on its subjects to behave according to Confucian ideals. A citizen whose behavior reflects Confucian virtues is held up as an example to others. Chinese newspapers frequently carry contemporary stories about selfless public servers, such as Yuan Jingliang. He is a doctor at a time when that profession earns little money in return for long hours of hard work. *China Daily* describes him and his work in ways that still reflect the idealization of Confucian virtues:

> Tall, thin, and with glistening, kind eyes, Yuan, 50, looks the model of the Chinese intellectual of his generation....
> Yuan doesn't take advantage of the loopholes in the hospital's administration, common in hospitals, to loaf on the job. He makes his rounds conscientiously, always looking to his patients' needs. He generally finds time for a comforting word or two.

Living Confucianism

Ann-ping Chin grew up in Taiwan, the daughter of parents from the northern part of mainland China. She teaches Confucianism and Taoism at Wesleyan University and has visited China five times to do research on the continuing changes in that society. Of the contemporary situation there with regard to traditional values she says:

"Lots of things are changing in China. First of all, the economic boom is changing women's perceptions of themselves and of their family. For instance, if a woman is determined to have a profession of her own, in this huge marketplace of China this implies that she would become involved in a private enterprise or begin one herself. If she does that, this means that she would have to consider child-rearing as secondary. Usually these women depend on their parents or in-laws to bring up their children, in their own homes.

Divorce is very common. Family units are breaking up and children have less security — there are all the problems that we associate with divorce in the West. The woman simply says, 'Look — I'm going to leave or you leave.'

Making money is now the most important thing for the Chinese. It's finally a free market. Even though it's economic freedom, it's some kind of freedom. 'So,' they feel, 'why not make the most of that sort of freedom? Political freedom can wait. Let's make the most of this that we have, and not ask too much.'

From an initial impression, perhaps you can say that the fundamental Confucian values are disappearing. Through more than two thousand years of Chinese history, both in traditional Confucian teachings and in Taoist teachings as well, you find a tremendous deprecation of the idea of making money — of taking advantage or making a profit, be it in money or in human relationships. Now unless you have the determination to make money, you are not considered a true man in Chinese society.

On the other hand, if you really delve into their private lives, and try to understand what is really important to the Chinese, I would say that the very basic relationships of parents and children, and of friends to friends are still very strong. The Chinese have given up their relationship with the ruler; that's really a joke. The relationship between husband and wife is much more complicated. Men love the idea of having a very devoted wife. They know that is perhaps impossible, but they still yearn for it. And they still value the traditional qualities that you find in the biographies of virtuous women. If they can find that in their mothers, they still appreciate those values.

Other values have been abandoned. I'm very disturbed and saddened, pained, by what is happening to the Chinese scholars. They cannot go out and do private enterprise, for they are scholars. They get paid a very pathetic amount of money each month, not enough to make ends meet. Scholars have always been really respected even though people didn't understand them. But now there isn't even that respect since the society is placing so much emphasis on making money.

My parents both came from very scholarly backgrounds. They passed down to us the traditions without the formalities, without the rigidities, so we were extremely fortunate. I think my father passed down to us his love of students, his love of teaching, and of the very special relationship between teachers and disciples. That relationship is a very special one in Chinese tradition. If you are lucky, you can still see that between an elderly teacher and his disciples. It's not obedience — rather, it's a concern that the disciple expresses toward the teacher.

In looking at what I've absorbed from my parents, there's also the matter of character. My father's character had a profound effect on me. I just intuitively know that he always tried to do the right thing. And to do the right thing sometimes can be so difficult. This was the only way that he could live — to always try to do the right thing, whether it was for a friend, or for us, for my mom, for his own parents, or for strangers. He would never compromise that."

"His voice is always so gentle and his face looks caring and sympathetic," said Wu Qihong [a patient].[39]

Conferences have recently been held on the mainland in China and also in Taiwan and Singapore to discuss Confucianism; it is becoming the conscious property of intellectuals once again.

In Korea, where few people now consider themselves adherents of Confucianism as a religion, lectures and special events are being sponsored by the 231 local Confucian institutes to promote Confucian teachings. They tend to be conservative, opposing women's groups who advocate revision of family laws. The Korean Overseas Information Service advocates a flexible, liberal version of the tradition, open to other cultures and to all religions but still providing a firm foundation for social order:

Confucianism can present contemporary Koreans with a set of practical standards of conduct in the form of rituals and etiquette. Extensive introduction of Western modes of behavior led to the confusion and adulteration of Korea's native behavior pattern. Civility and propriety in speech and deportment enhance the dignity of man. Rites and conduct befitting to a civilized people should be refined and adjusted to the conditions of the time....

Confucianism reinforces the fabric of society.... A sense of family which bolsters social integration, rather than impeding rational operation of community, ought to be stressed and developed for the good of society....

Confucian morality and character may contribute greatly to the humanization of contemporary industrial society. Obsession with efficiency and material value in an industrial society can suffocate humanity.... Korea should, through its Confucian heritage, sustain the tradition of propriety and modesty and defend the intrinsically moral nature of man from submergence in economic and materialistic considerations.[40]

Confucian thought has played a significant role in Japan as well. It entered Japan during the seventh century when Chinese political thought and religious ideas first began to have significant influence there. It left its mark on the first constitution of Japan, on the arrangement of government bureaucracy, and in the educational system. From the twelfth to the sixteenth century, Confucianism was studied in Zen Buddhist monasteries. Then from the seventeenth to nineteenth century, Confucianism began to spread more widely among the people of Japan because of its adoption as an educational philosophy in public and private schools. Confucian moral teachings became the basis for establishing proper human relationships in the family and in Japanese society.

Both Confucianism and Shinto were manipulated by the military during the pre-war period to inculcate a nationalist expansionist ideology. More in keeping with the original motives of Confucianism, some scholars have observed that Japan's notably effective modernization in the last one hundred years is due, in parts to various values derived from Confucianism. These values include a high regard for diligence, consensus, education, moral self-cultivation, frugality, and loyalty.

Suggested reading

de Bary, William Theodore, *East Civilizations: A Dialogue in Five Stages*, Cambridge: Harvard University Press, 1988. A masterful overview of three thousand years of East Asian civilization including the classical legacy, the Buddhist age, the Neo-Confucian stage and East Asia's modern transformation.

de Bary, William Theodore, Chan, Wing-tsit, and Watson, Burton, eds., *Sources of Chinese Tradition*, New York: Columbia University Press, 1960. Useful commentaries and extensive texts from Confucian and Taoist schools.

Fingarette, Herbert, *Confucius — The Secular as Sacred*, New York: Harper and Row, 1972. Sensitive analysis of Confucian philosophy, for a Western audience.

The *I Ching*, translated into German by Richard Wilhelm and thence into English by Cary Baynes, third edition, Princeton, New Jersey: Princeton University Press, 1967. Fascinating insights into the multiple possibilities of the interplay of yin and yang in our lives.

Mencius, trans. by D. C. Lau, New York: Viking Penguin, 1970.

Robinet, Isabelle, *Taoist Meditation: the Mao-shan Tradition of Great Purity*, trans. Julian Pas and Norman Girardot, Albany, New York: State University of New York Press, 1993. A careful analysis of the central scriptures and practices used by elite Taoists to become immortals.

Schipper, Kristofer M., *The Taoist Body*, trans. Karen Duvall, Berkeley: University of California Press, 1992. Explores integration of religious and philosophical Taoism within the Celestial Masters movement, from the Han Dynasty to contemporary Taiwan.

Tao-te Ching, attributed to Lao-tzu, available in numerous translations, including the English translation by D. C. Lau, London: Penguin Books, 1963.

Taylor, Rodney, *The Religious Dimensions of Confucianism*, Albany: State University of New York Press, 1990. A collection of essays dealing with the central question of whether Confucianism is a religion.

Tu Wei-ming, *Confucian Thought: Selfhood as Creative Transformation*, Albany: State University of New York Press, 1985. A collection of Tu's seminal essays on his concern that Confucian humanity be understood as a living tradition with something distinctive to contribute to contemporary discussions in philosophy and comparative religions.

Watson, Burton, *Chuang Tzu: Basic Writings*, New York: Columbia University Press, 1964. An engaging translation of major writings by Chuang Tzu, with an introduction that is particularly helpful in dealing with this paradoxical material.

Welch, Holmes H., (with Anna Seidel) ed., *Facets of Taoism*, New Haven: Yale University Press, 1979. A collection of essays that shows the diversity of Taoist movements up to the present.

CHAPTER 7

SHINTO

The way of the Kami

Japan has embraced and adapted many religions that originated in other countries, but it also developed its own unique path: Shinto. It is an organized version of the indigenous religion of the country, closely tied to nature and the unseen world. Of those modern Japanese who are religious, many combine practices from several religions, for each offers something different. Confucianism informs organizations and ethics, Buddhism and Christianity offer ways of understanding suffering and the afterlife, traditional veneration of ancestors links the living to their family history, and Shinto harmonizes people with the natural world.

The origins of Shinto

Shinto has no founder, no orthodox canon of sacred literature, and no explicit code of ethical requirements. It is so deep-seated and ancient that the symbolic meanings of many of its elaborate rituals have been forgotten by those who practice them. It seems to have begun as the local religion of agricultural communities and had no name until Buddhism was imported in the sixth century CE. To distinguish the indigenous Japanese way from the foreign one, the former was labeled "shin" (divine being) "do" (way). During one period it was used by the central government to inspire nationalism, but since the forced separation of church and state after World War II Shinto has quietly returned to its roots. They can be described through three central aspects of the path: affinity with natural beauty, harmony with the spirits, and purification rituals.

KINSHIP WITH NATURE Before industrial pollution and urbanization, Japan was a country of exquisite natural beauty, and to a certain extent, it still is. The islands marry mountains to sea, and the interiors are laced with streams, waterfalls, and lush forests. Even the agriculture is beautiful, with flowering fruit trees and terraced fields. The people lived so harmoniously with this environment that they had no separate word for "nature" until they began importing modern Western ideas late in the nineteenth century.

Living close to nature, the people experienced life as a continual process of change and renewal. They organized their lives around the turn of the seasons, honoring the roles of the sun, moon, and lightning in their rice farming. Mount Fuji, greatest of the volcanic peaks that formed the islands, was honored as the sacred embodiment of the divine creativity that had thrust the land up from the sea. It has never been called Mount Fuji by the Japanese, but rather, *Fuji-san,*

The Japanese people have traditionally honored the natural beauty of their land and have considered Mt. Fuji to be its most sacred peak. Pilgrims have long made the arduous climb up Fuji seeking purification and good fortune.

indicating a friendship and intimacy with the mountain. The sparkling ocean and rising sun so visible along the extensive coastlines were loved as earthly expressions of the sacred purity, brightness, and awesome power at the heart of life.

> *To be fully alive is to have an aesthetic perception of life because a major part of the world's goodness lies in its often unspeakable beauty.*
>
> Rev. Yukitaka Yamamoto, Shinto priest[1]

Although industrialization and urbanization have blighted some of the natural landscape, the sensitivity to natural beauty survives in small-scale arts. In traditional rock gardening, flower arranging, the tea ceremony, and poetry, Japanese artists continue to honor the simple and natural. If a rock is placed just right in a garden, it seems alive, radiating its natural essence. In a tea ceremony, great attention is paid to each natural sensual delight, from the purity of water poured from a wooden ladle to the genuineness of the clay vessels. These arts are often linked with Zen Buddhism, but the sensitivities seem to derive from the ancient Japanese ways.

HONORING THE KAMI Surrounded by nature's beauty and power, the Japanese people found the divine all around them. In Shinto, the sacred is both immanent and transcendent. In Japanese mythology, the divine originated as one essence:

> *In primeval ages, before the earth was formed, amorphous matter floated freely about like oil upon water. In time there arose in its midst a thing like a sprouting reedshoot, and from this a deity came forth of its own.*[2]

This deity gave birth to many **kami**, or spirits, two of whom — the Amatsu Kami — were told to organize the material world. Standing on the Floating Bridge of Heaven, they stirred the ocean with a jeweled spear. When they pulled it out of the water, it dripped brine back into the ocean, where it coagulated into eight islands, with mountains, rivers, plants, and trees (these may be interpreted either as Japan or the whole world). To rule this earthly kingdom they created the Kami Amaterasu, Goddess of the Sun. Through their union, the Amatsu Kami also gave birth to the ancestors of the people of Japan. All of the natural world — land, trees, mountains, waters, animals, people — is thus joined in kinship as the spiritual creation of the kami.

Although the word *kami* (a way of pronouncing the character "shin") is usually translated as "god" or "spirit," these translations are not exact. *Kami* can be either singular or plural, for the word refers to a single essence manifesting in many places. Rather than evoking an image, like the Hindu or Mahayana Buddhist god-idols, *kami* refers to a quality. It means that which evokes wonder and awe in us. The kami harmonize heaven and earth and also guide the solar system and the cosmos. It/they tend to reside in beautiful or powerful places, such as mountains, certain trees, unusual rocks, waterfalls, whirlpools, and animals. In addition, it/they manifest as wind, rain, thunder, or lightning. Kami also appears in abstract forms, such as the creativity of growth and reproduction. In general, explains Sakamiki Shunzo, kami include:

Shinto shrines are set apart by a torii, an ever-open sacred gateway at the entrance to all shrine precincts. This floating torii is the symbolic gate to Itsukushima Jjinja shrine, Miyajima.

... all things whatsoever which deserve to be dreaded and revered for the extraordinary and preeminent powers which they possess.... [Kami] need not be eminent for surpassing nobleness, goodness, or serviceableness alone. Malignant and uncanny beings are also called kami, if only they are the objects of general dread.[3]

SHRINES Recognizing the presence of kami, humans have built shrines to honor it/them. There are even now approximately eighty thousand Shinto shrines in Japan. Shrines may be as small as bee-hives or elaborate temple complexes covering thousands of acres. Some honor kami protecting the area; some honor kami with special responsibilities, such as protecting crops from insects. The shrines are situated on sites thought to have been chosen by the kami for their sacred atmosphere. At one time, every community had its own guardian kami.

It is thought that the earliest Shinto places of worship were sacred trees or groves, perhaps with some enclosure to demarcate the sacred area. Shrine complexes which developed later also have some way of indicating where sacred space begins: tall gate-frames known as *torii*, walls, or streams with bridges which must be crossed to enter the holy precinct of the kami. Water is a purifying influence, and basins of water are also provided for washing one's mouth and hands. Statues of guardian lions further protect the kami from evil intrusions, as do ropes with pendants hanging down.

In temple compounds, one first comes to a public hall of worship, behind which is an offering hall where priests conduct rites. Beyond that is the scared sanctuary of the kami, which is entered only by the high priest. Here the spirit of the kami is invited to come down to dwell within a special natural object or perhaps a mirror which reflects the revered light of brightness and purity, considered the natural order of the universe. If there is a spiritually powerful site already present — a waterfall, a crevice in a rock, a hot spring, a sacred tree — the spirit of the kami may dwell there. Some shrines are completely empty at the center. In any case, the eyes of the worshippers do not fall on the holy of holies; their worship is imageless. As Kishimoto Hideo explains,

A faithful believer would come to the simple hall of a Shinto sanctuary, which is located in a grove with a quiet and holy atmosphere. He may stand quite a while in front of the sanctuary, clap his hands, bow deeply, and try to feel the deity in his heart. He would not try to build up rational proof for the existence of an invisible deity. For him, the proof of divine existence depends on whether or not he can feel the deity directly in his heart. Shinto being a polytheistic religion, each sanctuary has its own particular deity. But seldom do the believers know the individual name of the deity whom they are worshipping. They do not care about that.... The more important point for them is whether or not they feel the existence of the deity directly in their hearts.[4]

The kami of a place may be experienced as energies. They are not necessarily pictured as forms, and at times Shintoism has been strongly iconoclastic. In the eighteenth century, for instance, a famous Shinto scholar wrote:

Never make an image in order to represent the Deity. To worship a deity is directly to establish a felt relation of our heart to the living Divinity through sincerity or truthfulness on our part. If we, however, try to establish a relation between Deity

Modern Japanese visit Shinto shrines for many purposes, asking the blessing of kami on the patterns of their lives. Most Shinto shrines are built with an appreciation for simple natural materials, and the larger ones are periodically rebuilt with great ceremony.

and man indirectly by means of an image, the image will itself stand in the way and prevent us from realizing our religious purpose to accomplish direct communion with the Deity. So an image made by mortal hands is of no use in Shinto worship.[5]

Ceremonies

To properly encourage the spirit of the kami to dwell in the holy sanctuary, long and complex ceremonies are needed. In some temples, it takes ten years for the priests to learn them. The priesthood was traditionally hereditary. One temple has drawn its priests from the same four families for over a hundred generations. Not uncommonly, the clergy are women priestesses. Neither priests nor priestesses live as ascetics; it is common for them to be married, and they are not traditionally expected to meditate. Rather, they are specialists in the arts of maintaining the connection between the kami and the people.

Everything has symbolic importance, even when people do not remember quite what it is, so rites are conducted with great care. The correct kind of wood, cloth, and clay in temple furnishings, the nine articles held by priests during ceremonies (such as branch, gourd, sword, and bow), the bowing, the sharp clapping of hands, beating of drums, the waving of a stick with paper strips — everything is established by tradition and performed with precision. Traditionally, there are no personal prayers to the kami for specific kinds of help, but rather a reverent recognition of the close relationship between the kami, the ancestors, the people, and nature. When people have made a pilgrimage to a special shrine, they often take back spiritual mementos of their communion with the kami, such as a paper symbol of the temple encased within a brocade bag.

Followers of the way of the kami may also make daily offerings to the kami in their home. Their place of worship usually consists of a high shelf on which rests a miniature shrine, with only a mirror inside. The daily home ritual may begin with greeting the sun in the east with clapping and a prayer for protection for the household. Then offerings are placed before the shrine: rice for health, water for cleansing and preservation of life, and salt for the harmonious seasoning of life. When a new house is to be built, the blessings of the kami are ceremonially requested.

To acknowledge and follow the kami is to bring our life into harmony with nature, Shintoists feel. The word used for this concept is *kannagara*, which is the same word used for the movements of the sun, moon, stars, and planets. Yukitaka Yamamoto, 96th Chief Priest of the Tsubaki Grand Shrine, says kannagara could be translated as "Natural Religion":

> *The life of man is located in Daishizen, Great Nature, the vast cosmic setting into which we are born, where we live and within which our lives find any meaning. Natural Religion is the spontaneous awareness of the Divine that can be found in any culture.... The Spirit of Great Nature may be a flower, may be the beauty of the mountains, the pure snow, the soft rains or the gentle breeze. Kannagara means being in communion with these forms of beauty and so with the highest level of experiences of life. When people respond to the silent and provocative beauty of the natural order, they are aware of* kannagara. *When they respond in life in a similar way, by following ways "according to the kami," they are expressing* kannagara *in their lives. They are living according to the natural flow of the universe and will benefit and develop by so doing.*[6]

Purification

In traditional Shinto, there is no concept of sin. The world is beautiful and full of helpful spirits. Sexuality per se is not sinful; the world was created by mating deities, and people have traditionally bathed together communally in Japan. However, there is a great problem of ritual impurity that may offend the kami and bring on calamities such as drought, famine, or war.

The quality of impurity or misfortune is called *tsumi*. It can arise through defilement by corpses or menstruation, by unkind interaction between humans, between humans and the environment, or through natural catastrophes. In contrast to repentance required by religions that emphasize sin, tsumi requires purification. Followers of the way of the kami have various means of removing tsumi. One is paying attention to problems as they arise:

> *To live free of obstructing mists, problems of the morning should be solved in the morning and those of the evening should be solved by evening. Wisdom and*

Purification by Waterfall

The cleansing powers of waters, plentiful in natural Japan, is often used. One may take a ritual bath in the ocean, source of life. Or, in a lengthy ritual called **misogi,** a believer may stand beneath a waterfall, letting its force hit the shoulders and carry impurities and tensions away. Before even entering the waterfall, those seeking purification must undergo preliminary purification practices because the waterfall itself is kami. The women put on white kimonos and headbands, the men white loincloths and headbands.

The misogi ritual proceeds with shaking the soul by bouncing the hands up and down in front of the stomach, to help the person become aware of the soul's presence. Next comes a form of warm-up calisthenics called Bird Rowing. Following a leader, the participants then shout invocations that activate the soul, affirm the potential for realizing the infinite in one's own soul, and unify the people with the kami of earth, guidance, water, life, and the **ki** energy (which the Chinese know as *ch'i*).

Before entering the waterfall, the participants raise their metabolism and absorb as much ki as possible by practicing a form of deep breathing. They are sprinkled with purifying salt and are given sake to spray into the stream in three mouthfuls.

The leader counts from one to nine, to symbolize the impurity of the mundane world and then cuts the air and shouts "Yei!" to dispel this impurity. With ritual claps and shouts the participants then enter the waterfall, continually chanting *"Harae-tamae-Kiyome-tamae-ro-kon-sho-jo!"* This phrase requests the kami to wash away all tsumi from the six elements that form the human being, from the senses, and from the mind. This part of the ritual has been scientifically proven to lower the blood pressure.

After this powerful practice, participants dry off, spend time in meditation to calm the soul, and share a ceremonial drink to unify themselves with the kami and with each other. The whole misogi ceremony is designed to restore one's natural purity and sense of mission in life. As Rev. Yamamoto explains:

> As imperfect beings, we often fail to recognize our mission. These failures come about because we have lost something of our natural purity. This is why purification, or misogi, is so central to Shinto. It enables man to cultivate spirituality and to restore his or her natural greatness.[7]

knowledge should be applied like the sharpness of an axe to the blinding effect of the mists of obstruction. Then may the kami purify the world and free it of tsumi.[8]

The kami of the high mountain rapids will carry the tsumi to the sea, where the whirlpool kami will swallow it and the wind kami will blow it to the netherworld, where kami of that place absorb and remove it.

After this has been completed, the heavenly kami, the earthly kami and the myriad of kami can recognise man as purified and everything can return to its original brightness, beauty and purity as before since all tsumi has wholly vanished from the world.[9]

People may also be purified spontaneously by a kind of grace that washes over them, often in nature, bringing them into awareness of unity with the universe. Hitoshi Iwasaki, a young Shinto priest, says that he likes to look at the stars at night in the mountains where the air is clear:

When I am watching the thoroughly clear light of the stars, I get a pure feeling, like my mind being washed. I rejoice to think this is a spiritual Misogi [purification ritual].… Master Mirihei Ueshiba, the founder of Aikido, is said to have looked upon the stars one night, suddenly realized he was united with the universe, and burst into tears, covering his face with his hands. We human beings, not only human beings but everything existing in this world, are one of the cells which form this great universe.[10]

Misogi is ritual purification by standing beneath a waterfall.

In addition to these personal ways of cleansing, there are ritual forms of purification. One is **oharai**, a ceremony commonly performed by Shinto priests which includes the waving of a piece of wood from a sacred tree, to which are attached white streamers (the Japanese version of the shaman's medicine fan of feathers or the Hindu yak-tail whisk, all used to sweep through the air and thus purify an area). This ceremony is today performed on cars and new buildings. A version used to soothe a kami who is upset by an impurity was called for in 1978 when there was a rash of suicides in a Tokyo housing complex by residents jumping off roofs.

Festivals

In addition to elaborate regular ceremonies, Shintoism is associated with numerous special festivals throughout the year and throughout a person's life. They begin four months before the birth of a baby, when the soul is thought to enter the fetus.

Then thirty-two or thirty-three days after the infant's birth, its parents take it to the family's temple for initiation by the deity. In a traditional family, many milestones — such as coming of age at thirteen, or first arranging one's hair as a woman at age sixteen, marriage, turning sixty-one, seventy-seven, or eighty-eight — are also celebrated with a certain spiritual awareness and ritualism.

The seasonal festivals are reminders to the people that they are descendants of the kami. This means remembering to live in gratitude for all that they have received. Festivals became exuberant affairs in which the people and the kami join in celebrating life. Many have an agricultural basis, ensuring good crops and then giving thanks for them. Often the local kami is carried about the streets in a portable shrine.

Among the many local and national Japanese festivals with Shinto roots, one of the biggest is New Year's. It begins in December with ceremonial housecleaning, the placing of bamboo and pine "trees" at doorways of everything from homes to offices and bars to welcome the kami, and dressing in traditional kimonos. On December 31, there is a national day of purification. On New Year's day, people may go out to see the first sunrise of the year and will try to visit a shrine as well as friends and relatives.

Many ceremonies honor those reaching a certain age. For instance, on January 15, those who are twenty years old are recognized as full-fledged adults, and on November 15, children who are three, five, or seven years old (considered delicate ages) are taken to a shrine to ask for the protection of the kami. On February 3, the end of winter, people throw beans to toss out bad fortune and invite good, and at shrines the priests shoot arrows to break the power of misfortune. A month-long spring festival is held from March to April, with purification rites and prayers for a successful planting season. The month of June is devoted to rites to protect crops from insects, blights, and bad weather. Fall brings thanksgiving rites for the harvest, with the first fruits offered to the kami and then great celebrating in the streets.

Buddhist and Confucian influences

Over time, the essence of Shinto has been blended with other religions imported into Japan. The two religions with which Shinto has been most blended are Buddhism, first introduced into Japan in the sixth century CE, and Confucianism, which has been an intimate part of Japanese culture since its earliest contact with Chinese influences.

Buddhism is still practiced side-by-side with Shinto. The fact that their theologies differ so significantly has been accepted by the people as covering different kinds of situations. The Japanese often go to Shinto shrines for life-affirming events, such as conception, birth, and marriage, and to Buddhist temples for death rites. Shingon Buddhist monks tried long ago to convince the Japanese that the Shinto kami were actually Buddhist deities. The two religions were therefore closely interwoven in some people's minds until the Meiji government extricated its version of Shinto from Buddhism in the nineteenth century. But the parallel worship of the two paths continues, with some villages having stone monuments to the kami and statues of Nichiren placed next to each other.

As for Confucianism, seventeenth-century Japanese Confucian scholars attempted to free themselves from Buddhism and to tie the Chinese beliefs they were importing to the ancient Japanese ways. One, for instance, likened *li* to the way of the kami as a means of social cohesion. Another stressed reverence as the common ground of the two paths and was himself revered as a living kami. The neo-Confucianists' alliance with Shinto to throw off the yoke of Buddhism actually revived Shinto itself and made the ancient, somewhat amorphous tradition more self-conscious. Scholars began to study and interpret its teachings. The combination of Confucian emphasis on hierarchy and Shinto devotion helped pave the way for the establishment in 1868 of the powerful Meiji monarchy.

State Shinto

The Meiji regime distinguished Shinto from Buddhism and took steps to promote Shinto as the spiritual basis for the government. Shinto, amplifying the Japanese traditions of ancestor veneration, had long taught that the emperor was the offspring of Amaterasu, the Sun Goddess. *Naobi no Mitma* ("Divine Spirit of Rectification"), written in the eighteenth century, expressed this ideal:

Left *On November 15, or the nearest Sunday, boys of five and girls of three and seven dress up in traditional clothes and visit a Shinto shrine to pray for health and good fortune. This is called the Seven-Five-Three Festival or Shichi-go-san.*
Right *Contemporary Japanese often honor both the Shinto kami and deceased relatives at their home shrines.*

> *This great imperial land, Japan, is the august country where the divine ancestral goddess Amaterasu Omikami was born, a superb country.... Amaterasu deigned to entrust the country with the words, "So long as time endures, for ten thousand autumns, this land shall be ruled by my descendants."*
>
> *According to her divine pleasure, this land was decreed to be the country of the imperial descendants, without disturbances from harsh gods, without any unsubmissive person. It is a land where, for ten thousand autumns, to the end of time, the emperors, as descendants of Amaterasu Omikami, would make theirs the mind of the heavenly gods, so that even now, without deviation from the divine age, the land might continue in tranquility and in accord with the will of the kami, a country ruled in peace.[11]*

It had been customary for the imperial family to visit the shrine to the Sun Goddess at Ise to consult the supreme kami on matters of importance. But the Emperor Meiji carried this tradition much farther. He decreed that the way of the kami should govern the nation. The way, as it was then interpreted, was labeled **State Shinto**. It was administered by government officials rather than bona fide Shinto priests, whose objections were silenced, and many of the ancient spiritual rituals were suppressed. State Shinto became the tool of militaristic nationalists as a way to enlist popular support for guarding the throne and expanding the empire.

By the time that Japan was defeated in World War II, the emperor Hirohito, Meiji's grandson, may have been little more than a ceremonial figurehead. But he had been held up as a god, not to be seen or touched by ordinary people. At the end of the war he officially declared himself human. The traditional spiritual Shinto, however, was left with the stigma built up by State Shinto. It was also confused with new religious sects that often had little to do with Shinto traditions but were nonetheless labeled *Sect Shinto* by the Meiji regime. One of these new sects, Tenrikyo, will be considered separately in Chapter 13.

Shinto today

In general, Shintoism is an indigenous Japanese faith, and it remains so. Outside Japan, it is a common faith only in Hawaii and Brazil, because many Japanese have settled there. Shintoism has not been a proselytizing religion.

Within Japan, reaction to the horrors of the war and desire for modernization threatened to leave Shinto in the shadows of the past. As Hitoshi Iwasaki notes (see Interview), for a time it was difficult for young people to learn about Shintoism. But the shrines remain and are visited by over eighty million Japanese at New Year. People often visit more as tourists than as believers, but many say they experience a sense of spiritual renewal when they visit a shrine. Long-established households still have their kami shelf, often next to the Buddhist family altar, which combines tablets memorializing the dead with scrolls or statues dedicated to a manifestation of the Buddha. In Japan, Shinto also survives as the basis for the seasonal holidays.

Despite the fact that Japan is now one of the most technologically advanced countries in the world, with business its primary focus, there still seems to be a place for ritual — and in some cases, heart-felt — communion with the intangible kami that, in Shinto belief, permeate all of life. Rapid and extreme urbanization

Living Shinto

Hitoshi Iwasaki is a young Shinto priest struggling to educate himself in the suppressed ancient ways of his people. He has officiated at the new Shinto shrine in Stockton, California, and at its parent shrine in Japan, Tsubaki Grand Shrine in the Mie Prefecture, where a fine waterfall is used for misogi.

"We Japanese are very fortunate. We are grateful for every natural phenomenon and we worship the mountain, we worship the river, we worship the sea, we worship the big rocks, waterholes, winds.

Unfortunately, after World War II, we were prohibited from teaching the Shinto religion in schools. We never learned about Shinto at school. Many young Japanese know the story of Jesus Christ, but nothing about Shinto. The government is not against Shinto. [The silence comes from] newspapers, the media, and the teachers' union, because they were established just after World War II. They have a very left-wing attitude [and associate Shinto with State Shinto]. Ordinary Japanese people don't link Shinto with politics nowadays, but the teachers' union and newspapers never give credence to religion, Shinto, or Japanese old customs.

Against this kind of atmosphere, we learned in the school that everything in Japan was bad. Shinto and Japanese customs were bad. Many young people are losing Japanese customs. But I went to Ise Shrine University, where I learned that Shinto is not just State Shinto. Some young people like me study Japanese things and they become super-patriots. That's the problem. There is no middle, just super-left or super-right.

I learned Shinto partly by learning aikido. The founder was a very spiritual person who studied in one of the Shinto churches. In Shinto we don't have services, we don't preach, we don't do anything for people who want to be saved. But I want to introduce the idea of Shinto to the people of the United States and young Japanese and I can do it through aikido. I think I learned the way of nature through aikido practice. We are born as a child of kami, which means we are part of the universe, like a tree. People practice aikido not to fight but to be a friend, to unite.

In Japan some people are going to Shinto. They were all doing Zen before, but Zen is very difficult. In waterfall purification there is no choice, just standing under the waterfall.

My friend, a Shinto priest, went to the Middle East, in complete desert. He says it was difficult to explain Shinto there. For them, nature is the enemy. They have to fight nature.

In Japan we have water everywhere. Now the big rivers and streams are polluted. But people come to the shrines. People gather because this is a sacred place from ancient times where people have come to pray. And other people want to go where people are gathered, so some of the shrines become vacation places, surrounded by souvenir shops. Many come to Shinto shrines and pray Buddhist prayers. Why not? Buddha is one of the kami. Everything has kami."

and industrialization in twentieth-century Japan have also brought extremes of pollution and disease. Minamata disease, for example, has since mid-century brought paralysis and painful suffering in an area of southern Japan where a chemical factory had been dumping mercury into the bay, contaminating the fish eaten by the residents. In another area of southern Japan, iron and steel factories had so polluted the air that children developed severe respiratory diseases and the sky was never blue. However, citizens' groups — many of them led by concerned mothers — are intervening to protest the despoliation of the environment and of human health and to urge a new appreciation of the natural beauty of the islands. Such actions can perhaps be seen as practical applications of Shinto sentiments.

Some Shintoists now explain their path as a universal natural religion, rather than an exclusively Japanese phenomenon, and try to explain the way of harmony with the kami to interested non-Japanese, without striving for conversions. A Shinto shrine has been built in California, offering ritual ways of experiencing one's connection with nature and learning to see the divine in the midst of life.

Within Japan, the Association of Shinto Shrines feels that it can play a role in helping people to remember the natural world. The Association recently stated,

> [Traditionally] the Japanese viewed nature not as an adversary to be subdued, but rather as a sacred space overflowing with the blessings of the kami, and toward which they were to act with restraint.... While the Japanese have loathed environmental destruction, the advance of civilization centered on science and technology, and the rush toward economic prosperity has created a tidal wave of modernization that has frequently resulted in the loss of that traditional attitude handed down from ancestors. This has, in turn, produced the unfortunate spectacle of profit-centered and hastily considered development plans which ignore the preservation of the natural environment. We Shintoists feel a great responsibility for this state of affairs, and are giving great efforts to programs meant to preserve the sacred groves and natural forests of Shinto shrines. By reconsidering the role of the sacred groves possessed by the some eighty thousand shrines in Japan, we hope to heighten Japanese consciousness, and expand the circle of active involvement in environmental preservation.[12]

Suggested reading

Hebert, Jean, *Shinto: At the Fountain-head of Japan*, New York: Stein and Day, 1967. A classic survey of the intricacies of Shinto practice.

Hori, Ichiro, *Folk Religion in Japan*, Chicago and London: University of Chicago Press, 1968. A lively study of Japanese folk traditions such as shamanism and mountain worship which contributed to Shinto.

Kitagawa, Joseph M., *On Understanding Japanese Religion*, Princeton, New Jersey and Guildford, Surrey: Princeton University Press, 1987. A scholarly history including Shinto and "new religions."

Mason, J. W. T., *The Meaning of Shinto: The Primaeval Foundation of Creative Spirit in Modern Japan*, Port Washington, New York: Kennikat Press, Inc., 1967.

Moore, Charles A., ed., *The Japanese Mind: Essentials of Japanese Philosophy and Culture*, Honolulu: The University Press of Honolulu, 1967, 1971. A valuable collection of essays covering Shinto and Buddhism as well as secular aspects of Japanese lifeways.

Picken, Stuart D. B., *Shinto: Japan's Spiritual Roots*, Tokyo: Kodansha International, 1980. An appreciative and well illustrated view of Shinto by a minister of the Church of Scotland who is also a practitioner of misogi.

Smith, Robert J., *Ancestor Worship in Contemporary Japan*, Stanford, California: Stanford University Press, 1974. A sociological study of the continuing tradition of venerating family ancestors in contemporary Japan, including historical chapters which are of help in understanding the roots of State Shinto.

Yamamoto, Yukitaka, *Way of the Kami*, Stockton, California: Tsubaki American Publications, 1987. A highly accessible introduction to Shinto, seen as a universal natural way.

CHAPTER 8

ZOROASTRIANISM

"May we be the perfectors of the world,
O Lord Mazda!"

From East Asia, we move to the Middle East, cradle of three major living religions, Judaism, Christianity, and Islam, and another religion of few living representatives but considerable historical significance, Zoroastrianism. For more than a thousand years, it was the official religion of the vast Iranian empire, which extended from Iraq or Turkey to India. It is in some ways a bridge between Eastern and Western religions. Its origins are synchronous with, and similar to, Hinduism, it is thought to have influenced Buddhism, and it introduced beliefs which were later integrated into Jewish, Christian, and Muslim religions, including heaven and hell, an evil force, judgment of the individual and resurrection of the body after death, and a dramatic apocalyptic end of the world with final resurrection of the dead.

The theology of ancient Zoroastrianism itself is subject to debate, for over the centuries a large portion of its sacred scriptures was destroyed or forgotten and the meanings of the old language were lost. Nevertheless, Zoroastrianism is of great interest to scholars of the history of religion and to the remaining practitioners of this ancient way.

Origins in ancient Iran

In Iran, this faith is called **Mazdayasna** — "the worship of Ahura Mazda," or the Wise Lord. Westerners label it Zoroastrianism after its great prophet Zarathushtra (called Zoroaster by the Greeks). Some scholars think he lived about 1100 to 550 BCE, although some historical references place him much earlier. In either case, it is clear that some elements of the faith pre-dated Zarathushtra. He was considered the last and greatest of numerous reformers who came to restore pure religion whenever its practice had lapsed, and the first to teach the perfectibility of humanity.

The early elements came from the faith of the Indo–Iranians, a branch of the same Aryan tribes who made their way down from the steppes of southern Russia into the Indian subcontinent. Semi-nomadic pastoralists from a cold climate, they seem to have revered fire, which they tried to keep ever burning. Like the Indian Aryans, they honored the divinities of nature in daily priestly rituals called *yasna* (known as *yagya* in India). These rituals, held on an open-air plot like the early Brahmanic rituals, included use of a sacred drink called *haoma*, comparable to the mysterious Vedic *soma* potion. Libations were offered to the god of fire and the goddesses of water, the two most precious sustainers of life.

When people died, their bodies were offered to the birds to be picked clean, to avoid contaminating the earth with decaying flesh. The bones were then buried and the memorial treated with special care by the next generation, for it was believed that at some point the person would be resurrected bodily.

The Indo–Iranian people also worshipped a pantheon of gods representing the elements, aspects of nature, and abstract principles, such as justice and obedience. These often corresponded with those worshipped by the Vedic Indians. As a group they were called **Daevas** (Sanskrit: **Devas**), or "Shining Ones," with the highest gods called **Ahuras** ("Lords"). The ritual worship conducted by the priests was designed, as in India, to maintain the natural order, truth, and righteousness of the universe by re-enacting the original sacrifice which led to its creation.

Zarathushtra's mission

Information about Zarathushtra's life is not easily reconstructed. It is thought that he was trained as a priest in the Indo–Iranian tradition. He was also apparently a mystical seeker who spent many years in spiritual retreat, asking for revelations of spiritual truth. He is said to have had a great vision at the age of thirty. After wading into a river up to his neck, he was symbolically purified of all lower aspects of his being. Radiant, he returned to the bank, where according to legend he saw a great shining being — Vohu Manah, the embodiment of the good mind, or the loving mind. Vohu Manah led him into the presence of Ahura Mazda, the creator God. Ahura Mazda was surrounded by angelic presences manifesting six attributes of the divine.

Scholars suggest that these attributes represent earlier Indo–Iranian deities, transformed by Zarathushtra to suit his monotheistic belief but still retaining their association with forces of nature — the earth, the arch of the sky, water, plants, cattle, and fire.

Zarathushtra said he experienced communion with Ahura Mazda and his attributes on many occasions. From these direct contacts with the divine, Zarathushtra reportedly determined that in contrast to the multiplicity of gods worshipped by the Indo–Iranians, Ahura Mazda was the Supreme Lord, from whom all good things flowed. The prophet had been troubled by violent aspects of the old religion, perhaps those carried by nomads worshipping the warlike Indra and plundering the pastoralists' settlements. He is also said to have disapproved of the worship of the nature spirits through fear, accompanied by requests for personal benefits. Zarathushtra denounced all cruelty, selfishness, distortion, and hypocrisy in the name of religion. He insisted that Ahura Mazda creates only goodness and should be worshipped by good thoughts, words, and deeds.

He poured forth his adoration for the Supreme in divine songs called **Gathas**. These hymns are the only words of the prophet that have been retained over centuries of vicissitudes. "Speak to me as friend to friend," he implores Ahura Mazda. "Grant us the support which friend would give to friend."[1] The Gathas are the major existing source of information about Zarathushtra's life and theology, but they are written in an ancient language whose meanings are now obscure. Scholars see close linguistic and thematic links between the Gathas and the earliest of the Rig Vedas.

In devotional art, the prophet Zarathushtra is often portrayed in communion with the divine, which he knew as the Lord of Life and Wisdom, Ahura Mazda.

Despite his ecstatic visions, Zarathushtra was long unable to convince anyone else to follow him in honoring Ahura Mazda above all others. He did not seek to extricate people from the older religion but rather to appeal to them to use their Good Mind, to think for themselves, rather than blindly following anyone. Priests of the ancestral religion denounced him as a heretic. After ten years, his only convert was his cousin. Some of the Gathas seem to refer to his despair at being unable to fulfill his divine mission:

> To what land shall I bend my steps? Whither shall I turn for homage? They have separated me from the Strong in Spirit and the Friend. Neither does the Fellow-worker seek to rejoice me, nor, by any chance, the cruel despots of the country who are Followers of the Druj [the Lie]. How then shall I rejoice Thee, O Mazda Ahura? ...[2]

At last Zarathushtra journeyed to another kingdom whose exact location is now unknown and convinced its king, Vishtaspa, of the truth of his understanding. A legend created long after Zarathushtra's death has it that the other priests of the court tried to frame the newcomer as a sorcerer. He revealed their deception and performed a miraculous healing on the king's ailing horse to demonstrate the truth of his faith. King Vishtaspa adopted Zarathushtra's creed and proclaimed it the state religion. Zarathushtra is said to have preached for almost fifty years until his death by assassination at a fire temple at the age of seventy-seven.

Post-Zarathushtran history

It is very difficult to trace the later spread of Zarathushtra's teachings. The Magi — a tribe of priestly specialists in western Iran — seem to have become involved with transmission of Zoroastrianism some time after Zarathushtra died, but they may have altered it significantly. Ahura Mazda was apparently revered by the Achaemenid kings of the great Persian Empire. The Persian Empire was the largest the world had known. It was built in the mid-sixth century BCE by King Cyrus, who seems to have been a follower of Ahura Mazda. He and the succeeding Achaemenid kings left no written mention of the prophet Zarathushtra. However, there are remnants of Zoroastrian-like fire holders and some references in inscriptions to Ahura Mazda. Darius the Great, a successor to Cyrus, claimed that Ahura Mazda had created the earth, the sky, and humans, and had made Darius the king to protect the world against wrongdoing. Cyrus's reign was noted for its religious tolerance as well as its power and wealth. The Jewish poet Second Isaiah (Isaiah 45:1) proclaimed him "God's anointed," for he released the Jews from their Babylonian exile, authorized their return to Judea, and even gave them resources with which to rebuild their Temple.

The empire Cyrus created by far-reaching conquests stretched from the Indus Valley to what is now Greece. The Jews within this territory were allowed to practice their own religion but seem to have adopted certain Zoroastrian beliefs, such as the belief that there is an evil aspect in life, an immortal soul, reward or punishment in an afterlife, and final resurrection of the body at the apocalypse — for these doctrines were absent from earlier Judaic religion. From Judaism, they may have passed indirectly into Christianity and Islam.

The spiritual tradition of devotion to Ahura Mazda was severely threatened by the 331 BCE invasion of Alexander, known as "The Great" in the West but "The Accursed" in Iran. According to Zoroastrian traditions, he ransacked the beautiful capital of Persepolis, destroying fire temples, burning the library containing the holy scriptures of Zarathushtra, and killing so many Zoroastrian priests that oral transmission of many scriptures was lost. It is thought that the Gathas of Zarathushtra survived only because many people knew them by heart.

Two centuries later Zoroastrianism was re-established in a shrunken Iranian empire by the Parthians, who ruled for almost four hundred years to 224 CE. Under the Parthians the surviving revealed teachings of Zoroastrianism were reassembled as the **Avesta**, or "holy texts." Then under the Sassanids of the third to mid-seventh centuries CE, Zoroastrianism came to the fore as the state religion, serving the aristocracy of Iran, and was thus one of the major religions of the ancient world.

However, a major threat to Zoroastrianism came from the spread of Islam. Arabic Muslims defeated the Zoroastrian Iranian forces, and when Mongols also invaded from the east, beginning in the thirteenth century, they were gradually converted to Islam rather than Zoroastrianism. Islam is said to have had the appeal of a new and living faith.

A number of Persian Zoroastrians avoided conversion to Islam by migrating to western India, whose spiritual origins were similar to their own. In India they were called **Parsis** (people from Pars province in Iran). The sacred fire they consecrated on reaching India is said to have been kept burning continuously ever since. Its temple in Udwada near Bombay is a major pilgrimage spot for Parsis. Some also migrated to what is now Pakistan.

The numbers of Zoroastrians remaining in Iran dwindled over the centuries under Muslim dominance. Even when Zoroastrians had become a minority in Iran, detailed instructions about the rituals and customs of the faith were preserved in a vast new literature, the **Pahlavi** texts written or translated in Middle Persian from about the ninth century CE. A small community of believers still survives in Iran.

Today, India — particularly the Bombay area — is the major center of Zoroastrian population, but whether it is also the repository of the purest surviving Zoroastrian teachings is a matter of debate. From the fifteenth to seventeenth centuries, the Parsis sent emissaries with many questions to their remaining counterparts in Persia, for those in India were unsure of numerous aspects of their religious tradition. Zoroastrianism in India seems to have been affected by surrounding religious traditions — such as Hinduism, Buddhism, and Christianity — and from the nineteenth century onward, by modern spiritual movements such as theosophy. The degree to which Parsis — as well as contemporary Zoroastrians elsewhere — still carry the original teachings of Zarathushtra is a subject of considerable debate.

Zoroastrian teachings

After Zarathushtra's death, his teachings seem to have been merged with earlier polytheistic trends. Today there is uncertainty about exactly what he taught, but enough is known that his theology can be sketched, along with its later transformations.

The primacy of Ahura Mazda

Zarathushtra is considered the first of the monotheists of the Western traditions, in the sense that he elevated one god above all others worshipped by the earlier Iranians. His mystical visions convinced him that there is only one divine being who creates and orders the universe. This God, Ahura Mazda, is referred to as masculine. It is he who creates all good things, gives life, "pours out His Holy Wisdom on every thing that lives," is eternal, mighty, and bountiful, "most worthy to be loved, radiant in action, Lord of Life and Truth."[3]

In the *Gathas* Zarathushtra makes impassioned pleas to Ahura Mazda to make him a more fit spiritual vehicle, so that he can "dedicate to Mazda the life-breath of his whole being."[4] He asks for Ahura Mazda's guidance in the mission of protecting the selfless, voluntarily poor devotees, "the poor in spirit, the meek and lowly of heart, who are Thine." He particularly emphasizes the need for clear thought in this mission:

O Lord of Life, we long for Thy mighty Fire of Thought which is an enduring, blazing Flame bringing clear guidance and joy to the true believer, but as for the destruction-loving, this quickening Flame overcomes his evil in a flash.[5]

O Lord of Life and Wisdom, I will forever uphold Thy Divine Law and Thy Good Mind. Teach me Thyself, through Thy spoken Word which springs from the Spirit, and with Thy very own Mouth, whence life first came into being.

Gatha Ahunavaiti, Yasna 28:11

Although Zarathushtra perceived Ahura Mazda as the one Eternal Being, he also described six divine powers that radiate from the godhead. They are Vohu Manah (The Good Mind), Asha Vahishta (Order, Eternal Truth, Righteousness), Khshathra Vairya (Absolute Power), Armaiti (Devotion), Haurvatat (Perfection), and Ameretat (Immortality).

After the prophet's death, these six attributes were personified as beautiful luminous beings, and uttering their names was thought to bring great power. These "Holy Immortals," or **Amesha Spenta**, are chief among the **Yazata**, or angels, who bring light to the earth, and thus are referred to as archangels by some scholars. The Amesha Spenta preside over specific aspects of the material world, which is created and ruled by Ahura Mazda — the people, animals, fire, metals, earth, water, and plants. To draw closer to Ahura Mazda and the radiant Amesha Spenta, humans are encouraged to curb their greed for consuming more of everything, to be moderate in their behaviors, to be unselfish, and to develop a feeling of kindness toward all, as "supporters and helpers of the world."[6]

The Yazata also include many of the deities worshipped by the earlier Iranians. Prominent among the Yazata is Sraosha, the guardian spirit of humankind, the messenger carrying prayers from humans to Ahura Mazda, and the model of obedient listening and service to the Divine. In the Gathas Zarathushtra invokes this quality of divine obedience as the highest of all traits. Another frequently mentioned Yazata is the popular Mithra, guardian of the light, protector of the truth, and bestower of wealth.

The choice between good and evil

In addition to adoring the good creator, Zarathushtra wrestled with the problem of evil. Precisely where evil comes from and whether it is a being, such as Satan, is controversial in contemporary interpretations of the Gathas. Many Western scholars describe Zarathushtra's theology as cosmic dualism, with Ahura Mazda opposed by a dark force of equal power. Others feel that this is a later development in Zoroastrianism and that the original teaching was that all life is naturally subject to creation and destruction. Both activities are under the control of Ahura Mazda, of whom one pole is the **Spenta Mainyu**, which sustains life, and the other pole is **Angra Mainyu**, which destroys. According to these scholars, during the Sasanian period (226–631 CE) Ahura Mazda became totally identified with the sustaining, increasing, life-giving power, leaving the destroying, chaos-producing power as a separate force. But even in this view, Angra Mainyu's destructive power is limited and will last only until the final resurrection of the people and renovation of the world. At that time, all evil will be destroyed. Zarathushtra seemed to feel that Ahura Mazda had revealed truth to him so that people could be empowered to work toward the final triumph of good. In this ultimate battle, the Gathas suggest, a supremely good man will come to embody righteousness and drive evil from the earth. Evil, Zarathushtra asserts, is not all-powerful or eternal, but to assure the victory of good over evil, humans must dedicate themselves as spiritual warriors on the side of Spenta Mainyu.

Yasna 30 is Zarathushtra's sermon on the origin of evil. In part, he states:

Yes, there are two fundamental spirits, twins which are renowned to be in conflict. In thought and in word, in action, they are two: the good and the bad. And between these two, the beneficent have correctly chosen, not the maleficent.

Furthermore, when these two spirits first came together, they created life and death, and how, at the end, the worst existence shall be for the deceitful but the best thinking for the truthful person....

The gods did not at all choose correctly between these two, since the deceptive one approached them as they were deliberating. Since they chose the worst thought, they then rushed into fury, with which they have afflicted the world and mankind.[7]

From the theosophical point of view, the Twin Mainyu are allegories for the two aspects of the human mind, rather than actual beings. In either interpretation, human beings are given the free will and mental capacity to choose between the two powers. In their thoughts, words, and deeds, they can grow in love, devotion, and service, or they can contribute to evil.

Zarathushtra felt that non-loving acts in the name of religion aided the cause of evil. He railed against worship of the Daevas, using the old word for the "shining gods" for what he considered dark forces and magic, and selfish ritualism. It is not clear precisely what gods and practices he was referring to, but the cult of Indra, for instance, was often bloody and violent. The *Gathas* include verses such as these directed at followers of what he termed the *Druj* (the Lie):

Let none of you, therefore, give ear to the unholy incantations and evil doctrines of the Follower of the Druj, for in truth he will sacrifice the home, the town, the province and the country to destruction and death.[8]

Ahura Mazda is symbolically represented as a human-like figure with the wings of a great bird, holding a ring representing authority with one hand and giving blessings with the other. The same image is often used to indicate humanity's spiritual nature.

Heaven and hell

At death, Zoroastrians believe each of us is judged according to the total goodness or evilness of our thoughts, words, and deeds. The greater the goodness, the wider the bridge to heaven, the House of Heavenly Song, the Kingdom of Light where the souls of the righteous reside. The greater the accumulated evil, the narrower the bridge, until it is so narrow that souls cannot cross. They fall into hell, House of the Lie, a murky, woeful place.

Some Zoroastrians interpret this scenario allegorically and feel that it applies to this life as well as the next. Tehmurasp Rustamji Sethna, for instance, explains that:

> When a man's actions are good he has self confidence and usually people say he has nothing to worry, his road is clear. On the other hand, if a man's actions are bad, it is usually said he is following a precarious path and any moment he will fall.[9]

Those who cross the bridge to arrive at the gates of heaven are met by the light and truth of Ahura Mazda, symbolically represented as angels. Once the soul's evil actions are weighed against the good ones, it is conducted to the appropriate grade of heaven by a young woman whose beauty corresponds to the degree of one's goodness. She represents the sum of one's actions. It is not Ahura Mazda who judges and metes out reward or punishment. By the natural law, Asha, good deeds bring their own reward and evil deeds their just punishment. This doctrine is similar to that of karma in Hinduism, Jainism, and Buddhism, but rather than shifting the effects of one's life to reincarnation in another life, Zoroastrians feel that the effects of their actions will be felt in the present and in an after-life.

The final resurrection

There is no eternal hell in Zoroastrianism, for good is ultimately victorious. With the help of all individuals who choose goodness over evil, the world will gradually reach a state of perfection in which all souls, living or dead, are liberated forever from evil. This time is the **Frashokereti**, the "renovation" of the world in which all of creation is resurrected into perfected immortality. Thenceforth the world will:

> never grow old and never die, never decay and never perish, ever live and ever increase, and be master over its wish, when the dead will rise, when life and immortality will come, and the world will be restored.[10]

This renovation of the world is not the work of a single savior; it requires the contributions of many, many people. Zoroastrianism therefore places great emphasis on the moral responsibility of each person, for the good of the whole.

Environmental ethics

From ancient times, Zoroastrians have been taught a respect for the created world that is highly relevant today in the face of environmental destruction. Dr. Homi Dhalla explains:

> The devout Zoroastrian regards the elements of nature with the most profound

reverence. The Avestan texts clearly reflect this veneration for the earth, the air, the waters, and even plant life. In his daily prayers, he is reminded of the beauty and majesty of nature, and from nature he turns to nature's God. The Zoroastrian child, taught to revere nature, is aware of any act that could defile the elements.[11]

Harmony with all people and all of creation is an essential virtue and a source of strength, according to Zoroastrian teachings. One of the daily prayers is to the four directions. Turning in reverence to each of the compass points, Zoroastrians acknowledge that Ahura Mazda is present everywhere. Another daily prayer praises the energy pervading the earth, teaching which things bring it joy and which things cause it to suffer. Water is considered sacrosanct and essential to all of life; sacred texts detail requirements for maintaining its purity. Another text asserts reverence for the energy found in animals and humans, and proclaims the holiness of feeding and safeguarding the health of animals who help in agriculture and are

TEACHING STORY

The Fate Of The Soul After Death

After death, the soul hovers about the head of the body for three days and nights. The demons that seek to prey upon it are kept away by the purifying rituals the person had undertaken during its life. But if the person was impure and unrighteous, its soul cries in agony, "To what place shall I flee?" For the wicked soul there is no escape. Into its nostrils, as it were, blows a wretched stench. On the fourth day demons bind the wicked soul roughly and drag it to the Chinvat Bridge — the bridge of the separator. There a tribunal of divinities review its deeds. The bridge is like a sword, broad on one side and sharp on the other. If the soul's evil deeds outweigh its good deeds, the bridge turns sharp-side-up, and the soul falls into the abyss of hell to await the final day of judgment.

A hideous hag confronts the soul of the evil person. "O wicked one," she says, "I am the image of your own bad thoughts, bad words, and bad deeds — your own evil inner being. In life, you served evil gods. You gave no hospitality to the good people who were helping others; instead, you hated them and tried to humiliate them. When you saw others speaking piously, bearing true witness, and not taking bribes, you did the opposite. This foulness is your fate: Your food will be poisonous, and you cannot escape from this foul smell."

And what of the good and pure soul? As it hovers about the head of the body for three days after death, it experiences great joy and inhales the sweetest of fragrances, as if from flowering meadows. It, too, is conducted to the fearful Chinvat Bridge, but it is accompanied by Sraosha, the divinity of obedience, who protects it from the demons. When the soul reaches the bridge, the bridge presents its broad side — in fact, it becomes so broad that the soul crosses easily. On the other side it is met by the fairest of girls. When questioned by the soul, the girl answers, "I am your own good inner self — the beauty of your own thoughts, words, and deeds. When you saw those who mocked truth, worshipped evil gods, and oppressed others, you sat chanting the Gathas, worshipping Ahura Mazda, and giving hospitality to the just. You thus raised me to a higher place, making me even more beautiful." The soul then advances into the great happiness of Endless Light.

(A composite of accounts from many Zoroastrian texts)

In a fire temple, a Zoroastrian priest performs rites over a sacred fire, revered since ancient times, and wears a mask to avoid contaminating it with his breath.

themselves used as food. Frequent references are made to gratitude for the gifts of healing plants, and in one prayer the faithful ask these plants' forgiveness for any harm done to them. Yet other prayers speak appreciatively of the purity of air and wind. Throughout the Avesta, Zoroastrians are reminded to be careful trustees of nature, and the sacred recitations themselves are thought to carry powerful earth-purifying energy.

Spiritual practices

Zoroastrians do not have an ascetic tradition. They are called to work in the world to increase goodness, to hasten the Frashokereti. It is not sufficient to be good oneself. A Zoroastrian must actively resist evil and try to guide others toward good thoughts, words, and deeds, as Zarathushtra did, although not necessarily to convert them to the Zoroastrian religion. One scripture says, "The three greatest duties of mankind are to make an enemy a friend, to make a wicked person righteous, and to make an ignorant person wise."[12]

Rituals are major elements of Zoroastrian practice. One that is particularly important is the act of tying the sacred cord (**kusti**) around one's mid-section, traditionally performed at least five times a day. Symbolically, the faithful are girding themselves as soldiers for Ahura Mazda, strengthening their resolve to follow the spiritual path. All children are invested with the kusti and **sudreh** (sacred shirt) in a "New Birth" ceremony before the age of puberty, affirming their membership in the Zoroastrian community. The inclusion of both males and females in this ritual constrasts with the male-only Hindu tradition of the sacred thread, for women and men are treated equally in many ways within Zoroastrianism.

Untied, the kusti is shaken to discard all negative thoughts and experiences. While tying the kusti, the faithful recite a prayer to keep evil at bay, and also chant the most ancient and powerful of Mazdayasnan prayers: the *Ahuna-Vairya*. It pre-dated Zarathushtra, and according to legend, the prophet recited it to protect himself from the temptations of Angra Mainyu:

> *As the Master, so is the Judge to be chosen in accord with truth. Establish the power of acts arising from a life lived with good purpose, for Mazda and for the lord whom they made pastor of the poor.*[13]

In addition to dedication to the good and protection from evil, Zoroastrian rituals emphasize purification. Menstruating women are considered impure and cannot participate. Water is venerated as a means or symbol of purification, and the devout will often dip their fingers into water, apply it to their eyes and forehead, and raise their hands in prayer to Ahura Mazda. Parsis in Bombay do this with ocean water at the beaches; Zoroastrians living inland honor springs and even wells. It is a great sin to pollute water or to place anything dead in it.

As of old, the other element emphasized in Zoroastrian rituals is fire, long used in Indo–Iranian tradition for its purifying, transformative power. The physical fire is worshipped as a symbol of the divine Light of Ahura Mazda, for the Avesta states that Ahura Mazda is Light. Dastur (High Priest) Framroze A. Bode explains this symbolic worship:

Zoroastrians tie the sacred cord (kusti) over the sacred shirt (sudreh) for protection against evil, within and without.

Zarathushtra's followers are ordinarily known as fire-worshippers, but they do not worship the physical fire of wood. Athra-Fire is universal ethereal energy, breath, life, heat and radiance. It is the flame of consciousness which burns in each and every heart. It is the light of reason in every mind and the glow of the pure emotion of love. In the symbol of Fire is the reverence for all life. The outer symbol of Fire reminds one of the inner Divine Spark in the true temple of God in the human heart.[14]

Living Zoroastrianism

Tina Mehta, mother of two grown children, grew up in Calcutta in a Zoroastrian family but only later began to understand the deeper meanings of her religion. In London, she taught Zoroastrian Studies and worked as a counselor to AIDS patients and drug addicts. She and her husband escaped from Kuwait the day before its occupation by Iraq; they are now living in Calcutta again.

"As children, we were taken once a year to the river to revere the waters. There is an angel for the waters; there's an angel for the plants. Each of God's seven creations — the sky, the waters, the earth, the plants, the animals, man, and fire — each has a fravashi (eternal spirit). They also have specific angelic spiritual aspects. And all together, they make up the realm of Ahura Mazda. We see them through God's creations.

Because we are brought up revering these various creations, we are very reluctant to pollute them, because we would then be polluting the angels, and therefore God. When I went swimming with my other friends who were non-Zoroastrians and they wanted to have a pee in the water, I couldn't because I was brought up believing that I shouldn't pollute the water. It was a joke to them: 'How is your pee going to destroy the whole river?' But I had been brought here to revere the water and I knew it just wasn't right somehow.

I used to resent being taken to the river to pay reverence. I thought, 'This is ridiculous.' And yet now I am very grateful I did that, because now I can understand when they are talking about environmental issues how important it is to actually revere the river because we would be less likely to pollute it. The same with the air and the plants. There are prayers where we apologize to animals and plants when we actually use them for food or for rituals. We do have to eat, but we eat with respect for the animal or plant that is giving its life to us.

As in the old days, we recognize that there are lots of creatures outside that could do you harm. Zoroastrian homes today still put lime powder — or things like Ajax — in little designs near the doorstep, to remind us that anything that is hurtful to the body, mind, or spirit should stay away and that whatever enters should enter with a good thought. When we've had a bad day, say at work, we see this marking and we remember that when we enter the home we don't bring that bad thought and bad feeling inside.

Sounds are also very important to us. That is why prayers in the Zoroastrian tradition are recited aloud. If there have been any bad sounds we overcome them with good sounds. If we have had a row in the house, then we counteract that aura of the row with good thoughts and good words. The mantric words act as a deterrent to evil sounds that have been uttered.

I think the work that is going on now (studying the historic links between Zoroastrianism and Judaism, Christianity, and Islam) will unify people. We have to realize that our antecedent is really one. Somehow that hasn't got through — we are in a state of considering each one as being different and separate. It's like three brothers just looking the other way. It must be very painful to the Father."

To be in the presence of fire is also thought to be a powerful meditative and purifying practice. Ervad Godrej Dinshawji Sidhwa, a Pakistan-based lecturer on Zoroastrian theology and history, explains from a theosophical perspective:

We focus our wandering thoughts and concentrate our mind on Fire when offering our daily prayers. We merely regard Fire as a real emblem of His refulgence, glory and light. The Sacred Fire burning in a Fire-Temple serves as a perpetual monitor to a Zoroastrian standing before it to preserve piety, purity, truthfulness, humility and brotherhood. It purifies everything. Bathed in its rays, we can purify our own body, mind and soul thereby.[15]

Only Zoroastrians can enter a fire temple, and within the temple, certain areas are accessible only to priests in a highly elevated state of purity. This restriction is explained as necessary to preserve the purity of the spiritual vibrations and to protect the unprepared from their power.

When the physical body dies, Zoroastrians consign it to a Tower of Silence, a special circular building open at the top so that vultures can alight on the corpses to pick the bones clean. This is done to avoid polluting the earth with decaying flesh, which the birds dispose of within an hour or two. Once the bones are also bleached clean by exposure to the sun, they are placed in a central pit with no monuments, no distinctions between rich and poor, as together they crumble into dust. But the survivors do pray for the departed and continue to observe death anniversaries at which the *fravashi* of the deceased person is invoked. The fravashi is "the transcendental divine essence in a human,"[16] or "the highest and the eternal 'principle' in a human being."[17] It is thought to continually evolve toward perfection. The fravashi of the righteous help the living in their good works.

At seasonal festivals, the fravashis of all the great Zoroastrians of the past are honored by the community, and this continuing remembrance by the living is coveted as a kind of immortality. One of the most popular celebrations is the Festival of All Souls, when homes are cleaned for visits from the fravashis and the people celebrate both the birth and the revelation of Zarathushtra.

Towers of Silence – such as the one on this hilltop in Iran – are open to the sky so that carrion-eating birds can clean the bones of the dead to avoid polluting the earth with decaying flesh.

Zoroastrianism today

Few followers remain of this ancient way of combating evil with goodness. There are thought to be only about 130,000 living Zoroastrians. Conversion to the faith is not emphasized, partly because of a desire not to dilute the teachings or the identity as a distinct faith community. This issue is often debated, and there is some agreement that it is all right for outsiders to "accept" the Zoroastrian faith, if not to convert to it. In contemporary Iran, there is little incentive to convert, for Zoroastrians, like Jews and Christians (all "People of the Book" — of revealed scriptures), are tolerated but limited in their privileges under Muslim rule. Historically, however, many Muslims converted to Zoroastrianism during the last years of the Pahlavi dynasty. The International Mazdayasnan Order, centered in Eugene, Oregon, accepts converts, but it is an eclectic group founded by a Muslim Sufi. Some Zoroastrians in North America favor active conversion of non-Zoroastrians to the faith; others are opposed to proselytizing but favor the acceptance of those who are truly moved by personal religious experience to join the faith. It is the community that decides whether to accept converts.

During the twentieth century, there has been a significant migration of Zoroastrians out of both India and Iran to other countries. London, New York, Chicago, Boston, Los Angeles, and Vancouver are now home to groups of Zoroastrians who mingle socially and professionally with people of other religions but generally do not intermarry with them. Training is still available in Iran and India for the hereditary line of Zoroastrian priests, and there is considerable interest in preserving and understanding the tradition.

When the Parsis were influenced by Westernization and Protestant missionary activity, they became somewhat embarrassed about the mystical aspects of their faith. Some began reciting their prayers in English rather than the ancient Avestan language, and interpreting what they were doing as talking to God rather than uttering powerful sacred mantras. They tended to de-emphasize rituals and beliefs in an evil spirit and the end of the temporal world in favor of the more abstract philosophy and ethical standards of the *Gathas*.

The pendulum now seems to be swinging in the other direction. Twentieth-century religious historians, metaphysicians, and linguists have attempted to translate the ancient language, uncover the deeper significance behind the rituals, and sift out the origins of the tradition from the thousands of years of later accretions. Such efforts have brought a renewed sense of pride and appreciation within Zoroastrianism. It now appears unlikely that the Zoroastrian religion will soon disappear from the face of the earth it has so long tried to serve.

Suggested reading

Bode, Dastur Framroze Ardeshir, and Nanavutty, Piloo, *Songs of Zarathushtra: The Gathas*, translated from the *Avesta*, London: George Allen and Unwin, 1952. A theosophically oriented translation of the *Gathas* into English.

Boyce, Mary, *Zoroastrians: Their Religious Beliefs and Practices*, London: Routledge and Kegan Paul, 1985. Detailed historical information, beginning with the pre-Zarathushtran roots of the tradition.

Boyce, Mary, ed. and trans., *Textual Sources for the Study of Zoroastrianism*, Manchester, U.K.: Manchester University Press, 1984. Useful extracts from many sources, with a concise general introduction and interpretative material for each text.

Choksy, Jamsheed K., *Purity and Pollution in Zoroastrianism: Triumph over Evil*, Austin: University of Texas Press, 1989. A very readable analysis of purifying rituals as a key to the Zoroastrian view of life.

Hinnells, John R., *Zoroastrianism and the Parsis*, London: Ward Lock International, 1981. A readable, straightforward portrayal of Zoroastrian history, beliefs, and practices, with illustrations.

Insler, Stanley, *The Gathas of Zarathustra*, Leiden: E. J. Brill, 1975. An English translation approved by many current scholars.

Mehr, Farhang, *The Zoroastrian Tradition: An Introduction to the Ancient Wisdom of Zarathushtra*, New York: Amity House, 1989. Good discussion of the principles of the Gathic and Pahlavi texts by an Iranian economist living in the United States.

Mirza, Dastur Hormazdyar Kayoji, *Outlines of Parsi History*, Bombay: Dastur Hormazdyar Mirza, 1987. A scholarly summary of Zoroastrian religion, literature, ritual, and art from the Indian Parsi perspective.

Taraporewala, I. J. S., *The Religion of Zarathushtra*, Madras, India: Theosophical Publishing House, 1926. A mystical interpretation of Zoroastrian spirituality.

CHAPTER 9

JUDAISM

A Covenant with God

Judaism, which has no single founder, no central leader or group making theological decisions, is the diverse tradition associated with the Jewish people. This family can be defined either as a religious group or a national group.

In religious terms, Jews are those who experience their long and often difficult history as a continuing dialogue with God. According to one tradition, God offered to share the divine law with seventy nations, but the semi-nomadic tribes of Israel were the only people in the world to answer God's call, to enter into a living covenant with their creator. This call is still available to all peoples, Jews feel. In a religious sense, "Israel" refers to all those who answer the call, who acknowledge and strive to obey the one God, through the *Torah*, or "teaching," given to the patriarchs, Moses, and the prophets.

As a nation, "Israel" is a people who have been repeatedly dispersed and oppressed. After the horrors of the Holocaust, some Jews founded a homeland in the land of Israel where their ancestors had once walked. Other Jews live in communities around the world. Many who consider themselves Jews have been born into a Jewish ethnic identity but do not feel or practice a strong connection to Jewish religious traditions.

In this chapter we will focus on Judaism as that which Mordecai Kaplan calls "an evolving religious civilization," first by taking an overview of the history of the Jewish people and then by examining the religious concepts and practices that generally characterize the followers of Torah today.

A history of the Jewish People

The Jewish sense of history begins with the stories recounted in the Hebrew Bible or **Tanakh** (which Christians call "the Old Testament"). Biblical history begins with the creation of the world by a supreme deity, or God, and progresses through the patriarchs, matriarchs and Moses who spoke with God and led the people according to God's commandments, and the prophets who heard God's warnings to those who strayed from the commandments. But Jewish history does not end where the stories of the Tanakh end, about the second century BCE. After the holy center of Judaism, the Temple of Jerusalem, was captured and destroyed by the Romans in 70 CE, Jewish history is that of a dispersed people, finding unity in their evolving teachings and traditional practices, which were eventually codified in the great compendium of Jewish law and lore, the **Talmud**.

TORAH	The Five Books of Moses	NEVI'IM	The Prophets
בראשית	GENESIS	יהושע	JOSHUA
שמות	EXODUS	שופטים	JUDGES
ויקרא	LEVITICUS	שמואל א	I SAMUEL
במדבר	NUMBERS	שמואל ב	II SAMUEL
דברים	DEUTERONOMY	מלכים א	I KINGS
		מלכים ב	II KINGS
		ישעיה	ISIAH
		ירמיה	JEREMIAH
		יחזקאל	EZEKIEL

KETHUVIM	The Writings		
תהילים	PSALMS		The Twelve Minor Prophets
משלי	PROVERBS	הושע	HOSEA
איוב	JOB	יואל	JOEL
שיר השירים	THE SONG OF SONGS	עמוס	AMOS
רות	RUTH	עבדיה	OBADIAH
איכה	LAMENTATIONS	יונה	JONAH
קהלת	ECCLESIASTES	מיכה	MICAH
אסתר	ESTHER	נחום	NAHUM
דניאל	DANIEL	חבקוק	HABAKKUK
עזרא	EZRA	צפניה	ZEPHANIAH
נחמיה	NEHEMIAH	חגי	HAGGAI
דברי הימים א	I CHRONICLES	זכריה	ZECHARIAH
דברי הימים ב	II CHRONICLES	מלאכי	MALACHI

The Jewish Scriptures consist of the Torah (or Pentateuch), the Prophets, and the Writings. These books date roughly from the 12th to 2nd century BCE, and were written mostly in classical Hebrew. They are often referred to as Tanakh, an acronym from the first syllables of each division – Torah, Nev'im, Kethurim.

Biblical stories

Although knowledge of the early history of the children of Israel is based largely on the narratives of the Tanakh, scholars are uncertain of the historical accuracy of the accounts. Some of the people, events, and genealogies set forth cannot be verified by other evidence, such as archaeological findings or references to the Israelites in the writings of neighboring peoples. It may be that the Israelites were too small and loosely organized a group to be noted by historians of other cultures. No mention of Israel appears in other sources until about 1230 BCE, but biblical narratives and genealogies place Abraham, said to be the first patriarch of the Israelites, at about 1700 to 1900 BCE.

Jews hold the **Pentateuch**, the "five books of Moses" which appear at the beginning of the Tanakh, as the most sacred part of the scriptures. Traditionalists believe that these books were divinely revealed to Moses and written down by him as a single document. Some contemporary biblical researchers disagree. On the basis of clues such as the use of variant names for God, they speculate that these books were oral traditions reworked and set down later by several different sources with the intent of interpreting the formation of Israel from a religious point of view, as the results of God's actions in human history. The Pentateuch seems to have assumed its final form in the days of Ezra the Scribe (fifth century BCE).

JUDAISM

	2000 BCE — Abraham, the first patriarch 1900–1700 BCE?
	1800
	1600
	1400
Moses leads the Israelites out of bondage in Egypt 12th C BCE	**1200**
	1000 — David, King of Judah and Israel 1010–970 BCE?
	800 — King Solomon builds the First Temple 961–931 BCE
	600 — First Temple destroyed; Jews exiled to Babylon 586 BCE
	400 — Second Temple built 515 BCE
	Torah established 430 BCE: Ezra the Scribe
	200
	Hillel the Elder 30 BCE –10 CE
Development of rabbinic tradition 1st–4th C	**CE**
	200 — Jerusalem falls to the Romans 70 CE / Jewish Canon fixed c.90 / Mishnah compiled c.200
	400
	600 — Babylonian Talmud completed mid 6th C
	800
	1000
	1200 — Maimonides 1135–1204
	1400
The Inquisition begins 1480 / Mass expulsion of Jews from Spain 1492	Ghettos of Italy and Germany 1555 onward
	1600
The Baal Shem Tov 1700–1760 / The Enlightenment in Europe 1800s	**1800**
The Holocaust 1940–1945 / The Six-Day War 1967	**2000** — Nuremberg laws strips Jews of rights 1935 / Death camps established 1942 / Israel declared an independent state 1948

Some of the stories in the Pentateuch, such as the Creation, the Garden of Eden, the great flood, and the Tower of Babel, are similar to earlier Mesopotamian legends. In the narratives of the continuing history of the Israelites, only the last four books (First and Second Samuel and First and Second Kings) are thought to be edited directly from contemporary sources. Although the accuracy of many of the stories has not yet been independently documented, they are of great spiritual significance in Christianity and Islam as well as Judaism. They are also politically important, for along with the Talmud they later gave a scattered people a special sense of group identity.

FROM CREATION TO THE GOD OF ABRAHAM   The Hebrew Scriptures begin with a sweeping poetic account of the creation of heaven and earth by God in six days, from the time of "the earth being unformed and void, with darkness over the surface of the deep and a wind from (or: the spirit of) God sweeping over the water."[1] After creating the material universe, God created man and woman in the divine "image" or "likeness", placing them as masters of the earth, rulers of "the fish of the sea, the birds of the sky, and all the living things that creep on the earth."[2] In this account, God is portrayed as a transcendent Creator, without origins, gender, or form, a being utterly different from what has been created. Since Hebrew has no gender neuter pronouns, God is generally—though not always — described in male singular terms. This creation story (in Genesis 1 and 2:1–4) is attributed by scholars to the "priestly source," thought to be editors writing after the exile of the Jews to Babylon in 586 BCE.

A second, probably earlier, version of the creation story follows, beginning in Genesis 2:4. It is thought to be a contribution to the Scriptures from the "Yahwist Source," which used the word transliterated as "Yahweh" for the supreme male deity. Instead of presenting woman as the equal of man, it portrays her as an offshoot of Adam, the first man; she was formed from one of Adam's ribs to keep him company. This version has commonly been interpreted as blaming woman for the troubles of humanity, although this reading is not supported in the Hebrew manuscripts. According to the legend of Adam and Eve, originally God placed the first two humans in a garden paradise. The woman Eve ("mother of all the living") was promised wisdom by a serpent (later often interpreted as a symbol of Satan) to tempt her to taste the fruit of the tree of knowledge of good and evil, against God's command. She gave some to Adam as well. According to the legend, this ended their innocence. God cursed the serpent and the land and banished them from their garden; their lives were no longer paradisical nor were they immortal, for they no longer had access to the "tree of life."

The theme of exile reappears continually in the Hebrew Bible, and in later Jewish history the people are rendered homeless again and again. The biblical narratives emphasize that the people risk God's displeasure every time they stray from God's commands. They are repeatedly exiled from their spiritual home and continually seek to return to it.

A more optimistic interpretation developed later, however. This was the feeling that the Jewish people were spread throughout the world by God's will, for a sacred purpose: to be good citizens of whatever land they reside in, and to help raise the imperfect world back up to the condition of perfection in which God had created it. Israel would only find its way home when all of creation was lifted up. The

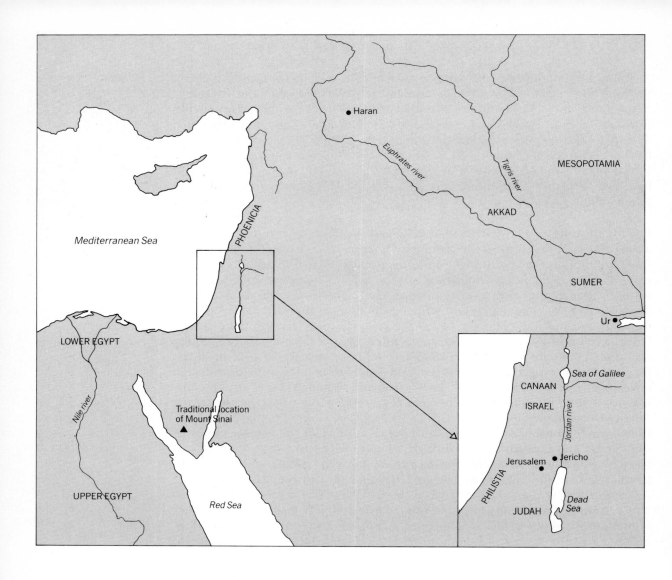

The map shows the ancient Near East, including the Mediterranean Sea, Phoenicia, Lower Egypt, Upper Egypt, Nile river, Red Sea, Traditional location of Mount Sinai, Mesopotamia, Akkad, Sumer, Haran, Ur, Euphrates river, Tigris river, and an inset of Canaan, Israel, Judah, Philistia, Jerusalem, Jericho, Jordan river, Sea of Galilee, and Dead Sea.

The Israelites identify themselves as a people whose ancestors Abraham and Sarah moved from Ur and Haran in Mesopotamia to Canaan; Abraham's grandson Jacob, called "Israel," resettled his large family in Egypt, where the Israelites were eventually treated as slaves.

rabbinic tradition which began in the first century CE and shaped Jewish theology into the modern period emphasized that the way out of exile was through wisdom and righteous living. Ethical commandments have their origin in God and if followed, will lead humanity back to a life in harmony with God.

Again and again, however, according to the scriptural stories, the people disobey God's will. One of the legends recounted concerns Noah, the sole righteous man of his generation. According to the narrator, who attributes thoughts and emotions to God, God despairs of the general wickedness of humans, regrets having created them, and sends a great flood "to destroy all flesh under the sky."[3] But with Noah, God establishes a covenant and gives directions for the building of an ark which saves Noah's family and two of each of God's creatures. God promises never again to destroy the created world or interfere with the established natural order, with the rainbow as a sign of this covenant "between me and all flesh that is on earth."[4]

God does, however, continue to intervene in history, according to the narrators. Many generations after Noah, for instance, the people are becoming so strong and ambitious that, according to the legend of the Tower of Babel, God limits their power by confounding their speech and scattering them across the earth.

After the legend of Noah, the narrative focuses on Abraham, Isaac, and Jacob (the "patriarchs"), and their wives, Sarah, Rebecca, Leah, and Rachel (the "matriarchs"). They were perhaps actual historical figures who seem to have lived as semi-nomadic pastoralists within a relatively small area of what is now called the Middle East. According to the biblical narratives, Abraham was called by God to leave his home in Ur and then in Haran, Mesopotamian trading centers, to journey with his wife Sarah to Canaan. He left the land of his father and also the religion of his father, whom oral tradition describes as not only a worshipper of the old gods but also a maker of statues devoted to them.

Abraham is held up as an example of obedience to God's commands. Without hesitation, he is said to undergo *circumcision* (cutting away of the foreskin of the penis) as an initiatory sacrifice, a sign of the covenant in which God agrees to be the divine protector of Abraham and his descendants, with all males to be likewise circumcised on the eighth day after birth.

After Abraham has a son, Ishmael, by the Egyptian slave woman Hagar, God blesses the one-hundred-year-old Abraham's ninety-year-old wife Sarah, saying that she will become the "mother of nations: the kings of many people shall spring from her." (Genesis 17:16). According to the biblical account, Sarah does indeed give birth to a son, Isaac, and then insists that Ishmael and Hagar be banished to the wilderness. God supports this demand, assuring Abraham that he will be father of two nations — one line through Isaac (to become the Israelites) and one through Ishmael (whom Muslims consider their ancestor).

God then tests Abraham by asking him to sacrifice his son Isaac. When the patriarch prepares to comply, the Lord stops him, satisfied that "now I know that you fear God."[5] The Hebrew word *yirah*, usually translated as "fear" of God, also means "awe of God's greatness," or what Rabbi Lawrence Kushner calls "trembling in the presence of ultimate holiness."[6]

Scholars disagree on whether pure monotheism — the worship of a single God of the universe, exclusive of any other divine beings — was encouraged by the early patriarchs, or "fathers," as they are simply called in Hebrew. Many names for divinity are used in the early scriptures, and some researchers consider them names of separate gods. It is known that the religion of the Canaanites had some influence on that of the Israelites. The Canaanites were polytheistic, with highly developed mythology and ritual directed largely to agricultural fertility.

As is common in the growth of any new religion, elements of the older faiths of the area were incorporated into or adapted to the new one. However, the ultimate thrust of Judaism was rejection of the gods of surrounding peoples. The Israelites came to see themselves as having been chosen by a single divine Patron. In their patriarchal culture, this God was perceived as a ruler in a close relationship to the people, like a parent to children, or a sovereign to vassals. At first Israel's God may have been perceived as a private tribal god, later known as the supreme and only deity of the universe.

ISRAEL'S BIRTH IN STRUGGLE It is also unclear who the people of the biblical narratives were. Some scholars think the word "Hebrew" is derived from the generic term *habiru*, used for the low-class landless people who lived as outlaws and were

The settled agricultural peoples of Canaan paid homage to a high male god, called El, and an earlier Great Mother Goddess (Ishtar, disguised as his consort). The Goddess (shown here), associated with vegetation, agricultural knowledge, and abundance, was worshipped at asherahs, sacred tree-symbol altar poles, which the Israelites destroyed.

often hired as mercenaries. Others point to *ibri* as the biblical word for Hebrew, meaning "children of Eber," an ethnic term. But because of frequent moving and inter-marrying, the Israelites were actually of mixed ethnic stock, including Hebrew, Aramean, and Canaanite. The word **Semite** is a modern linguistic term applied to Jews, Arabs, and others of eastern Mediterranean origin whose languages are classified as Semitic; it is often inaccurately used as a racial designation.

According to the genealogies set forth in the Pentateuch, the people who became known as Israelites were the offspring of Israel (first called Jacob), grandson of Abraham. Jacob received the new name after wrestling all night with a being who turned out to be an angel of God. "Israel" means "the one who struggled with God."

This story in which a human being struggles and finally is reborn at a higher level of spirituality has been taken as a metaphor for the spiritual evolution of the people Israel. As a result of the struggle, Israel the patriarch receives not only a new name but also the promise that many nations will be born from him. The nation Israel — "the smallest of peoples"[7] — is perceived as the spiritual center for the world to grow toward God. This is its destiny, though Jews do not feel that it has yet been fulfilled.

EGYPT: BONDAGE AND EXODUS Jacob is said to have had one daughter and twelve sons by his two wives and their two maidservants. The twelve sons became the heads of the twelve tribes of Israel. The whole group left Canaan for Goshen in Egypt during a famine. At first they were well treated, but their numbers multiplied as prophesied, and the Egyptian Pharaohs are said to have become worried that they might pose an internal political threat. To keep them from becoming too powerful, the reigning Pharaoh ordered that they be turned into slaves for massive construction projects. To further curb the population, the Pharaoh ordered midwives to kill all boy babies born to the Israelite women.

One who escaped this fate was Moses, who was raised in the palace by the Pharaoh's own daughter. He is said to have fled the country after killing an Egyptian overseer who was beating an Israelite worker. While he lived in exile in Midian, the oppression of the Israelites in Egypt grew worse and worse.

According to the scriptural book of Exodus, Moses was chosen by God to defy the Pharaoh and lead the people out of bondage, out of Egypt. While he was tending his father-in-law's flocks on Mount Sinai, an angel of God appeared to him from within a bush blazing with fire but not consumed by it. God called to him out of the bush and yet cautioned, "Do not come closer. Remove your sandals from your feet, for the place on which you stand is holy ground."[8] When God told Moses to go rescue "My people, the Israelites, from Egypt,"[9] Moses demurred, but God insisted, "I will be with you."[10] And when Moses asked how to explain to the Israelites who sent him to rescue them, God said:

> *Thus you shall say to the Israelites, "Ehyeh [I Am] sent me to you. … The Lord, the God of your fathers, the God of Abraham, the God of Isaac, and the God of Jacob, has sent me to you."*[11]

The word given in this biblical translation as "Lord" is considered too sacred to be pronounced. In the ancient scriptures it is rendered only in consonants as YHWH or YHVH; the pronunciation of the vowels is not known. According to the scriptures, this ineffable name and this identity were first revealed to Moses.

According to the legend of Exodus, God empowered Moses to hold back the waters of the Red Sea to let the children of Israel pass through, and then drown the pursuing Egyptians in the returning waters. (Hebrew ms 6 Haggadah.)

With his brother Aaron to act as spokesperson, Moses did indeed return to Egypt. Many chapters of Exodus recount miracles used to convince the stubborn Pharaoh to let the people go into the wilderness to worship their God. These signs included a rod that turned into a serpent, plagues of locusts, flies and frogs, animal diseases, a terrible storm, lasting darkness, and finally, the killing by the Lord of all firstborn children and creatures. The Israelites were spared this fate, marking their doors with the blood of a slaughtered lamb so that the Lord would pass over them. At this, the Pharaoh at last let the Israelites go. The redemption from bondage by the special protection of the Lord has served ever since as a central theme in Judaism.

A stone inscription, the Merneptah Stele, written for the Egyptian Pharaoh Merneptah, places the Hewbrews as being either in the desert between Egypt and Canaan or in Canaan during the years 1250–1300 BCE. According to the scriptural account, the Lord's presence led the Israelites, manifesting as a pillar of cloud by day and a pillar of fire by night. The armies of the deceitful Pharaoh pursued them until the famous scene in which Moses stretched his rod toward the sea and God caused an east wind to blow all night, dividing the waters so that the Israelites could pass through safely on a dry seabed. As the Egyptians tried to follow, God told Moses again to hold out his arm over the sea, and the walls of water came crashing down on them, drowning every one.

FROM THE WILDERNESS TO CANAAN According to the Pentateuch, God told Moses that he would lead the people back to Canaan. First, however, it was necessary to travel to the holy Mount Sinai to re-establish the covenant between God and the people. The Lord is said to have descended to its summit in a terrifying show of lightning, thunder, fire, smoke, and trumpeting. God is said to have then given the people through Moses a set of rules for righteous living, later called the **Torah**. Among them are the Ten Commandments. God also gave a set of social norms, prescribed religious feasts, and detailed instructions for the construction of a portable tabernacle with a holy ark, **The Ark of the Covenant**, in which to keep the stone tablets on which God inscribed the commandments.

THE TEN COMMANDMENTS

"I am the Lord your God who brought you out of Egypt, out of the land of slavery. You shall have no other god to set against me.

You shall not make a carved image for yourself nor the likeness of anything in the heavens above, or on the earth below, or in the waters under the earth.

You shall not bow down to them or worship them; for I, the Lord your God, am a jealous god. I punish the children for the sins of the fathers to the third and fourth generations of those who hate me. But I keep faith with thousands, with those who love me and keep my commandments.

You shall not make wrong use of the name of the Lord your God; the Lord will not leave unpunished the man who misuses his name.

Remember to keep the sabbath day holy. You have six days to labor and do all your work. But the seventh day is a sabbath of the Lord your God; that day you shall not do any work, you, your son or your daughter, your slave or your slave-girl, your cattle or the alien within your gates; for in six days the Lord made heaven and earth, the sea, and all that is in them, and on the seventh day he rested. Therefore the Lord blessed the sabbath day and declared it holy.

Honor your father and your mother, that you may live long in the land which the Lord your God is giving you.

You shall not commit murder.

You shall not commit adultery.

You shall not steal.

You shall not give false evidence against your neighbor.

You shall not covet your neighbor's house; you shall not covet your neighbor's wife, his slave, his slave-girl, his ox, his ass, or anything that belongs to him."

Exodus 20: 2–17

During the forty-day period while Moses was on the mountain receiving these instructions, the people who had just agreed to a holy covenant with God became disturbed and impatient. The biblical account says that under Aaron's reluctant supervision, they melted down their gold jewelry and cast it into the form of a golden calf, practicing what the authors of the biblical narratives considered idol-worship, which had been explicitly forbidden by God. Moses is said to have been so outraged by their idolatry that he smashed the stone tablets and destroyed the idol. He ordered the only people still siding with YHWH, the Levites, to slay three thousand of those who had strayed.

God's presence abided with the Israelites, wandering or stationary, in the portable Ark of the Covenant, which was said to house the tablets of Moses. This third century CE painting from the Dura Europos Synagogue shows the Ark leaving the land of the Philistines. They had captured the Ark but sent it back after being cursed by bubonic plague.

After another forty-day meeting with God on the summit of Mount Sinai, Moses again returned with stone tablets on which God had inscribed the commandments. Moses's face was said to be so radiant from his encounter with God that he had to veil his face. Aaron and his sons were invested as priests, the tabernacle was constructed as directed, and the people set off for the land of Canaan, with the Presence of the Lord filling the tabernacle.

Even with the powerful presence of the Ark they carried, the Israelites had to wander forty years through the desert before they could re-enter the promised land, fertile Canaan, which at that time belonged to other peoples. The long sojourn in the wilderness is a familiar metaphor in the spiritual search. Faith is continually tested by difficulties. But even in the wilderness, the Israelites' God did not forsake them. Every day they found their daily bread scattered on the ground, in the form of an unknown food which they named *manna*.

Through the miraculous help of God, they at last captured the walled city of Jericho and fought many battles against the kings and tribes of Canaan. Archaeological evidence indicates that every Canaanite town was destroyed from one to four times between the thirteenth and eleventh centuries BCE, though the identity of the conquerors is not known. At Sinai, God had vowed to oust the inhabitants of the lands into which the Israelites advanced, warning them against adopting the local spiritual practices: "No, you must tear down their altars, smash their pillars, and cut down their sacred posts."[12] The editors of the scriptures clearly considered the "heathen" religions of other people spiritually invalid and morally inferior to their own. But the Israelites' attention to their God was not absolute.

From The Hewbrew Bible: David and Goliath

David, the youngest son of Jesse of Bethlehem, was just a bright-eyed, ruddy-cheeked shepherd, but from the time that he was secretly anointed by the prophet Samuel as the future king of Israel, the Power of the living God was with him. His father had become feeble, so David was tending Jesse's flocks while his three elder brothers were doing battle with the Philistines in King Saul's Israelite army.

One day Jesse asked David to carry some food to his brothers and their commanding officer and to bring back news from the front. When David arrived at the battlefield, he learned that every day, Goliath, the champion of the Philistines, came out of the Philistine encampment to challenge the Israelites to send one man out to do battle with him. Goliath's challenge: If any Israelite could kill him in a fair one-to-one fight, the Philistines would surrender to the Israelites and become their slaves. If the Israelite lost, the Israelites would become slaves of the Philistines.

No Israelite had dared to take up this challenge, for Goliath was a giant of a man. He stood over nine feet tall, wore heavy bronze armor, and carried a massive spear. David alone was undismayed. He presented himself to King Saul and said, according to the biblical account,

"Do not lose heart, sir, I will go and fight this Philistine." Saul answered, "You cannot go and fight with this Philistine; you are only a lad, and he has been a fighting man all his life." David said to Saul, "Sir, I am my father's shepherd; when a lion or bear comes and carries off a sheep from the flock, I go after it and attack it and rescue the victim from its jaws. Then if it turns on me, I seize it by the beard and batter it to death. Lions I have killed and bears, and this uncircumcised Philistine will fare no better than they; he has defied the army of the living God. The Lord who saved me from the lion and the bear will save me from this Philistine." "Go then," said Saul, "and the Lord will be with you." He put his own tunic on David, placed a bronze helmet on his head and gave him a coat of mail to wear; he then fastened his sword on David over his tunic. But David hesitated, because he had not tried them, and said to Saul, "I cannot go with these, because I have not tried them." So he took them off. Then he picked up his stick, chose five smooth stones from the brook and put them in a shepherd's bag which served as his pouch. He walked out to meet the Philistine with his sling in his hand.

The Philistine came on towards David, with his shield-bearer marching ahead; and he looked David up and down and had nothing but contempt for this handsome lad with his ruddy cheeks and bright eyes. He said to David, "Am I a dog that you come out against me with sticks?" And he swore at him in the name of his god. "Come on," he said, "and I will give your flesh to the birds and the beasts." David answered, "You have come against me with sword and spear and dagger, but I have come against you in the name of the Lord of Hosts, the God of the army of Israel which you have defied. The Lord will put you into my power this day; I will kill you and cut your head off and leave your carcass and the carcasses of the Philistines to the birds and the wild beasts; all the world shall know that there is a God in Israel. All those who are gathered here shall see that the Lord saves neither by sword nor spear; the battle is the Lord's, and he will put you all into our power."

When the Philistine began moving towards him again, David ran quickly to engage him. He put his hand into his bag, took out a stone, slung it, and struck the Philistine on the forehead. The stone sank into his forehead, and he fell flat on his face on the ground. So David proved the victor with his sling and stone; he struck Goliath down and gave him a mortal wound, though he had no sword. Then he ran to the Philistine and stood over him, and grasping his sword, he drew it out of the scabbard, dispatched him and cut off his head. The Philistines, when they saw that their hero was dead, turned and ran [but were killed by the pursuing Israelites]. … David took Goliath's head and carried it to Jerusalem.[13]

According to the scriptures, whenever they turned away from YHWH, forgetting or worshipping other gods, surrounding peoples found them easy prey.

THE FIRST TEMPLE OF JERUSALEM   It was David, who is remembered as Israel's greatest king, who brought the Ark to Jerusalem (former home of the old high god). As an obscure shepherd, David was chosen by the prophet Samuel to be anointed on the head and beard with oil, for thus were future kings found and divinely acknowledged in those times. Composer and singer of many famous Psalms, David was summoned to the court of the reigning king, Saul, to play soothing music whenever an evil spirit seized the king and to bear the king's arms. When Saul and his son were killed in battle, David was made king. By defeating or making allegiances with surrounding nations, David created the beginnings of a secure, prosperous Israelite empire. He made the captured city of Jerusalem its capital.

Under the reign of King Solomon (son of David), a great Temple was built in Jerusalem. It was to be a permanent home for the Ark of the Covenant, which was housed in the innermost sanctum, and a place for making the burnt offerings of animals, grain, and oil to the divine. There already existed an ancient practice among pre-Israelite peoples of using high places for altars where sacrifices were made to the gods. The Canaanite high god El had been worshipped thus on a rocky prominence just north of Jerusalem. Before David's death, he charged his son Solomon with the task of building a monumental temple to Yahweh there. According to the biblical account in 1 Kings, the great Temple erected under Solomon's supervision by 183,300 men was 90 feet (27.5 m) long, 30 feet (9 m) wide, and 45 feet (13.7 m) high, in a style similar to those found in nearby Canaanite shrines. After centuries of wandering worship, the Israelites now had a central, stationary place where God would be most present to them.

According to the scriptural account, Solomon dedicated the Temple by praying that God would grant all manner of serious requests (such as national prayers for forgiveness of sins and relief from famine, and even the prayers of foreigners), if the requests were made by sincere turning to God at the Temple or even in the direction of the Temple by captives in other countries. According to the biblical account, Solomon prayed:

> I have now built for You
> A stately House,
> A place where You
> May dwell forever....
> But will God really dwell on earth? Even the heavens to the uttermost reaches cannot contain You, how much less this House that I have built! Yet turn, O Lord my God, to the prayer and supplication of Your servant, and hear the cry and prayer which Your servant offers before You this day. May Your eyes be open day and night toward this House, toward the place of which You have said, "My name shall abide there."[14]

God is said to have appeared to Solomon after the fourteen-day Temple dedication ceremony and pledged, "I consecrate this House which you have built and I set My name there forever. My eyes and My heart shall ever be there."[15]

With this feeling of God's special presence, the Temple became the central focus of Judaism. But its builder, Solomon, also accumulated great personal wealth, at

A model of the Second Temple after enlargements by Herod, shortly before its destruction by the Romans. Once it was destroyed, images of the temple's facade expressed the messianic hope of the restoration of the holy land.

the expense of the people, and built altars to the gods of his wives, who came from other nations. This so angered the Lord, according to the scriptures, that he divided the kingdom after Solomon's death into Judah, with Jerusalem its capital, and Israel, to the north of Judah, with no permanent capital. Divided, neither prospered, and war became commonplace.

Under Ahab, a king of Israel who made his capital in Samaria, the situation became particularly grim, from the point of view of the scriptures. Ahab married the Phoenician princess Jezebel, an ardent worshipper of the Canaanite god Baal, and built altars to Baal and other Canaanite gods around the land. Jezebel herself is said to have destroyed altars to the God of Israel and to have attempted to slaughter all those who were faithful to this God.

At that point, the prophet Elijah appeared to demonstrate the supreme power of the Lord YHWH and to warn the people against worshipping other gods. The message from God that the people should worship him and end their evil ways was repeated by many prophets over the centuries. These prophets were men and women who had undergone transformational ordeals which made them instruments for the word of God. The "early prophets" such as Elijah focused on the sin of idolatry; the "later prophets" warned that social injustice and moral corruption would be the ruin of the Jewish state.

By the reign of King Hoshea of Israel, the kingdom was so corrupt and idolatrous that, in the scriptural interpretation, God permitted the strong kingdom of Assyria to overtake what was left of the small country. To sustain the population needs for its empire-building and keep Israel from rising again as a nation, Assyria carried off most of the Israelites to exile among the **Gentiles** (non-Jewish people, from the Latin word for nation). Most of the Israelites became dispersed within Assyria; these people who thenceforth lost a distinct ethnic identity are known as the "Ten Lost Tribes of Israel."

Judah maintained its independence, declining and continually warned of impending doom by its prophets, until King Nebuchadnezzar of Babylonia (which by then had taken over the Assyrian empire) captured Jerusalem. In 586 BCE the great walls of the holy city were battered down, and its buildings put to the torch by the Babylonians. The great Temple was emptied of its sacred treasures, the altar dismantled, and the building destroyed. Many Judeans were taken to exile in Babylonia, where they were thenceforth known as "Jews," since they were from Judah.

The prophets interpreted these events as reasonable punishment by God for Judah's wickedness. Nevertheless, Isaiah and a later anonymous prophet (known to historians as "Second Isaiah" or "Deutero-Isaiah") prophesied that God would soon usher in a new era of peace and justice among all peoples, from his holy temple in Jerusalem.

> *I never could forget you.*
> *See, I have engraved you*
> *On the palms of My hands...*
>
> *Isaiah 49: 15–16*

Return to Jerusalem

After fifty years of exile in Babylon, a small group of devoted Jews, probably fewer than fifty thousand, returned to their holy city. They were allowed to do so by the Persian King Cyrus. Second Isaiah called him the Messiah ("anointed one"). Cyrus authorized the rebuilding of the Temple, and it was completed in 515 BCE. He returned the thousands of vessels of silver and gold that Nebuchadnezzar had earlier stripped from the First Temple and these sacred treasures were used to adorn the Second Temple.

The Temple became the central symbol to a scattered Jewish nation, most of whom did not return to Jerusalem from Babylon, which was now their home (and were thenceforth said to be living in the *Diaspora*, from the Greek word for "disperse"). A new emphasis on Temple rites developed, with an hereditary priesthood tracing its ancestry to Aaron.

The priestly class, under the leadership of Ezra, a priest and a scribe, also undertook to revise, or redact, the stories of the people, editing the Pentateuch to reveal the hand of God. Some scholars think that it was these priestly editors who wrote the book of Genesis, glorifying the greatness and omnipotence of their God as creator of the universe.

The Torah was now established as the spiritual and secular foundation of the dispersed nation. In approximately 430 BCE, Ezra the scribe set the precedent of reading for hours from the Torah scrolls in a public square. These "five books of Moses" were accepted as a sacred covenant.

As the Jews lived under foreign rule — Persian, Greek, Parthian, and then Roman — Judaism became somewhat open to cross-cultural religious borrowings. Concepts of Satan, the angelic hierarchy, bodily resurrection, and the Day of Judgment are thought by some scholars to have made their way into Jewish belief from Zoroastrianism but were not uniformly accepted. Greek lifeways and thought were introduced into the Middle East by Alexander the Great in the fourth century BCE. Alexander had a friendly relationship with the Jews within his domain, and the rationalistic, humanistic influences of Hellenism led many wealthy and intellectual Jews, including the priests in Jerusalem, to adopt a Hellenistic attitude of scepticism rather than unquestioning belief.

Tension between traditionalists and those embracing Greek ways came to a head during the reign of Antiochus of Syria, the nation which then held political sovereignty over the land of Israel. Antiochus seems to have tried to emphasize political unity by forcing a single Hellenistic culture on all his subjects, insisting that they all worship the Greek god Zeus, of whom he was the worldly embodiment. He reportedly tried to force Greek ways on all Judea by abolishing the Torah as the Jewish constitution, burning copies of the Torah, killing families who circumcised their sons, building an altar to Zeus in the Temple in Jerusalem, and sacrificing a hog on it (in defiance of the Mosaic law against eating or touching dead pigs as unclean). The Maccabean rebellion, a revolt led by the Hasmon family of priests, won a degree of independence for Judea in 140 BCE, but the establishment of the kingdom of God on earth remained a dream.

Under the Hasmonean kings three main groups of Jews stood out in Judea. One was the **Sadducees**, priests and wealthy businesspeople, conservatives intent on preserving the letter of the law. The **Pharisees** were more liberal citizens from all classes who sought to study the applications of Torah to everyday life. A third group was uncompromising in their piety and their disgust with what they considered a corrupted priesthood. Some of them seem to have retreated to the desert wilderness next to the Dead Sea, where they joined or formed the **Essene** Brotherhood. Their leader was "The Teacher of Righteousness," a priest, reformer, and mystic whose name was not uttered. Scrolls discovered in Qumran at the northwest end of the Dead Sea in 1947 suggest that the Essenes emphasized monastic discipline, communal living, obedience, study, and spiritual preparation for the Day of Judgment they anticipated, the New Age when the "sons of light" would be victorious over the "sons of darkness."

Eventually the disagreements between the Sadducees and the Pharisees erupted into civil war. The Roman general Pompey was called in from Syria in 63 BCE to arbitrate the dispute, but he took over the country instead. There followed a period of oppressive Roman rule of Judea, with the colonized people heavily taxed.

Under Roman rule, popular belief grew that a Messiah would come at last to rescue the people from their sufferings. For example, a vision had reportedly been given to Daniel when the Jews were in exile in Babylon (but recorded centuries later in 164–167 BCE under the coercive rule of Antiochus). Daniel foresaw that one "like a human being" would come on heavenly clouds, and on him the white-haired, fiery-throned "Ancient of Days" would confer "everlasting dominion" over all people, a kingship "that shall not be destroyed."[16] By the first century CE, expectations had developed that through this Messiah, God would gather the chosen people and not only free them from oppression but also reinstate Jewish political sovereignty in the land of Israel. Then all nations would recognize that Israel's God is the God of all the world. The messianic end of the age, or end of the world, would be heralded by a period of great oppression and wickedness. Many felt that this time was surely at hand. As indicated below, there were some who felt that Jesus was the long-awaited Messiah.

The Essenes seem to have lived communally and ascetically, awaiting the final judgment in settlements such as this one excavated at Qumran, where ancient biblical scrolls were found hidden in caves.

Suffering from intolerable Roman oppression the Jews rose up in armed rebellion. After heroic resistance, the Jewish patriots were slaughtered in the holy walled city of Jerusalem in 70 CE. A second disastrous revolt followed in 132–136 CE. Ultimately, Jerusalem, including the second Temple, was reduced to ruins, along with all Judean towns. Those remaining Jews who had not been executed were forbidden to read Torah, observe the Sabbath, or circumcise their sons. None were allowed to enter Jerusalem when it was rebuilt as the Roman city Aelia Capitolina, except on the anniversary of the destruction of the Temple, when they could pay to lean against all that remained of it — the western wall — and lament the loss of their sacred home. Judea was renamed Palestine after the ancient Philistines. Judaism no longer had a physical heart or a geographic center.

Christianity diverges from Judaism

Judaism could have died then, as its people scattered throughout the Mediterranean countries and western Asia. One of the groups who survived the destruction of Judea were the rabbis, inheritors of the Pharisee tradition. They are the founders of the rabbinic, or post-biblical, direction in Judaism, which has defined virtually all forms of Jewish practice over the last two thousand years. Another was the messianic movement that had grown up around Jesus of Nazareth, later known as Christianity. Between them they have kept the teachings of the Tanakh vibrantly alive. Both Christianity and rabbinic Judaism used the Hebrew Bible as a foundation document, but from it they have developed in their own ways.

Little is known of how Jews responded to the life and teachings of Jesus during his lifetime. He was a Jew and frequently referred to biblical stories and points of view. The Christian Gospels portray him as a follower of the Jewish commandments; he taught in synagogues and in the Temple of Jerusalem. His followers called him the Messiah (meaning "anointed," and therefore "king"). Jews used this term for a longed-for charismatic leader whom they believed would cast off the yoke of foreign oppression and restore the kingdom of Israel to the heights it had known under King David.

The person most often considered a potential candidate for this role was Bar Kokhba, who led a brave but abortive attempt to free Judea after the destruction of the Sacred Temple. Jews were not looking for a savior in the sense that Christians pictured Jesus: as a suffering servant who was ushering in the spiritual kingdom of God. They continued to expect a human descendent of David who would literally restore Jewish political sovereignty and usher in an age of universal peace and brotherhood.

As time went on, the Christian tradition diverged farther and farther from its parent, which also continued to evolve separately, just as Buddhism diverged from Hinduism. Over the centuries, Christian–Jewish relationships have been strained by Christians' interpretation of Jesus's identity and also by anti-Jewish statements in the New Testament. Many contemporary biblical scholars feel that these statements were later interpolations which the followers of Jesus used to help distinguish Christianity from Judaism (a possibility to which we return in the next chapter). Christians who now seek to harmonize Christian–Jewish relationships feel that it is inappropriate to "blame" the Jews for not regarding Jesus as the Messiah, for it is possible that he may not have claimed that role for himself either. In any case, some Christian theologians are now willing to take into consideration the Jewish feeling that to put heavy emphasis on the person of Jesus takes attention away from Jesus's message and from God. Furthermore, Jesus's teachings had much in common with his Jewish context and links can also be inferred to reforms introduced by the Pharisees. For instance, the Pharisees did not see God as belonging only to Israel, but rather as the parent watching over and taking care of every individual. They addressed God by new names, such as *Abinu She-Bashamayim* ("Our Father who art in Heaven"), the same form of address by which Jesus reportedly taught his followers to pray to God (Matthew 6:9). The great Jewish thinker Martin Buber (1878–1965), speaking to Christians, reminds them that they worship the same God celebrated in the Tanakh:

> To you the book is a forecourt; to us it is the sanctuary. But in this place we can dwell together, and together listen to the voice that speaks there.[17]

The rabbinic tradition

The other group that survived the loss of Jerusalem were the inheritors of the Pharisee tradition: the **rabbis**, who were teachers, religious decision-makers, and creators of liturgical prayer. No longer were there priests or Temple for offering sacrifices. The substitute for animal sacrifice was liturgical prayer and ethical behavior. Without the Jerusalem Temple, the community itself gained new importance. The people met in **synagogues**, which simply means "meeting places," to read the

Torah and to worship communally, praying simply and directly to God, with little ceremony. A *minyan* — a quorum of ten adult males — had to be present for community worship.

Everyone was taught the basics of Torah as a matter of course, but many men also occupied themselves with deep study of the scriptures, from the age of five or six. Women were excluded from formal Torah study, because of notions of men's and women's different roles. Women's family responsibilities at home were considered primary for them; elsewhere they were to be subordinate to men. Literacy was highly valued for men, and this characteristic persisted through the centuries even in the midst of largely illiterate societies. It is said that in the afterlife one can see the Jewish sages still bent over their books studying. This is Paradise.

The revealed scriptures were closed; what remained was to interpret them as indications of God's word and will in history. This process continues to the present, giving Judaism a continually evolving quality in tandem with unalterable roots in the ancient books of Moses. Centering the religion in books and teachings rather than in a geographical location or a politically vulnerable priesthood has enabled the dispersed community to retain a sense of unity across time and space, as well as a common heritage of law, language, and practice.

The rabbis set themselves the task of thoroughly interpreting the Hebrew Scriptures. Their process of study, called **midrash**, yielded two types of interpretation: legal decisions, called **halakhah** ("the way to walk"), and non-legal teachings, called **haggadah** (folklore, sociological and historical knowledge, theological arguments, ritual traditions, sermons, and mystical teachings).

In addition to delving into the meanings of the written Torah, the rabbis undertook to apply the biblical teachings to their contemporary lives, in very different cultural circumstances than those of the ancients, and to interpret scripture in ways acceptable to contemporary values. The model for this delicate task of living interpretation had been set by Hillel the Elder, who lived from about 30 BCE to 10 CE, probably overlapping with the life of Jesus. He was known as a humble and pious scholar who stressed loving relationships, good deeds, and charity toward the less-advantaged. He also established a valuable set of rules for flexible interpretation of Torah.

What is hateful to you, do not do to your neighbor:
that is the entire Torah;
the rest is commentary;
go and learn it.

Hillel the Elder[18]

This process of midrash yielded a vast body of legal and spiritual literature, known in Jewish tradition as the oral Torah. According to rabbinical tradition, God gave Moses two versions of the Torah at Sinai: the written Torah, which appears in the five books of Moses, and the oral Torah, a larger set of teachings which was memorized and passed down through the generations all the way to the early rabbis. After the fixing of the Jewish canon — the scriptures admitted to the Tanakh, in about 90 CE — the rabbinical schools set out to systematize all the commentaries and the oral tradition, which was continually evolving on the basis of expanded and updated understandings of the original oral Torah. In about 200 CE, Judah the Prince completed a terse edition of legal teachings of the oral Torah which was thenceforth known as the **Mishnah**. Several centuries later, the Mishnah plus rabbis' commentaries on it were organized into the **Talmud** (meaning "study").

Midrash is still open-ended, for significant commentaries and commentaries upon commentaries have continued to arise over the centuries. No single voice has dominated this continual study of the Torah and its interpretations. Rabbis often disagreed in their interpretations. These disagreements, sometimes between rabbis from different centuries, are presented together. This continual interweaving of historical commentaries, as if all Jewry were present at a single marathon Torah-study event, has been a significant unifying factor for the far-flung, often persecuted Jewish population of the world.

In the hearty process of exegesis, the rabbis have actually introduced new ideas into Judaism, while claiming that they were merely revealing what already existed in the scriptures. Notions of the soul are not found in the Tanakh, but they do appear in the Talmud and Midrash. The way in which God is referred to and perceived also changes. In the early biblical narratives, the Lord appears to the patriarchs and Moses in dramatic forms, such as the burning bush and the smoking mountain. Later, the prophets are visited by angelic messengers and sometimes hear a divine inner voice speaking to them. In the rabbinical tradition God is presented in even more transcendent, less anthropomorphic ways. God's presence in the world, in relationship to the people, is called the **Shekhinah**, a feminine noun which often represents the nurturing aspect of God.

According to midrash, the Shekhinah came to the earth at creation but as a result of human wickedness she withdrew to the heavens, to be brought down by human acts of faithfulness, charity, and loving-kindness. God spoke to Moses from a burning thorn-bush, rather than some more lofty object, to demonstrate that there is no place where the Shekhinah cannot dwell. Sometimes the loving protection of the Shekhinah is depicted as a radiant, winged presence.

Judaism in the Middle Ages

In the early centuries of the Common Era, the land of Israel declined in population. While some Jews settled in other regions of the Roman Empire (North Africa, Egypt, Italy, Spain, Germany), larger numbers established themselves beyond the boundaries of Rome among the Zoroastrian Persians in Mesopotamia. The city of Babylon, which already had a sizeable Jewish population dating back to the biblical exile, became the major center of Jewish intellectual activity, a position it would hold well into the tenth century. While the Exilarch (the hereditary "ruler of the exiles"), a descendant of King David, served as political intermediary between his community and the non-Jewish authorities, the religious leadership was held by the Geonim, the appointed leaders of the two great Babylonian rabbinic academies. Under the leadership of the Geonim, the authoritative Babylonian Talmud received its final editing in the middle of the sixth century CE. A second Talmud, the Talmud of the Land of Israel, had been developed somewhat earlier, but since it is incomplete and relatively brief, this document is usually seen as secondary to the Babylonian Talmud.

Even when the Talmud was complete, the rabbinic enterprise continued. Seen as the pre-eminent legal authorities, the Geonim were often appealed to with difficult questions from far-flung Jewish communities. Their answers, which were considered binding on all Jews, and the questions themselves, became a new and enduring form of legal writing, *Responsa* literature, which continues up to the present. Under the leadership of the Geonim, the prayerbook also first took form, and Jewish learning was democratized through semi-annual public convocations at the academies.

The Babylonian Jewish community continued to flourish after the Muslim conquests of the late seventh century, and when Baghdad became the capital city of the great Abassid empire in the eighth century, Jewish life concentrated around that city as well. Jews were treated relatively well under Muslim rule. Like Christians, they were recognized as a "People of the Book," and were allowed to maintain their religious traditions and run their communities autonomously as long as they paid a substantial head tax in acknowledgment of their subordinate status. In Baghdad, as throughout the Muslim Middle East, many Jews were prosperous merchants, professionals and craftsmen. In the early Middle Ages, in fact, Jews tended to dominate international trade between Muslim and Christian realms because of their facility with languages and their ability to find supportive co-religionists in virtually any community.

Life under Muslim rule was also intellectually exciting for the Jewish community, which had rapidly adopted Arabic as its spoken language. During its early centuries, Islam was far advanced beyond Christian Europe in its explorations of science, medicine, philosophy, poetry, and the fine arts. Jews living in Muslim countries benefited from an atmosphere of cultural creativity and toleration, and themselves developed Jewish religious philosophy and Hebrew secular poetry. Many Jews were well-known physicians. Muslim Spain, in particular, where some Jews rose to high political position in Muslim courts, is renowned for its outstanding Hebrew poets and major philosophical and scientific Jewish writers.

From time to time, however, Jews were threatened by intolerant Muslim rulers and were forced to flee to other territories. The great scholar and physician Maimonides was forced to leave his ancestral home of Cordoba, Spain in the mid-twelfth century; he and his family eventually settled in Egypt. Considered one of the greatest of all Jewish intellectuals, Maimonides is particularly famous for his synthesis between reason and faith. In writings such as his *Guide of the Perplexed* he spoke on behalf of the rationality that had characterized Judaism since the dawning of the rabbinic age:

> *What is man's singular function here on earth? It is, simply, to contemplate abstract intellectual matters and to discover truth ... And the highest intellectual contemplation that man can develop is the knowledge of God and his unity.*[19]

Jews who lived in Christian countries were not exposed to the intellectual energy so vibrant in the Muslim world between the seventh and twelfth centuries. Christian Europe in those centuries was primarily a feudal agricultural society in which literacy mainly belonged to the Church. Jews, who were primarily merchants, were among the few town dwellers, and generally lived under charters of protection from the ruler of the area. In France and Germany, Jewish intellectual life flourished, but Christians assumed the financial functions. Jews became expendable, and throughout the later Middle Ages there is a steady pattern of expulsions of Jews from countries in which they had long lived.

The ultimate event of this kind was the expulsion of the Jews from Spain in 1492, when tens of thousands of Jews were forced to leave a country in which they had lived for over a thousand years. Some Jews fled to safety in Portugal or Italy, or in the Muslim realms of North Africa and the Ottoman Empire of Turkey. Others chose to convert to Christianity rather than to leave their homeland even though staying in Spain as *conversos* (converted Jews, also known to "old" Christians as *marranos*, or swine) would expose them to the dreaded Inquisition which had been established in Spain in 1482. The Inquisition represented the Roman Catholic Church, and its mission was to discover perceived heretics within the Christian community. It had no power over Jews, but it did have jurisdiction over the large numbers of Jews who had converted to Christianity, whether voluntarily or by force, and who might be practicing their religion in secret. The Inquisition, which had the power to torture the accused and to execute the convicted, continued to function in Spain and in Spanish territories, including those in the New World, well into the eighteenth century.

There was further deterioration of Jewish life in Western Europe in the sixteenth and seventeenth centuries. After 1555, those Jews who still remained in some cities of Italy and Germany were forced to live in **ghettos**, special Jewish-only quarters often walled in and locked at night and during Christian holy days to limit mixing between Christians and Jews. Despite the constriction and crowding, Jewish leaders ran the ghettos according to talmudic law, providing for the needs of the poor, and fostering Jewish study and scholarship.

During the later Middle Ages, Poland had become a haven for the expelled Jews of Western Europe. Jews were welcomed by Poland's feudal leaders who needed a middle class for economic development of their agricultural country. Jews were allowed freedom of residence and occupation in Poland, and they rapidly grew in numbers, finding in their new home an enclave of peace and prosperity. By the

According to the Spanish Inquisitors, the murder of hundreds of thousands of people – many of them marranos, *or "secret Jews" –* was an auto da fe, *an "act of faith" to rid the church of heretics.*

sixteenth and early seventeenth century Eastern Europe had become the major European center of Jewish life and scholarship. Jews lived an intensely religious life in villages and towns that were almost completely Jewish, speaking Yiddish, a distinctive Jewish language, based on the medieval German they had spoken in Western Europe, and written in Hebrew characters. In 1648, the situation changed drastically with the revolt against Polish rule by the Cossack peasants of the Ukraine. Associating Jewry with their Roman Catholic Polish oppressors, the Russian Orthodox Cossacks led terrible massacres against the Jews, which were followed by even more killing as Poland collapsed and passed from one foreign ruler to another.

In this time of despair in both Eastern and Western Europe, Jews were heavily taxed and ill-treated. Their longing for deliverance from danger, poverty, and oppression fueled the old messianic dream. Among the "pseudo-Messiahs" who rose to the occasion, the most famous was Shabbatai Tzevi (1626–1676) of Smyrna, a Turkish port. A rather unstable personality, he became convinced that it was his calling to be the Messiah. A young man named Nathan, who became his enthusiastic prophet, sent letters to Jews throughout Europe, Asia, and Africa announcing that the Messiah had at last appeared in his master. Many believed him and made provisions for their return to the Holy Land. However, when Tzevi entered the Ottoman Empire, he was arrested and put in jail. Given the choice of converting to Islam or being executed, he chose conversion and was given a government position. The shock to his supporters was terrible.

Enlightenment

The eighteenth-century European movement called the Enlightenment brought better conditions for the Jews in Western Europe. It played down tradition and authority in favor of tolerance, reason and material progress. In such a rational atmosphere, restrictions on Jews began to decrease. The French Revolution brought equality for the masses, including Jews living in France, and in the course of the nineteenth century this trend slowly spread to other European nations. For the first time since the period of the Roman Empire, Jews were granted citizenship rights in some Western European countries. Ghettos were torn down and some Jews even ascended to positions of prominence in Western European society. The Rothschild family, for instance, became international financiers, benefactors, and patrons of the arts. Moses Mendelssohn (1729–1786), a German Jew, founded a movement known as the Jewish Enlightenment, whose goal was to integrate Jews more fully into European culture. In his book *Jerusalem*, Mendelssohn urged his fellow Jews to learn German and to dress and comport themselves as non-Jews, at the same time as he urged the governments of his time to separate Church and State, and to tolerate differences in beliefs among their citizens. Mendelssohn believed that one could be a Jew at home and a German in the street, without weakening loyalty to Jewish tradition.

In the midst of such modernizing influences, some Jews began to revise Jewish worship to remove what were seen as antiquated and "oriental" practices. Hymns and sermons in the vernacular language instead of Hebrew began to replace the traditional liturgy, while references to a return to the land of Israel and the rebuilding of the Temple were removed from the service. Leaders of this new Reform Judaism saw their religion as continually evolving and harmonizing with the times; they believed that Jews could best accomplish "the mission of Israel" as loyal citizens of the countries in which they lived.

Kabbalah and Hasidism

Mystical yearning has always been a part of Jewish tradition. The fervent experience of and love for God is an undercurrent in several writings of the biblical prophets, and is incorporated into the Talmud as well. Some mystical writings are found outside the biblical canon, in the extra-biblical collections of texts known as the *Apocrypha* and the *Pseudepigrapha*. The apocryphal Book of Enoch describes the ascent to God as a journey through seven heavenly spheres to an audience with the King of the celestial court. The core mystical encounter with indescribable sanctity is based on the vision of the prophet Isaiah (Isaiah 6), and includes the chant of the heavenly court, *"Kadosh, Kadosh, Kadosh"* ("Holy, Holy, Holy"), which is included in all Jewish communal prayer.

A central Kabbalistic image is the Tree of God, a representation of the emanation of the qualities of the infinite Ein Sof into revealed aspects, the sephiroth.

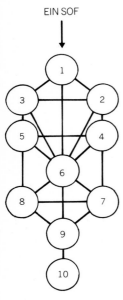

EIN SOF

1 Kether (Supreme Crown)
2 Hokhmah (Wisdom)
3 Binah (Intelligence)
4 Hesed (Love)
5 Gevura (Might)
6 Tifereth (Beauty)
7 Netsah (Eternity)
8 Hod (Splendor)
9 Yesod (Foundation)
10 Malkuth (Kingdom)

In the Middle Ages, Jewish mystical traditions, known as **Kabbalah**, began to be put into writing. The most important of these books is *The Zohar* ("Way of Splendor"). The Zohar is a massive and complex offering of stories, explanations of the esoteric levels of the Torah, and descriptions of visionary practice and experiences. It depicts the world we perceive with our senses as but a lower reflection of a splendid higher world. Mystics held the Hebrew Bible in great esteem, but felt that it was not to be interpreted literally. During the sixteenth century Kabbalah's most influential leader was Isaac Luria. He explained creation as the beaming of the divine light into ten special vessels, some of which were shattered by the impact because they contained lower forces that could not bear the intensity of the light. The breaking of the vessels spewed forth particles of evil as well as fragments of light into the world. According to Lurianic teachings, only the coming of the Messiah will bring **tikkun** ("correction" or "repair" of this situation), ending chaos and evil in the world. Although only God will decide when this will happen, humans have a great responsibility to prepare by regathering the "sparks of holiness" in the unclean realms to repair the holy vessels. To this end, Luria asked his followers to follow strict ascetic purification practices, prayer, observance of the mitzvot of the Torah, and chanting of sacred formulas.

Lurianic Kabbalism resurfaced in a very different form in the eighteenth century as **Hasidism**, the path of ecstatic piety. It developed in Ukraine and Poland, where Jews were subject to legal limitations, poverty-stricken and fearing for their lives from riots and murders. The rabbis had little to offer them, retreating into academic debates about legal aspects of the Torah.

Into this grim setting came the Baal Shem Tov (1700–1760), a beloved healer and Hasidic teacher offering a joyful version of Jewish holiness. To him, Torah study and obedience to the letter of the law were no better than deep-felt, pure-hearted prayer; everyone is capable of the highest enlightenment. He asserted that the divine could be found everywhere, in the present, thereby de-emphasizing the perennial waiting for a future Messiah. "Leave sorrow and sadness," he cried; "man must live in joy and contentment, always rejoicing in his lot."[20] Followers of the Baal Shem Tov worshipped through joyous songs and ecstatic, swaying prayer, and found God in the midst of the ghetto.

In an Hasidic school, preservation of traditional ways is maintained in the teacher's dark dress, beard and side curls.

God can be found everywhere, emphasizes the Baal Shem Tov, but can only be seen by those who are not taken in by surface appearances and who really want to find him. God is here in the midst of even the most mundane everyday activities; if carried out in remembrance of God, even eating, drinking, and working become holy acts. It is through the ups and downs of everyday life that the soul advances toward God. The highest goal is **devekut**, "cleaving" to God, free of the egotism and vanity that separate humans from the Holy One.

As the hand held before the eye conceals the greatest mountain, so the little earthly life hides from the glance the enormous lights and mysteries of which the world is full, and he who can draw it away from before his eyes, as one draws away a hand, beholds the great shining of the inner worlds.

attributed to Reb Nachman of Bratzlav

Soon an estimated half of all Eastern European Jews were followers of the Hasidic path. Spread of the teachings is credited to Dov Ber, who emphasized the importance of the *tzaddik*, or enlightened saint and teacher, called *rebbe* (or Reb) when ordained as a Hasidic spiritual guide. Ber urged Hasidim to take spiritual shelter with a tzaddik, whose prayers and wisdom would be more powerful than their own because of the tzaddik's personal relationship with God. This idea stirred enormous opposition from non-Hasidic leaders who believed that each Jew should be his or her own tzaddik. While the position of tzaddik became hereditary and was sometimes subject to exploitation by less-than-holy lineage carriers, such charismatic leadership remains a central element and perhaps one of the enduring attractions of modern Hasidism. The religious fervor associated with Hasidism clearly continues as an influence within Judaism.

American Judaism

The first Jewish community in North America was established by descendants of Jewish exiles from Spain in the Dutch colony of New Amsterdam in 1654. Substantial Jewish immigration to the United States, however, did not begin until the mid-nineteenth century when large numbers of Jews were part of the massive influx of immigrants from German-speaking Europe. By 1880, there were 250,000 Jews in the United States, mostly of German origin, spread across the continent. Middle class in occupations and attitudes, they were primarily affiliated with Reform synagogues.

Between 1881 and the early 1920s, Jewish immigration to the United States totalled two million, mainly Jews from Eastern Europe. This exodus was prompted by virulent anti-semitism in Czarist Russia, particularly following the assassination of Czar Alexander II in 1881, and endemic Jewish poverty in both Russia and eastern provinces of Austria–Hungary. This new immigration was far more diverse than that of the German Jews, religiously, politically, and socially. If the new immigrants were religious, they tended to be extremely orthodox; if they were political, their politics were far to the left; socially, they tended to be craftsmen and laborers.

Today, the United States, with approximately six million Jews, has the largest Jewish population in the world. It continues to be a highly diverse and highly acculturated population, consisting of Jews who are religiously affiliated and those who are not. Of those who are identified with a synagogue (perhaps half), ten percent are Orthodox, with almost equal numbers of the rest identifying as either Reform or Conservative.

Holocaust

For many the defining event of the twentieth century is the Holocaust, the murder of almost six million European Jews by the Nazi leadership of Germany during the Second World War. These Jews constituted over a third of the Jewish people in the world and half of all Jews in Europe. Holocaust is the overwhelmingly tragic event of Jewish history, and an indelible marker for all time of the depths of twentieth-century inhumanity and evil.

Although anti-semitism was part of Greco–Roman culture and had been present in Europe since the Roman Empire first adopted Christianity as its state religion in the fourth century CE, new and virulent strains of this disease appeared in Western Europe at the end of the nineteenth century. It began to be suggested that Jews differed from non-Jews not only in religious convictions but also in essential, racial qualities. Racist theories spread that those of "pure" Nordic blood were genetically ideal, while Jews were a dangerous "mongrel" race.

Reactionary anti-Jewish feelings also resurfaced late in the nineteenth century in Russia and Eastern Europe, where Jews formed a sizeable minority of the population and were growing in wealth and presence in higher educational circles. Jews were increasingly associated with left-wing movements pushing for social change, even though many Jewish socialists were non-observant Jews. Leon Trotsky, for example, was religiously indifferent but of Jewish blood. His leadership in the violent Bolshevik Revolution and the Red Army brought terrible reprisals, called *pogroms*, against Jewish communities by the White Russians in the civil war. In a thousand separate incidents, up to seventy thousand Jews were killed by unrestrained rioting mobs. Even after the Bolshevik Revolution, continuing social chaos in Russia led to massacres of an estimated quarter-of-a-million Jews.

In the aftermath of Germany's defeat in World War I, and the desperate economic conditions that followed, Adolf Hitler's Nazi party bolstered its popular support by blaming the Jews for all of Germany's problems. Germany, they claimed, could not regain its health until all Jews were stripped of their positions in German life or driven out of the country. Demands to eliminate the Jews for the sake of "racial hygiene" were openly circulated.

Hitler came to power in 1933, and began to issue anti-Jewish legislation. Seeing the writing on the wall, many Jews, including eminent professionals, managed to emigrate, leaving their homes, their livelihood, and most of their possessions behind. Others stayed, hoping that the terrifying signs would be short-lived.

Beginning in 1935, German Jews were deprived of their legal and economic rights by the Nuremberg Laws, and when Hitler invaded Austria in 1938, Austrian Jews fell under the same laws. Jewish businesses were forcibly taken over by "Aryans." Polish Jews living in Germany were rounded up into trucks and conveyed to the Polish border, where Polish officials refused to take them in. In November, 1938, in one night, *Kristallnacht*, the "night of broken glass," synagogues and Jewish businesses throughout Germany were smashed and burnt. Others were appropriated by the government, and numerous Jews were arrested.

By 1939, 300,000 of Germany's 500,000 Jews, together with another 150,000 from Austria, had fled. Few countries, however, would allow them to enter. The United States government's attempts to arrange for systematic emigration were abandoned when Germany invaded Poland and then in rapid succession Denmark, Norway, Belgium, Holland, and France, thereby placing several million more Jews under Nazi control.

World War II began with the German invasion of Poland. Immediately, systematic oppression began with orders to all Polish Jews to move into the towns, where walled ghettos were then created to confine them. Jews were made to wear a yellow or white badge with the Star of David on it to reveal their stigmatized status, and since all other jobs were taken away from them, they could do only menial labor.

A young Jewish man wears a star of David armband for identification in Nazi Germany.

Along the Russian front, special groups (*Einsatzgruppen*, or "Action Groups") were assigned to slaughter Jews, gypsies, and commissars as the German troops advanced and to incite the local militia to do the same. The Einsatzgruppen would locate the presiding rabbi and leaders of the Jewish intelligentsia in each town, tell them to round up all their people for relocation in a "Jewish region," and then herd them outside of town to ravines or dugouts and machine-gun them all down. Sometimes the people were drowned instead, or gassed by poison in traveling vans. The Jews were unsuspecting, for news of this activity was forbidden. One cannot comprehend the numbers of men, women, and children killed in these mass murders — 34,000 at Babi Yar, 26,000 at Odessa, 32,000 at Vilna — probably totalling hundreds of thousands.

In the Eastern European ghettos, Jewish Councils (*Judenrat*) were set up as intermediaries between the Jewish people and the Nazis. By 1942 large-scale death camps had been set up by the Nazis to facilitate the "Final Solution" — total extermination of all Jews in Europe, a population the Nazis estimated at eleven million.

The Judenrat in Warsaw, the largest of the ghettos, was ordered to select 6000 Jews a day to be "resettled" (exterminated). After two days of this, the head of the Judenrat committed suicide, but the mass round-ups continued. In 1943 there was a heroic resistance effort in the Warsaw ghetto, with defenders holding out for five weeks against overwhelming Nazi forces until virtually every Jewish fighter was killed.

From the ghettos Jews were transported by cattle cars (in which many suffocated to death) from all over Europe to concentration camps. There they were starved, worked to death as slaves, tortured, "experimented" on, and/or shipped to extermination camps. The industrial-scale gas chambers were found to be the most efficient means of killing and also an impersonal way to get around the increasing unwillingness of Germans to kill so many Jewish men, women, and children.

Hitler was the architect and the motivating force behind the genocide, but he was not the only one responsible. There were tremendous numbers of people throughout Western and Eastern Europe whose active or passive participation was needed to carry out the killings.

The governments of some countries, to a greater or lesser extent, tried to protect their Jews; also some individuals, at great personal risk, in every part of Europe, hid Jews or tried to help them escape. But there was little outcry from the outside world. The Vatican was silent, though it sheltered 477 Jews and several thousand more found refuge in monasteries and convents. The Allies took no special action to save the Jews during the war. Bombing the gas chambers was militarily feasible and urged by Winston Churchill, who called the killing "probably the greatest and most horrible crime ever committed in the whole history of the world." But he had no support from his own government or from the United States. In the United States, the government even asked Jewish organizations not to publicize the exterminations, to avoid interference with the war effort — and lest the country be besieged with Jewish refugees. Reversing its policy in 1943 through pressure and financial support from American Jews, the United States managed to save 200,000 Jews. In hindsight, many historians have concluded that Hitler's hideous policy could have been slowed by determined resistance from free Allied countries.

No modern Jewish thinker can ignore the challenge which the Holocaust poses to traditional Jewish beliefs of an omnipotent and caring God. Some, such as Eliezer Berkovits, have suggested that God is not responsible for the evil human beings commit. Rather he looks to a

> dimension beyond history in which all suffering finds its redemption through God.... The Jew does not doubt God's presence, though he is unable to set limits to the duration and intensity of His absence. This is no justification for the ways of providence, but its acceptance. It is not a willingness to forgive the unheard cries of millions, but a trust that in God the tragedy of man may find its transformation.[21]

Over half a century later, the Holocaust is still a raw wound in the minds of survivors. Even Jews who were not directly affected by the Holocaust include its terrors in their feeling of what it means to be Jewish. Elie Wiesel, a survivor of Auschwitz, feels that the painful memories must be continually rekindled. He says that we cannot turn away from the questions about how it could happen, how the world could allow such genocide to occur, for genocidal actions are being undertaken against other minority groups in our times as well. As Wiesel points out:

> According to Jewish tradition, the death of one innocent person tarnishes the cosmos. Other people's tragedies are our tragedies. We must study the past, the horrors of the past and the melancholy of the past, if we are to be sensitive in the present. [In this] there are eternities of distress — the terrifying power of evil over innocence — but also some strength in the resolve of the victim never to become a killer.[22]

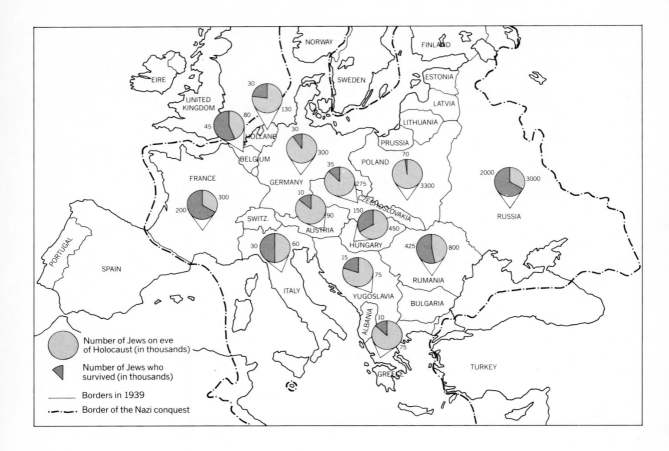

Number of Jews on eve
of Holocaust (in thousands)

Number of Jews who
survived (in thousands)

Borders in 1939

Border of the Nazi conquest

Hitler's Final Solution was to herd Jews into concentration camps throughout Nazi-occupied Europe and then ship the survivors east into extermination camps in Poland. The pie charts show the number of Jews in each country who were left after the Holocaust, relative to their previous populations.

The philosopher Emil Fackenheim insists that the "Voice of Auschwitz" commands Jewish commitment:

Jews are forbidden to hand Hitler posthumous victories. They are commanded to survive as Jews, lest the Jewish people perish. They are commanded to remember the victims of Auschwitz, lest their memory perish. They are forbidden to despair of man and his world, and to escape into either cynicism or otherworldliness, lest they cooperate in delivering the world over to the forces of Auschwitz. Finally, they are forbidden to despair of the God of Israel, lest Judaism perish.[23]

What unites all the disparate responses to this nightmare in history is the religious search for an ultimate meaning in the Jewish experience that transcends the moment, while still bearing witness to those whose lives were so mercilessly taken.

Let this place remain for eternity as a cry of despair, and a warning to humanity. About one and a half million men, women, children and infants, mainly Jews from different countries of Europe, were murdered here. The world was silent. Auschwitz Birkenau, 1940–1945.

Inscription at Auschwitz–Birkenau, Poland

Zionism

Zionism is the Jewish movement dedicated to the establishment of a politically viable, internationally recognized Jewish state in the biblical land of Israel. While political Zionism was a reaction to increasing anti-semitism in both Western and Eastern Europe in the late nineteenth century, just at a time when Jews had appeared to have achieved emancipation and cultural acceptance, it is a movement with deep roots in Judaism and Jewish culture. The desire to end the centuries-long exile from Zion (the site of the Jerusalem Temples) was a central theme in all of Jewish prayer and in many religious customs. Jewish messianism is focused around a descendant of King David who will return his united people to the land of Israel, where Jewish sovereignty will be eternally re-established in an atmosphere of universal peace.

Although groups of young people dedicated to building agricultural settlements in Palestine began to form in Eastern Europe in the 1880s, Zionism became an organized international political movement under the leadership of the Viennese journalist, Theodor Herzl. He believed that the Jews could never be "normal" people until they had their own nation. Herzl worked to provide political guarantees for Jewish settlement and offer institutional support through the formation of various Zionist organizations. Simultaneously, pioneers, mainly secular Jews from Eastern Europe, began establishing a Jewish presence on the land. The 1917 Balfour Declaration stated Britain's support for limited Jewish settlement in Palestine following World War I and the defeat of Turkey, when Britain expected to take over control of the region. While most Jews worldwide also applauded this Zionist victory, not all supported the movement. Most Reform Jews of that time believed the destiny of Jews was to be lived out among the Gentiles, where the Enlightenment had fueled hopes of a freer future and where Jews hoped they could be recognized as legitimate citizens of the countries in which they lived. Some support for Zionism came from traditional Orthodox Jews, but not all of the traditional community

Much of the Promised Land to which the Jews wanted to return was a desert. This group is celebrating the founding of Tel Aviv, now a modern city, on sand dunes in 1909.

Members of a Kibbutz at Kfar Rupin, Israel, wait with soldiers from a nearby army camp in an underground shelter. A four hour artillery battle takes place overhead between Israel and Jordan (April 26, 1969).

embraced the idea. Many felt it was up to God to end the exile, for it was God who had punished the people for their unfaithfulness by sending them away from the promised land.

By United Nations decision in 1947, Palestine was partitioned into two areas, one to be governed by Jews and the other by Arabs. Political tensions between the two groups have been violently expressed again and again in the area. Israel declared the Law of Return, which welcomed all Jews who chose to resettle in their homeland, and continues to resettle Jews to this day. Israel has established itself as a sovereign state in the Middle East, yet it still faces the hostility of many of its Arab neighbors. The large Palestinian population of the territories occupied in 1967 have also presented Israel with both military and moral dilemmas. Many Jews are unhappy with the bitterness of the relations between two peoples who have so much in common. Some feel that Israel's Jews must not forget their own history of oppression and must maintain their compassion for the oppressed people among them.

In addition to pressures from neighbors, tensions exist within Israel, where some Jewish factions believe that the land has been promised to them by God and should never be given into Arab hands. In late 1995, as attempts were underway to restore some political sovereignty and territory to Palestinians, Prime Minister Yitzhak Rabin was assassinated at a peace rally in Tel Aviv by a right-wing Jewish extremist. The Prime Minister had just said to the one hundred thousand Israelis who had gathered, "I want to thank each of you for coming to demonstrate for peace and against violence."[24] Reactions to his death have strengthened the fragile peace process.

Torah

It is difficult to outline the tenets of the Jewish faith. As we have seen, Jewish spiritual understandings have changed repeatedly through history. Rationalists and mystics have often differed. Since the nineteenth century, there has been disagreement between liberal and traditional Jews, to be discussed at the end of the chapter.

Nevertheless, there are certain major themes that can be extricated from the vast history and literature of Judaism. Jewish teachings are known as **Torah**, which literally means "the Guidance, the Teachings." In its narrowest sense, Torah refers to the Five Books of Moses. On the next level, it means the entire Hebrew Bible and the Talmud, the written and the oral law. For some, it is all sacred Jewish literature. At the highest level, Torah is God's will, God's wisdom.

The One God

The central Jewish belief is monotheism. It has been stated in different ways in response to different cultural settings (emphasizing the divine Unity when Christians developed the concept of the Holy Trinity; emphasizing that God is formless and ultimate holiness in opposition to the earthly local gods; de-emphasizing the willful deliverer-of-all-suffering aspect of God after the Holocaust). But the central theme is that there is one Creator God, the "cause of all existent things."[25]

God is everywhere, even in the darkness, as David sings in Psalms:

Where can I escape from Your spirit?
Where can I flee from your presence?
If I ascend to Heaven, You are there:
if I descend to Sheol [the underworld],
You are there too.

If I take wing with the dawn
to come to rest on the western horizon,
even there Your hand will be guiding me,
Your right hand will be holding me fast.
Psalm 139:7–14

This metaphysical understanding of God's oneness is difficult to explain in linear language, which refers to the individual objects perceived by the senses. As the eleventh-century Spanish poet and mystical philosopher Ibn Gabirol put it, "None can penetrate … the mystery of Thy unfathomable unity."[26]

One of the most elegant attempts to "explain" God's oneness has been offered by the great twentieth-century thinker, Abraham Joshua Heschel. Unity is in a sense another word for "eternity," Heschel says. "One" also refers to the state of perfection, which is the sole reality, and toward which all existence is drawn. "One" also means "the same," the unity of all qualities which appear to be opposites on the earth plane. God is both immanent and transcendent, both loving and powerful, both known and hidden, both personal Father and impersonal Eternal. God is revealed in nature — the heavens and earth glorify God (although Heschel sadly notes that "the awareness of grandeur and the sublime is all but gone from the modern mind"[27]). But God is not the same as nature; God is its creator. "The earth is our sister, not our mother,"[28] Heschel states.

> *Plurality is incompatible with the sense of the ineffable. You cannot ask in regard to the divine: Which one? There is only one synonym for God: One.*
> *Abraham Joshua Heschel*[29]

In traditional Judaism, God is often perceived as a loving Father who is nonetheless infinitely majestic, sometimes revealing divine power when the children need chastising.

Love for God

The essential commandment to humans is to love God. The central prayer in any Jewish religious service and the inscription on the *mezuza* at the doorpost of every traditional Jewish home is the *Shema Israel*:

Hear, O Israel! The Lord is our God, the Lord alone. You shall love the Lord your God with all your heart and with all your soul and with all your might. Take to heart these instructions with which I charge you this day. Impress them upon your children. Recite them when you stay at home and when you are away, when you lie down and when you get up. Bind them as a sign on your hand and let them serve as a symbol on your forehead; inscribe them on the doorposts of your house and on your gates.

Deuteronomy 6:4–9

Even Maimonides, the great proponent of reason and study, asserted the primacy of love for God. He emphasized that one should not love God from selfish or fearful motivations, such as receiving earthly blessings or avoiding problems in the life after death. One should study Torah and fulfill the commandments out of sheer love of God.

The sacredness of human life

Humans are the pinnacle of creation, created in the "image" of God, according to the account of Creation in Genesis 1. Jews do not take this passage to mean that God literally looks like a human. It is often interpreted in an ethical sense: that humans are so wonderfully endowed that they can mirror God's qualities, such as justice, wisdom, righteousness, and love.

All people are potentially equal; they are said to be common descendants of the first man and woman. But they are also potentially perfectable, and in raising themselves they uplift the world. God limited the divine power by giving humans free will, involving them in the responsibility for the world's condition, and their own. If we are suffering, according to the Talmud, we should examine our own deeds.

Martin Buber describes the relationship between God and humans as reciprocal:

> You know always in your heart that you need God more than everything; but do you not know too that God needs you – in the fulness of His eternity needs you? How would man exist, how would you exist, if God did not need him, did not need you? You need God, in order to be – and God needs you, for the very meaning of your life.... There is divine meaning in the life of the world ... of human persons, of you and of me.... We take part in creation, meet the Creator, reach out to him, helpers and companions.[30]

Human life is sacred, rather than lowly and loathsome, Judaism celebrates the body. Sexuality within marriage is holy, and the body is honored as the instrument through which the soul is manifested on earth. Indeed, according to some thinkers, body and soul are an inseparable totality.

Jewish theology has been shaped by the most compelling thinkers of each era. In the 20th century, Martin Buber described the cherished human-divine encounter as an I-Thou relationship, in which the self experiences its wholeness.

> I praise You, for I am awesomely, wondrously made.   Psalm 139:14

Law

Because of the great responsibility of humankind, traditional Jews give thanks that God has revealed in the written and oral Torah the laws by which they can be faithful to the divine will and fulfill the purposes of Creation by establishing a Kingdom of God here on earth, in which all creatures can live in peace and fellowship. In the words of the biblical prophet Isaiah, speaking for God,

> The wolf and the lamb shall graze together,
> And the lion shall eat straw like the ox,
> And the serpent's food shall be earth.
> In all my sacred mount
> Nothing evil or vile shall be done.[31]

To the extent that traditional Jews act according to the Torah, they feel they are upholding their part of the ancient covenant with God. The Hebrew word for transgression or sin means literally to "miss the mark"; the word for righteousness literally means "straight," not deviating from the right path because of stress or desire.

The Torah, as indicated through rabbinic literature, is said to contain 613 commandments, or **mitzvot** (singular: **mitzvah**). Judaism makes no distinction between spirit and matter, sacred and secular life, so these include general ethical guidelines such as the Ten Commandments and the famous saying in Leviticus 29:18 — "Love your fellow as yourself" — plus detailed laws concerning all aspects of life, such as land ownership, civil and criminal procedure, family law, sacred observances, diet, and ritual slaughter. A Sabbath prayer, "Ahavat Olam," thanks the Lord for this guidance, a token of the divine love:

> *With everlasting love You have loved Your people Israel. You have taught us the Torah and its Mitzvot. You have instructed us in its laws and judgments.*
>
> *Therefore, O Lord our God, when we lie down and when we rise up we shall speak of Your commandments and rejoice in Your Torah and Mitzvot.*
>
> *For they are our life and the length of our days; on them we will meditate day and night.*[32]

The biblical book of Genesis also sets forth what is called the *Noahide Code* of seven universal principles for a moral and spiritual life: idolatry (worshipping many gods or images of God), blasphemy against God, murder, theft, sexual behaviors outside of marriage, and cruelty to animals are all prohibited, and the rule of law and justice in society is affirmed as a positive value.

From the time of its final editing in Babylonia in the mid-sixth century CE, the Talmud, together with its later commentaries, has served as a blueprint for Jewish social, communal, and religious life. Through the rabbinic tradition, law became the main category of Orthodox Jewish thought and practice, and learned study of God's commandments one of the central expressions of faith.

Suffering and faith

In the Hebrew Bible, it was emphasized that people who lived by God's command-ments would be protected by God. If not, they deserved to suffer. Jewish tradition depicts the universe as being governed by an all-powerful, personal God who intervenes in history to reward the righteous and punish the unjust. Within this context, Jews have had considerable difficulty in answering the eternal question: Why must the innocent suffer? This question has been particularly poignant since the Holocaust.

The Hebrew Bible itself brings up the issue with the challenging parable of Job, a blameless, God-fearing, and wealthy man. The story involves Satan, depicted as an angel beneath God, who creates both darkness and light. In a conversation with God, Satan predicts that Job will surely drop his faith and blaspheme the Lord if he is stripped of all his possessions. With God's assent, Satan creates a test, fomenting incidents that destroy everything, including Job's children. On hearing the news:

> *Job arose, tore his robe, cut off his hair, and threw himself on the ground and worshipped. He said, "Naked came I out of my mother's womb, and naked shall I return there; the Lord has given, and the Lord has taken away, blessed be the name of the Lord."*[33]

With an itchy inflammation covering him from head to foot, Job begins to curse his life and to question God's justice. In the end, Job acknowledges not only God's power to control the world but also his inscrutable wisdom, which is beyond human understanding. God then rewards him with long life and even greater riches than he had before the test.

Debate over the meanings of this story, which came from the esoteric wisdom tradition, has continued over the centuries. One rabbinical interpretation is that Satan was cooperating with God in helping Job grow from fear of God to love of

God. Another is that faith in God will finally be rewarded in this life, no matter how severe the temporary trials. Another is that those who truly desire to grow toward God will be asked to suffer more, that their sins will be expiated in this life so they can enjoy the divine bliss in the life to come. Such interpretations assume a personal, all-powerful loving God doing what is best for the people, even when they cannot understand God's ways. In such belief, God is seen as always available, like a shepherd caring for his sheep, no matter how dark the outer circumstances.

> *Though I walk through a valley of deepest darkness,*
> *I fear no harm, for You are with me;*
> *Your rod and Your staff – they comfort me.*
>
> *Psalm 23:4*

On the other hand, oppression and then the Holocaust have led some Jews to complain to God in anguish. They, too, feel close to God, but in a way that allows them to scream at God, as it were. In questioning the justice of history, they hold God responsible for what is inexplicably monstrous. But even in the Holocaust, there were those who held fast to hope for better times. As they walked to their death in Nazi gas chambers, some were reciting the hymn *Ani maamin*: "I believe with complete faith in the coming of the Messiah, and even though he may delay, nevertheless I anticipate every day that he will come."[34]

Sacred practices

The ideal is to remember God in everything one does, through prayer and keeping the commandments. These commandments are not other-worldly. Many are rooted in the body, and spiritual practices often engage all the senses in awareness of God.

Boys are ritually circumcised when they are eight days old, to honor the seal of God's commandment to Abraham. Orthodox Jews consider women ritually unclean during their menstrual periods and for seven days afterwards. They are not to have sexual intercourse with their husbands and at the end of this forbidden period Othodox Jewish women undertake complete immersion in a **mikva**, a special deep bath structure, symbolizing their altered state. Marital sex is sacred, with the Sabbath night the holiest time for making love. By contrast, adultery is strictly forbidden as one of the worst sins against God, for Jewish tradition is extremely concerned with maintaining pure lines of descent.

What one eats is also of cosmic significance, for according to Torah, some foods are definitely unclean. For example, the only ritually acceptable, or **kosher**, meats, are those from warmblooded animals, with cloven hoofs who chew their cuds, such as cows, goats, and sheep. Poultry is kosher, except for birds of prey, but shellfish are not. Meat is also kosher only if it has been butchered in the traditional humane way with an extremely sharp, smooth knife by an authorized Jewish slaughterer. Great pains are taken to avoid eating blood; meat must be soaked in water and then drained on a salted board before cooking. Meat and milk cannot be eaten together, and separate dishes are maintained for their preparation and serving.

Living Judaism

Herman Taube is a poet, Professor Emeritus of Jewish Studies and Yiddish Literature, and volunteer chaplain to nursing home patients. He emigrated to the United States in 1947 from Poland with his wife, who had earlier been sent to a concentration camp where her younger sister and mother died. During World War II, Herman was a medic working side by side with Russian Orthodox and Muslim doctors in Uzbekhistan to aid people in a refugee camp. He says,

"If you do charitable work — if you help in clinics, if you help unfortunate children, if you go into the jails to help inmates — this is God's work. It is not the responsibility of the rich only to help the poor. Even the poorest man has to give charity. This is the law in Jewish religion.

Maimonides says, and Jews are saying every morning in their prayers, that a human being has to believe every day in the coming of the Messiah. Messiah does not come with a long beard and a donkey. Messiah can be you. Messiah can be a man on the street who helps a fellow human being. In the Hebrew Bible, in the Talmud, there are quotations indicating that the Messiah will come in a generation which is full of innocence or full of guilt — one of the two. And he will spiritually lead the people away from evil. I think this will become a messianic era.

Look at the fall of communism, the fall of fascism in our generation. Something is changing. You don't have to go far — look at Washington. You see good people living in the streets, with no roof over their head. They cannot make a meal. On the other side, you see those big parties where people spend millions. There is a need for a messianic age, a need for a better world.

A reporter asked me, 'Can you believe in God after the Holocaust?' Belief is not something static. My wife and I sometimes ask, 'Where was God?' A million and a half Jewish children were killed. Little boys and girls who were just learning how to say, 'Mama,' and the grandmother said, 'How big is the baby?' and tried to pick up their hands. And this child was taken and thrown into a lamppost. So yes, there are questions. We have no answers.

Why did Polish people, nuns and plain peasants risk their lives to save Jewish people, when they knew that for saving a Jew's life their house would be burned down? And their children were taken into forced labor. Why did the people of Assisi save sixty Jewish people under the noses of the Nazis? The Vatican wasn't too helpful, didn't speak up, but they, the simple people, risked their lives. So there is goodness in the world, too. There is goodness and Godness in the hearts of those people.

The Talmud says God said, 'You don't believe in me? So you don't believe in me. But keep my commandments. Care for the poor and for the widows.' This is exactly what a lot of those Messiahs are doing.

About chosenness: My grandfather was a really Orthodox Jew. He prayed three times a day, studied, studied the Bible, was always praying, always reciting Psalms, a really generous man. He found time to give charity. He did the same thing that I do now: He volunteered to go to the hospitals. Some of the people couldn't afford to go to the hospital, so he went to their homes, on the fifth floors in Poland, with no elevators, sitting with somebody sick all night. On the way home he would go to services. Then at home, something to eat — dry bread, a piece of herring, imitation coffee. This is the way he lived. This man, this chosen man, was one of the first Jews of the Lodz ghetto to be taken to the concentration camp. The Nazis used gas to kill them, and then disposed of them. If this is the chosenness that God wants us for — thank you, choose another people.

My wife doesn't like to be interviewed. It's like pulling off a bandage from an open wound. Even after forty-five years, comes to the holidays and she's missing her mother and her sister. That unbelievable guilt feeling: Why did we survive and they die?

I believe in God. There is a Power above us that rules our life. We do not see it, we cannot comprehend it. But there is something. I do not deny Him — or Her; maybe it's a Her. And I don't deny my roots."

These dietary instructions are laid out in the biblical book of Leviticus, which quotes God as saying to Moses and Aaron, "For I the Lord am He who brought you up from the land of Egypt to be your God: you shall be holy, for I am holy."[35] The rules of diet, if strictly followed, give Jews a feeling of special sacred identity and link them to the eternal authority of Torah.

Some contemporary Jews feel that consciousness about what they eat can be extended to environmental considerations. To them, the styrofoam box in which a cheeseburger is sold at fast-food places is as much a problem as the mixing of meat and milk. Nuclear power-generated electricity used for cooking might itself be non-kosher, so long as there is no safe provision for disposing of nuclear waste.

For traditional Jews, the morning begins with a prayer before opening one's eyes, thanking God for restoring one's soul. The hands must then be washed before reciting blessings and, for all traditional male Jews, putting a special fringed rectangle of cloth around the neck. It is usually worn under the clothes as a reminder of the privilege of being given divine commandments. For weekday morning prayers men also put on **t'fillin**, or phylacteries, small leather boxes containing biblical verses about the covenant with God, including the "Shema." One is tied on the forehead and the other on the upper arm, held against the heart, in fulfillment of the Shema commandment; as literally understood: "Bind them (the Shema's words about the primacy of love for God) as a sign on your hand and let them serve as a symbol on your forehead." Traditional Jewish men also wear a fringed prayer shawl (**talit**) whose fringes act as reminders of God's commandments, and keep their heads covered at all times, if possible.

Before praying, traditional Jewish men bind t'fillin to their arm and forehead in remembrance of their covenant with God.

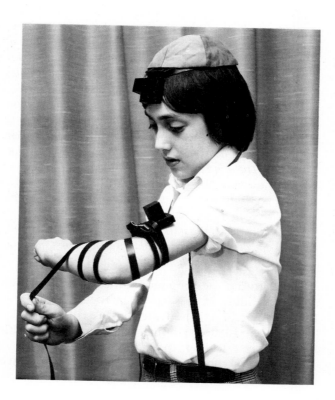

Traditionally, prayers are recited on waking and at bedtime. In addition, three prayer services are chanted daily in a synagogue by men if there is a minyan (quorum of ten). Women can say them also, but they are excused from rigid schedules because their household responsibilities are considered important.

Jews are also expected to give thanks continually. One should recite a hundred benedictions to God every day. To this end, there is a blessing to be said every time one takes a drink of water. There is even a blessing to be recited after using the toilet:

> *Blessed art thou, our God, Ruler of the universe, who hast formed (human) beings in wisdom, and created in them a system of ducts and tubes. It is well known before thy glorious throne that if but one of these be opened, or if one of those be closed, it would be impossible to exist in thy presence. Blessed art thou, O God, who healest all creatures and doest wonders.[36]*

The Jewish **Sabbath** runs from sunset Friday night to sunset Saturday night, because the Jewish "day" begins with nightfall. The Friday night service welcomes the Sabbath as a bride and is often considered an opportunity to drop away the cares of the previous week so as to be in a peaceful state for the day of rest. Just as God is said to have created the world in six days and then rested on the seventh, all work is to cease when the Sabbath begins. Ruth Gan Kagan describes the experience:

> *The most amazing and wonderful thing about the Sabbath is that peace is just there. From the moment the Sabbath enters (forty minutes before sunset on Friday afternoon) her presence is immediately felt, upon me, upon my city — Jerusalem — and upon all Jews who welcome her. I am aware of a wave of peace flooding my heart and that transparent veils of tranquility are covering the World around me. A moment before I would probably be rushing around trying to finish all the preparations, getting dressed in a hurry, shouting at the children to complete their pre-Sabbath chores, setting the candles, laying the table, checking the food, fixing the lights ... but all this tension and rush vanishes when the fixed moment arrives; not a second earlier nor a second later. The moment I light the Sabbath candles and usher in the Sabbath spirit everything undergoes a magical transformation.*
>
> *The Queen has arrived. In Her presence there are not even talks of weekday matters. The mind quiets down leaving business, plans and worries behind as one quietly walks to the synagogue for services; the sky is aglow with the colours of sunset; the bird-song is suddenly more present; the people of the congregation gather to welcome in the Sabbath in song, prayer and silence.*
>
> *Coming home, the stars are out; in a religious neighborhood, no travelling cars break the descended peace; children are holding their parents' hands, walking in the middle of the road without fear of death.[37]*

The Saturday morning service incorporates public and private prayers, singing, and the reading of passages from the Pentateuch and Prophets sections of the Hebrew Bible. Torah scrolls are kept in a curtained ark on the wall facing Jerusalem. They are hand-lettered in Hebrew and are treated with great reverence. It is a great honor to be "called up" to read from the Torah.

More liberal congregations may place emphasis on an in-depth discussion of the passage read. Often it is examined not only from an abstract philosophical perspective but also from the point of its relevance to political events and everyday attempts to live a just and humane life. Torah study, and study of all Jewish literature, is highly valued as a form of prayer in itself, and synagogues usually have libraries for this purpose, sometimes in the same space that is used for worship.

In Hasidic congregations, the emphasis falls on the intensity of praying, or **davening**, even in saying fixed prayers from the prayer book. Some sway their bodies to induce the self-forgetful state of ecstatic communion with the Loved One. Others quietly shift their attention from earthly concerns to "cleave to God." The rabbinical tradition states the ideal in prayer: "A person should always see himself as if the Shekhinah is confronting him."[38]

In addition to or instead of going to a service welcoming the Sabbath, observant families usually begin the Sabbath eve with a special Friday night dinner. The mother lights candles to bring in the Sabbath light; the father recites a blessing over the wine. Special braided bread, *challah*, is shared as a symbol of the double portions of manna in the dessert. The rituals help to set a different tone for the day of rest, as do commandments against working, handling money, traveling except by foot, lighting a fire, cooking, and the like. The Sabbath day is set aside for public prayer, study, thought, friendship, and family closeness, with the hope that this renewed life of the spirit will then carry through the week to come. Saturday evening, there is a ceremony, the *havdala* ("separation"), to mark the shift back from holy to secular time.

It is customary to recognize coming of age, at thirteen, in Jewish boys by the **Bar Mitzvah** ("son of the commandment") ceremony. The boy has presumably undertaken some religious instruction, including learning to pronounce Hebrew, if not always to understand it. He is called up to read a portion from the Torah scroll and recite a passage from one of the books of the prophets, in Hebrew, and then perhaps to give a short teaching about a topic from the reading. Afterwards there may be a simple *kiddush*, a celebration with blessing of wine and sweet bread or cake, but a big party is more likely. This custom of welcoming the boy to adult responsibilities has been extended to girls in non-Orthodox congregations in the **Bat Mitzvah** ("daughter of the commandment").

Holy days

Like other peoples, Jews honor the circle of the seasons with special ceremonies. For Jews, many of these times are also linked to special events in history. Judaism follows a 354-day lunar calendar consisting of twelve months following the cycles of the moon. Seven times in a nineteen-year cycle, an additional or leap month is added to keep the calendar in synchronization with the seasons and the solar year of 365 days. This is why the dates of Jewish holy days vary against the solar calendar by as much as four weeks from year to year.

The spiritual year begins with the High Holy Days of Rosh Hashanah and Yom Kippur. **Rosh Hashanah**, a time of spiritual renewal, is celebrated on the first two days of the seventh month (around the fall equinox). For thirty days prior to Rosh Hashanah, each morning synagogue service brings blowing of the *shofar* (a ram's horn that produces an eery, unearthly blast) to remind the people that they stand before God. At the service on the eve of Rosh Hashanah, a prayer is recited asking

Rosh Hashanah brings the blowing of the shofar in three ways: a note of alarm, three wails, and nine sobbing blasts of contrition.

that all humanity will remember what God has done, that there will be honor and joy for God's people, and that righteousness will triumph while "all wickedness vanishes like smoke."[39]

Yom Kippur follows ten days later. It honors and renews the sacred covenant of the Jewish people with God, but does so in the spirit of atonement. Historically, this was the only time when the high priest entered the Holy of Holies in the Temple of Jerusalem, and the only time that he would pronounce the sacred name of the Lord, YHWH, in order to ask for forgiveness of the people's sins. Today, there is an attempt at personal inner cleansing and individuals must ask pardon from everyone they may have wronged during the past year. If necessary, restitution for damages should be made. Congregations also confess their sins communally, ask that their negligence be forgiven, and pray for their reconciliation to God in a new year of divine pardon and grace.

Sukkot is a fall harvest festival. A simple outdoor booth is built and decorated as a dwelling place of sorts for seven days. The fragile home reminds the faithful that their real home is in God, who sheltered their ancestors on the way from Egypt to the promised land of Canaan. Some contemporary groups also pray for peace amid our vulnerability to nuclear war. Participants hold the *lulav* (a bundle made of a palm branch, myrtle twigs, and willow twigs) in one hand and the *etrog* (a citrus fruit) in the other and wave them together toward the four compass directions, earth and sky, praising God and acknowledging him as the unmoving center of creation. There is an offering of water, precious in the desert lands of the patriarchs, and great merrymaking. During the Second Temple days, the ecstatic celebration even included burning of the priests' old underclothes. The last day of the seven-day Sukkot festival is **Simhat Torah** ("Joy in Torah"), ending the yearly cycle of Torah readings, from Creation to the death of Moses, and beginning again.

Near the winter solstice, the darkest time of the year, comes **Hanukkah**, the Feast of Dedication. Each night for eight nights, another candle is lit on a special candle holder. The amount of light gradually increases like the lengthening of sunlight. Historically, Hanukkah was a celebration of the victory of the Maccabean Rebellion against the attempt by Antiochus to force non-Jewish practices on the Jewish people. According to legend, when the Jews regained access to the Temple, they found only one jar of oil left undefiled, still sealed by the high priest. It was only enough to stay alight for one day, but by a miracle, the oil stayed burning for eight days. Many Jewish families also observe the time by nightly gift-giving, as rewards for Torah study. The children have their own special Hanukkah pastimes, such as "gambling" for nuts with the *dreidel*. It is a spinning top with four letters on its sides as an abbreviation of the sentence "A great miracle happened there."

As the winter rainy season begins to diminish in Israel, Jews everywhere celebrate the reawakening of nature on **Tu B'shvat**. Observances lavish appreciation on a variety of fruits and plants. In Israel, the time is now marked by planting of trees to help restore life to the desert.

On the full moon of the month before spring comes **Purim**. It theoretically commemorates the legend of Esther, queen of Persia, and Mordecai, who saved their fellow Jews from destruction by the evil viceroy Haman. It has been linked to Mesopotamian mythology about the goddess Ishtar, whose spring return brings joy and fertility. Purim is a bawdy time of dressing in costumes and mocking life's seriousness, and the jokes frequently poke fun at sacred Jewish practices. As the story of Esther is read from an ornate scroll, the congregation responds with noisy stomping, rattles, horns, and whistles whenever Haman's name is read.

Simhat Torah is a joyous celebration of the Torah, with everyone joining in the dancing and singing. This one is taking place at the western "Wailing Wall," where for nearly two thousand years Jews have made pilgrimages to pray.

For children of all ages, the lighting of Hannukah candles is a special event in the darkness of winter.

The next major festival is **Pesach**, or **Passover**, which celebrates the liberation from bondage in Egypt and the spring-time advent of new life. It was the tenth plague, death to all first-born sons of the Egyptians, which finally brought the Pharoah to relent. The Israelites were warned to slaughter a lamb for each family and mark their doors with its blood so that the angel of death would pass over them. They were to roast the lamb and eat it with unleavened bread and bitter herbs. So quickly did they depart that they didn't even have time to bake the bread, which is said to have baked in the sun as they carried it on their heads. The beginning of Pesach is still marked by a **Seder** dinner with the eating of unleavened bread (*matzah*), to remember the urgency of the departure, and bitter herbs as a reminder of slavery, so that they would never impose it on other peoples. Also on the table are *charoset* (a sweet fruit and nut mixture, a reminder of the mortar that the enslaved Israelites molded into bricks) and salt water (a reminder of the tears of the slaves) into which parsley or some other plant (a reminder of spring life) is dipped and eaten. Children ask ritual questions about why these things are done, as basic religious instruction. A movement for contemporary liturgical renewal has yielded many new scripts for the Seder — such as special liturgies for feminists, for secular Zionists, and for co-celebration of Pesach with Muslims.

Several new holidays have been established in the period that follows Pesach. One is Holocaust Memorial Day, **Yom Hashoah**, in April or May. Observances often include the singing in Yiddish of a song from the Jewish Resistance Movement. In part:

תסדר ליל פסח

Part of the Pesach Seder, celebrated here by a Polish family, is the drinking of wine four times, in remembrance of the four promises of freedom that God allegedly made to the people during the Exodus from Egypt.

Never say that you are going your last way, though leaden skies blot out the blue of day. The hour for which we long will certainly appear.[40]

Another new holiday is Israel Independence Day, **Yom Haatzma-ut**, honoring May 14, 1948, when Israel was affirmed as a sovereign state.

Early summer brings **Shavuot**, traditionally identified with the giving of the Torah to Moses at Mount Sinai and the people's hearing of the voice of God. It is likely that Shavuot was initially a summer harvest festival that later was linked with the revelation of the Torah. In Israeli kibbutzim the old practice of bringing the first fruits to God has been revived. Elsewhere, the focus is on reading of the Ten Commandments and on presenting the Torah as a marriage contract between God and Israel. In some congregations, Shavuot is a time to celebrate children's graduation from religious school.

Then come three weeks of mourning for the Temples, both of which were destroyed on the ninth day of the month of Av (July or August), **Tisha Be-Av**. This is traditionally a time of fasting and avoidance of joyous activities. Some feel that there is no longer cause for mourning because even though the Temple has not been rebuilt, the old city of Jerusalem has been recaptured. Others feel that we are all still in exile from the state of perfection.

Contemporary Judaism

Within the extended family of Judaism, there are many groups, many different focuses, and many areas of disagreement. Currently disputed issues include the degree of adherence to Torah and Talmud, requirements for conversion to Judaism, the extent of the use of Hebrew in prayer, and the full participation of women in religious obligations including the synagogue service.

Among those who champion the rights of women to participate equally with men in ritual and prayer, there is also an ongoing effort to revise liturgical language in gender-neutral and gender-inclusive ways, both in reference to worshippers, and in reference to God. The Hebrew scriptures describe God as both female and male, validating new translations from the Hebrew which use gender-neutral language. As an example of the shift from male-centered to gender-neutral language, the biblical passage:

> *And God created man in his own image, in the image of God created He them; male and female created He them....*[41]

has been re-translated thus:

> *Thus God created us in the divine image, creating us in the image of God, creating us male and female.*[42]

Judaism, like all modern religions, has struggled to meet the challenge of secularization: the idealization of science, rationalism, industrialization, and materialism. The response of the **Orthodox** has been to stand by the Hebrew Bible as the revealed word of God and the Talmud as the legitimate oral law. Orthodox Jews feel that they are bound by the traditional rabbinical halakhah, as a way of achieving closeness to God. But within this framework there are great individual differences, with no central authority figure or governing body. Orthodoxy includes mystics and rationalists, Zionists and anti-Zionists. The Orthodox also differ greatly in their tolerance for other Jewish groups and in their degree of accommodation of the surrounding secular environment. Thus, while some Hasidic groups practice complete withdrawal from the secular world and the rest of the Jewish community, others, such as the *Lubavich Hasidim* (originally from Lithuania, with strong communities in many countries), are devoted to extending their message to as many Jews as possible, using all the tools of modern technology for their sacred purpose. The Lubavich, who offer highly structured and nurturing communities in which male-female roles are strictly defined and an all-embracing piety and devotion to a charismatic leader are universally shared, have had considerable success in attracting young Jews to their way of life. They are seen as strong role models, and present themselves as true Jews. This return to a structured practice of Judaism has surprised many observers. When the seventh Lubavich rabbi came to the United States, he was discouraged by other Jewish rabbis from trying to interest people in Torah in a country where so many had abandoned their tradition and were living secular lives. To the contrary, the emphasis on Torah proved to have great appeal and has encouraged many to return to their Jewish roots.

The **Reform** movement, at the other end of the religious spectrum from Orthodoxy, began in eighteenth-century Germany as an attempt to help modern Jews appreciate their religion rather than regarding it as antiquated, meaningless, or even repugnant. In imitation of Christian churches, synagogues were redefined as places for spiritual elevation, with choirs added for effect, and the Sabbath service was shortened and translated into the vernacular. The liturgy was also changed to eliminate references to the hope of return to Zion and animal sacrifices in the Temple. Halakhic observances were re-evaluated for their relevance to modern needs, and Judaism was understood as an evolving, open-ended religion rather than one fixed forever by the revealed Torah. Reform congregations are numerous in North America where they are continually engaged in a "creative confrontation with modernity." Rather than exclusivism, Reform rabbis cultivate a sense of the universalism of Jewish values. It is felt that only by making Judaism meaningful to modern tastes and modern minds can it survive.

Given this approach, it is not surprising that Reform Judaism, particularly in North America, has been at the forefront in the establishment of inter-faith dialogue and civic cooperation with non-Jewish groups. Reform Judaism is not fully accepted in Israel, where the Israeli Rabbinate, which has considerable civil

Rabbi Pauline Bebe with the Torah scroll.

and political power, does not recognize the authority of non-Orthodox rabbis. For example, Israeli religious officials are reluctant to acknowledge Reform converts as true Jews who can be Israeli citizens.

Traditionalist objections notwithstanding, the liberalization process has also given birth to other groups with intermediate positions. **Conservative** Judaism is the largest Jewish movement in the United States (which now has the world's largest Jewish population). While Conservative Jews feel they are totally dedicated to traditional rabbinical Judaism, at the same time they are restating and restructuring it in modern terms so that it is not perceived as a dead historical religion. To appeal to intelligent would-be believers, Conservative Judaism has sponsored critical studies of Jewish texts from all periods in history. They believe that Jews have always searched and added to their laws, liturgy, midrash, and beliefs to keep them relevant and meaningful in changing times. Some of the recent changes introduced are acceptance of riding to a synagogue for Sabbath services and acceptance of women into rabbinical schools as candidates for ordination as rabbis. These changes are not forced on local congregations, which have the right to accept or reject them.

Rabbi Mordecai Kaplan, a highly influential American thinker who died in 1983, branched off from Conservatism (which initially rejected his ideas as too radical), and founded a movement called **Reconstructionism**. Kaplan held that the Enlightenment had changed everything and that strong measures were needed to preserve Judaism in the face of rationalism. Kaplan asserted that "as long as Jews adhered to the traditional conception of Torah as supernaturally revealed, they would not be amenable to any constructive adjustment of Judaism that was needed to render it viable in a non-Jewish environment."[43] He defined Judaism as an "evolving religious civilization," both cultural and spiritual, and asserted that the Jewish people are the heart of Judaism. The traditions exist for the people, and not vice versa, he said. Kaplan denied that the Jewish people were specially chosen by God, an exclusivist idea. Rather, they had chosen to try to become a people of God. Kaplan created a new prayer book, deleting traditional portions he and others found offensive, such as derogatory references to women and Gentiles, references to physical resurrection of the body, and passages describing God as rewarding or punishing Israel by manipulating natural phenomena such as rain. Women were accepted fully into synagogue participation.

There are also numerous small *havurot*, or communities of Jews, who are not affiliated with any formal group but get together on a regular basis to worship and celebrate the traditions. They favor a democratic organization and personal experience, and are often engaged in trying to determine what parts of the traditions to use and how. Some incorporate study groups continuing the ancient intellectual tradition of grappling with the ethical, philosophical, and spiritual meanings of the texts. Such groups are indicative of a developing spirit of Jewish renewal among many younger Jews who are attempting to enrich their religious lives through intellectual and spiritual explorations of their tradition.

In addition to those who affiliate with a religious movement, there are many Jews who identify themselves as secular Jews, affirming their Jewish origins and maintaining various Jewish cultural traditions while eschewing religious practice. There are also significant numbers of people of Jewish birth, particularly in North America and Western Europe, whose Jewish identity is vestigial at best, and unlikely to survive in future generations. The possibilities for total assimilation into Western culture are evident in statistics indicating that over fifty percent of Western Jews marry non-Jews. In most cases, neither spouse in such a marriage converts, and research indicates that it is highly unlikely that their children will identify as Jews. Thus, one of the great ironies of the liberty offered to the Jewish people by democratic secular societies is the freedom to leave Judaism as well as to affirm it.

Although anti-semitism continues to flare up here and there, many non-Jews are developing sensitivity against negative stereotyping of Jews. The Evangelical Lutheran Church in America has issued an historic public apology for the anti-Jewish writings of Martin Luther, the father of Protestant Christianity. In part, they declared:

> As did many of Luther's own companions in the sixteenth century, we reject this violent invective, and yet more do we express our deep and abiding sorrow over its tragic effects on subsequent generations. In concert with the Lutheran World Federation, we particularly deplore the appropriation of Luther's words by modern anti-Semites for the teaching of hatred toward Judaism or toward the Jewish people in our day.... We recognize in anti-Semitism a contradiction and an affront to the Gospel, a violation of our hope and calling, and we pledge this church to oppose the deadly working of such bigotry.[44]

In post-Soviet Russia, where under Stalin Jews had been so persecuted that only a few rabbis remained in all of Russia, there are now Jewish seminaries and universities, schools, and kindergartens. Rabbi Dovid Karpov, whose congregation serves one hundred and fifty free hot meals a day in Moscow, says that Judaism is beginning to flourish again after years of secrecy and danger:

> Now we can celebrate holidays such as Hannukah openly. It is not yet a mass movement, but there are more people than you can count on your fingers. We feel that soon we will see the fruit of our work. Judaism survives despite all the persecutions. The new world is coming very soon and it will have a very different form. The Messiah is coming. The time will soon come when we will have the peace that everyone is waiting for. It will happen sooner than anyone can imagine.[45]

For many Jews, the future continues to hold messianic promise. Some look toward a messianic era of social justice, as called for long ago by the Hebrew prophet Amos:

> Let justice roll on like a river
> and righteousness like an ever-flowing stream.[46]

Suggested reading

Ariel, David S., *The Mystic Quest: An Introduction to Jewish Mysticism*, Northvale, New Jersey: Jason Aronson, 1988. An accessible introduction to mystical Jewish thinking.

Baskin, Judith R., ed., *Jewish Women in Historical Perspective*, Detroit: Wayne State University Press, 1991. Twelve pioneering essays by modern scholars explore Jewish women and their activities in a variety of times and places.

Ben-Sasson, H. H., ed., *A History of the Jewish People*, Cambridge, Massachusetts: Harvard University Press, 1976. Leading scholars of the Hebrew University in Jerusalem offer a comprehensive, scholarly analysis of Jewish history which assumes some knowledge of the tradition.

Braybrooke, Marcus, *Time to Meet: Towards a deeper relationship between Jews and Christians*, London: SCM Press, 1990. Information about both Christianity and Judaism which helps to remove historic ill feelings between them.

Cohen, Arthur A. and Mendes-Flohr, Paul, eds., *Contemporary Jewish Religious Thought*, New York: Charles Scribner's Sons, 1987. Brief essays on all aspects of Jewish belief, from Aesthetics to Zionism, by writers from all Jewish schools.

Encyclopedia Judaica, Jerusalem: Keter Publishing House Jerusalem Ltd., 1972. The authoritative, multi-volume reference on all aspects of Judaism, as seen from a broad spectrum of points of view.

Glatzer, Nahum N., ed., *The Judaic Tradition*, Boston: Beacon Press, 1969. A useful compilation of writings from all periods of Jewish history.

Grossman, Susan and Haut, Rivka, eds., *Daughters of the King: Women and the Synagogue*, Philadelphia: Jewish Publication Society, 1992. An excellent anthology of history, *halakhah*, and contemporary testimonies concerning women and synagogue participation.

Heschel, Abraham J., *Between God and Man: An interpretation of Judaism*, ed. Fritz A. Rothschild, New York: The Free Press, 1959. An intimate exploration of the relevance of traditional Judaism for today's world, by a great twentieth-century theologian.

Holtz, Barry W., ed., *The Schocken Guide to Jewish Books*, New York: Schocken Books, 1992. Fifteen fascinating bibliographical chapters by experts in their fields provide entry to all major historical, literary, philosophical, and mystical areas of Jewish study.

Jacobs, Louis, *Principles of the Jewish Faith*, Northvale, New Jersey: Jason Aronson, 1964, 1988. Many commentaries spanning the centuries are brought to bear on thirteen central principles of Judaism as set forth by Maimonides.

Schachter-Shalomi, Zalman, with Donald Gropman, *The First Step: A Guide for the New Jewish Spirit*, New York: Bantam Books, 1983. A modern explanation of the essence of Judaism, of special interest to non-observant Jews who want to find their way back into the faith.

Scholem, Gershom G., *Major Trends in Jewish Mysticism*, New York: Schocken Books, 1974. The classic scholarly work on the development of mystical Judaism.

Seltzer, Robert, *Jewish People, Jewish Thought: The Jewish Experience in History*, New York: Macmillan, 1980. An excellent comprehensive one-volume history of the Jewish people, with a particular emphasis on philosophy, mysticism, and religious thought.

Tanakh: The Holy Scriptures, The New JPS Translation according to the Traditional Hebrew Text, Philadelphia: The Jewish Publication Society, 1988. The preferred translation of the Hebrew Scriptures, in graceful and spiritually sensitive modern English.

Wiesel, Elie, *Night*, New York: Bantam, 1960. Short, searing memoir of a teenage boy's Holocaust experience.

Wouk, Herman, *This is my God*, Boston: Little, Brown, 1959, 1988. A very readable personal description of a lived faith.

CHAPTER 10
CHRISTIANITY

"Jesus Christ is Lord"

Christianity is a faith based on the life, teachings, death, and resurrection of Jesus. He was born as a Jew about two thousand years ago in Roman-occupied Palestine. He taught for fewer than three years and was killed on charges of sedition. Nothing was written about him at the time; some years after his death attempts were made to record what he had said and done. Yet his birth is now celebrated around the world and since the sixth century used as the major point from which time is measured in the West. The religion centered around him has more followers than any other.

In studying Christianity we will first examine what can be said about the life and teachings of Jesus, based on accounts in the Bible and historians' knowledge of the period. We will then follow the evolution of the religion as it spread to all continents and became theologically and liturgically more complex. This process continues in the present, in which there are not one but many different versions of Christianity.

The Christian Bible

The Christian Bible consists of the Hebrew Bible (called the "Old Testament") plus the twenty-seven books of the "New Testament" written after Jesus's earthly mission. What we know about Jesus's life and teachings is derived largely from the first four books of the New Testament. They are called the **gospels** ("good news"). On the whole, they seem to have been originally written about forty to fifty years after Jesus's death. They are based on oral transmission of the stories and discourses, which may have been influenced by the growing split between Christians and Jews. The documents are now thought to have been anonymous, but they are given the names of four of Jesus's followers: Matthew, Mark, Luke, and John. The gospels were first written down in Greek and perhaps Aramaic, the common spoken languages of the day, and then copied and translated in many different ways over the centuries. They offer a composite picture of Jesus as seen through the eyes of the Christian community.

How do Christians approach the gospels? Traditionally, the holy scriptures have been reverently regarded as the Word of God, divinely inspired. Furthermore, in Eastern Orthodox Christianity, "the Gospel is not just Holy Scripture but also a symbol of Divine Wisdom and an image of Christ Himself."[1] Nonetheless, some Christians have attempted to clarify what Jesus taught and how he lived, so that people might truly follow him. In general, interpretations of the stories and sayings of Jesus may be literal, allegorical, mystical, or moral. In the nineteenth century, critical study of the Bible from a rationalist point of view began in Western Europe. This approach, now accepted by many Roman Catholics and Protestants, is based on the literary method of interpreting ancient writings in their historical context, with their intended audience and desired effect taken into account. There have thus been many attempts to analyze the gospel books in comparison with each other and with reference to non-Biblical writings of the time.

Three of the gospels, Matthew, Mark, and Luke, are so similar that they are called the **synoptic** gospels, referring to the fact that they can be "seen together" as presenting rather similar views of Jesus's career, though they are organized somewhat differently. Most historians think that they draw from a basic source, most likely an early version of the shortest gospel called Mark. This hypothesized source would probably be a compilation of oral traditions, circulated anonymously at first. Its intended audience may have been non-Palestinian Christians who were converts from polytheistic faiths.

The other two synoptic gospels often parallel Mark quite closely but add additional material. The gospel entitled "Matthew" (one of Jesus's original disciples, a tax collector) is sometimes called a Jewish Christian gospel. It represents Jesus as a second Moses as well as the Messiah ushering in the kingdom of heaven, with frequent references back to the Old Testament. Matthew's stories emphasize that the Gentiles accept Jesus, whereas the Jews reject him as savior.

Luke, to whom the third gospel is attributed, is traditionally thought to have been a physician referred to by Paul the apostle. The gospel seems to have been written with a Gentile (i.e., non-Jewish) Christian audience in mind. Luke presents Jesus's mission in universal rather than exclusively Jewish terms and accentuates the importance of his ministry to the underprivileged and lower classes.

The Gospel of John, traditionally thought to have been written by "the disciple Jesus loved," is of a very different nature than the other three. It concerns itself less with following the life of Jesus than with seeing Jesus as the eternal Son of God, the incarnation of God on earth.

Other gospels circulating in the early Christian church were not included in the official canon of the Bible. They include magical stories of Jesus's infancy, such as an account of his making clay birds and then bringing them to life. The Gospel According to Thomas, one of the long-hidden manuscripts discovered in 1945 by a peasant in a cave near Nag Hammadi, Egypt, is of particular interest. Some scholars feel that it may have been written as early or even earlier than the canonical gospels. It contains many sayings in common with the other gospels but places the accent on mystical concepts of Jesus:

Jesus said: I am the Light that is above
them all. I am the All,
the All came forth from me and the All
attained to me. Cleave a (piece of) wood, I
am there; lift up the stone and you will
find Me there.[2]

The life and teachings of Jesus

It is not possible to reconstruct from the gospels a single chronology of Jesus's life or to account for much of what happened before he began his ministry. Nevertheless, the stories of the New Testament are important to Christians as the foundations of their faith. And after extensive analysis some scholars have concluded on grounds of linguistics and regional history that many of the sayings attributed to Jesus by the gospels may be authentic.

No one now knows what Jesus, the founder of the world's largest religion, looked like. Rembrandt used a young European Jewish man as his model for this sensitive "portrait" of Jesus.

Birth

Historians think Jesus was probably born several years before or after the first year of what is now called the Common Era. When sixth-century Christian monks began figuring time in relationship to the life of Jesus, they may have miscalculated slightly. Traditionally, Christians have believed that Jesus was born in Bethlehem. This detail fulfills the rabbinic interpretation of the Old Testament prophecies that the Messiah would be born in Bethlehem, the home of David the great king, and in the lineage of David. Both Matthew and Luke offer genealogies tracing Jesus to David, but the people in their lists are different. Some scholars suggest that Jesus was actually born in or near Nazareth, his own home town in Galilee. This region, whose name meant "Ring of the Gentiles" (non-Jews), was not fully Jewish; it was also scorned as somewhat countrified by the rabbinic orthodoxy of Judaea. Both Judaea and Galilee were ruled by Rome at the time.

According to the gospels Jesus's mother was Mary, who was a virgin when she conceived him by the Holy Spirit; his father was Joseph, a carpenter from Bethlehem. Luke states that they had to go to Bethlehem to satisfy a Roman ruling that everyone should travel to their ancestral cities for a census. When they had made the difficult journey, there was no room for them in the inn, so the baby Jesus was born in a manger in the animals' quarters. He was named Jesus, which means "God saves." This well-loved birth legend exemplifies the humility that Jesus taught. According to Luke, those who came to pay their respects were poor shepherds to whom angels had appeared with the glad tidings that a Savior had been born to the people. Matthew tells instead of Zoroastrian Magi from "the east" who brought the Christ child symbolic gifts of gold and frankincense and myrrh, confirming his kingship and his adoration by Gentiles.

Preparation

No other stories are told about Jesus's childhood in Nazareth until at twelve he came of age and accompanied his parents on their yearly trip to Jerusalem for Passover. Left behind by mistake, he was said to have been discovered by his parents in the Temple discussing the Torah with the rabbis; "all who heard him were amazed at his understanding and his answers." When scolded, he reportedly replied, "Did you not know that I must be in my Father's house?"[3] This story is used to demonstrate his sense of mission even as a boy, his knowledge of Jewish tradition, and the close personal connection between Jesus and God. In later accounts of his prayers, he spoke to God as "Abba," a very familiar word for father which had never been used in Jewish prayers.

Jesus is often pictured as a divine child, born in a humble stable, and forced to flee on a donkey with his parents. (Monastere Benedictin de Keur Moussa, Senegal, Fuite en Egypte.)

The New Testament is also silent about the years of Jesus's young manhood. What is described, however, is the ministry of John the Baptist, a prophet citing Isaiah's prophecies of the coming kingdom of God. He was conducting baptism according to Jewish practice in the Jordan River in preparation for the Kingdom. Apocalyptic expectations were running high at the time, with Israel chafing under Roman taxation and rule.

According to all four gospels, at the age of about thirty Jesus appeared before John to be baptized. John was calling people to repent of their sins and then be spiritually purified and sanctified by immersion in the river. He felt it improper to perform this ceremony for Jesus, whom Christians consider sinless, but Jesus insisted. How can this be interpreted? One explanation is that, for Jesus, this became a ceremony of his consecration to God as the Messiah. The Gospel writer reports,

> *When he came up out of the water, immediately he saw the heavens opened and the Spirit descending upon him like a dove; and a voice came from heaven. "Thou art my beloved Son; with thee I am well pleased."*[4]

Another interpretation is that Jesus's baptism was the occasion for John's publicly announcing that the Messiah had arrived, beginning his ministry. A third interpretation is that by requesting baptism, Jesus identified himself with sinful humanity. Even though he had no need for repentence and purification, he accepted baptism on behalf of all humans.

At some point, Jesus reportedly undertook a forty-day retreat in the desert wilderness, fasting. During his retreat, the gospel-writers say he was tempted by Satan to use his spiritual power for secular ends, but he refused.

John the Baptist is said to have baptized Jesus only reluctantly, saying that he was unworthy even to fasten Jesus's shoes. When he did so, the Spirit allegedly descended upon Jesus as a dove. (Painting by Esperanza Guevara, Solentiname, Nicaragua.)

Ministry

In John's gospel, Jesus's baptism by John the Baptist was followed by his gathering of the first disciples, the fisherman Simon (called Peter), Andrew (Peter's brother), James, and John (brother of James), who recognized him as the Messiah. First of all Jesus warned his disciples that they would have to leave all their possessions and human attachments to follow him — to pay more attention to the life of the spirit than to physical comfort and wealth. He said that it was extremely difficult for the wealthy to enter the kingdom of heaven. God, the Protector, takes care of physical needs, which are relatively unimportant anyway:

Is not life more than food, and the body more than clothing? Look at the birds of the air; they neither sow nor reap nor gather into barns, and yet your heavenly Father feeds them. Are you not of more value than they? And which of you by being anxious can add one cubit to his span of life?[5]

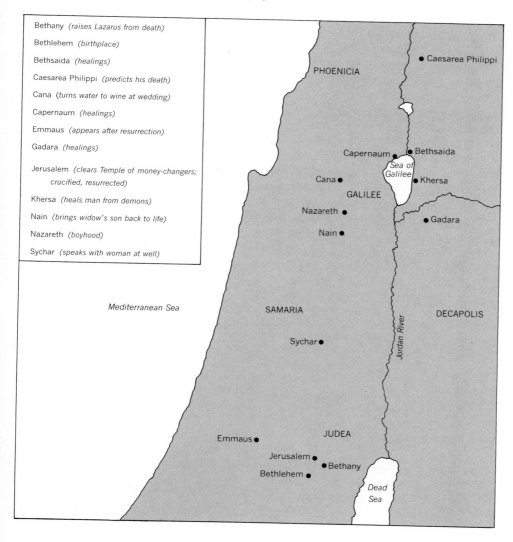

Bethany *(raises Lazarus from death)*

Bethlehem *(birthplace)*

Bethsaida *(healings)*

Caesarea Philippi *(predicts his death)*

Cana *(turns water to wine at wedding)*

Capernaum *(healings)*

Emmaus *(appears after resurrection)*

Gadara *(healings)*

Jerusalem *(clears Temple of money-changers; crucified, resurrected)*

Khersa *(heals man from demons)*

Nain *(brings widow's son back to life)*

Nazareth *(boyhood)*

Sychar *(speaks with woman at well)*

From north to south, the area covered by Jesus during his ministry was no more than 100 miles (161 km). Yet his mission is now worldwide, with more followers than any other religion.

CHRISTIANITY

	0 CE — Jesus c.4 BCE–30 CE
	Paul organizes early Christians c.50–60 CE
	100 — Gospels written down c.70–95 CE
	200
Constantine Emperor of Roman Empire 306–337	**300** — Canon of New Testament set 367
	400 — Life of Augustine 354–430
	500 — Life of Benedict and creation of his monastic rule c.480–542
	600
	700
Middle Ages in Europe; centralization of papal power 800–1300	**800**
	900
	1000 — Split between Western and Eastern Orthodox Church 1054
The Crusades 1095–1350	**1100** — St. Francis of Assisi 1182–1226
	1200
Proliferation of monastic orders 1300s	**1300**
	1400
	1500 — Martin Luther posts 95 Theses 1517
Church of England separates from Rome 1534	The Council of Trent; Roman Catholic Reformation 1545–1563
	1600
	1700
The Enlightenment in Europe 1800s	**1800**
World Council of Churches formed 1948	**1900** — Discovery of the Nag Hammadi manuscripts 1945
Freedom of religion granted in USSR 1980s	**2000** — The Second Vatican Council 1962

Jesus taught that his followers should concentrate on laying up spiritual treasures in heaven, rather than material treasures on earth, which are short-lived. Because God is a generous parent, those who love God and want to follow the path of righteousness should pray for help, in private: "Ask, and it will be given you; seek, and you will find; knock, and it will be opened to you."[6]

As Jesus traveled, speaking, he is said to have performed many miracles, such as turning water into wine, healing the sick, restoring the dead to life, walking on water, casting devils out of the possessed, and turning a few loaves and fish into enough food to feed a crowd of thousands, with copious leftovers. Jesus reportedly performed these miracles quietly and compassionately; the gospels interpreted them as signs of the coming kingdom of God.

The stories of the miracles performed by Jesus have symbolic meanings taken from the entire Jewish and early Christian traditions. In the sharing of the loaves and fishes, for instance, it may have been more than physical bread that Luke was talking about when he said, "and all ate and were satisfied."[7] The people came to Jesus out of spiritual hunger, and he fed them all, profligate with his love. Bread often signified life-giving sustenance. Jesus was later to offer himself as "the bread of life."[8]

On another level of interpretation, the story may prefigure the Last Supper of Jesus with his disciples, with both stories alluding to the Jewish tradition of the Great Banquet, the heavenly feast of God, as a symbol of the messianic age. The fish were a symbol of Christ to the early Christians; what he fed them was the indiscriminate gift of himself.

Theological interpretations of the biblical stories are based on the evidence of the Bible itself, but people also bring their own experiences to them. To William, a twentieth-century Nicaraguan peasant, the miracle was not the multiplication of the loaves but the sharing: "The miracle was to persuade the owners of the bread to share it, that it was absurd for them to keep it all while the people were going hungry."[9]

Jesus preached truly radical ethics, extending the application of Jewish laws: "You have heard that it was said to the men of old," Jesus began, "You shall not kill; and whoever kills shall be liable to judgment. But I say to you that every one who is angry with his brother shall be liable to judgment...."[10] Not only should a man not commit adultery; it is wrong even to look at a woman lustfully. Rather than revenging an eye for an eye, a tooth for a tooth, respond with love. If a person strikes you on one cheek, turn the other cheek to be struck also. If anyone tries to rob you of your coat, give him your cloak as well. And not only should you love your neighbor, Jesus says:

> Love your enemies and pray for those who persecute you, so that you may be sons of your Father who is in heaven; for he makes his sun rise on the evil and on the good, and sends rain on the just and on the unjust.[11]

The extremely high ethical standards of the *Sermon on the Mount* (Matthew 5 to 7), may seem impossibly challenging. Who can fully follow them? And Jesus said these things to people who had been brought up with the understanding that to incompletely fulfill even one divine commandment is a violation of the Law. But when people recognize their helplessness to fulfill such commandments, they are ready to turn to the divine for help. Jesus pointed out, "With man this is impossible,

Many miracles are associated with Jesus, such as the miraculous healing of a crippled man to whom he said, "Pick up your bed and walk."

but not with God; all things are possible with God." (Mark 10: 27).

The main thing Jesus taught was love. He stated that to love God and to "love your neighbor as yourself"[12] were the two great commandments in Judaism, upon which everything else rested. To love God means placing God first in one's life, rather than concentrating on the things of the earth. To love one's neighbor means selfless service to everyone, even to those despised by the rest of society. Jesus often horrified the religious authorities by talking to prostitutes, tax-collectors, and the poorest and lowliest of people. He set an example of loving service by washing his disciples' feet. This kind of love, he said, should be the mark of his followers, and at the last judgment, when the Son of man judges the people of all time, he will grant eternal life in the kingdom to the humble "sheep" who loved and served him in all:

> *Then the righteous will answer him, "Lord, when did we see thee hungry and feed thee, or thirsty and give thee drink? And when did we see thee a stranger and welcome thee, or naked and clothe thee? And when did we see thee sick or in prison and visit thee?" And the King will answer them, "Truly, I say to you, as you did it to one of the least of these my brethren, you did it to me."[13]*

Jesus preached that God is forgiving to those who repent. He told a story likening God to the father who welcomed with gifts and celebration his "prodigal son" who had squandered his inheritance and then humbly returned home. He told story after story suggesting that those who considered themselves superior were less beloved by God than those whom society had rejected. The hated toll-collectors and prostitutes, the ignorant common people, are more likely to receive God's merciful forgiveness through repentance than are the learned and hypocritically self-righteous. Indeed, Jesus said, it was only as children that people could enter the kingdom of heaven. In a famous series of statements about supreme happiness called the **Beatitudes**, Jesus is quoted as having promised blessings for the "poor in spirit,"[14] the mourners, the meek, the seekers of righteousness, the pure in heart, the merciful, the peacemakers, and those who are persecuted for the sake of righteousness and of spreading the gospel.

Jesus's stories were typically presented as **parables**, in which earthly situations familiar to people of his time and place were used to make a spiritual point. He spoke of parents and children, of masters and servants, of sowing seeds, of fishing. For example,

> *The kingdom of heaven is like a dragnet cast into the sea that brings in a haul of all kinds. When it is full, the fishermen haul it ashore; then, sitting down, they collect the good ones in a basket and throw away those that are no use. This is how it will be at the end of time: the angels will appear and separate the wicked from the just to throw them into the blazing furnace where there will be weeping and grinding of teeth.[15]*

As we have seen, messianic expectations were running very high among Jews of that time, oppressed as they were by Roman rule. They looked to a time when the people of Israel would be freed and the authority of Israel's God would be

---

TEACHING STORY

The Good Samaritan

On one occasion a lawyer came forward to put this test question to Jesus: "Master, what must I do to inherit eternal life?" Jesus said, "What is written in the Law? What is your reading of it?" He replied, "Love the Lord your God with all your heart, with all your soul, with all your strength, and with all your mind; and your neighbor as yourself." "That is the right answer," said Jesus; "do that and you will live."

But he wanted to vindicate himself, so he said to Jesus, "And who is my neighbor?" Jesus replied, "A man was on his way from Jerusalem down to Jericho when he fell in with robbers, who stripped him, beat him, and went off leaving him half dead. It so happened that a priest was going down by the same road; but when he saw him, he went past on the other side. So too a Levite came to the place,

and when he saw him went past on the other side. But a Samaritan (a person from a region against whom the Jews of Judaea had developed religious and racial prejudice) who was making the journey came upon him, and when he saw him was moved to pity. He went up and bandaged his wounds, bathing them with oil and wine. Then he lifted him on to his own beast, brought him to an inn, and looked after him there. Next day he produced two silver pieces and gave them to the innkeeper, and said, 'Look after him; and if you spend any more, I will repay you on my way back.' Which of these three do you think was neighbor to the man who fell into the hands of the robbers?" He answered, "The one who showed him kindness." Jesus said, "Go and do as he did."[16]

recognized throughout the world. Jesus reportedly spoke to them again and again about the fulfillment of these expectations: "The time is fulfilled, and the kingdom of God is at hand; repent, and believe in the gospel"[17]; "I must preach the good news of the kingdom of God … for I was sent for this purpose."[18] He taught them to pray for the advent of this kingdom: "Thy kingdom come, Thy will be done on earth as it is in heaven."[19] However, in contrast to expectations of secular deliverance from the Romans, Jesus seems to refer to the kingdom as manifestation of God's full glory, the consummation of the world.

> *Every one who drinks of this water will thirst again, but whoever drinks of the water that I shall give him will never thirst; the water that I shall give him will become in him a spring of water welling up to eternal life.[20]*
> *(Jesus, as quoted in The Gospel of John, 4:13–14)*

True to the apocalyptic Jewish writings of the time, Jesus said that things would get much worse right before the end. He seemed to foretell the destruction of Jerusalem by the Romans that began in 70 CE. But:

> *then will appear the sign of the Son of man in heaven, and then all the tribes of the earth will mourn, and they will see the Son of man coming on the clouds of heaven with power and great glory; and he will send out his angels with a loud trumpet call, and they will gather his elect from the four winds, from one end of heaven to the other.[21]*

It was his mission, he said, to gather together everyone who could be saved.

Challenges to the authorities

As Jesus traveled through Galilee, many people gathered around him to be healed. Herod Antipas, a Jew who had been appointed by the Romans as ruler of Galilee, had already executed John the Baptist and may have been concerned that Jesus might be a trouble-maker, perhaps one of the Zealots of Galilee who were stirring up support for a political uprising against the Romans. Jesus therefore moved outside Herod's jurisdiction for a while, to carry on his work in Tyre and Sidon.

According to the gospels, Jesus was also regarded with suspicion by prominent Jewish groups of his time — the emerging Pharisees (the shapers of rabbinic Judaism, deriving from the written and oral traditions), Sadducees (the priests and upper class) and the scribes (specially trained laymen who copied the written law and formulated the oral law of Judaism). Jesus seems not to have challenged Mosaic law, but rather, its interpretations in the evolving rabbinic traditions and the hypocrisy of those who claim to be living by the law. It is written in the gospel of Matthew that the Pharisees and scribes challenged Jesus:

> *"Why do your disciples break away from the tradition of the elders? They do not wash their hands when they eat food."*
> *"And why do you," he answered, "break away from the commandment of God for the sake of your tradition? For God said: 'Do your duty to your father and mother' and: 'Anyone who curses father or mother must be put to death.'[22] But you*

At the Last Supper, Jesus foretold his death and instructed his disciples to maintain mystic communion with him through a ceremony with bread and wine.

say, 'If anyone says to his father or mother: Anything I have that I might have used to help you is dedicated to God,' he is rid of his duty to father or mother. In this way you have made God's word null and void by means of your tradition. Hypocrites! It was you Isaiah meant when he so rightly prophesied: 'This people honors me only with lip service / while their hearts are far from me. / The worship they offer me is worthless; / the doctrines they teach are only human regulations."[23]

He called the people to him and said, "Listen, and understand. What goes into the mouth does not make a man unclean; it is what comes out of the mouth that makes him unclean.... For things that come out of the mouth come from the heart,

and it is these that make a man unclean. For from the heart come evil intentions....
But to eat with unwashed hands does not make a man unclean."[24]

Then addressing the people and his disciples Jesus said, "The scribes and the
Pharisees occupy the chair of Moses. You must therefore do what they tell you and
listen to what they say; but do not be guided by what they do: since they do not
practice what they preach....

Alas for you, scribes and Pharisees, you hypocrites! You who are like
whitewashed tombs that look handsome on the outside, but inside are full of dead
men's bones and every kind of corruption. In the same way you appear to people
from the outside like good honest men, but inside you are full of hypocrisy and
lawlessness."[25]

Many seemingly anti-Jewish statements in the New Testament are suspected by
some modern scholars as additions or interpretations dating from the period after
Jesus's death, when rabbinic Judaism and early Christianity were competing
for followers. Nevertheless, more universal teachings are apparent in such
stories attributed to Jesus. For instance, in all times and all religions there have
been those who do not practice what they preach when claiming to speak with
spiritual authority.

Jesus also confronted the commercial interests in the Temple of Jerusalem, those
who were making a living by charging a profit when exchanging money for Temple
currency and selling animals for sacrificial offerings:

So they reached Jerusalem and he went into the Temple and began driving out those
who were selling and buying there; he upset the tables of the money changers and
the chairs of those who were selling pigeons. Nor would he allow anyone to carry
anything through the Temple. And he taught them and said, "Does not scripture
say; 'My house will be called a house of prayer for all the peoples?'[26] *But you have*
turned it into a robbers' den."[27] *This came to the ears of the chief priests and the*
scribes, and they tried to find some way of doing away with him; they were afraid of
him because the people were carried away by his teaching.[28]

According to the gospel accounts, Jesus appropriated to himself the messianic
prophecies of Second Isaiah. In private, he asked his disciples, "Who do you say
that I am?" Peter answered, "You are the Christ."[29] **"Christ"** is Greek for "anointed
one," which in Aramaic (*M'shekha* or *Messiah*) also means "perfected" or "enlightened
one." Contemporary Biblical scholars have concluded that Jesus rejected the title
of Messiah, for it might have been misunderstood. His disciples later spoke of him
as the Messiah after he died and was resurrected. But during his lifetime as well,
they were convinced of his divinity. His follower Martha, sister of Lazarus whom
Jesus reportedly raised from the dead, is quoted as having said to Jesus, "I now
believe that you are the Messiah, the Son of God who was to come into the world."[30]

A spectacular event, "The Transfiguration," was witnessed by three disciples.
Jesus had climbed a mountain to pray, and as he did:

He was transfigured before them, and his face shone like the sun, and his garments
became white as light. And behold, there appeared to them Moses and Elijah,
talking with him.... When lo, a bright cloud overshadowed them, and a voice
from the cloud said, "This is my beloved Son, with whom I am well pleased;
listen to him."[31]

The presence of Moses and Elijah (who in Jewish apocalyptic tradition were expected to return at the end of the world) placed Jewish law and prophecy behind the claim that Jesus is the Christ. They were representatives of the old covenant; Jesus brought a new dispensation of grace.

Jesus claimed that John the Baptist was Elijah come again. The authorities had killed John the Baptist and, Jesus prophesied, they would attack him, too, not recognizing who he was. John's gospel is particularly intent on portraying him as the Christ. John quotes Jesus as saying things like "My teaching is not mine, but his who sent me"; "I am the light of the world"; "You are from below, I am from above; you are of this world, I am not of this world"; and "Before Abraham was, I am."[32]

Jesus characterized himself as a good shepherd who is willing to lay down his life for his sheep. Foreshadowing the crucifixion, he said he would offer his own flesh and blood as a sacrifice for the sake of humanity. His coming death would mark a "new covenant" in which his blood would be "poured out for many for the forgiveness of sins."[33]

It is possible that such passages defining Jesus's role were later interpolations by the early Christians as they tried to explain the meaning of their Master's life and death in new terms during the decades when the New Testament was in formation.

Crucifixion

The anti-institutional tenor of Jesus's teachings did not endear him to those in power. Jesus knew that to return to Jerusalem would be politically dangerous. But eventually he did so, at Passover. He entered the town on a donkey, accompanied by multitudes who cried:

"Hosanna! Blessed be he who comes in the name of the Lord! Blessed be the kingdom of our father David that is coming! Hosanna in the highest!"[34]

However, Jesus warned his disciples that his end was near. At "the Last Supper," a meal during the Passover season, he is said to have given them instructions for a ceremony with bread and wine to be performed thenceforth to maintain a mystical communion with him. However, one of the disciples would betray him, he said. This one, Judas, had already done so, selling information leading to Jesus's arrest for thirty pieces of silver.

Jesus took three of his followers to a garden called Gethsemane, on the Mount of Olives, where he is said to have prayed intensely that the cup of suffering would pass away from him, if it be God's will, "yet not what I will, but what thou wilt."[35] The gospels often speak of Jesus's spending long periods in spontaneous prayer to God, whom he addressed very personally as "Abba." It is possible to interpret Jesus's prayer at Gethsemane as a confirmation of his great faith in God's mercy and power. In the words of New Testament theologian Joachim Jeremias:

Jesus takes into account the possibility that God may rescind his own holy will ... The Father of Jesus is not the immovable, unchangeable God who in the end can only be described in negations. He is not a God to whom it is pointless to pray. He is a gracious God, who hears prayers and intercessions, and is capable in his mercy of rescinding his own holy will.[36]

Jesus's crucifixion was interpreted by many later Christians as the sacrifice of an innocent lamb as atonement for the sins of humanity. A different interpretation was that God gave "himself or herself" in love, drawing the world into a loving relationship with the divine. (Rembrandt van Rijn, The Three Crosses, 1653.)

Nevertheless, after this period of prayer Jesus said, according to Mark's gospel, "It is all over. The hour has come."[37] A crowd led by Judas approached with swords and clubs; they led Jesus away to be questioned by the chief priest, elders and scribes.

Then followed several trials of sorts. The high priest, Caiaphas, asked Jesus several questions to establish that he was a blasphemer. One concerned the claim that he was the Son of God. Jesus answered:

You have said so. But I tell you, hereafter you will see the Son of man seated at the right hand of Power, and coming on the clouds of heaven.[38]

Caiaphas pronounced this statement blasphemy, and they took him to Pilate, the Roman governor, for sentencing. To Pilate's leading question, "Are you King of the Jews?" Jesus is said to have replied, "You have said so."[39]

For this potentially seditious "statement," they took Jesus to a hill called Golgotha and nailed him to a cross, as was the Roman executionary custom. The accusation — "This is Jesus, King of the Jews" — was set over his head, and two robbers were crucified alongside him. The authorities, the people, and even the robbers mocked him for saying that he could save others when he could not even save himself.

Jesus hung there for hours until, according to the Gospels, he cried out, "My God, my God, why hast thou forsaken me?"[40] This is the first line of Psalm 22, which is actually a great proclamation of the faith in God of one who is persecuted. Then Jesus died. This event is thought to have happened on a Friday some time between

27 and 33 CE. A wealthy Jewish disciple called Joseph of Arimathea asked Pilate for Jesus's body, which he wrapped in a linen shroud and placed in his own tomb, with a large stone against the door. A guard was placed at the tomb to make sure that no followers would steal the body and claim that Jesus had risen from the dead.

Resurrection

That seemed to be the end of it. Jesus's disciples were terrified, so some of them hid, mourning and disheartened. The whole religious movement could have died out, as did Shabbatai Tzevi's Jewish messiahship centuries later. However, what happened next, according to varying gospel accounts, seemed to change everything.

The resurrected Jesus displays his wounds, symbolizing the ongoing wounding of God by human actions. At the same time that God confronts humans with their sins, God also offers total forgiveness, according to some Christian theologians. (Grunewald, detail from The Isenheim Altarpiece, c. 1510–15.)

Some of the women who had been close to Jesus visited the tomb on Sunday to prepare the body for a proper burial, a rite which had been postponed because of the Sabbath. Instead, they found the tomb empty, with the stone rolled away. Angels then appeared and told them that Jesus had risen from death. The women ran and brought two of the male disciples, who witnessed the empty tomb with the shrouds folded.

Then followed numerous reports of appearances of the risen Christ to various disciples. He dispelled their doubts about his resurrection, having them touch his wounds and even eating a fish with them. He said to them, as recounted in the gospel of Matthew:

> *All authority in heaven and on earth has been given to me. Go therefore and make disciples of all nations, baptizing them in the name of the Father and of the Son and of the Holy Spirit, teaching them to observe all that I have commanded you; and lo, I am with you always, to the close of the age.*[41]

The details of the appearances of the resurrected Jesus differ considerably from gospel to gospel. Some scholars think that to have women as the first witnesses to the empty tomb suggests that there must be some historical truth in the claims of Jesus's resurrection, for no one trying to build a case would have rested it on the testimony of women, who had little status in a patriarchal society.

It was the resurrection that presumably turned defeat into victory for Jesus, and discouragement into powerful action for his followers. As the impact of all they had seen set in, the followers came to believe that Jesus had been God in human form, walking among them.

The Early Church

Persecution became the lot of Jesus's followers. But within three hundred years, despite strong opposition, Christianity had become the official religion of the vast Roman Empire. As it became the establishment, rather than a tiny, disorganized handful of heretics within Judaism, Christianity continued to define and organize itself from the first century onward.

From persecution to empire

The earliest years of what became the mainstream of Christianity are described in the New Testament books that follow the gospel accounts of the life of Jesus. "The Acts of the Apostles" was presumably written by the same person who wrote the gospel of Luke, for the language is the same, both books are addressed to the same person named Theophilus, and Acts refers back to the gospel of Luke as an earlier part of a single history of the rise of Christianity. Acts is followed by letters to some of the early groups of Christians, most of them apparently written by Paul, a major organizer and apostle (missionary), in about 50 to 60 CE.

Like the gospel accounts, the stories in these biblical books are examined by many contemporary scholars as possibly romanticized, idealized documents, used to convert, to increase faith, to teach principles, and to establish Christian theology, rather than to accurately record historical facts.

According to Acts, an event called **Pentecost** galvanized the early Christians into action. At a meeting of the disciples, something that sounded like a great wind came down from the sky, and what looked like tongues of fire swirled around to touch each one's head. The narrative states that they all began speaking in languages they had never studied. Some mocked them, saying they were drunk, but Peter declared that they had been filled with the Spirit of God, as the Old Testament prophet Joel had prophesied would happen in the last days before the onset of the kingdom of God. He testified that the Jesus whom the people had crucified had been raised up by God, who had made him "both Lord and Christ."[42] Reportedly, three thousand people were so convinced that they were baptized that day.

One of the persecutors of Christians was Saul. He was a Pharisee tentmaker who lived during the time of Jesus but never met him. Instead, after Jesus died, he helped to throw many of his followers into prison and sentence them to death. Acts relates that on the way to Damascus in search of more heretics, he saw a light brighter than the sun and heard the voice of Jesus asking why Saul was persecuting him. This resistance was useless, said the vision of Jesus, who then appointed him to do the opposite: to go to both Jews and Gentiles:

to open their eyes, that they may turn from darkness to light and from the power of Satan to God, that they may receive forgiveness of sins and a place among those who are sanctified by faith in me.[43]

Saul was baptized and immediately began promoting the Christian message under his new name, Paul. His indefatigable work in traveling about the Mediterranean world was of great importance in shaping and expanding the early Christian church. He was shipwrecked, stoned, imprisoned, and beaten, and probably died as a martyr in Rome, but nothing short of death deterred him from his new mission.

Paul tried to convince Jews that Jesus's birth, death, and resurrection had been predicted by the Old Testament prophets. This was the messiah they had been waiting for, and now, risen from death, he presided as the cosmic Christ, offering God's forgiveness and grace to those who trust in God rather than in themselves. Some Jews were converted to this belief, but the Jewish authorities repeatedly accused Paul of leading people away from Jewish law and tradition. Judaism had many variations, but those who emphasized that Jews had been especially chosen by God were confronted by interpretations of Jesus's life and teachings which saw Christianity as a universal mission of salvation for all peoples. These interpretations made the new sect, Christianity, seem irreconcilable with exclusive versions of Judaism, and the gap between the two became deep and bitter. The New Testament writings reflect the criticisms of the early Christians against Jews who did not accept Jesus as their Messiah. These polemics exaggerate the differences between Christians and Jews and have contributed to centuries of anti-Semitism.

Paul also tried to sway Gentiles: worshippers of the old gods whose religion was in decline, supporters of the emperor as deity, ecstatic initiates of mystery cults, and followers of dualistic Greco-Roman philosophers who regarded matter as evil and tried to emancipate the soul from its corrupting influence. He taught them that God did not reside in any idol but yet was not far from them, "For in him we live and move and have our being."[44] For Gentiles embracing Christianity, Paul and others argued that the Jewish tradition of circumcision should not be required of them. As Paul interpreted the gospel, salvation came by repentant faith in the grace of Christ, rather than by observance of a traditional law. In Romans, Paul's letter to the church in Rome, he argues that Abraham himself was **justified**, or absolved of sin, by God because of his great faith in God rather than by his circumcision.

Christianity spread rapidly. Soon it departed from its status as one of many unorthodox Jewish sects and became largely non-Jewish in membership. By 200 CE, it had spread throughout the Roman Empire and into Mesopotamia, despite sometimes fierce opposition. Some Christians were subject to imprisonment, torture, and confiscation of property, because they were intolerant toward polytheistic beliefs in the Roman Empire. They themselves were suspected of being revolutionaries, with their talk of a messiah, and of strange cultic behaviors, such as their secret rituals of symbolically drinking Jesus's blood and eating his flesh. Persecution did not sway the most ardent of Christians, for it united them intimately to the passion and death of Christ.

With the rise of Constantine to the imperial throne early in the fourth century CE, opposition lapsed and then turned to official embracing of Christianity. Constantine said that God showed him a vision of a cross to be used as a standard in battle. After he used it and won, he instituted tolerance of Christianity alongside the state cult, of which he was the chief priest. Just before his death, Constantine was baptized as a Christian.

By the end of the fourth century CE, people of other religions were stripped of all rights, and ordered into Christian churches to be baptized. Some paid outward service to Christianity but remained inwardly faithful to their old traditions. As Christianity became the favored religion, many converted for secular reasons.

By the end of the fifth century CE, Christianity was the faith claimed by the majority of people in the vast Roman Empire. It also spread beyond the empire, from Ireland on the west to India and Ceylon on the east, with a partial, tense presence in Mesopotamia, where Zoroastrianism prevailed.

Evolving organization and theology

During its phenomenal growth from persecuted sect to state religion throughout much of the ancient world, Christianity was developing organizationally and theologically. By the end of the first century CE it had a bureaucratic structure which carried on the rites of the church and attempted to define true Christianity.

One form that was judged to be outside the mainstream was Gnostic Christianity, which appeared as a movement in the second century CE. **Gnosticism** means mystical perception of knowledge. The Nag Hammadi library found in Egypt presents Jesus as a great Gnostic teacher. His words are interpreted as the secret teachings given only to initiates. "He who is near to me is near to the fire," he says in the Gospel According to Thomas.[45] The gnostics held that only spiritually mature individuals could apprehend Jesus's real teaching: that the kingdom of heaven is a present reality experienced through personal realization of the Light.

When the New Testament canon of twenty-seven officially sanctioned texts was set and translated into Latin in the fourth century, the Gnostic Gospels were not included. Instead, the Church treated possession of Gnostic texts as a crime against church law because it considered Gnostic teaching fundamentally at odds with Jesus's teachings. The Christian faith community felt that Jesus had not taught

The Nag Hammadi manuscripts found in Egypt were buried about 400 CE. They contain copies and translations of early Christian texts condemned as heretical by the Church.

an elitist view of salvation, and had not discriminated against the material aspect of creation.

What became mainstream Christianity is based not only on the life and teachings of Jesus, as set forth in the gospels selected for the New Testament, but also on the ways that they have been interpreted over the centuries. One of the first and most important interpreters was Paul. His central contribution — which was as influential as the four gospels in shaping Christianity — was his interpretation of Jesus's death and resurrection. This came to him directly as a revelation from the risen Christ, he said.

Paul spoke of *agape* — altruistic, self-giving love — as the center of the Christian ideal. He placed it above adherence to law, thereby departing from rabbinic Judaism. He also placed it above spiritual wisdom, asceticism, faith, and supernatural "gifts of the Spirit," such as the ability to heal, prophesy, or spontaneously speak in unknown tongues.

Let all that you do be done in love.

The First Letter of Paul to the Corinthians, 16:14

Love was applied not only to one's neighbors but also to one's relationship with the divine. It was love plus gnosis — knowledge of God, permeated with love — that became the basis of contemplative Christianity, as it was shaped by the "Fathers" of the first centuries.

The cross, with or without an image of Jesus crucified on it, became a central symbol of Christianity. It marked the path of suffering service, rather than political domination, as the way of conquering evil and experiencing union with a compassionate God. To participate in Jesus's sacrifice, people could repent of their sins, be baptized, and be reborn to new life in Christ. In the early fifth century CE the bishop Augustine, one of the most influential theologians in the history of Christianity, described this spiritual rebirth thus:

CHRISTIANITY

Where I was angry within myself in my chamber, where I was inwardly pricked, where I had sacrificed, slaying my old man and commencing the purpose of a new life, putting my trust in Thee — there hadst Thou began to grow sweet unto me and "hadst put gladness in my heart."[46]

Twentieth-century theologian Rowan Williams explains this repentance and spiritual resurrection as:

the refusal to accept that lostness is the final human truth. Like a growing thing beneath the earth, we protest at the darkness and push blindly up in search of light, truth, home — the place, the relation where we are not lost, where we can live from deep roots in assurance. "Because I live, you will live also."[47]

The feeling of expectation of the coming of God's Kingdom, so prevalent in Jesus's time, began to wane as time went by. The notion of the kingdom of God began to shift to the indefinite future, with emphasis placed on a preliminary judgment at one's death. There was nevertheless the continuing expectation that Christ would return in glory to judge the living and the dead and bring to fulfillment the "new creation." This belief in the *Second Coming* of Christ is still an article of faith today.

The Holy Trinity, depicted as three angels in a famous icon by Rublev, is a distinctively Christian view of God. God is One as a communal plurality, an endless circle sharing the love intrinsic to the godhead, inviting all to be healed and saved by this love.

Another early doctrinal development was the doctrine of the **Holy Trinity**. Christians believed that the transcendent, invisible God — the Father — had become immanent in the person of Jesus, God the Son. Furthermore, after his physical death Jesus promised to send the Holy Spirit to his followers. This makes three aspects of God, or three "persons" within the one divine being: Father, Son, and Holy Spirit. Christian theologians believed that the mystery of God was one, expressed in three ways. The Father is envisioned as the almighty transcendent creator of heaven and earth. The Son is the incarnation of the Father, the divine in human form, who returned at the ascension to live with the Father in glory, though he remains fully present in and to his "mystical body" on earth — the community of believers. The Holy Spirit or Holy Ghost is the power and presence of God, actively guiding and sustaining the faithful.

Although Jesus had spoken in parables with several levels of meaning, the evolving Church found it necessary to articulate some of its beliefs more openly and systematically. A number of **creeds**, or professions of faith, were composed for use in religious instruction, baptism, to define who Jesus was and his relationship to God, and to provide clear stands against the challenge of various heresies. For example, one early creed was known as the Roman Creed:

I believe in God the Father Almighty,
And in Jesus Christ, his only Son, our Lord,
Who was born by the Holy Ghost, of the Virgin Mary, was crucified under
*   Pontius Pilate, and was buried.*
The third day he rose from the dead,
He ascended into heaven and sits on the right hand of the Father;
From thence he will come to judge the quick and the dead.
And in the Holy Ghost, the Holy Church, the forgiveness of sins, the
*   resurrection of the body.*

As theological debates proliferated, more phrases were added to affirm the Church's position in contrast to beliefs that were determined to be heresies. For example, the Gnostic heresy that God did not create this often evil physical world was countered in later creeds by the phrase "Maker of heaven and earth" after "God the Father Almighty." The early creeds were developed by global councils of representatives of all area churches. The first of these gatherings for all areas to discuss church matters together was held in 325 CE in Nicea as Christianity was just emerging from persecution to empire.

Early monasticism

Alongside the development of doctrine and the consolidation of church structure, another trend was developing. Some Christians were turning away from the world to live in solitary communion with God, as ascetics. There had been a certain amount of asceticism in Paul's writings. He himself was celibate, as he believed avoiding family entanglements helped one to concentrate on the Lord.

By the fourth century CE, there were Christian monks living simply in caves in the Egyptian desert with little regard for the things of the world. They had no central organization but tended to learn from the examples of sincere monks. Avoiding emphasis on the supernatural powers that often accompany the ascetic life, they told stories demonstrating the virtues they valued, such as humility, submission, and the sharing of food. For example, an earnest young man was said to have visited one of the desert fathers and asked him how he was faring. The old man sighed and said, "Very badly, my child." Asked why, he said, "I have been here forty years doing nothing other than cursing my own self each day, inasmuch as in the prayers I offer, I say to God, 'Accursed are those who deviate from Your commandments.'"[48] The young seeker was moved by such humility and made it his model.

> *The carefree man, who has tested the sweetness of having no personal possessions, feels that even the cassock which he wears and the jug of water in his cell are a useless burden, because these things, too, sometimes distract his mind.*
>
> *A Desert Father*[49]

The desert monks were left to their own devices at first. In Christian humility, they avoided judging or trying to teach each other and attempted to be, at best, harmless. But by the fifth century CE, the monastic life shifted from solitary, unguided practice, to formal spiritual supervision. Group monasteries and structures for guidance by an abbot or abbess were set up and rules devised to help monks persevere in their calling. The Rule of St. Benedict became a model for all later monastic orders in the West, with its emphasis on poverty, chastity, and obedience to the abbot, and insistence that each monastery be economically self-sufficient through the labor of the monastics. The Benedictines have been famous over the centuries for their practice of hospitality to pilgrims and travelers, and are today active participants in inter-religious monastic dialogue.

The Eastern Orthodox Church

Christianity's history has been marked by internal feuds and divisions. One of the deepest schisms occurred in 1054, when the Western Catholic Church and the Eastern Orthodox Church split apart.

The history of the Orthodox Church

Late in the third century CE, the Roman Empire had been divided into an eastern and a western section. In the fourth century CE, Constantine established a second imperial seat in the east, in Constantinople (now Istanbul, Turkey). It was considered a "second Rome," especially after the sack of Rome by the Goths in 410. The two halves of the Christian world grew apart from each other, divided by language (Latin in the west, Greek in the east), culture, and religious differences.

In the western half, religious power was becoming more and more centralized in the Roman pope and other high officials; after the barbarian invasions, the clergy were often the only educated people. The Byzantine east was more democratic, with less distinction between clergy and laypeople. Its highest official, the patriarch of Constantinople, was largely a titular head, a symbol of Christian unity, and the east did not recognize the Roman pope's claim to universal authority in the Church.

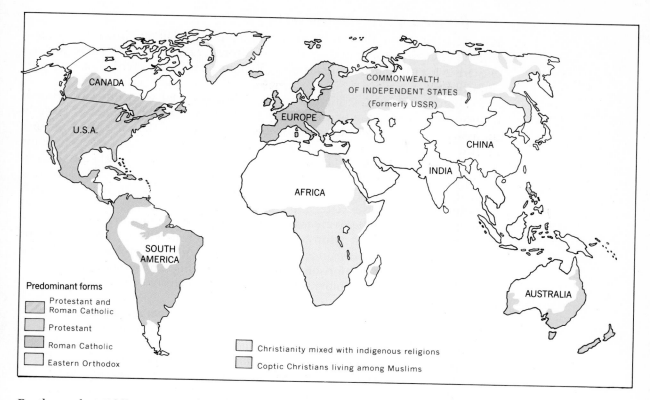

Predominant forms

- Protestant and Roman Catholic
- Protestant
- Roman Catholic
- Eastern Orthodox

- Christianity mixed with indigenous religions
- Coptic Christians living among Muslims

By the early Middle Ages, there were also doctrinal disagreements. In its version of the Nicene-Constantinople Creed, the western church professed that the Holy Spirit came from both the Father and the Son; the eastern church retained what it considered the original understanding, that the Holy Spirit proceeds only from the Father.

In 1054, leaders of the eastern and western factions excommunicated each other over the disagreement about the Holy Spirit, and also over the papal claim, celibacy for priests (not required in the eastern church), and whether the Eucharistic bread should be leavened or unleavened. To the eastern church, the last straw was its treatment by Crusaders.

From 950 to 1350, loosely organized waves of Christians poured out of Europe in what were presented as "holy Crusades" to recapture the holy land of Palestine from Muslims, to defend the Byzantine Empire against Muslim Turks, and in general wipe out the enemies of Christianity. It was a tragic and bloody time. One of the many casualties was the already tenuous relationship between the eastern and western churches. When Crusaders entered Constantinople in 1204, they tried to intervene in local politics. Rebuffed, they were so furious that they ravaged the city. They destroyed the altar and sacred icons in Hagia Sophia, the awesome Church of the Holy Wisdom (later taken over as a Muslim mosque), and placed prostitutes on the throne reserved for the Patriarch of the region. Horrified by such profanity, the Orthodox Church ended its dialogue with Rome and proceeded on its own, claiming to be the true descendant of the apostolic church. Despite periodic attempts at reconciliation the eastern and western churches are still separate.

Map showing the approximate distribution of Christians in the world today.

The Russian Orthodox Church

When the Ottoman Turks took Constantinople in the fifteenth century, Russia became more prominent in the Orthodox Church, calling itself the "third Rome." The Orthodox Church had spread throughout the Slavic and eastern Mediterranean countries.

Russian Orthodox Christianity was closely associated with Russian national history since its adoption by the royalty in the tenth century. But it was severely repressed by the Soviet government during the twentieth century. Lenin saw institutionalized religion as a divisive, backward force in society, an apology for oppression which should wither away in the socialist state. With the 1917 Revolution, anti-Church propaganda was broadcast, and many intellectuals who sincerely wanted the good of society left the Church. Lenin proclaimed that all church property belonged to the state, and church properties were seized. Thousands of monasteries and churches were taken over during the Revolution and in the early 1920s thousands of priests, nuns, and lay Christians were killed. During the 1930s more monasteries were disbanded, multitudes of churches were closed, and great numbers of clergy were imprisoned. Bishops who refused to accept Soviet control issued what is called the Solovky Memorandum, which stated in part,

> *The Church recognizes spiritual principles of existence; communism rejects them. The Church believes in the living God, the Creator of the world, the leader of its life and destinies; communism denies his existence. Such a deep contradiction in the very basis of their Weltanschauungen precludes any intrinsic approximation or reconciliation between the Church and state, ... because the very soul of the Church, the condition of her existence and the sense of her being, is that which is categorically denied by communism.*[50]

The bishops were imprisoned in the Solovky labor camp; many were killed there. It is estimated that some forty thousand priests were killed from 1918 to 1940. Out of almost eighty thousand churches and chapels in the Russian Empire in 1914, only a few hundred or a thousand remained by the beginning of World War II. Under Krushchev, a new campaign against religion was unleashed, and perhaps two-thirds of the remaining Orthodox churches were closed.

Nevertheless, the Orthodox Church did not die, for it was deeply rooted in the minds and hearts of the people, and was closely linked to national identity. In the mid-1980s, the Russian Orthodox Church had an estimated fifty million members. Most of those who dared to worship publicly were the babushkas — the faithful old women who were apparently not regarded as politically dangerous.

After decades of severe oppression, the Russian Orthodox Church witnessed a great change in government policy in 1988, the celebration of its first millennium in Russia and Ukraine. Mikhail Gorbachev's government approached the Orthodox Church leaders, asking their help in perestroika, returning some church buildings which had been turned into museums or warehouses. Some seventeen hundred churches were reopened in 1988 and 1989, and each was immediately filled with worshippers again. Seminaries where new clergy are trained report a great increase in enrollment. Late in 1989, Soviet President Mikhail Gorbachev ended seven decades of suppression of religion, pronouncing the right of the Soviet faithful to "satisfy their spiritual needs."[51]

Nevertheless, many people are disillusioned with the contemporary Russian Orthodox Church because it, like all other institutions in the former Soviet Union, was riddled with KGB informants, at all levels. Some of its leaders felt that they had to make certain compromises in order to survive at all as a religion under Soviet rule. Since the early days of the Soviet Union, there have also been Orthodox Christians who refused to collaborate or compromise with the government. At the risk of their jobs and lives, some Christian laypeople and priests began to worship secretly in what became known as catacomb churches, just as the early Christians had worshipped in underground catacombs to evade persecution. Father Alexey Vlasov, a catacomb priest, explains:

> Members of this catacomb Church were risking their lives by worshipping. They tried to live by the Ten Commandments and live by love within society. It was not their intention to oppose the Orthodox Church but to bring Christ's love into society.[52]

As recently as 1990, as the Soviet Union's attempts to restrict religion were diminishing, dissent had one more famous martyr, Alexander Men. His charismatic teachings on the search for truth won him so many followers that the state authorities had him transferred to remote locations. He was murdered with an ax on his way to church. Speculation as to motives for his killing include possible racial hatreds (for he was the son of a Jewish father and a mother who had converted to Christianity), antagonism from the Russian Orthodox Church of whose reported collaboration with the state he was openly critical, and the KGB's desire to demonstrate its continuing control.

Even today, some Orthodox Christians continue to worship in secret rather than subject their congregations to the registration requirements of the state and disapproval of the official Church. Bishop Feodor, Bishop of underground Christians in Moscow, Riga, and the Far East, says that groups within the Russian Orthodox Church are divided by

> hatred that comes from the sin of internal pride. If the Church has pride, it has no holy power. We are all brothers in Adam and in Christ. We are all baptized by God. This is true for each Christian. If you cannot love your brother who is next to you, how can you love one you cannot see, such as Christ, who has not been with us for two thousand years?[53]

The Orthodox world today

There are now fifteen self-governing Orthodox Churches worldwide, each having its own leader, known as patriarch, metropolitan, or archbishop. The majority of Orthodox Christians now live in the CIS, Balkan states, and eastern Europe, in formerly atheistic communist countries where the teaching and propagation of Christianity had been severely restricted. Autocephalous churches there include the large Church of Russia dominated by the Moscow Patriarchate, plus the Churches of Serbia, Bulgaria, Romania, Albania, Poland, and the Czech Republic. The original and still central Patriarchate of Constantinople is based within Turkey, as a small minority within a Muslim country. This Patriarchate also includes islands in the Aegean and the precipitous Mount Athos peninsula. The latter was historically a great center of Orthodox monasticism but its population of monks has

Contemporary Russian Orthodox worship in Zagorsk before an elaborate iconostasis, where St. Sergei of Radonezh once built a small chapel in the forest to worship the Holy Trinity.

declined considerably in the twentieth century with prohibition of emigration of monks from formerly communist countries.

The Patriarchate of Alexandria is based in Egypt and includes all of Africa, where Orthodoxy arose independently in Uganda and has been embraced with considerable enthusiasm. The Patriarchate of Antioch consists mostly of Orthodox Christian Arabs in Syria and Lebanon. The Patriarchate of Jerusalem is charged with guarding the Holy Places of Christianity. Before the strictures of atheistic communism, thousands of Russian Orthodox pilgrims used to appear in the holy city yearly at Easter time after an extremely arduous journey of thousands of miles by foot and ship.

The Greek Orthodox Church dominates religious life in Greece and is assisting in the revival of interest in the classical books and arts of Orthodox spirituality. In the Church of Cyprus, the Archbishop is also traditionally the political leader of the people. The Church of Sinai consists only of one monastery.

Extensive emigration, particularly from Russia during the first few years of communist rule, has also created large Orthodox populations in western countries. Some retain direct ties to their home patriarchate, such as the New York-based Archdiocese of the Greek Orthodox Church in North and South America. Alongside that, the Orthodox Church in America was granted its independence in 1970, and now claims over four million members in a country where Protestantism and Roman Catholicism are the predominant forms of Christianity. Missionary activity by the Russian Orthodox Church also established Orthodoxy in China and Korea, and Japan, but its practice is restricted under communist regimes.

Christians light candles around a Christmas tree in Bucharest, December 25, 1989.

Distinctive features of Orthodox spirituality

Over the centuries, the individual Orthodox Churches have probably changed less than have the many descendants of the early western church. There is a strong conservative tradition, attempting to preserve the pattern of early Christianity. Even though hierarchs can make local adaptations suited to their region and people, they are united in doctrine and sacramental observances. Any change that will affect all churches is decided by a **synod** — a council of officials, trying to reach common agreements as did the early church. Although women are important in local church affairs, they cannot be ordained as priests or serve in hierarchical capacities.

In addition to the Bible, Orthodox Christians honor the writings of the saints of the Church. Particularly important is a collection called *The Philokalia*. It consists of texts written by Orthodox masters between the fourth and fifteenth centuries. "Philokalia" means love of the exalted, excellent, and beautiful, in other words, the transcendent divine source of life and truth.

The Philokalia is essentially a Christian guide to the contemplative life for monks but is also for laypeople. A central practice is called "unceasing prayer"; the continual remembrance of Jesus or God, often through repetition of a verbal formula that gradually impresses itself on the heart. The most common phrase is the "Jesus prayer": "Lord Jesus Christ, Son of God, have mercy on me, a sinner." The repetition of the name of Jesus brings purification of heart and singularity of desire. To call upon Jesus is to experience his presence in oneself and in all things.

The Orthodox Church has affirmed that humans can approach God directly. Some may even see the light of God and be utterly transformed by it:

> *He who participates in the divine energy, himself becomes, to some extent, light: he is united to the light, and by that light he sees in full awareness all that remains hidden to those who have not this grace; … for the pure in heart see God … who, being Light, dwells in them and reveals Himself to those who love Him, to His beloved.*[54]

Most icon painters, such as this monk at Mt. Athos, Greece, use the ancient Byzantine style in creating sacred icons, which represent Christian stories and open windows to the divine.

Another distinctive feature of Orthodox Christianity is its veneration of **icons**. These are stylized paintings of Jesus, his mother Mary, and the saints. They are created by artists who prepare for their work by prayer and ascetical training. There is no attempt at earthly realism, for icons are representations of the reality of the divine world. They are beloved as windows to the eternal. In addition to their devotional and instructional functions, some icons are reported to have great spiritual powers, heal illnesses, and transmit the holy presence. Believers enter into the grace of this power by kissing the icon reverently and praying before it.

Some of the major icons in an Orthodox church are placed on an *iconostasis*. This is a screen separating the floor area for the congregation from the Holy of Holies, the sanctuary which can be entered only by the clergy. On either side of the opening to the altar are icons of Jesus and the Virgin Mary ("Mother of God," often venerated as Protectress and Ruler of Russia).

Orthodox choirs sing the divine liturgy in many-part harmony, producing an ethereal and uplifting effect as the sounds echo and re-echo around each other. Everything strives toward that beauty to which the Philokalia refers. Archimandrite Nathaniel of the Russian Othodox Pskova-Pechorsky Monastery, which has been a place of uninterrupted prayer for almost six hundred years despite eight hundred attacks on its walls and numerous sieges, speaks of the ideal of beauty in Orthodox Christianity:

The understanding of God is the understanding of beauty. Beauty is at the heart of our monastic life. The life of prayer is a constant well of beauty. We have the beauty of music in the Holy Liturgy. The great beauty of monastic life is communal life in Christ. Living together in love, living without enmity, as peaceful with each other as one dead body is peaceful with another dead body, we are dead to enmity.[55]

Russian Orthodox Kenoticism

A great mystical spiritual tradition emerged on Russian soil. The *kenotic* pattern of loving and world-directed monastic work was set by the eleventh-century saint Theodosius, who attempted to imitate the poverty and self-sacrificing humility of Jesus. He ate nothing but dry bread and herbs, spent his nights in prayer and his days in work. He dressed in the rough clothes of a peasant, patiently bore insults, worked with his own hands — chopping wood, spinning thread, baking bread, comforting the sick — and refused to present himself as an authority, even though he became the revered leader of this monastic community.

It is recorded that once, after Theodosius had visited a distant prince, the prince sent his own coach to take the saint home in comfort. The coachman, seeing Theodosius's crude clothing, assumed he was a beggar, and asked him to mount the horse so that the coachman could sleep. The saint humbly did so and thus drove the coach all night, with the coachman sleeping inside. When St. Theodosius became too sleepy to drive, he dismounted and walked; when he became weary of walking, he rode again. As the morning sun rose, the noblemen of his area recognized him, dismounted, and bowed to him, whereupon the saint gently said to the coachman, "My child, it is light. Mount your horse." The coachman was amazed and terrified as he saw the great reverence paid to the saint as they proceeded. Rather than chastizing him, Theodosius led him by the hand to the refectory, ordered that he should be given all the food and drink that he wanted, and paid him for the journey.

In the thirteenth century, Russia suffered from Mongolian invasions. Even though the Mongol khans nominally protected the Christians' freedom of religious practice when they themselves adopted Islam, spiritual and social life were in disarray. Monasticism shifted from urban settlements to the wilderness of the great forests of northern Russia. Hermit monks lived there in silence and solitary prayer until so many of the faithful gathered that thriving communities developed around them.

One of the most celebrated of the forest monks was St. Sergius. As a boy, Sergius retreated to the forest and built a small chapel for his intense devotions. Despite his noble lineage, he dressed like a peasant and did manual work. Even when he was abbot of the community that grew up around him, he was asked by one of his monks to build a cell, for which labor he was given a bit of mouldy bread. In his contemplations, Sergius was said to be graced with visions of Mary, Mother of Christ, and of angels, fire, and light. He was nonetheless socially engaged with the national effort to resist foreign rule, and his blessing of the first victorious battle of Russians against the Tartars set the precedent for the future close links between church and state in Russia. The relics of St. Sergius's body still lie undecayed in the huge and ornate Holy Trinity Lavra beyond Moscow where once he had built his simple chapel, and among his followers were seventy famous saints of Russia.

Medieval Roman Catholicism

In the west, the old Roman Empire gradually fell to non-Christian invaders from the sixth to tenth centuries CE. Islam also made spectacular advances in areas previously converted to Christianity. Arabs took Palestine, Syria, Mesopotamia, Egypt, North Africa, and part of Spain. However, the Angle and Saxon invaders of England were new converts to Christianity, with whole tribes joining the faith at the behest of their chiefs. By the fourteenth century, most of central and western

Europe was claimed for Christianity, and missionaries spread the faith to isolated areas of Asia.

Western Europe became de-centralized into feudal kingdoms, with the Christian Church the major force uniting Europe. The chief forces sustaining Christianity through these chaotic centuries were its centralized organization and the periodic refreshing of its spiritual wellsprings through monasticism and mysticism.

Papal power

During the late first and early second centuries CE, some men and women had followed a charismatic Christian life, leaving home to preach, baptize, prophesy, and perhaps die as martyrs; others had moved toward an institutionalized Church modeled on the patriarchal family. By the beginning of the second century CE, a consolidation of spiritual power had begun with the designation of specific people to serve as clergy and bishops (superintendents) to administer the church affairs of each city or region. While some women served as deacons ministering to women, the clergy and bishops had to be male, with wife and children. The bishops of the chief cities of the Roman Empire had the greatest responsibilities and authority, with the greatest prestige being held by the Bishop of Rome, eventually known as the **pope**. By the fifth century CE, Pope Leo I argued that all popes were apostolic successors to Peter, the "rock" on which Jesus reportedly said he would found his church. On Leo's behalf, the Roman Emperor passed an edict requiring all Christians to submit to the authority of the Bishop of Rome, the successor to Peter.

The strongest of Church administrators during these early centuries was Gregory I ("the Great"), who died in 604 CE. Wealthy by birth but ascetic by choice, he devoted his personal fortune to founding monasteries and feeding the poor. Suffering from health problems and longing for the quiet life of a monk, he was reluctantly convinced to be pope at a time of pestilence, floods, and military invasions. Even in this setting, he managed to provide for the physical needs of the poor, promote the discipline of the clergy (including the Western ideal that priests should be celibate), revamp the liturgy (Gregorian chanting is named after him), and to re-establish the Church as a decent, just institution carrying high spiritual values.

The papacy began to wield tremendous secular power. Beginning in the eighth century, the approval of the papacy was sought as conferring divine sanction on feudal kings. In the ninth century the Church produced documents old and new establishing the hierarchical authority of the papacy over the Church, and the Church over society, as the proper means of transmitting inspiration from the divine to humanity. Those who disagreed could be threatened with **excommunication**. This exclusion from participation in the sacraments was a dread ban cutting a person off from the redemption of the Church (blocking one's entrance to heaven in the afterlife), as well as from the benefits of the Church's secular power. Crusades were launched under the auspices of the Church, with war used ostensibly in defense of the faith, with no humane restraints on treatment of the "infidel."

Late in the eleventh century, Pope Gregory VII set forth unprecedented claims for the papacy. The pope, he asserted, was divinely appointed and therefore could be ruled by no human. The pope had the right to depose emperors; the princes of the world should kiss his feet.

This centralization of power became a major unifying element in Europe of the early Middle Ages. Kingdoms broke up between 800 and 1100 as Vikings invaded from the north and Magyars from the east. For the sake of military protection, peasants gave up their freedom to feudal lords. The feudal lords in turn began to war among themselves. In the midst of the ensuing chaos, people looked to the pope as an orderly wielder of power.

Church and states were at times locked in a mutual struggle for dominance, with popes alternately supporting, dominating, and being deposed by secular rulers. The power of the papacy was also somewhat limited by the requirement that the pope be elected by a council of cardinals. The position could not become hereditary. But it was nonetheless open to intrigue, scandal, and power-mongering.

The thirteenth century saw the power of the papacy placed behind the **Inquisition**, an ecclesiastical court set up in 1229 to investigate and suppress heresy. This instrument of terror was based on Augustine's concept that heretics should be controlled for the sake of their own eternal salvation, out of love for their souls. But whereas Augustine saw fines and imprisonment as reasonable coercion to help people change their minds, in some cases the medieval Inquisitors had them tortured and burned to deter others from dangerous views. For example,

Although the Roman Catholic Pope wields enormous power, he is also expected to carry out a rite of humility dating from the 7th century or earlier: lovingly washing the feet of the less powerful, as Jesus did for his disciples.

in northern Italy and southern France a sect arose which was later called Cathari ("the pure"), for its members lived ascetically, emphasizing poverty and mutual aid. Though similar to Christianity in organization and worship, the movement denied that Jesus was the incarnation of God, and saw spirit as good but matter as bad. Such beliefs were proclaimed heretical by the papacy; the Cathari sect, attacked by the Inquisition, disappeared.

Though strong, the papacy was often embroiled in its own political strife. During the fourteenth century, the popes left their traditional seat in turbulent Rome for the more peaceful climate of Avignon, France. There they built up an elaborate administrative structure, increasingly involved in worldly affairs. After the papacy was persuaded to return to Rome, a would-be reformer, Pope Urban, turned to terror tactics to get his way. At one point he had five cardinals tortured and killed. Many people refused to follow him; for a while they followed an "anti-pope" they established in Avignon.

Intellectual revival and monasticism

Although the papacy was subject to abuses, mirrored on a lesser scale by the clergy, Christian spirituality was vigorously revived in other quarters of medieval society. During the twelfth and thirteenth centuries great universities developed in Europe, often from cathedral schools. Theology was considered the greatest of the sciences, with Church ideals permeating the study of all areas of life. Soaring Gothic cathedrals were built to uplift the soul to heavenly heights, for God was perceived as being enthroned in the heavens, far above the workaday world.

The yearning for spiritual purity was particularly pronounced in monasticism. It was largely through monks and nuns that Christian spirituality survived and spread. Monasteries also became bulwarks of western civilization. In Ireland, particularly, they were the centers of larger communities of laypeople, and places of learning within illiterate societies.

During the twelfth century many new monastic orders appeared in the midst of a massive popular re-invigoration of spiritual activity. A major influence was a new community in Cluny, France. Its monks specialized in liturgical elaborations and prayer, leaving agricultural work to serfs. An alternative direction was taken by the Cistercians, Gregorians, and Carthusians. They returned to St. Benedict's Rule of combining manual work and prayer; "to labor is to pray," said the monks. The Carthusians lived cloistered lives as hermits, meeting each other only for worship and business matters. Despite such austere practices, people of all classes flocked to monastic life as a pious refuge from decadent society.

> *It is not only prayer that gives God glory but work.... He is so great that all things give Him glory if you mean they should.*   *Gerard Manley Hopkins*[56]

In contrast to monks and nuns living cloistered lives, mendicant friars, or brothers, worked among the people. The Dominican Order was instituted primarily to teach and refute heresies. A famous Dominican scholar, Thomas Aquinas, created a monumental work, *Summa Theologica*, in which rational sciences and spiritual revelations were joined in an immense, consistent theological system.

Franciscans, following the lead of the beloved St. Francis of Assisi (see below), wandered about without personal property or established buildings, telling people about God's love and accepting charity for their meager needs. The mendicant Dominicans and Franciscans, still noted as missionaries today, became one of the major features of medieval Christianity.

In addition to organized orders of nuns, there was a grassroots movement among thirteenth-century German and Flemish women to take private vows of chastity and voluntary simplicity. These women, who were called *beguines*, lived frugally by their own work. Because they were not organized into a religious order, they chose their own lifestyles, with their chief intention being simply to live "religiously." At times persecuted because it did not fit into any traditionally sanctioned pattern, the movement persisted, drawing tens of thousands of women. Eventually they built small convents for themselves; by the end of the fourteenth century, there were 169 beguine convents in Cologne, the heart of the movement.

Medieval mysticism

Mysticism also flowered during the middle ages, renewing the spiritual heart of the Church. Especially in cloistered settings, monks and nuns sat in contemplation of the meanings of the scriptures for the soul. Biblical stories of battles between heroes and their enemies were, for instance, interpreted as the struggle between the soul and one's baser desires. Beyond this rational thought, some engaged in quiet non-conceptual prayer, simply resting receptively in the presence of God.

St. Francis statues often show birds perched on him, representing his kinship with the natural world.

In thirteenth-century Italy, there was the endearing figure of St. Francis of Assisi (1182–1226). The carefree, dashing son of a merchant, he underwent a radical spiritual transformation. He traded his fine clothes for simple garb and "left the world"[57] for a life of total poverty, caring for lepers and rebuilding dilapidated churches, since Jesus supposedly spoke to him from the cross: "Repair my Church." Eventually Francis understood that his real mission was to rebuild the Church by re-emphasizing the Gospel and its commands of love and poverty. A band of brothers and then of sisters, led by the saintly Clare, gathered around him. The Friars preached, worked, begged, tended lepers, and lived a simple life of penance and prayer while wandering from town to town. This ascetic life was permeated with mystical joy, one of St. Francis's hallmarks. He was also known for his rapport with wild animals and is often pictured with birds resting lovingly on his shoulders.

Two years before his death, Francis received the *stigmata*, replicas on his own body of the crucifixion wounds of Jesus. This miracle was interpreted as a sign of the saint's union with Christ by suffering, prayer, holiness, and love.

The flowering of English mysticism during the fourteenth century included Julian of Norwich. As a girl, she had prayed that when she reached the age of thirty (the age at which Jesus began his public mission) she would have an illness that would bring her an understanding of his *Passion* (the sufferings of his final days). As requested, she did indeed become so ill when she was thirty that she almost died. During this crisis, she had visions and conversations with Christ which revealed the boundless love with which he continually offers himself for humanity. Her writings delve into the perennial problem of reconciling the existence of evil with the experience of a loving God, whom she sometimes referred to as "God our Mother."

The young Catherine of Siena, "mother of thousands of souls," had a vision in which Christ, in the company of the Virgin Mary and other saints, gave her a wedding ring, the sign of the mystical marriage.

An anonymous fourteenth-century English writer contributed a volume entitled *The Cloud of Unknowing*. Christianity then and now largely follows what is called the *affirmative way*, with art, liturgy, scriptures, and imagery to aid devotion. But the author of *The Cloud* spoke to those who were prepared to undertake the *negative way* of abiding in sheer love for God, with no thoughts. God cannot be known through ideas or physical images; "a naked intent toward God, a desire for him alone, is enough."[58] In the silence of wordless prayer, the light of God may pierce the cloud of human unknowing that obscures the divine from the seeker.

Fourteenth-century Italy witnessed a period of unprecedented degradation among the clergy, while the papacy occupied itself with organizational matters in Avignon. In this spiritual vacuum, laypeople gathered around saintly individuals to imbibe their atmosphere of genuine devotion. One of the most celebrated of these was the young Catherine of Siena. In her persistent efforts to restore spiritual purity and religious discipline to the Church, she gained the ear of Pope Gregory XI, helping to convince him to return to Rome. She was called "mother of thousands of souls," and people were said to be converted just by seeing her face.

The Protestant Reformation

Despite the genuine piety of individuals within the Catholic Church, some who clashed with its authority claimed that those in power seemed often to have lost touch with their own spiritual tradition. With the rise of literacy and printing in the late fifteenth century, many Christians were rediscovering early Christianity and comparing it unfavorably with what the Roman Catholic Church had made of it. Roman Catholic fund-raising or church-building financial activities were particularly criticized. These included **indulgences** (services or payments for official absolution of sin by the clergy), the sale of relics, purchases of masses for the dead, spiritual pilgrimages, and the earning of spiritual "merit" by donating to the Church.

The person who emerged as leader of the reform movement was Martin Luther. Luther was a monk and priest who lectured at the University of Wittenberg. He struggled personally with the question of how one's sins could ever be totally atoned

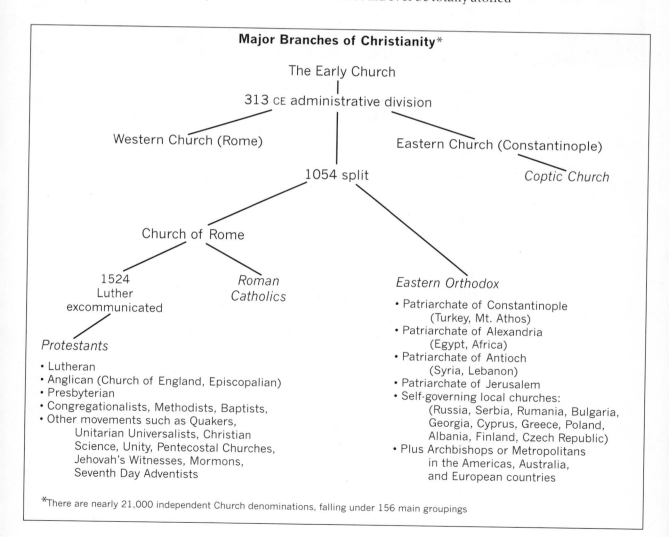

Major Branches of Christianity*

The Early Church

313 CE administrative division

Western Church (Rome)

Eastern Church (Constantinople)

1054 split

Coptic Church

Church of Rome

Eastern Orthodox

1524
Luther
excommunicated

*Roman
Catholics*

- Patriarchate of Constantinople
      (Turkey, Mt. Athos)
- Patriarchate of Alexandria
      (Egypt, Africa)
- Patriarchate of Antioch
      (Syria, Lebanon)
- Patriarchate of Jerusalem
- Self-governing local churches:
      (Russia, Serbia, Rumania, Bulgaria,
      Georgia, Cyprus, Greece, Poland,
      Albania, Finland, Czech Republic)
- Plus Archbishops or Metropolitans
      in the Americas, Australia,
      and European countries

Protestants

- Lutheran
- Anglican (Church of England, Episcopalian)
- Presbyterian
- Congregationalists, Methodists, Baptists,
- Other movements such as Quakers,
      Unitarian Universalists, Christian
      Science, Unity, Pentecostal Churches,
      Jehovah's Witnesses, Mormons,
      Seventh Day Adventists

*There are nearly 21,000 independent Church denominations, falling under 156 main groupings

Martin Luther's political influence and prolific writings led to a deep split in the western church, severing Protestant Reformers from the Roman Catholic Church. (Lucas Cranach the Elder, Martin Luther, *1533.)*

by one's own actions. The Roman Catholic Church's position was that to be forgiven of post-baptismal sins, people should repent and then confess their sins to a priest and be pardoned. In addition, the temporal punishment due to sins could be remitted either for the performance of prescribed penances or through granting of an indulgence. Indulgences could even be procured to make sure that the souls of those who had died repentant were freed from **Purgatory** (the intermediate place of purifying suffering for those who died in a state of repentance and grace but who were not yet sufficiently stainless to enter heaven). To this end, the Castle Church at Wittenberg housed an immense collection of relics, including hairs from the Virgin Mary and a thorn from the "crown" of thorns placed on Jesus's head before he was crucified. This relic collection was said to be so powerful and extensive that those who viewed them on the proper day and contributed sufficiently to the church could receive indulgences from the pope freeing themselves or their loved ones from almost two million years in Purgatory.

By intense study of certain writings of the early Church fathers, Luther began to emphasize a different approach. Both Paul and Augustine could be interpreted as saying that God, through Jesus, offered salvation to sinners in spite of their sins. This salvation was offered by the "Uncreated Grace" of God and claimed through the conviction of sinfulness and absolute faith in salvation, rather than through the "created graces" offered by the Church. The "good works" prescribed by Catholics to earn merit in heaven were not the original Christian way to salvation, Luther argued. Salvation from sin comes from faith in God, which itself comes from God, by grace. This gift of faith brings "**justification**" (being found righteous in God's sight) and then flowers as unselfish good works, which characterize the true Christian:

> *From faith flows love and joy in the Lord, and from love a joyful, willing and free mind that serves one's neighbor willingly and takes no account of gratitude or ingratitude, of praise or blame, of gain or loss…. As our heavenly father has in Christ freely come to our help, we also ought freely to help our neighbor through our body and its works, and each should become as it were a Christ to the other.*[59]

In 1517 Luther invited the university community to debate this issue with him, by the established custom of nailing his theses to the door of the church. He apparently had no intention of splitting with the Church. But in 1521 the Roman Catholic Church chose to excommunicate him.

Cut off from Rome, Luther sought support from the secular princes of Germany. For reasons sometimes more political than spiritual, many came over to his side and helped to enforce his ideas. Although there were some attempts at compromise by followers of both Luther and Rome, conciliatory efforts collapsed.

Luther's evolving theology took him farther and farther from the institutions of the Roman Catholic Church. He did not think that the Bible supported the Roman Catholic tradition that pope, bishops, priests, and monks should have spiritual authority over laypeople; instead, he asserted that there is "a priesthood of all believers." He also felt that the sacred rites, or sacraments, of the Church were ways of nourishing faith instituted by Jesus and included baptism and the Eucharist.

Another major reformer who eventually broke with Rome was the Swiss priest Ulrich Zwingli (1484–1531). He rejected practices not mentioned in the Bible, such as abstaining from meat during Lent, veneration of relics and saints, religious pilgrimages, and celibacy for monks and priests. Zwingli asserted that the Lord's Supper, or mass, should be celebrated only as a memorial of Jesus's sacrifice; he did not believe in the myserious presence of Jesus's blood and body in the consecrated wine and bread. He even questioned the spiritual efficacy of rituals such as masses for the dead and confession of one's sins to a priest:

The truly sacred writings know of no other confession than that by which a man comes to know himself and to throw himself upon the mercy of God.... As, therefore, it is God alone who remits sins and puts the heart at rest, so to Him alone ought we to ascribe the healing of our wounds, to Him alone display them to be healed.[60]

The ideals of these reformists were adopted by many Christians. The freedom of scriptural interpretation which they opened turned out to be a Pandora's box. **Protestantism**, as the new branch of Christianity came to be called, was never as monolithic as the Roman Catholic Church had been in the west. Branches began springing up immediately.

A major seat of Protestantism developed in Geneva, under John Calvin (1509–1564). He shared the reform principles of salvation by faith alone, the exclusive authority of the Bible, and "the priesthood of all believers." But Calvin carried the doctrine of salvation by faith to a new conclusion. To him, the appropriate response to God is a zealous piety and awe-struck reverence in which one "dreads to offend him more than to die."[61] Human actions are of no eternal significance because God has already decided the destiny of each person. By grace, some are to be saved; for God's own reasons, others are predestined to be damned eternally. Although there was therefore nothing that people could do about it, their behavior would reveal which fate awaited them.

Although only God absolutely knew who was saved, there are three signs which humans could recognize: profession of faith, an upright life, and participation in the sacraments. Calvin felt that the church has the right to chastize and in some extreme situations, excommunicate those who seemed to violate the sanctity of the church. Calvin envisioned a holy commonwealth in which the church, government, and citizens all cooperate to create a society dedicated to the glory and mission of God.

Calvin's version of Christianity made its followers feel that they should fear no one except God. Convinced that they were predestined to do God's will, they were impervious to worldly obstacles to the spread of their faith. **Calvinism** became the state religion of Scotland and also had a following in England.

Concurrently, the Church of England separated from the Church of Rome when Henry VIII separated from the Church of Rome in order to have a marriage annulled which had produced him no sons.

As this Protestant Reformation progressed, political entities in Europe chose specific forms of Christianity as their official religion. Spain, France, and Italy remained largely Roman Catholic. Germany was largely Lutheran. Ireland split between Catholicism and Protestantism, leading to wars that continue today. The Calvinist Church of Scotland called itself **Presbyterian**, a reference to its form of organization. Some Polish and Hungarian communities adopted a form of **Unitarianism**, which rejected the ideas of original sin, the Trinity, and Jesus's divinity, in favor of a simple theism and imitation of Jesus.

Intense emotional intimacy with Jesus is displayed during a service at Mount Vernon Baptist Church in Indianapolis.

These ideas later found a home in America, as some Protestant groups that were outlawed by the Church of England emigrated to new colonies in North America. These offshoots included such **denominations** (organized groups of congregations) as Baptists, Congregationalists, Quakers, and Methodists. One of the major denominations in terms of numbers is **Baptists**, a denomination which baptizes people as conscious adult believers rather than as infants. **Congregationalists** emphasize the independence of each local church and the "priesthood" of all members. **Quakers** (formally known as The Religious Society of Friends) worship without any liturgy or minister, in the hope that as they sit in worshipful silence, God would speak through any one of their members. **Methodists** are followers of the evangelist John Wesley, who traveled an average of 8000 miles (12,874 km) a year by horseback to promote "vital practical religion and by the grace of the life of God to beget, preserve, and increase the life of God in the souls of men."[62]

Mainstream Anglicans (members of the Church of England) were called **Episcopalians** in the New World after the American Revolution. During the nineteenth century, yet more Protestant churches sprang up in the United States. **Mormons** (The Church of Jesus Christ of Latter-Day Saints) believe that Jesus taught for a time in America after his resurrection and that The Book of Mormon, the revelation given to their founder Joseph Smith (1805–44) is to be treated as holy scripture alongside the Bible. **Evangelical** churches — those emphasizing salvation by explicit, personal faith in Jesus, personal conversion, the importance of the Bible, and preaching instead of ritual — have proliferated in North America. **Seventh Day Adventists** believe that the Second Coming of Christ will soon occur, and they regard the Bible as an absolute guide to faith and spiritual practice in anticipation of the return of Jesus. **Jehovah's Witnesses** criticize other Christian churches as having developed false doctrines from the second century onwards, and they urge people to leave these "false religions" and prepare for a coming time when all who do not hold true belief will be destroyed. Fundamentalist evangelical sects are also gaining strongholds in South America, which had been largely Roman Catholic since the Spanish conquests of these countries. Protestant missionaries have also carried the gospel to Asia, Africa, and Eastern Europe.

Despite the great diversity among Protestant denominations, most share several characteristics that distinguish them somewhat from Orthodoxy and Roman Catholicism, though the Catholic Church's positions are now much closer to those of Protestants as a result of the profound changes introduced in 1962 by the Second Vatican Council. First, Protestants place their emphasis on the Bible rather than on the authority of the Church, though they differ in how the Bible should be interpreted. Second, they emphasize individual relationship to Jesus and God rather than the mediation of God's grace through the Church. Instead of priests, most Protestant churches have ministers, whose role emphasizes preaching and building the community rather than acting as vehicles of God's grace. The Quakers have gone even farther in rejecting human spiritual authority. They follow the example of George Fox (1624–1691), who experienced in the inner light the certainty of the divine; these "Children of the Light" utterly rejected any outer religious forms and instead simply sit in the silence, surrendered to God.

The Roman Catholic Reformation

As the Protestant reformers were defining their positions, so was the Roman Catholic Church. Because reform pressures were underway in Catholicism before Luther, Catholics refer to the movement as the Catholic Reformation, rather than the "Counter-Reformation," as Protestants call it. However, the Protestant phenomena provoked the Roman Catholic Church to clarify its own position, largely through the Council of Trent (1545 to 1563). It attempted to legislate moral reform among the clergy, to tighten the church administration, and to recognize officially the absolute authority of the pope as the earthly vicar of God and Jesus Christ. The Council also took historic stands on a number of issues, emphasizing that its positions

The Virgin of Guadalupe, who reportedly appeared in the 16th century to an indigenous convert to Catholicism, speaking the native language Nahuatl, has been embraced as patron saint of the Americas.

were **dogmas**, or authoritative truths. For example, one of the fundamental doctrines of the Roman Catholic Church is the dogma of *original sin*. All humans are said to be morally defective, having inherited a sinful nature from the first human ancestors. They can be saved from this condition only by the grace of God, as mediated through the death and resurrection of Jesus.

The Council of Trent ruled that salvation requires "good works" as well as faith. These works include acts of mercy, veneration of the saints, relics, and sacred images, and participation in the sacraments. In the sacrament of the Eucharist, the Council reiterated the doctrine of **transubstantiation**: what appear to be ordinary bread and wine are mysteriously transformed into the body and blood of Christ.

In addition to the actions of the Council of Trent, the Roman Catholic Church gradually chose more virtuous popes than in the past, and several new monastic orders grew out of the desires for reform. The Jesuits offered themselves as an army for God at the service of the pope. The Society of Jesus, as the order was formally called, was begun by Ignatius Loyola in the sixteenth century. His *Spiritual Exercises* is still regarded as an excellent guide to meditation and spiritual discernment. However, it was as activists and educators in the everyday world that Jesuits were highly influential in the Reformation, and they pioneered in carrying Roman Catholicism to Asia.

Roman Catholicism was also carried to the western hemisphere and the Philippines by Spanish conquistadores. At home, Spain was host to a number of outstanding mystics during the sixteenth and seventeenth centuries. St. Teresa of Avila (1515–1582), a Carmelite nun, became at mid-life a dynamo of spiritual activity, in an order of ascetic Reformed (or Discalced) Carmelite nuns and monks. Discalced Carmelites usually pray much, and eat and sleep little. Despite her organizational activity, St. Teresa was able to maintain a calm sense of deep inner communion with God. In her masterpiece entitled *Interior Castle*, she described the state of "spiritual marriage":

> *Here it is like rain falling from the heavens into a river or a spring; there is nothing but water there and it is impossible to divide or separate the water belonging to the river from that which fell from the heavens.*[63]

St. Teresa's great influence fell onto a young friend, now known as St. John of the Cross. He became a member of one of the Carmelite houses for men; when imprisoned by other Carmelites who opposed the reforms, he experienced visions and wrote profound spiritual poetry. For John, the most important step for the soul longing to be filled with God is to surrender all vestiges of the self. This state he called the "dark night of the soul," a relinquishing of human reasoning into a state of not-knowing into which the pure light of God may enter without resistance. St. John of the Cross is still considered one of the great masters of the spiritual life.

The impact of the Enlightenment

Major potential threats to Christianity arose during the eighteenth-century "Enlightenment" in Europe. Intellectual circles exalted human reason and on this basis rejected faith in Biblical miracles and revelations. Some people felt that nineteenth-century scientific advances undermined the biblical story of the creation of the world. However, most of the major nineteenth-century scientists were deeply believing Christians who thought that rather than contradicting Christianity, science brought people closer to faith.

Such views spread rapidly. Many Protestant theologians tried to support the tenets of their faith in "rational" terms, but with an emphasis on "reasonableness" and usefulness, and an aversion to dogmatic insistence on orthodox conformity in religious belief. Individuals were encouraged to judge religious beliefs by their own experience.

Undaunted, and in some cases invigorated, by these challenges to traditional faith, Protestantism developed a strong missionary spirit, joining Roman Catholic efforts to spread Christianity to every country, along with colonialism. John Wesley, the founder of Methodism, explained:

> I looked upon all the world as my parish; … that in whatever part of it I am, I judge it meet, right, and my bounden duty to declare unto all that are willing to hear, the glad tidings of salvation.[64]

The "social gospel" movement brought Protestant churches to the forefront of efforts at social and moral reform. Women, long excluded from important positions in the church, played major roles in church-related missionary and reform efforts, such as abolition of slavery; they cited certain biblical passages as supporting equality of the sexes. When Sarah Grimke and other women were criticized by their Congregational church for speaking publicly against slavery, Grimke asserted, "All I ask of my brethren is that they will take their feet from off our necks and permit us to stand upright on that ground which God has designed us to occupy."[65]

Liberal trends in Protestant theology led to biblical criticism — that is, to efforts to analyze the Bible as literature. What, for instance, were the earliest texts? Who wrote them? How did they relate to each other? Such questions would have been unthinkable to generations raised to regard the Bible as the revealed word of God.

Vatican Councils I and II

In the meantime, the Roman Catholic and Eastern Orthodox Churches had continued to defend tradition against the changes of modern life. A general council of the Roman Catholic hierarchs was held in 1868. It found itself embroiled chiefly in the question of papal infallibility, a doctrine which it upheld. The Pope, proclaimed the bishops of the council, can never err when he speaks *ex cathedra*, from the seat of authority, on matters of faith and morals.

In 1962 Pope John XXIII, known for his holiness and friendliness, convened the Second Vatican Council for the express purposes of updating and energizing the Church and making it serve the people better as a living force in the modern world rather than being an old, embattled citadel. When questioned about his intentions, he demonstrated by opening a window to let in fresh air. With progressives and traditionalists often at odds, the majority nevertheless voted for major shifts in the Church's mission.

Many of the changes involved the liturgy of the **mass**, or the Eucharist. Rather than celebrate it in Latin, which most people did not understand, much of the liturgy was to be translated into the local languages. Rites were to be simplified.

The large and august Second Vatican Council convened by Pope John XXIII in 1962 came to historic conclusions. Their recommendations turned Catholicism in a new direction, bringing the hierarchy closer to the common people in a compassionate partnership.

Greater use of sacred music was encouraged, and not just formal organ and choir offerings. For the first time the laity were to be invited to participate actively. After Vatican II thus unleashed creativity and simplicity in public worship, entirely new forms appeared, such as informal folk masses — with spiritual folk songs sung to guitar accompaniment.

Another major change was the new emphasis on **ecumenism**, in the sense of rapprochement among all branches of Christianity. The Roman Catholic Church acknowledged that the Holy Spirit is active in all Christian churches, including Protestant denominations and the Eastern Orthodox churches. It pressed for a restoration of unity among all Christians, proclaiming that each could preserve its traditions intact. It also extended the concept of revelation, increasing the hope of dialogue with Jews, with whom Christians share "spiritual patrimony"[66] and with Muslims, upon whom the Church "looks with esteem," for they "adore one God" and honor Jesus as a prophet.

Appreciative mention was also made of other world religions as ways of approaching the same One whom Christians call God. Specifically described were Hinduism ("through which men contemplate the divine mystery") and Buddhism ("which acknowledges the radical insufficiency of this shifting world").[67]

Vatican II clearly marked major new directions in Catholicism. Its relatively liberal, pacificistic characteristics are still meeting with some opposition within the Church decades later. In the late twentieth century, conservative elements in the

Vatican seemed to be reversing the direction taken by Vatican II to some extent, to the dismay of liberal Catholics. In the final section of this chapter, concerning current trends in Christianity, we will note several ways in which the renewed conservatism in the Vatican is being expressed.

Central beliefs in contemporary Christianity

The history of Christianity is characterized more by divisions than by uniformity among Christian groups. The Church is vast and culturally diverse, and Christian theologies are complex and intricate. Nevertheless there are a few basic motifs on which the majority of people who are faithful Christians would probably agree today.

A central belief is the divine Sonship of Jesus — the assertion that Jesus is the incarnation of God. According to the Gospel of John, before Jesus's death he told his disciples that he would be going to "my Father's house ... to prepare a place for you." When they asked how they would find the way to that place, Jesus reportedly said:

> I am the way, I am the truth and I am life. No one comes to the Father except by me.... Anyone who has seen me has seen the Father.... It is the Father who dwells in me doing his own work.[68]

Throughout most of Christian history, there has been the feeling that Jesus was the only incarnation of God. Theologian Paul Knitter is one of the contemporary voices calling for a less exclusive approach which still honors the unique contribution of Jesus:

> What Christians do know, on the basis of their praxis of following Jesus, is that his message is a sure means for bringing about liberation from injustice and oppression, that it is an effective, hope-filled, universally meaningful way of realizing Soteria (human welfare and liberation of the poor and oppressed) and promoting God's kingdom.... Not those who proclaim "only Lord, only Lord," but those who do the will of the Father will enter the kingdom (Matthew 7:21–23).[69]

For Christians, Jesus is the Savior of the world, the one whom God sent to redeem people from their sins and reconcile them with God. Matthew reports that Jesus said he "did not come to be served, but to serve, and to give up his life as a ransom for many."[70] His own suffering and death are regarded as a substitute sacrifice on behalf of all those who follow and place their faith in him. According to the Gospel of John,

> God loved the world so much that he gave his only Son, that everyone who has faith in him may not die but have eternal life. It was not to judge the world that God sent his Son into the world, but that through him the world might be saved.[71]

According to Christian belief, humanity has a sinful character, illustrated metaphorically in the Old Testament by the fall of Adam and Eve. We have lost our original purity. Given free will by God, we have chosen disobedience rather than surrender to the will of God. We cannot save ourselves from our fallen condition; we can only be forgiven by the compassion of a loving God.

Through fully surrendered faith in Jesus, Christians hope to be washed of their egotistical sinfulness, regenerated, made righteous, adopted by God, sanctified, and glorified in the life to come. These are the blessings of **salvation** which Christians feel Jesus won for them by his sacrifice.

Although Christians worship Jesus as Savior, as the incarnation of a merciful God, they also see him as a human being showing fellow human beings the way to God. His own life is seen as the perfect model for human behavior. Archbishop Desmond Tutu of South Africa emphasizes Jesus's identification with the human condition:

God does not occupy an Olympian fastness, remote from us. He has this deep, deep solidarity with us. God became a human being, a baby. God was hungry. God was tired, God suffered and died. God is there with us.[72]

This is the central mystery of Christianity: that God became human in order to lead people back to God.

The human virtue most often associated with Jesus is love. Many Christians say they experience Jesus's love even though he is no longer walking the earth in human form. And in turn, they have deep love for Jesus. Those who are experiencing problems in life are comforted to feel that Jesus is a living presence in their lives, standing with them spiritually, supporting them, loving them even in the darkest of times. Reverend Larry Howard, the African–American pastor of Hopps Memorial Christian Methodist Episcopal Church in Syracuse, New York, declares:

We found a Jesus. A Jesus who came in the midnight hour. A Jesus that was able to rock babies to sleep. A Jesus that stood in the midst and walked the miles when the freedom train rode through the South all the way through Syracuse. Jesus brought us through the mighty trials and tribulations. Why did Jesus do that? Jesus loved us and through that love and because of that love we stand here today. Not because the world has been so good to us. Not because we have been treated fair. Not because we have been able to realize the dream that God has given every man, woman, and child. But we stand here because we love Jesus. We love him more and more and more each day.[73]

> *The basic thrust of Jesus' message is to invite us into divine union, which is the sole remedy for the human predicament.*   *Father Thomas Keating*[74]

In addition to being the paragon of love, Jesus also provides a model of sinlessness. To become like God, humans must constantly be purified of their lower tendencies. This belief has led some Christians to extremes of penance, such as the monks who flogged themselves and wore hairshirts so that their conscience might always be pricked. In a milder form, confession of one's sinfulness is a significant part of Christian tradition. There is an emphasis on self-discipline to guard against temptations, on examination of one's own faults, and on rituals such as baptism that help to remove the contamination that is innate in humanity. Although one must make these efforts at purification, most Christians believe that it is only through the grace of God — as mediated by the saving sacrifice of Jesus — that one can be delivered from sin and rise above ordinary human nature toward a divine state of sinlessness.

Mother Teresa's Missionaries of Charity

The love of which Christ spoke is not an intellectual abstraction. According to the diminutive nun loved around the world as Mother Teresa, love must be put into action.

Mother Teresa was born in 1910 in Albania, to a wealthy family which lost all its money when her father died. She entered a convent of the Loretto Sisters when she was eighteen and never saw her mother and sisters again before their deaths. She felt called to India, where she initially taught at a girls' school in Calcutta. Then came an even more difficult inner calling "to be God's love in action to the poorest of the poor." At a time when India was in turmoil after the shooting of Gandhi and the separation into Hindu and Muslim states, Calcutta was crowded with refugees. With no resources, Mother Teresa simply walked through the streets, with only loving care to give to those who had been abandoned by society, beggars, lepers, the dying. She wanted to live and serve the poor like Jesus, claiming nothing for herself, not even the security of knowing where she would sleep. She says, "There is but one person in the poor — Jesus. To be able to love him with undivided love we take a vow of poverty which frees us from all material possessions. We bind ourselves to be one of (the poor), to depend solely on divine providence, to have nothing, yet possess all things in possessing Christ."[75]

To assist in this work, Mother Teresa eventually received permission to found a new order, the Missionaries of Charity. Some of the first sisters were her former pupils. They wore simple white saris with blue stripes, the colors of the Virgin Mary and the garment of Indian women; they lived in poverty, without possessions or grand institutions, to help them understand the poor. In training them

to work without the assurance of financial backing or physical safety, Mother Teresa emphasized that the most important thing is to pray and pray and pray; divine providence will always give what is needed.

As her work has expanded around the globe to 230 houses on all continents, the results of her faith have been demonstrated again and again. There is no plan, no fundraising organization (although the Missionaries of Charity do accept individual donations). Wherever the sisters go, they try to help the poorest of the poor in whatever ways are needed. In each person they care for, they see the face of Jesus. In Calcutta, the Missionaries have picked up tens of thousands of sick, starving, and dying people from the streets and given them tender personal care, hand-feeding them a special formula made from soybeans. In New York City, they feed the homeless, shop and clean for the elderly poor, and care for those with AIDS.

During a period of intense mortar-bombing between Christian and Muslim militia in Beirut, Mother Teresa learned that a home for sixty spastic children had been stranded without caretakers on the Muslim side of the battle lines. When she insisted on crossing the lines to get them, the local clergy assured her that it was impossible. With utter faith, she said that she had asked the Virgin to arrange a cease-fire, which did indeed happen the next day, giving her time to rescue the terrified, helpless children. Within a day, the children were smiling. Mother Teresa says: "The Missionaries do small things with great love. It is not how much we do, but how much love we put into doing it. To God there is nothing small. The moment we have given it to God, it becomes infinite."

Sacred practices

Imitation of the model set by Jesus in his own life is the primary practice of Christians. In the widely-read fourteenth-century book *The Imitation of Christ*, people are encouraged to aspire to Jesus's own example as well as his teachings:

> *O how powerful is the pure love of Jesus, which is mixed with no self-interest, nor self-love!.... Where shall one be found who is willing to serve God for naught?*[76]

In addition to the inner attempt to become more and more like Jesus, Christians have developed a variety of spiritual practices. Although forms and understandings of the practices vary among the branches of Christendom, they may include public worship services with sermons and offering of the sacraments, celebrations of the liturgical year, private contemplation and prayer, and devotions to Mary and the saints.

Worship services and sacraments

Christian worship typically takes place in a church building which may be revered as a sacred space. The late nineteenth-century Russian Orthodox Saint Ioann Kronshtadtsky (d. 1908) explains,

> *Entering the church you enter some special realm which is not like the visible one. In the world you hear and see everything earthly, transient, fragile, liable to decay, sinful. In the church you see and hear the heavenly, the non-transient, the eternal, the holy. A temple is the threshold of heaven. It is like the heaven itself, because here is God's throne, the service of angels, the frequent descent of the Holy Spirit....*
> *Here everything from icons to censer and the priests' robes fills you with veneration and prayer; everything tells you that you are in God's shrine, face to face with God himself.*[77]

The word **sacrament** can be translated as "mystery." In Christianity, the sacraments are the sacred rites that are thought capable of transmitting the mystery of Christ to worshippers. Roman Catholic and Eastern Orthodox Churches observe seven sacraments: baptism (initiation and symbolic purification from sin by water), confirmation (of membership in the Church), Eucharist (the ritual meal described below), penance (confession and absolution of sins), extreme unction (anointing of the sick with oil, especially before death), Holy Orders (consecration as a deacon, priest, or bishop), and matrimony. In general, Protestant Churches recognize only baptism and the eucharist as sacraments.

The ritual of public worship, or **liturgy**, usually follows a set pattern, though in some churches the actions of the Holy Spirit are thought to inspire spontaneous expressions of faith.

In most forms of Christianity, the central sacrament is the **Holy Eucharist** (also called Holy Communion). It is a mystery through which the invisible Christ is thought to grant communion with himself. Believers are given a bit of bread to eat, which is received as the body of Christ, and a sip of wine or grape juice, understood as his blood. The priest or minister may consecrate the bread and wine in ritual fashion and share them among the people. In Roman Catholic or Orthodox masses, the cup of wine and the bread are thought to be mystically transformed

The sacrament of Eucharist, celebrated here in the Philippines, engages believers in a communal mystical encounter with the presence of Christ.

by the Holy Spirit into the blood and body of Christ. They are treated with profound reverence. In sharing the communion "meal" together, the people are united with each other as well as with Christ. The traditional ideal was to take communion every day and certainly every Sunday (the day set aside as the Sabbath).

Jesus is pictured in the Bible as having set the pattern for this sacrament at what is called The Last Supper, the meal he shared with his inner circle before his capture by the authorities in Jerusalem. The body and blood of Christ are seen as the spiritual nourishment of the faithful, that which gives them eternal life in the midst of earthly life.

Mother Julia Gatta, Anglican priest, describes this sacred experience from the point of view of the clergy who preside at the liturgy:

> To be the celebrant of Eucharist is, I think, the most wonderful experience on earth. In a sense, you experience the energy flowing both ways.... One experiences the Spirit in them offering their prayer through Christ to the Father. But at the same time, you experience God's love flowing back into them. When I give communion to people, I am aware that I am caught in that circle of love.[78]

The partaking of sacred bread and wine is the climax of a longer liturgy of Holy Communion. The Communion service, often called a **mass** in Catholicism, begins with liturgical prayers, praise, and confession of sinfulness. A group confession chanted by some Lutheran congregations enumerates these flaws:

> *Most merciful God, we have sinned against you in thought, word, and deed, by what we have done and by what we have left undone. We have not loved you with our whole heart; we have not loved our neighbors as ourselves.*[79]

Catholics were traditionally encouraged to confess their sins privately to a priest before taking communion, in the sacrament of **penance**, or "reconciliation." After hearing the confession, the priest pronounces forgiveness and blessing over the penitent, or perhaps prescribes a penance. Orthodox Christians were also traditionally expected to spend several days in contrition and fasting before receiving communion. The reason for the emphasis on purification is that during the service the church itself is perceived as the kingdom of God, in which everything is holy. In Orthodox services, the clergy walk around the church, swinging an incense censer to set apart the area as a sacred space and to lift the prayers of the congregants to God.

In all Christian churches, passages from the Old and New Testaments may be read and the congregation may sing several *hymns*, songs of praise or thanksgiving to God. The congregation may be asked to recite a credal statement of Christian beliefs, and to make money offerings. There may be an address by the priest or minister (called a sermon or a homily) on the readings for the day. These parts of the liturgy constitute the Liturgy of the Word, in which Christ is thought to be present as the living Word addressing the people through scripture and preaching. In Protestant churches, the Liturgy of the Word is often offered by itself, without the communion service.

In both Protestantism and Roman Catholicism, there are now attempts at updating the liturgy to make it more meaningful and personally relevant for twentieth-century Christians. One innovation that seems to have taken hold everywhere is the "sharing of the peace." Partway through the worship service, congregants turn to everyone around them to hug or shake hands and say, "The Peace of Christ be with you" — "and also with you."

In addition to regular liturgies and the sacrament of the mass or communion, there are special events treated in sacred ways. The first to be administered is the sacrament of **baptism**. Externally, it involves either immersing the person in water or, more commonly, pouring sanctified water (representing purification) on the candidate's head, while invoking the Holy Trinity. In a recent ecumenical document, the World Council of Churches defined the general meaning of the practice:

> *By baptism, Christians are immersed in the liberating death of Christ where their sins are buried, where the "old Adam" is crucified with Christ, and where the power of sin is broken ... They are raised here and now to a new life in the power of the resurrection of Jesus Christ.*[80]

Aside from adult converts to Christianity, the rite is usually performed on infants, with parents taking vows on their behalf. There are arguments that infant baptism has little basis in the Bible and that a baby cannot make the conscious repentance of sin and "conversion of heart" implied in the ceremony. Baptists and several other Protestant groups therefore reserve baptism for adults.

A second ceremony — **confirmation** — is often offered in early adolescence in Roman Catholicism and Protestantism. After a period of religious instruction, a group of young people are allowed to make a conscious and personal commitment to the Christian life.

Some Christians observe special days of fasting. Russian Orthodox Old Believer priest Father Appolinari explains fasting as a way of *soprichiastna*, of becoming part of something very large, the spiritual aura of the Lord. He says,

> *More and more ordinary people are seeking a comfortable life. More and more we leave spirituality. We try to fill this vacuum with material things. I told my students that there was a fast coming up. They groaned, "Why?" I said that we fast for spiritual reasons. The rule is that you should fast not with a spirit of suffering but with such elevated spirit that your soul sings.*
>
> *When we limit our physicality, as in limiting our food intake, then we grow in our spirituality. I advise my students to notice whether their brain works better when their stomach is full or when it is almost empty. Monks refuse physical things in order to get spiritual benefits. We look at them and see their lives as dark, but for them, it is light.*[81]

The liturgical year

Just as Christians repeatedly enact their union with Christ through participation in the Eucharist sacrament, the Church every year celebrates a cycle of celebrations leading the worshipper through the life of Jesus and the gift of the Spirit. As the faithful repeat this cycle year after year, they hope to enter more deeply into the mystery of God in Christ, and the whole body of believers in Christ theoretically grows toward the kingdom of God.

CHRISTMAS AND EPIPHANY There are three major events in the church calendar, each associated with a series of preparatory celebrations. The first is the season of light: Christmas and Epiphany. **Christmas** is the celebration of Jesus's birth on earth. **Epiphany** means "manifestation" or "showing forth." It celebrates the recognition of Jesus's spiritual kingship by the three Magi (in the Western Church), his acknowledgement as the Messiah and the beloved Son of God when he is baptized by John the Baptist, and his first recognized miracle: the turning of water into wine at the wedding in Cana.

In early Christianity, Epiphany was more important than the celebration of Jesus's birth. The actual birth date is unknown. The setting of the date near the winter solstice allowed Christianity to take over the older "pagan" rites celebrating the return of longer periods of daylight at the darkest time of year. In the gospel of John, Jesus is "the true light that enlightens every man,"[82] the light of the divine appearing amid the darkness of human ignorance.

Advent, the month preceding Christmas, is supposed to be a time of joyous anticipation. But in industrialized countries, it is more likely a time of frenzied marketing and buying of gifts, symbolizing God's gift to the world in the person of Jesus. Attempts are being made to sidestep the extreme commercialization of the season and to return to simpler, more sacred ways of honoring the birth of the Christ child.

In some countries churches stage pageants re-enacting the birth story, with people taking the parts of Mary, Joseph, the innkeeper who has no room, the shepherds, and the three Magi. It is traditional to cut or buy an evergreen tree (symbol of eternal life, perhaps borrowed from pagan ceremonies) and erect it in one's house, decorated with lights and ornaments. On Christmas Eve some Christians gather for a candlelit "watch-night" service, welcoming the turn from midnight to a new day in which Christ has come into the world. On Christmas Day, Catholic and Protestant children are sometimes told that presents have been magically brought by St. Nicholas, a fourth-century bishop noted for his great generosity. Exchange of gifts may be followed by a great feast.

EASTER The second major focus of the liturgical year is **Easter**. This is the commemoration of Jesus's death (on "Good Friday") and Resurrection (on Easter Sunday, which falls in the spring but is celebrated at different times by the eastern and western churches). Like Christmas, Easter is a continuation of earlier rites — those associated with the spring solstice, celebrating the regeneration of plant life and the return of warm weather after the cold death of winter. It is also related to Pesach, the Hebrew Passover, the Jewish spring feast of deliverance.

Liturgically, Easter is preceded by a forty-day period of repentance and fasting, called **Lent**. Many Christians are called to acts of asceticism, prayer, and charity, to join in Jesus's greater sacrifice. In the Orthodox Church, the last Sunday before Lent is dedicated to asking forgiveness. People request forgiveness from each other, bowing deeply. In the West, Lent begins with Ash Wednesday, when many Christians have ash smudges placed on their foreheads by a priest who says, "Remember, man, thou art dust and unto dust thou shalt return." On the Sunday before Easter, Jesus's triumphal entry into Jerusalem is honored by the waving of palm or willow branches in churches and the proclaiming of Hosannas. His death is mourned on "Good Friday." The mourning is jubilantly ended on Easter Sunday, with shouts of "Christ is risen!"

In Russia, the Great Vigil welcoming Easter morning lasts from midnight until dawn, with the people standing the entire time. Jim Forest describes such a service in a church in Kiev, with two thousand people crowding into the building and as many more standing outside:

> *The dean went out the royal doors into the congregation and sang out, "Christos Voskresye!" [Christ is risen!] Everyone responded in one voice, "Veyeastino voskresye!" [Truly he is risen!] It is impossible to put on paper how this sounds in the dead of night in a church overheated by crowds of people and hundreds of candles. It is like a shudder in the earth, the cracking open of the tomb. Then there was an explosion of ringing bells.[83]*

PENTECOST Fifty days after the Jewish Passover (which Jesus is thought to have been celebrating at the Last Supper with his disciples) comes the Jewish celebration, Shavuot (which commemorates the giving of the Torah to Moses, as well as the first fruits of the harvest). Jews nicknamed it **Pentecost**, which is Greek for "fiftieth." Christians took over the holiday season but gave it an entirely different meaning.

In Christianity, Pentecost commemorates the occasion described in Acts when the Holy Spirit descended upon the disciples after Jesus's death and resurrection, filling them with the Spirit's own life and power, and enabling them to speak in foreign tongues they had not known. In early Christianity, Pentecost was an occasion for baptisms of those who had been preparing for admission to the church.

THE TRANSFIGURATION AND ASSUMPTION Some Christian churches also emphasize two other special feast days. On August 6, the people honor the Transfiguration of Jesus on the mountain, revealing his supernatural radiance. On August 15, they celebrate the Assumption of Mary, known as "The Falling Asleep of the Mother of God." These feasts are prominent in the Eastern Church, which generally places more emphasis on the ability of humanity to break out of its earthly bonds and rise into the light, than on the heaviness and darkness of sin.

Contemplative prayer

The contemplative tradition within Christianity is beginning to re-emerge. The hectic pace and rapid change of modern life make periods of quietness essential, if only for stress relief. Many Christians, not aware of a contemplative way within their own church, have turned to Eastern religions for instruction in meditation.

One of the most influential twentieth-century Christian contemplatives was the late Thomas Merton (1915–1968). He was a Trappist monk who received a special dispensation to live as a hermit in the woods near his abbey in Kentucky. Merton lived simply in nature, finding joy in the commonplace, experienced attentively in silence. He studied and tried to practice the great contemplative traditions of earlier Christianity and reintroduced them to a contemporary audience through his writings.

The Christian monk Thomas Merton and the Tibetan Buddhist Dalai Lama, two great ecumenical figures of the 20th century, met right before Merton died during his trip to visit the monks of the Eastern traditions.

Two scenes from the passion of Christ – Jesus falling as he is forced to carry the cross and the Virgin Mary's grief after Jesus's death. Of these Stations of the Cross, falling under the weight of the cross is not mentioned in the Bible.

In meditative "prayer of the heart," or "contemplative prayer," he wrote:

> *We seek first of all the deepest ground of our identity in God. We do not reason about dogmas of faith, or "the mysteries." We seek rather to gain a direct existential grasp, a personal experience of the deepest truths of life and faith, finding ourselves in God's truths.… Prayer then means yearning for the simple presence of God, for a personal understanding of his word, for knowledge of his will and for capacity to hear and obey him.[84]*

Before he became a Christian monk, Merton had studied Eastern mysticism, assuming that Christianity had no mystical tradition. He became friends with a Hindu monk who advised him to read St. Augustine's *Confessions* and *The Imitation of Christ*. These classical works led Merton toward a deep appreciation of the potential of the Christian inner life, aligned with a continuing openness to learn from Eastern monasticism. He died by accident while in Asia visiting Buddhist and Hindu monastics.

Spiritual renewal through inner silence has become an important part of some Christians' practice of their faith. Syrian Orthodox Bishop Paulos Mar Gregorios of India, past-President of the World Council of Churches, concludes from the Bible evidence that Jesus himself was a contemplative:

> *Christ spent seventy percent of his whole life in meditation. He would sleep rarely. All day he gave himself to healing the sick. At night he would pray, sometimes all night. He was not seeking his own self-realization. His meditation and prayer were*

not for himself but for the world — for every human being. He held the world in his consciousness through prayer, not with attachment but with compassion. He groaned and he suffered with humanity. To follow Jesus in the way of the cross means to say, "I lay aside all personal ambition and dedicate myself to God: 'Here I am, God. I belong to you. I have no idea where to go. It matters not what I am, so long as You lead me.' "[85]

A form of Christian meditation that was instituted by the Franciscan monks and is still practiced in many Catholic and Anglican churches is following the *Stations of the Cross*. These are fourteen plaques or paintings placed on the walls of the church depicting scenes from the death of Jesus. As one sees him taking up the Cross, falling three times under its weight, being stripped of his clothes and being nailed to the cross, one becomes painfully and humbly aware of the suffering that God's son experienced in manifesting as a human redeemer.

Contemplation of the humanness of Jesus is used to help believers identify with him and thence to aspire to his divine model. Theology professor and spiritual director Kathleen Dugan says that when she teaches devotions on the deep humanity of Jesus:

my students have difficulty assimilating it. "You mean to say that he felt sorrow like I do?" "Yes." "That he cried?" "Yes." "That he felt joy?" "Yes." The Gospel examples show that he wept before Lazarus's tomb. He wept at the sorrow of Martha and Mary over their brother. He rejoiced with the couple that were being married at the wedding of Cana. He felt terrible isolation; so many things in the Gospels speak of that. He said on the cross, "My God, my God, why have you forsaken me?" There is no human emotion that he did not experience. He did suffer. Crucifixion was a long, lingering death, with great agony. Jesus is our brother, our spouse, our son. When students think about these things, it is often transforming.

Here is a living, breathing image of what it means to be God. We are called to imitate the saints, but primarily we are called to imitate Jesus.[86]

In Orthodoxy, the central contemplative practice is repetition of the Jesus Prayer. Eventually its meaning imbeds itself in the heart and one lives in a state of unceasing prayer.

Devotions to Mary

Thus far in this chapter, little has been said about Mary, the mother of Jesus, for she has not been in the forefront of historical theological disputes. Veneration of Mary has come more from the grassroots than from the top. Drawings of her were found in the catacombs in which the early Christians met; explicit devotion to her was well developed by the third or fourth century CE. Despite the absence of detailed historical information, she serves as a potent and much-loved spiritual symbol. She is particularly venerated by Roman Catholics, Eastern Orthodoxy, and Anglicans.

Some researchers feel that devotion to Mary is derived from earlier worship of the Mother Goddess. They see her as representing the feminine aspect of the Godhead. She is associated with the crescent moon, representing the receptive willingness to be filled with the Spirit. In the story of the **Annunciation** — the appearance of an angel who told her she would have a child conceived by the Holy Spirit — her reported response was "Behold, I am the handmaid of the Lord; let it be to me according to your word."[87] This receptivity is not seen as utter powerlessness, however. Mary, like Christ, embodies the basic Christian paradox: that power is found in "weakness."

Whether or not devotion to Mary is linked to earlier Mother Goddess worship, oral Christian traditions have given her new symbolic roles. One links her with Israel, referred to as the daughter of Zion or daughter of Jerusalem in Old Testament passages. God comes to her as the overshadowing of the Holy Spirit, and from this love between YHWH and Israel, Jesus is born to save the people of Israel.

Mary is also called the New Eve. The lengendary first Eve disobeyed God and was cast out of the garden of Eden; Mary's willing submission to God allows birth of the new creation, in which Christ is in all.

In the Orthodox and Catholic traditions, she is referred to as the Mother of God. In Russia, she is also revered as the protectress of all humanity, and especially of the Russian people. Before he died on the cross, Jesus is said to have told John, the beloved disciple, that thenceforth Mary was to be his Mother. The story is interpreted as meaning that thenceforth all humanity was adopted by Mary.

Another symbolic role ascribed to Mary is that of the immaculate virgin. According to the gospels of Matthew and Luke, she conceived Jesus by heavenly intervention rather than human biology. Roman Catholicism asserts that at the Immaculate Conception, she was freed by God from all the "original sin" traced back to Adam and Eve's disobedience. Even in giving birth to Jesus, she remained a virgin.

Orthodoxy does not insist on these doctrines, nor on the Catholic dogma that Mary ascended bodily to heaven after her physical death. The emphasis on virginity is a spiritual sign of being dedicated to God alone, rather than to any temporal attachments.

According to the faithful, Mary is not just a symbol but a living presence, like Christ. She is appealed to in prayer and is honored in countless paintings, statues, shrines, and churches dedicated to her name. Catholics are enjoined to repeat the "Hail Mary" prayer:

> Hail, Mary, full of grace, the Lord is with thee. Blessed art thou among women, and blessed is the fruit of thy womb, Jesus. Holy Mary, Mother of God, pray for us sinners, now and at the hour of our death.

Theologians are careful to point out, however, that veneration of Mary is really directed toward God; Mary is not worshipped in herself but as the mother of Christ, reflecting his glory. If this were not so, Christians could be accused of idolatry.

Be this as it may, Mary has been said to appear to believers in many places around the world. At Lourdes, in France, it is claimed that she appeared repeatedly to a young peasant girl named Bernadette in the nineteenth century. A spring found where she indicated has been the source of hundreds of medically authenticated healings from seemingly incurable diseases. In 1531, in Guadalupe (within what is now Mexico City), Mary appeared to a converted Aztec, Juan Diego. She asked him to have the bishop build a church on the spot. To convince the skeptical bishop, Juan filled his cloak with the out-of-season roses to which she directed him. When he opened the cloak before the bishop, the petals fell away to reveal a large and vivid image of Mary, with Indian features. The picture is now enshrined in a large new church with moving walkways to handle the crowds who come to see it, and the Virgin of Guadalupe has been declared Celestial Patroness of the New World.

Veneration of saints and angels

Roman Catholics and Orthodox Christians honor their spiritual heroes as saints. These are men and women who are recognized as so holy that the divine life of Christ is particularly evident in them. After their death, they are carefully judged by the Church for proofs of exalted Christian virtue, such as tolerance under extreme provocation, and of miraculous power. Those who are canonized by this process are subject to great veneration.

> Each saint is a unique event, a victory over the force of evil. So many blessings can pour from God into the world through one life.
>
> Father Germann, Vladimir, Russia[88]

Orthodox Christians are given the name of a saint when they are baptized. Each keeps an icon of this patron saint in his or her room and prays to the saint daily. Icons of many saints fill an Orthodox Church, helping to make them familiar presences rather than names in history books. Saints are often known as having special areas of concern and power. For instance, St. Anthony of Padua is invoked for help in finding lost things. **Relics,** usually parts of the body or clothes of saints, are felt to radiate the holiness of the saints' communion with God. They are treasured and displayed for veneration in Catholic and Orthodox churches. It is said that saints' physical bodies were so transformed by divine light that they do not decay after death, and that they continue to emit a sweet fragrance.

Roman Catholics and Orthodox Christians also pray to the angels for protection. **Angels** are understood as spiritual beings who serve as messengers from and adoring servants of God. They are usually pictured as humans with wings. In popular piety, each person is thought to have a guardian angel for individual protection and spiritual help.

Contemporary trends

Christianity is gaining membership and enthusiastic participation in some quarters and losing ground in others. In Egypt, Orthodox *Coptic* Christians, heirs to the ancient tradition of the Desert Fathers, have long been submerged under Muslim rule, but the monasteries have begun to flourish again. The sixteen million Coptic Christians have their own pope; he and the Roman Catholic pope recognize each other's authority.

Roman Catholicism is torn by divisions between conservatives and liberals. After the liberal tendencies of Vatican II, Pope John Paul II reaffirmed certain traditional stands and strengthened the position of the right wing of the Church. In a 1995 encyclical, he emphatically insisted upon what he called the fundamental right to human life as opposed to the "culture of death," condemning abortion and euthanasia as "crimes which no human law can claim to legitimise" and condemning the death penalty.[89] Despite the public attention paid to the pope as a person, the priesthood is dwindling in some countries (it is estimated that by the year 2000, there will be only half as many active Catholic priests in the United States as there were in 1966, partly because of the requirement that priests be celibate). There is also increased interest in participation by women (who are not allowed by the Vatican to be priests), and widespread disregard of papal prohibitions on effective birth control, abortion, test-tube conception, surrogate motherhood, genetic experimentation, divorce, and homosexuality. Although four million Filipinos turned out to greet the pope in 1995, polls indicate that sixty-one percent of Filipinos regard family planning as a matter of private choice.

While cautioning against a recreational view of sexuality, Sean McDonagh SSC emphasizes that the environmental and social consequences of unlimited population growth require a rethinking of traditional Catholic proscriptions on birth control:

> The pro-life argument needs to be seen within the widest context of the fragility of the living world. Is it really pro-life to ignore the warnings of demographers and ecologists who predict that unbridled population growth will lead to severe hardship and an increase in the infant mortality rate for succeeding generations? Is it pro-life to allow the extinction of hundreds of thousands of living species which will ultimately affect the well-being of all future generations on the planet?[90]

The Vatican has responded to these trends by insisting on the value of tradition and authority. But many American Catholic leaders are concerned that, in the words of Father Frank McNulty of Newark, New Jersey, "people often do not perceive the church as proclaiming integral truth and divine mercy, but rather as sounding harsh, demanding."[91] Acting as a group, Roman Catholic bishops in the United States have issued statements deploring sexism as a "sin" (recommending that spiritual positions of responsibility and authority be opened to women and that non-sexist language be used in liturgy), supporting peace efforts, and insisting on the morality of economic social justice.

In Protestantism, traditional denominations in Europe and the United States are declining in membership. According to a Gallup poll, only a minority of the "unchurched" actually disagree with their denomination's teachings. They are more likely to drop away because of apathy, a lack of services, or a lack of welcome on the part of the minister. The numbers of women in the ministry are increasing, however; the National Council of Churches predicts that by the year 2000 some twenty-five percent of all Protestant clergy in the United States will be women. Gender-inclusive language is increasingly common in liturgies.

Although many traditional Christian churches are losing members, other groups and trends are taking vigorous root. These include evangelical and charismatic groups, non-Western Christian churches, liberation theology, creation-centered Christianity, and the ecumenical movement.

Barbara Harris became the first female bishop in the history of the Anglican Church, February 11, 1988, at a ceremony in Boston.

Evangelicalism

To evangelize is to preach the Christian gospel and convert people to Christianity. Evangelical theology, with its emphasis on experiencing the grace of God, has been important throughout the history of American Protestantism. The current evangelical movement has its roots in the Fundamentalist–Modernist controversy of the early twentieth century.

The Fundamentalists were reacting against the liberal or modern movement in Christianity that sought to reconcile science and religion and to use historical and archaeological data to understand the Bible. This movement had an optimistic view of human nature and stressed reason, free will, and self-determination. In response, a group of Christians called for a return to the "Fundamentals" which they identified as 1) the inspiration and authority of scripture (and sometimes its inerrancy); 2) an emphasis on the virgin birth of Christ and other miracles; 3) the deity of Christ and the bodily resurrection as a literal historical event; 4) Christ's atoning and substitutionary death; and 5) an emphasis on the literal and imminent second coming of Christ. The controversy between these two groups received its most famous public expression in the Scopes trial in 1925 when John Thomas Scopes, a high school teacher in Tennessee, challenged a state law forbidding the teaching of evolution in schools.

Beginning in the 1930s and with waves of enthusiasm in the 1950s and late twentieth century, heirs of this movement, who can broadly be called **"evangelicals,"** have become a vigorous movement in many Protestant denominations. Evangelicals study the Bible together and value being "born again" in Christ. They vary from conservative to liberal on other theological and ethical issues (such as literal interpretation of the Bible and involvement in social issues such as the peace movement and alleviation of poverty).

The message of some forms of evangelicalism has become particularly visible and effective through books sold in exclusively Christian bookstores and through

Televised evangelism on Memorial Day, from the Crystal Cathedral, California.

the medium of television. Television evangelism, with its accompanying pleas for continuing financial donations to the cause, has suffered a number of scandals as certain top evangelists have been exposed for sexual and financial transgressions. Howard Cleinbell, a theology professor, speaks of this indulgence in the forbidden:

> *The person who is the clergy has to deny his shadow side. He's put on a pedestal by followers, and as such he puts himself on a pedestal. So when his gutsy, earthy, sensual side is denied or hidden, the pressure builds up on a subconscious level, which often results in acting out in secret ways.*[92]

Despite disillusionment with some forms of evangelical Christianity in North America, it continues to be an important part of Protestantism. The movement is also making great strides in South America, in areas that were largely Roman Catholic as a result of colonization by Spain centuries ago. In the early 1990s, an average of five evangelical churches were being established each week in Rio de Janeiro, most of them in the slum areas, in an attempt to offer food, job training, day care, and perhaps conversion to the very poor.

Charismatics

Overlapping somewhat with the evangelical surge, there is a rising emphasis on *charismatic* experience — that is, divinely inspired powers — among Christians of all classes and nations. While Christian fundamentalists stress the historical Jesus,

Young children re-enact the Christmas story, adoring Jesus as a baby.

charismatics feel they have also been touched by the "third person" of the Trinity, the Holy Spirit. These include members of Protestant Pentecostal churches but also Roman Catholics and members of mainline Protestant denominations. Under the influence of the Spirit, they speak in tongues, pray and utter praises spontaneously, heal by the laying on of hands and prayer, and bear witness to spiritual miracles. Dogma and religious authority are usually less important in these groups than personal spiritual experience.

Mainstream Christian churches, which have often rejected emotional spiritual experience in favor of a more orderly piety, are gradually becoming more tolerant of it. Among Roman Catholics the movement is often called "Charismatic Renewal," for it claims to bring true life in the Spirit back to Christianity.

Pentecostal Christians have been active in the former Soviet Union since the 1920s. Speaking of the descent of the Holy Spirit, Roman Bilas, Moscow head of the Union of Pentecostal Christians of Evangelical Faith, says passionately,

This moment when you really feel God's power in yourself brings so much peace and joy within you. It transforms you and society. There comes a sense of total forgiveness for your sins, and the ability in you to forgive others. At that moment, you start to speak in different languages, maybe such that no one can understand.

We may also receive the gift of prophecy. When we were persecuted during Soviet rule, we received inner spiritual messages to change our appointments in order to avoid capture by the KGB. We are always very careful about such inner messages,

Ecstatic experience of the Holy Spirit at a Baptist Church.

because it is possible that they may come from the person himself rather than from God. We check to see if the message is consistent with the Bible. If it is, then we will listen. Otherwise, the person is told not to speak publicly because he would create confusion in the Church.

The main thing is that the person should be filled with God's Power. A nice-looking car will not move unless it is fueled. God's Power will only fill those who are pure. That is why in the early Church people went into the wilderness to fast and repent. Then God could fill them with His Power. Each sermon should have this Power of God; then the people will really listen and repent of their sins.[93]

Cultural broadening

Although contemporary Christianity was largely shaped in Europe and its North American colonies, a large percentage of the Christian Church lies outside these areas. It has great numerical strength and vigor in Africa, Latin America, and parts of Asia.

As missionaries spread Christianity to these regions, they often assumed that European ways were culturally superior to indigenous ways and peoples. But some of these newer Christians have come to different conclusions. Theologians of the African Independent Churches, for instance, reject the historical missionary efforts to divorce them from their traditions of honoring their ancestors. This effort tore apart their social structure, they feel, with no scriptural justification:

> As we became more acquainted with the Bible, we began to realise that there was nothing at all in the Bible about the European customs and Western traditions that we had been taught. What, then was so holy and sacred about this culture and this so-called civilisation that had been imposed upon us and was now destroying us? Why could we not maintain our African customs and be perfectly good Christians at the same time?…
>
> We have learnt to make a very clear distinction between culture and religion.… [For instance], the natural customs of any particular nation or race must never be confused with the grace of Jesus Christ our Saviour, Redeemer and Liberator.[94]

Contemporary perceptions of Jesus have been deeply enriched by those from the inhabitants of poor Third World countries who have brought personal understanding of Jesus's ministry to the outcastes and downtrodden. In Asia, where Christians are usually in the minority, there is an emphasis on a Christ who is present in the whole cosmos and who calls all people to sit at a common table to partake of his generous love. In Latin America, Jesus is viewed as the liberator of the people from political and social oppression, from dehumanization, and from sin. In Africa, the African Independent Churches have brought indigenous traditions of drumming, dancing, and singing into community worship of a Jesus who is seen as functioning as the greatest of ancestors — a mediator carrying prayers and offerings between humans and the divine, and watchful caretaker of the people.

Liberation theology

Although many Christians make a distinction between the sacred and the secular, some have involved themselves deeply with social issues as an expression of their Christian faith. For instance, the late Baptist preacher, Martin Luther King Jr.,

For liberation theologians, the message of the gospel often entails down-to-earth physical help to the poor. Maryknoll lay sisters Norma Jejia, Julia Mamani, and Delia Gamboa are here lending a hand to the families of a Peruvian barrio.

became a great civil rights leader, declaring, "It was Jesus of Nazareth that stirred the Negroes to protest with the creative weapon of love."[95] This trend is now called **liberation theology** — a faith that stresses the need for concrete political action to help the poor. Beginning in the 1960s with the Vatican II, and the conference of Latin American bishops in Columbia in 1968, Roman Catholic priests and nuns serving in Latin America began to make conscious, voluntary efforts to understand and side with the poor in their struggles for social justice. Biblical basis for this approach is found in the Acts of the Apostles:

> *The group of believers was one in mind and heart. No one said that any of his belongings was his own, but they all shared with one another everything they had.... There was no one in the group who was in need. Those who owned fields or houses would sell them, bring the money received from the sale and turn it over to the apostles; and the money was distributed to each one according to his need.*
>
> *(Acts 4: 32–35)*

The Peruvian theologian Gustavo Gutierrez, who coined the expression "theology of liberation," explains the choice of voluntary poverty as:

> *a commitment of solidarity with the poor, with those who suffer misery and injustice.... It is not a question of idealizing poverty, but rather of taking it on as it is — an evil — to protest against it and to struggle to abolish it.[96]*

For their sympathetic siding with those who are oppressed, Catholic clergy have been murdered by political authorities in countries such as Guatemala. They have also been strongly criticized by conservatives within the Vatican. Cardinal Ratzinger, who heads the Congregation for the Doctrine of the Faith, has decried liberation theology. He says that it inappropriately emphasizes liberation from material poverty rather than liberation from sin. The movement has nevertheless spread to all areas where there is social injustice. Bakole Wa Ilunga, Archbishop of Kananga, Zaire, reminds Christians that Jesus warned the rich and powerful that it would be very difficult for them to enter the kingdom of heaven. By contrast, writes Ilunga:

> *Jesus liberates the poor from the feeling that they are somehow less than fully human; he makes them aware of their dignity and gives them motives for struggling against their lot and for taking control of their own lives.[97]*

Creation-centered Christianity

Another current trend in Christianity is an attempt to develop and deepen its respect for nature. In the Judeo–Christian tradition, humans are thought to have been given dominion over all the things of the earth. Sometimes this "dominion" was interpreted as the right to exploit, rather than the duty to care for, the earth. This view contrasts with indigenous beliefs that the divine resides everywhere, that everything is sacred, and that humans are only part of the great circle of life. Some Christians now feel that the notion of having a God-given right to control has allowed humans to nearly destroy the planet. In some cases, they are turning to indigenous spiritual leaders for help in extricating the planet from ecological destruction, as we will see in Chapter 13. Historian and passionate earth-advocate

Father Thomas Berry feels that "we need to put the Bible on the shelf for twenty years until we learn to read the scripture of life."[98]

A Christianity that would accord greater honor to the created world would also tend to emphasize the miracle that is creation, thus helping to unite science and religion. Creation-centered Christians — such as the late Jesuit priest and paleontologist Teilhard de Chardin — see the mind of God in the perfect, intricate balances of chemistry, biology, and physics that allow life as we know it to exist. This rejoicing in all of life as divine has been advanced by Dominican scholar Matthew Fox. Fox's teachings include appreciation of the feminine aspect of the divine and celebration of the human body as blessed.

Conscience and the fall of communism

Although communism is already beginning to make a comeback, the astonishingly fast fall of the huge communist bloc has been traced in part to the courageous personal decisions of individual Christians. They decided that to live by their faith, they must speak out against injustice and perhaps risk their careers and their own life in nonviolent resistance to oppression. In Poland, where the resistance began, theologian Jozef Tischner described this phenomenon as "a huge forest of awakened consciences."[99]

Throughout Eastern Europe, the practice of Christianity had been severely restricted under atheistic communism. In the Soviet Union, all religions, including the Russian Orthodox Church, had to be officially registered with the state. Registration meant that the group had to obey the regulations imposed by the government. A church was allowed only to hold worship services. All other activities — such as public speaking about Christianity, charitable service, and Christian teaching of children — were banned. Those who violated these regulations could be fired from their jobs, expelled from school, fined heavily, or sent to jail. Alexander Ogorodnikov explains, "By the norm of Soviet ideology, it was impossible for us to live our faith."[100]

In country after country, at first a few and then multitudes of Christians began to resist the oppressive regimes. In East Germany, where guards were required to shoot those trying to cross the border to the free West, thousands of people began attending "Prayers for Peace" meetings held in churches in Leipzig. The movement spread to other cities in a chain reaction, as people hearing others speak openly gained the courage to do so themselves. Those who congregated prayed for their countries, for justice, for nonviolent change. Gabriele Anger, a regular participant in the Prayers for Peace in Leipzig, says,

Inside the church, we had the most incredible feeling of security and warmth. People were changed somehow. You would notice it in a squeeze of the hand, or somebody giving you an unexpected hug and saying, "We have to stick together." They would look deep into your eyes just for a second longer than normally. It had a fascinating effect on all of us. We would go outside through the lines of police that had surrounded the church, and it was impossible to think "You pig." Instead I would think, "If you only knew how rich we are." And we would smile and go through the narrow path between the soldiers in a human wall to the left and the right of us, and look them in the eyes.[101]

Living Christianity

In contrast to their earlier cultural chauvinism, Western Christian missionaries now often recognize that they can learn and grow through their experiences in other cultures. Maryknoll, a missionary institution within the Roman Catholic Church, has developed a form of liberation theology based on strengthening leadership among the poor. Brother John Blazo served in Nicaragua for a year and in Guatemala for five years, sometimes with his life in danger from militarists opposing church help to the poor.

"In both of these places, the church has been focusing on local leadership. We encourage people in basic leadership skills — how to be self-supporting, how to make more decisions independently of us. When I first got to Nicaragua, the people's first response was always 'Tell us,' but I said, 'I'm not here to tell you what to do. I don't speak Spanish that well. This is your church, this is your village. I just got out of language school and I don't know what the customs are. You know that; you know what has happened in the past. You know what you want to do. I'm just asking you the questions to see if you want to do this or not.' It was a very slow process.

The idea is for the group to help itself to see what are their living situations, what is their reality, and then compare that to 'What does the Lord say about this?' And 'What does our Catholic church say about this?' Then they can make the necessary changes to bring about something else. The famous text we always use is Moses and the Red Sea — with the community and with the help of the almighty God, they put down their oppressor, they went through the armies and the Red Sea to a new light. But it took time to do all that. God is with those people who are suffering, who are trying to work and trying to improve their life; that's God's will. Some of the political structures are set up to keep people down — to provide cheap labor or cheap resources, to control. That's what humans did; that's certainly not God's will.

There's another element; evangelization, looking for people who aren't sacramentalized, who aren't Catholic. When Maryknoll was founded in 1911, the sense was that it was important to get them into your church. In the changing church, there are still elements of that. I'd love more people to come into the Catholic church, but I'm not going to try to bend people's necks, saying that things are perfect in the Catholic church and we have the only way. We certainly don't do that.

This work has helped me to be a broader person and to go deeper in my own religion. My constant question is 'What is basic Christianity and what is a cultural expression?' The cultural expression can always change, but the basics theoretically can't. There is the belief in one God, and I think the other thing we have to be really pushing is the idea of reconciliation amongst people. Those are basics which are obviously not limited to Christianity. There is also belief in the afterlife — belief in heaven and hell, belief in Jesus as God. Jesus died for us, Jesus showed a way of working, of having ways of forgiving our sins, so let's emphasize the positive, let's struggle toward doing better. You see people struggling to do good, especially the very poor people, and you say, 'The last thing I want to do is focus on what possible wrong they might be doing which might not even be wrong. It's just a different cultural way of doing something. You're making the effort — I can tell, because I know you.'"

This emboldening of the populace was often centered in Christian churches, drawing in many who had not been participating in religion previously. What drew them was perhaps not the historical Christian church, but the power of truth, as Jesus himself had lived and died by truth. Czechoslovakia's Vaclav Havel observes that "a single seemingly powerless person who dares to cry out the word of truth and to stand behind it with all his person and all his life, has surprisingly greater power, though formally disfranchised, than do thousands of anonymous voters."[102]

The courage of a few, and then hundreds of thousands, to maintain a fearless, nonviolent stand for truth, toppled seemingly powerful Communist regimes in country after country with amazingly little bloodshed. Pastor Christian Fuhrer of Leipzig explains this miraculous phenomenon as the spirit of Jesus at work:

Non-violence is clearly the spirit of Jesus. With these people who grew up with pictures of class enemies, and whose parents grew up with the Nazis and violence and racial hatred, you can prove that it didn't come from here. It's not a question of one's upbringing. And the few Christians that there are in this unchristian country — they didn't do it either. That was the spirit of God at work. We few people couldn't have done it. God honored us by letting us play this part in His plan.[103]

Ecumenical movement

The restoration of religious freedom to multitudes of Christians in formerly communist countries increases the great diversity of Christian ways of worshipping. Another contemporary trend is the attempt to unify all Christians around some point of agreement or at least fellowship with each other.

Vatican II asserted that the Roman Catholic Church is the one church of Christ but opened the way to dialogue with other branches of Christianity by declaring that the Holy Spirit was active in them as well. The Orthodox Church likewise believes that it is the "one, holy, Catholic, and Apostolic Church." Although it desires reunion of all Christians and denies any greed for organizational power, it insists on uniformity in matters of faith. Orthodox and Roman Catholic Churches therefore do not share Holy Communion with those outside their respective disciplines. Some Protestant denominations have branches that also refuse to acknowledge each other's validity.

There are, however, attempts to restore some bonds among all Christian churches. There are dozens of official ecumenical dialogues going on among them. The World Council of Churches, centered in Geneva, was founded in 1948 as an organizational body allowing Christian churches to cooperate on service projects even in the midst of their theological disagreements. Its Faith and Order Commission links three hundred culturally, linguistically, and politically, not to mention theologically, different Christian churches in working out the problems of Christian unity.

In 1995, Pope John Paul issued an encyclical entitled "That They May All Be One" urging Roman Catholics, Protestants, Anglicans, and Orthodox Christians to forgive each other for past mistakes so that the followers of Jesus could be reunified.

In June 1994 there was an historical gathering of representatives of many Christian churches at the Danilov Monastery in Moscow to discuss "Christian Faith and Human Enmity." They concluded,

We call upon the servants of all Christian Churches and confessions to be very careful in their actions and always resist the manifestations of chauvinism and cultural and national intolerance. The ideal of Christian love demands that we should show a special care and concern for national and cultural minorities and that we should never forget the commandment to love our neighbor.[104]

Suggested reading

Abbott, Walter M., ed., *The Documents of Vatican II*, New York: The America Press, 1966. Landmark conclusions of the Council Fathers, with special emphasis on the poor, religious unity and social justice.

Dillenberger, John and Welch, Claude, *Protestant Christianity Interpreted through its Development*, New York: Charles Scribner's Sons, 1954. The classic history and interpretation of Protestantism.

Fernando, Antony, *Christianity made Intelligible*, Eldeniya, Kadawata, Sri Lanka: Intercultural Book Promoters, 1990. A usefully concise and yet sensitive portrayal of Christianity for both Christians and people of other faiths.

Fosdick, Harry Emerson, ed., *Great Voices of the Reformation*, New York: Random House, 1952. Extensive quotations, with commentary, from major early Protestant leaders.

Jeremias, Joachim, *New Testament Theology: The Proclamation of Jesus*, New York: Charles Scribner's Sons, 1971. Extensive but highly readable analyses of the authenticity and meanings of key biblical passages.

Pope-Levison, Priscilla and Levison, John R., *Jesus in Global Contexts*, Louisville, Kentucky: Westminster/John Knox Press, 1992. Examinations of the question "Who is Jesus?" from poor cultures and feminist perspectives.

Price, James L., *Interpreting the New Testament*, second edition, New York: Holt, Rinehart and Winston, 1971. Excellent survey of the literature and interpretation of the New Testament.

Robinson, James M., ed., *The Nag Hammadi Library*, San Francisco: Harper and Row, 1977. A fascinating collection of early scriptures that are not included in the Christian canon.

Tugwell, Simon, *Ways of Imperfection*, London: Darton, Longman and Todd, 1984, and Springfield, Illinois: Templegate Publishers, 1985. Spirituality as a whole vision of life, as seen by a series of great Christian practitioners.

von der Heydt, Barbara, *Candles behind the Wall*, Grand Rapids, Michigan: William B. Eerdmans Publishing Co., 1993. Gripping stories of individual Christians whose courageous acts of conscience helped to topple communism in Eastern Europe.

Walker, Williston, Norris, Richard A., Lotz, David W., and Handy, Robert T., *A History of the Christian Church*, fourth edition, New York: Charles Scribner's Sons, 1985, and Edinburgh: T&T Clark, 1986. A classic history of Christianity, authoritatively updated.

Ware, Timothy, *The Orthodox Church*, Middlesex, England and Baltimore, Maryland: Penguin Books, 1984. An excellent overview of the history, beliefs, and practices of the Eastern Church.

CHAPTER 11
ISLAM

"There is no god but God"

In about 570 CE, a new prophet was born. This man, Muhammad, is considered by Muslims to be the last of a continuing chain of prophets who have come to restore the true religion. They regard the way revealed to him, Islam, as the final stage in the evolution of the Judeo-Christian-Islamic monotheistic tradition.

After carrying the torch of civilization in the West while Europe was in its Dark Ages, Islam is undergoing a great resurgence in the twentieth century. It is now the religion of an estimated one-fifth of the world's people. Its monotheistic creed is very simple: "There is no god but God, and Muhammad is his Messenger." Its requirements of the faithful are straightforward, if demanding. But beneath the simplicities of outward conformity to the teachings—and aggressive interpretations of them in some quarters — lie profundities and subtleties of which non-Muslims are largely unaware. Glimmers of appreciation for the faith are just beginning to appear outside Islam, partly as sincere Muslims attempt to counteract negative media portrayals of the faithful.

The Prophet Muhammad

Islam, like Christianity and Judaism, traces its ancestry to the patriarch Abraham. Ishmael was said to be the son of Abraham and an Egyptian slave, Hagar. When Abraham's wife Sarah also bore him a son (Isaac), Abraham took Ishmael and Hagar to the desert valley of Becca (Mecca) in Arabia to spare them Sarah's jealousy.

The sacred book of Islam, the Holy Qur'an, received as a series of revelations to Muhammad, relates that Abraham and Ishmael together built the holiest sanctuary in Islam, the *Ka'bah*. It was thought to be the site of Adam's original place of worship; the cornerstone of the cubic stone building is a venerated black meteorite. According to the Qur'an, God told Abraham that the Ka'bah should be a place of pilgrimage. It was regarded as a holy place by the Arabian tribes.

According to Muslim tradition, the region sank into historical oblivion, "the Age of Ignorance," as it turned away from Abraham's monotheism. For many centuries, the events of the rest of the world passed it by, aside from contact through trading caravans. Then into a poor clan of the most powerful of the tribes in the area was born a child named Muhammad ("the praised one"). His father died before he was born; his mother died during his infancy. He was nursed by a woman of another tribe and raised among them as a shepherd.

ISLAM

CE	
	Birth of Muhammad c.570 CE
600	Revelation of the Qur'an to Muhammad begins c.610
	The hijrah ("migration") from Mecca 622
	Muhammad's triumphant return to Mecca 630
700	Death of Muhammad, election of Abu Bakr as first caliph 632
	Written text Qur'an established 650

Rapid spread of Islam begins 633 — 600

Umayyad dynasty 661–750

Karbala massacre 680 — 700

European advance of Islam stopped at Battle of Tours 732

800

Islam reaches its cultural peak under Abbasid caliphs 750–1258 — 900

al-Hallaj killed 922

1000

al Ghazali 1058–1111

1100

Salah-al-Din recaptures Jerusalem from Crusaders 1171

1200

Christians take Spain, institute Inquisition 1300s — 1300

1400

Turks conquer Constantinople, renaming it Istanbul 1453

1500

Akbar becomes Mughal emperor in India 1556

1600

1700

Muslim areas fall under European domination 1800s–1900s — 1800

1900

Oil-rich Muslim states join OPEC and Muslim resurgence begins 1970s

Partition of Muslim Pakistan from Hindu India 1947

2000

Allah (God) is *the* focus in Islam, the sole authority, not Muhammad. But Muhammad's life story is important to Muslims, for his character is considered a model of the teachings in the Qur'an. The stories of Muhammad's life and his sayings are preserved in a vast, not fully authenticated literature called the **Hadith** which reports on the Prophet's **Sunnah** (sayings and actions). They indicate that the Prophet-to-be returned to live and travel with his uncle as a young teenager. On a trip to Syria, he was noticed by a Christian monk who recognized his deep spirituality. Another who appreciated his fine qualities was the beautiful, intelligent, and wealthy Khadijah, his employer. When she was forty and Muhammad twenty-five, she offered to marry him. Khadijah became Muhammad's strongest supporter during the difficult and discouraging years of his early mission.

With Khadijah's understanding of his spiritual propensities, Muhammad began to spend periods of time in solitary retreat. These retreats were not uncommon in his lineage. They were opportunities for contemplation, away from the world.

When Muhammad was forty years old, he made a spiritual retreat during the month called Ramadan. An angel in human-like form, Gabriel, reportedly came to him and insisted that he recite. Three times Muhammad demurred that he could not, for he was unlettered, and three times the angel commanded him. After the third time, Muhammad was able to recite the first words of what became the Qur'an, repeating them as the angel dictated:

Proclaim! (or Read!)
In the name
Of thy Lord and Cherisher,
Who created —
Created man, out of
A (mere) clot
Of congealed blood:
Proclaim! And thy Lord
Is Most Bountiful, —
He Who taught
(The use of) the Pen, —
Taught man that
Which he knew not.[1]

Muhammad returned home, deeply shaken. Khadijah comforted him and encouraged him to overcome his fear of the responsibilities and ridicule of prophethood. The revelations continued intermittently, asserting the theme that it was the One God who spoke and who called people to *Islam* (which means complete trusting surrender to God). According to tradition, Muhammad described the form of these revelations thus:

Revelation sometimes comes like the sound of a bell; that is the most painful way. When it ceases I have remembered what was said. Sometimes it is an angel who talks to me like a human, and I remember what he says.[2]

The Prophet shared these revelations with the few people who believed him: his wife Khadijah, his young cousin 'Ali, his friend the trader Abu Bakr, and the freed slave Zayd.

The Ka'bah in Mecca is Islam's holiest place of worship.

Muhammad allegedly undertook spiritual retreats in this cave on Mt. Hira outside Mecca. It was here that he received the revelations of the Qur'an.

After three years, Muhammad was instructed by the revelations to preach publicly. He was ridiculed and stoned by the Qurayshites, the aristocrats of his tribe who operated the Ka'bah as a pilgrimage center and organized profitable trading caravans through Mecca. Finally, according to some accounts, Muhammad and his followers were banished for three years to a desolate place where they struggled to survive by eating wild foods such as tree leaves.

The band of Muslims were asked to return to Mecca, but their persecution by the Qurayshites continued. Muhammad's fiftieth year, the "Year of Sorrows," was the worst of all: he lost his beloved wife Khadijah and his protective uncle. With his strongest backers gone, persecution of the Prophet increased.

According to tradition, at the height of his trials, Muhammad experienced the Night of Ascension. He is said to have ascended through the seven heavens to the far limits of the cosmos, and thence into the Divine Proximity. There he met former prophets and teachers from Adam to Jesus, saw paradise and hell, and received the great blessings of the Divine Presence.

Pilgrims to Mecca from Yathrib, an oasis to the north, recognized Muhammad as a prophet. They invited him to come to their city to help solve its social and political problems. Still despised in Mecca as a potential threat by the Qurayshites, Muhammad and his followers left Mecca secretly. Their move to Yathrib, later called al-Medina ("The City [of the Prophet]"), was not easy. The Prophet left last, accompanied (according to some traditions) by his old friend Abu Bakr. To hide from the pursuing Meccans, it is said that they took refuge in a cave, where the Prophet taught his friend the secret practice of the silent remembrance of God.

The **hijrah** ("migration") from Mecca took place in June 622 CE. The Muslim era is calculated from the beginning of the year in which this event took place, for it marked the change from persecution to appreciation of the Prophet's message.

Faithful Muslims pray five times a day, no matter where they are. The prayer rug provides a sacred precinct from which one can turn toward Mecca, the center of the faith.

In Medina, he drew up a plan for solving community tensions that later served as a model for Muslim social administration. In a battle between the young community and Meccans at Badr near Medina, the small group of Muslims was victorious.

According to the Qur'anic revelations, God sent a thousand angels to help Muhammad. Furthermore, Muhammad threw a handful of pebbles at the Meccans and this turned the tide, for it was God who threw, and "He will surely weaken the designs of the unbelievers."[3] The Meccans repeatedly tried to attack the Medinans, but the latter held fast, inspired by revelations to Muhammad about the battle against oppression.

The Qur'anic revelations to Muhammad emphasize the basic religious unity of Jews, Christians, and Muslims, members of the same monotheistic tradition of Abraham. But Jews refused to accept Islam since it recognized Jesus and claimed to complete the Torah. In addition, they were politically allied to those who opposed the Prophet. Eventually their farms were appropriated by increasing numbers of Muslim converts; some Jews were killed as political opponents. The Qur'an taught that the Jews and Christians had distorted the pure monotheism of Abraham; Muhammad had been sent to restore and supplement the teachings of the apostles and prophets. He was instructed to have the people face Mecca rather than Jerusalem during their prayers.

In 630 CE the Prophet returned triumphant to Mecca with such a large band of followers that the Meccans did not resist. The Ka'bah was purged of its idols, and from that time to the present it has been the center of Muslim piety. Acquiescing to Muhammad's political power and the Qur'anic warnings about the dire fate of those who tried to thwart God's prophets, many Meccans converted to Islam. Former opponents were reportedly treated leniently.

The Prophet then returned to Medina, which he kept as the spiritual and political center of Islam. From there, campaigns were undertaken to spread the faith. In addition to northern Africa, the Persian states of Yemen, Oman, and Bahrain came into the fold. As the multi-cultural, multi-racial embrace of Islam evolved, the Prophet declared that the community of the faithful was more important than the older tribal identities that had divided people. The new ideal was a global family, under God. In his "Farewell Sermon," Muhammad stated, "You must know that a Muslim is the brother of a Muslim and the Muslims are one brotherhood."[4]

In the eleventh year of the Muslim era Muhammad made a final pilgrimage to the Ka'bah to demonstrate the rites that were to be followed thenceforth. Then he became very ill. As he recognized that the end was near, he gave final instructions to his followers, promising to meet them at "the Fountain" in Paradise. But he left no clear instructions as to who should succeed him. In the confusion that followed, his steadfast friend Abu Bakr was elected the first **caliph** (political successor to the Prophet). Another possible successor was the trustworthy and courageous 'Ali, the Prophet's cousin and husband of his favorite daughter, Fatima. Tradition has it that the Prophet Muhammad actually transferred his spiritual light to Fatima before his death, but that in the midst of funeral arrangements, neither she nor 'Ali participated in the selection of the first caliph. The Shi'ite faction would later claim 'Ali as the legitimate heir. Abu Bakr and Umar, who became the second caliph upon Abu Bakr's death, put military pressure on the Byzantine and Persian Empires. Soon, Persia, Egypt, and the Fertile Crescent were within the Muslim fold.

Muhammad's own life has continued to be very precious to Muslims, and it is

Although representations of humans, including himself, were forbidden by the Prophet to avoid idolatry, Persian artists later gave imaginative expression to Muslim stories, such as the Miraj, *or Ascension, of the Prophet.*

his qualities that a good Muslim tries to emulate. He always denied having any superhuman powers, and the Qur'an called him "a human being like you," just "a servant to whom revelation has come."[5] The only miracle he ever claimed was that though unlettered, he had received the Qur'anic revelations in extraordinarily eloquent and pure Arabic. He did not even claim to be a teacher — "God guides those whom He will,"[6] he was instructed to say.

Nevertheless, all who saw the Prophet remarked on his touching physical beauty, his nobility of character, the fragrance of his presence, his humility, and his kindness. In his devotion to God, he quietly endured poverty so extreme that he tied a stone over his stomach to suppress the pangs of hunger. He explained, "I eat as a slave eats, and sit as a slave sits, for I am a slave (of God)." Although his people regarded him as the perfect model for humanity, the purest vehicle for God's message, he himself perpetually prayed for God's forgiveness. When he was asked how best to practice Islam, he said, "The best Islam is that you feed the hungry and spread peace among people you know and those you do not know."[7]

TEACHING STORY

The Humility of the Prophet

The Prophet Muhammad's followers had such reverence for him that they caught the very water dripping from his arms when he did his ablutions, in order to rub it on themselves as a blessing. But he himself was so humble that he asked for God's forgiveness at least seventy times a day.

Once the Prophet asked his companions to prepare goat's meat for the group as they were traveling. One said he would kill the goat; another said he would skin it; another volunteered to cook it. The Prophet said he would gather the wood for the fire. His companions immediately protested: "You are God's Messenger. We will do everything." "I know you would," said the Prophet, "but that would be discrimination. God does not want His servants to behave as if they were superior to their companions."

When the Prophet was the recognized head of Medina, he borrowed some money from Zaid ibn Sana'a. Several days before the repayment of the loan, Zaid came to the Prophet, grabbed his clothes, and roughly demanded his money, saying, "Your relatives are always late in paying their debts." Umar, the Prophet's supporter, voiced his outrage and prepared to manhandle the moneylender. The Prophet merely said to Zaid, "Three days remain for the fulfillment of my obligation." He reserved his strong words for Umar: "You should have treated us both better. You should have told me to be better at repaying my debts, and you should have told him to be better at demanding payment. Pay him the amount due and give him 40 kilograms extra of dates as compensation for the alarm that you have caused him."

The Qur'an

The heart of Islam is not the Prophet but the revelations he received. Collectively they are called the *Qur'an* ("reading" or "reciting"). He received the messages over a period of twenty-three years, with some later messages replacing earlier ones. At first they were striking affirmations of the unity of God and the woe of those who did not heed God's message. Later messages also addressed the organizational needs and social lives of the Muslim community.

As Muhammad heard the revelations, he dictated them to a scribe; many of his companions then memorized them. They are said to have been carefully safeguarded against changes and omissions. Recited, the passages have a lyrical beauty and power that Muslims believe to be unsurpassed; these qualities cannot be translated. The recitation is to be rendered in what is sometimes described as a sad, subdued tone, because the messages concern God's sadness at the waywardness of the people. Muhammad said, "Weep, therefore, when you recite it."[8]

Recitation of the Qur'an is thought to have a healing, soothing effect, but can also bring protection, guidance, and knowledge, according to Muslim tradition. It is critical that one recite the Qur'an only in a purified state, for the words are so powerful that the one who recites it takes on a great responsibility. Ideally, one learns the Qur'an as a child, when memorization is easiest and when the power of the words will help to shape one's life.

During the life of the Prophet, his followers attempted to preserve in writing the oral tradition as an additional way of safeguarding it from loss. The early caliphs continued this effort until a council was convened by the third caliph around 650 CE to establish a single authoritative written text. This is the one still used. It is divided into 114 *suras* (chapters). The first is the **Fatiha**, the opening sura which reveals the essence of the Qur'an:

In the name of God, Most Gracious, Most Merciful.
Praise be to God,
The Lord of the Worlds;
Most Gracious, Most Merciful;
Master of the Day of Judgment.
Thee do we worship,
And Thine aid we seek.

Show us the straight way,
The way of those on whom
Thou hast bestowed Thy Grace
Those whose portion
Is not wrath,
And, who go not astray.

The verses of the Qur'an are terse, but are thought to have multiple levels of meaning. Translator and commentator Abdullah Yusuf Ali notes that in the mystical early passages there are often three layers: 1 a reference to a particular person or situation, 2 a spiritual lesson, and 3 a deeper mystical significance. He offers interpretation of these three levels in the first two verses of Sura 74 ("O thou wrapped up / [In a mantle]! / Arise and deliver thy warning!"):

As to 1, the Prophet was now past the stage of personal contemplation, lying down or sitting in his mantle; he was now to go forth boldly to deliver his Message and publicly proclaim the Lord … As to 2, similar stages arise in a minor degree in the life of every good man, for which the Prophet's life is to be a universal pattern. As to 3, the Sufis understand, by the mantle and outward wrappings, the circumstances of our phenomenal existence, which are necessary to our physical comfort up to a certain stage; but we soon outgrow them, and our inner nature should then boldly proclaim itself.... [9]

The Qur'an makes frequent mention of figures and stories from Jewish and Christian sacred history, all of which is considered part of the fabric of Islam by Muslims. Islam — surrender to God — is the original religion, according to Qur'an. Submission has existed as long as there have been humans willing to submit. Adam was the first prophet. Abraham was not exclusively a Jew nor a Christian; he was a monotheistic, upright person who had surrendered to Allah. Jesus was a very great prophet, though different in kind from Muhammad. As Khalid Duran explains:

For Muslims, Jesus is an extreme, a heartrending as well as heartwarming example, but one who is to be imitated only under the most extraordinary circumstances — unlike Muhammad, who is for Muslims primarily the good exemplar, for all times and climes. [10]

The Jewish prophets and Jesus all brought the same messages from God, Muslims believe. However, Qur'an teaches that God's original messages have been added to and distorted by humans. For instance, Muslims do not accept the idea developed historically in Christianity that Jesus has the authority to pardon or atone for our sins. The belief that this power lies with anyone except God is considered a blasphemous human interpolation into what Muslims understand as the basic and true teachings of all prophets of the Judeo-Christian-Islamic tradition: belief in one

Enjoined against pictorial representation, Muslim artists lavished great devotion on elaborate calligraphy and decoration for the word of God, revealed in the Holy Qur'an. The illuminations express the luminous flowing outward from the Sacred Word.

God and in our personal moral accountability before God on the Day of Judgment. In the Muslim view, Qur'an was sent as a final corrective in the continuing monotheistic tradition. Muslims believe that Jesus prophesied the coming of Muhammad when he promised that the **Paraclete** ("one who would be called to help the people") would come to assist humanity after him.

The Qur'an revealed to Muhammad is understood as a final and complete reminder of the prophets' teachings, which all refer to the same God. For example, in Sura 42, Muhammad is told:

Say: "I believe in whatever Book Allah has sent down; and I am commanded to judge justly between you. Allah is our Lord and your Lord! For us is the responsibility for our deeds, and for you for your deeds. There is no contention between us and you. Allah will bring us together, and to Him is our final goal."[11]

Living Islam

Trained as a doctor of pharmacy, Khaled aly Khaled of Egypt did not appreciate his Muslim heritage when he was a child. He explains that his faith grew slowly as he became aware of the scientific accuracy and literary genius of the Qur'an.

"For a very long time in Egypt, we had the idea that it is better for you not to stick to a religion. If you stuck to a religion, people looked at you as just a fool. They thought there is a correlation between the success in the real life and the religion. If you have success in the real world, you didn't have to do these things that were religious. If you pray and fast and talk about Qur'an, the people start to think that you are not having any success.

Ten years ago I could not even read Qur'an. So I started from the very end, very far from religion, but I am getting back to it. For me, maybe the most important thing is scientific interpretation of the Qur'an. I can just believe what I can see, what I can feel, and just try to make interpretation of what I can collect from data. I started to read about the planets and their movement, from the scientific point of view. It is hard to believe these kind of things come just from blind nature. But a Big Mind behind this system? I could not believe that. That's against the science. But it cannot come as an accident. If you change one part out of one hundred million parts, the whole universe will collapse. So you cannot be accurate unless you have some mind or some knowledge to control the whole thing.

Now I'm sure that someone is behind the universe, is creating it, is creating me. You cannot feel the miracle of the universe unless you work in science. The human body cannot come from a primary cell reacting to another primary cell to create a creature from two cells and construct the body. It is beyond probability. Some supreme power created everything.

Some of the statements in the Qur'an had no meaning at that time, fourteen hundred years ago, but they have meaning now. For example, 'We have created this universe and we have made it expanding.' 'We have made the earth look like an egg.' Such statements cannot come from just an average person living fourteen hundred years ago. Among ancient Egyptians, ancient Syrians, we cannot find this information. I started to believe that someone was giving the knowledge to Muhammad. I'm not a very good believer — don't ask me to believe just because there is a book. But this information cannot come from any source except One Source.

As for the language of the Qur'an, scholars who speak Arabic have tried to write just one statement similar to this book in beauty. They could not. One computer scientist did a computer analysis of the Qur'an. He found that the number of chapters, the number of statements, and the number of times each letter is used are all multiples of nineteen (which is the number of angels in the Hellfire). Then he tried to see if he could write a book about any subject, using multiple numbers of any figure. No one could do it. The beauty of the Qur'an is pure, supreme.

If you compare the speech of Muhammad to the Qur'an, there is a big difference in beauty. He himself cannot make even one statement like that. He cannot write, he doesn't have knowledge, he just was taking care for the sheep. From this, I started to believe that there is a God."

The central teachings

On the surface, Islam is a very straightforward religion. Its teachings can be summed up very simply, as in this statement by the Islamic Society of North America:

Islam is an Arabic word which means peace, purity, acceptance and commitment. As a religion, Islam calls for complete acceptance of the teachings and guidance of God.

A Muslim is one who freely and willingly accepts the supreme power of God and strives to organize his life in total accord with the teachings of God. He also works for building social institutions which reflect the guidance of God.[12]

This brief statement can be broken down into a number of articles of faith.

The Oneness of God and of humanity

The first sentence chanted in the ear of a traditional Muslim infant is the **Shahadah** — "*La ilaha illa Allah.*" Literally, it means "There is no god but God." Exoterically, the phrase supports absolute monotheism. As the Qur'an reveals in Sura 2:163,

Your God is One God:
There is no god but He,
Most Gracious, Most Merciful.

Esoterically, the Shahadah means that ultimately there is only one Absolute Reality; the underlying essence of life is eternal unity rather than the apparent separateness of things in the physical world. Muslims think that the Oneness of God is the primordial religion taught by all prophets of all faiths. Muhammad merely served to remind people of it.

It has been estimated that over ninety percent of Muslim theology deals with the implications of Unity. God, while One, is called by ninety-nine names in the Qur'an. These are each considered attributes to the One Being, such as *al-Ali* ("The Most High") and *ar-Raqib* ("The Watchful"). **Allah** is the name of God that encompasses all the attributes. Each of the names refers to the totality, the One Being.

Unity applies not only to the conceptualization of Allah (God), but also to every aspect of life. In the life of the individual, every thought and action should spring from a heart and mind intimately integrated with the divine. Islam theoretically rejects any divisions within itself; all Muslims around the globe are supposed to embrace as one family. All humans, for that matter, are a global family; there is no one "chosen people," for all are invited into a direct relationship with God. Science, art, and politics are not separate from religion in Islam. Individuals should never forget Allah; the Oneness should permeate their thoughts and actions. Abu Hashim Madani, an Indian Sufi sage, is said to have taught, "There is only one thing to be gained in life, and that is to remember God with each breath; and there is only one loss in life, and that is the breath drawn without the remembrance of God."[13]

Muslims express their belief in the Oneness of the divine by saying the Shahadah ("There is no god but Allah"), the sentence emblazoned on this Turkish plaque.

> *"The 'remembrance of God' is like breathing deeply in the solitude of high mountains: here the morning air, filled with purity of the eternal snows, dilates the breast; it becomes space and heaven enters our heart."*
>
> *Frithjof Schuon[14]*

Prophethood and the compass of Islam

Devout Muslims feel that Islam encompasses all religions. Islam honors all prophets as messengers from the one God:

> *Say ye: We believe*
> *In God, and the revelation*
> *Given to us, and to Abraham,*
> *Isma'il, Isaac, Jacob,*
> *And the Tribes, and that given*
> *To Moses and Jesus, and that given*
> *To (all) Prophets from their Lord:*
> *We make no difference*
> *Between one and another of them:*
> *And we bow to God in surrender.*[15]

Muslims believe that the original religion was monotheism, but that God sent prophets from time to time as religions decayed into polytheism. Each prophet came to renew the message, in a way specifically designed for his or her culture and time. Muhammad, however, received messages meant for all people, all times. The Qur'anic revelations declared him to be the "Seal of the Prophets," the last and ultimate authority in the continuing prophetic tradition. The prophets are mere humans; none of them are divine, for there is only one Divinity.

Islam is thought to be the universal religion in its pure form. All scriptures of all traditions are also honored, but only the Qur'an is considered fully authentic, because it is the direct, unchanged, untranslated word of God. Whatever exists in other religions that agrees with the Qur'an is divine truth.

Human relationship to the divine

> *We are nearer to him than his jugular vein.*
>
> *The Holy Qur'an, Sura 50:16*

In Muslim belief, God is all-knowing and has intelligently created everything for a divine purpose, governed by fixed laws which assure the harmonious and wondrous working of all creation. Humans will find peace only if they know these laws and live by them. They have been revealed by the prophets, but the people often have not believed. To believe is to totally surrender to Allah. As Qur'an states,

> *None believes in Our revelations save those who, when reminded of them, prostrate themselves in adoration and give glory to their Lord in all humility; who forsake their beds to pray to their Lord in fear and hope; who give in charity of that which We have bestowed on them. No mortal knows what bliss is in store for these as a reward for their labors.*[16]

Qur'an indicates that human history provides many "signs" of the hand of God at work bestowing mercy and protection on believers. Signs such as the great flood which was thought to have occurred at the time of Noah illustrate that nonbelievers and evil-doers ultimately experience great misfortune in this life or the afterlife. None are punished without first being warned by a messenger of God to mend their ways. Creation itself is a sign of God's compassion, as well as of God's omnipotent will.

According to Islam, the two major human sins involve one's relationship to God. One is **shirk** (associating anything else with divinity except the one God). The other is **kufr** (ungratefulness to God, atheism). Furthermore, a major human problem is forgetfulness of God. As Professor Seyyed Hossein Nasr explains:

> It is a going to sleep and creating a dream world around us which makes us forget who we really are and what we should be doing in this world. Revelation is there to awaken man from this dream and remind him what it really means to be man.[17]

According to Muslim belief, angels are everywhere; they come to our help in every thought and action. A group of angels is here shown helping the 8th-century Sufi ascetic, Ibrahim ibn Adham.

God has mercifully sent us revelations as reminders. The veils that separate us from God come from us, not from God; Muslims feel that it is ours to remove the veils by seeking God and acknowledging the omnipresence, omniscience, and omnipotence of the Divine. For the orthodox, the appropriate stance is a combination of love and fear of God. Aware that God knows everything and is all-powerful, one wants to do everything one can to please God, out of both love and fear. This paradox was given dramatic expression by the caliph 'Umar ibn al-Khattab:

> If God declared on the Day of Judgment that all people would go to paradise except one unfortunate person, out of His fear I would think that I am that person. And if God declared that all people would go to hell except one fortunate person, out of my hope in His Mercy I would think that I am that fortunate person.[18]

The unseen life

Muslims believe that our senses do not reveal all of reality. In particular, they believe in the angels of God. These are nonphysical beings of light who serve and praise God day and night. They are numerous, and each has a specific responsibility. For instance, certain angels are always with each of us, recording our good and bad deeds. Qur'an also mentions four archangels, including Gabriel, highest of the angelic beings, whose main responsibility is to bring revelations to the prophets from God. But neither he nor any other angel is to be worshipped, according to strict monotheistic interpretation of Islam, for the angels are simply utterly submissive servants of God. By contrast, according to Islamic belief, there is a non-submissive being called Satan. He was originally one of the **jinn** — immaterial beings of fire, whose nature is between that of humans and angels. He proudly refused to bow before Adam and was therefore cursed to live by tempting Adam's descendants— all of humanity, in other words — to follow him rather than God. According to Qur'an, those who fall prey to Satan's devices will ultimately go to hell.

Popular Muslim piety also developed a cult of saints. The tombs of mystics known to have had special spiritual powers have become places of pilgrimage. Many people visit them out of devotion and desire for the blessings of the spirit which is thought to remain in the area. This practice is frowned upon by some reformers, who assert that Muslim tradition clearly forbids worship of any being other than God.

The Last Judgment

In the polytheistic religion practiced by Arabs before Muhammad, the afterlife was only a shadow, without rewards or punishments. People had little religious incentive to be morally accountable. By contrast, Qur'an emphasizes that after a period of repose in the grave, all humans will be bodily resurrected and assembled for a final accounting of their deeds. At that unknown time of the Final Judgment, the world will end cataclysmically: "The earth will shake and the mountains crumble into heaps of shifting sand." (Sura 73:14). Then comes the terrible confrontation with one's own life:

> The works of each person We have bound about his neck. On the Day of Resurrection, We shall confront him with a book spread wide open, saying, "Read your book. Enough for you this day that your own soul should call you to account."[19]

Hell is the grievous destiny of unrepentant nonbelievers — those who have rejected faith in and obedience to Allah and His Messenger, who are unjust and who do not forbid evil. Hell also awaits the hypocrites who even after making a covenant with Allah have turned away from their promise to give in charity and to pray regularly:

> It is a flaming Fire. It drags them down by their scalps; and it shall call him who turned his back and amassed riches and covetously hoarded them.[20]

Muslim piety is ever informed by this belief in God's impartial judgment of one's actions, and of one's responsibility to remind others of the fate that may await them.

Basically, Islam says that what we experience in the afterlife is a revealing of our tendencies in this life. Our thoughts, actions, and moral qualities are turned into our outer reality. We awaken to our true nature, for it is displayed before us. For the just and merciful, the state after death is a Garden of Bliss. Those who say, "Our Lord is God … shall have all that your souls shall desire…. A hospitable gift from One Oft-Forgiving, Most Merciful!" (Sura 41:30–32) The desire of the purified souls will be for closeness to God, and their spirits will live in different levels of this closeness. For them, there will be castles, couches, fruits, sweetmeats, honey, houris (beautiful virgin women), and immortal youths serving from goblets and golden platters. Such delights promised by the Qur'an are interpreted metaphorically to mean that human nature will be transformed in the next life to such an extent that the disturbing factors of this physical existence will no longer have any effect.

People are asleep, but when they die, they wake up.
Hadith of the Prophet Muhammad

By contrast, sinners and nonbelievers will experience the torments of Hell, fire fueled by humans, boiling water, pus, chains, searing winds, food that chokes, and so forth. It is they who condemn themselves; their very bodies turn against them "on the Day when their tongues, their hands, and their feet will bear witness against them as to their actions." (Sura 24:24) The great medieval mystic Al-Ghazzali speaks of spiritual torments of the soul as well: the agony of being separated from worldly desires, burning shame at seeing one's life projected, and terrible regret at being barred from the vision of God. Muslims do not believe that hell can last forever for any believer, though. Only the nonbelievers will be left there; the others will eventually be lifted to paradise, for God is far more merciful than wrathful.

The Sunni-Shi'ite Split

The preceding pages describe beliefs of all Muslims, but groups within Islam differ somewhat on other issues. After Muhammad's death, resentments over the issue of his succession began to divide the unity of the Muslim community into factions. The two main opposing groups have come to be known as the **Sunni**, who now comprise about eighty percent of all Muslims worldwide, and the **Shi'ite**.

As discussed earlier, a series of caliphs was elected to lead the Muslim community after Muhammad's death. The fourth caliph was 'Ali, the Prophet's cousin and son-in-law. He was reportedly known for his holy and chivalrous qualities, but the opposition party, the Umayyads, never accepted him as their leader, and he was assassinated by a fanatic from his own party. His son Husayn, grandson of the Prophet, challenged the authority of the next Umayyad caliph, Mu'awiyya, and his son and designated successor Yazid, and in return was massacred by Yazid's troops in the desert of Karbala along with many of his relatives, who were also members of the Prophet's own family. This horror unified Shi'ite opposition to the elected successors and they broke away, claiming their own legitimate line of succession through the direct descendants of the Prophet, beginning with 'Ali. Nearly fourteen hundred years later the two groups are still separate.

Sunnis

Those who follow the elected caliphs are "the people of the Sunnah." They consider themselves traditionalists who emphasize the authority of the Qur'an and the Hadith and Sunnah (the sayings and practices of the Prophet, as collected under the Sunni caliphs). They believe that Muhammad died without appointing a successor and left the matter of successors to the **ummah**, the Muslim community. The caliph is not a replacement of the Prophet; he is the leader of worship and the administrator of the **Shari'ah**, the sacred law of Islam.

The Shari'ah consists of teachings and practices for everything in Muslim life, from how to conduct a war to how to pray. Like Torah for Jews, the Shari'ah sets the pattern for all individual actions and theoretically bonds them into a coherent, divinely regulated, peaceful community.

The Shari'ah is based chiefly on the Qur'an and Sunnah of Muhammad, who was the first to apply the generalizations of the Qur'an to specific life situations. The revelations of the Qur'an include not only human-divine relationships but also humans' relationships with each other. Religion is not a thing apart; all of life is to be integrated into the spiritual unity which is the central principle of Islam. For example, the faithful are enjoined to be kind to their parents and kin, children and strangers, to protect orphans and women, to exercise justice and honesty in their relationships and business interactions, to stop killing infants, to manage their wealth carefully, and to avoid adultery and arrogance.

In the second century of Islam, the Abbasid dynasty replaced the Umayyads, who had placed more emphasis on empire-building and administration than on spirituality. At this point, there was a great concern for purifying and regulating social and political life in accord with Islamic spiritual tradition. Mechanisms for establishing the Shari'ah were developed. Since then, Sunnis have felt that as life circumstances change, laws in the Qur'an, Hadith, and Sunnah should be continually interpreted by a consensus of opinion and the wisdom of learned men and jurists. For example, the twentieth-century Muslim faces new ethical questions not specifically addressed in the Qur'an and Hadith, such as whether or not test-tube fertilization is acceptable (some think yes, on condition that the sperm is the father's and the egg the mother's). Divorce has always been addressed by the Shari'ah, but the conditions under which a wife may petition for divorce has been closely examined in recent years.

Shi'ites

Shi'ites are ardently devoted to the memory of Muhammad's close relatives: 'Ali, Fatima (the Prophet's beloved daughter), and their sons Hasan and Husayn. The martyrdom of Husayn at Karbala in his protest against the alleged tyranny, oppression, and injustice of the Umayyad caliphs is held up as a symbol of the struggle against human oppression. It is commemorated yearly, as *Muharram*, with participants in mourning processions crying and beating their chests or, in some areas, offering cooling drinks to the populace in memory of the martyred Husayn. Shi'ite piety places great emphasis on the touching stories told of 'Ali and Husayn's dedication to truth and integrity, even if it leads to personal suffering, in contrast to the selfish power politics ascribed to their opponents.

Rather than recognize the Sunni caliphs, Shi'ites pay their allegiance to a string of seven or twelve **Imams** ("leaders," "guides"). The first three were 'Ali, Hasan, and Husayn. According to a saying of the Prophet acknowledged by both Sunni and Shi'a:

> I leave two great and precious things among you: the Book of Allah and my Household. If you keep hold of both of them, you will never go astray after me.[21]

"Twelver" Shi'ites believe that there were a total of twelve Imams, legitimate hereditary successors to Muhammad. The twelfth Imam, they believe, was commanded by God to go into an occult hidden state in 940 CE, to continue to guide the people and return publicly at the Day of Resurrection as the Mahdi. A minority of Shi'ites, the Isma'ilis and "Seveners" recognize a different person as the seventh and last Imam, and believe that it is he who is hidden and still living. There must always be an Imam. As Muhammad Rida al-Muzaffar explains:

> The Imamate must continue uninterrupted, although the Imam may live hidden among mankind until Allah wills that he reappear on a certain day, a Divine mystery known only to Him. The fact that he has lived for such a long time is a miracle granted to him by Allah…. Even though medical science is not yet able to prolong human life as much as possible,… Allah can, for He is All-Powerful and Omnipotent. For the Qur'an states that Nuh [Noah] lived to a very old age, and that 'Isa [Jesus] is alive now, and once one has accepted Islam, there can be no denying what the Qur'an says.[22]

Unlike the Sunni Caliph, the Imam combines political leadership (if possible) with continuing the transmission of Divine Guidance. This esoteric religious knowledge was given by God to Muhammad, from him to 'Ali, and thence from each Imam to the successor he designated from 'Ali's lineage. It includes both the outer and inner meanings of the Qur'an. The Shari'ah is therefore interpreted for each generation by the Imam, for he is closest to the divine knowledge. When the Imam is not in a position to assert political power, those in positions of authority are expected to carry out his decisions. This assumption of spiritual authority has at times been carried to autocratic, violent extremes by Isma'ilis in power.

Aside from the issue of succession to Muhammad, Sunnis and Shi'ites are in general agreement on most issues of faith. Shi'ites follow the same essential practices as Sunnis, but, as discussed in a later section on spiritual practices, add several that express their ardent commitment to re-establishing what they see as the true spirit of Islam in a corrupt, unjust world.

Sufism

In addition to these two main groups within Islam, there is also an esoteric tradition which is said to date back to the time of the Prophet. He himself was at once a political leader and a contemplative with a deep prayer life. He reportedly said that every verse of the Qur'an has both an outside and an inside. Around him were gathered a group of about seventy people. They lived in his Medina mosque in voluntary poverty, detached from worldly concerns, praying night and day. After the time of the first four caliphs, Muslims of this deep faith and piety, both Sunni and Shi'ite, were distressed by the increasingly secular, dynastic, wealth-oriented characteristics of Muhammad's Umayyad successors. The mystical inner tradition of Islam, called **Sufism** (Arabic: *tasawwuf*), also involved resistance to the legalistic, intellectual trends within Islam in its early development.

Sufis have typically understood their way as a corrective supplement to orthodoxy. They consider their way a path to God that is motivated by longing for the One. In addition to studying the Qur'an, Sufis examine their own hearts and the world around them. They feel that the world is a book filled with "signs" — divine symbols and elements of beauty that speak to those who understand. The intense personal journeys of Sufis and the insights that have resulted from their truth-seeking have periodically refreshed Islam from within. Much of the allegorical interpretation of the Qur'an and devotional literature of Islam is derived from Sufism.

The early Sufis turned to asceticism as a way of deepening their piety. In this, they may have been influenced by ascetics from other traditions with which they came into contact, particularly Christianity. The Christian ascetics were following Jesus's advice not to worry about material life because God would take care of their physical needs; the Prophet had said something very similar to his followers: "If ye had trust in God as ye ought He would feed you even as He feeds the birds."[23] Muhammad himself had lived in poverty, reportedly gladly so. Complete trust in and surrender to God became an essential step in the journey. **Dervishes** (poor mendicant mystics) with no possessions, no attachments in the world, were considered holy people like Hindu sannyasins. But Sufi asceticism is based more

Sufi dervishes enter a state of ecstatic unity with the divine by repeating the Shahadah.

on inner detachment than on withdrawal from the world; the ideal is to live with feet on the ground, head in the heavens.

To this early asceticism was added fervent, selfless love. Its greatest exponent was Rabi'a, the eighth-century saint. A famous mystic of Iraq, she scorned a very rich man's offer of marriage, saying that she did not want to be distracted for a moment from God. All her attention was placed on her Beloved, which became a favorite Sufi name for God. Rabi'a emphasized disinterested love, with no selfish motives of hope for paradise or fear of hell. "I have served Him only for the love of Him and desire for Him."[24] Any other motivation is a veil between lover and Beloved. When no veils of self exist, the mystic dissolves into the One she loves.

> *The Beloved is all, the lover just a veil.*
> *The Beloved is living, the lover a dead thing.*   *Jalal al-Din Rumi*[25]

In absolute devotion, the lover desires *fana*, total annihilation in the Beloved. This Sufi ideal was articulated in the ninth century CE by the Persian Abu Yazid al-Bistami. He is said to have fainted while saying the Muslim call to prayer. When he awoke, he observed that it is a wonder that some people do not die when saying it, overwhelmed by pronouncing the name Allah with the awe that is due to the One. In his desire to be annihilated in God, al-Bistami so lost himself that he is said to have uttered pronouncements such as "Under my garment there is nothing but God,"[26] and "Glory be to Me! How great is My Majesty!"

The authorities were understandably disturbed by such potentially blasphemous statements. Sufis themselves knew the dangers of egotistical delusions inherent in the mystical path. There was strict insistence on testing and training by a sufficiently trained, tested, and illumined **murshid** ("teacher") or **shaykh.** Advanced practices were taught only to higher initiates. It was through the shaykh that the *barakah* ("blessing," sacred power) was passed down, from the shaykh of the shaykh, and so on, in a chain reaching back to Muhammad, who is said to have transmitted the barakah to 'Ali.

A number of esoteric orders (**tariqas**) evolved, most of which traced their spiritual lineage back to Junayd of Baghdad (who died in 910 CE). He taught the need for constant purification, a continual serious examination of one's motives and actions. He also knew that it was dangerous to speak openly of one's mystical understandings; the exoteric-minded might find them blasphemous, and those who had not had such experiences would only interpret them literally and thus mistakenly. He counseled veiled speech, and much Sufi literature after his time is couched in metaphors accessible only to mystics.

Despite such warnings, the God-intoxicated cared little for their physical safety and exposed themselves and Sufism to opposition. The most famous case is that of Mansur al-Hallaj. After undergoing severe ascetic practices, he is said to have visited Junayd. When the master asked, "Who is there?", his disciple answered, *"ana'l-Haqq"* ("I am the Absolute Truth," i.e., "I am God"). After Junayd denounced him, al-Hallaj traveled to India and throughout the Middle East, trying to open hearts to God. He wrote of the greatness of the Prophet Muhammad, and introduced into the poetry of divine love the simile of the moth that flies ecstatic into the flame and, as it is burned up, realizes Reality.

Political maneuverings made a possible spiritual revival a threat to authorities back home, and they imprisoned and finally killed al-Hallaj in 922 CE for his "ana'l-Haqq." Now, however, al-Hallaj is considered by many to be one of the greatest Muslim saints, for it is understood that he was not speaking in his limited person. Like the Prophet, who had reportedly said, "Die before ye die,"[27] al-Hallaj had already died to himself so that nothing remained but the One.

> *What's in your head — toss it away! What's in your hand — give it up! Whatever happens — don't turn away from it.... Sufism is the heart standing with God, with nothing in between.*
>
> *Abu Sa'id Abu al-Khayr[28]*

A more moderate Sufism began to make its way into Sunni orthodoxy through Abu Hamid al-Ghazzali. He had been a prominent theologian but felt compelled to leave his prestigious position for a life of spiritual devotion. Turning within, he discovered mystical truths which saved him from his growing scepticism about the validity of religion. His persuasive writings combined accepted Muslim theology with the assertion that Sufism is needed to keep the mystical heart alive within the tradition. By the fourteenth century, three sciences of religion were generally accepted by the orthodoxy: jurisprudence, theology, and mysticism.

Over the centuries, other elements have been added to Sufism. Some Sufis have embraced teachings from various religions, emphasizing that the Qur'an clearly states that the same Voice has spoken through all prophets. Shihabuddin Suhrawardi (1153–1191 CE), for instance, combined many currents of Islam with spiritual ideas from the Zoroastrians of ancient Iran and the Hermetic tradition from ancient Egypt. His writings are full of references to the divine light and hierarchies of angels. We humans have descended from the angels and realms of light, he wrote; we are in exile here on earth, longing for our true home, searching for that radiant purity, dimly remembered, in this dark world of matter.

Although Sufi teachings and practices have been somewhat systematized over time, they resist doctrinal, linear specification. They come from the heart of mystical experiences which defy ordinary logic. Paradox, metaphor, the world of creative imagination, of an expanded sense of reality — these characteristics of Sufi thought are better expressed through poetry and stories. A favorite character in Sufi teaching tales is Mulla Nasrudin, the wise fool. An example, as told by Idries Shah:

> *One day Nasrudin entered a teahouse and declaimed, "The moon is more useful than the sun." Someone asked him why. "Because at night we need the light more."[29]*

These "jokes" boggle the mind, revealing the limitations of ordinary thinking at the same time that they offer flashes of metaphysical illumination for those who ponder their deeper significances.

Poetry has been used by Sufis as a vehicle for expressing the profundities and perplexities of relationship with the divine. Jalal al-Din Rumi, the thirteenth-century founder of the Mevlevi Dervish Order in Turkey (famous for its "Whirling Dervishes" whose dances lead to transcendent rapture), was also a master of mystical poetry. He tells the story of a devotee whose cries of "O Allah!" were finally answered by God:

Pilgrimage to the tombs of the Sufi saints is a popular form of piety. Women are not allowed to enter this tomb of a Chisti Sufi saint in Delhi, so they tie bits of fabric with their prayers to the grillework outside.

Was it not I that summoned thee to service?
Did not I make thee busy with My name?
Thy calling "Allah!" was My "Here am I,"
Thy yearning pain My messenger to thee.
Of all those tears and cries and supplications
I was the magnet, and I gave them wings.[30]

The aim of Sufism is to become so purified of self that one is a perfect mirror for the divine attributes. The central practice is called *dhikr*, or "remembrance." It consists of stirring the heart and piercing the solar plexus, seat of the ego, by movements of the head, while continually repeating *la ilaha illa Alla*, which Sufis understand in its esoteric sense: There is nothing except God. Nothing in this ephemeral world is real except the Creator; nothing else will last. As the seventy thousand veils of self — illusion, expectation, attachment, resentment, egocentrism, discontent, arrogance — drop away over the years, this becomes one's truth, and only God is left to experience it.

The Five Pillars and jihad

While Sufism carries the inner practice of Islam, the outer practice is set forth in the *Shari'ah*, the straight path of the Divine Law. It specifies patterns for worship (known as **The Five Pillars of Islam**) as well as detailed prescriptions for social conduct, to bring remembrance of God into every aspect of daily life and practical ethics into the fabric of society. These prescriptions include injunctions against drinking intoxicating beverages, eating certain meats (including pork, rodents, predatory animals and birds, and improperly slaughtered animals), gambling and vain sports, sexual relations outside of marriage, and sexually provocative dress, talk, or actions. They also include positive measures, commanding justice, kindness, and charity. Women are given many legal rights, including the right to own property, to divorce (according to certain schools of law), to inherit, and to make a will. These rights divinely decreed during the time of the Prophet, fourteen hundred years ago, were not available to Western women until the nineteenth century. Polygyny is allowed for men who have the means to support several wives, to bring all women under the protection of a husband. Women are allowed to inherit only half as much as men because men have the obligation to support women financially.

The Shari'ah is said to have had a transformative effect on Muhammad's community. Before Muhammad, the people's highest loyalty was to their tribe. Tribes made war on each other with no restraints. Women were possessions like animals. Children were often killed at birth either because of poverty or because they were females in a male-dominated culture. People differed widely in wealth. Drunkenness and gambling were commonplace. Within a short time, Islam made great inroads into these traditions, shaping tribes into a spiritual and political unity with a high sense of ethics.

A Muslim must do his or her best to fulfill the Five Pillars because they are considered God's commandments.

Belief and witness

The first pillar of Islam (the **Shahadah**) is believing and professing the unity of God and the messengership of Muhammad: "There is no god but God, and Muhammad is his Messenger." The Qur'an requires the faithful to tell others of Islam, so that they will have the information they need to make an intelligent choice. However, it rules out the use of coercion in spreading the message:

> Let there be [or: There is] no compulsion
> In religion: Truth stands out
> Clear from Error: whoever
> Rejects Evil and believes
> In God hath grasped
> The most trustworthy
> Hand-hold, that never breaks.[31]

The Qur'an insists on respect for all prophets and all revealed scriptures.

Daily prayers

The second pillar is the performance of a continual round of prayers. Five times a day, the faithful are to perform ritual ablutions with water (or sand or dirt if necessary), face Mecca, and recite a series of prayers and passages from the Qur'an, bowing and kneeling. Around the world, this joint facing of Mecca for prayer unites all Muslims into a single world family. When the prayers are recited by a congregation, all stand and bow shoulder to shoulder, with no distinctions of social standing. In a mosque, women and men pray in separate groups, with the women

At a Muslim mosque, there are no social distinctions, as all worshippers line up shoulder to shoulder to pray together.

behind a screen, to avoid sexual distractions. There may be an **imam**, or prayer-leader, but no priest stands between the worshipper and Allah. On Friday afternoon, there is usually a special prayer service in the mosque, but Muslims observe no sabbath day. Remembrance of God is an everyday obligation; invoking the Name of Allah continually polishes the rust from the heart.

Repeating the prayers is thought to strengthen one's belief in God's existence and goodness and to carry this belief into the depths of the heart and every aspect of external life. Praying thus is also expected to purify the heart, develop the mind and the conscience, comfort the soul, encourage the good and suppress the evil in the person, and awaken in the believer the innate sense of higher morality and higher aspirations. The words of praise and the bowing express continual gratefulness and submission to the One. At the end, one turns to each of the two guardian angels on one's shoulders to say the traditional Muslim greeting — *"Assalamu Alaykum"* ("Peace be on you") — and another phrase adding the blessing, "and mercy of God."

While mouthing the words and performing the outer actions, one should be concentrating on the inner prayer of the heart. The Prophet reportedly said, "Prayer without the Presence of the Lord in the heart is not prayer at all."[32] Internal prayer of the heart should actually continue at all times, keeping it pure of negativity, humbled to God, and growing in realization of the One.

Fasting

The third pillar is fasting. Frequent fasts are recommended to Muslims, but the only one that is generally obligatory is the fast during Ramadan, commemorating the first revelations of the Qur'an to Muhammad. For all who are beyond puberty, but not infirm or sick or menstruating or nursing children, a dawn-to-sunset abstention from food, drink, sexual intercourse, and smoking is required for the whole month of Ramadan.

Because Muslims use a lunar calendar of 354 days, the month of Ramadan gradually moves through all the seasons. When it falls in the summer, the period of fasting is much longer than in the shortest days of winter. The hardship of abstaining even from drinking water during these long and hot days is an unselfish surrender to God's commandment and an assertion of control over the lower desires. The knowledge that Muslims all over the world are making these sacrifices at the same time builds a special bond between haves and have-nots, helping the haves to experience what it is to be hungry, to share in the condition of the poor. Those who have are encouraged to be especially generous in their almsgiving during Ramadan.

Fasting is expected to allow the body to burn up impurities and provide one with "a Transparent Soul to transcend, a Clear Mind to think and a Light Body to move and act."[33] Many people feel that they are spiritually more sensitive and physically more healthy during Ramadan fasting, and they look forward eagerly to this period each year. Esoterically, it is believed that the external fast is prescribed to help people grow in internal fasting. That is, control of the body's desires also builds the mastery needed to control the lower emotions, such as anger and jealousy.

Zakat

The fourth pillar is **zakat**, or spiritual tithing and almsgiving. At the end of the year, all Muslims must donate at least two and a half percent of their income (after basic expenses) to needy Muslims. This provision is designed to help even out inequalities in wealth and to prevent personal greed. Its literal meaning is "purity," for it purifies the distribution of money, helping to keep it in healthy circulation.

Saudi Arabia devotes fifteen percent of its kingdom's GDP to development and relief projects throughout the world. The Islamic Relief Organization which it funds makes a point of helping people of all religions, without discrimination, where there is great need following disasters such as earthquakes, floods, and wars. Many stories from the life of the Prophet Muhammad are cited as teaching that one should help others whether or not they are Muslims. For example, the Prophet's neighbor was Jewish. The Prophet reportedly gave him a gift every day, even though the neighbor daily left garbage at his door. Once the neighbor was sick, and the Prophet visited him. The neighbor asked, "Who are you to help me?" The Prophet replied, "You are my brother. I must help you."

In addition to zakat, Shi'ites are obligated to give one-fifth of their disposable income to the Imam. Because the Imam is now hidden, half of this now goes to the deputy of the Imam to be used however he thinks appropriate; the other half goes to descendants of the Prophet as a gift of love and honor, to spare them the humiliation of poverty.

Hajj

The fifth pillar is **hajj**, the pilgrimage to Mecca. All Muslims who can possibly do so are expected to make the pilgrimage at least once in their lifetime. It involves a series of symbolic rituals designed to bring the faithful as close as possible to God. Male pilgrims wrap themselves in a special garment of unsewn cloths, rendering them all alike, with no class distinctions. The garment is like a burial shroud, for by dying to their earthly life they can devote all their attention to God. It is a time for *dhikr*, the constant repetition of the Shahadah, the remembrance that there is no god but God.

Pilgrims walk around the ancient Ka'bah seven times, like the continual rotation around the One by the angels and all of creation, to the seventh heaven. Their hearts should be filled only with remembrance of Allah.

Another sacred site on the pilgrimage is the field of 'Arafat. It is said to be the place where Adam and Eve were taught that humans are created solely for the

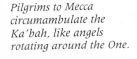

Pilgrims to Mecca circumambulate the Ka'bah, like angels rotating around the One.

worship of God. Here pilgrims pray from noon to sunset to be forgiven of anything that has separated them from the Beloved. In addition, pilgrims carry out other symbolic gestures, such as sacrificing an animal and throwing stones at the devil, represented by pillars. The animal sacrifice reminds the hajjis of Abraham's willingness to surrender to God that which was most dear to him, his own son, even though in God's mercy he was allowed to substitute a ram for the sacrifice. Most of the meat is distributed to the needy, a service for which Saudi Arabia has had to develop huge preservation and distribution facilities. Hajjis also perform symbolic acts at the holy well of Zamzam, the spring which God is said to have provided for Hagar when she and Ishmael were left alone in the desert.

Hajj draws Muslims from all corners of the earth together for this intense spiritual experience. Because Islam is practiced on every continent, it is truly an international gathering. The crowds are enormous. During the month of Dhu'l-hijjah, the time for the pilgrimage, an estimated two million pilgrims converge upon Mecca. To help handle the crowds, the Saudi government has built the immense King Abdul Aziz International Airport near Jedda, with a special terminal just for hajj pilgrims. The journey was once so hazardous that many people and camels died trying to cross the desert in fulfillment of their sacred obligation.

Throughout Muslim history, hajj has brought widely diverse people together, consolidating the center of Islam, spreading information and ideas across cultures, and sending pilgrims back into their communities with fresh inspiration.

Jihad

In addition to these Five Pillars of Islam, there is another important injunction: **jihad**. Commonly mistranslated as "holy war," it means "striving," resisting evil both individually and collectively. The Greater Jihad, Muhammad said, is the struggle against the lower self. It is the internal fight between wrong and right, error and truth, selfishness and selflessness, hardness of heart and an all-embracing love. As Seyyed Hossein Nasr explains, the inner jihad is:

> an inner battle against that which the soul has become, in order to transform it into that which it "is" and has never ceased to be if only it were to become aware of its own nature.... Through inner jihad, the spiritual man dies in this life in order to cease all dreaming, in order to awaken to that Reality which is the original of all realities, in order to behold that Beauty of which all earthly beauty is but a pale reflection, in order to attain that Peace which all men seek but which can in fact be found only through this practice.[34]

Whatever good, (O man!)
Happens to thee, is from God
But whatever evil happens
To thee, is from thy (own) soul.   *The Holy Qur'an, Sura 4:79*

On the external level, the Lesser Jihad is exerting effort to protect the Way of God against the forces of evil. This jihad is safeguarding of one's life, faith, livelihood, honor, and the integrity of the Muslim community. It is not to be undertaken for

The Prophet's Mosque in Medina has been enlarged to allow room for over one million praying pilgrims.

personal gain. The Qur'anic revelations that apparently date from the Medina period when the faithful were being attacked by Meccans make it clear that

> *To those against whom*
> *War is made, permission*
> *Is given (to fight), because*
> *They are wronged; — and verily,*
> *God is Most Powerful*
> *For their aid;*
>
> *(They are) those who have*
> *Been expelled from their homes*
> *In defiance of right,*
> *(For no cause) except*
> *That they say, "Our Lord*
> *Is God."*[35]

The Qur'an gives permission to fight back under such circumstances, but also gives detailed limitations on the conduct of war and the treatment of captives, to prevent atrocities.

Muhammad is the prototype of the true **mujahid**, or fighter in the Path of God, one who values the Path of God more than life, wealth, or family. He is thought to have had no desire for worldly power, wealth, or prestige. By fasting and prayer, he continually exerted himself toward the One, in the Greater Jihad. In defending the Medina community of the faithful against the attacking Meccans, he was acting from the purest of motives. It is believed that a true mujahid who dies in defense of the faith goes straight to paradise, for he has already fought the Greater Jihad, killing his ego.

The absolute conviction which characterizes jihad derives from recognition of the vast disparity between evil and the spiritual ideal, both in oneself and in society. Continual exertion is thought necessary in order to maintain a peaceful equilibrium in the midst of changing circumstances. Traditionalists and radicals have differed in how this exertion should be exercised in society.

In terms of the lesser jihad, support can be found in Qur'an both for a pacifist approach and for active opposition to unbelievers. The Qur'an asserts that believers have the responsibility to defend their own faith as well as to remind unbelievers of the truth of God and of the necessity of moral behavior. In some passages, Muslims are enjoined simply to stand firm against aggression. For example, "Fight for the sake of Allah those that fight against you, but do not be aggressive. Allah does not love the aggressors."[36] In other passages, Qur'an suggests active opposition to people who do not believe in the supremacy of the one God:

> *Tumult and oppression are worse than slaughter.*
> *Nor will they cease fighting you*

Until they turn you back from your faith
If they can....
Fight them on
Until there is no more tumult or oppression
And there prevail justice and faith in God.[37]

The ultimate goal and meaning of Islam, and of Jihad, is peace through devoted surrender to God. A peaceful society is like paradise. Sri Lankan Sufi Shayk M. R. Bawa Muhaiyaddeen observes:

If one knows the true meaning of Islam, there will be no wars. All that will be heard are the sounds of prayer and the greetings of peace. Only the resonance of God will be heard. That is the ocean of Islam. That is unity. That is our wealth and our true weapon. Not the sword in your hand.[38]

The spread of Islam

In the time of Muhammad, Islam combined spiritual and secular power under one ruler. This tradition, which helped to unify the warring tribes of the area, was continued under his successors. Islam expanded phenomenally during the centuries after the Prophet's death, contributing to the rise of many great civilizations. The **Ummah** became a family that spread from Africa to Indonesia. Non-Muslims have the impression that it was spread by the sword, but this does not seem to be the

Only one hundred years after Muhammad's death, Islam had spread around the Mediterranean. Its diffusion continued for centuries and the numbers of converts are still increasing, making Islam the fastest-growing religion today. Of areas previously converted to Islam, all remain Muslim except Spain and Sicily.

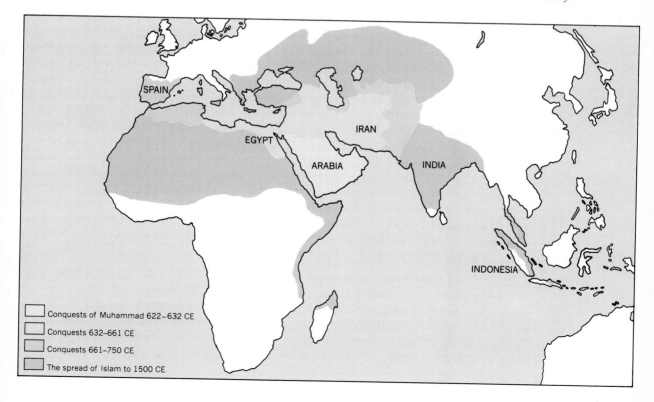

SPAIN

EGYPT

IRAN

ARABIA

INDIA

INDONESIA

☐ Conquests of Muhammad 622–632 CE
☐ Conquests 632–661 CE
☐ Conquests 661–750 CE
☐ The spread of Islam to 1500 CE

general case. The Qur'an forbids coercion in religion, recommending instead that Muslims invite others to the Way by their wisdom, beautiful teaching, and personal example. Islam spread mostly by personal contacts: trade, attraction to charismatic Sufi saints, appeals to Muslims from those feeling oppressed by Roman and Persian rule, unforced conversions. There were some military battles conducted by Muslims over the centuries, but they were not necessarily for the purpose of spreading Islam, and many Muslims feel that wars of aggression violate Muslim principles. Non-Muslim citizens of newly-entered territories were asked to pay a poll tax entitling them to Muslim defense against enemies and exempting them from military service.

Muhammad's non-violent takeover of Mecca occurred only two years before he died. It was under his successors that Islam spread through what is commonly known today as the Middle East and far beyond. Only a year after he died, a newly-converted Qurayshite, Khalid ibn al-Walid, began a series of campaigns that within seven years had claimed the entire Arabian peninsula and Syria as well for Islam. Another group of converts quickly swept through the elegant Persian Empire, which had stood for twelve centuries. Within ten years of the Prophet's death, a mere four thousand horsemen commanded by Amr ibn al-As took the major cities of Egypt, centers of the brilliant Byzantine Empire. Another wave of Islamization soon penetrated into Turkey and Central Asia, North Africa, and north through Spain, to be stopped in 732 CE in France at the battle of Tours. At this point, only a hundred years after Muhammad died, the Muslim Ummah under the Umayyad caliphs was larger than the Roman Empire had ever been.

Muslims cite the power of the divine will to establish a peaceful, God-conscious society as the reason why this happened. By contrast with their strong convictions, the populations they approached were often demoralized by border fighting among themselves and by grievances against their rulers. Many welcomed them without a fight. For example, the Christians of Damascus expected Muslim rule to be more bearable than Byzantine rule, so they opened the city gates to the Muslim armies. Jerusalem and Egypt accepted the Muslims in similar fashion. Syrian Christians at Shayzar under Byzantine rule reportedly went out to meet the Muslim commander and accompanied him to their city, singing and playing tambourines. In Spain, Visigoth rule and taxation had been oppressive; the persecuted Jews were especially glad to help Islam take over. Both Christians and Jews often converted to Islam.

Some historians cite economic factors as an underlying motive for Arabs' expansion beyond their original territory. Although Islamic civilization did become quite opulent, the central leadership did not always support the far-reaching adventures. The conquered peoples were generally dealt with in the humane ways specified in the Qur'an and modeled by Muhammad in his negotiations with tribes newly subjected to Muslim authority. The terms offered by Khalid to the besieged Damascans were these:

> *In the name of God, the merciful, the compassionate. This is what Khalid would grant the inhabitants of Damascus when he enters it. He shall grant them security for their lives, properties and churches. Their city wall shall not be demolished, neither shall any Moslem be quartered in their homes. Thereunto we give them the pact of God and the protection* (dhimmah) *of His Messenger, upon whom be God's blessing and peace, the caliphs and the Believers. So long as they pay poll-tax nothing but good shall befall them.*[39]

Monotheistic followers of revealed traditions, Christians and Jews, who like Muslims were "people of the book," were treated as **dhimmis**, or protected people. They were allowed to maintain their own faith, but not to try to convert others to it. The Dome of the Rock was built on the site of the old Temple of the Jews in Jerusalem, honoring Abraham as well as Muhammad in the city that is still sacred to three faiths: Judaism, Christianity, and Islam.

The Umayyad caliphs had their hands full administering this huge Ummah from Damascus, which they had made its capital. They tended to focus more on organizational matters than on the spiritual life. Some were also quite worldly, such as Walid II, who is said to have enjoyed a pool filled with wine so that he could swim and drink at the same time. In 750 CE a rival to the caliphate is said to have invited eighty of the princes of the line to a banquet, where he had them all killed. Four years after "the bloodshedder," a new series of caliphs took over: the Abbasids. They held power until 1258 CE.

Islamic culture

Under the Abbasids, Muslim rule became more Persian and cosmopolitan and Islamic civilization reached its peak. The capital was moved to the new city of Baghdad. No more territories were brought under centralized rule, and merchants, scholars, and artists became the cultural heroes. A great House of Wisdom was built, with an observatory, a famous library, and an educational institution where Greek and Syriac manuscripts on subjects such as medicine, astronomy, logic, mathematics, and philosophy were translated into Arabic. In Cairo, Muslims built in 972 CE a great university and mosque, Al-Azhar, which is still the center of Muslim scholarship.

In its great cities, Islam went through a period of intense intellectual and artistic activity, absorbing, transmitting, and expanding upon the highest from other cultures. For instance, from Persia, which was to become a Shi'ite stronghold, it adopted a thousand-year-old tradition of exquisite art and poetry. To these avid cultural borrowings Islam added its own innovations. The new system of nine Arabic numerals and the zero derived from Indian numbers revolutionized mathematics by liberating it from the clumsiness of Roman numerals. Muslim philosophers were highly interested in Aristotelian and Neo-Platonic thought, but in their unique synthesis these intellectual ways were harmonized with revealed religion. Muslim scholars' research into geography, history, astronomy, literature, and medicine lifted these disciplines to unprecedented heights.

The pivotal institution of Islamic society was the **ulama**, whose primacy and influence was unchallenged. The ulama were not only guardians of the faith but were also the pervasive force holding together Islamic society. They were *qadis* (judges), *muftis* (jurisconsults), guides and pastors of the artisans' guilds, spiritual leaders, mosque imams, the sole teachers of the civil and military schools, state scribes, and market inspectors. The major source of their economic power and their independence from the state was religious endowments and private endowments, run and controlled by the ulama.

Although Baghdad was the capital of the Abbasids, independent caliphates were declared in Spain and Egypt. Muslim Spain was led by successors to the Umayyads and became a great cultural center. Cordoba, the capital, had seven

Whereas non-Muslims tend to think of Islam as a religion carried by the sword, Muslims believe their faith spread by its innate appeal and its reputation for humane, just government. The inhabitants of a besieged city are depicted welcoming the Muslim conquerors.

hundred mosques, seventy libraries, three hundred public baths, and paved streets. Europe, by contrast, was in its Dark Ages; Paris and London were only mazes of muddy alleys.

Tunisia and Egypt comprised a third center of Islamic power: the Shi'ite Fatimid imamate (so-named because they claimed to be descendants of Muhammad's daughter Fatima). Under the deranged Fatimid caliph Al-Hakim, the Fatimids broke with Islamic tradition and persecuted dhimmis; they also destroyed the Church of the Holy Sepulchre in Jerusalem, provoking European Christian crusades to try to recapture the Holy Lands.

The Islamic period in Spain was known for its tolerance of Judaism. But during the thirteenth century, Christians took Spain and instituted the dread Inquisition against those not practicing Christianity. By the beginning of the sixteenth century, an estimated three million Spanish Muslims had either been killed or had left the country.

Crusading Christians also fought their way down to Jerusalem, which they placed under a month-long seige in 1099. When the small Fatimid garrison surrendered, the Crusaders slaughtered the inhabitants of the holy city. Severed hands and feet were piled everywhere. Anti-Crusading Muslims led by the famous Salah-al-Din (known in the West as Saladin) retook Jerusalem in 1171 and treated its Christian population with the generous leniency of Islam's highest ideals for the conduct of war. But widespread destruction remained in the wake of the Crusaders, and a reservoir of ill-will against Christians lingered, to be exacerbated centuries later by European colonialism in Muslim lands.

Eastward expansion

Its westward advance stopped at Europe, Islam carried its vitality to the north, east, and south. Although Mongolian invasions threatened from Central Asia, the Mongols were converted to Islam; so were the Turks. It is noteworthy that while Uzbek Khan, Mongol leader from 1313 to 1340, zealously desired to spread Islam throughout Russia, he nonetheless maintained tolerance toward the Christians in the conquered lands. He granted a charter to the Orthodox Metropolitan concerning treatment of Christians: "Their laws, their Churches; their monasteries and chapels shall be respected; whoever condemns or blames this religion, shall not be allowed to excuse himself under any pretext but shall be punished with death."[40]

Similar tolerance toward other religions was practiced by the Muslim Turks, but in 1453, the Turks conquered Constantinople, the heart of the old Byzantine Empire, and renamed it Istanbul; Hagia Sophia was turned into a mosque even though it did not face Mecca. At its height, the Turkish Ottoman Empire dominated the eastern Mediterranean as well as the area around the Black Sea.

Farther east, Islam was carried into northern India, where Muslims destroyed many Hindu idols and temples but allowed the Hindu majority a protected dhimmi status. The Chishti Sufi saints drew people to Islam by their great love for God. "The heart of a mystic is a blazing furnace of love which burns and destroys

A Muslim mosque hugs the earth, for Islam attempts to establish just, godly societies in this world and conceives of God as being everywhere. Al-Azhar, a venerable institution in Cairo, combines a mosque with a major university.

The Mughal Emperor
Akbar initiated
interfaith dialogue
among spiritual leaders
of different religions
during his reign in India
in the 16th century.

everything that comes into it because no fire is stronger than the fire of love," declared Khwaja Muinuddin Chishti.[41]

Under the Muslim Mughals, the arts and learning flourished in India. The Emperor Akbar, who rose to the Mughal throne in 1556, made yearly pilgrimages to the shrine of the Sufi saint, Muinuddin Chishti. In his ecumenical spiritual curiosity, he created a house of worship where representatives from many traditions — Hindu, Zoroastrian, Jain, Christian — were invited to the world's first interfaith dialogues. Eventually he devised a new religion that was a synthesis of Islam and all these other religions, with himself as its supposedly enlightened head, but it died with him and Muslim orthodoxy returned.

Under British colonization of India, tensions between Hindus and Muslims were inflamed, partly to help England divide and rule. India gained its independence under Gandhi, who was unable to end the enmity between the two faiths. In 1947, West and East Pakistan (now the independent nation of Bangladesh) were partitioned off to be Muslim-ruled and predominantly populated by Muslims, while India was to be run by Hindus. Millions lost their lives trying to cross the borders, and the strife between the two faiths continues. In December 1992, militant Hindus set off renewed communal violence by destroying a mosque in Ayodhya, India, in the belief that it had been built by the Mughals on the site of an ancient temple to Lord Rama.

The greatest concentration of Muslims developed even farther east, in Indonesia, where Muslim traders and missionaries may have first landed as early as the tenth century CE. Many centuries later, large segments of the population embraced Islam, at least partly to shore up their defense against European colonialism. About ninety percent of the people are now Muslim, but the government refuses to establish Islam as a state religion; President Suharto stated in 1989, "We want each and all religions existing and developing in our country to achieve progress in an atmosphere of unity and mutual respect."[42] China and the former Soviet Union encompass tens of millions of Muslims.

To the south, Islam spread into Africa along lines of trade — salt from the north for gold and slaves from the south. In competition with Christianity, Islam sought the hearts of Africans and eventually won in many areas. Many converted to Islam; many others maintained some of their indigenous ways in combination with Islam. The prosperous Mali empire was headed by a Muslim, who made an awe-inspiring pilgrimage to Mecca with a gold-laden retinue of eight thousand in 1324. As the spread of Islam encompassed an increasing diversity of cultures, hajj became important not only for individuals but also for the religion as a whole, holding its center in Mecca in the midst of worldwide variations.

Relationships with the West

Although Islam honors the prophets of all traditions, its own religion and prophet were denounced by medieval Christian Europe. Christianity had considered itself the ultimate religion and had launched its efforts to bring the whole world under its wings. Islam felt the same way about its own mission. Northern Christians were aghast as the Mediterranean area where Christianity began converted to Islam instead. In the struggle for souls, the Church depicted Muhammad as an idol-worshipper, an anti-Christ, the Prince of Darkness. Islam was falsely portrayed as a religion of many deities, in which Muhammad himself was worshipped as a god (thus the inaccurate label "Muhammadanism"). Europeans watched in horror as the Holy Lands became Muslim and the "infidel" advanced into Spain. Even though it was Muslim scholars and artists who preserved, shared, and advanced the classic civilizations while Europe was benighted, the wealth of Arabic culture was interpreted in a negative light.

By the nineteenth century, Western scholars began to study the Arabic classics, but the ingrained fear and loathing of Muhammad and Muslims remained. The ignorance about, and negative stereotyping of, Muslims continues today. Western cartoonists, for instance, inevitably draw Muslims as wild-eyed radicals dressed in desert robes and brandishing scimitars. Annemarie Schimmel, Professor of Indo-Muslim Culture, Harvard University, explains:

> The idea that the Muslims conquered everything with fire and sword was unfortunately deeply ingrained in the medieval mind. All these misconceptions about Islam as a religion and the legends and lies that were told about it are really unbelievable. I have often the feeling that this medieval image of Islam as it was perpetuated in ever so many books and even scholarly works is part of our subconscious. When someone comes and says, "But real Islam is something completely different," people just will not believe it because they have been indoctrinated for almost fourteen hundred years with the image of Islam as something fierce and something immoral. Unfortunately, some of the events of our century have revived this medieval concept of Islam.[43]

Borrow the Beloved's eyes. Look through them and you'll see the Beloved's face everywhere....
Let that happen, and things you have hated will become helpers.

Jalal al-Din Rumi[44]

Although it had enjoyed great heights of culture and political power, the Muslim world fell into decline. It seems that the Mongol invasions were at least partly responsible, for they eradicated irrigation systems and libraries and killed scholars and scientists, erasing much of the civilization that had been built up over five hundred years. Some Muslims today feel that spiritual laxness was the primary reason that some of the previously glorious civilizations became impoverished third world countries. Another theory is that Muslim culture was no longer dynamic. As it rigidified and stagnated, it was overwhelmed by cultures both less civilized than itself (the Mongols) and more civilized (the Europeans, who were becoming major world powers on the strength of their industrialization and colonizing navies).

During the late eighteenth and early nineteenth centuries, many Muslim populations fell under European domination. From the mid-twentieth century onward, most gained their independence as states that had adopted certain Western ideals and practices. In many cases, they had let go of some aspects of their Muslim heritage, considering it a relic that prevented them from success in the modern world. Arabic was treated as an unimportant language; Western codes of law had replaced the Shari'ah in social organization. But yet they were not totally Westernized, and they resumed local rule with little training for twentieth-century self-government and participation in a world economy dominated by industrial nations.

Societies which had been structured along traditional lines fragmented from the mid-nineteenth century onward, as wide-ranging programs of reforms and modernization were unleashed throughout the Muslim world. The local autonomy of the traditional Islamic society was swept away and replaced by centralized regulations of Western origin. Traditional schools, markets, guilds, and courts into which the societies had been organized lost much of their reason for being.

Before the colonial forces moved out, foreign powers led by Britain helped to introduce a Jewish state in the midst of the Middle East. After long and terrible persecution in many countries, Jewish Zionists sought resettlement in what they considered their ancient homeland. But some historians allege that the chief motive of the countries supporting this claim was to protect European interests. Lord Palmerston of Britain suggested that a wealthy Jewish population transplanted to Palestine, and highly motivated to protect itself, would prop up the decaying Ottoman Empire so that it could serve as a bulwark against Russian imperialism; the new Jewish presence in Palestine would also serve as a check against the attempts of the Egyptian leader Mehemet Ali to create a pan-Islamic state encompassing Egypt, Syria, and the Arabian peninsula.

Islam in the United States

Even as Muslims were feeling humiliated by foreign domination elsewhere, they were growing in numbers and self-pride within the United States. Islam is the fastest-growing religion in the United Sates, and may soon become the second largest religion in the country. Two-thirds of American Muslims are immigrants from the Middle East, who began to arrive at the end of the nineteenth century. One-third of American Muslims are converts, most of them African–Americans.

Conversion to Islam by African–Americans was encouraged early in the twentieth century as a form of separatism from white oppression. The Christianity espoused by the dominant white population was interpreted as part of the pattern of oppression. Under the leadership of Elijah Muhammad, who proclaimed himself a messenger of Allah, tens of thousands of African–Americans became "Black Muslims." However, faith in Elijah Muhammad himself was shaken by allegations about his sexual relationships with his secretaries. Some followers — especially the influential leader Malcolm X and Warith Deen Muhammad, son of Elijah Muhammad — developed contacts with mainstream Muslims in other countries and came to the conclusion that Elijah Muhammad's version of Islam was far removed from Muslim orthodoxy. They steered converts toward what they perceived as the true traditions of the world brotherhood of Islam. Today these American converts are simply called "Muslims" rather than "Black Muslims."

Others of African–American heritage, especially Minister Louis Farrakhan, maintain a more political focus on black separatism as a central aspect of their belief in Islam, despite its strong tradition of non-racism. However, politicization of Islamic identity is probably not the main aspect of the growth of Islam. Many American Muslims embrace their religion as a bulwark of discipline and faith against the degradations of materialism.

Muslim resurgence

The Muslim world had lost its own traditional structure and was also generally helpless against manipulations by foreign nations until it found its power in oil. In the 1970s, oil-rich nations found that by banding together they could control the price and availability of oil. OPEC (The Organization of Petroleum Exporting Countries) brought greatly increased revenues into previously impoverished countries and strengthened their self-image as well as their importance in the global balance of power. Of the thirteen OPEC nations, most are predominantly Muslim (Algeria, Libya, Saudi Arabia, Kuwait, Qatar, the United Arab Emirates, Iraq, Iran, Indonesia, and half-Muslim Nigeria). Other predominantly Muslim oil-exporting countries who are not members of OPEC (Egypt, Tunisia, Syria, Malaya, Oman, Bahrain and Brunei) have also benefited from oil price controls.

As the wealth suddenly poured in, it further disrupted established living patterns. Analysts feel that some people may have turned back to a fundamentalist version of Islam in an effort to restore a personal sense of familiarity and stability amid the chaos of changing modern life; the increase in literacy, urbanization, and communications helped to spread revived interest in Islam. There was also the hope that Islam would provide the blueprint for enlightened rule, bringing the spiritual values into community and politics just as Muhammad had done in Medina.

Return to Shari'ah

The resurgence of Islam takes several forms. One is a call for return to Shari'ah rather than secular law derived from European codes. The feeling of the orthodox is that the world must conform to the divine law, rather than diluting the law to accommodate it to the material world. For example, Egypt has made it illegal for its Muslim citizens to drink alcoholic beverages in public. In Saudi Arabia, morality squads actively enforce the obligatory prayers. In post-Revolutionary Iran, an attempt has been made to shape every aspect of life according to Shari'ah. Fasting during Ramadan is strictly enforced in Saudi Arabia and Iran, and restaurants in many Muslim countries close during the fasting hours.

Private behaviors are also becoming more traditional. In particular, to honor the Qur'anic encouragement of physical modesty to protect women from being molested, many Muslim women have begun covering their bodies except for hands, face, and feet, as they have not done for decades. Many Muslim women assert that they like dressing more modestly so that men will view them as persons, not as sex objects. Others feel that men are simply treating women as slaves. Noor Grant, publisher of *Islamic Canada Reflections*, says that to expect all Muslim women to dress "like the oppressed women of Saudi Arabia is indeed a travesty of Islam."[45]

In some largely Muslim countries, such as Egypt, it is the possibility of employment which motivates women to adopt **hijab** (veiling for the sake of modesty). Women are allowed to join the work force only if they are veiled.

Shari'ah has been locally adapted to various societies over the centuries; to attempt to restore its original form designed for Muhammad's time or any other form from another period is to deny the usefulness of its flexibility. Some customs thought to be Muslim are actually cultural practices not specified in the basic sources; they are the result of Islamic civilization's assimilation of many cultures

Veiling of Muslim women is a complex phenomenon, only partly associated with religious disapproval of revealing clothing. Some modern women choose to cover their hair in a return to traditional values; for others veiling is a sign of high social status.

in many places. Muhammad worked side-by-side with women, and the Qur'an encourages equal participation of women in religion and in society. Veiling and seclusion were practices absorbed from conquered Persian and Byzantine cultures, particularly the upper classes; peasant women could not carry out their physical work under encumbering veils or in seclusion from public view. The authenticity of hadith relegating women to subordinate status has been questioned in recent years by certain scholars, but cultural determinations of the role of women continue to be practiced and to be commonly considered part of Islam.

Another problem with applying Shari'ah as civil law is that some ethical issues which arise today either did not exist in their present form at the time of Muhammad or were not specifically addressed by the Qur'an or Hadith. Artificial birth control methods, for example, were not available then. However, infanticide and abortion were mentioned by the Qur'an: "Do not kill your children for fear of poverty. We will provide for them and for you." Does this mean that all forms of population control should be considered forbidden by Islam, or should the overpopulation of the earth be a major contemporary consideration? According to Islamic legal reasoning, the accepted method for determining such ambiguous issues is to weigh all the benefits and disadvantages that might result from a course of action and then discourage it if the likely disadvantages outweigh the advantages. Many Muslim leaders joined with the Catholic Church in criticizing the agenda of the 1994 UN Conference on Population and Development in Cairo. They felt that sexual promiscuity would be encouraged and traditional Muslim family and social values undermined if Western methods of family planning and sex education were imposed on their countries.

Professor Sajida Sultana Alvi states that a rigid approach to Shari'ah is contrary to the spirit of Islam. She says,

Change is actually the essence of Islam — a very dominant and central feature. If you rob Islam of that dynamism and that capacity for change, then it becomes static. That is why there are so many difficulties in the minds of Muslims all over the world: They are trying to cope with the demands of modernity and looking for the solutions within the scriptures. I don't mean that we should ignore the scriptures, but we are to interpret them in a way that supports changing with the times, in a way that would adapt and integrate the Muslim community. Of course we cannot ignore the fundamentals in Islam, but that should not make us bigots. That should not make us intolerant of any change.[46]

The global family of Islam is not a political unit; its unity under Arab rule broke up long ago. There is as yet no consensus among Muslim states about how to establish a peaceful, just, modern society based on basic Muslim principles. But there is widespread recognition that there are problems associated with modern Western civilization that should be avoided, such as crime, drug abuse, and unstable family life.

Today everyone cries for peace but peace is never achieved, precisely because it is metaphysically absurd to expect a civilization that has forgotten God to possess peace.
Seyyed Hossein Nasr[47]

Outreach and education

Another sign of Muslim resurgence is the increase in outreach, as Muslims become more confident of the value of their faith. Islam is the fastest-growing of all world religions, with one billion two hundred million followers. New mosques are going up everywhere, including a $25 million Islamic Cultural Center in the heart of Manhattan, with Kuwait, Saudi Arabia, and Libya as major contributors to the project. Muslims who constitute a minority in their countries are beginning to assert their rights to practice their religion. They no longer feel they have to be secretive about praying five times a day or apologetic about leaving work to attend Friday afternoon congregational worship.

A third sign of Muslim resurgence is the increasing attention being given to developing educational systems modeled on Islamic thought. Islam is not anti-scientific or anti-intellectual; on the contrary, it has historically bridged reason and faith and placed a high value on developing both in order to tap into the fullness of human potential. Western education has omitted the spiritual aspects of life, so Muslims consider it incomplete and imbalanced. The 1977 First World Conference on Muslim Education defined the goals of education thus:

Education should aim at the balanced growth of the total personality of Man through the training of Man's spirit, intellect, his rational self, feelings and bodily senses. Education should cater therefore for the growth of Man in all its aspects: spiritual, intellectual, imaginative, physical, scientific, linguistic, both individually and collectively and motivate all aspects toward goodness and the attainment of perfection. The ultimate aim of Muslim education lies in the realisation of complete submission to Allah on the level of the individual, the community and humanity at large.[48]

Islam in politics

In addition to return to Shari'ah, numerical growth, and attention to Muslim-based education, governments are becoming Islamicized. There are more frequent references to Islam and Qur'anic statements by political leaders. Some use it to support the status quo and glorify Islam's past heights. In Arabic countries, others have used Muslim idealism to rally opposition to ruling elites with ties to the West or who are perceived as corrupt. Pahlavi Shahs of predominantly Shi'ite Iran had tried to rapidly modernize their country, turning it into a major military and industrial power. In the process, they eroded the authority of the *ulama*, the clerics and expounders of the Shari'ah. A revolutionary leader emerged from this disempowered group, the Ayatollah Khomeini, and swept the Shah from power in 1979. Once in power, however, the ulama had no clear program for reorganizing society according to Muslim principles. Shari'ah has never specified a single political or economic system as best. Attempts to redistribute wealth in revolutionary Iran

In secular societies, where they are in the minority, some Muslims have set up their own schools for Qur'an-centered education to counter the mass culture's influence. This group is studying the Qur'an in Birmingham, England.

were muddled, and Khomeini made some drastic changes in interpretation of Islam in order to justify violent revolutionary behavior.

The Ayatollah also attempted to export his revolution to other Muslim countries with Shi'ite populations that could carry on the work. He conducted a war against "atheist" Iraq (where the fifty percent of citizens who are Shi'ites are ruled by the forty-five percent who are Sunni), denounced predominantly Sunni Saudi Arabia for its ties to the West, and inspired some Lebanese Shi'ites to see their political struggle against Christians and Jews as part of a great world battle between Islam and the satanic forces of Western imperialism and Zionism. He issued a legal opinion that Indian-born British author Salman Rushdie could be sentenced to death under Islamic law, because his novel, *Satanic Verses*, seemed to defame the Prophet and his wives. In resultant riots over the controversial book, hundreds of people died.

Khomeini's call for governmental change was not heeded, so radicals resorted to sabotage and terrorism as their most powerful weapons. Their surprise attacks on civilians tended to turn world opinion against Islam, rather than promoting its ideals. Little is known of the clandestine radical groups; the Muslim governments they oppose control the media and have portrayed them as mindless fanatics, supporting Western fears and stereotyping of Islam. When Saddam Hussein of Iraq tried to unseat the royalty of Kuwait, Islam was again cast as a political football by both sides in the Gulf war. Hussein, an Arab nationalist, resorted to Islam as a means of mass mobilization against what he saw as a foreign Western intrusion in the Gulf.

An unusual side-effect of the negative publicity about Muslim extremists has been a widespread attempt by moderate Muslims to share positive information about their faith. Interest has grown rapidly: Muslim speakers are now in great demand by non-Muslim communities who want to understand and appreciate Islam, rather than remain ignorant about it. Jews are surprised to discover how closely it parallels their own faith; Christians are gradually undoing centuries of sensationalist misinformation about Islam bred by fear.

Nevertheless, in contemporary nationalistic struggles, Muslims have often been the losers, to such an extent that some eighty percent of the world's huge refugee population is Muslim. In Czechnya, where an indigenous movement by the largely Muslim populace was pitted against the power of the central Russian government, joint teams of Christians, Muslims, and Buddhists visited areas of fighting and hospitals to bring help and food supplies. Mufti Magomed-Khaji Albogachiev, Chairman of the Religious Center of Muslims of Ingushetia Republic (which borders Czechnya), said of these efforts,

> *Unfortunately, only disasters have brought us together. We have a lot of opportunities to cooperate. We do not use all the opportunities which we have. As Allah taught us, we are to help each other in doing good things.*[49]

Mufti Albogachiev speaks of the recent past, in which Muslims, along with people of other religions, were imprisoned and killed by the communist state:

> *We should remember that there is nothing more horrible, more dangerous, than to live without God. When religious people were considered criminals for their belief, only for the fact that they had religious books in their home, when only seventy mosques survived from a previous count of fourteen thousand mosques in one region*

of Russia, when tens of thousands of religious leaders were imprisoned and sent to hard labor camps where they died, when hundreds of tons of religious books were burned in Soviet fires, I want to remind you that there is nothing more dangerous than atheism and life without God. But God heard our prayers and this regime was destroyed by itself, because nothing could divide it, except by God's will.[50]

Until recently, Muslims tended to point to their glorious past as proof of the value of their tradition. But the newest thought is forward-looking, exploring how Islam can help to shape a better world. Mahmoon-al-Rasheed, Founder of the Comprehensive Rural Educational, Social, Cultural and Economic Center in Bangladesh, maintains that there is violence within and between nations because people have not developed a sense of duty toward each other and have not recognized how inseparably all people of the earth are related to each other. He proposes that Islamic values are not aimed at creating a political state but rather a harmoniously integrated world society, for:

We cannot begin to realize our full potential until we have achieved a community which knows no limit but that of human society and renders all obedience to a Law common to all.[51]

Dr. Ahmad Kamal Abu'l Majd, an ex-Minister of Culture in Egypt, looks toward the future:

I'm glad and proud I'm a Muslim. I carry on my shoulders a scale of values, a code of ethics that I genuinely believe is good for everybody.... I even venture sometimes to say that Islam was not meant to serve the early days of Islam when life was primitive and when social institutions were still stable and working. It was meant to be put in a freezer and to be taken out when it will be really needed. And I believe that time has come. But the challenge is great because not all Muslims are aware of this fact: That the mission of Islam lies not in the past but in the future.[52]

Suggested reading

Abdalati, Hammudah, *Islam in Focus*, Indianapolis, Indiana: American Trust Publications, 1975. A thorough, non-sectarian explanation of Muslim ideals and practices.

Dessouki, Ali E. Hillal, ed., *Islamic Resurgence in the Arab World*, New York: Praeger Publishers, 1982. A scholarly study of the contemporary Islamic resurgence in specific Arab nations.

Esposito, John L., *Islam: The Straight Path*, New York, Oxford: Oxford University Press, 1988. A scholarly, clear introduction to historical and contemporary Islam.

The Holy Qur'an. Although the Qur'an is considered untranslatable, numerous translations from the Arabic have been attempted. Many Muslims' favorite English translation is by Abdullah Yusuf Ali, (Durban, South Africa: Islamic Propagation Center International, 1946). It gives the Arabic, an English translation, introductions to each Sura, and helpful commentaries on the verses that reveal their deeper meanings. The King Fahd Holy Qur'an Printing Complex in Medina has published a very helpful revision based on Yusuf Ali's translation, with extensive thematic index. Thomas Ballantine Irving (Al-Hajj Ta'lim'Ali) has prepared "The First American Version" of the Qur'an (translation and commentary, Brattleboro, Vermont: Amana Books, © 1985), an effort which is receiving considerable attention. One of the useful English interpretations of the meaning of the Qur'an has been prepared by a committee of Muslim scholars in Lebanon under the direction of Mahmud Y. Zayid.

Kramer, Martin, ed., *Shi'ism, Resistance, and Revolution*, Boulder, Colorado: Westview Press, 1987. Perceptive analyses of recent revolutionary developments in Shi'ism, in the context of Muslim tradition.

Lings, Martin, *Muhammad*, London: George Allen and Unwin, and Islamic Text Society, 1983. Highly regarded biography of the Prophet.

Lings, Martin, *What is Sufism?* Berkeley and Los Angeles: University of California Press, 1975 and London: Unwin Paperbacks, 1981. An excellent introduction to the inner experience of Islam.

Nasr, Seyyed Hossein, *Ideals and Realities of Islam*, second edition, London: Unwin Hyman Ltd., 1985. Thoughtful presentation of both esoteric and exoteric features of Islam.

Nasr, Seyyed Hossein, ed., *Islamic Spirituality I: Foundations*, New York: Crossroad Publishing Company, 1987 and London: SCM Press, 1989. Excellent chapters on key features of Muslim spirituality, from fasting to angels, with sections on Sunnism, Shi'ism, and Sufism.

Nasr, Seyyed Hossein, Dabashi, Hamid, and Nasr, Seyyed Vali Reza, *Shi'ism: Doctrines, Thought, and Spirituality*, Albany, New York: State University of New York Press, 1988. To balance the predominant media attention to Shi'ite politics, a set of thoughtful essays on aspects of Shi'ite spirituality.

Paige, Glenn D., Satha-Anand, Chaiwats, and Gilliatt, Sarah, *Islam and Nonviolence*, Honolulu: University of Hawaii, Center for Global Nonviolence Planning Project, 1993. Strong essays on theories and practice of nonviolence stemming from Muslim values.

Pinault, David, *The Shiites: Ritual and Popular Piety in a Muslim Community*, New York: St. Martin's Press, 1992. Sensitive discussions of Shi'ite interpretations of Muslim history and how these inform communal life and action.

Rumi, Jalal al-Din, *We Are Three*, translations of Rumi poems by Coleman Barks, Athens, Georgia: Maypop Books, 1987. Free contemporary renderings of Rumi's startling, passionate poetry of the love between humans and the divine.

Schimmel, Annemarie, *Mystical Dimensions of Islam*, Chapel Hill, North Carolina: University of North Carolina Press, 1975. A classic survey of Sufi history, teachings, and saints.

Schimmel, Annemarie, *And Muhammad is His Messenger: The Veneration of the Prophet in Islamic Piety*, Chapel Hill, North Carolina: University of North Carolina Press, 1985. Extensive exploration of Muslims' love for the Prophet.

Schuon, Frithjof, *Understanding Islam*, London: George Allen and Unwin, 1963. Profound and lyrical observations about the way of Islam.

CHAPTER 12
SIKHISM

"By the guru's grace shalt thou worship Him"

Another great teacher made his appearance in northern India in the fifteenth century CE. This was Guru Nanak, whose followers were called **Sikhs**, meaning "disciples, students, seekers of truth." Sikhs understand their path not as another sectarian religion but as a statement of the universal truth within, and transcending, all religions. Many of their beliefs have been interpreted as a synthesis of the Hindu and Muslim traditions of northern India, but Sikhism has its own unique quality, independent revelation, and history.

This spiritual essence of Sikhism is little known to the outside world, which tends to equate the word "Sikh" with the military and political aspects of the Punjabis' struggle for independence. As awareness of Sikh spirituality spreads, Sikhism is becoming a global religion, although it does not actively seek converts. Instead, it emphasizes the universality of spirituality.

The sant tradition

Before Guru Nanak, Hinduism and Islam had already begun to draw closer to one another in northern India. One of the foremost philosophers in this trend was the Hindu saint, Ramananda, who held theological arguments with teachers from both religions. But a deeper marriage occurred in the hearts of **sants**, or "holy people," particularly Sufi mystics such as Shaikh Farid and Hindu bhaktas such as Sri Caitanya. They shared a common cause in emphasizing devotion to the Beloved above all else.

The most famous of the bridges between Hindu and Muslim is the fifteenth-century weaver Kabir (1440–1518). He was the son of Muslim parents and the disciple of the Hindu guru, Ramananda. Rather than taking the ascetic path, he remained at work at his loom, composing songs about union with the Divine that are at once earthly and sublime. He could easily transcend theological differences between religions, for he was opposed to outward forms, preferring ecstatic personal intimacy with God. Speaking for the One, he wrote:

Are you looking for me? I am in the next seat.
My shoulder is against yours.
You will not find me in stupas, not in Indian shrine rooms, nor in synagogues, nor
*   in cathedrals:*
not in masses, nor kirtans, not in legs winding around your own neck, nor in eating
*   nothing but vegetables.*

When you really look for me, you will see me instantly —
you will find me in the tiniest house of time.
Kabir says: Student, tell me, what is God?
He is the breath inside the breath.[1]

Guru Nanak

When Guru Nanak was born in 1469, the area of Northern India called the Punjab was half-Muslim, half-Hindu, and ruled by a weak Afghan dynasty. For centuries, the Punjab had been the lane through which outer powers had fought their way into India. In 1398, the Mongolian leader Tamerlane had slaughtered and sacked Punjabis on his way both to and from Delhi. Toward the end of Nanak's life, it was the Mughal Emperor Babur who invaded and claimed the Punjab. This casting of the Punjab as a perpetual battleground later became a crucial aspect of Sikhism.

Nanak was reportedly little concerned with things of the earth in general. As a child he was of a contemplative nature, resisting the appurtenances of his Hindu religion. Even after he was married, it is said that he roamed about in nature rather than working and gave away any money he had to the poor. At length he took a job as an accountant, but his heart was not in material gain.

When Nanak was thirty, his life was transformed after immersion in a river, from which it is said he did not emerge for three days. Some people now think he was meditating on the opposite side, but at the time he could not be found until he suddenly appeared in town, radiant. According to one account, he had been taken into the presence of God, who gave him a bowl of milk to drink, saying that it was actually nectar (**amrit**) which would give him "power of prayer, love of worship, truth and contentment."[2] The Almighty charged him to go back into the tainted world to redeem it from **Kali Yuga** (the darkest of ages).

After his disappearance in the river in 1499, Nanak began traveling through India, the Himalayas, Afghanistan, Sri Lanka, and Arabia, teaching in his own surprising way. When people asked him whether he would follow the Hindu or Muslim path, he replied, "There is neither Hindu nor Mussulman [Muslim], so whose path shall I follow? I shall follow God's path. God is neither Hindu nor Mussulman ..."[3] Nanak mocked the Hindu tradition of throwing sacred river water east toward the rising sun in worship of their ancestors — he threw water to the west. If Hindus could throw water far enough to reach their ancestors thousands of miles away in heaven, he explained, he could certainly water his parched land several hundred miles distant in Lahore by throwing water in its direction. Another tradition has it that he set his feet toward the Ka'bah when sleeping as a pilgrim in Mecca. Questioned about this rude conduct, he is said to have remarked, "Then kindly turn my feet toward some direction where God is not." He espoused the inner rather than the outer path. In Muslim terms:

Make mercy your mosque and faith your prayer mat,
  righteousness your Qur'an;
Modesty your circumcising, goodness your fasting,
  for thus the true Muslim expresses his faith.

A painting of Guru Nanak and the words "Ik Onkar" ("One God") adorn this Sikh gurdwara in Coventry, England.

*Make good works your Ka'bah, take truth as
  your Master, pious deeds your creed and your prayer.
Let mental equanimity be the beads which you tell
  and God will exalt you to glory.[4]*

Again and again, Guru Nanak emphasized three central teachings as the straight path to God: working hard in society to earn one's own honest living (rather than withdrawing into asceticism and begging), sharing from one's earnings with those who are needy, and remembering God at all times as the only Doer, the only Giver.

Nanak's commitment to practical faith, as opposed to external adherence to religious formalities, won him followers from both Hinduism and Islam. Before he died, they argued over who would bury him. He reportedly told Muslims to place flowers on one side of his body, Hindus on the other; the side whose flowers remained fresh the next day could bury him. The next day they raised the sheet that had covered his body and reportedly found nothing beneath it; all the flowers were still fresh, leaving only the fragrance of his being.

---

*Oh my mind, love God as a fish loves water:
The more the water, the happier is the fish,
  the more peaceful his mind and body.
He cannot live without water even for a moment.
God knows the inner pain of that being without water.*   *Guru Nanak[5]*

The succession of gurus

Before Nanak's death, he appointed a spiritual successor, his devoted disciple Angad Dev. This Second Guru strengthened the new Sikh tradition and developed a script for setting down its memorized teachings, which had been given orally in the common language.

There were eventually a total of ten Sikh gurus. The Second Guru, who accepted the guruship most reluctantly after the death of his beloved master, Guru Nanak, emphasized by his own example the central Sikh virtues of humility and service. The Third and Fourth Gurus developed organizational structures for the growing Sikh church while also setting personal examples of humility. The Fourth Guru founded the holy city of Amritsar, within which was built the religion's most sacred shrine, the Golden Temple. The Fifth Guru compiled the sacred scriptures of the Sikhs, the *Adi Granth* ("original holy book"), from devotional hymns composed by Guru Nanak, the other gurus, and Hindu and Muslim saints, including Kabir and many spiritual figures of low caste. When a copy was sent to the Emperor Akbar on his demand, he was so pleased with its universalism that he offered a gift of gold to the Book. But apparently because of suspicions that the Fifth Guru supported a rival successor to Akbar's throne, he was tortured and executed by Akbar's son and successor, Jehangir, in 1606. It is said that the Fifth Guru remained calmly meditating on God as he was tortured by heat, with his love and faith undismayed. His devotional hymns include words such as these:

There were ten Sikh Gurus from Guru Nanak (top center) to Guru Gobind Singh (bottom middle). Then Guru Gobind Singh told his disciples to consider the sacred scripture their Guru: the Guru Granth Sahib (center).

Merciful, merciful is the Lord.
Merciful is my master.
He blesses all beings with His bounties.
Why waverest thou, Oh mortal? The Creator Himself shall protect you.
He who has created you takes care of you....
Oh mortal, meditate on the Lord as long as there is breath in your body.[6]

From that point on, Sikhism took measures to protect itself and to defend the weak of all religions against tyranny. The Sixth Guru built a Sikh army, carried two swords (one symbolizing temporal power, the other, spiritual power), and taught the people to defend their religion. The tender-hearted Seventh Guru taught his Sikhs not only to feed anyone who came to their door, but moreover to:

do service in such a way that the poor guest may not feel he is partaking of some charity but as if he had come to the Guru's house which belonged to all in equal measure. He who has more should consider it as God's trust and share it in the same spirit. Man is only an instrument of service: the giver of goods is God, the Guru of us all.[7]

A pacifist, the Seventh Guru never used his troops against the Mughals. The Eighth Guru became successor to Guru Nanak's seat when he was only five years old and died at the age of eight. When taunted by Hindu pandits the "Child Guru" reportedly touched a lowly deaf and dumb Sikh watercarrier with his cane, whereupon the watercarrier expounded brilliantly on the subtleties of the Hindu scripture, Bhagavad-Gita.

The Ninth Guru was martyred in 1675. According to Sikh tradition, he was approached by Hindu pandits who were facing forced conversion to Islam by the Mughal Emperor Aurangzeb. The Emperor viewed Hinduism as a totally corrupt, idolatrous religion which did not lead people to God; he had ordered the destruction of Hindu temples and mass conversion of Hindus throughout the land, beginning in the north with Kashmir. Reportedly, one of the Kashmiri pandits dreamed that only the Ninth Guru, the savior in Kali Yuga, could save the Hindus. With the firm approval of his young son, Guru Teg Bahadur told the Hindu pandits to inform their oppressors that they would convert to Islam if the Sikh Guru could be persuaded to do so. Imprisoned and forced to witness the torture and murder of his aides, the Ninth Guru staunchly maintained the right of all people to religious freedom. Aurangzeb beheaded him before a crowd of thousands. But as his son later wrote, "He has given his head, but not his determination."[8]

The martyred Ninth Guru was succeeded by his young son, who became the tenth master, Guru Gobind Singh. It was he who turned the intimidated Sikhs into saint-warriors for truth.

In 1699 he reportedly told a specially convened assembly of Sikhs that the times were so dangerous that he had developed a new plan to give the community strength and unity. Total surrender to the master would be necessary, he said, asking for volunteers who would offer their heads for the cause. One at a time, five stepped forward. Each was escorted into the Guru's tent, from which the Tenth Guru emerged alone with a bloody sword. After this scene was repeated five times, the Guru brought all the men out of the tent, alive. Some say the blood was that of a goat, in a test of the people's loyalty; others say that Guru Gobind Singh had actually killed the men and then resurrected them. At any rate, their willingness to serve and bravely to sacrifice themselves was dramatically proven, and the Five Beloved Ones became models for Sikhs.

Guru Gobind Singh instituted a special baptismal initiation using water stirred with a double-edged sword to turn his followers into heroes, mixed with sugar candies symbolizing that they would also be compassionate. After baptizing the Five Beloved Ones, he established a unique Guru-Sikh relationship by asking that they baptize him — thus underscoring the principle of equality among all Sikhs. The baptized men were given the surname *Singh* ("lion"); the women were all given the name *Kaur* ("princess") and treated as equals. Together, they formed the **Khalsa** ("Pure Ones"), a fraternity pledged to a special code of personal discipline. They were sworn to wear five distinctive symbols of their dedication: long unshorn hair bound under a turban or a veil, a comb to keep it tidy, a steel bracelet as a personal reminder that one is a servant of God, short underbreeches for modesty, and a sword for dignity and the willingness to fight for justice and protection of the weak. These "5 K's" clearly distinguished Sikhs from Muslims and Hindus, supporting the assertion that they constituted a third path with its own right to spiritual sovereignty. All of these innovations were designed to turn the meek into warriors capable of shaking off Mughal oppression and protecting freedom of religion; the distinctive dress made it impossible for the Khalsa to hide from their duty by blending with the general populace. In Sikh history, their bravery was proven again and again. For example, it is reported that the Tenth Guru's own teenage sons were killed as they single-handedly engaged several thousand Mughal soldiers in battle.

In addition to transforming the Sikh faithful into a courageous, unified community, Guru Gobind Singh ended the line of bodily succession to guruship. As he was dying in 1708, he transferred his authority to the Adi Granth rather than to a human successor. Thenceforth, the Granth Sahib (another name for the Adi Granth, with Sahib an expression of veneration) was to be the **Guru Granth Sahib** — the living presence of the Guru embodied in the sacred scriptures, to be consulted intuitively by the Khalsa for spiritual guidance and decision-making.

As the Mughal Empire began to disintegrate and Afghans invaded India, the Sikhs fought for their own identity and sovereignty. In the eighteenth century under Maharaja Ranjit Singh, they formed the Sikh Empire — a secular government noted for its generous tolerance toward Muslims, despite the earlier history of oppression by the Muslim rulers. The Sikh Empire attempted to create a pluralistic society, with social equality and full freedom of religion. They also blocked the Khyber Pass against invaders. The Empire lasted only half a century, for the British took over in 1849.

Resistance to oppression had become a hallmark of Sikhism, for the times were grim for India's people. Despite heavy losses, Guru Gobind Singh's outnumbered Sikhs began the protection of the country from foreign rule, a process which continued into the twentieth century. High praise of the Guru's military effect has been offered by Dr. S. Radhakrishnan, a highly respected former President of India:

For one thousand years, after the defeat of Raja Jaipal, India had lain prostrate. The raiders and invaders descended on India and took away the people, to be sold as slaves. People watched and had not the courage to strike a blow in defence of their weeping, wailing, sobbing, groaning mothers, sisters and daughters. Alas, poor India suffered unfathomable anguish. Guru Gobind Singh raised the Khalsa to defy religious intolerance, religious persecution and political inequality. It was a miracle that heroes appeared out of straws and common clay. Those who grovelled in the dust rose proud, defiant and invincible in the form of the Khalsa. They bore all sufferings and unnamable tortures cheerfully and unflinchingly.... India is at long last free. This freedom is the crown and climax and a logical corollary to the Sikh Guru's and Khalsa's terrific sacrifices and heroic exploits.[9]

In addition to the bravery evident in Sikh history, stories of the Gurus are full of miracles which reportedly happened around them such as the Child Guru's empowering a lowly watercarrier to give a profound explanation of the *Bhagavad-Gita*. Neither age nor caste is thought to have any relevance in Sikh spirituality.

Although the Sikh Gurus gave their followers no mandate to convert others, their message was spread in a nonsectarian way by the Udasis. These are renunciates who do not withdraw from the world but rather practice strict discipline and meditation while at the same time trying to serve humanity. Their missionary work began under Baba Siri Chand, the ascetic elder son of Guru Nanak. He had a close relationship with the Sikh Gurus and was highly respected by people of all castes and creeds because of his spiritual power, wisdom, and principles. During the reign of the Mughal Emperor Shah Jahan, a census showed that Baba Siri Chand had the largest following of any holy person in India. Nevertheless, he directed all attention and praise to his father, Guru Nanak, and never claimed to be a guru himself. Udasi communities and educational institutions are still maintained in many parts of the Indian subcontinent, and old Udasi inscriptions have been discovered in Baku, Azerbaijan.

Baba Siri Chand, elder son of Guru Nanak, combined the power of intense meditation with the power of hard work.

TEACHING STORY

Guru Arjun Dev's Devotion

Throughout his life, Guru Arjun Dev, the Fifth Sikh Guru, responded with calm faith in God to jealous machinations against him. His martyrdom by torture was the ultimate demonstration of his devotion.

The Mughal Emperor Jehangir claimed that the Adi Granth — the sacred scripture which Guru Arjun Dev had compiled — was negative toward Hindus and Muslims, even though both were becoming followers of the gentle Guru. Jehangir ordered that all references to Hinduism and Islam be deleted from the holy book and that the Guru be fined 200,000 rupees. The Guru reportedly replied that the hymns of the Sikh Gurus and Muslim and Hindu saints were inspired praises of God and that no one could change them. Furthermore, monies were not his own property but rather belonged to the Sikh community, to be used for the welfare of those in need. Even though his Sikhs started collecting money to pay the fine, the Guru stopped them, saying that he had not done anything wrong and that compromising with wrong is irreligious.

Ostensibly for his refusal to follow the Emperor's orders — but more likely to end his popular influence — the Guru was subjected to terrible tortures by heat, during the already terrible heat of summer. He was made to sit on a hot iron sheet.

Hot sand was dumped onto his body and he was placed into boiling water.

As these tortures were being inflicted, Mian Mir, an established saint of Islam who laid the foundation stone of the Holy Temple at Amritsar, pleaded with the Guru to let him use his mystical power against the persecutors. Guru Arjun Dev refused, telling Mian Mir to patiently accept the reality that everything is under God's control; every leaf that moves does so by God's will.

The daughter-in-law of Chandu, the rich man of Delhi who had turned the Emperor against the Guru, tried to offer sherbet to the Guru to ease his agony. But just as he had refused attempts to wed her to his son, saying that a rich man's daughter would not be happy in the home of a dervish, he refused her food, saying that he would accept nothing. Nonetheless, he blessed her for her devotion.

Through five days of torture, Guru Arjun Dev persisted in calm faith in God. His torturers then forced him to bathe in the river alongside the Mughal fort. His followers wept to see the blisters covering his body. As he walked on blistered feet, he repeated again and again, "Your will is sweet, Oh God; I only seek the gift of Your Name." Calmly, he walked into the water and breathed his last.

Central beliefs

Sikhism's major focus is loving devotion to one God, whom Sikhs recognize as the same One who is worshipped by many different names around the world. God is formless, beyond time and space, the only truth, the only reality. This boundless concept was initially set forth in Guru Nanak's *Mool Mantra* ("basic sacred chant"), which prefaces the Guru Granth Sahib, and *Jap Ji*, the first morning prayer of Sikhs:

There is One God
Whose Name is Truth,
The Creator,
Without fear, without hate,
Eternal Being,

Beyond birth and death,
Self-existent,
Realized by the Guru's grace.[10]

Following Guru Nanak's lead, Sikhs often refer to God as *Sat* ("truth") or as *Ik Onkar*, the One Supreme Being. God is pure being, without attributes.

Guru Gobind Singh, a great custodian of scholars who kept many poets in his court, offered a litany of praises of this boundless, formless One. His inspired composition, *Jaap Sahib*, includes 199 verses such as these:

Immortal
Omnipotent
Beyond Time
And Space
Invisible
Beyond name, caste, or creed
Beyond form or figure
The ruthless destroyer
Of all pride and evil
The Salvation of all beings ...
The Eternal Light
The Sweetest Breeze
The Wondrous Figure
The Most Splendid.[11]

The light of God shines fully through the Guru, the perfect prophet. The light of God is also present in the Guru Granth Sahib, the Holy Word (**shabd**) of God, and in all of creation, in which the Holy Name (**Nam**) of God dwells. God is not separate from this world. God pervades the cosmos and thus can be found within everything. As the Ninth Guru wrote:

Why do you go to the forest to find God? He lives in all and yet remains distinct. He dwells in you as well, as fragrance resides in a flower or the reflection in a mirror. God abides in everything. See him, therefore, in your heart.[12]

Sikhism does not claim to have the only path to God, nor does it try to convert others to its way. As Ralph Singh, founder of the Sikh-based community Gobind Sadan in the United States explains, "When you have a beacon of light, those who are of that light see no divisions."[13] The respected Muslim mystic, Said Mian Mir, was invited to lay the cornerstone of the Golden Temple in Amritsar. It was constructed with four doors, inviting people from all traditions to come in to worship. When Guru Gobind Singh created an army to resist tyranny, he admonished Sikhs not to feel enmity toward Islam or Hinduism, the religions of the oppressors. The enemy, he emphasized, was oppression and corruption. Sikh soldier-saints are pledged to protect the freedom of all religions. Sikhism is, however, opposed to empty ritualism and affirms the universality of all religions.

According to the Sikh ideal, the purpose of life is to realize God within the world, through the everyday practices of work, worship, and charity, of sacrificing love. All people are to be treated equally, for God's light dwells in all and ego is a major hindrance to God-realization. From Guru Nanak's time on, Sikhism has refused to acknowledge the traditional Indian caste system.

The Guru Granth Sahib is treated with great reverence by Sikhs, who place it on pillows, cover it with beautiful cloth, and carry it on their heads in profound respect.

The Golden Temple in Amritsar, holiest of Sikh shrines.

Like Hinduism, Sikhism conceives a series of lives, with karma (the effects of past actions on one's present life) governing transmigration of the soul into new bodies, be they human or animal. The ultimate goal of life is **sahaj**, mystical union with the divine, reflected in one's way of living.

> *I was separated from God for many births, dry as a withered plant,*
> *But by the grace of the Guru, I have become green.*
>
> Guru Arjun, the Fifth Guru[14]

Sacred practices

To be a true Sikh is to live a very disciplined life of surrender and devotion to God, with hours of daily prayer, continual inner repetition of the Name of God, and detachment from negative, worldly mind-states. At the same time that one's mind and heart are joined with God, one is to be working hard in the world, earning an honest living, and helping those in need. Of this path, the Third Sikh Guru observes:

> *The way of devotees is unique; they walk a difficult path.*
> *They leave behind attachments, greed, ego, and desires, and do not speak much.*
> *The path they walk is sharper than the edge of a sword and thinner than a hair.*
> *Those who shed their false self by the grace of the Guru are filled with the fragrance*
> *of God.*[15]

The most dedicated of Sikhs are those who have taken initiation as Khalsa, "the pure." The standards set by Guru Gobind Singh for Khalsa are so high that few people can really meet them. In addition to outer disciplines such as abstaining from drugs, alcohol, and tobacco, the person who is Khalsa, said the Guru, will always recite the Name of God:

> *The Name of God is light, the Light which never extinguishes, day or night. Khalsa*
> *recognizes none but the One. I live in Khalsa; it is my body, my treasure store.*[16]

The one who is Khalsa does not criticize anybody. He fights on the very front line against injustice and vanquishes the five evils [lust, anger, greed, attachment, and ego] in himself. He burns his karmas and thus becomes egoless. Not only does he not take another person's spouse; he doesn't even look at the things that belong to others. Reciting Nam is his joy, and he falls in love with the words of the Gurus. He faces difficulties squarely, always attacks evil, and always helps the poor. He always recites Nam and joins other people with the Nam also. He is not bound within the forts of narrow-mindedness.[17]

The Sikh gurus created several institutions to help erase caste distinctions. One is **langar**, the communal kitchen which is freely offered to all who come, regardless of caste. This typically takes place at a **gurdwara**, the building where the Guru Granth Sahib is enshrined and public worship takes place. During communal worship as well as langar, all strata of people sit together, though men and women may sit separately, as in the Indian custom. People of all ethnic origins, ideologies, and castes, including Untouchables, may bathe in the tank of water at Sikh holy places. Baptism into the Khalsa does away with one's former caste and makes a lowly person a chief. Many Sikh officials were originally Shudras, of the lowest caste in India. At least one-tenth of one's income is to be contributed toward the welfare of the community. In addition, the Sikh gurus glorified the lowliest forms of manual labor, such as sweeping the floor and cleaning shoes and dirty pots, especially when these are done as voluntary service to God.

The morning and evening prayers take about two hours a day, starting in the very early morning hours. The first morning prayer is Guru Nanak's **Jap Ji**. *Jap*, meaning "recitation," refers to the use of sound, especially the Name of God (*Nam*), as the best way of approaching the divine. Like combing the hair, hearing the sacred word combs all negative thoughts out of the mind. Much of the Jap Ji is devoted to the blessings of Nam. For example,

The devotees are forever in bliss, for by hearing the Nam their suffering and
sins are destroyed.
Hearkening to the Nam bestows Truth, divine wisdom, contentment.
By hearing the Nam, the blind find the path of Truth and
realize the Unfathomable.[18]

> *"The Lord is stitched into my heart and never goes out of it even for a moment."*
> *Fifth Guru, Jaitsri*

The second morning prayer is Guru Gobind Singh's universal *Jap Sahib*. It names no prophet, nor creates any religion. It is sheer homage to God. The Guru addresses God as having no form, no country, and no religion but yet as the seed of seeds, song of songs, sun of suns, the life force pervading everywhere, ever merciful, ever giving, indestructible. Complex in its poetry and profound in its content, *Jap Sahib* asserts that God is the cause of conflict as well as of peace, of destruction as well as of creation; God pervades in darkness as well as in light. In verse after verse, devotees learn that there is nothing outside of God's presence, nothing outside of God's control.

In addition to recitation of prayers, passages from the Guru Granth Sahib are chanted or sung as melodies, often with musical accompaniment. This devotional tradition of **kirtan** was initiated by Guru Nanak. But great discipline is required to attend the pre-dawn songs and recitations every day, and in contrast to the pride developed by Guru Gobind Singh in the Khalsa, worshippers humble themselves before the sacred scriptures. The Granth is placed on a platform, with a devotee waving a whisk over the sacred book to purify the atmosphere around it. Worshippers bow to it, bring offerings, and then sit below, on the floor. Every morning and evening, the spirit of God reveals its guidance to the people as an officiant opens the scripture at random, intuitively guided, and reads a passage that is to be a special spiritual focus for the day.

Some gurdwaras — including the Golden Temple in Amritsar — have previously allowed only men to read publicly from the Guru Granth Sahib, to preach, to officiate at ceremonies, or to sing sacred songs. This has been a cultural custom, however, for nothing in the Sikh scriptures bars women from such privileges. In 1996, the central body settling policies for Sikh gurdwaras ruled that women should also be allowed to perform such sacred services.

In addition to group chanting, singing, and listening to collective guidance from the Guru Granth Sahib, devout Sikhs are encouraged to begin the day with private

There are now Indian Sikh communities in many countries. These Sikhs are dedicating a new temple in Kenya, with Khalsa members representing the Five Beloved Ones.

meditations on the name of God. As one advances in this practice and abides in egoless love for God, one is said to receive guidance from the inner guru, the living word of God within each person.

Sikhism today

Despite its politically precarious position within India, Sikhism is still a vibrant religion and is becoming a global faith. The center of Sikhism remains the Punjab. The area of this territory, which is under Indian rule, was dramatically shrunk by the partition of India in 1947, for two-thirds of the Punjab was in the area thenceforth called Pakistan. The two million Sikhs living in that part were forced to migrate under conditions of extreme hardship. Some managed to migrate to Western countries and parts of India other than the Punjab. Emigration continued, and there are now large Sikh communities in England, western Canada, and the west coast of the United States.

In India, Sikhs and Hindus have lived side-by-side in mutual tolerance until recent years, when violent clashes have begun between Hindus and Sikhs. Sikh separatists want to establish an independent Sikh state, called Khalistan, with a commitment to strong religious observances. Another purpose of Khalistan would be to protect Sikhs from oppression and exploitation by the much larger Hindu community. In 1984, Prime Minister Indira Gandhi chose to attack the Golden Temple, Sikhism's holiest shrine, for Sikh separatists were thought to be using it as a shelter for their weapons. The attack seemed an outrageous desecration of the holy place, and counter-violence increased. The Prime Minister herself was killed

The Punjab at the end of the reign of the Mughal Emperor Akbar. The 1947 partition of India left two-thirds of the Punjab, including many of its Sikh temples, inside Pakistan, a Muslim state.

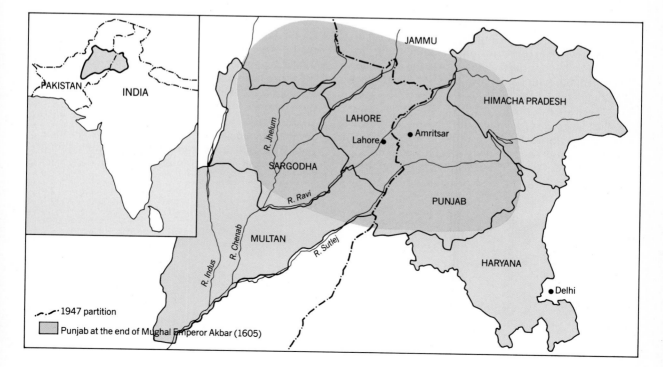

1947 partition

Punjab at the end of Mughal Emperor Akbar (1605)

Living Sikhism

G. S. Jauhal is a Punjabi Sikh, a commandant in the Indian military service and a disciple of the contemporary Sikh teacher, Baba Virsa Singh. His words illustrate the humility which characterizes those who truly live the teachings of the Sikh gurus:

"I am not an authority. I'm just a student in the very beginning stage. I want to learn so much. I've been a Sikh since birth and I'm forty-seven now. But I think one needs many births and then the Guru's grace — then only can he learn Sikhism. It is so deep, so vast.

We can only get something if first of all Guru's grace is there. Then we keep on endeavoring sincerely, from the core of our heart, and keep on learning. Again and again reading, reciting Guru Granth Sahib, trying to understand what it means. I myself feel that I am one of those who, without understanding ourselves, we try to teach others. This is a pity. Whatever the Guru has given in the Granth Sahib, we are supposed to practice so that everyone knows that what we say, we do. Otherwise people will not take us as true persons. This is the teaching of Guru Granth Sahib — whatever you do outwardly, the same thing should be in your heart. I do try to recite and follow Gurbani, but I am far, far away from the goal which is desired by the Guru.

There are five things which we should not have — lust, anger, greed, attachment to worldly things, ego. These things take us toward the worldly side and away from the true path. The difficult path is chosen by the Gurus. Once man is trying from his inner being to follow that path, and he prays to his Gurus to help him to achieve that path, the Guru always helps this small being, and there is nothing difficult in the world. As the Guru described, to perfect ourself is a very thin path the Sikh is supposed to walk.

When I was young, I learned from my mother. She was totally uneducated. She knew some sabds from Guru Granth Sahib which she learned verbally from her brother. She used to recite when I was just a small child; she used to put me on her lap and recite the Name. Still I remember today some of the words recited by my mother, so it has gone deep into my mind.

I think Sikhism is a unique religion, and the latest. All the good things of all the religions have been combined in one. It is meant to be spread all over the world. We should understand other religions also; there are so many good things in other religions. But I find that the work toward spreading our religion in other parts of the world has not been done as much as it should have been. That could have been possible if the message of the Gurus had been printed in all the languages and then taken to the doorsteps of the other people. People will not come to you to learn your religion in your language. So it was our duty to make it convenient, to translate our Guru Granth Sahib and Guru's teachings into simple speaking language and take it to the people in their own languages. It is a world religion, and we should not have kept it in our closed doors."

later in 1984, and her Sikh bodyguards were suspected. In retribution, terrible killings of Sikhs followed. At least eight thousand Sikhs were murdered by mobs in Delhi alone.

Many Sikhs have "disappeared" in the Punjab, allegedly at the hands of both separatists and police terrorists. Guru Gobind Singh himself emphasized that one should resort to the sword only after all other means of effecting change have failed. Sikhs long for an end to the violence.

Historical tensions have also arisen within Sikhism, as it became institutionalized and used by some factions for their own ends, such as acquiring the landholdings of the gurdwaras. However, peace is now returning to Punjab. Sri Surendra Nath, the Arya Samaj Hindu who was Governor of the Punjab as peace re-emerged, attributed the growing harmony to the blessings of God and to the fact that in the Governor's Mansion itself, Guru Granth Sahib was enshrined and read and Guru Gobind Singh's *Jaap Sahib* was continually recited on the recommendation of his Sikh teacher, Baba Virsa Singh. The Governor himself continually affirmed the Sikh Gurus' nonsectarian principles of selfless devotion to God and to dharma as the ethical basis of society and of government.

In 1994, the large-scale celebration of Baba Siri Chand's five hundredth birth anniversary drew together Sikhs of all factions, from villagers to scholars and government leaders, and also people of other faiths, to affirm the nonsectarian message of the Sikh Gurus. Baba Virsa Singh, whose life and work are shaped by Baba Siri Chand's model of meditation and service, proclaimed then that

> No one who came to Baba Siri Chand remained rigidly exclusive and ritualistic in their religious views. Hindus, Muslims, Sikhs, Nawabs, kings, and commoners all came to him, and all were affected by Baba Siri Chand's teaching that there should be no boundaries between people of different religions, because all are worshippers of the same Formless One.[19]

Baba Virsa Singh's own communities, known collectively as Gobind Sadan ("House of God") are regarded as spiritual oases by spiritual seekers from all social levels, all religions, and many countries. These communities which "Babaji" has developed in India and the United States are farm-based, on land reclaimed from barren wastes by volunteers in order to benefit the poor. They are becoming globally renowned as holy places of ecumenical devotion, with worship of such holy figures as Jesus, Mary, Lord Krishna, Lord Shiva, Durga, Mata Ganga, and Muslim pirs carried on as well as devotions to the Sikh Gurus. Babaji preaches that all prophets have brought the same basic message and that all have come from the same all-pervading Light, so there need be no clashes between people of different religions. However, until a person has gained some enlightenment through meditation, Babaji observes, he may not fully understand the messages of the Prophets and may be misguided by self-seeking religious figures who have "no connection with God." Of Sikhism, Baba Virsa Singh says:

> That which we call dharma, that which we call Sikhism, that which we call the religion of Guru Nanak, that which we call the command of Guru Gobind Singh is this: That we should not forget God even for one breath.
>
> Guru Nanak prepared a lovely ship, in which all the seats were to be given to those who were doing both manual work and spiritual practice.

The contemporary teacher, Baba Virsa Singh, demonstrates the practical results of combining intense meditation, great faith in God, and hard work in the world for the sake of others.

The religion of Guru Gobind Singh, of Guru Nanak was not given to those of one organization, one village, one country. Their enlightened vision was for the whole cosmos. Guru Granth Sahib is not for some handful of people. It is for everyone.[20]

During the years when Sikhs were asserting their distinct identity, lest they be subsumed under Hinduism, the ecumenical nature of Sikhism was not generally emphasized. Now, however, Sikh scholars are concluding that this is indeed the Sikh Gurus' message to the world. As Baba Virsa Singh explains,

The words of the Prophets have been a continuing strand of revelation from God. But we have cut them into little pieces, making walled sects of religion. These divisions are created by humans, reflecting their own policies. The Sikh Gurus never broke the circle of religion. They never tried to place any boundaries on God.[21]

In the words of Guru Gobind Singh:

*Same are the temple and the mosque
And same are the forms of worship therein.
All human beings are one though apparently many,
Realize, therefore, the essential unity of mankind.*[22]

Suggested reading

Cole, W. Owen, and Sambhi, Piara Singh, *The Sikhs: Their Religious Beliefs and Practices*, London: Routledge and Kegan Paul, 1978. A clearly-written survey of the Sikh tradition.

Macauliffe, Max Arthur, *The Sikh Religion: Its Gurus, Sacred Writings, and Authors*, sixteen vols., Oxford: Oxford University Press, reprinted in Delhi: S. Chand and Company, 1963. The most respected general account of Sikhism in English, even though its author was not Sikh.

McLeod, W. H., trans. and ed., *Textual Sources for the Study of Sikhism*, Totowa, New Jersey: Barnes and Noble Books, 1984 and Manchester: Manchester University Press, 1984. Interesting compilation of Sikh literature, from selections from the Adi Granth to rules for the Khalsa initiation ceremony, all with explanatory comments.

Singh, Dr. Gopal, *A History of the Sikh People 1469–1978*, New Delhi: World Sikh University Press, 1979. Thorough and scholarly history of the Sikhs to modern times.

Singh, Khushwant, trans., *Hymns of Guru Nanak*, New Delhi: Orient Longmans Ltd., 1969. Stories about Guru Nanak's life and selections from his sacred songs.

Singh, Manmohan, trans., *Sri Guru Granth Sahib*, eight vols., Amritsar: Shromani Gurdwara Parbandhak Committee, 1962. A good English translation of the Sikh sacred scripture.

Singh, Ralph, *Sikhism: A Distinct, Universal Religion*, Central Square, New York: Gobind Sadan, U.S.A. A succinct pamphlet about central Sikh beliefs and practices.

Singh, Trilochan, Singh, Jodh, Singh, Kapur, Singh, Bawa Harkishen, and Singh, Khushwant, trans., *The Sacred Writings of the Sikhs*, New York: Samuel Weiser, 1973. Selections from the Adi Granth and hymns by Guru Gobind Singh.

CHAPTER 13

NEW RELIGIOUS MOVEMENTS

"That yielding of the human mind to the divine"

The history of religions is one of continual change. Each religion changes over time, new religions appear, and some older traditions disappear. Times of rapid social change are particularly likely to spawn new religious movements, for people seek the security of the spiritual amidst worldly chaos. In the period since World War II, thousands of new religious groups have sprung up around the world. In sub-Saharan Africa, there are now over seven thousand different religions; every Nigerian town of several thousand people now has up to fifty or sixty different kinds of religion.[1] In Japan, an estimated thirty percent of the population belongs to one of hundreds of new religious movements. Imported versions of ancient traditions, such as Hinduism and Buddhism, have made many new converts in countries such as the United States, Canada, and Russia, where they are seen as "new religions." The United States seems a particularly fertile breeding ground for new religious movements, for religious freedom is a constitutionally guaranteed right and many people are seeking alternatives to the spiritual emptiness of secular industrial life.

New religious movements have always met with resistance from previously organized religions. As Hare Krishna devotees or Jain meditation groups move into old Christian church buildings, the newcomers are branded with labels such as "cults" or "sects." These words have specific, neutral meanings: a **cult** is a religion devoted to a single person or deity, often representing a distinct break from the prevailing tradition, while a **sect** is a splinter group or a subgroup associated with a larger tradition, such as the Theravada sect within Buddhism. The word "sect" is often used to indicate a nonmainstream splinter group. Both "cult" and "sect" have sometimes been used imprecisely and pejoratively to distinguish new religions from older ones, each of which already claims to be the best or only way. The word "cult" has often been used to signify a group temporarily gathered around a charismatic leader whose influence may be dangerous to his or her followers.

The label **new religious movement** seems more neutral at this time and is becoming widely used to avoid such negative connotations. However, the word "new" is itself imprecise, for many of these groups have a rather lengthy history and have survived long after the death of the original founder.

In addition to negative reactions from previously organized religions, new religious movements usually meet with opposition from family members of those who join. In the United States, the "anti-cult" movement employs special agents who capture and "deprogram" followers of new religions, at the request of their parents. Mental health professionals warn about the psychological dangers of some of the new ways. For instance, Dr. Marc Galanter of New York University Medical School has concluded from interviews with thousands of members of new religious movements with charismatic leaders that those most likely to join such a group are already lonely and alienated from the mainstream culture. Those who most feel a sense of belonging within the new group are those who share its distrust of outsiders. The "shared paranoia" that holds the group together may be exacerbated in the case of apocalyptic groups. Dr. Galanter explains,

> The only source of information becomes what the leader tells you. They have to rebuff any external reality that would undermine their beliefs. Then, if outsiders actually appear to threaten the group, it bonds them more closely and validates their view that it's better to die together than to submit to evil outside forces.[2]

As indicated in Chapter 1 of this book, there are both potential dangers and potential benefits associated with giving power over one's life to any religion, new or old. After members of the Aum Shrinrikyo movement were suspected of launching a poison gas attack on a Tokyo subway, Japanese asked themselves how their intelligent countrymen could have been drawn to the movement. It had been associated with secret meditation training, but after the subway attack, the movement was described in the media as a doomsday cult making chemical weapons. Japanese observers have looked at their modern society and concluded that it creates a susceptibility to blind obedience. Author Reiko Hatsumi writes:

> I think most of my countrymen are honest and hardworking, yet also gullible, with a childlike naivete and a disinclination to think on their own. Japanese education has always encouraged this. Students are taught to absorb knowledge but not to judge or rationalize....
>
> By being childlike, we also demand emotional security, a guiding hand. Unfortunately, we no longer have a family system. Fathers have abdicated their position as head of the family. They are too busy working late and commuting. The mothers spur their children to get into good schools.... The children don't have much to look forward to, except a struggle to get ahead in a crowded, competitive society.
>
> So when someone such as Asahara [leader of Aum Shrinrikyo] comes along and takes time to listen and to give advice that seems to resolve dilemmas and solve problems, the young hand over their hearts and follow.[3]

Nevertheless, in religion, as in other life commitments such as marriage, there are potential benefits in dedication and obedience. Many religions, including the largest world religions, teach self-denial and surrender as cardinal virtues which help to vanquish the ego and allow one to approach ultimate reality. The question for a sincere person of faith is where to place one's faith.

All of the major religions we have examined were once new, were once resisted by more entrenched institutions. Will any of today's new religious movements last more than a few generations? Those who study the sociology of religion are researching the secular factors that seem to predispose a new religious movement to become widespread and longlasting. One of these is a balance between similarities to existing beliefs (making it attractive and nonthreatening to potential converts) and differences compelling enough for people to convert. A second factor is organization, personal commitment, and bonds between members that will survive the death of the prophet and the original followers. Third is the social setting: Times of great social change, places which allow freedom of choice in matters of religion, and societies with fragmented relationships between people are most conducive to the recruitment of new members. Fourth is the status of prevailing religions; if they have become merely institutional with little spiritual life, they are susceptible to being supplanted by more vibrant new faiths. Fifth is the younger generations: Children must be continually born or recruited into the faith, taught its values, and given responsible parts to play in keeping the faith alive.

Spiritual aspects of new religions are also of major importance but they cannot easily be quantified. Among these are the genuine spirituality of the founder or spreader of the message, and the ability of the new teachings and their presentation to capture people's hearts, change their lives, motivate them to act collectively, and give them the courage to face social opposition. Finally, there is the necessity of divine assistance, in the parlance of theistic religions, or alliance with absolute truth, from the point of view of nontheistic religions.

In this chapter we will survey some representative examples of new religious movements that have developed in the nineteenth and twentieth centuries. All have some link with previous traditions but are sufficiently different to be studied independently. Previous chapters included groups which are modern and perhaps exported versions of older ways with which they are still identified (such as the Hare Krishna movement, which is clearly allied with the sixteenth-century Hindu bhakti tradition of Sri Caitanya). The pages that follow provide a sampling of more distinct manifestations of the current burgeoning of spiritual vitality. The headings do not delineate separate categories, but rather ways of understanding aspects of the new religious movements.

Apocalyptic expectations

As we approach the beginning of the twenty-first century, according to Christian dating, speculations abound that some major change is about to occur in the world. Some people prophesy forthcoming planetary disaster; some see better times ahead.

The expectation of major world changes appears in many religions, including Hinduism, Zoroastrianism, Judaism, Christianity, Islam, and some indigenous religions. In Christianity, for instance, the last book in the Bible, Revelation, predicts a world war between the forces of Satan and the forces of God, with great destruction, followed by the **millennium**, a thousand-year period of special holiness in which Christ rules the earth. Hindus anticipate that Kali Yuga, the worst of times, will be followed by the return of Sat Yuga, when dharma will again prevail over evil. However, when members of less established new religious movements genuinely anticipate a doomsday or a new world order, they tend to be regarded as eccentrics by the rest of their society. To maintain their faith, they may isolate themselves from mainstream society and try to prepare for the coming changes. This was the strategy of the Branch Davidians, whose devotional community in Waco, Texas, was attacked by federal officials on weapons charges (even though Texas has twice as many guns per capita as was apparently the case within the community), with the result that over eighty of the members died a fiery death. Alternatively, those who anticipate the end of the present world may accept social scorn and try to share their prophecies with others in order to save them from the anticipated coming destruction. Two examples of the latter approach — Rastafarians and Jehovah's Witnesses — demonstrate some ways in which people may try to engage others in their expectations.

Rastafarianism

In Jamaica, millennarian expectations have been expressed as **Rastafarianism**. In 1895, Alexander Bedward of the Baptist Free Church in Jamaica prophesied a coming holocaust in which all the white people would be killed, leaving the blacks, "the true people," to celebrate the new world. He sat in his special robes as the predicted date came and went; eventually he was placed in an asylum for the insane. A more generalized hopeful vision was spread by Marcus Garvey, who saw a fundamental change in society that would be led by blacks. Garvey linked these dreams to the return of blacks to Africa, from which their ancestors had been taken as slaves; there they would rebuild a great civilization. A prophecy attributed to Garvey — "Look to Africa when a black king shall be crowned, for the day of deliverance is near"[4] — was thought to have been realized when Ras (Prince) Tafari of Ethiopia was crowned as Haile Selassie, Emperor of Ethiopia.

An elaborate mystique was built up around Haile Selassie as the living God (though neither Selassie nor Garvey shared this view). Hopeful lore was based on interpretations of Selassie's statements and of passages from the Old Testament and the New Testament book of Revelation. Poor Jamaicans (who likened themselves to the Jews in captivity in Babylon) repeatedly prepared to be given free passage back to Africa.

Haile Selassie's reign (until his death in 1974) did nothing to liberate Jamaican Africans, but blacks in Jamaica have nevertheless developed a new religious movement around these ideals. They intend to revive the "Way of the Ancients,"

Rastafarian male musicians carry the message of reasserting black spiritual and social rights.

their concept of the lost civilization of pre-colonial Africa, and to free people of African extraction from subservience. "Babylon," the oppressor, is the United States, Britain (the former colonial power in Jamaica), the state of Jamaica, and the Christian Church. In protest against Babylon, Rastafarians wear their hair in long uncombed curls, called "dreadlocks," a symbol of the natural non-industrial life. Some give use of marijuana (*ganja*) religious significance as a sacrament. A distinctive music, *reggae*, has evolved as an expression of black pride, social protest, and Rastafarian millennarian ideals.

The Rastafarian movement has spread beyond Jamaica to blacks and a few whites elsewhere in the Caribbean, North America, Europe, Southern Africa, Australia, and New Zealand. It is a very localized and diverse movement. Rastas insist that the truths they espouse are not just for people of African descent. However, in many areas the movement has developed mostly through men; they consider women incapable of experiencing Rasta awareness except through their husbands.

Jehovah's Witnesses

Those who call themselves **Jehovah's Witnesses** foresee a new world in which people of all races (including many raised from the dead) will join hands in peace. They believe that this will happen only after the majority of humanity is destroyed for not obeying the Bible. In the understanding of Jehovah's Witnesses, God will not let anyone, including "false Christians," ruin the earth. Those who are of the true religion will be saved from the general destruction, reunited with their dead loved ones in a paradise on earth (except for 144,000 who will live with God in heaven). In the earthly paradise there will be no pain, no food shortages, no sickness, no death, according to the teachings.

The nineteenth-century founder of Jehovah's Witnesses, Charles Taze Russell, predicted that 1914 would be the date of this apocalypse. When 1914 passed, the

The baptism of Jehovah's Witness followers in a portable pool during their International Convention.

prophecy was changed: 1914 was the date when Jesus began to rule in heaven, but his rule is not yet visible on earth. In the meantime, Jehovah's Witnesses go from door to door, encouraging people to follow their program of studying the Bible as an announcement of the millennium. They encourage people to leave politics and "false religions." The latter include mainstream Christian churches, who, the Witnesses feel, began to deviate from Jesus's message in the second and third centuries by developing untrue doctrines: that God is a Trinity, that the soul is resurrected after death, and that the unrepentant wicked endure eternal torment (rather than the utter annihilation which the Witnesses predict for them). Emphasis on the immediacy of the millennium is waning as 1914 recedes, but the movement's statisticians claim that it is continuing to grow rapidly. By 1993 there were said to be almost four and a half million Jehovah's Witnesses at work in 229 countries, all of them considered ministers of the faith.

Supernatural powers and revelations

Numerous new religious movements operate in the realm of that which is supernatural, beyond the experiences of the senses and therefore mysterious to most people. Those who are interested in penetrating these mysteries may do so to attain personal power, or they may seek to use their presumed contacts with invisible realities to bring healing to those who are suffering and insights for those who want to understand what they cannot see.

Many founders of these new religions are women with shamanistic gifts. Miki Nakayama, nineteenth-century founder of the **Tenrikyo** movement, was acting as a trance medium for the healing of her son when she was reportedly possessed

Sathya Sai Baba of South India, one of the gurus whose personal following constitutes a new religious movement of sorts.

In the syncretism of Santeria, the Yoruba river goddess Oshun is merged with the Christian Our Lady of La Caridad del Cobre, patron saint of Cuba.

by ten kami, including the chief God the Parent. They proclaimed through her, "Miki's mind and body will be accepted by us as a divine shrine, and we desire to save this three-thousand-world through this divine body."[5] It is said that she later spontaneously composed 1711 poems under divine inspiration, and that these became the sacred scriptures of a new religion. Tenrikyo has continued to be popular since her death, with Miki revered as the still-living representative of the divine will.

The **Mahikari** movement was founded in Japan in 1959 by Sukui Nushi Sama, who believes he is the successor to Buddha and Christ as God's representative on earth. The path he taught has become popular in the Caribbean. Although it does not claim to be a religion in itself, but rather to bring all religions together, it involves certain distinctive practices centering on spiritual "light." Mahikirians are taught to heal by radiating light out of their hands, to send light to disturbed ancestral spirits to help them find peace, and to spread the divine civilization through the world by transmitting light. Inverting the conventional opinion of such practices, Mahikirians are taught that the spiritual realm is the only reality; science and medicine are ignorant superstitions.

In the Caribbean and Latin America, many mixtures of African and Catholic traditions have evolved, with a prevailing interest in contacting and cooperating with spirits. **Santeria**, which literally means "the way of the saints," blends some of the Yoruba gods of ex-Nigerian slaves in Cuba with images of Catholic saints. **Voodoo**, meaning "spirit," developed in Haiti as a blending of West African and French Catholic teachings. Specialists in these traditions have techniques for "magical" intervention in people's lives to help solve problems that cannot be fixed by ordinary means. The santeros, for example, say they are able to clear away negative spiritual influences around people, help them get jobs, heal sickness, attract mates, block their enemies, and get ahead financially.

Where remnants of slave populations have coalesced, renewed practice of African traditions has given the people a link with their cultural heritage, a sense of inner integrity, and a means of sheer survival. But these African traditions have been viewed with some suspicion by the dominant societies. For instance, traditional African methods of communicating with the spirits include divination and consecrated slaughter of animals, in the context of a community meal. The latter practice was outlawed in Hialeah, Florida, as "animal sacrifice," but in a landmark judgment in 1993, the United States Supreme Court overruled the ban as an unconstitutional barrier to religious freedom.

Communication with spirits of the dead has also surfaced within a Christian context in the United States as **Spiritualism**. The National Spiritualist Association of Churches defines Spiritualism as "The science, philosophy, and religion of continuous life." Its services resemble Christian worship services, with a sermon and the singing of devotional hymns, but without the focus on Jesus or sinfulness. They include periods of spiritual healing in which trained "healing vehicles" are believed to serve as channels for God's healing power by placing their hands on or near the head and shoulders of a seated person. Equally important are messages transmitted by a medium who delivers messages to members of the congregation from deceased relatives "on the other side." Spiritualist medium Sandra Pfortmiller explains:

> The gift and faculty of mediumship is to prove that life continues, that our loved ones are only a prayer away, that we do have help, guidance, communication and inspiration from another Plane of existence. It shows that we should not fear death but rather understand that the personality continues, always growing.[6]

Spiritualist doctrine includes a version of karma — "We affirm the moral responsibility of the individual, and that he makes his own happiness or unhappiness as he obeys or disobeys Nature's physical and spiritual laws" — with infinite possibility for positive change — "We affirm that the doorway to reformation is never closed against any human soul here or hereafter."[7]

Throughout human history, certain people have felt that they are receiving revelations from unseen spiritual powers. Some of them, such as the Prophet Muhammad, have become the founders of major religions as others became convinced of the truth of their revelations. This process continues today with great numbers of people around the world feeling that they are serving as "channels" for divine wisdom.

One well-established example that has now survived over a century and has spawned its own splinter groups is the **Theosophical Society**. "Theosophy" means "divine wisdom," as revealed to Madame Helena Blavatsky (1831–1891) by unseen Ascended Masters. Born into a noble Russian family, she was a holy terror with notable psychic powers. She traveled around the globe studying with masters of esoteric schools and said she had undergone initiations with Tibetan masters. She founded the Theosophical Society with the motto, "There is no religion higher than truth." It was an attempt, she said, "to reconcile all religions, sects and nations under a common system of ethics, based on eternal verities."[8]

An early meeting of The Theosophical Society in Madras, 1884. Fourth from the left in the back is its founder, Madame H. P. Blavatsky, who wrote of the boundless eternal Principle, innumerable universes, and the identity of souls with the Universal Oversoul.

The Theosophical Society introduced ancient Eastern ideas to Western seekers, especially Hindu beliefs such as karma, reincarnation, and subtle energies. Madame Blavatsky was particularly interested in the secret esoteric teachings of each religion, which collectively she called the "Wisdom Religion" or the "secret doctrine." Her book *The Secret Doctrine* describes an elaborate cosmology of levels or "rays" through which humans can rise by consciousness-expanding initiation from spiritual Masters.

Early in the twentieth century, Mrs. Annie Besant, who was then President of the Theosophical Society, proclaimed that the long-awaited World Teacher had arrived in the person of the Indian mystic Jiddu Krishnamurti (1895–1986). A large international organization called The Order of the Star of the East was set up with Krishnamurti as its head. He practiced intense meditation and is said to have been in communion with the invisible Masters of the Theosophical hierarchy. However, twenty years after the Order of the Star was organized, Krishnamurti's beloved younger brother became very ill. Krishnamurti pleaded with the Masters to save him, but his brother died. Utterly disillusioned and saddened, he dissolved the organization and began his own independent investigation of truth without reference to any earlier scriptures or religious traditions. People continued to follow him, but he refused the role of guru, insisting that the discovery of truth is "essentially an individual process."[9]

Although it lost its World Teacher, the Theosophical Society itself has continued its work and now has members in seventy countries. The movement has splintered into several factions using the same name, and has also spawned other groups, such as the Roerich Society. Nicholas Roerich was an early twentieth-century

Russian painter, philosopher, and humanitarian who traveled in the Himalayas with his wife, Helena. He painted the spiritual light he perceived in those mountains and placed in his paintings holy figures from many religious traditions. After his death, Helena encouraged students to revere unseen Masters from India as well as Jesus.

Another contemporary spinoff from Madame Blavatsky's work is <u>The Church Universal and Triumphant</u>. It is one of the groups which claims to link members with an invisible **Great White Brotherhood** ("white" refers to the light surrounding them, rather than their skin color). Elizabeth Claire Prophet, one of the "messengers" of these "Ascended Masters," explains that they include:

> *Gautama Buddha, Confucius, Moses, Mohammed, Jesus Christ, Saint Germain [a mysterious eighteenth-century European count believed to be the Master of the "Seventh Ray"], Mother Mary, to name but a few, who have mastered outer conditions and earned the right to ascend into the very Presence of God.... The Brotherhood is a spiritual fraternity of lightbearers.... They work hand in hand with their disciples in every nation, and of every race and religious persuasion.... As immortal, God-free beings living in the joy of the Eternal Now, they would lovingly, wisely, and safely guide you on the path to soul freedom.*[10]

Prophet's group, called the *Church Universal and Triumphant*, owns a huge range next to Yellowstone National Park in Montana. People are invited to bring their recreational vehicles or tents for international conferences in which they work with practices such as visualization of the "violet flame" for healing and purification and "receive initiations from the Ascended Masters."[11] Yet the environmental impact of the camp and its alleged arsenal of weapons have invoked serious criticism. The CUT claims that the Church itself owns no weapons and has no arsenal, although its members, like many people in the area, own guns for hunting and self-defense. The earlier I AM tradition, founded in 1930 by Guy Ballard, envisions the United States as the potential spiritual salvation of the planet and teaches members to concentrate spiritual power to dissipate the power of "enemies of America."

Offshoots and combinations of older religions

In previous chapters we have looked at contemporary versions of ancient religions, such as Hare Krishna in Hinduism and Soka Gakkai in Buddhism. Mixtures of more than one religion also arise in many places. This process is referred to as **syncretism** — the combining of normally differing beliefs. For example, a number of "new" religions in West Africa combine ritual elements of indigenous and Christian traditions. They take seriously problems with the spirit world, such as retaliations from spirits who have not been treated respectfully, and mix Christian prayers and incense with fetishes, talismans, divining, chanting, and drumming. This syncretistic mixture gives a sense of power against evil spirits and is also applied to contemporary, this-worldly problems. These groups are most popular in urban areas, where they offer a refuge from unpleasant aspects of city life. Those such as The Brotherhood of the Cross and Star are deeply committed to serving the people in areas where the governments have failed them. They therefore operate their own schools, food shops, industries, health care centers, and transportation services. Those who say they once felt like nobodies, alienated within modern impersonal culture, now feel recognized as important individuals within a loving group. The movements revive the traditional African community spirit as a stable support network within a changing society. They may also build a sense of African pride and spiritual destiny. Rev. William Kingsley Opoku of Ghana, International Coordinator of African Council of Spiritual Churches and member of the Brotherhood of the Cross and Star asserts:

> *African Scriptures confirm that the world peace process will finally be founded in Africa, and the whole world will come and help build it, to signify the unity of mankind under the Government of God on earth.*[12]

Some new religions profess certain aspects of older religions but eschew other features of those religions, perhaps also adding new elements of their own to the extent that they may no longer be considered within the mainstream of the earlier tradition. These days there are many groups promoting personal growth, with a basis in Christianity or in Eastern meditation.

New Thought

Emphasis on self-improvement through positive thinking has burgeoned in the United States into a number of new religious movements such as the **United Church of Religious Science** and, the **Unity School of Christianity**, sometimes referred to collectively as "**New Thought**." Although they resemble Christianity in some aspects, these groups do not see God as separate from humans nor believe in humankind's innate sinfulness. Rather, they emphasize that our real inner selves are emanations of God — that we have access to the infinite divine potential if only we can learn to tap into it. We can create anything we choose and heal ourselves and others if we use the power of mind wisely. Many of these groups use daily affirmations to train the mind to remember its divine context. An affirmation by Ernest Holmes, founder of the United Church of Religious Science, illustrates the method:

> *I am energized by the vitality of the living Spirit. All the Power there is, with all the energy and vitality It has, is mine, and I experience enthusiasm for life, the glad expectation of the more yet to be, and give gratitude for what has been and now is. Every weight or burden of thought or feeling falls from me and I am lifted up into the atmosphere of that Divine Presence which knows only the vitality, the joy, and the strength of Its own being. I am one with all this.*[13]

Many New Thought groups are spinoffs of **Christian Science**, founded by Mary Baker Eddy in the late nineteenth century. Christian Science differs significantly from New Thought in two major ways: Christian Science is centered on the Bible and on Jesus (Mrs. Eddy sought to reinstate what she considered "primitive Christianity"), and it maintains the conviction that human sinfulness is what stands between humans and the loving God. When humans live in moral and spiritual sinfulness — including states such as hatred, fear, selfishness, and envy — these qualities obscure the true reality. When one squarely faces these manifestations of

The "Mother Church" of Christian Science, founded by Mary Baker Eddy in Boston in the 19th century. Eddy revealed the loving maternal aspect of God as Holy Comforter, referring to the motherhood as well as the fatherhood of the divine.

mental darkness and surrenders oneself prayerfully to the reality which is God, Christian Scientists affirm that healing naturally takes place as one's true being emerges. Not only are states such as hatred and fears "errors of the mortal mind"; so also are organic diseases and physical deformities. Only God is real; the physical body, with its ailments, is not. In their faith, Christian Scientists usually refuse medical treatment, turning instead to prayer. Christian Scientist Tom Johnson explains:

> This is not positive thinking or psychological training, and it is not beseeching God. Prayer is so much more than that. It is a yielding of heart and being to God, to divine love. It affirms truth. When there is that yielding of the human mind to the divine, the body naturally manifests that reality, and healing takes place, as in the New Testament. Healing is not magical, not just an occasional lightning bolt from on high. Health is the natural and very normal result when one's whole being grasps and is grasped by one's relationship to God.[14]

Christian Science publishes a respected newspaper, *The Christian Science Monitor*, but the movement has been jarred in recent years by legal claims on behalf of children whose parents refuse medical care for them.

Radhasoami

The **Radhasoami** movement is an outgrowth of Sikhism in India. Its leaders often have Sikh backgrounds, but while orthodox Sikhs believe in a succession of masters

In the Radhasoami tradition, the living master is seen as one's beloved and essential guide to the divine. Master Sant Darshan Singh died in 1989; his position was filled by Rajinder Singh, who is standing in the background in this photograph.

that stopped with the Tenth Guru and was transferred to the holy scripture, Radhasoamis believe in a continuing succession of living masters. The first of the Radhasoami gurus was Shiv Dayal Singh. In 1861 he offered to serve as a spiritual savior, carrying devotees into Radhasoami, the ineffable Godhead. Some ten thousand took initiation under him. After his death, the movement eventually split into what are now over thirty branches, each with its own living master, although there is theoretically only one of these at a time on the earth. The Punjabi branches are known collectively as **Sant Mat**, or Path of the Masters.

Radhasoami is primarily an esoteric path, without exoteric ceremonies. Initiates are taught a secret yoga practice of concentrating on the third eye with attention to the inner sound and inner light in order to commune with the all-pervading power of God, called the "Word," or *Naam*. The faithful are told that the experience must be both initiated and guided by a perfected being. Sant Mat masters teach respect for all earlier Perfect Masters for they feel they are of the same continuing lineage that includes Buddha, Mahavira, Jesus, Muhammad, Kabir, and the Sikh saints.

The Radhasoami approach to the Godhead now claims an estimated 1.7 million initiates. Those in the Agra area of India have created whole spiritual suburbs who live and work as well as worship together. Outside of India, devotees gather in **satsangs** (spiritual congregations), who are supposed to support each other in the path. They are required to be vegetarians, to meditate every day, to forego alcohol and, if possible, tobacco, and to be employed.

Sant Rajinder Singh, the contemporary "god-man" in one Sant Mat lineage, emphasizes universal harmony among people of different religions and different countries. He says his aim is to "take the mystery out of mysticism, to help people put mysticism into action in their own lives. By doing so, they will help themselves as well as those around them attain bliss and universal love."[15] Sant Rajinder Singh travels widely teaching meditation on inner light and sound. His version of Radhasoami is now called "The Science of Spirituality."

Brahma Kumaris

Brahma Kumaris is a recent development of Hinduism, in the sense that its founder, an Indian jeweler known as Brahma Baba, considered that the light of Siva had become manifest in him. From the age of sixty until his death in 1969 at the age of ninety-three, Brahma Baba taught simplified versions of ancient Indian meditation practices and lifestyle which he called Raja Yoga. Their purpose is to help a person become conscious of the power, purity, and wisdom of the soul, and physically and mentally healthy. The students of the Brahma Kumaris World Spiritual University, a majority of whom are women, with largely female leadership, dress in spotless white saris. They conduct courses in meditation, vegetarianism, improving karma, self-development, and cooperation skills. Centered in Rajasthan, India, the organization now has three thousand centers in sixty-two affiliated countries. It is also an NGO to the United Nations and has initiated several global projects such as "Visions of a Better World," to which thousands of people from 130 countries contributed their ideas of what the world could be. Testimonies of change in their own lives as a result of spiritual study with Brahma Kumaris include these words from Lucy, a management consultant in the Philippines:

Brahma Kumaris in England welcome their administrative head, Dadi Prakashmani, after her world tour.

There have been great changes in my life: from a feeling of unworthiness to a sense of fulfillment; from a cyclical pattern of joy and depression to a constant feeling of loving and being genuinely loved; from an erratic way of dealing with family, friends and colleagues, to a quality of relationship filled with happiness.[16]

The Unification Church

The spread of the Unification Church despite prolonged criticism of its founder, Sun Myung Moon, provides a contemporary case history for the creation and spread of new religious movements. Followers of Reverend Moon are commonly called "Moonies," but they prefer to be called "Unificationists."

The Unification Church began in the 1950s in Korea. In 1905, Korea had been occupied by Japan, and Christians who refused to bow to the Shinto kami were martyred. Christianity was therefore practiced secretly and became associated with Korean nationalism. Christians met underground, hiding from the Japanese authorities and then from the communists, who began to suppress religion in North Korea in 1945. Many of the Christian churches had strong messianic expectations.

Sun Myung Moon, who has proclaimed himself and his wife Hak Ja Han to be collectively the Messiah, was born in 1920 in what is now North Korea into a family of farmers. As a boy he studied at a Confucian school. His parents converted to Christianity, and the young Moon became a Sunday school teacher. Reverend Moon says that on Easter 1935, while he was praying in the mountains, Jesus appeared to him in a vision. Jesus reportedly told him that it had not been God's desire that he be crucified, for his mission on earth was left unfinished. By Moon's account, Jesus asked him to complete the task of establishing God's kingdom on earth. Moon says that he tried to determine what Jesus had left undone. Gradually he developed the teachings which were later systematized into the "Unification Principle."

According to the Unification Principle, God created the universe in order to manifest true love. The family is considered the primary institution for the growth of love. Parents are to live for their children and children for their parents; husbands should live for their wives and wives for their husbands. Based on spiritual and moral education in the family, people are to live for the sake of others in all situations. However, concludes Moon, humans do not live according to God's design; selfishness prevails in human relationships and in relationships between ethnic groups and nations.

Moon traces this situation to the story of the fall of Adam and Eve. In Moon's unique interpretation, Eve lost her purity through an illicit relationship with Satan, symbolized as a serpent, and she in turn seduced Adam. They never grew to the spiritual maturity whereby they could have manifested true love. Instead, Moon teaches, their son Cain murdered his brother Abel because he inherited a false and selfish kind of love from his parents. According to Moon's theology, false love has thence been passed down from generation to generation, infecting the whole human race.

In 1945, after the liberation of Korea from Japanese rule, Moon began his ministry in Korea. He contacted other Christian ministers and offered to share his teachings with them, with the idea that his theology would help to end the quarrels among different Christian denominations. However, they refused to work with him. He began to develop a "Home Church" movement based in family life, preaching that one could be a self-sacrificing good Christian without going to church.

Moon says that God then directed him to teach publicly in North Korea, where communist leaders were seeking to quash religious activity. He was arrested and tortured, and his apparently lifeless body was thrown into a snowdrift. After followers found him and nursed him back to health, he continued preaching in public, was arrested again, and sentenced to five years of hard labor in a concentration camp. He reports that when he prayed to God during this time, "I could only tell Him that I would never be defeated by my suffering."[17]

Moon was liberated when American forces bombed the prison, and he moved into a shanty made from discarded army ration boxes.

In 1954 Moon founded the Holy Spirit Association for the Unification of World Christianity, or Unification Church. When members stayed overnight to listen to his teaching, rumors spread that there were sex orgies in the church. As the Unification Church grew, it continued to be dogged by controversy.

In the 1970s, the Unification Church staged a series of well-publicized rallies in the United States and saw a rapid growth in membership. Middle-class youths put aside their careers, gave up their worldy possessions, broke off from their girlfriends and boyfriends, and devoted themselves to the religious path. They saw their sacrificial and ascetic way of life as a rejection of the materialistic and hedonistic American lifestyle. However, alarmed parents accused the church of brainwashing their adult children. The church was viewed with suspicion by the established Christian churches and vilified by the political left because of its anti-communist activities.

In 1981, the American government indicted Reverend Moon for income tax evasion. The government offered to waive his prison sentence if he would leave America, but he refused and was imprisoned for thirteen months. Leaders of some established churches protested the conviction, asserting that religious freedom had been attacked.

There are now approximately one hundred thousand active Unification Church members around the world. Some young unmarried Unificationists live together in communal centers, but most live as nuclear families. The family is the central worshipping unit, with formal home rites celebrated weekly. There are also Protestant Christian-style public services with hymns and sermon. The central rite is called the "Blessing." These are mass weddings in which thousands of couples matched by Reverend Moon, often from different countries, plus non-Unificationists renewing their marriage vows, pledge to create families dedicated to loving and serving others. Some 360,000 couples were wed simultaneously in 1995, in a ceremony originating in the Olympic Stadium in Seoul with satellite link-ups to groups of betrothed couples around the world. Unificationists view these mass weddings as a demonstration of the desire to create one human family, with couples of all races and nationalities being "engrafted" onto "God's lineage of true love."

Unification members are taught that they have a responsibility to transform the outer world through practical activities and public service. They have thus developed international organizations working in various fields — academic, political, cultural, and business — which include many people who are not Unification Church members. For instance, the Unification-sponsored Inter-Religious Federation for

Reverend and Mrs. Sun Myung Moon conclude a Blessing Ceremony in Seoul for thirty thousand couples from around the world.

World Peace and the Religious Youth Service have created international interreligious dialogues and service projects. On the fiftieth anniversary of the end of World War II, the Unification-sponsored Women's Federation for World Peace promoted a "Sisters of Peace" program to join in sisterhood over 300,000 women from former enemy nations — Japan and the United States, and Japan and Korea. Such expensive projects, including air travel and hotel accommodations for participants in blue-ribbon conferences, are financially supported by members' door-to-door sales and their establishment of business companies such as industrial-scale fishing ventures.

Reverend and Mrs. Moon are now undertaking global speaking tours, giving the same prepared speeches in many countries to announce that they are the True Parents of all humankind, come to establish the reign of true love. Whereas Moon was once regarded as a notorious lunatic, some high officials now consent to appear with him, such as US ex-President George Bush. At the same time, there is continual attrition among those who have tentatively become involved in his blue-ribbon international organizations but cannot tolerate his theology or his messianic claims. Yet in his 1995 speech, "The True Family and I," Reverend Moon told his audiences in various countries, "The entire world did everything it could to oppose and put an end to me, yet I did not die and today I am firmly standing on top of the world."[18]

Living New Religions

Ursula is German, matched by the Unification Church to David McLackland from England; they have three children and live in New Delhi, India, where Ursula is now Regional Director for South Asia for the Unification Church. Her spiritual search took her first into Ananda Marga, a yoga-based movement emphasizing social work which has declined somewhat following the death of its founder, but she was born as a Christian:

"I was raised in a Protestant church, but I was not interested in religion. I just learned whatever prayers by heart, but I had never any experience. When I was fifteen I followed my elder sister and left the church. I went to the government and officially said, 'I am not a Christian any more.' When I was a student I joined the communist movement at the university. But I soon became disappointed in the difference between theory and practice of the communists.

Maybe the most motivating experience was when I was in a project trying to help drug addicts overcome their internal spiritual addiction to drugs. I was confronted with them with the question 'What is the purpose of life?' They said, 'I don't care if I die in two years or twenty years so why?' So then I felt if I want to help drug addicts, I must give them the purpose of life — why they could have hope. I felt if I want to help them, I have to invest the same sincerity as they do. A friend had by that time introduced me to a yoga group. I felt the love among the people, the sacred singing, the meditation was what really drew and completely changed my life. Through the moral principles and starting a disciplined lifestyle, many questions in my life were answered, and I felt my mind got cleared up.

When I met the Unification Movement, that is the point which really attracted me, because they had a very clear logical explanation about the relationship between man and woman, and they were teaching about the ideal of the family. I could see in their own members that even though they were married, now as a family they were sacrificing for society and for the world, not just an individual living for the sake of the world.

David and I were matched and then engaged for one and a half years. We got to know each other through writing letters. When I met him after one and a half years, I felt tremendous love from God for my husband.

This feeling was really immense. I felt this love is not me for him; it is God's love coming through us.

[In contrast to criticisms that the 'Moonies' are being exploited as cheap labor by the higher-ups in the movement], I see that the higher people are in the hierarchy, the more loving, the more sacrificial they are. I couldn't live like Reverend Kwak (Reverend Moon's direct assistant) or Reverend Moon. Literally, they sleep just a few hours a day, and all day they are active and busy. They are always loving, they are always there for you, they are always supporting you. I want to become like them because they really show me what is a parent's heart, what is a father's or mother's love.

For us, of course it's true that we are not looking for job security in that sense of money or savings. I think our members come because all of them are very idealistic, that we look for internal satisfaction. Maybe what is most commonly accused is that our members start with sales to support our projects. But some of my most beautiful and wonderful experiences are doing these sales. When I go out and work hard all day to sell, I can really feel God's love, because I do this to do some good work. This money is not for me it is to help others. I have such beautiful experiences where I can just feel actually it is God who is selling it. It is not me. Actually I could not sell by myself. I think that is for all of our members who have these experiences: We have the most beautiful and wonderful experiences with God doing this.

We feel that through this type of experience, for example going door to door, you meet all kinds of people in all levels of society. Normally we would meet maybe people from our background — that's it. As a laborer, you wouldn't meet a manager. As a manager you wouldn't get involved with laborers or academics. But through this we meet all kinds of people, and that is really Reverend Moon's internal motivation: To give members broad experience and to train them to get to know all kinds of people and relate to them and love them and understand them.

When I met the movement, I felt, 'Wow — here are people who are more sincere than I am, people who are more sacrificial, who are more sincere to live for others.' I felt I want to become like them. I think that is really the motive of our members — we don't want to live for ourselves, we really want to live for others."

Nature spirituality

If religion is defined in the broadest sense as that which ties us back to the sacred, one of the strongest trends in our time is that of the religion of nature. Many who are experiencing a reconnection with the natural world do not think of this path as a religion, for it has no clear structure. It is growing spontaneously, from within. Its power as a global "religion" was illustrated by the 1992 UN Earth Summit in Rio de Janeiro, Brazil, to which tens of thousands of people from all religions and all countries flocked to voice and coordinate their mutual concerns for the ways in which we humans are destroying our planetary home. The effects of unchecked industrialization are gruesome in formerly communist countries. The unique ecosystem of Lake Baykal, for instance, was highly contaminated by the production of cellulose on its shores and by the discharge into the lake of millions of tons of waste water from industrial and agricultural projects. Some industrial areas are nearly dead ecologically, with high rates of birth defects and disease among their human inhabitants.

Revival of old models

Some who seek to practice a nature-oriented spirituality look to the past for models. This trend is sometimes called **Neo-Paganism**, although many who practice these ways would not think of applying this label (with its old pejorative connotations) to what they are doing. It is an attempt to return to the spiritual ways of ancient peoples who were suppressed by more powerful organized religions. Some, particularly women, believe that the divine was once worshipped as a female power. They feel that by worshipping the Goddess they are reviving an ancient tradition, rejecting what they see as the negative aspects of patriarchal religions. They may call their way **Witchcraft**. As Starhawk, minister of the Covenant of the Goddess, explains:

> Modern Witches are thought to be members of a kooky cult, … lacking the depth, the dignity and seriousness of purpose of a true religion. But Witchcraft is a religion, perhaps the oldest religion extant in the West … and it is very different from all the so-called great religions. The Old Religion, as we call it, is closer in spirit to Native American traditions or to the shamanism of the Arctic. It is not based on dogma or a set of beliefs, nor on scriptures or a sacred book revealed by a great man. Witchcraft takes its teachings from nature, and reads inspiration in the movements of the sun, moon, and stars, the flight of birds, the slow growth of trees, and the cycles of the seasons.[19]

Some Neo-Pagans honor pantheons such as the Egyptian gods and goddesses, balancing "masculine" and "feminine" qualities. Some try to reproduce some of the sacred ways of earlier European peoples, such as the Celts in the British Isles or the ancient Scandinavians. Reconstructing these ways is difficult, for they were largely oral rather than written traditions. After religions such as Christianity were installed, the remaining practitioners of the old ways were often tortured and killed as witches, blamed for social ills such as the plague. They were said to be in league with the devil against God, but the pagan pantheons had no devil; he was introduced by the Judeo-Christian-Muslim traditions.

Teachers from life-affirming religions that were never totally destroyed, such as certain Native American sacred ways, are highly valued as guides to worship for the natural world. From them, contemporary seekers have learned to use traditions such as vision quests, sweat lodges, and medicine wheels. But the traditions are complex, requiring life-long training and interwoven with ways of life that have passed; Neo-Pagans from non-native backgrounds usually cannot experience them in their original fullness. What remains is the intent: to honor and cooperate with the natural forces, to celebrate the circle of life rather than destroy it, as "civilization" has done.

In the absence of sure knowledge of ancient ways of honoring Spirit, Neo-Pagans often make up their own forms of group ritual, attempting to draw on divine inspiration for these new ceremonies. Usually they are held outside, with the trees and rocks and waters, the sun, moon, and stars as the altars of the sacred. Speakers may invoke the pantheistic Spirit within all life or the invisible spirits of the place. At ceremonies dedicated to a phase of the moon or the change of the seasons, worshippers may be reminded of how their lives are interwoven with and affected by the natural rhythms. Prayers and ritual may be offered for the healing of the earth, the creatures, or the people.

Certain spots have traditionally been known as places of high energy, as indicated in Chapter 2, and these are often used for ceremonies and less structured sacred experiences. Ancient ceremonial sites in the British Isles, such as Stonehenge and Glastonbury Tor, draw a new breed of tour groups wanting to experience the atmosphere of the places. In New Zealand, the traditional Maori people know of the revivifying power of running water, such as waterfalls (now understood by scientists as places of negative ionization, which do indeed have an energizing effect). The Maori elders have told the public of the healing power of a certain waterfall on the North Island; the area is dedicated to anyone who needs healing. The government has built a special parking area and walkway for access to the falls, explicitly for spiritual healing purposes.

Left *Fountain International members invoke the Earth spirit at the Merry Maiden's stone circle, Land's End, Cornwall, England.* **Right** *The NASA photograph of the earth from space has been called "the spiritual symbol of our times." It has helped to inspire an amorphous but growing "religion" of personal dedication to the earth.*

Deep ecology

In addition to groups that are looking to replicate or re-invent past ways of earth-centered worship, many people in non-traditional societies are now feeling their way toward new ways of connecting themselves with the cosmos. What is called deep ecology is the *experience* of oneness with the natural world. By contrast, most Western religions have cast humans as controllers of the natural world, of a different order of being than bears and flowers, mountains and rivers. Australian deep ecologist John Seed calls this attitude **anthropocentrism** — "human chauvinism, the idea that humans are the crown of creation, the source of all value, the measure of all things."[20]

> *What is man without the beasts? If all the beasts were gone, men would die from a great loneliness of spirit. For whatever happens to the beasts soon happens to the man.... The earth does not belong to man; man belongs to the earth. This we know. All things are connected like the blood which unites one family.*
>
> *attributed to Chief Seattle*[21]

Many of us came to a new awareness of our planetary home when we first saw it photographed from space. Rather than a globe divided by natural political boundaries, it appeared as a beautiful being, its surface mostly covered by oceans, wreathed in clouds, floating in the darkness of space. Some scientists have taken up this metaphor of the earth as a being and are finding evidence of its scientific plausibility. Biogeochemist James Lovelock proposed in 1969 that the *biosphere* ("the entire range of living matter on Earth, from whales to viruses, and from oaks to algae") plus the earth's atmosphere, oceans, and soil can be viewed as "a single living entity, capable of manipulating the Earth's atmosphere to suit its overall needs and endowed with faculties and powers far beyond those of its constituent parts."[22] Lovelock named this complex, self-adjusting entity **Gaia**, after the Greek name for the Earth Goddess. In more recent elaborations of his *Gaia Theory*, Lovelock emphasizes the "feminine" and divine characteristics of this being:

> *Any living organism a quarter as old as the Universe itself and still full of vigour is as near immortal as we ever need to know. She is of this Universe and, conceivably, a part of God. On Earth she is the source of life everlasting and is alive now; she gave birth to humankind and we are part of her.*[23]

"New Age" planetary consciousness

A corollary to the Gaia hypothesis is the concept that humans are becoming the global brain of the planet, its mode of conscious evolution. In the "body" of Gaia, the tropical rainforests function as the liver and/or lungs, the oceans as the circulatory system, and so on. As the evolving brain of the planet, we are becoming conscious of the dangers our activities pose to these other parts of "our body." Peter Russell, author of *The Global Brain*, warns that we have little time to become fully conscious of our potential destructiveness, our connectedness to everything else, and to take appropriate action to forestall environmental disaster:

As a species we are facing our final examination; ... it is in fact an intelligence test – a test of our true intelligence as a species. In essence we are being asked to let go of our self-centred thinking and egocentric behaviour. We are being asked to become psychologically mature, to free ourselves from the clutches of this limited identity, and express our creativity in ways which benefit us all.[24]

Russell acknowledges that "the wisdom of the human psyche" is already embodied in many of our religions, philosophies, and psychologies. But he feels that this understanding of our sacred oneness must be re-interpreted in contemporary language and scientific terms if it is to be grasped by enough people to make a difference.

How many people does it take to shift the consciousness of the earth? Many believers in planetary consciousness now think in terms of the **Hundredth Monkey Effect**. That is, they believe that there is some mechanism by which the consciousnesses of all members of our species are interlinked, and if enough of us change our way of thinking, the rest of us will spontaneously change as well. The "Harmonic Convergence," August 16 and 17, 1987, seemingly predicted by the Mayan calendars as a time of major transition in the consciousness of humanity toward less anthropocentric thinking, drew hundreds of thousands of people to gatherings and sacred power spots around the earth. They were attempting to raise their own awareness above self-centeredness to planetary and even cosmic conciousness, in the hope that this mental/spiritual energy would have an impact on the whole globe.

In addition to group meditations, what has been called the "New Age" spirituality often blossoms in individual mystical experiences of union with the cosmos. Some people find that if they commune non-verbally in a friendly spirit of oneness, they transcend the cultural boundaries between humanity and the rest of nature. It seems that those who have such experiences have often prepared themselves by spiritual disciplines, such as meditation practices, but the mystical experience itself comes spontaneously. Dorothy Maclean studied with Sufi masters, learning how

The Findhorn Community in Scotland draws people from all around the world to share in its spiritual ways of listening to and cooperating with nature.

to receive "inner guidance," before joining with Eileen and Peter Caddy in developing **Findhorn** — a transformation of desolate dunes on the coast of Scotland into an extraordinarily lush farming community. Dorothy's role was to receive communications from the energies that she called the plant "devas," after the Hindu term for the invisible "shining ones." Dorothy developed a cooperative relationship with the devas, asking for their "advice" on matters such as what nutrients the plants needed.

Those who have opened to the oneness of all life are often inspired to take political action to protect other members of the earth's body. Many support "Green" political agendas on behalf of the environment. In Australia and the United States, people have chained themselves to giant trees to try to keep loggers from cutting them down. In 1974, the women and children of Reni, a Himalayan village, wrapped themselves around trees to protect them from woodcutters seeking wood for the cities. They knew that the trees' roots were like hands that kept the hillside from washing away, that they provided shade for the plants they used for medicine and homes for the animals and birds. They said, "The trees are our brothers and sisters."[25] Although some view such actions as romantically naive and hopeless, the "Tree Hugging" movement grew to such proportions in northern India that the government stopped commercial wood-cutting in Uttar Pradesh, a heavily populated state.

Universalist religions

At the same time that an amorphous new religious movement toward "Green" spirituality is bringing humans into connection with all beings, there are efforts being made to harmonize the world's religions. To cite some examples, the

The Dances of Universal Peace ("Sufi dancing") are often used to bring people into harmony with each other and with the divine during Universal Worship services. Rahima Dziubany (left) led the dances at a British community of handicapped adults and said: "I met their hearts in the very first moment, and from that place we danced."

Theosophical Society encourages study of all religions and maintains interfaith libraries. Their books are made available to all who are interested in world religions, not just to Theosophists. Many Protestant ministers are trained at interfaith theological seminaries. A number of temples are being built to honor all religions, such as the Light of Truth Universal Shrine at the Satchidananda Ashram in Virginia. In addition, several groups have religious unity as their major focus.

Universal Worship

The Sufi Order of the West trains ministers who offer Universal Worship services, at which the scriptures of all the major religions (including indigenous ways and worship of the "Divine Feminine Principle") are placed side-by-side on an altar. Candles are lit for each tradition from one light, representing what is believed to be the common source of all religions, all life. Participants share scriptural readings, songs, stories, and meditations from all the religions on a particular theme, such as the idea of spiritual sacrifice. Murshid Hazrat Inayat Khan, who initiated the Universal Worship early in the twentieth century, explained:

> Instead of giving a new form of worship, it collects all forms in one, so that no one may say, "My form of worship is left out." It gives examples so that the followers of all religions may worship at the same time. It also brings all teachers known and unknown to the world as different beads in the same rosary. Imagine this idea spreading and penetrating through those separated because of differences of faith!... This is the fulfillment of the prayer of Moses, the aspiration of Jesus Christ, the desire of Muhammad, the dream of Abraham. They all desired that one day there would come a time when humanity would no longer be divided into different sections.[26]

Baha'i

One new religion has been developed that attempts to unite all of humanity in the belief that there is only one God, the foundation of all religions. This is the **Baha'i** faith. It was foreshadowed in Persia in 1844 when a young man called the Bab ("Gate") announced that a new messenger of God to all the peoples of the world would soon appear. Because he proclaimed this message in a Muslim state, where Muhammad was considered the Seal of the Prophets, he was arrested and executed. Some twenty-two thousand of his followers were reportedly massacred as well. One of his imprisoned followers was Baha'u'llah, a member of an aristocratic Persian family. He was stripped of his worldly goods, tortured, banished to Baghdad, and then finally imprisoned for life in Palestine by the Turks. From prison, he revealed himself as the messenger proclaimed by the Bab. He wrote letters to the rulers of all nations, asserting that humanity was becoming unified and that a single global civilization was emerging.

Despite vigorous initial persecution, this new faith has by now spread to over five million followers in 233 countries and territories around the world, involving people from a great variety of racial and ethnic groups. They have no priesthood but they do have their own sacred scriptures, revealed to Baha'u'llah. Baha'is compare this new messenger to previous great prophets, such as Abraham, Moses, Jesus, Muhammad, Zarathustra, Krishna, and Buddha. In fact, they see Baha'u'llah as the fulfillment of the prophecies of all religions. He did not declare himself to be the ultimate messenger, however. Rather, he prophesied that another would follow in a thousand years.

The heart of Baha'u'llah's message appears in the *Kitab-i-Iqan* ("The Book of Certitude"). God, Baha'u'llah says, is unknowable. Mere humans cannot understand God's infinite nature with their limited minds. However, God has become known through divine messengers, the founders of the great world religions. All are manifestations of God, pure channels for helping humanity to understand God's will. The spiritual education of humans has been a process of *progressive revelation*, said Baha'u'llah. Humanity has been maturing, like a child growing in the ability to grasp complex ideas as it grows in years and passes through grade school and college. Each time a divine messenger appeared, the message was given at levels appropriate to humanity's degree of maturity. Baha'u'llah proclaimed his own message as the most advanced and the one appropriate for this time. It contains the same eternal truths as the earlier revelations, but with some new features which humanity is now ready to grasp, such as the oneness of all peoples, prophets, and religions, and a program for universal governance for the sake of world peace and social justice.

Baha'is' efforts are partly devotional and partly worldly, such as the sponsorship of a radio station in Ecuador. Its programs range from information about vaccination of livestock to revitalization of traditional Quechua music.

The Baha'i Model for Governance of the World

One of the most unusual features of the Baha'i faith is its own organization, which it sees as a good model for democratic governance of the whole world. Everywhere that people have converted to Baha'i faith, there is a highly organized framework designed not only to propagate the faith but also to democratize its leadership. Campaigning, electioneering, and nominations are prohibited, thus avoiding the empty promises to voters, corruption, and negative campaigning which tarnishes elections in contemporary worldly democracies.

In the Baha'i "administrative order," each local group yearly elects nine or more people to a local Spiritual Assembly. Each local member is asked to pray and meditate and then write down the names of nine adults from the local Baha'i community who seem best qualified to lead the community. The necessary qualities are those of "unquestioned loyalty, of selfless devotion, of a well-trained mind, of recognized ability and mature experience."[27] By this simple and unusual process, Baha'is feel they usually choose leaders who are mature and humble rather than politically bold and egotistical. By the same process, the Local Spiritual Assemblies elect the National Spiritual Assemblies, and by the same process, the National Spiritual Assemblies choose

the nine members of the Universal House of Justice, seated in Haifa. Baha'is feel that this framework allows both grassroots access to decision-making and a superstructure for efficient international coordination of activities.

Within these elected groups — and also within business, school, and family settings — Baha'is attempt to reach decisions by a non-adversarial process of "consultation." The point of the process is to investigate truth in depth and to build consensus rather than struggle for power. Participants are enjoined to gather information from as many sources as possible and to be at once truthful and courteous to each other. Any idea once proposed is thereafter considered group property; it does not belong to one person or group to cling to, but rather is investigated impartially. As Svetlana Dorzhieva, Executive Secretary of the National Spiritual Assembly of Baha'is of Russia, Georgia, and Armenia, explains, "What is wonderful is that when a person says his opinion, he just forgets that it belonged to him. It is offered and then it is discussed."[28] Attempts are made to reach unanimous consensus, but failing that, a majority vote may be taken. The success of this process is demonstrated in the fact that people from very diverse backgrounds manage to work and worship together.

Baha'i Houses of Worship are open to all, with nine doors and a central dome symbolizing the simultaneous diversity and oneness of humanity. Devotional services include readings from the scriptures of all religions, meditations, unaccompanied singing, and prayers by the Bab, Baha'u'llah, and his successor 'Abdu'l-Baha, his oldest son. 'Abdu'l-Baha describes the unified world which Baha'is envision:

The world will become the mirror of the Heavenly Kingdom.... All nations will become one, all religions will be unified ... the superstitions caused by races, countries, individuals, languages and politics will disappear; and all men will attain to life eternal under the shadow of the Lord of Hosts ... The relations between the countries, the mingling, union and friendship of the people ... will reach to such a degree that the human race will be like one family ... The light of heavenly love will shine, and the darkness of enmity and hatred will be dispelled from the world. Universal peace will raise its tent in the centre of the earth and the blessed Tree of Life will grow and spread to such an extent that it will overshadow the East and the West.[29]

Islam opposes Baha'i as theological heresy, for Baha'i denies that Muhammad is the final prophet. Baha'i also finds theological legitimacy in religions such as Hinduism and Buddhism, which Islam does not consider acceptable God-worshipping traditions of revealed scriptures. Baha'is in Iran have been subjected to persecution since the 1979 Revolution, and 170 were reportedly killed in the first five years after the revolution. Baha'is' attempts to unite the earth in faith do extend into the political sphere, where they actively support the United Nations' efforts to unify the planet. Their goal is the building of a unified, peaceful global society. To this end, they work for these principles:

1 The end of prejudice in all forms.
2 Equality for women.
3 Acceptance of the relativity and unity of spiritual truth.
4 Just distribution of wealth.
5 Universal education.
6 The individual responsibility to seek truth.
7 Development of a world federation.
8 Harmony of science and true religion.[30]

> *If the religions are true it is because each time it is God who has spoken, and if they are different it is because God has spoken in different "languages" in conformity with the diversity of the receptacles. Finally, if they are absolute and exclusive, it is because in each of them God has said "I."*
>
> *Frithjof Schuon*[31]

Not only Baha'is but also an increasing number of people within all faiths are coming to the conclusion that we have allowed our religious preferences to divide us so that we no longer recognize ourselves as members of one species, of one human family. The final chapter of this book will examine efforts to draw closer across religious boundaries, as well as other trends in religion as a whole at the turn of the century.

Suggested reading

Barker, Eileen, *New Religious Movements — A Practical Introduction*, London: Her Majesty's Stationery Office, 1989. A sociological study on the effects of new religious movements on people's lives.

Beckford, James A., ed., *New Religious Movements and Rapid Social Change*, Paris: UNESCO and London: Sage Publications, 1986. Descriptions and sociological analyses of many new religious movements, from the Unification Church to sects in Nigeria, the Caribbean, and Sri Lanka.

Blavatsky, H.P., *The Key to Theosophy*, Los Angeles: The United Lodge of Theosophists, 1920. A wide-ranging survey of esoterica from many of the world's religions.

Bromley, David G. and Hammond, Phillip E., eds., *The Future of New Religious Movements*, Macon, Georgia: Mercer University Press, 1987. Interesting sociological analyses of the likelihood of longrun success of some contemporary movements.

Bryant, M. Darrol and Dayton, Donald W., *The Coming Kingdom*; Essays in American Millennialism and Eschatology, Barrytown, New York: International Religious Foundation, 1983. Studies of Christianity-based movements such as Jehovah's Witnesses and Mormons which foretell a dramatic coming of the kingdom of God on earth.

Ellwood, Robert S. and Partin, Harry B., *Religious and Spiritual Groups in Modern America*, Englewood Cliffs, New Jersey: Prentice Hall, 1988. Useful source of information and appreciation of new religions that have flourished in the United States.

Gaver, Jessyca Russell, *The Baha'i Faith: Dawn of a New Day*, New York: Hawthorn Books, Inc., 1967. The history and beliefs of Baha'is, in appreciative detail.

Melton, J. Gordon, *Encyclopedic Handbook of Cults in America*, New York: Garland Publications, 1992. History and criticism of new religious movements which are considered controversial in North America.

Miller, Timothy, ed., *When Prophets Die: The Postcharismatic Fate of New Religious Movements*, Albany, New York: State University of New York Press, 1991. Contemporary case studies of how the followers of strong founders have or have not succeeded in keeping the faith alive.

Miller, Timothy, *America's Alternative Religions*, Albany: State University of New York Press, 1995. A lengthy survey of the major alternative traditions in America, with chapters written by scholars specializing in specific groups.

Seed, John, Macy, Joanna, Fleming, Pat, Naess, Arne, *Thinking Like a Mountain: Towards a Council of All Beings*, Philadelphia: New Society Publishers, 1988. Some of the leaders of the deep ecology movement offer a collection of thoughts and exercises leading one into the experience of kinship with all life.

Starhawk, *The Spiral Dance: A Rebirth of the Ancient Religion of the Great Goddess*, San Francisco and London: Harper and Row, 1979. A lyrical, experimental introduction to the interweaving of the God and Goddess principles.

CHAPTER 14
RELIGION AT THE TURN OF THE CENTURY

As we enter the twenty-first century, the global landscape is a patchwork of a multitude of faiths. Religion as a whole is heading in various directions at the same time. Yet as we conclude this book, it is helpful to look at the overall scene to get a sense of how religion is affecting human life now and what impact it may have in the near future.

Religious pluralism

A major feature of religious geography is that no single religion dominates the world. Although authorities from many faiths have historically asserted that theirs is the best and only way, in actuality new religions and new versions of older religions continue to spring up and then divide, subdivide, and provoke reform movements. Christianity claims the most members of any global religion, but yet Christianity is not a monolithic faith. Thousands of forms of Christianity are now being professed.

With migration, missionary activities, and refugee movements, religions have also shifted from their country of origin. It is no longer so easy to show a world map in which each country is assigned to a particular religion. In Russia live not only Russian Orthodox Christians but also Muslims, Catholics, Protestants, Jews, Buddhists, Hindus, shamanists, and members of new religions. At the same time, there are now sizeable Russian Orthodox congregations in the United States. Or, for example, Buddhism arose in India but now is most pervasive in East Asia. Islam arose in what is now Saudi Arabia, but there are more Muslims in Indonesia than in any other country. There are large Muslim populations in Central Asia, and growing Muslim populations in the United States, with over fifty mosques in the city of Chicago alone.

Professor Diana Eck, Chairman of the Pluralism Project at Harvard University, describes what she terms the new "geo-religious reality":

Our religious traditions are not boxes of goods passed intact from generation to generation, but rather rivers of faith — alive, dynamic, ever-changing, diverging, converging, drying up here, and watering new lands there.

*We are all neighbors somewhere, minorities somewhere, majorities somewhere.
This is our new geo-religious reality. There are mosques in the Bible Belt in
Houston, just as there are Christian churches in Muslim Pakistan. There are
Cambodian Buddhists in Boston, Hindus in Moscow, Sikhs in London.*[1]

Hardening of religious boundaries

As religions proliferate and interpenetrate geographically, one common response
has been the attempt to deny the validity of other religions. In many countries
there is tension between the religion which has been most closely linked with
national history and identity and other religions also practiced or introduced into
the country. Protestant congregations are rushing to offer Bibles and religious tracts
to citizens of formerly atheistic communist countries, with the idea that they are
restoring Christianity there. But some Christians had managed to maintain the
faith under communist oppression, even though the church structures were limited
and controlled by the state. People from the more established religions seek to find
a balance between freedom of religion for all and the threat they perceive to their
traditional values, customs, and sense of national identity.

The issue arises of which religions will receive state funding. In Ontario, Canada,
for instance, the government has given partial funding to Roman Catholic Schools
for a hundred years and full funding for the past ten years. Yet thus far such funds
have been denied to Jewish, Muslim, and Protestant Chrisitan schools. In some

*This chart shows current
followers of the world's
religions. Percentages of
the world's population
following each religion or
none, and approximate
numbers of followers (in
brackets) are based on
statistics in* The World
Almanac 1996.

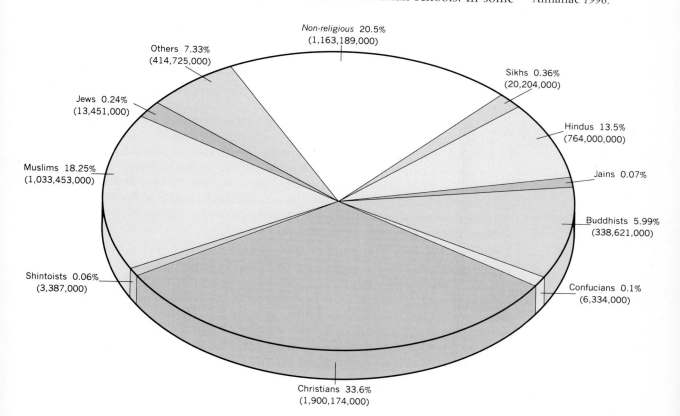

Non-religious 20.5%
(1,163,189,000)

Others 7.33%
(414,725,000)

Sikhs 0.36%
(20,204,000)

Jews 0.24%
(13,451,000)

Hindus 13.5%
(764,000,000)

Muslims 18.25%
(1,033,453,000)

Jains 0.07%

Buddhists 5.99%
(338,621,000)

Shintoists 0.06%
(3,387,000)

Confucians 0.1%
(6,334,000)

Christians 33.6%
(1,900,174,000)

countries, there is resistance to offering such public funds to new groups which are organized and well financed from abroad.

Registration requirements are another means used to help control or at least track the introduction of religions into countries where they did not originate. Another is to warn that if one is attracted into the new religions, one may be cutting onself off from one's previous religion. In 1994, the Sanctified Council of Higher Church Orders in Russian Orthodoxy issued a decree warning its followers against new religions, referring to them in Biblical language as false prophets in sheep's clothing who are actually predatory wolves (Matthew 7:15). It spoke of the teachings of the more newly-introduced religions as destroying "the traditional order of life which grew under the influence of the Orthodox Church, our common spiritual and moral ideal, and threaten the integrity of national self-conscience and cultural identity." The Council declared that all those who share or promote the teachings of sects and new religious movements which it listed had thus excommunicated themselves from the Orthodox Church.

In areas that have recently seen the collapse of atheistic communism, newly arrived or newly created religions are an especially sensitive subject. From the point of view of the newcomers, they are helping to fill a vacuum, to meet the long suppressed desire for vibrant faith. But those religious groups which existed in some form even under communist rule — sometimes by collaboration with the oppressive authorities, sometimes by sheer devotion in the midst of hardship — do not perceive any vacuum. Archpriest Victor Petluchenko, Deputy Chairman of the Department for External Church Relations of the Moscow Patriarchate, Russian Orthodox Church, asserts:

They say that they are bringing God back to our society, but on the contrary, Jesus Christ always lives in the hearts of people. The official church structure was limited and controlled by the state, but the churches simply moved to the hearts and to families. Churches became a family affair. Tradition was passing on from generation to generation on a family level.

The ecumenical idea is very sensitive and tense now. You know why? Because with so many people with different faiths, with different ideas of preaching, coming and using their possibilities and opportunities and economical foundations, it becomes very easy for every confession in the world to come to our country and to profess and to found every organization. What do they need? They need only ten followers, which can be bought very easily, to register. Sometimes minority is more active than majority. Sometimes missions come and give you a piece of paper saying that "The best way to the Lord is our way."[2]

In some previously communist countries, old hatreds between people of different ethnic groups have often resurfaced with great violence once totalitarian regimes toppled. These intense ethnic and political struggles often pit people of different faiths against each other, as in former Yugoslavia. Where there had been a seemingly rather peaceful society, horrifying atrocities arose among largely Orthodox Christian Serbs, Roman Catholic Croats, and the Muslims living mainly in Bosnia and Hercegovina. Gyorgy Bulanyi, founder of the Hungarian Bokor Movement, charges that religious leaders were instigators rather than abettors of the violence:

Neither the cardinal in Zagreb nor the Patriarch of Belgrade nor the Great Mufti of Sarajevo preaches to his people that Serbians — or Croats or Muslims — are also created by God, and that it is therefore a cardinal sin to kill them. This is not the line we hear from them, but rather another one: "It is a human right and duty to defend one's family and nation against attack."[3]

The twentieth-century rush for materialism and secular values has also fanned an increase in fundamentalism. Fundamentalists do not want their values and life patterns to be despoiled by contemporary secular culture, which they see as crude and sacreligious. They may try to withdraw socially from the secular culture even while surrounded by it. Or they may actively try to change the culture, using political power to shape social laws or lobbying for banning of textbooks which they feel do not include their religious point of view. As described by The Project on Religion and Human Rights,

Fundamentalists' basic goal is to fight back — culturally, ideologically, and socially — against the assumptions and patterns of life that are taken for granted in contemporary secular society and culture, refusing to celebrate them or to embrace them fully. They keep their distance and refuse to endorse the legitimacy of any culture that opposes what they perceive as fundamental truths. Secular culture, in their eyes, is base, barbarous, crude, and essentially profane. It produces a society that respects no sacred order and ignores the possibility of redemption.[4]

Although fundamentalism is based on religious motives, it has often been politicized and turned to violent means. Political leaders have found the religious loyalty and absolutism of some fundamentalists an expedient way to mobilize political loyalties, and fundamentalists have themselves attempted to control the political arena in order to bring the social changes they prefer. Thus, Hindu fundamentalists in India have been encouraged to demolish Muslim mosques built on the foundation of older Hindu temples and to rebuild Hindu temples in their place. Hindu and Sikh communities which had long lived side-by-side in India, in mutual tolerance and even admiration, have been encouraged to view each other as enemies. The United States, which had prided itself on being a "melting pot" for all cultures, with full freedom of religion and no right of government to promote any specific religion, is witnessing attempts by Christian fundamentalists to control education and politics, and a simultaneous rise in violence against ethnic and religious minorities.

Interfaith movement

At the same time that boundaries between religions are hardening in some areas, they are softening in other areas around the world as the interfaith movement gains momentum. There has been a rapid acceleration of **interfaith dialogue —** the willingness of people of all religions to meet, explore their differences, and appreciate and find enrichment in each other's ways to the divine. This approach has been historically difficult, for many religions have made exclusive claims to being the best or only way. Professor Ewert Cousins, editor of an extensive series of books on the spiritual aspects of major religions, comments, "I think all the religions are overwhelmed by the particular revelation they have been given and are thus blinded to other traditions' riches."[5]

However, many people of broad vision have noted that many of the same principles reappear in all traditions. Every religion teaches the importance of setting one's own selfish interests aside, loving others, and harkening to the divine.

Responses to other faiths

Diana Eck, Professor of Comparative Religion and Indian Studies of Harvard Divinity School and Chair of the World Council of Churches committee on interfaith dialogue, observes that there are three responses to contact between religions. One is **exclusivism**: "Ours is the only true way." In Christianity, for instance, a few lines of the New Testament have been interpreted thus. There are passages such as John 14:6: "I am the way, the truth, and the life; no one comes to the Father but by me." But some Christian scholars now feel that it is inappropriate to take this line out of its context (in which Jesus's disciples were asking how to find their way to him after they died) and to interpret it to mean that the ways of Hindus and Buddhists are invalid. Relationships with other faiths was not the question being answered. Nevertheless, Eck feels that the first essential step in interfaith dialogue is faith, deep personal commitment to one's own faith.

Eck sees the second response to interfaith contact as **inclusivism**. This may take the form of trying to create a single world religion, such as Baha'i. Or it may appear as the belief that our religion is spacious enough to encompass all the others, that it supersedes all previous religions, as Islam said it was the culmination of all monotheistic traditions. In this approach, the inclusivists do not see other ways as a threat. They feel that all diversity is included in a single world view — their own.

The third way Eck discerns is **pluralism** — to hold one's own faith and at the same time ask people of other faiths about their path, about how they want to be understood. As Eck sees it, this is the only point from which true dialogue can take place. And it is a place from which true cooperation, true relationship can happen.

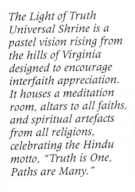

The Light of Truth Universal Shrine is a pastel vision rising from the hills of Virginia designed to encourage interfaith appreciation. It houses a meditation room, altars to all faiths, and spiritual artefacts from all religions, celebrating the Hindu motto, "Truth is One, Paths are Many."

Uniformity and agreement are not the goals — the goal is to collaborate, to combine our differing strengths for the common good. For effective pluralistic dialogue, people must have an openness to the possibility of discovering sacred truth in other religions. This is the premise on which this book has been written.

Raimundo Panikkar, a Catholic/Hindu/Buddhist doctor of science, philosophy, and theology, has written extensively on this subject. He speaks of "concordant discord":

We realize that, by my pushing in one direction and your pushing in the opposite, world order is maintained and given the impulse of its proper dynamism ...One animus does not mean one single theory, one single opinion, but one aspiration (in the literal sense of one breath) and one inspiration (as one spirit). Consensus ultimately means to walk in the same direction, not to have just one rational view.... To reach agreement suggests to be agreeable, to be pleasant, to find pleasure in being together. Concord is to put our hearts together.[6]

Guidelines for Interreligious Understanding

1 The world religions bear witness to the experience of the Ultimate Reality to which they give various names: Brahman, the Absolute, God, Allah, Great Spirit, the Transcendent.

2 The Ultimate Reality surpasses any name or concept that can be given to it.

3 The Ultimate Reality is the source (ground of being) of all existence.

4 Faith is opening, surrendering, and responding to the Ultimate Reality. This relationship precedes every belief system.

5 The potential for human wholeness — or in other frames of reference, liberation, self-transcendence, enlightenment, salvation, transforming union, moksha, nirvana, fana — is present in every human person.

6 The Ultimate Reality may be experienced not only through religious practices but also through nature, art, human relationships, and service to others.

7 The differences among belief systems should be presented as facts that distinguish them, not as points of superiority.

8 In the light of the globalization of life and culture now in process, the personal and social ethical principles proposed by the world religions in the past need to be re-thought and re-expressed. For example:

a In view of the inceasing danger of global destruction, the world religions should emphasize the corresponding moral obligation of nations and ethnic groups to make use of nonviolent methods for the resolution of conflicts.

b The world religions should encourage civil governments to respect every religion without patronizing one in particular.

c The world religions should work for the practical acceptance of the dignity of the human person; a more equitable distribution of material goods and of opportunities for human development; the cause of human rights, especially the right to choose and practice one's own religion or no religion; the solidarity and harmony of the human family; the stewardship of the earth and its resources; the renewal of their respective spiritual traditions; and interreligious understanding through dialogue.[7]

Father Thomas Keating

Interfaith meetings

People of all faiths have begun to put their hearts together. Initially, ecumenical conferences involved pairs of related religions who were trying to agree to disagree, such as Judaism and Christianity. Now interfaith meetings draw people from all religions in a spirit of mutual appreciation.

In 1986 Pope John Paul II invited 160 representatives of all religions to Assisi in honor of the humble St. Franics, to pray together for world peace. "If the world is going to continue, and men and women are to survive in it, it cannot do without prayer. This is the permanent lesson of Assisi," declared the pope.[8]

Two years later, the Assisi idea was extended to include governmental leaders, scientists, artists, business leaders, and media specialists as well as spiritual leaders. Some two hundred of them from around the globe met in Oxford, England, in 1988 at the Gobal Forum of Spiritual and Parliamentary Leaders on Human Survival. They held their plenary sessions beneath an enormous banner with the image of the earth as seen from space. Statements of concern for the environment brought participants to the conclusion that the ecological dangers now threatening the entire human race may be the key that draws us together. But it was spiritual camaraderie rather than shared fear that brought the participants together. Dr. Wangari Maathai, leader of the Green Belt movement in Kenya, observed:

> *All religions meditate on the Source. And yet, strangely, religion is one of our greatest divides. If the Source be the same, as indeed it must be, all of us and all religions meditate on the same Source.*[9]

Yearly International Human Unity conferences have been convened for the general public by various spiritual groups. The first was held in India in 1974, sponsored by Sant Kirpal Singh. Over one hundred thousand people gathered

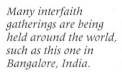

Many interfaith gatherings are being held around the world, such as this one in Bangalore, India.

to explore and honor spiritual ways to peace, unity, and service. Since then, similar conferences have been held in Brazil, Mexico, Canada, Great Britain, and the United States.

In January, 1990, an astonishing assembly of spiritual leaders of all faiths with scientists and parliamentarians took place in what, until a few years before, would have been the most unlikely place in the world for such a gathering — Moscow, capital of the previously officially atheistic Soviet Union. The final speaker was Mikhail Gorbachev, who called for a merging of scientific and spiritual values in the effort to save the planet. This vision has been furthered, at least on paper, by the "Scientists' Appeal on the Environment," a document signed by spiritual leaders of many religions from eighty-three countries. In part, it states:

> We are close to committing — many would argue we are already committing — what in religious language is sometimes called Crimes against Creation.
>
> By their very nature these assaults on the environment were not caused by any one political group or any one generation. Intrinsically, they are transnational, transgenerational, and transideological. So are all conceivable solutions. To escape these traps requires a perspective that embraces the peoples of the planet and all the generations yet to come.[10]

The interfaith movement has become so strong that there are now well over eight hundred interfaith organizations in the world. Some are global, some local.

Throughout 1993, special interfaith meetings were held around the world to celebrate the one hundredth anniversary of the 1893 Parliament of the World's Religions in Chicago. In 1893, the figure who most captured world attention was Swami Vivekananda, a learned disciple of Sri Ramakrishna. He brought appreciation of Eastern religions to the West, and made these concluding remarks:

> If the Parliament of Religions has shown anything to the world it is this: It has proved to the world that holiness, purity, and charity are not the exclusive possessions of any church in the world, and that every system has produced men and women of the most exalted character. In the face of this evidence, if anybody dreams of the exclusive survival of his own religion and the destruction of others, I pity him from the bottom of my heart.[11]

TEACHING STORY

The Frog in the Well

A frog lived in a well. It had lived there a long time. One day another frog, that lived in the sea, came and fell into the well. "Where are you from?" the first frog asked. "I am from the sea," the second one said. "The sea! What is it like? Is it as big as my well?" The second tried to describe how impossibly big was the sea and leapt to the other side of the well and said to the other frogs, "What nonsense this frog is speaking to compare the sea with your well." But the frog in the well retorted, "Nothing can be bigger than my well. There can be nothing bigger than this. This fellow is a liar, so turn him out."

as told by Swami Vivekananda to the 1893 Parliament of the World's Religions, Chicago

Among the 1993 celebrations was a gathering at Kanyakumari, the southernmost tip of India where three seas meet. Participants walked to the point where the seas merged, carrying symbols and reciting prayers from their various religions. They formed a circle, joining hands and singing, "We shall overcome, we shall overcome. Wherever you go, I shall go, your people will be my people and your God will be my God. We will be together forever."

The largest 1993 centenary celebration of the Parliament of the World's Religions was again held in Chicago. It gathered hundreds of well-known teachers from all faiths and thousands of participants to consider the critical issues facing humanity. It included an attempt to define and then use as a global standard for behavior the central ethical principles common to all religions. The provisional conference document signed by many of the leaders included agreement on what has been called the Golden Rule:

There is a principle which is found and has persisted in many religious and ethical traditions of humankind for thousands of years: What you do not wish done to yourself, do not do to others. Or in positive terms: What you wish done to yourself, do to others! This should be the irrevocable, unconditional norm for all areas of life, for families and communities, for races, nations, and religions.[12]

"Spirituality is not merely tolerance.... It is the absolute recognition of the other's faith in God as one's own."

Sri Chinmoy

Marcus Braybrooke, Chairman of the International Interfaith Organizations Co-ordinating Committee, said of the 1993 gatherings:

The tragic increase of extremism and of violence in the name of religion make all efforts for inter-religious understanding and co-operation vital. My hope is that the gatherings ... will send a message of hope across the world to recall people to those spiritual values on which a world society needs to be based.[13]

Gordon Kaufman, Harvard professor and Mennonite Christian minister, sees interfaith dialogue as crucial in solving the problems of the planet:

The problems with which modernity confronts us — extending even to the possibility that we may obliterate mankind completely in a nuclear holocaust — demand that we bring together all the wisdom, devotion, and insight that humanity has accumulated in its long history.... We simply cannot afford not to enter into conversation with representatives of other traditions, making available to each other whatever resources each of our traditions has to offer, and learning from each other whatever we can.[14]

To make a difference in the world, interfaith dialogue must not be just armchair scholarship. In some places, it is being applied directly to difficult real-life situations, such as the fighting between Protestants and Catholics in Northern Ireland and between Muslims and Christians in parts of Africa. In Mayfair, a neighborhood of Washington, D.C., people lived in fear of drug dealers armed with semi-automatic weapons. A group of African–American Muslims went into the area and chased

Baba Virsa Singh prays to the one Light that shines through all the prophets and pervades all Creation.

out the drug dealers, making Mayfair a safe place to live. Then, rather than consolidating their own power, they invited African–American Baptist ministers to come in and help teach the people of Mayfair about the spiritual life.

In India, where communal violence between people of varying religions is daily news, the Sikh-based interfaith work of Gobind Sadan is bringing together volunteers of all religions in practical farm work on behalf of the poor. Baba Virsa Singh, the spiritual inspiration of Gobind Sadan, continually quotes from the words of all the Prophets and says:

All the Prophets have come from the same Light; they all give the same basic messages. None have come to change the older revealed scriptures; they have come to remind people of the earlier Prophets' messages which the people have forgotten. We have made separate religions as walled forts, each claiming one of the Prophets as its own. But the Light of God cannot be confined within any manmade structures. It radiates throughout all of Creation. How can we possess it?[15]

Religion and social issues

Within every religion, there are contemporary attempts to bring religious perspectives to bear on the critical issues facing humanity. Many religious groups sent representatives to the huge Earth Summit in Rio de Janeiro, lobbying for careful stewardship of the natural environment. At the 1994 Cairo Conference on Population and Development, Christian and Muslim delegations took strong stands on behalf of just economic development and education and health care for women rather than forced population control or abortion as means of stabilizing population. Poverty and injustice in societies are being addressed by many religious groups. The Catholic liberation theologian Gustavo Gutierrez asserts,

> In the last analysis, poverty means an unjust and early death. Now everything is subordinated to market economies, without taking into consideration the social consequences for the weakest. People say, for example, that in business there are no friends. Solidarity is out of fashion. We need to build a culture of love, through respect of the human being, of the whole of creation. We must practice a justice inspired by love. Justice is the basis of true peace. We must, sisters and brothers, avoid being sorry for or comforting the poor. We must wish to be friends of the poor in the world.[16]

South Africa, long known for oppression and injustice, has become an inspiring example of peace and forgiveness under its new leadership, with an overtly spiritual basis. And for eight months in 1994 and 1995, Buddhists of the Nipponzan Myohoji order sponsored an Interfaith Pilgrimage for Peace and Life, in which approximately one hundred people from many countries and many faiths walked over twelve miles (twenty km) a day from Auschwitz in Poland, to Hiroshima and Nagasaki in Japan to commemorate the fiftieth anniversary of the end of World War II with personal witness to the need for nonviolence and respect for all of life. The group walked and chanted through many areas of conflict, including former Yugoslavia, Israel, Iraq, and Cambodia, with considerable impact both on the participants and those they met along the way. Martha Penzer, a Quaker from Boston who made the pilgrimage, reflects:

> This pilgrimage gathered support in awesome measure. I think what united us in this was our hunger, our yearning, our searching to find a better way, our acknowledgement that in the fifty years since that war humanity had to face itself and make reckoning with the demonic forces in us, that in those fifty years since that time of destruction, since we saw what hatred and what fear, what prejudice can take us to, we have continued to support militarism as a way of life — against the will of the people. We should never forget that there are people struggling for reconciliation. I have the highest regard for people who by accident of birth find themselves in places of conflict able to behave with nobility. Living as an interfaith, intercultural community, we [pilgrims] have had the supreme challenges of getting along with one another. The supreme grace of it is when we don't run away and get stuck in our own enmities, when we allow God to enter into those enmities and transform them. I think that is the task of religious people — not that we are perfected, by any means, but that we are willing to say to God, "I am just a work in progress and I need Your help." I guess a religious person is a confessing person, a person who is continuously holding his or her life up in accountability to God. Not someone who has it all figured out.[17]

Religion and materialism

All religions teach that one should not hurt others, should not lie, should not steal, should not usurp others' rights, should not be greedy, but rather should be unselfish, considerate and helpful to others, and humble before the Unseen. These universal spiritual principles have been swamped by the expansion of capitalism in the twentieth century, as the profit motive has triumphed as the most important value in economies around the world.

Many people live by material greed alone, with no further meaning to their lives. As Vaclav Havel, now President of the Czech Republic, wrote to his wife Olga when he was imprisoned for his courageous human rights work,

> The person who has completely lost all sense of the meaning of life is merely vegetating and doesn't mind it; he lives like a parasite and doesn't mind it; he is entirely absorbed in the problem of his own metabolism and essentially nothing beyond that interests him: other people, society, the world, Being — for him they are all simply things to be either consumed or avoided or turned into a comfortable place to make his bed. Everything meaningful in life, though it may assume the most dramatic form of questioning and doubting, is distinguished by a certain transcendence of individual human existence. Only by looking outward ... does one really become a person, a creator of the "order of the spirit," a being capable of a miracle: the re-creation of the world.[18]

Now, at the turn of the century, many individuals and corporations have stepped back to consider how to reconcile spiritual motives with earning a living. Professor Syed Anwar Kabir, a faithful Muslim on the faculty of the Management Development Institute in New Delhi, India, teaches his managerial students to do mind-stilling meditation daily in order to listen to their own conscience and make ethical choices from a base of inner tranquility. He observes,

> In our days, a great deal of power and wealth is being wielded by business enterprises. There is also a close interaction between business enterprises and bureaucracy of the political machinery. When there is power, when these three things — bureaucracy, political machinery, and business enterprises — come together, ethics and values take a back seat. One finds an increasing number of scandals, white-collar crimes, and ethically questionable practices.
>
> We managers are confronted with many ethical dilemmas in everyday situations — in hiring employees, in creating substandard products which are known to cause harmful side effects, in making tall claims in advertising, in trying to create a demand for our products. Whether a company is ethical or unethical depends on its senior managers. When a company is ethical, it means that their managers or managerial system is ethical.
>
> A company may be having written ethical codes, but many ethical situations are not written down in black and white. No amount of intellectual talk about a topic is going to help unless and until we turn within ourselves to understand our feelings and thoughts. The ethical transformation one needs in management can be brought about only at the personal level.
>
> The realization of the importance of values and ethics in business has come from businessmen themselves. Businessmen themselves say that the uninhibited, reckless way in which you accumulate wealth will not give you a good name. If you forget your values and ethics, perhaps you will gain in the short run. But for a company to

survive in a highly competitive world in the long term means creating an image in the mind of the public, creating good will, creating its own impact and niche in the market. The company's values and ethics are manifest in how it treats its employees, how it respects their individuality and freedom and feelings. If you treat human beings not as means but also as ends, naturally it is reflected in your products and services and creates an impact in the world of consumers so that they also come to respect the company's principles and strategies.[19]

Although a sense of ethics is arising in some businesses, it is not so apparent in governments at the turn of the century. Power-mongering, self-interest, and corruption are at the forefront of political activities; honesty, altruism, sacrifice, service, harmony, justice, and the public good are not the primary motivating forces in most government actions. Here and there — in South Africa, for instance — there are glimmers of religious principles in government. But in general, attempts to practice religious principles seem more evident in the common people than in their political leaders.

Individual acts of conscience have emerged as a quiet but very potent force on the political scene. Most spectacularly, the astonishingly fast fall of totalitarian communist regimes seems to have been aided by the courageous individual actions of great numbers of unsung heroes who decided that they had to put their faith into practice, even if it meant facing torture or death. In Christianity alone, it is speculated that there have been more martyrs of faith in the twentieth century than in all preceding centuries. Beginning in 1976, the Christian Committee for Defense of the Rights of Religious Believers smuggled more than three thousand pages of documents to the West describing religious persecution in the former Soviet Union. Zoya Krakhmalnikova was one of those imprisoned and tortured for writing about this twentieth-century religious persecution and its myriad martyrs. Like others, she was moved to heroic refusal to cooperate with what she described as "the tragedy of mankind which rose against God."[20]

In Latvia, Ukraine, Poland, Czechoslovakia, East Germany, Russia, throughout the former Communist bloc, individual choices to stand up for one's faith led to an informal but extremely powerful network of people whose opposition to totalitarian oppression — including religious repression — brought down massively powerful and entrenched regimes. Journalist Barbara von der Heydt, who interviewed many such people for her book *Candles Behind the Wall*, concludes:

What was it that rumbled across the European continent, bringing Communist governments heaving and crashing to the ground in 1989 and 1991? Even the most astute political observers concede that there is no purely political explanation for the unexpected way this phenomenon occurred. It was a revolt of staggering proportions that freed about four hundred million people — and it was remarkably peaceful. In the end, one of the earth's greatest powers simply groaned, staggered, and collapsed. But why?

When tanks surrounded the Russian parliament building in the attempted coup of August 1991, what gave a young woman the courage to walk up to a tank and speak to its driver, urging him not to fire? Why did a young border guard stationed at the Berlin Wall refuse to shoot at anyone attempting to escape? What motivated tens of thousands to risk their lives on the streets of Leipzig in the fall of 1989, armed with nothing but candles? ... The most important aspect of the collapse was a moral and spiritual revolution.[21]

Religion and the future of humanity

Freedom of religion does not automatically mean that religion is fully practiced, however. The worst excesses of materialistic greed, crime, and ethnic hatreds having erupted wherever repressive governments have fallen. Amorality is widespread. Many religious "leaders" themselves operate religion as a business, rather than a living spiritual experience.

The negative signs of our times are interpreted by some as the darkness before the dawn, chaos from which will emerge a new and greater order. As Yasuhiro Nakasone, former Prime Minister of Japan, optimistically states, "Perhaps we are undergoing a trial — a test that will facilitate the rebirth of the human race."[22]

Baba Virsa Singh confidently asserts that sweeping change in the hearts and actions of humanity is not difficult at all for the One who has created the entire cosmos. He reminds people of the value of practicing the eternal spiritual teachings and advises them to ignore self-styled religious leaders who do not practice what they preach and who have led people away from the truth because they themselves are not connected to it. He says that truth and love are ultimately very powerful, even if they are not in the majority. He counsels people to find within themselves the Light whose power pervades everywhere:

After being closed for decades, the Church of Saints Cosmas and Damian in Moscow is being renovated and fervent worship is taking place.

Anticipate that day when God transforms the world, and the Truth, which is now hidden, comes out and starts working among the people again. That day is upon us.[23]

At the turn of the century, the world stage is ready for a true moral and spiritual revolution, in which people of every faith truly begin to practice in their own lives what their prophets have taught. The words of the late French sage Teilhard de Chardin are often quoted in these millennial days:

Some day, after mastering the winds, the waves, the tides, and gravity, we shall harness for God the energies of love. And then, for the second time in the history of the world, man will have discovered fire.

Suggested reading

Beversluis, Joel V., ed., *A Sourcebook for Earth's Community of Religions*, second edition, Grand Rapids, Michigan: 1995. A tasty banquet of tidbits from each religion, with essays on contemporary issues, reflections on how religious people might come together in harmony, and resources guides for religious education, first prepared for the 1993 Chicago Parliament of the World's Religions.

Clark, Francis, ed., *Interfaith Directory*, New York: International Religious Foundation, 1987. Detailed listings of some seven hundred organizations, groups, and institutions engaged in interfaith dialogue around the world.

Forward, Martin, *Ultimate Visions: Reflections on the Religions we Choose*, Oxford: One World Publications, 1995. Interesting personal essays by scholars and leaders of many religions, reflecting upon why they like their religion and how it can contribute to a future of harmony among all religions.

Kelsay, John and Sumner, B. Twiss, eds., *Religion and Human Rights*, New York: The Project on Religion and Human Rights, 1994. A sensitive introduction to conflicts caused by religious "fundamentalism," with positive suggestions as to the potential of religions for insuring human rights.

Khan, Hazrat Inayat, *The Unity of Religious Ideals*, New Lebanon, New York: Sufi Order Publications, 1927, 1979. A master of Sufi mysticism explores the underlying themes in the religious quest which are common to all religions.

Storey, Celia and David, eds., *Visions of an Interfaith Future*, Oxford: International Interfaith Centre, 1994. Rich gleanings from Sarva-Dharma-Sammelana, a global interfaith gathering celebrating the centenary of the World's Parliament of Religions, held in Bangalore and Delhi, India.

Swidler, Leonard, ed., *Toward a Universal Theology of Religion*, Maryknoll, New York: Orbis Books, 1988. Leaders in the evolving interfaith dialogue grapple with the issues of transcending differences.

World Scripture: A Comparative Anthology of Sacred Texts, New York: Paragon House/International Religious Foundation, 1991. A thematic compendium of appealing excerpts from the scriptures and oral traditions of many religions, in excellent translations selected by major scholars.

NOTES

CHAPTER ONE
THE RELIGIOUS RESPONSE

1 Karl Marx, from "Contribution to the Critique of Hegel's Philosophy of Right," 1884, *Karl Marx, Early Writings*, translated and edited by T. B. Bottomore, London: C. A. Watts and Co., 1963, pp. 43–44; *Capital*, vol. 1, 1867, translated by Samuel Moore and Edward Aveling, ed. F. Engels, London: Lawrence and Wishart, 1961, p. 79; "The Communism of the Paper 'Rheinischer Beobachter'," *On Religion*, London: Lawrence and Wishart, undated, pp. 83–84.

2 Jiddu Krishnamurti, *The Awakening of Intelligence*, New York: Harper and Row, 1973, p. 90.

3 Buddha, *The Dhammapada*, translated by P. Lal, 162/92 Lake Gardens, Calcutta, 700045 India. (Originally published by Farrar, Straus and Giroux, 1967, p. 97.) Reprinted by permission of P. Lal.

4 Mahatma Gandhi, quoted in Eknath Easwaran, *Gandhi the Man*, Petaluma, California: Nilgiri Press, 1978, p. 121.

5 *The Bhagavad-Gita*, portions of Chapter 2, translated by Eknath Easwaran, quoted in Easwaran, op. cit., p. 121–122.

6 Excerpted from Agnes Collard, in "The Face of God," *Life*, December 1990, p. 49.

7 Philippians 4: 7, *The Holy Bible*, King James Version.

8 *Brihadaranyaka Upanishad*, Fourth Adhyaya, Fourth Brahmana, 20, 13, translated by F. Max Muller, *Sacred Books of the East*, vol. 15, Oxford: Oxford University Press, 1884, pp. 178–179.

9 William James, *The Varieties of Religious Experience*, New York: New American Library, 1958, p. 49.

10 From *The Kabir Book* by Robert Bly, copyright 1971, 1977 by Robert Bly, copyright 1977 by Seventies Press. Reprinted by permission of Beacon Press.

11 William Wordsworth, "Ode on Intimations of Immortality."

12 St. Francis of Assisi, "Canticle to all Creation," quoted in Rosemary Ruether, *Women-Church: Theology and Practice of Feminist Liturgical Communities*, San Francisco: Harper and Row, 1985, p. 271.

13 Pierre Teilhard de Chardin, *The Heart of Matter*, translated by Rene Hague, New York and London: Harcourt Brace Jovanovich, 1978, pp. 66–67.

14 AE (George William Russell), *The Candle of Vision*, Wheaton, Illinois: The Theosophical Publishing House, 1974, pp. 8–9.

15 John White, "An Interview with Nona Coxhead: The Science of Mysticism — Transcendental Bliss in Everyday Life," *Science of Mind*, September 1986, pp. 14, 70.

16 William James, op. cit., p. 298.

17 Dr. Anand Mohan, personal communication, October 27, 1995.

18 Lucien Cuenot, *Invention et finalité en biologie*, translated by Robert Augros and George Stanciu, Paris: Flammarion, 1941, pp. 240–241.

19 Robert Augros and George Stanciu, *The New Biology*, Boston: Shambhala, New Science Library, 1987, pp. 209, 213.

20 Quoted in John Gliedman, "Mind and Matter," *Science Digest*, March 1983, p. 72.

21 Albert Einstein, *The World as I See It*, New York: Wisdom Library, 1979; *Ideas and Opinions*, translated by Sonja Bargmann, New York: Crown Publishers, 1954.

22 The Holy Qur'an, Surah 42:15.

23 Martin Luther, as quoted in Gordon Rupp, "Luther and the Reformation," in Joel Hurstfield, ed, *The Reformation Crisis*, New York: Harper and Row, 1966, p. 23.

24 Abu Yazid, as quoted in R. C. Zaehner, *Hindu and Muslim Mysticism*, London: University of London, The Athalone Press, 1960, p. 105.

25 Sallie McFague, *Models of God: Theology for an Ecological, Nuclear Age*, Philadelphia: Fortress Press, 1987, p. 133.

26 *Marx and Engels on Religion*, Introduction by Reinhold Niebuhr, New York: Schocken Books, 1964, pp. viii–ix.

27 As quoted by Huston Smith, "The Future of God in Human Experience," *Dialogue and Alliance*, vol. 5, no. 2, Summer 1991, p. 11.

28 Maimonides, "Guide for the Perplexed," 1, 59, as quoted in Louis Jacobs, *Jewish Ethics, Philosophy, and Mysticism*, New York: Behrman House, 1969, p. 80.

29 Guru Gobind Singh, *Jaap Sahib*, English translation by Surendra Nath, New Delhi: Gobind Sadan, 1992, verses 7, 29–31.

30 Bede Griffiths, *Return to the Center*, Springfield, Illinois: Templegate, 1977, p. 71.

31 Pir Vilayat Inayat Khan, "The Significance of Religion to Human Issues in the Light of the Universal Norms of Mystical Experience," *The World Religions Speak on the Relevance of Religion in the Modern World*, ed. Finley P. Ounne, Jr., The Hague: Junk, 1970, p. 145.

32 Antony Fernando, "Outlining the Characteristics of the Ideal Individual," paper for the Inter-Religious Federation for World Peace conference, Seoul, Korea, August 20–27, 1995, p. 9.

33 Joseph Campbell, *The Hero with a Thousand Faces*, second edition, Princeton, New Jersey: Princeton University Press, 1972, p. 29.

34 Quoted in Merlin Stone, *When God was a Woman,* San Diego, California: Harcourt Brace Jovanovich, 1976, p. x.

35 Rosemary Radford Ruether, *Woman-Church: Theology and Practice of Feminist Liturgical Communities,* San Francisco: Harper and Row, 1985, p. 3.

36 Rev. Valson Thampu, "Religious Fundamentalisms in India Today," *Indian Currents,* November 2, 1995, p. 3.

37 Dr. Syed Z. Abedin, "Let There be Light," *Saudi Gazette,* Jeddah, June 1992, reprinted in Council for a Parliament of the World's Religions Newsletter, Vol. 4, no. 2, August 1992, p. 2.

38 Jonathan Edwards, sermon in Enfield, Connecticut, July 8, 1741. Reproduced in Charles Hurd, *A Treasury of Great American Speeches,* New York: Hawthorn Books, 1959, pp. 19–20.

39 John Welwood, "Principles of Inner Work: Psychological and Spiritual," *The Journal of Transpersonal Psychology,* 1984, vol. 16, no. 1, pp. 64–65.

40 Declaration of The World Conference of Religions on Religious and Human Solidarity, Kochi, Kerala, India, October 1–6, 1991.

CHAPTER TWO
INDIGENOUS SACRED WAYS

1   Vine Deloria, Jr., *God is Red,* New York: Grosset and Dunlap, 1973, p. 267.

2   Lorraine Mafi Williams, personal communication, September 16, 1988.

3   Gerhardus Cornelius Oosthuizen, "The Place of Traditional Religion in Contemporary South Africa," in Jacob K. Olupona, *African Traditional Religions in Contemporary Society,* New York: Paragon House, 1991, p. 36.

4   Quoted by Bob Masla, "The Healing Art of the Huichol Indians," *Many Hands: Resources for Personal and Social Transformation,"* Fall 1988, p. 30.

5   Dhyani Ywahoo, personal communication, May 31, 1988.

6   George Tinker, *Missionary Conquest: The Gospel and Native American Genocide,* Minneapolis: Fortress Press, 1993, p. 122.

7   Ywahoo, op. cit.

8   Williams, op. cit.

9   John (Fire) Lame Deer and Richard Erdoes, *Lame Deer – Seeker of Visions,* New York: Pocket Books, 1972, p. 100.

10 Knud Rasmussen, *Across Arctic America,* New York: G. P. Putnam and Sons, 1927, p. 386.

11 Interview with Rev. William Kingsley Opoku, August 1992.

12 Adapted from a Yoruba story told by Diedre L. Badejo. Deidre L. Badejo, "Osun Seegesi: The Deified Power of African Women and the Social Ideal," paper presented at the Inter-Religious Federation for World Peace Conference, Seoul, Korea, August 20–27, 1995.

13 Jo Agguisho/Oren R. Lyons, spokesman for the Traditional Elders Circle, Wolf Clan, Onondaga Nation, Haudenosaunee, Six Nations Iroquois Confederacy, from the speech to the Fourth World Wilderness Conference, September 11, 1987, p. 2.

14 Bill Neidjie, *Speaking for the Earth: Nature's Law and the Aboriginal Way,* Washington: Center for Respect of Life

and Environment, 1991, pp. 40–41. Reprinted from *Kakadu Man* by Big Bill Neidjie, Stephen Davis, and Allan Fox, Northryde, New South Wales, Australia: Angus and Robertson.

15 Jaime de Angulo, "Indians in Overalls," *Hudson Review,* II, 1950, p. 372.

16 Kahu Kawai'i, interviewed by Mark Bochrach in *The Source,* as quoted in *Hinduism Today,* Dec. 1988, p. 18.

17 Quoted in Matthew Fox, "Native teachings: Spirituality with power," *Creation,* January/February 1987, vol. 2, no. 6.

18 Lame Deer with Richard Erdoes, op. cit., p. 116.

19 Tlakaelel, talk at Interface, Watertown, Massachusetts, April 15, 1988.

20 Ibid.

21 As quoted in Georges Niangoran-Bouah, "The Talking Drum: A Traditional African Instrument of Liturgy and of Meditation with the Sacred," in Jacob K. Olupona, ed., *African Traditional Religions in Contemporary Society,* New York: Paragon House, 1991, pp. 86–87.

22 Leonard Crow Dog and Richard Erdoes, *The Eye of the Heart,* unpublished manuscript, quoted by Joan Halifax, *Shamanic Voices: A Survey of Visionary Narratives,* New York: E. P. Dutton, 1979, p. 77.

23 Quoted in John Neihardt, *Black Elk Speaks,* op. cit., pp. 208–209.

24 Mado (Patrice) Somé, interviewed Sept. 14, 1989.

25 Lame Deer with Richard Erdoes, op. cit., pp. 145–146.

26 Uvavnuk, in Knud Rasmussen, *Across Arctic America,* report of the Fifth Thule Expedition, 1921–1924, trans. W. E. Calvert, ed. from *Fra Groland till Stillehavet,* Copenhagen, 1925, reprint New York: Greenwood Press, 1969, p. 34.

27 From an interview conducted for this book by Tatiana Kuznetsova.

28 Igjugarjuk, in Knud Rasmussen, *Intellectual Culture of the Hudson Bay Eskimos,* report of the Fifth Thule Expedition, 1921–1924, trans. W. E. Calvert, vol. 7, Copenhagen: Gylendal, 1930, p. 52.

29 Ruth M. Underhill, *Papago Woman,* New York: Holt, Rinehart and Winston, 1979, p. 9.

30 Dhyani Ywahoo, personal communication, May 31, 1988.

31 Dhyani Ywahoo, *Voices of our Ancestors,* Boston: Shambhala Publications, 1987, p. 89.

32 Leonard Crow Dog and Richard Erdoes, in Joan Halifax, *Shamanic Voices,* op. cit., p. 77.

33 Interview with Wande Abimbola, August 6, 1992.

34 Tlakaelel, op. cit.

35 Quoted by Black Elk in Joseph Epes Brown, *The Sacred Pipe,* op. cit., p. 71.

36 Jameson Kurasha, "Plato and the Tortoise: A Case for the death of ideas in favour of peace and life?", paper presented at Assembly of the World's Religions, Seoul, Korea, August 1992, pp. 4–5.

37 "Declaration of Vision: Toward the Next 500 Years," from the Gathering of the 1993 United Indigenous Peoples at the Parliament of the World's Religions, Chicago, Illinois, 1993.

38 Excerpted from Traditional Circle of Indian Elders and Youth, *Communique No. 12,* Haida Gwaii, Queen Charlotte Islands, June 14, 1989, pp. 5–6.

39 Rigoberta Menchú, quoted in Art Davidson, *Endangered Peoples,* San Francisco: Sierra Club Books, 1994, p. ix.

CHAPTER THREE
HINDUISM

1   English transliteration of the Sanskrit s as "s" or "sh" varies widely and is by no means consistent. In accordance with the inconsistencies long found, this chapter follows existing usage and does not try to standardize it, to conform with popular though inconsistent English usage.

2   Sukta-yajur-veda XXVI, 3, as explained by Sai Baba in *Vision of the Divine* by Eruch B. Fanibunda, Bombay: E. B. Fanibunda, 1976.

3   Excerpted from Sri Aurobindo, *The Immortal Fire*, Auroville, India: Auropublications, 1974, pp. 3–4.

4   *The Upanishads*, translated by Swami Prabhavananda and Frederick Manchester, The Vedanta Society of Southern California, New York: Mentor Books, 1957.

5   Chandogya Upanishad, ibid., p. 46.

6   Brihadaranyaka Upanishad, ibid.

7   T. M. P. Mahadevan, *Outlines of Hinduism*, second edition, Bombay: Chetana Ltd., 1960, p. 24.

8   A condensation by Heinrich Zimmer of the Vishnu Purana, Book IV, Chapter 24, translated by H. H. Wilson, London, 1840, in Zimmer's *Myths and Symbols in Indian Art and Civilization*, New York: Pantheon Books, 1946, p. 15.

9   From the Ramayana, as quoted in P. Thomas, *Epics, Myths and Legends of India*, Bombay: D. B. Taraporevala Sons and Co., 1961, p. 30.

10   Uttara Kandam, *Ramayana*, third edition, as told by Swami Chidbhavananda, Tiriuuparaitturai, India: Tapovanam Printing School, 1978, pp. 198–199.

11   Chapter III: 30, p. 57. All quotes from the *Bhagavad-Gita* are from *Bhagavad-Gita as It Is*, translated by A. C. Bhaktivedanta Swami Prabhupada, New York: Copyright 1972, The Bhaktivedanta Book Trust. Reproduced with permission of The Bhaktivedanta Book Trust International.

12   Ibid., III: 30, p. 57.

13   Ibid., IV: 3, p. 64.

14   Ibid., IV: 7–8, pp. 68–69.

15   Ibid., VII: 7–8, 12, pp. 126, 128.

16   Ibid., IX: 26, p. 157.

17   Ibid., X: 10, p. 167.

18   *Srimad-Bhagavatam*, second canto, "The Cosmic Manifestation," part one, chapter 6:3 and 1:39, translated by A. C. Bhaktivedanta Swami Prabhupada, New York: Bhaktivedanta Book Trust, 1972, pp. 275–276 and 59.

19   *Thus Spake Sri Ramakrishna*, fifth edition, Madras: Sri Ramakrishna Math, 1980, p. 54.

20   Swami Prajnananda, introduction to *Light on the Path*, Swami Muktananda, South Fallsburg, New York: SYDA Foundation, 1981, p. x.

21   Swami Satchidananda, ed. Philip Mandelkorn, *To Know Your Self*, Garden City, New York: Anchor Press/Doubleday, 1978, p. 42.

22   Swami Sivananda, *Dhyana Yoga*, fourth edition, Shivanandanagar, India: The Divine Life Society, 1981, p. 67.

23   Ramana Maharshi, *The Spiritual Teaching of Ramana Maharshi*, Boston: Shambhala, 1972, pp. 4, 6.

24   Swami Vivekananda, *Karma-Yoga and Bhakti-Yoga*, New York: Ramakrishna-Vivekananda Center, 1982, p. 32.

25   *Bhagavad-Gita as It Is,* op. cit., Chapter 2:49 (p. 36), Chapter 5:8, p. 12.

26   Saint Nam Dev, as included in Sri Guru Granth Sahib, p. 693, adapted from the translation by Manmohan Singh, Amristsar, India: Shiromani Gurdwara Parbandhak Committee, 1989.

27   Saint Ravi Das, as included in Sri Guru Granth Sahib, p. 694, op. cit.

28   Ramakrishna, quoted in Carl Jung's introduction to *The Spiritual Teaching of Ramana Maharshi*, op. cit., p. viii.

29   Leela Arjunwadkar, "Ecological Awareness in Indian Tradition (Specially as Reflected in Sanskrit Literature)," paper presented at Assembly of the World's Religions, Seoul, Korea, August 24–31, 1992, p. 4.

30   Swami Sivasiva Palani, personal communication, October 26, 1989.

31   Gerard Blitz, April 2, 1988, talk at Satchidananda Ashram, Yogaville, Virginia.

32   Swami Palani, op. cit.

33   Robert N. Minor, "Sarvepalli Radhakrishnan and 'Hinduism': Defined and Defended," in Robert D. Baird, ed., *Religion in Modern India*, New Delhi: Manohar Publications, 1981, p. 306.

34   *Condensed Gospel of Sri Ramakrishna*, Mylapore, Madras: Sri Ramakrishna Math, 1911, p. 252.

35   Ramakrishna, as quoted in Swami Vivekananda, *Ramakrishna and His Message*, Howra, India: Swami Abhayananda, Sri Ramakrishna Math, 1971, p. 25.

36   Lectures delivered by Shastriji Pandurang Vaijnath Athavale at the Second World Religious Congress held at Shimizu City, Japan in October, 1954.

37   Shri Pandurang Vaijnath Athavale Shastri, *Nivedanam*, third edition, Bombay, 1973, p. 6.

38   Rev. Pandurang Shastri Athavale, discourse on January 10, 1988, Bombay, on the occasion of Diamond Jubilee Celebration of Shrimad Bhagvad Geeta Pathshala by Sagar-Putras of the Fishing Community, p. 5.

39   John S. Hagelin et al., "Results of the National Demonstration Project to Reduce Violent Crime and Improve Governmental Effectiveness in Washington, D.C.," Institute of Science, Technology, and Public Policy, Sept. 1994.

40   "US studies back meditation as substance abuse therapy," *Indian Express*, January 21, 1995, p. 1.

41   Krishna Kaumar Das, interviewed Oct. 1994.

42   Paraphrased from brochure from Vedanta Centre, Ananda Ashram, Cohasset, Massachusetts.

43   Karan Singh, *Essays on Hinduism*, second edition, New Delhi: Ratna Sagar, 1990, p. 43.

CHAPTER FOUR
JAINISM

1   Akaranga Sutra, translated by Padmanabh S. Jaini in *The Jaina Path of Purification*, Berkeley: University of California Press, 1979, p. 26.

2   Akaranga Sutra, Fourth Lecture, First Lesson, in *Sacred Books of the East*, ed. F. Max Muller, vol. XXII, Gaina Sutras part 1, Oxford: Clarendon Press, 1884, p. 36.

3   Jaina Sutras, Akaranga Sutra, second book, lecture 1, *The Sacred Books of the East*, Max Muller, ed., Delhi: Motilal Banarsidass, 1964, vol. XXII, pp. 105–108.

4   Samani Sanmati Pragya, interviewed December 11, 1993, Rishikesh, India.
5   Address to the North American Assisi Interfaith Meeting in Wichita, Kansas, October 31, 1988.
6   Gurudev Shree Chitrabhanu, *Twelve Facets of Reality: The Jain Path to Freedom*, New York: Dodd Mead and Company, 1980, p. 93.
7   Lala Sulekh Chand, in "A Rare Renunciation," *The Hindustan Times*, New Delhi, February 17, 1992, p. 5.
8   Muni Amit Sagar, in "A Rare Renunciation," ibid.
9   Padma Agrawal, "Jainism: Mahavira as Man-God," *Dialogue and Alliance*, p. 13.
10 Acharya Kund Kund, *Barasa Anuvekkha* (Twelve Contemplations), ed. M. K. Dhara Raja, New Delhi: Kund Kund Bharati, 1990, p. 32.
11 Ibid., p. 11.
12 Acharya Shri Sushil Kumar, personal communication, October 30, 1989.
13 Acharya Mahapragya, as quoted in Prof. R. P. Bhatnagar, "Acharya Mahapragya: A Living Legend," in *Anuvibha Reporter*, January–March 1995, p. 8.

CHAPTER FIVE
BUDDHISM

1   Muhaparinibbana Sutta, Digha Nikaya, 2.99f, 155–56, quoted in *Sources of Indian Tradition*, ed. William Theodore de Bary, New York: Columbia University Press, 1958, pp. 110–111.
2   *Gopakamoggallana Sutta*, Middle Length Sayings III, p. 59.
3   "A message from Buddhists to the Parliament of the World's Religions," Chicago, September 1993, as quoted in *World Faiths Encounter* no. 7, February 1994, p. 53.
4   Majjhima-Nikaya, "The Lesser Matunkyaputta Sermon," Sutta 63, translated by P. Lal in the introduction to *The Dhammapada*, op. cit., p. 19.
5   Walpola Sri Rahula, *What the Buddha Taught*, revised edition, New York: Grove Press, 1974, p. 17.
6   Ven. Ajahn Sumedho, "Now is the Knowing," undated booklet, pp. 21–22.
7   Sigalovada Sutta, Dighanikaya III, pp. 180–193, quoted in H. Saddhatissa, *The Buddha's Way*, New York: George Braziller, 1971, p. 101.
8   *The Dhammapada*, translated by P. Lal, op. cit., p. 152.
9   Ibid., p. 49.
10 Achaan Chah, *A Still Forest Pool*, eds. Jack Kornfield and Paul Breiter, Wheaton, Illinois: Theosophical Publishing House, 1985.
11 *The Dhammapada*, translated by P. Lal, op. cit., pp. 71–72.
12 Samyutta Nikaya, quoted in the introduction to *The Dhammapada*, translated by P. Lal, op. cit., p. 17.
13 Vinaya-pitaka I., 20–21, quoted in *Buddhist Texts Through the Ages*, ed. Edward Conze, New York: Philosophical Library, 1954, p. 33.
14 So Mouy, quoted in Coalition for Peace and Reconciliation newsletter, Phnom Penh, Cambodia, July 1995.
15 Joko Beck, as quoted in Lenore Friedman, *Meetings with Remarkable Women*, Boston: Shambhala, 1987, p. 119.
16 "Khandhaparitta, The Group Protection," from *Pali Chanting with Translations*, Bangkok, Thailand: Mahamakut Rajavidyalaya Press, pp. 18–19.
17 His Holiness the Fourteenth Dalai Lama, speaking on February 15, 1992, in New Delhi, India, Ninth Dharma Celebration of Tushita Meditation Centre.
18 As quoted in Lenore Friedman, *Meetings with Remarkable Women*, op. cit., p. 75.
19 Roshi Jiyu Kennett, as quoted in Lenore Friedman, *Meetings with Remarkable Women*, op. cit., p. 168.
20 His Holiness the Fourteenth Dalai Lama, February 15, 1992, op. cit.
21 David W. Chappell, personal communication, July 26, 1995.
22 Tarthang Tulku, *Openness Mind*, Berkeley, California: Dharma Publishing, 1978, pp. 52–53.
23 *Stories and Songs from the Oral Tradition of Jetsun Milarepa*, translated by Lama Kunga Rimpoche and Brian Cutillo in *Drinking the Mountain Stream*, New York: Lotsawa, 1978, pp. 56–57.
24 His Holiness Tentzin Gyato, the Fourteenth Dalai Lama, "I know I am a Human Being," interview by Suma Varughese, *Society*, Sept. 1994, unpaginated.
25 Platform Scripture of the Sixth Patriarch, Hui-neng, quoted in *World of the Buddha*, ed. Lucien Stryk, New York: Doubleday Anchor Books, 1969, p. 340.
26 From "Hsin hsin ming" by Sengtsan, third Zen patriarch, translated by Richard B. Clarke.
27 Roshi Philip Kapleau, *The Three Pillars of Zen*, New York: Anchor Books, 1980, p. 70.
28 Bunan, quoted in *World of the Buddha*, Stryk, op. cit., p. 343.
29 Zen Master Seung Sahn, personal communication, January 18, 1990.
30 Genshin, *The Essentials of Salvation*, quoted in ed. William de Bary, *The Buddhist Tradition in India, China, and Japan*, New York: Modern Library, 1969, p. 326.
31 Taitetsu Unno, personal communication, March 28, 1988.
32 The Most Venerable Nichidatsu Fujii, quoted in a booklet commemorating the dedication for the Peace Pagoda in Leverett, Massachusetts, October 5, 1985.
33 "Introduction to NSA" (Nichiren Shoshu Soka Gakkai of America).
34 Ibid.
35 "Rissho Kosei-kai, Practical Buddhism and Interreligious Cooperation," brochure from Rissho Kosei-kai, Tokyo.
36 Richard B. Clarke, personal communication, October 2, 1981.
37 Walpola Rahula, "The Social Teachings of the Buddha," in *The Path of Compassion*, ed. Fred Eppsteiner, Berkeley, California: Parallax Press, 1988, pp. 103–104.
38 *Metta Sutta*, as translated by Maha Ghosananda, in "Invocation: A Cambodian Prayer," *The Path of Compassion*, op. cit., p. xix.
39 Sulak Sivaraksa, "Buddhism in a World of Change," in *The Path of Compassion*, op. cit., p. 16.
40 Thich Nhat Hanh, "The Individual, Society, and Nature," in *The Path of Compassion*, op. cit., pp. 42–43.

CHAPTER SIX
TAOISM AND CONFUCIANISM

1   *The I Ching*, translated by Richard Wilhelm (German)/ Cary F. Baynes (English), Princeton, New Jersey: Princeton University Press, 1967, pp. 620–621.

2 Excerpt from verse 1 in *Tao-te Ching,* translated by Stephen Mitchell. Translation copyright 1988 by Stephen Mitchell. Reprinted by permission of Harper and Row, Publishers, Inc.

3 *Tao-te Ching,* translated by Lin Yutang, New York: Modern Library, 1948, verse 1, p. 41.

4 Lao-tzu, *Tao-te Ching,* translated by D. C. Lau, London: Penguin Books, 1963, verse 25, p. 82.

5 Ibid.

6 Chang Chung-yuan, *Creativity and Taoism,* New York: Harper Colophon, 1963, p. 5.

7 Chuang-tzu, *Basic Writings,* translated by Burton Watson, New York: Columbia University Press, 1964, p. 40.

8 Chuang-tzu, *Basic Writings,* translated by Burton Watson, op. cit., p. 36.

9 *The Way to Life: At the Heart of the Tao-te Ching,* non-literal translation by Benjamin Hoff, New York/Tokyo: Weatherhill, 1981, p. 52, chapter 78.

10 *Tao-te Ching,* translated by Stephen Mitchell, op. cit., Chapter 15.

11 Lao-tzu, *Tao-te Ching,* translated by D. C. Lau, op. cit., Chapter 20:47, p. 77.

12 *The Way to Life,* translated by Benjamin Hoff, op. cit., p. 33, chapter 35.

13 *Tao-te Ching,* translated by Stephen Mitchell, op. cit., Chapter 15.

14 *The Secret of the Golden Flower,* translated by Richard Wilhelm/Cary Baynes, New York: Harcourt Brace Jovanovich, 1962, p. 21.

15 Chuang-tzu, op. cit., p. 59.

16 Excerpted from Huai-Chin Han, translated by Wen Kuan Chu, *Tao and Longevity: Mind-Body Transformation,* York Beach, Maine: Samuel Weiser, 1984, pp. 4–5.

17 Quoted in *T'ai-chi,* Cheng Man-ch'ing and Robert W. Smith, Rutland, Vermont: Charles E. Tuttle, 1967, p. 106.

18 Ibid., p. 109.

19 Excerpted from Al Chung-liang Huang, *Embrace Tiger, Return to Mountain,* Moab, Utah: Real People Press, 1973, pp. 12, 185.

20 Quoted by Da Liu, *The Tao and Chinese Culture,* London: Routledge and Kegan Paul, 1981, p. 161.

21 "Brooms, Gourds, and the Old Ways, An Interview with Daoist Master An," *Heaven Earth: The Chinese Art of Living,* vol. 1, no. 1, May 1991, p. 2.

22 Yu Yingshi, "A Difference in Starting Points," *Heaven Earth,* ibid., p. 1.

23 *The Analects,* VII: 1, in *Sources of Chinese Tradition,* vol. 1, eds. William Theodore de Bary, Wing-tsit Chan, Burton Watson, p. 23.

24 Ibid. XIII: 6, p. 32, and Analects II: 1, as translated by Ch'u Chai and Winberg Chai in *Confucianism,* Woodbury, New York: Barron's Educational Series, 1973, p. 52.

25 Confucius, *The Analects,* translated by D. C. Lau, London: Penguin Books, 1979, VIII:19, p. 94.

26 *Great Learning,* in William Theodore de Bary, Wing-tsit Chan, and Burton Watson, *Sources of Chinese Tradition,* New York: Columbia University Press, 1960.

27 *Chung Yung* (The Doctrine of the Mean), translated by Ch'u Chai and Winberg Chai, *The Sacred Books of Confucius and Other Confucian Classics,* New Hyde Park, New York: University Books, 1965, pp. 11–12.

28 *The Analects,* XI—11, in Chai and Chai, ibid., p. 46.

29 *The Analects,* op. cit., X:25, p. 105.

30 Ibid., X:103.

31 The Mencius, in De Bary, op. cit., p. 91.

32 Ibid., p. 89.

33 From the Hsun Tzu, Chapter 17, in de Bary, op. cit., p. 101.

34 Chang Tsai's *Western Inscription,* in William Theodore de Bary et. al., *Sources of Chinese Tradition,* op. cit.

35 A prayer offered by the Ming dynasty emperor in 1538, in James Legge, *The Religions of China,* London, 1880, pp. 43–44.

36 *Quotations from Chairman Mao tse-Tung,* second edition, Peking: Foreign Language Press, 1967, pp. 172–173.

37 *China Daily,* January 30, 1989, p. 1.

38 Ann-ping Chin, personal interview, July 1992.

39 "Surgeon with pure heart," *China Daily,* January 19, 1989, p. 6.

40 Korean Overseas Information Service, *Religions in Korea,* Seoul, 1986, pp. 55–57.

CHAPTER SEVEN
SHINTO

1 Yukitaka Yamamoto, *Way of the Kami,* Stockton, California: Tsubaki America Publications, 1987, p. 75.

2 Adapted from the *Nihon Shoki* (Chronicles of Japan), I:3, in Stuart D. B. Picken, *Shinto: Japan's Spiritual Roots,* Tokyo: Kodansha International, 1980, p. 10.

3 Sakamiki Shunzo, "Shinto: Japanese Ethnocentrism," in Charles A. Moore, ed., *The Japanese Mind,* Hawaii: University of Hawaii Press, p. 25.

4 Kishimoto Hideo, "Some Japanese Cultural Traits and Religions," in Charles A. Moore, ed., *The Japanese Mind,* op. cit., pp. 113–114.

5 Ise-Teijo, *Gunshin-Mondo, Onchisosho,* vol. x., quoted in Genchi Kato, p. 185.

6 Yamamoto, op. cit., pp. 73–75.

7 Yamamoto, op. cit., p. 97.

8 Unidentified quotation, Stuart D. B. Picken, ed., *A Handbook of Shinto,* Stockton, California: The Tsubaki Grand Shrine of America, 1987, p. 14.

9 Ibid.

10 Hitoshi Iwasaki, "Wisdom from the night sky," Tsubaki Newsletter, June 1, 1988, p. 2.

11 Motoori Norinaga (1730–1801), *Naobi no Mitma,* quoted in Tsubaki Newsletter, November 1, 1988, p. 3.

12 Jinja-Honcho (The Association of Shinto Shrines), "The Shinto View of Nature and a Proposal Regarding Environmental Problems," Tokyo.

CHAPTER EIGHT
ZOROASTRIANISM

1 *The Hymns of Zarathushtra,* translated by Jacques Duchesne-Guillemin/Mrs. M. Henning, London: John Murray Publishers, 1952, p. 7.

2 Yasna 46: 1–2, *Songs of Zarathushtra,* The Gathas translated by Dastur Framroze Ardeshir Bode and Piloo Nanavutty, London: George Allen and Unwin, 1952, p. 83.

3 Yasna 31: 8, 45: 6, 46: 9, translated by Bode and Nanavutty, ibid., p. 33.

4 Yasna 33: 14, ibid., p. 66.

5 Yasna 34: 5, 4, p. 67.
6 Ahunavaiti Gatha.
7 Yasna 30, as translated by Stanley Insler, *The Gathas of Zarathustra*, Leiden: E. J. Brill, 1975, p. 34.
8 Yasna 31: 18, translated by Bode and Nanuvutty, op. cit., p. 55.
9 T. R. Sethna, *Book of Instructions on Zoroastrian Religion*, Karachi: Informal Religious Meetings Trust Fund, 1980, p. 87.
10 Zamyad Yasht, quoted in Rustom Masani, *Zoroastrianism: The Religion of the Good Life*, New York: Macmillan, 1968, pp. 75–76.
11 Dr. Homi Dhalla, "The Avestan View of Ecology," paper presented at the World Conference of Religions, Kochi, India, October 1–6, 1991, extract in souvenir of the conference, pp. 60–61.
12 *Shayest ne-Shayest* xx.6.
13 I. J. S. Taraporewala, *The Religion of Zarathushtra*, Madras, India: Theosophical Publishing House, 1926, p. 70.
14 Dr. Framroze A. Bode, "Mazdayasna Today," Eugene, Oregon: Mazdayasnan Anjoman Press, p. 5.
15 From Ervad Godrej Dinshawji Sidhwa, *Discourses on Zoroastrianism*, second edition, Karachi: Ervad G. D. Sidhwa, p. 52.
16 Dr. Homi Dhalla.
17 I.J. Taraporewala, *The Religion of Zarathushtra*, Bombay: B.I. Taraporewala, , 1979, p. 62.

CHAPTER NINE
JUDAISM

1 Genesis 1: 1. *Tanakh — The Holy Scriptures*: The New JPS Translation According to the Traditional Hebrew Text, Philadelphia: The Jewish Publication Society, 1985. This translation is used throughout this chapter.
2 Genesis 1: 28.
3 Genesis 6: 17.
4 Genesis 9: 17.
5 Genesis 22: 12.
6 Personal communication, March 24, 1989.
7 Deuteronomy 7: 7.
8 Exodus 3: 5.
9 Exodus 3: 10.
10 Exodus 3: 12.
11 Exodus 3: 14–15.
12 Exodus 34: 13.
13 I Samuel 17: 32–54, and the Ten Commandments on p. 224, Exodus 20: 2–17, *New English Bible*, © Oxford University Press and Cambridge University Press, 1961, 1970.
14 I Kings 8: 12–13, 27–29.
15 I Kings 9: 3.
16 Daniel 7: 13–14.
17 Martin Buber, "Jews and Christians," in *The Way of Response: Martin Buber*, selections from his writings, ed. N. N. Glatzer, New York: Schocken Books, 1966, p. 149.
18 From the Talmud and Midrash, quoted in *The Judaic Tradition*, ed. Nahum N. Glatzer, Boston: Beacon Press, 1969, p. 197.
19 Maimonides, *Guide of the Perplexed*.
20 Quoted in S. A. Horodezky, *Leaders of Hasidism*, London:

Ha-Sefer Agency for Literature, 1928, p. 11.
21 Eliezer Berkovits, *Faith After the Holocaust* (1973), quoted in Francine Klagsbrun, *Voices of Wisdom: Jewish Ideals and Ethics for Everyday Living*, New York: 1980, p. 436.
22 Elie Wiesel, speech for the UConn Convocation, September 7, 1988, University of Connecticut, Storrs, Connecticut.
23 Emil Fackenheim, *God's Presence in History* (1970), quoted in Klagsbrun, *Voices of Wisdom*, op. cit., p. 435.
24 Yitzhak Rabin, as quoted in "The Peace of the Brave," *Indian Currents*, November 9, 1995, p. 1.
25 Maimonides' "First Principles of Faith," as quoted in Louis Jacobs, *Principles of Jewish Faith*, Northvale, New Jersey: Jason Aronson, 1988, p. 33.
26 Ibn Gabirol, *Keter Malkhut*, quoted in Abraham J. Heschel, "One God," in *Between God and Man: An Interpretation of Judaism, from the Writings of Abraham J. Heschel*, ed. Fritz A. Rothschild, New York: Free Press, 1959, p. 106.
27 Heschel, ibid., p. 37.
28 Ibid., p. 105.
29 Ibid., p. 104.
30 Martin Buber, in *The Way of Response: Martin Buber – Selections from His Writings*, ed. Nahum N. Glatzer, New York: Schocken Books, 1968, p. 53.
31 Isaiah 65:25, JPS *Tanakh*.
32 Translated from the Hebrew by Rabbi Sidney Greenberg, *Likrat Shabbat*, Bridgeport, Connecticut: Media Judaica/The Prayer Book Press, 1981, p. 61.
33 Job 1: 20–21.
34 The Jewish Prayer Book, as quoted by Jocelyn Hellig, "A South African Jewish Perspective," in Martin Forward, ed., *Ultimate Visions*, Oxford: Oneworld Publications, 1995, p. 136.
35 Leviticus 11:45.
36 Talmud Berakhoth 11a, in *Ha-Suddur Ha-Shalem*, translated by Philip Birnbaum, New York: Hebrew Publishing Company, 1977, p. 14.
37 Excerpted from Ruth Gan Kagan, "The Sabbath: Judaism's Discipline for Inner Peace," paper presented at the Assembly of the World's Religions, Seoul, Korea, August 24–31, pp. 3, 7.
38 Sanhedrin 22a, quoted in *The Second Jewish Catalog*, eds. Sharon Strassfeld and Michael Strassfeld, Philadelphia: The Jewish Publication Society, 1976.
39 Rabbi Yochanan ben Nuri, Rosh Hashanan prayer quoted by Arthur Waskow, *Seasons of Our Joy*, New York: Bantam Books, 1982, p. 11.
40 Ibid., p. 175.
41 Genesis 1:26 from *The Torah*, Philadelphia: The Jewish Publication Society, 1962.
42 *The Gates of Repentance*, New York: Central Conference of American Rabbis, p. 197.
43 Mordecai M. Kaplan, "The Way I Have Come," in *Mordecai M. Kaplan: An Evaluation*, eds. I. Eisenstein and E. Kohn, New York, 1952, p. 293.
44 "Declaration of the ELCA to the Jewish Community," as quoted in Joel Beversluis, *A Sourcebook for Earth's Community of Religions*, revised edition, Grand Rapids, Michigan: CoNexus Press-Sourcebook Project, 1995, p. 170.
45 Rabbi Dovid Karpov, interviewed October 24, 1994.
46 Amos 5:24.

CHAPTER TEN
CHRISTIANITY

1   Publishing Department of Moscow Patriarchate, *The Russian Orthodox Church*, Moscow, 1980, p. 239 in English translation by Doris Bradbury, Moscow: Progress Publishers, 1982.

2   *The Gospel According to Thomas*, Coptic text established and translated by Guilloaumont et al., Leiden: E. J. Brill; New York: Harper and Row, 1959, verse 77.

3   Luke 2: 47, 49. Most Biblical quotations in this chapter are from the Revised Standard Version of the Bible, copyright 1946, 1952, 1971 by The Division of Christian Education of the National Council of the Churches of Christ in the USA. Used by permission.

4   Mark 1: 10–11.

5   Matthew 6: 25–27.

6   Matthew 7: 7.

7   Luke 9: 17.

8   John 6: 48.

9   William, quoted in *The Gospel in Art by the Peasants of Solentiname*, eds. Philip and Sally Scharper, Maryknoll, New York: Orbis Books, 1984, p. 42.

10   Matthew 5: 21–22.

11   Matthew 5: 44–45.

12   Matthew 22: 39.

13   Matthew 25: 37–40.

14   Matthew 5: 3.

15   Matthew 13: 47–50, The New English Bible, Cambridge, England: Cambridge University Press, corrected impression, 1972.

16   Luke 10: 25–37, The New English Bible.

17   Mark 1: 15.

18   Luke 4: 43.

19   Matthew 6: 10.

20   John 4: 13–14.

21   Matthew 24: 29–31.

22   Leviticus 20: 9.

23   Isaiah 29: 13, The New English Bible.

24   Matthew 15: 1–20, The New English Bible.

25   Matthew 23: 1–3, 27–28, The New English Bible.

26   Isaiah 56: 7.

27   Jeremiah 7: 11.

28   Mark 11: 15–18, The New English Bible

29   Mark 8: 29–30.

30   John 11: 27.

31   Matthew 17: 2–5.

32   John 7: 16, 8: 12, 8: 23, 8: 58.

33   Matthew 26: 28.

34   Mark 11: 10.

35   Mark 14: 36.

36   Joachim Jeremias, *New Testament Theology: The Proclamation of Jesus*, translated by John Bowden, New York: Charles Scribner's Sons, 1971, p. 40.

37   Mark 14: 41.

38   Matthew 26: 64.

39   Matthew 27: 11.

40   Matthew 27: 46.

41   Matthew 28: 18–20.

42   Acts 2: 36.

43   Acts 26: 18.

44   Acts 17: 28.

45   *The Gospel According to Thomas*, op. cit., 82.

46   *Confessions of St. Augustine*, translated by Edward Bouverie Pusey, Chicago: Encyclopedia Britannica, vol. 18 of Great Books of the Western World, 1952, p. 64.

47   Rowan Williams, *Resurrection*, New York: The Pilgrim Press, 1984, p. 46 with quotations from John 14:19.

48   Archimandrite Chrysostomos, *The Ancient Fathers of the Desert*, Brookline, Massachusetts: Hellenic College Press, 1980, p. 78.

49   Ibid., p. 80.

50   The Solovky Memorandum, as quoted in Barbara von der Heydt, *Candles Behind the Wall*, Grand Rapids, Michigan: William B. Eerdmans Publishing Company, 1993, p. 46.

51   Mikhail S. Gorbachev, quoted in Michael Dobbs, "Soviets, Vatican to Establish Ties," *The Hartford Courant*, December 2, 1989, p. 1.

52   Father Alexey Vlasov, interviewed October 26, 1994.

53   Father Feodor, interviewed October 29, 1994.

54   St. Gregory Palamas, "Homily on the Presentation of the Holy Virgin in the Temple," ed., Sophocles, *22 Homilies of St. Gr. Palamas*, Athens, 1861, pp. 175–177, quoted in Vladimir Lossky, *The Mystical Theology of the Eastern Church*, New York: St. Vladimir's Seminary Press, 1976, p. 224.

55   Jim Forest, *Pilgrim to the Russian Church*, New York: Crossroad Publishing Company, 1988, p. 50.

56   From *A Hopkins Reader*, ed. John Pick, New York: Oxford University Press, 1953, quoted in D. M. Dooling, ed., *A Way of Working*, New York: Anchor Press/Doubleday, 1979, p. 6.

57   St. Francis, *Testament*, April 1226, p. 3, quoted in eds. Jean Leclerc, Francois Vandenbroucke, and Louis Bouyer, *The Spirituality of the Middle Ages*, vol. 2 of *A History of Christian Spirituality*, New York: Seabury Press, 1982, p. 289.

58   *The Cloud of Unknowing and The Book of Privy Counseling*, Garden City, New York: Image Books, 1973 edition, p. 56.

59   Martin Luther, *A Treatise on Christian Liberty*, quoted in John Oillenberger and Claude Welch, *Protestant Christianity*, New York: Charles Scribner's Sons, 1954, p. 36.

60   Ulrich Zwingli, "On True and False Religion," quoted in ed. Harry Emerson Fosdick, *Great Voices of the Reformation*, New York: Random House, 1952, p. 169.

61   John Calvin, "Instruction in Faith," quoted in Fosdick, op. cit., p. 216.

62   John Wesley, as quoted in F. L. Cross and E. A. Livingstone, eds., *The Oxford Dictionary of the Christian Church*, Oxford: Oxford University Press, 1983, p. 1467.

63   St. Teresa of Avila, *Interior Castle*, translated by E. Allison Peers from the critical edition of P. Silverio de Santa Teresa, Garden City, New York: Image Books, 1961, p. 214.

64   John Wesley, as quoted in John Dillenberger and Claude Welch, *Protestant Christianity*, New York: Charles Scribner's Sons, 1954, p. 134.

65   Sarah Grimke, "Letters on the Equality of the Sexes and the Condition of Women" (1836–37), in *Feminism: The Essential Historical Writings*, ed., M. Schneir, New York: Vintage, 1972, p. 38.

66   The Documents of Vatican II, ed. Walter M. Abbott, New York: Guild Press, 1966, p. 665.

67   Ibid., pp. 661–662.

68 John 14: 2–10, The New English Bible.

69 Paul Knitter, in John Hick and Paul F. Knitter, eds., *The Myth of Christian Uniqueness: Toward a Pluralistic Theology of Religions*, Maryknoll, New York: Orbis Books, 1987, pp. 192–193.

70 Matthew 20: 28.

71 John 3: 16–17, The New English Bible.

72 Archbishop Desmond Tutu, "The Face of God," *Life*, December 1990, pp. 49–50.

73 Rev. Larry Howard, interfaith service, Syracuse, New York, October 25, 1992.

74 Thomas Keating, *The Mystery of Christ: The Liturgy as Spiritual Experience*, Amity, New York: Amity House, 1987, p. 5.

75 From Mother Teresa, as quoted in Malcolm Muggeridge, *A Gift for God*, London: Collins, 1975, pp. 37–38.

76 (Thomas a Kempis), *The Imitation of Christ*, p. 139.

77 F. Ioann Kronshtadtsky, as quoted in F. Veniamin Fedchenkov, *Heaven on Earth*, Moscow: Palmnik, 1994, p. 70.

78 Julia Gatta, personal communication, July 22, 1987.

79 "Brief Order for Confession and Forgiveness," *Lutheran Book of Worship*, Prepared by the churches participating in the Inter-Lutheran Commission on Worship, Minneapolis, Minnesota: Augsburg Publishing House, 1978, p. 56.

80 World Council of Churches, *Baptism, Eucharist and Ministry*, Faith and Order Paper No. 111, Geneva, 1982, p. 2.

81 Father Appolinari, interviewed October 28, 1994.

82 John 1: 9.

83 Jim Forest, *Pilgrim to the Russian Church*, op. cit., p. 72.

84 Thomas Merton, *Contemplative Prayer*, Garden City, New York: Image Books, 1969, p. 67.

85 Father Paulos Mar Gregorios, World Congress of Spiritual Concord, Rishikesh, India, December 11, 1993.

86 Interview with Professor Kathleen Dugan, February 4, 1993.

87 Luke 1: 38.

88 Quoted in Jim Forest, *Pilgrim to the Russian Church*, New York: Crossroad Publishing Company, 1988, p. 63.

89 *New York Times*, as reprinted in "The Gospel of Life," *Indian Currents*, April 8, 1995, p. 1.

90 Sean McDonagh, *The Greening of the Church*, Maryknoll, New York: Orbis Books, p. 65.

91 Quoted in Don A. Schanche and Russell Chandler, Los Angeles Times, "Tensions confront pope in U.S.," *The Hartford Courant*, September 11, 1987, p. 1.

92 Quoted by Geraldine Baum, "Fallen fundamentalists: solving the puzzle," *The Hartford Courant*, March 8, 1988, p. C1.

93 Roman I. Bilas, interviewed October 25, 1994.

94 Members of African Independent Churches Report on their Pilot Study of the History and Theology of their Churches, "Speaking for Ourselves," Braamfontein, South Africa: Institute for Contextural Theology, 1985, pp. 23–24.

95 Martin Luther King, Jr., "An Experiment in Love," in *A Testament of Hope: The Essential Writings of Martin Luther King, Jr.*, ed. James Melvin Washington, San Francisco: Harper and Row, 1986, p. 16.

96 Gustavo Gutierrez, quoted in Phillip Berryman, *Liberation Theology*, New York: Pantheon Books, 1987, p. 33.

97 Bakole Wa Ilunga, *Paths of Liberation: A Third World Spirituality*, Maryknoll, New York: Orbis Books, 1984, p. 92.

98 Thomas Berry, remarks at "Seeking the True Meaning of Peace" conference in San Jose, Costa Rica, June 27, 1989.

99 Jozef Tischner, as quoted in Barbara von der Heydt, *Candles Behind the Wall*, Grand Rapids, Michigan: William B. Eerdmans Publishing Company, 1993, p. 197.

100 Alexander Ogorodnikov, as quoted in von der Heydt, op. cit., p. 28.

101 Gabriele Anger, as quoted in von der Heydt, op. cit., p. 175.

102 Vaclav Havel, as quoted by Timothy Garton Ash, "Does Central Europe Exist?" in *The Uses of Adversity: Essays on the Fate of Central Europe*, Cambridge: Granta Books, 1989, p. 179.

103 Christian Fuhrer, as quoted by von der Heydt, op. cit., pp. 186–187.

104 Interconfessional Conference, "Christian Faith and Human Enmity," St. Daniel's Monastery, Moscow, 21–23 June 1994, Final Document, pp. 2–4.

CHAPTER ELEVEN
ISLAM

1 *The Holy Qur'an*, XCVI: 1–5, English translation by Abdullah Yusuf Ali, Durban, R.S.A.: Islamic Propagation Center International, 1946. This translation is used throughout this chapter, by permission.

2 Abu Abdallah Muhammad Bukhari, *Kitab jami as-sahih*, translated by M. M. Khan as *Sahih al-Bukhari*, Lahore: Ashraf, 1978–80, quoted in Annemarie Schimmel, *And Muhammad is His Messenger*, Chapel Hill, North Carolina: University of North Carolina Press, 1985, p. 11.

3 Sura 8: 18.

4 Maulana M. Ubaidul Akbar, *The Orations of Muhammad*, Lahore: M. Ashraf, 1954, p. 78.

5 Sura 41: 6.

6 Sura 28: 56.

7 Hadith quoted by Annemarie Schimmel, *And Muhammad is His Messenger*, Chapel Hill, North Carolina: University of North Carolina Press, 1985, pp. 48 and 55.

8 Quoted by Mahmoud Ayoub, *The Qur'an and its Interpreters*, Albany: State University of New York Press, 1984, vol. 1, p. 14.

9 Footnote 5778, Sura 74: I, p. 1640.

10 Khalid Duran, "Interreligious Dialogue and the Islamic 'Original Sin,'" in Leonard Swidler, ed., *Toward a Universal Theology of Religion*, Maryknoll, New York: Orbis Books, 1988, p. 213.

11 Sura 42: 15.

12 Islamic Society of North America, "Islam at a Glance," Plainfield, Indiana: Islamic Teaching Center.

13 Abu Hashim Madani, quoted in Samuel L. Lewis, *In the Garden*, New York: Harmony Books/Lama Foundation, 1975, p. 136.

14 Frithjof Schuon, *Understanding Islam*, translated by D. M. Matheson, London: George Allen and Unwin, 1963, p. 59.

15 Sura 2: 136.

16 Sura 32: 16–17.

17 Seyyed Hossein Nasr, *Ideals and Realities of Islam,* second edition, London: Unwin Hyman Limited, 1985, p. 23.

18 Quoted by Abdur-Rahman Ibrahim Doi, "Sunnism," *Islamic Spirituality: Foundations,* ed. Seyyed Hossein Nasr, New York: Crossroad, 1987, p. 158.

19 Sura 17: 13–14.

20 Sura 70:16–18.

21 Quoted by Muhammad Rida al-Muzaffar, *The Faith of Shi'a Islam,* London: The Muhammadi Trust, 1982, p. 35.

22 Ibid., p. 42.

23 Hadith # 535 cited in Badi'uz-Zaman Furuzanfar, *Ahadith-i Mathnawi,* Tehran, 1334 sh./1955, in Persian, quoted in Annemarie Schimmel, *Mystical Dimensions of Islam,* Chapel Hill: University of North Carolina Press, 1975, p. 118.

24 Rabi'aal-'Adawiyya al-Qaysiyya, quoted in Abu Talib, *Qut al-Qulub,* II, Cairo, A. H. 1310, p. 57, as quoted in Margaret Smith, *Rabi'a the Mystic and her Fellow-Saints in Islam,* Cambridge: Cambridge University Press, 1928, 1984, p. 102.

25 Mevlana Jalal al-Din Rumi, opening lines of the *Mathnawi,* as translated by Edmund Helminski, *The Ruins of the Heart: Selected Lyric Poetry of Jelaluddin Rumi,* Putney, Vermont: Threshold Books, 1981, p. 20.

26 Jalal al-Din Rumi, *Mathnawi-i ma'nawi,* ed. and translated by Reynold A. Nicholson, London, 1925–40, vol. 4, line 2102.

27 Hadith of the Prophet, #352 in Zam Furuzanfar, *Ahadith-i Mathnawi,* op. cit.

28 Quoted in Javad Nurbakhsh, *Sufism: Meaning, Knowledge, and Unity,* New York: Khaniqahi-Nimatullahi Publications, 1981, pp. 19, 21.

29 Idries Shah, *The Sufis,* London: Jonathan Cape, 1964, p. 76.

30 Rumi, *Mathnawi,* VI, 3220–3246, as translated by Coleman Barks in *Rumi: We are Three,* Athens, Georgia: Maypop Books, 1987, pp. 54–55.

31 Sura 2: 256.

32 Hadith quoted by Syed Ali Ashraf, "The Inner Meaning of the Islamic Rites: Prayer, Pilgrimage, Fasting, Jihad," in *Islamic Spirituality: Foundations,* op. cit., p. 114.

33 Hammudah Abdalati, *Islam in Focus,* Indianapolis, Indiana: American Trust Publications, 1975, p. 88.

34 Seyyed Hossein Nasr, *Traditional Islam in the Modern World,* London: KPI Ltd., 1987, p. 33.

35 Sura 22: 39–40.

36 Sura 2: 190.

37 Sura 2: 217, 192.

38 M. R. Bawa Muhaiyaddeen, "Islam's Hidden Beauty: The Sufi Teachings of M. R. Bawa Muhaiyaddeen," tape from New Dimensions Foundation, San Francisco, 1989, side 1.

39 Treaty cited in Philip K. Hitti, *Islam and the West,* Princeton, New Jersey: D. Van Nostrand, 1962, p. 112.

40 Uzbek Khan, 1313 charter granted to Metropolitan Peter, as quoted in *Al Risala,* June 1994, p. 12.

41 Dalil-ul-Arifin, p. 37, as quoted in W. D. Begg, *The Holy Biography of Hazrat Khwaja Muinuddin Chishti,* Botswana, Africa: G. N. Khan, 1979, p. 41.

42 Indonesian President Suharto, quoted in *Hinduism Today,* July 1989, p. 20.

43 Annemarie Schimmel, speaking in "Islam's Hidden Beauty," tape from New Dimensions Foundation, San Francisco, 1989, side 1.

44 Jalal al-Din Rumi, *Mathnawi,* IV, in *Rumi: We are Three:* op. cit., Barks, p. 52.

45 Noor Grant, as quoted in *Islam in America,* vol. 2, no. 2, Summer 1995, p. 41.

46 Interview with Sajida Sultana Alvi, June 15, 1992.

47 Seyyed Hossein Nasr, "The Pertinence of Islam to the Modern World," *The World Religions Speak on the Relevance of Religion in the Modern World,* ed. Finley P. Dunne Jr., The Hague: Junk, 1970, p. 133.

48 The First World Conference on Muslim Education, quoted in Syed Ali Ashraf, *New Horizon in Muslim Education,* Cambridge, England: Hodder and Stoughton/The Islamic Academy, 1985, p. 4.

49 Mufti Magomed-Khaji Albogachiev, remarks at The Inter-Religious Federation for World Peace Conference, Seoul, Korea, 1995.

50 Ibid.

51 Mamoon-al-Rasheed, "Islam, Nonviolence, and Social Transformation," ed. by Glenn D. Paige, Chaiwat Satha-Anand, Sarah Gilliatt, Honolulu: University of Hawaii, Center for Global Nonviolence Planning Project, 1993, p. 70.

52 Dr. A. K. Abu'l Majd, quoted in the video "Islam," Smithsonian World series, Smithsonian Institution and WETA, Washington, D.C., originally broadcast July 22, 1987, transcript pp. 6, 17.

CHAPTER TWELVE
SIKHISM

1 Kabir, in modern translation by Robert Bly, *The Kabir Book: Forty-four of the Ecstatic Poems of Kabir,* Copyright 1971, 1977 by Robert Bly, copyright 1977 by Seventies Press. Reprinted by permission of Beacon Press, p. 33.

2 Puratan, quoted in Khushwant Singh, *Hymns of Guru Nanak,* New Delhi: Orient Longmans Ltd., 1969, p. 10.

3 Guru Nanak, as quoted in W. Owen Cole and Piara Singh Sambhi, *The Sikhs: Their Religious Beliefs and Practices,* London: Routledge and Kegan Paul, 1978, p. 39.

4 Var Maji 7: 1, *Adi Granth,* quoted in *Textual Sources for the Study of Sikhism,* translated and edited by W. H. McLeod, Totowa, New Jersey: Barnes and Noble, 1984, p. 43.

5 Sri Rag, p. 59, quoted in Trilochan Singh, Jodh Singh, Kapur Singh, Bawa Harkishen Singh, and Kushwant Singh, trans., *The Sacred Writings of the Sikhs,* reproduced by kind permission of Unwin Hyman Ltd., 1973, p. 72.

6 Guru Granth Sahib 724.

7 Guru Har Rai, as quoted in Dr. Gopal Singh, *A History of the Sikh People,* New Delhi: World Sikh University Press, 1979, p. 257.

8 Guru Gobind Singh, *Bachittar Natak,* autobiography.

9 From Dr. S. Radhakrishnan, letter in the Baisakhi edition of "The Spokesman," 1956, reprinted as introduction to Giani Ishar Singh Nara, *Safarnama and Zafarnama,* New Delhi: Nara Publications, 1985, pp. iv-v.

10 Mool Mantra, quoted in *Hymns of Guru Nanak,* op. cit., p. 25.

11 *Jaap Sahib,* verses 84, 159, English translation by Harjett Singh Gill, New Delhi: Gobind Sadan Institute for Advanced Studies in Comparative Religion.

12 Adi Granth 684, quoted in Cole and Sambhi, op. cit., p. 74.

13 Ralph Singh, interview October 30, 1988.
14 Guru Arjun, Rag Majh, p. 102, quoted in Singh et al, *Sacred Writings of the Sikhs*, op. cit., p. 180.
15 *Anand Sahib*, verse 14.
16 Excerpted from Guru Gobind Singh, *Rahitnamas*, as translated by Gurden Singh.
17 Ibid.
18 Jap Ji verses 9–10.
19 Baba Virsa Singh, September 13, 1994, speech in Gobind Sadan, New Delhi.
20 Baba Virsa Singh, "News from Gobind Sadan," May 1994, p. 4.
21 Baba Virsa Singh, personal communication, December 1, 1992.
22 Guru Gobind Singh, *Dasam Granth*.

CHAPTER THIRTEEN
NEW RELIGIOUS MOVEMENTS

1 Friday M. Mbon, "The Social Impact of Nigeria's New Religious Movements," in ed. James A. Beckford, *New Religious Movements and Rapid Social Change*, Paris and London: Unesco/Sage Publications, 1986, p. 177.
2 Dr. Marc Galanter, in Daniel Coleman, "A Cultist's Mind," *New York Times*, April 21, 1993, p. A21.
3 Reiko Hatsumi, "In a spiritual vacuum anything can flourish, even destruction," *Asian Age*, May 28, 1995, p. 9.
4 Quoted in Ernest Cashmore, *Rastaman*, London: Unwin Paperbacks, 1983, p. 22.
5 *Tenri kyoso den* ("Life of the Founder of the Tenri-kyo Sect") compiled by the Tenri-kyo doshi-kai, Tenri, 1913, quoted in Ichiro Hori, *Folk Religion in Japan*, Chicago: University of Chicago Press, 1968, p. 237.
6 Sandra Pfortmiller, "Messages," *The National Spiritualist Summit*, January 1989, p. 31.
7 Principles 7 and 8 of the Declaration of Principles, National Spiritualist Association of Churches.
8 H. P. Blavatsky, *The Key to Theosophy*, Los Angeles: The United Lodge of Theosophists, 1920, p. 3.
9 J. Krishnamurti, as quoted in "J. Krishnamurti, An Extraordinary Mystic," Usha John, *Indian Perspectives*, March 1994, p. 23.
10 Elizabeth Claire Prophet, brochure from The Summit Lighthouse, Livingston, Montana.
11 "The Chart of Your Divine Self," Summit University, Livingston, Montana.
12 Rev. William Kingsley Opoku, personal communication, February 6, 1993.
13 Ernest Holmes, excerpt from "I am Vitalized by the Strength of God," reprinted in *Science of Mind*, October 1981, p. 59.
14 Tom Johnson, personal communication, February 19, 1990.
15 "A Brief Biography of Rajinder Singh," Delhi: Sawan Kirpal Publications Spiritual Society, p. 11.
16 Brahma Kumaris World Spiritual University, "Women and Spirituality in a Changing World," brochure.
17 Rev. Sun Myung Moon, in W. Farley Jones, ed., *A Prophet Speaks Today*, New York: HSA-UWC, 1975, p. 157.
18 Rev. Sun Myung Moon, "The True Family and I," speech in New Delhi, India, November 25, 1995, p. 11.
19 Starhawk, *The Spiral Dance: A Rebirth of the Ancient Religion of the Great Goddess*, San Francisco: Harper and Row, 1979, pp. 2–3.
20 John Seed, "Anthropocentrism," *Awakening in the Nuclear Age*, Issue #14 (Summer/Fall 1986), p. 11.
21 Chief Seattle, "Chief Seattle's Message," quoted in eds. John Seed, Joanna Macy, Pat Fleming, Arne Naess, *Thinking Like a Mountain: Toward a Council of All Beings*, Santa Cruz, California: New Society Publishers, 1988, p. 71.
22 J. E. Lovelock, *Gaia: A new look at life on Earth*, Oxford: Oxford University Press, pp. 9, 11.
23 James Lovelock, *The Ages of Gaia*, New York: Bantam Books, 1990, p. 206.
24 Peter Russell, "Endangered Earth: Psychological roots of the environmental crisis," *Link Up*, Issue #38 (Spring 1989), pp. 7–8.
25 David Albert, "A Children's Story: Gaura Devi Saves the Trees," *Awakening in the Nuclear Age*, op. cit., p. 15.
26 Hazrat Inayat Khan, "A New Form," *Addresses to Cherags*, Lebanon Springs, New York: Sufi Order, p. 75.
27 "The Baha'is: A Profile of the Baha'i Faith and its Worldwide Community," Leicestershire, UK: Baha'i Publishing Trust, p. 42.
28 Svetlana Dorzhieva, interviewed October 26, 1994.
29 'Abdu'l -Baha', as quoted in "One World, One Faith," New Delhi: National Spiritual Assemblies of the Baha'is of India, 1979, p. 3.
30 Adapted from "The Baha'i Faith," New York: Baha'i International Community (unpaginated).
31 Frithjof Schuon, *Understanding Islam*, London: George Allen and Unwin Ltd., translated from French, 1963, p. 41.

CHAPTER FOURTEEN
RELIGION AT THE TURN OF THE CENTURY

1 Diana Eck, "A New Geo-Religious Reality," paper presented at the World Conference on Religion and Peace Sixth World Assembly, Riva del Garda, Italy, November 1994, p. 1.
2 Archpriest Victor Petluchenko, interviewed October 31, 1994.
3 Gyorgy Bulanyi, "Church and Peace: Vision and Reality," address at Overcoming Violence, a Church and Peace Conference in Pecel, Hungary, April 1995, as printed in *Church and Peace*, Spring 1995, p. 4.
4 Charles Strozier et al., "Religious Militancy or 'Fundamentalism'," *Religion and Human Rights*, New York: The Project on Religion and Human Rights, 1994, p. 19.
5 Ewert Cousins, Speech at North American Interfaith Conference, Buffalo, New York, May 1991.
6 Raimundo Panikkar, "The Invisible Harmony: A Universal Theory of Religion or a Cosmic Confidence in Reality?", *Toward a Universal Theology of Religion*, ed. Leonard Swidler, Maryknoll, New York: Orbis Books, 1987, p. 147.
7 By Father Thomas Keating, as reprinted in Susan Walker, ed., *Speaking of Silence: Christians and Buddhists on the Contemplative Way*, Boulder, Colorado: Naropa Institute, 1987. Used by permission of Paulist Press.

8   Pope John Paul II, quoted in Richard N. Ostling,
    "A Summit for Peace in Assisi," *Time*, November 10,
    1986, p. 78.

9   Wangari Maathai, speaking at the Oxford Global Survival
    Conference, quoted in *The Temple of Understanding
    Newsletter*, Fall 1988, p. 2.

10 "Preserving and cherishing the Earth: An Appeal for
    Joint Commitment in Science and Religion," as quoted
    in Carl Sagan, "To Avert a Common Danger," *Parade
    Magazine*, March 1, 1992, p. 14.

11 Swami Vivekananda, speech for The Parliament of the
    World's Religions, Chicago, 1893.

12 "Towards a Global Ethic," Assembly of Religious and
    Spiritual Leaders, at The Parliament of World Religions,
    Chicago, 1993.

13 Marcus Braybrooke, letter prior to the Sarva-Dharma-
    Sammelana in Bangalore, India, June 28, 1993, p. 2.

14 Gordon Kaufman, *The Myth of Christian Uniqueness*,
    Maryknoll, New York: Orbis Books, 1987.

15 Baba Virsa Singh, in Mary Pat Fisher, ed., *Loving God: The
    Practical Teachings of Baba Virsa Singh*, New Delhi: Gobind
    Sadan Institute for Advanced Studies in Comparative
    Religion, pp. 7–8.

16 Gustavo Gutierrez, address to The World Conference on
    Religion and Peace, Riva del Garda, Italy, November
    1994.

17 Martha Penzer, interviewed March 31, 1995, in New
    Delhi.

18 Vaclav Havel, *Letters to Olga*, translated by Paul Wilson,
    London and Boston: Faber and Faber, 1988 edition of
    1983 original, pp. 236–237.

19 Professor Syed Anwar Kabir, interviewed April 12, 1995.

20 Zoya Krakhmalnikova, "Once Again about the Bitter
    Fruits of a Sweet Captivity," Thomastown, Victoria,
    Australia: Orthodox Action, 1989, p. 7.

21 Barbara von der Heydt, *Candles Behind the Wall*, Grand
    Rapids, Michigan: William B. Eerdmans Publishing
    Company, 1993, p. xiii.

22 Yasuhiro Nakasone, speech at the Sixth World
    Conference on Religion and Peace, Riva del Garda, Italy,
    November 4, 1994, p. 3.

23 Baba Virsa Singh, *Loving God*, New Delhi: Gobind Sadan
    Institute for Advanced Studies in Comparative Religion,
    second edition, 1995, p. 60.

GLOSSARY

In the glossary, most words are accompanied by a guide to pronunciation. This guide gives an accepted pronunciation as simply as possible. Syllables are separated by a space and those that are stressed are underlined. Letters are pronounced in the usual manner for English unless they are clarified in the following list.

a *as in* flat
aa father
aw saw
ay pay
ai there
ee see
e let
ī pity
i high
o not
ŏŏ book
oo food
oy boy
ō no
ow now
u but
ă, ĕ, ŏ, ŭ, about (unaccented vowels represented by " " in some phonetic alphabets)
er, ur, ir fern, fur, fir

ch church
j jet
ng sing
sh shine
wh where
y yes
kh guttural aspiration (ch in Welsh and German)

Agni (ag nee) The god of fire in Hinduism.

agnosticism (ag nos ti siz ĕm) The belief that if there is anything beyond this life, it is impossible for humans to know it.

ahimsa (ă him să) Non-violence, a central Jain principle.

Ahura (ă hŏŏ ră) In Indo-Iranian tradition, one of the highest deities.

Allah (aa lă) The one God, in Islam.

Amesha Spenta (aa mesh aa spen taa) The luminous deities of Zoroastrianism.

Amida (ă mee dă) (Sanskrit: Amitabha) The Buddha of infinite light, the personification of compassion whom the Pure Land Buddhists revere as the intermediary between humanity and Supreme Reality; esoterically, the Higher Self.

anatta (ă nat ă) In Buddhism, the doctrine that nothing in this transient existence has a permanent self.

anekantwad (ă nay kant wăd) The Jain principle of relativity or open-mindedness.

angel In the Zoroastrian–Jewish–Christian–Islamic traditions, an invisible servant of God.

Angra Mainyu (aan graa mīn yoo) The evil spirit or mental tendency in Zoroastrianism.

anicca (ă ni chă) In Buddhism, the impermanence of all existence.

animism (a nim izĕm) The belief in usually invisible spirits present within things and people.

Annunciation (ă nun see ay shun) In Christianity, the appearance of an angel to the Virgin Mary to tell her that she would bear Jesus, conceived by the Holy Spirit.

anthropocentrism (an thro po sen triz ĕm) The assumption that the whole universe revolves around the human species.

aparigraha (ă paa ree gră hă) The Jain principle of non-acquisitiveness.

apocalypse (ă paw kă lips) In Judaism and Christianity, the dramatic end of the present age.

Arhant (aar hănt) (Sanskrit; Pali: arhat or arahat) A "Worthy One" who has followed the Buddha's

Eightfold Path to liberation, broken the fetters that bind us to the suffering of the Wheel of Birth and Death, and arrived at Nirvana; the Theravadan ideal.

Ark of the Covenant In Judaism, the shrine containing God's commandments to Moses.

Aryans (ayr ee ăns) The Indo-European pastoral invaders of many European and Middle Eastern agricultural cultures during the second millennium BCE.

asana (aa să nă) A yogic posture.

ashram (ash ram) In Indian tradition, a usually ascetic spiritual community of those who have gathered around a guru.

atheism (ay thee is em) Non-belief in any deity.

Atman (aat man) In Hinduism, the soul.

Avesta (ă ves ta) The texts assembled of Zarathushtra's teachings.

baptism A Christian sacrament by which God cleanses all sin and makes one a sharer in the divine life, and a member of Christ's body, the Church.

baraka (bă raa ka) In Islamic mysticism, the spiritual wisdom and blessing transmitted from master to pupil.

Bar Mitzvah (baar mitz vă) The coming-of-age ceremony for a Jewish boy.

Bat Mitzvah (bat mitz vă) The coming-of-age ceremony for a Jewish girl in some modern congregations.

Beatitudes (bee at ě toods) Short statements by Jesus about those who are most blessed.

Bhagavad-Gita (ba gă văd gee tă) A portion of the Hindu epic Mahabarata in which Lord Krishna specifies ways of spiritual progress.

bhakti (bak tee) In Hinduism, intense devotion to a personal aspect of the Deity.

bhikkhu (bi koo) (Sanskrit: bhikshu; feminine; bhikkuni or bhikshuni). A Buddhist monk or nun who renounces worldliness for the sake of following the path of liberation and whose simple physical needs are met by lay supporters.

Bodhisattva (boo dee sat vă) In Mahayana Buddhism, one who has attained enlightenment but renounces Nirvana for the sake of helping all sentient beings in their journey to liberation from suffering.

Brahman (braa măn) The impersonal Ultimate Principle in Hinduism.

Brahamanas (braa mă năs) The portion of the Hindu Vedas concerning rituals.

Brahmin (braa min) (brahman) A priest or member of the priestly caste in Hinduism.

Buddha-nature A fully awakened consciousness.

caliph (kay lif) In Sunni Islam, the successor to the Prophet.

caste (kast) Social class distinction on the basis of heredity or occupation.

catholic Universal, all-inclusive. Christian churches referring to themselves as Catholic claim to be the representatives of the ancient undivided Christian church.

chakra (chuk ră) An energy center in the subtle body, recognized in kundalini yoga.

ch'i (chee) (ki) The vital energy in the universe and in our bodies, according to Far Eastern esoteric traditions.

ch'i-kung (chee kung) A Taoist system of harnessing inner energies for spiritual realization.

Communion See "Eucharist."

cosmogony (kos mog ŏn ee) Model of the evolution of the universe.

creed A formal statement of the beliefs of a particular religion.

cult Any religion that focuses on worship of a particular person or deity.

darsan (daar shan) Visual contact with the divine through encounters with Hindu images or gurus.

davening (daa věn ing) In Hasidic Judaism, prayer.

deity yoga (dee i tee yō gă) In Tibetan Buddhism, the practice of meditative concentration on a specific deity.

denomination (di nom ě nay shun) One of the Protestant branches of Christianity.

dervish (der vish) A Sufi ascetic, in the Muslim tradition.

Deva (day vă) In Hinduism, a deity.

Dhammapada (dam ă pă dă) A collection of short sayings attributed to Buddha.

Dharma (daar mă) (Pali: Dhamma) The doctrine or law, as revealed by the Buddha; also the correct conduct for each person according to his or her level of awareness.

dhimmi (dě hem ee) A person of a non-Muslim religion whose right to practice that religion is protected within an Islamic society.

dogma (dog mă) A system of beliefs declared to be true by a religion.

dualism The separation of reality into two categories, particularly the concept that spirit and matter are separate realms.

dukkha (doo kă) According to the Buddha, a central fact of human life, variously translated as discomfort, suffering, frustration, or lack of harmony with the environment.

Durga (do͝or ga) The Great Goddess as destroyer of evil, and sometimes as sakti of Siva.

ecumenism (ek yoo mĕ niz ĕm) Rapprochement between branches of Christianity or among all faiths.

Essenes (es eenz) Monastic Jews who were living communally, apart from the world, about the time of Jesus.

Eucharist (yoo kă rist) The Christian sacrament by which believers are renewed in the mystical body of Christ by partaking of bread and wine, understood as his body and blood.

evangelism (i van jĕ liz ĕm) Ardent preaching of the Christian gospel.

exclusivism The idea that one's own religion is the only valid way.

Fatiha (fat haa) The first sura of the Qur'an.

Frashokereti (fraa show ke re tee) In Zoroastrianism, the final resurrection of humanity into perfection and eternal life.

fundamentalism (fun dă men tăl iz ĕm) Insistence on what people perceive as the historical form of their religion, in contrast to more contemporary influences. This ideal sometimes takes extreme, rigidly exclusive, or violent forms.

Gathas (gaa tăs) The hymns of Zarathushtra.

Gayatrimantra (gī ă tree man tră) The daily Vedic prayer of upper-caste Hindus.

Gentile (jen tīl) Any person who is not of Jewish faith or origin.

ghetto Urban area occupied by those rejected by a society, such as quarters for Jews in some European cities.

Gnosticism (nos ti sizĕm) Mystical perception of spiritual knowledge.

gospel In Christianity, the "good news" that God has raised Jesus from the dead and in so doing has begun the transformation of the world.

gunas (goo năs) In Yoga, the three states of the Cosmic Substance: sattva, rajas, tamas.

gurdwara (go͝or dwa ră) A Sikh temple.

guru (goo roo) In Hinduism, an enlightened spiritual teacher.

Guru Granth Sahib (goo roo granth sa heeb) The sacred scripture compiled by the Sikh Gurus.

Hadith (had ith) In Islam, a traditional report about a reputed saying or action of the Prophet Muhammad.

haggadah (hă gaa dă) The non-legal part of the Talmud and midrash.

hajj (haj) The holy pilgrimage to Mecca, for Muslims.

halakha (haa laa khaa) Jewish legal decision and the parts of the Talmud dealing with laws.

haoma (hō ma) An intoxicating drink used by Indo–Iranian worshippers (see soma).

Hasidism (has ĭd iz ĕm) Ecstatic Jewish piety, dating from eighteenth-century Poland.

hatha yoga (ha thă yō gă) Body postures, diet, and breathing exercises to help build a suitable physical vehicle for spiritual development.

heretic (hair i tik) A member of an established religion whose views are unacceptable to the orthodoxy.

heyoka (hay yō kă) "Contrary" wisdom or a person who embodies it, in some Native American spiritual traditions.

hijab (hay jab) The veiling of women for the sake of modesty in Islam.

hijrah (hij ră) Muhammad's migration from Mecca to Medina.

Hinayana (hee nă ya nă) In Mahayana Buddhist terminology, the label "lesser vehicle," given to the orthodox Southern tradition now represented by Theravada; in Tibetan terminology, one of the three vehicles for salvation taught by the Buddha.

Holocaust (haw lō cawst) The genocidal killing of six million Jews by the Nazis during World War II.

Holy Trinity In many branches of Christianity, the idea that there is one God with three aspects: Father, Son, and Holy Spirit.

icon (ī kon) A sacred image, a term used especially for the paintings of Jesus, Mary, and the saints of the Eastern Orthodox Christian Church.

Imam (i maam) A leader of Muslim prayer; in Shi'ism, the title for the person carrying the initiatic tradition of the Prophetic Light.

immanent Present in Creation.

incarnation Physical embodiment of the divine.

indigenous (in dij ĕ nĕs) Native to an area.

Indra (in dră) The old Vedic thunder god in the Hindu tradition.

infidel (in fid ĕl) The Muslim and Christian term for "non-believer," which each of these traditions often applied to the other.

Inquisition (in kwi zi shun) The use of force and terror to eliminate heresies and nonbelievers in the Christian Church starting in the thirteenth century.

interfaith dialogue Appreciative communication between people of different religions.

Jap Ji (jap jee) The first morning prayer of Sikhs, written by Guru Nanak.

jen (yen) Humanity, benevolence – the central Confucian virtue.

jihad (ji had) The Muslim's battle against the inner forces that prevent God-realization and the outer barriers to establishment of the divine order.

Jina (ji nă) In Jainism, one who has realized the highest, omniscient aspect of his or her being and is therefore perfect.

jinn (jin) In Islam, an invisible being of fire.

Jiva (ji vă) The soul in Jainism.

jnana yoga (ya na yō gă) The use of intellectual effort as a yogic technique.

Juchiao (jee tzŭ yow) The Chinese term for the teachings based on Confucius.

justification In Christianity, being absolved of sin in the eyes of God.

Kabbalah (kă baa lă) The Jewish mystical tradition.

Kali (kaa lee) Destroying and transforming Mother of the World, in Hinduism.

Kali Yuga (kaa lee yō gă) In Hindu world cycles, an age of chaos and selfishness, including the one in which we are now living.

kami (kaa mee) The Shinto word for that invisible sacred quality which evokes wonder and awe in us, and also for the invisible spirits throughout nature that are born of this essence.

kannagara (kă nă gă ră) Harmony with the way of the kami in Shinto.

karma (kaar mă) (Pali: kamra) In Hinduism and Buddhism, our actions and their effects on this life and lives to come.

karma yoga (kaar mă yō gă) The path of unselfish service in Hinduism.

kenoticism (ki not ik iz ĕm) In Russian Orthodox Christianity, the monastic pattern of ascetic poverty combined with service in the world.

kensho (ken shō) Sudden enlightenment, in Zen Buddhism.

kevala (ka vă lă) The supremely perfected state in Jainism.

Khalsa (kal să) The body of the pure, as inspired by the Sikh Guru Gobind Singh.

kirtan (keer tan) Devotional singing of hymns from the Guru Granth Sahib in Sikhism.

kosher (kō sher) Ritually acceptable, applied to foods in Jewish Orthodoxy.

kshatriya (ksha tree ă) A member of the warrior or ruling caste in traditional Hinduism.

kufr (kōō fer) In Islam, the sin of atheism, of ingratitude to God.

kundalini (koon dă lee nee) In Hindu yogic thought, the life force that can be awakened from the base of the spine and raised to illuminate the spiritual center at the top of the head.

kusti (koos tee) The sacred cord Zoroastrians tie around their waists as armoring against evil within and without.

lama (laa mă) A Tibetan Buddhist monk, particularly one of the highest in the hierarchy.

langar (lan găr) A free communal meal without caste distinctions, in Sikh tradition.

li (lee) Ceremonies, rituals, and rules of proper conduct, in the Confucian tradition.

liberation theology Christianity expressed as solidarity with the poor.

lingam (ling ăm) A cylindrical stone or other similarly shaped natural or sculpted form, representing for Saivite Hindus the unmanifest aspect of Siva.

liturgy (lit ĕr jee) In Christianity, the rites of public worship.

Mahabarata (mă haa baa ră tă) A long Hindu epic which includes the *Bhagavad-Gita*.

Mahayana (maa hă ya nă) The "greater vehicle" in Buddhism, the more liberal and mystical Northern School which stressed the virtue of altruistic compassion rather than intellectual efforts at individual salvation.

mandala (man daa lă) A symmetrical image, with shapes emerging from a center, used as a meditational focus.

mantra (m) (man tră) A sound or phrase chanted to evoke the sound vibration of one aspect of creation or to praise a deity.

mass The Roman Catholic term for the Christian Eucharist.

maya (mī yă) In Indian thought, the attractive but illusory physical world.

Mazdayasna (maaz daa yaas naa) Iranian term for Zoroastrianism.

medicine Spiritual power, in some indigenous traditions.

messiah The "anointed," the expected king and deliverer of the Jews, a term later applied by Christians to Jesus.

metaphysics A branch of philosophy that deals with the systematic investigation of ultimate reality.

metta (met ă) In Buddhist terminology, loving-kindness.

midrash (<u>mid</u> rash) The literature of delving into the Jewish Torah.

mikva (<u>mik</u> vă) A deep bath for ritual cleansing in Judaism.

millennium One thousand years, a term used in Christianity and certain newer religions for a hoped-for period of a thousand years of holiness and happiness, with Christ ruling the earth, as prophesised in the book of Revelation.

minyan (<u>min</u> yăn) The quorum of ten adult males required for Jewish communal worship.

misogi (mee sō gee) The Shinto waterfall purification ritual.

mitzva (<u>mitz</u> vă) (plural: mitzvot) In Judaism, a divine commandment or sacred deed in fulfillment of a commandment.

moksha (<u>mōk</u> shă) Liberation of the soul from illusion and suffering, in Hinduism.

monism (<u>mon</u> iz ĕm) The concept of life as a unified whole, without a separate "spiritual" realm.

monotheism (mon ō <u>thee</u> iz ĕm) The concept that there is one God.

mujahid (<u>moo</u> jă hid) In Islam, selfless fighter in the path of Allah.

muni (<u>moo</u> nee) A Jain monk.

murshid (<u>moor</u> shid) A spiritual teacher, in esoteric Islam.

mystic One who values inner spiritual experience in preference to external authorities and scriptures.

naga (<u>naa</u> gă) A snake, worshipped in Hinduism.

Nam (naam) The holy Name of God reverberating throughout all of Creation, as repeated by Sikhs.

Nirvana (ner <u>va</u> nă) (Pali: Nibbana) In Buddhism, the ultimate egoless state of bliss.

occult Involving the mysterious, unseen, supernatural.

OM (ōm) In Hinduism, the primordial sound.

original sin The Christian belief that all human beings are bound together in prideful egocentricity. In the Bible, this is described mythically as an act of disobedience on the part of Adam and Eve.

orthodox Adhering to the established tradition of a religion.

Pahlavi (<u>paa</u> lă vee) The Iranian language of Persia under the Sassanids.

Pali (<u>paa</u> lee) The Indian dialect first used for writing down the teachings of the Buddha, which were initially held in memory, and still used today in the Pali Canon of scriptures recognized by the Theravadins.

pantheism (<u>pan</u> thee iz ĕm) The concept that One Absolute Reality is everywhere.

parable (<u>par</u> ă bŭl) An allegorical story.

Paraclete (<u>par</u> ă kleet) The entity that Jesus said would come after his death to help the people.

Parsi (<u>paar</u> see) A Zoroastrian settled in India.

Parvati (<u>paar</u> vă tee) Siva's spouse, sweet daughter of the Himalayas.

Pentateuch (<u>pen</u> tă took) The five books of Moses at the beginning of the Hebrew Bible.

Pentecost (<u>pen</u> tĕ kost) The occasion when the Holy Spirit descended upon the disciples of Jesus after his death.

Pharisees (<u>fair</u> ĕ seez) In Roman-ruled Judea, liberals who tried to practice Torah in their lives.

pluralism An appreciation of the diversity of religions.

polytheism (<u>pol</u> ĕ thee iz ĕm) Belief in many deities.

pope The Bishop of Rome and head of the Roman Catholic Church.

Prakriti (<u>praak</u> ri tee) In Samkhya Hindu philosophy, the cosmic substance.

prana (<u>praa</u> nă) In Indian thought, the invisible life-force.

pranayama (<u>praa</u> nă ya mă) Yogic breathing exercises.

prasad (pră <u>saad</u>) In Indian traditions, blessed food.

puja (<u>poo</u> jă) Hindu ritual worship.

Puranas (pŏŏ <u>raa</u> năs) Hindu scriptures written to popularize the abstract truths of the Vedas through stories about historical and legendary figures.

Pure Land A Buddhist sect in China and Japan that centers on faith in Amida Buddha, who promised to welcome believers to the paradise of the Pure Land, a metaphor for enlightenment.

Purgatory (<u>pur</u> gă tōr ee) In some branches of Christianity, an intermediate after-death state in which souls are purified from sin.

Purusha (poo <u>roo</u> shă) The Cosmic Spirit, soul of the universe in Hinduism.

rabbi (<u>rab</u> ī) Historically, a Jewish teacher; at present, the ordained spiritual leader of a Jewish congregation.

rajas (<u>raa</u> jăs) The active state, one of the three gunas in Hinduism.

Ramayana (raa <u>maa</u> yă nă) The Hindu epic about Prince Rama, defender of good.

reincarnation The transmigration of the soul into a new body after death of the old body.

relic In some forms of Christianity, part of the body or clothing of a saint.

Rig Veda (rig <u>vay</u> dă) Possibly the world's oldest scripture, the foundation of Hinduism.

rishi (<u>rish</u> ee) A Hindu sage.

Sabbath (<u>sab</u> ăth) The day of the week set aside for rest and worship in Judaism and Christianity.

sacrament Outward and visible signs of inward and spiritual grace in Christianity. Almost all churches recognize baptism and the Eucharist as sacraments; some churches recognize five others as well.

sacred thread In Hinduism, a cord worn over one shoulder by men who have been initiated into adult upper-caste society.

Sadducees (<u>saj</u> ŭ seez) In Roman-ruled Judea, wealthy and priestly Jews.

sadhana (<u>saad</u> hă nă) In Hinduism, especially yoga, a spiritual practice.

sadhu (<u>sad</u> oo) An ascetic holy man, in Hinduism.

Saivite (<u>sīv</u> īt) A Hindu worshipper of the Divine as Siva.

Sakta (<u>sak</u> ta) A Hindu worshipper of the female aspect of Deity.

sakti (<u>sak</u> tee) The creative, active female aspect of Deity in Hinduism.

samadhi (sa <u>maa</u> dee) In yogic practice, the blissful state of superconscious union with the Absolute.

Samkhya (<u>saam</u> khyă) One of the major Hindu philosophical systems, in which human suffering is characterized as stemming from the confusion of Prakriti with Purusha.

samsara (săm <u>saa</u> ră) The continual round of birth-and-death existence, in Hinduism, Jainism, and Buddhism.

Sanatana Dharma (să <u>na</u> tă nă <u>daar</u> mă) The "eternal religion" of Hinduism.

Sangha (<u>sung</u> ă) In Theravada Buddhism, the monastic community; in Mahayana, the spiritual community of followers of the Dharma.

sannyasin (sun <u>yaa</u> sin) In Hinduism, a renunciate spiritual seeker.

Sanskrit (<u>san</u> skrit) The literary language of classic Hindu scriptures.

sati (<u>sa</u> tee) The Hindu tradition of live cremation of a widow with her dead husband.

sativa (<u>sa</u> tee vă) The state of purity and illumination, one of the three gunas in Hinduism.

satori (să <u>taw</u> ree) Enlightenment, realization of ultimate truth, in Zen Buddhism.

sect A sub-group within a larger tradition.

Semitic (sem <u>i</u> tik) Referring to Jews, Arabs, and others of eastern Mediterranean origin.

shabd (shaabd) The Sikh term for a Name of God that is recited or a hymn from the Guru Granth Sahib, considered the Word of God.

Shahadah (shă <u>haa</u> dă) The central Muslim expression of faith: "There is no god but God."

shaktipat (<u>shak</u> tă pat) In the Siddha Yoga tradition of Hinduism, the powerful, elevating glance or touch of the guru.

shaman (<u>shaa</u> man) A "medicine person," a man or woman who has undergone spiritual ordeals and can communicate with the spirit world to help the people in indigenous traditions.

Shari'ah (shă <u>ree</u> ă) The divine law, in Islam.

shayk (shaik) A spiritual master, in the esoteric Muslim tradition.

Shekhinah (shĕ <u>kī</u> nă) God's presence in the world, in Judaism.

Shi'ite (<u>shee</u> īt) A follower of the minority branch of Islam which feels that Muhammad's legitimate successors were 'Ali and a series of Imams.

shirk (shirk) The sin of believing in any divinity except the one God, in Islam.

shudra (<u>shoo</u> dră) A member of the manual laborer caste in traditional Hinduism.

Sikh (seek) "Student," especially one who practices the teachings of the ten Sikh Gurus.

Siva (<u>shee</u> vă) In Hinduism, the Supreme as lord of yogis, absolute consciousness, creator, preserver, and destroyer of the world; or the destroying aspect of the Supreme.

soma (<u>sō</u> ma) An intoxicating drink used by early Hindu worshippers.

Spenta Mainyu (<u>spen</u> taa <u>mīn</u> yoo) The good spirit or power of mind in Zoroastrianism.

stupa (<u>stoo</u> pă) A rounded monument containing Buddhist relics or commemorative materials.

Sufism (<u>soo</u> fis ĕm) The mystical path in Islam.

Sunnah (<u>soo</u> nă) The behavior of the Prophet Muhammad, used as a model in Islamic law.

Sunni (<u>soo</u> nee) A follower of the majority branch of Islam which feels that successors to Muhammad are to be chosen by the Muslim community.

sunyata (<u>soon</u> yă tă) Voidness, the transcendental ultimate reality in Buddhism.

Sura (<u>sōō</u> ră) A chapter of the Qur'an.

sutra (<u>soo</u> tră) (Pali: Suta) Literally, a thread on which are strung jewels – the discourses of the Buddha.

synagogue (<u>sin</u> ă gog) A meeting place for Jewish study and worship.

syncretism (<u>sing</u> kri tis ĕm) A form of religion in which otherwise differing traditions are blended.

synoptic (sin <u>op</u> tik) Referring to three similar books of the Christian Bible: Matthew, Mark, and Luke.

T'ai-chi chuan (tī chee hwaan) An ancient Chinese system of physical exercises which uses slow movements to help one become part of the universal flow of energy.

talit (<u>ta</u> lit) A shawl traditionally worn by Jewish men during prayers.

Talmud (<u>tal</u> mŏŏd) Jewish law and lore, as finally compiled in the sixth century CE.

tamas (<u>tam</u> ăs) The dull state, one of the three gunas in Hinduism.

Tanakh (ta <u>nakh</u>) The Jewish scriptures.

Tantras (<u>tan</u> trăs) The ancient Indian texts based on esoteric worship of the divine as feminine.

Tantrayana (tăn tră <u>ya</u> nă) See Vajrayana.

Tao (Dao) (dow) The way or path, in Far Eastern traditions. The term is also used as a name for the Nameless.

Tao-chia (dow cheeă) The ancient philosophical Taoist tradition.

Tao-chiao (dow cheeow) The newer magically religious Taoist tradition.

t'fillin (tĕ <u>fil</u> in) A small leather box with verses about God's covenant with the Jewish people, bound to the forehead and arm.

thang-ka (tang ka) In Tibetan Buddhism, an elaborate image of a spiritual figure used as a focus for meditation.

theistic (thee <u>is</u> tik) Believing in a God or gods.

Theravada (<u>ter</u> ă vă dă) The remaining orthodox school of Buddhism, which adheres closely to the earliest scriptures and emphasizes individual efforts to liberate the mind from suffering.

third eye The center of spiritual insight thought to reside between and slightly above the physical eyes.

Tirthankaras (<u>tir</u> tăn kăr ăs) The great enlightened teachers in Jainism, of whom Mahavira was the last in the present era.

Torah (<u>tō</u> raa) The Pentateuch or the whole body of Jewish teaching and law.

transcendent Existing outside the material universe.

transpersonal Referring to an eternal, infinite reality, in contrast to the finite material world.

transubstantiation (<u>tran</u> sŭb stan shee ay shun) In some branches of Christianity, the idea that wine and bread are mystically transformed into the blood and body of Christ during the Eucharist sacrament.

Trinity The Christian doctrine that in the One God are three divine persons: the Father, the Son, and the Holy Spirit.

Triple Gem The three jewels of Buddhism: Buddha, Dharma, Sangha.

tsumi (tzoo mee) Impurity or misfortune, a quality that Shinto purification practices are designed to remove.

"twice-born" Upper-caste men who have been initiated into Aryan society in traditional Hinduism.

tzaddik (<u>tzaa</u> dik) An enlightened Jewish mystic.

ulama (oo lă <u>maa</u>) The influential leaders in traditional Muslim society, including spiritual leaders, imams, teachers, state scribes, market inspectors, and judges.

Ummah (ō <u>maa</u>) The Muslim community.

Upanishads (oo <u>pan</u> i shăds) The philosophical part of the Vedas in Hinduism, intended only for serious seekers.

Vaishnavite (<u>vīsh</u> nă vīt) (*Vaishnava*) A Hindu devotee of Vishnu, particularly in his incarnation as Krishna.

vaishya (<u>vīsh</u> ă) A member of the merchant and farmer caste in traditional Hinduism.

Vajrayana (văj ră <u>ya</u> nă) The ultimate vehicle used in Tibetan Buddhism, consisting of esoteric tantric practices and concentration on deities.

Varuna (<u>va</u> roo nă) The old thunder god of cosmic order in ancient Hinduism.

Vedanta (vi <u>dan</u> tă) A Hindu philosophy based on the Upanishads.

vipassana (vi <u>pas</u> ă nă) In Buddhism, meditation based in watching one's own thoughts, emotions, and actions.

Vishnu (<u>vish</u> noo) In Hinduism, the preserving aspect of the Supreme or the Supreme Itself, incarnating again and again to save the world.

vision quest In indigenous traditions, a solitary ordeal undertaken to seek spiritual guidance about one's mission in life.

Voodoo (<u>voo</u> doo) Latin American and Caribbean ways of working with the spirit world, a blend of West African and Catholic Christian teachings.

wu wei (woo way) In Taoism, "not doing," in the sense of taking no action contrary to the natural flow.

yagna (<u>yaj</u> nă) (Persian: yasna) Ancient religious rituals in Hinduism and Zoroastrianism.

yang (yang) In Chinese philosophy, the bright, assertive, "male" energy in the universe.

yantra (<u>yan</u> tră) In Hinduism, a linear cosmic symbol used as an aid to spiritual concentration.

yi (yee) Righteous conduct (as opposed to conduct motivated by desire for personal profit), a Confucian virtue stressed by Mencius.

yin (yin) In Chinese philosophy, the dark, receptive, "female" energy in the universe.

yoga (yō gă) Ancient techniques for spiritual realization, found in several Eastern religions.

Yoga (yō gă) A systematic approach to spiritual realization, one of the major Hindu philosophical systems.

yoni (yō nee) Abstract Hindu representation of the female vulva, cosmic matrix of life.

yuga (<u>yoo</u> gă) One of four recurring world cycles in Hinduism.

zakat (zak at) Spiritual tithing in Islam.

zazen (zaa <u>zen</u>) Zen Buddhist sitting meditation.

Zen (zen) (Chinese: Ch'an) A Chinese and Japanese Buddhist school emphasizing that all things have Buddha-nature, which can only be grasped when one escapes from the intellectual mind.

zendo (<u>zen</u> dō) A Zen meditation hall.

CREDITS

The authors and publishers wish to acknowledge, with thanks, the following photographic sources.

Half-title: Rex Features
Frontispiece: Panos Pictures/Marc Schlossman

Chapter 1
13 Barnaby's Picture Library
14 Panos Pictures/J. Holmes
16 Idemetsu Museum of Arts, Tokyo
17 Hirmer Fotoarchiv
19 Barnaby's Picture Library
20 Hirschhorn Museum and Sculpture Garden; Smithsonian Institution (Gift of Joseph H. Hirschhorn)
21 The Tate Gallery, London
22 Barnaby's Picture Library
26 Magnum Ltd., London/Ian Berry
29 JCK Archives
31 Werner Forman Archive
33 Trustees of the Victoria and Albert Museum, London

Chapter 2
40 Barnaby's Picture Library
43 Pygmy fund; Photo Jean-Pierre Hallet
48 © Elisabeth Sunday
50 Mary Pat Fisher
52 Mat Farbman © Life Magazine
53 Smithsonian Institution: National Anthropological Archives
55 (left) The Hutchison Library
55 (right) Topham Picture Source
57 (left) The Hutchison Library/Juliet Highet
57 (right) Courtesy Dept. of Library Services, American Museum of Natural History
59 © Prof JVW Megaw, Flinders University of South Australia
61 (top left) Elisofon Archives; Museum of African Art Washington DC
61 (top right) The Hutchison Library/Juliet Highet
61 (bottom) Photo: Dana Salvo
64 Werner Forman Archive
66 The Hutchison Library/Jeremy Horner

Chapter 3
71 Courtesy: Museum of Fine Arts, Boston (Charles Amos Cummings Bequest Fund)
73 The Mansell Collection
74 Mary Pat Fisher
79 Gurmeet Thukral
81 Trustees of the Victoria and Albert Museum, London
82 Gurmeet Thukral

84 Mary Pat Fisher
85 Ann and Bury Peerless
86 (left) Gurmeet Thukral
86 (right) Douglas Dickens
88 Photo of Paramhansa Yogananda, copyright © 1953 renewed 1981 Self-Realisation Fellowship. Copyright © 1984 Self-Realisation Fellowship. All rights reserved. Reprinted with permission.
89 (top) Ann and Bury Peerless
90 Mary Pat Fisher
91 Mary Pat Fisher
93 Trustees of the Victoria and Albert Museum, London
96 (right) Ann and Bury Peerless
96 (left) Gurmeet Thukral
97 Metropolitan Museum, New York (Harris Brisbane Dick Fund)
98 (top) JCK Archives
98 (bottom) Rex Features
99 Mary Pat Fisher
103 (top) Popperfoto
103 (bottom) The Hutchison Library/Nancy Durrell Mckenna
104 The Hutchison Library/Dave Brinicombe
107 Magnum Photos Ltd./Raghu Rai
111 Mary Pat Fisher

Chapter 4
115 Musée Guimet, Paris/Werner Forman Archive
117 Anne and Bury Peerless
122 Barnaby's Picture Library
124 Mary Pat Fisher

Chapter 5
128 (top) Sarnath Museum
128 (bottom) The Hutchison Library/Ivan Strasburg
131 The Hutchison Library
136 Trustees of the Victoria and Albert Museum, London
139 The Hutchison Library
141 Christine Osborne
143 Douglas Dickens
144 (left) Barnaby's Picture Library
144 (right) Barnaby's Picture Library
145 Barnaby's Picture Library
146 Trustees of the Victoria and Albert Museum, London
149 The Hutchison Library/Sarah Errington
150 Rex Features
151 (top) Barnaby's Picture Library
151 (bottom) Trustees of the Victoria and Albert Museum, London
152 Colorific!/Susan McCartney
155 Society for Educational Information, Tokyo
156 Teeksa Photography – Skip Schiel
159 Zen Mountain Monastery, Mount Trumper

INDEX

	2000 BCE	1500	1000	500	0 CE
Indigenous	←				
Hinduism	← *Vedas* heard	*Vedas* first written c. 1500		*Ramayana* and *Mahabharata* in present form 400+	Code of Manu compiled before 100 CE
					Pantanjali systematizes Yoga Sutras 200
Judaism	Abraham 1900-1700 BCE?	Moses 1300 BCE?	King David 1010-970		Jerusalem falls to Romans 70
				First temple destroyed; Jews exiled 586	
Taoism and Confucianism				Chuang-tzu c.400-300 or earlier Lao-tzu c. 600-500 Confucius c.551-479	
					Educational system based on Confucian Classics from 205
Buddhism				Gautama Buddha c. 563-483	King Asoka spreads Buddhism c. 258 Theravada Buddhism develops 200 BCE – 200 CE
Christianity					Jesus c.4 BCE – c.30 Paul organizes early Christians c.50-60 CE Gospels written down c.70-95 CE
Islam					
Zoroastrianism	Early elements of Zoroastrianism in Indo-Iranian tribes		Zarathushtra c.1100-550 BCE	State religion of Iranian Empire 131 BCE	
Jainism	Series of 23 Tirthankaras		Mahavira 599-527 BCE	Digambaras and Svetambaras diverge from 3rd C. BCE	
Shinto	Shinto begins in pre-history as local nature- and ancestor-based traditions				
Sikhism					
Interfaith					

cient ways passed down and adapted over millenia ⟶

Bhakti movement 600-1800 ⟶ Ramakrishna
1836-1886

bbinical tradition
veloped 1st – 4th C. CE
Maimonides 1135-1204

The Baal
Shem Tov
1700-1760

1940-1945
The Holocaust
1948 Israel's
independence

oist religion institutionalized
m 2nd C. CE

960-1280 Sung Dynasty revives ritualistic
Confucianism ("neo-Confucianism")

1966-1976 Cultural
Revolution attacks
religions
1989 Chinese
government limits
religious freedoms

c.500-600 Japan
imports Confucianism
to unite tribes into empire

hayana Buddhism
velops 1st C. CE

Buddhism declared
national religion
of Tibet 700s

Persecution
of Buddhism
begins in China
845

Ch'an Buddhism
to Japan as Zen
13th C.

Buddhism spreads
in the West 20th C.

Centralization of papal
power 800-1100

Western and Eastern
Churches split 1054

Monastic orders
proliferate 1300s

Protestantism begins
1521

Second Vatican
Council 1962

Spanish inquisition
established 1478

Muhammad c. 570-632
Spread of Islam begins 633
Sunni-Shi'ite split c. 682
Islam's cultural peak 750-1258

Mughal Emperor
Akbar 1556

European dominance
1800s-1900s
OPEC and Muslim
resurgence 1970s

Emigration of Parsis to
India 10th C.

Jain monks establish
Jain centers outside
India 1970s-80s

Shinto name adopted
6th C. CE

State Shinto
established 1868

Guru Nanak
1469-1504

At death of Guru
Gobind Singh, the
scriptures become the
guru 1708

Mughal Emperor
Akbar initiates
interfaith dialogues
1556-1605

First International
Human Unity
Conference 1974
Centenary Celebrations
1993